SEVENTH EDITION

Racial and Ethnic Relations

Joe R. Feagin

University of Florida

Clairece Booher Feagin

Upper Saddle River, New Jersey 07458

Library of Congress Cataloging-in-Publication Data

Feagin, Joe R.
Racial and ethnic relations/Joe R. Feagin, Clairece Booher Feagin.—7th ed.
p. cm.
Includes bibliographical references and index.
ISBN 0-13-099533-9
1. Minorities—United States. 2. United States—Race relations. 3. United States—Ethnic relations. I. Feagin, Clairece Booher. II. Title.

E184.A1 F38 2003
305.8'00973—dc21 2002066338

AVP, Publisher: Nancy Roberts
Managing editor: Sharon Chambliss
Editorial assistant: Lee Peterson
Marketing manager: Amy Speckman
Editorial/production supervision: Kari Callaghan Mazzola
Prepress and manufacturing buyer: Mary Ann Gloriande
Electronic page makeup: Kari Callaghan Mazzola and John P. Mazzola
Interior design: John P. Mazzola
Director, Image Resource Center: Melinda Reo
Manager, Rights and Permissions: Zina Arabia
Interior image specialist: Beth Boyd-Brenzel
Image permissions coordinator: Michelina Viscusi
Photo researcher: Clare Maxwell
Cover image specialist: Karen Sanatar
Cover director: Jayne Conte
Cover design: Bruce Kenselaar
Cover art: Sergio Baradat/Stock Illustration Source, Inc.

This book was set in 10/12 Palatino by Big Sky Composition
and was printed and bound by Von Hoffmann Press, Inc.
The cover was printed by Phoenix Color Corp.

Printed in the United States of America
10 9 8 7 6 5 4 3 2 1

ISBN 0-13-099533-9

Pearson Education LTD., London
Pearson Education Australia PTY, Limited, Sydney
Pearson Education Singapore, Pte. Ltd
Pearson Education North Asia Ltd, Hong Kong
Pearson Education Canada, Ltd., Toronto
Pearson Educación de Mexico, S.A. de C.V.
Pearson Education—Japan, Tokyo
Pearson Education Malaysia, Pte. Ltd
Pearson Education, Upper Saddle River, New Jersey

Contents

CHAPTER 2 Adaptation and Conflict: Racial and Ethnic Relations in Theoretical Perspective 22

CHAPTER 9 Puerto Rican and Cuban Americans 232

CHAPTER 10 Japanese Americans 265

CHAPTER 12 Arab Americans 323

Preface

OVER THE PAST FEW DECADES, NUMEROUS SCHOLARS, JOURNALISTS, AND POLITICIANS have argued that there is a "declining significance of race" or an "end to racism" in the United States. They have written or spoken optimistically about the decrease in discrimination and the improving character of racial and ethnic relations in this country. Over the same period of time, however, the scholarly journals and mass media have been filled with accounts of violent hate crimes targeting people of color, accounts of the violent views and actions of white supremacist groups, discussions of many lawsuits over racial discrimination in employment and public accommodations, studies showing widespread housing discrimination, descriptions of community rebellions against local police brutality incidents, and controversies over affirmative action and other anti-discrimination programs. In recent years, we have also seen intense debates about the character and impact of the recent immigrants to the United States, many of whom are immigrants of color from Latin American or Asian countries.

As we move into the new millennium, there is much scholarly and public discussion and argument about racial and ethnic discrimination, oppression, and conflict.

Contrary to what some scholars and journalists assert, this debate reflects the underlying social, economic, and political realities in the United States. Today, many Americans are well aware, or are becoming aware, of the continuing significance of "race," racism, and ethnicity, not only in this country but also in other countries—from the Republic of South Africa to Northern Ireland, the former Yugoslavia, the former Soviet Union, and the Middle East. Racial and ethnic oppression and conflict are extraordinarily important in the modern world and have the potential to tear apart any country, including highly industrialized countries.

One result of the reinvigorated interest in racial and ethnic issues in many areas of the United States is the creation of college and university courses that focus on racial and ethnic divisions, cultural diversity, and multicultural or multiracial issues. We have revised this seventh edition of *Racial and Ethnic Relations* with this growing interest in U.S. racial and ethnic heritages, developments, conflicts, and coalitions in mind. This textbook is designed for sociology courses, other social science courses, and education courses variously titled Racial and Ethnic Relations, Race Relations, Minority Groups, and Minority Relations, and also for various other courses on cultural diversity, multiculturalism, and racial and ethnic groups offered in college, university, business, and governmental settings.

One purpose of this book is to provide readers with access to the important literature on racial and ethnic groups in the United States and, to a lesser extent, in certain other countries around the globe. We have drawn on a broad array of sources, including articles, books, and other data analyses by sociologists, political scientists, social psychologists, anthropologists, historians, economists, investigative journalists, and legal scholars.

We have limited space, so we have not been able to deal with all the important racial and ethnic groups in the United States. Instead, we have focused on a modest number of major racial and ethnic groups, generally preferring to accent depth rather than breadth in the analyses. In recent decades, social science analyses have begun to dig deeper into the "what," "why," and "how" of racial and ethnic oppression and conflict. We draw heavily on this ever-growing research.

The introduction to Part I looks briefly at the origins of the racial and ethnic mosaic that is the United States. It serves as an introduction to Chapters 1 and 2, which discuss major concepts and theories in the study of racial and ethnic relations. The introduction to Part II sketches the political and economic history of the United States in order to provide the context for understanding the adaptation and oppression of the various immigrant groups that have come, voluntarily or involuntarily, to U.S. shores. Only one major group, Native Americans (Indians), cannot be viewed as such immigrants; indeed, as the original inhabitants of this continent, they were often the victims of actions by the early immigrants (colonists) from outside North America. The situations and experiences of Native American societies and the various groups that have immigrated to North America are considered in Chapters 3–13. In Part III, Chapter 14 moves away from the United States to look at patterns of racial and ethnic relations in several other countries around the world, including France, South Africa, and Brazil. In the latter two cases, we examine how global patterns of racial oppression and conflict have often been developed or fostered by the outside European colonizers and their descendants during the colonial and decolonization periods in the histories of such countries.

In this seventh edition of *Racial and Ethnic Relations* we have updated each chapter with much new material and research, such as that on housing discrimination facing Latinos in Chapters 8 and 9. We have added a new and timely chapter on Arab Americans, many of whom have recently immigrated from the Middle East. In several chapters we give expanded attention to new conceptual approaches to racial and ethnic relations. For example, in Chapter 2 and elsewhere, we explore how new theorizing about assimilation and racial and ethnic discrimination is forcing a deeper probing of the dimensions and variations in intergroup relationships and adaptation, including the sometimes negative consequences of group integration into the dominant culture. Where possible in the group chapters, we have given attention to current events and issues. In addition, in Chapter 13 we deal with the increasingly multiracial and multicultural character of U.S. society. We examine the implications of the forecasts by demographers that by the middle of the twenty-first century the United States will become a country whose population majority is composed of Latino, African, Asian, Middle Eastern, and Native Americans.

SUPPLEMENTS

Test Item File

This carefully prepared manual offers test questions in multiple-choice, true/false, and essay formats. All questions are keyed to the text.

MAC/WIN Prentice Hall Test Manager

This computerized software allows instructors to create their own personalized exams, to edit any or all test questions, and to add new questions. Other special features of this program, which is available for Windows and Macintosh, include random generation of an item set, creation of alternate versions of the same test, scrambling question sequence, and test preview before printing.

ABC News/Prentice Hall Video Library for Race and Ethnic Relations

Selected video segments from award-winning ABC News programs such as *Nightline*, *ABC World News Tonight*, and *20/20* accompany topics featured in the text. Please contact your Prentice Hall representative for more details.

Companion Website™

In tandem with the text, students can now take full advantage of the Internet to enrich their study of racial and ethnic relations. Features of the Website include chapter objectives, study questions, and links to *The New York Times* and the *USA Today Census 2000*, as well as other interesting links on the Web that can reinforce and enhance the content of each chapter. Use of the site is free to all students and faculty. Visit the Website at **http://www.prenhall.com/feagin**

A Prentice Hall Guide to Evaluating Online Resources, Sociology, 2003

This guide provides a brief introduction to navigating the Internet, along with references related specifically to the discipline of sociology. Also included with the guide is access to **ContentSelect**. Developed by Prentice Hall and EBSCO, the world leader in online journal subscription management, ContentSelect is a customized research database for students of sociology, and is free to students when packaged with this text.

Census2000 Interactive CD-ROM

Capturing the rich picture of our nation drawn by Census2000, this CD-ROM brings related census data—including audio, video, and actual reports in PDF format—into your classroom in a multimedia format. It is free when packaged with this text.

10 Ways to Fight Hate Brochure

Produced by the Southern Poverty Law Center, the leading crime-watch organization and authority on hate-crime in the United States, this brochure walks students through ten steps that they can take on their own campus or in their own neighborhood to fight hate every day. It is free when packaged with this text.

ACKNOWLEDGMENTS

In writing this and previous editions of this textbook, we have received useful comments and suggestions from numerous colleagues, students, teachers, correspondents, editors, and reviewers. We are indebted to those whose advice, suggestions, and insights have made this a better book. Among these are Leland Saito, Gary David, Amir Marvasti, Nijole Benokraitis, Nestor Rodríguez, Melvin Sikes, Hernán Vera, Joane Nagel, Howard Winant, Edna Bonacich, Karyn McKinney, Eileen O'Brien, Leslie Inniss, Richard Alba, Yanick St. Jean, Debra Van Ausdale, Robert Parker, Daniel Duarte, Teun Van Dijk, Harriett Romo, Alice Littlefield, Wendy Ng, John R. Sosa, Jaime Martinez, Bud Khleif, Howard Leslie, Larry Horn, Doris Wilkinson, Anthony Orum, James Button, Ward Churchill, Edward Múrguía, S. Dale McLemore, Gideon Sjoberg, Gilberto Cardenas, Nikitah Imani, David Roth, Joseph Lopreato, John Butler, Eric Woodrum, Andrew Greeley, Graham Kinloch, Lester Hill, Chad Oliver, Marcia A. Herndon, Rogelio Nuñez,

Tom Walls, Samuel Heilman, Phylis Cancilla Martinelli, José Limon, Devon Peña, Diana Kendall, Robena Jackson, Mark Chesler, David O'Brien, Bradley Stewart, and the reviewers of this seventh edition: John A. Arthur of the University of Minnesota, Barbara L. Mori of California Polytechnic State University, Robert E. Parker of the University of Nevada at Las Vegas, and William L. Smith of Georgia Southern University. We would also like to thank Leslie Houts for research assistance, and the students of several sociology colleagues, including Yanick St. Jean, for helpful comments on an earlier edition. We are also indebted to Pinar Batur for revising Chapter 14.

We hope that you find this seventh edition informative and intellectually stimulating. We welcome your comments. Please write to us at the Department of Sociology, Box 117330, University of Florida, Gainesville, FL, 32611-2036.

Joe R. Feagin
Clairece Booher Feagin

PART I

The Racial and Ethnic Mosaic

MORE THAN TWO HUNDRED YEARS AGO, the new United States severed its colonial ties with Europe. Born in revolution, this new nation was portrayed as centrally dedicated to freedom and equality. Over the next two centuries, a vigorous nation would emerge, with great racial and ethnic diversity. Yet the new society had its seamy side. Racial and ethnic oppression and conflict were also imbedded in the founding period and in the subsequent history of the new republic. The European immigrants often took the lands of Native Americans by force. By the end of the seventeenth century, the enslavement of Africans and African Americans was fundamental to the economy of the North American colonies, and resistance and revolt by these enslaved Americans were recurring problems for white slaveholders. In succeeding centuries other non-European peoples, such as Chinese, Japanese, and Mexican Americans, would suffer serious yokes of racial oppression. But non-Europeans were not the only ones to face oppressive conditions. Discrimination against white immigrant groups was part of the sometimes forgotten history of both the pre- and post-revolutionary periods.

In the earliest period, the colonial population on the prospering Atlantic coast was predominantly English in its origins and basic social institutions. Because of England's huge appetite for raw materials and new markets, English authorities encouraged non-English immigration to the colonies. Yet there was popular opposition, verbal and violent, to the long line of new white immigrants. "Foreigners" soon became a negative category for many colonists. "Despite the need for new settlers English colonials had mixed feelings about foreign arrivals. Anglo-Saxon mobs attacked Huguenots in Frenchtown, Rhode Island, and destroyed a Scotch-Irish frontier settlement in Worcester, Massachusetts."[1] In the 1700s, colonies such as Virginia, Pennsylvania, and Rhode Island attempted to restrict non-British immigrants.[2]

The basic documents of the new republic reflected its patterns of racial relations and racial subordination, and some of the republic's first laws were aimed at hampering groups of non-English origin. The otherwise radical Declaration of Independence, prepared mostly by Thomas Jefferson, originally contained language accusing King George of pursuing slavery, of waging "cruel war against human nature itself, violating its most sacred rights of life and liberty in the persons of a distant people who never offended him, captivating them and carrying them into slavery in another hemisphere, or to incur miserable death in the transportation thither."[3] Jefferson further noted that the English king had not attempted to prohibit the slave trade and had encouraged enslaved Africans to "rise in arms" against white colonists. But because of pressure from white slaveholding interests in the South and slave-trading interests in New England, this critique of slavery was omitted from the final version of the Declaration. Even in this revolutionary period, the doctrines of freedom and equality could not be extended to the African American population, for criticism of King George on the issue of slavery was in fact criticism of the North American social and economic system. Jefferson himself was a major slaveholder whose prosperity and wealth were closely tied to an oppressive, slaveholding agricultural system.

The U.S. Constitution explicitly recognized racial subordination in several places. First, as a result of a famous compromise between northern and southern representatives to the Constitutional Convention, Article I originally stipulated that three-fifths of a given state's enslaved population was to be counted among the total in apportioning the state's legislative representation—that is, each enslaved American was officially viewed as three-fifths of a person. Interestingly, in this case southern slave-owners pressed for full inclusion of the enslaved African Americans in the population count, while northern interests were opposed.

In addition, a section was added to Article I permitting the slave trade to continue until 1808. The Constitution also incorporated a fugitive slave provision that required the return of runaways to their owners, a provision opposed by few whites at the time.[4] Neither the statement in the Declaration of Independence that "all men are created equal" nor the Constitution's Bill of Rights was seen as applying to Americans of African descent. Slavery, ironically, would last much longer in the new "democratic" republic than in aristocratic Britain.[5]

African Americans were not the only group to suffer from government action. Numerous other non-English groups continued to find themselves less than equal under the law. Anti-immigrant legislation in the late 1700s and early 1800s included the Alien, Sedition, and Naturalization Acts.[6] Irish, German, and French immigrants were growing in number by the late eighteenth century, and concern with the liberal political sentiments of the new immigrants was great. The Naturalization Act stiffened residency requirements for citizenship from five to fourteen years; the Alien Act gave the president the power to expel foreigners. President John Adams was pressed to issue orders deporting immigrants under the Alien Act and did so in two cases. Shiploads of foreign immigrants left the country out of fear of exclusion.

Inequality in life chances and wealth along racial and ethnic lines was a fundamental fact of the new nation's institutions. At first, liberty and justice were for men of British descent only. This situation did not go unchallenged. By the late eighteenth century, many Irish and German immigrants had come into the colonies. Indeed, a significant proportion of the 4 million persons enumerated in the first U.S. census in 1790 were of non-English origins.

Over the next two centuries, English domination was modified by the ascendance of other northern Europeans, such as the Irish. These groups in turn were later challenged by southern and eastern European and non-European groups trying to move up in the social, economic, and political systems. Gradually, the new nation became an unprecedented mixing of diverse peoples.

Most in the non-British immigrant groups gradually came to adopt the English language and adjust to English institutions, seen by many as the core society and culture. All entering groups adapted, to some degree, to the dominant culture and ways. White immigrant groups eventually gained substantial power and status in the process.

In contrast to white immigrants, the voluntary and involuntary immigrants from Africa, Asia, and Latin America, as well as Native Americans, have generally remained subordinate to white Americans in political, cultural, and economic terms. Racial and ethnic inequality and oppression were and continue to be part of the foundation of U.S. society. Nonetheless, racially oppressed Americans have long challenged their subordinate status, and they continue to do so. If current demographic trends continue, Americans of color will become the majority of the U.S. population by the middle of the twenty-first century.

Today, as in the past, issues of immigration, adaptation, inequality, and oppression are at the heart of the sociological study of racial and ethnic relations in the United States. They will continue to be central issues for the foreseeable future. In the two chapters of Part I, we will define basic terms used by social scientists and examine these concepts from a critical perspective. Chapter 1 examines terms such as *race*, *racism*, *ethnic group*, and *prejudice*. Chapter 2 reviews major conceptual frameworks, including a variety of assimilation theories and power-conflict theories, for interpreting the complex structure and long-term development of racial and ethnic relations in the United States.

1 Basic Concepts in the Study of Racial and Ethnic Relations

IN THE 1980S SUSIE GUILLORY PHIPPS, THE WIFE OF A WHITE BUSINESSPERSON IN Louisiana, went to court to try to get the racial designation on her birth certificate at the Louisiana Bureau of Vital Records changed from "colored" to "white." A 1970 Louisiana "blood" law required that persons with one-thirty-second or more "Negro blood" (ancestry) were to be designated as "colored" on birth records; before 1970 "any traceable amount" of African ancestry had been used to define a person as colored. The light-skinned Phipps was the descendant of an eighteenth-century white plantation owner and an African American slave, and her small amount of African ancestry was enough to get her classified as "colored" on her official Louisiana birth certificate. Because other records supported the designation, Phipps lost her case against the state of Louisiana.[1]

This controversy raises the basic question of how a person comes to be defined as *white* or *not white* in U.S. society. It is only under racist assumptions that having one black ancestor makes one black while having one white ancestor does not make one white. If the latter were the law in Louisiana, of course, many *black* residents there—those who have at least one white ancestor (such as a white slaveholder)—would be classified as *white*! This story illustrates that racial categories are constructed and defined socially and politically, not scientifically.

A logical place to start making sense out of this system of racial definition is with basic terms and concepts. People have often used such terms as *racial groups* and *prejudice* without specifying their meaning. Since these are basic concepts in the study of intergroup relations, we will analyze them in detail.

ISSUES OF RACE AND RACISM

Racial Groups and Hierarchies

Both *racial group* and the more common term *race* have been used in a number of senses in social science and popular writings. *Human race, Jewish race, White race*—such terms in the literature suggest a range of meanings. In sixteenth- and early seventeenth-century Europe, the word *race* was used for descendants of a common ancestor, emphasizing kinship linkages rather than physical characteristics such as hair type or skin color. It was only in the late eighteenth century that the term *race* came to mean a category of human beings with distinctive physical characteristics transmitted by descent.[2]

In the 1600s François Bernier was one of the first Europeans to sort human beings into distinct categories. Soon a hierarchy of physically distinct groups (not yet termed *races*) came to be accepted, with white Europeans, not surprisingly, at the top. Africans were relegated by European observers to the bottom, in part because of (black) Africans' color and allegedly "primitive" culture, but also because Africans were often known to Europeans as slaves. Economic and political oppression resulted in a low position in the white classification system, or what can be termed "racial subordination."[3]

Immanuel Kant's use of the German phrase for "races of mankind" in the 1770s was one of the first explicit uses of the term "race" in the sense of biologically distinct categories of human beings. In 1795 Johann Blumenbach, a German anatomist, established a racial classification system that became an influential typology. At the top of his racial hierarchy were the Caucasians (Europeans), followed in order by the Mongolians (Asians), the Ethiopians (Africans), the Americans (Native Americans), and the Malays (Polynesians). Blumenbach was the first to use the term *Caucasian*; he felt that the Europeans in the Caucasus mountains of Russia were "the most beautiful race of men." Ever since, Europeans have been called by a term that originally applied only to a small and unrepresentative area of Europe. Blumenbach also chose the term Caucasian because he believed the earliest human beings came from there.[4]

The concept of race as a biologically distinctive category was developed by northern Europeans who, for much of their histories, had been largely isolated from contact with people who differed from them physically or culturally. Before the development of large sailing ships in the late 1400s, the Europeans had little contact with people from Asia, Africa, or the Americas. Soon, however, it was these northern Europeans who established slave systems in the Americas. The slave colonies were legitimated and rationalized by the northern Europeans, including the English, who classified African slaves as a lesser "race." The idea of race was not developed from scientific observations of all human beings. Rather, "race was, from its inception, a folk classification, a product of popular beliefs about human differences that evolved from the sixteenth through the nineteenth centuries."[5]

From the eighteenth century to the twentieth century, the use of *race* by most biologists, physical anthropologists, and other scientists increasingly drew on this folk classification of race in the sense of biologically distinctive groups. The scientists who used race in this sense reflected their own racial prejudices and those of the white public. "The scientists themselves undertook efforts to document the existence of the differences that the European cultural worldview demanded and had already created."[6] Basic to this increasingly prevalent view was the theory of a fixed number of biologically distinct "races" with differing physical characteristics and the belief that these characteristics were hereditary and thus created a natural hierarchy of groups. By the late nineteenth century, numerous European and U.S. scientists and popular writers were systematically downgrading all peoples not of northern European origin, especially southern Europeans and Jewish Europeans, as inferior "races."[7]

This singling out of people within the human species in terms of a biologized "race" hierarchy is a distinctively European and Euro-American idea. "Indigenous peoples ... have observed and appreciated cultural diversity as variations on cosmological themes. As a rule, the indigenous worldview encompasses all humanity."[8] In the view of M. Annette Jaimes, indigenous peoples around the globe typically emphasize building alliances across a variety of racial and ethnic groups. U.S. examples include the assistance in agricultural techniques given by Native Americans to early European settlers and later to Japanese Americans who were imprisoned during World War II (see Chapter 10) in concentration camps located near reservations in the western United States.[9]

Ideological Racism

The development of ideological racism is rooted in the European global expansion that began in earnest in the late 1400s. We can define *ideological racism* specifically as *an ideology that considers a group's unchangeable physical characteristics to be linked in a direct, causal way to psychological or intellectual characteristics and that, on this basis, distinguishes between superior and inferior racial groups.*[10] The "scientific racism" of such European writers as Count Joseph Arthur de Gobineau, a French diplomat in the mid-nineteenth century, was used to justify the spread of European colonialism in Asia, Africa, and the Americas. A long line of racist theorists followed in De Gobineau's footsteps, including the German Nazi leader Adolf Hitler. Sometimes they even applied the ideology of racial inferiority to culturally distinct white European groups, such as Jewish Europeans. In a racist ideology, real or alleged physical characteristics are linked to *cultural* traits that the dominant group considers undesirable or inferior.

Ideological racism has long been common in the United States. For example, in 1935 an influential white University of Virginia professor wrote:

> The size of the brain in the Black Race is below the medium both of the Whites and the Yellow-Browns, frequently with relatively more simple convolutions. The frontal lobes are often low and narrow. The parietal lobes voluminous, the occipital protruding. The psychic activities of the Black Race are a careless, jolly vivacity, emotions and passions of short duration, and a strong and somewhat irrational egoism. Idealism, ambition, and the co-operative faculties are weak. They love amusement and sport but have little initiative and adventurous spirit.[11]

This example of crude ideological racism links physical and personality characteristics. Although this type of racist portrait often passed for science before World War II—and in today's white supremacy organizations (for example, the Ku Klux Klan), some of it still does—it is, in fact, *pseudoscience*. Ideological racists have accepted as true the stereotyped characteristics traditionally applied by whites to various "outsider" groups.

Modern biologists and anthropologists have long demonstrated the wild-eyed irrationality of this racist mythology. The basic tenet of racist thinking is that physical differences such as skin color or nose shape are intrinsically and unalterably tied to meaningful differentials in basic intelligence or "civilization." Yet, despite periodic assertions of such a linkage by white supremacy groups and pseudoscientists, no scientific support for this assumed linkage exists.

Indeed, there is no distinctive biological reality called "race" that can be determined by objective scientific procedures. The social, medical, and physical sciences have demonstrated this fact.[12] Given the constant blending and interbreeding of human groups over many centuries and into the present, it is impossible to sort human beings into unambiguously distinctive "races" on genetic grounds. There is too much overlapping of genetic characteristics across the variety of human populations. Two randomly selected individuals from the world's population would have in common, on average, about 99.8 percent of their genetic material. Most of the genetic variation in regard to human populations "occurs *within* populations, not *between* them."[13] There are genetic differences between geographically scattered human populations, but these differences are slight. The racial importance of the slight dissimilarities is *socially*, not scientifically, determined.

Human populations singled out as "races" are simply groups with visible differences that people have decided to emphasize as important in their social, economic, and political relations. Such racial categorizing is neither objective nor scientific. Indeed, there are *many* different ways of classifying human populations in terms of genetic characteristics: "One such procedure would group Italians and Greeks with most African blacks. It would classify Xhosa—the South African 'black' group to which [South African] President Nelson Mandela belongs—with Swedes rather than Nigerians."[14] What physiologist

Jared Diamond has in mind here are the antimalarial genes that are not found among the light-skinned Swedes or dark-skinned southern African groups like the Xhosas, but are commonly found in northern African groups and among Europeans such as Italians and Greeks. These antimalarial genes may be more important for human beings than those determining skin color variations, yet they are not used by Europeans or Euro-Americans, including pseudoscientists, for their "racial" classifications.[15]

There is only one human race (Homo sapiens), to which we all belong. Every human being is in fact distantly *related* to every other human being. The indigenous view of human beings, previously noted, is now accepted by most scientists.[16] Nonetheless, the lack of scientific support has not lessened the popularity of racist ideologies in many areas. The scholar Ashley Montagu has noted the extreme danger of ideological racism, a view shaped in part by his observation of the consequences of the German Nazi ideology, according to which there were physically distinct Aryan and Jewish races.[17] That racist ideology lay behind the killing of millions of European Jews (and other Europeans) during the 1930s and 1940s.

Racial Group

Today, social scientists view "race" not as a given biological reality but as a socially constructed reality. Sociologist Oliver C. Cox, one of the first to underscore this perspective, defined a race as "any people who are distinguished, or consider themselves distinguished, in social relations with other peoples, by their physical characteristics."[18] Similarly, a *racial group* has been defined by Pierre van den Berghe as a "human group that defines itself and/or is defined by other groups as different from other groups by virtue of innate and immutable physical characteristics."[19]

A racial group is not something naturally generated as part of the self-evident order of the universe. A person's "race" is typically determined by, and important to, certain outsiders, although a group's own self-definition can also be important. In this book we define a *racial group* as a *social group that persons inside or outside the group have decided is important to single out as inferior or superior, typically on the basis of real or alleged physical characteristics subjectively selected.* Racial group distinctions are rooted in ideological racism, which, as we noted previously, links physical characteristics to "inferior" or "superior" cultural and intellectual characteristics.

In the United States, a number of groups would fit this definition. Asian Americans, African Americans, Native Americans, and Mexican Americans have had their physical characteristics, such as skin color and eye shape, singled out by dominant white Americans as badges of social and racial inferiority. Some groups once defined as racial groups—and as physically and mentally inferior groups—are no longer defined that way. In later chapters we will see that Irish and Italian immigrants were once defined as inferior "races" by native-born Anglo-Protestant Americans. Later, the social definition of these European immigrants as distinctive racial groups was replaced by a social construction of these groups as white and as *ethnic groups*, a term examined later in the text.

These examples of Irish and Italian Americans make it clear that racial definitions are not fixed essences that last forever, but instead are temporary constructions that are shaped in social and political struggles in particular times and in particular societies. Racial definitions can change and even disappear.

Why are some physical characteristics, such as skin color, selected as a basis for distinguishing racial groups, whereas other characteristics, such as eye color, seldom are? These questions cannot be answered in biological terms. They require historical and sociological analysis. Some have argued that such characteristics as skin color are "easily observed and ordered in the mind."[20] More important than ease of observation, however, is the way economic or political subordination creates a need to identify the powerless group in a certain way. In justifying exploitation, the dominant group often defines the real (or alleged) physical characteristics that are singled out to typify the exploited group as inferior racial characteristics. Technological differences in weaponry and firepower, for example, between European and African peoples facilitated the enslavement of Africans in the American colonies. In turn, the generally darker skin of the Africans and their descendants came to be used by white groups as an indicator of subordinate racial and cultural status. Skin-color characteristics have no inherent meaning; in group interaction they become important because they can be used to classify members of the dominant and subordinate groups.

In addition, knowledge of one's relatives sometimes affects one's assignment to a racial group, particularly for those who lack the emphasized physical characteristics. At various times in many societies, people have been distinguished not only on the basis of their own physical characteristics but also on the basis of a socially determined "rule of descent."[21] For example, in Nazi Germany Adolf Hitler's officials often identified Jewish Germans on the basis of their having one or more Jewish ancestors or relatives.

Ancestry and Multiracial Realities

The socially applied rules of descent have varied greatly from society to society. For example, in some countries there are special categories or designations for mixed-ancestry groups, such as the "Coloreds" for people with African and European ancestry in South Africa. Many Latin American countries recognize two or more mixed-ancestry categories. Mixed-ancestry distinctions have been rare in the United States. In the case of African Americans, interracial blending has, over time, caused dark skin color to become a less reliable characteristic for those making racial distinctions, and the rule of descent has gained more importance as a mechanism of racial identification to perpetuate discrimination. Today, black Americans "evidence an unusually wide range of physical traits. Their skin color extends from ebony to a shade paler than many 'whites.'"[22] Indeed, relatively few black Americans are literally "black." Most have a skin color that is some shade of brown.

In many U.S. communities, the social aspect of the defining process becomes obvious when a light-skinned person, say, of one-eighth African ancestry but with none of the physical traits most whites associate with African Americans, is regarded as "black" because one of his or her ancestors is known to be of African ancestry. Sometimes termed the "one drop of blood" rule, this odd rule of descent is unique to the United States. Indeed, in Caribbean nations such as Jamaica or in many parts of Africa, a person who is one-eighth African in ancestry and seven-eighths European would be considered "white."

Mixed racial ancestry does not fit neatly into the traditional U.S. system of racial categorizing. Today, there are millions of children in interracial families, and growing numbers of interracial marriages take place annually. The existence and experiences of these Americans underscore the social construction of racial identities. Consider the case of Tiger Woods, a talented golfer. In 1997, at the age of 21, Woods became the center of media attention when he won a number of major golf tournaments, including the Masters tourney, where he posted a record score.[23] Woods's ancestry is complex. He has described his ancestry as one-eighth white, one-eighth Native American, one-fourth African American, one-fourth Thai, and one-fourth Chinese. However, the mass media have usually portrayed Woods as African American. Following his major victories, his father also spoke of him as a black sports star, and Woods presented himself in some early commercials as black. Later Woods accented his mixed ancestry and seemed to some observers to play down his African American identity. After some criticism by African Americans who were proud of his achievements and his African ancestry, Woods issued a statement that he was proud of his African American *and* other ancestry.[24]

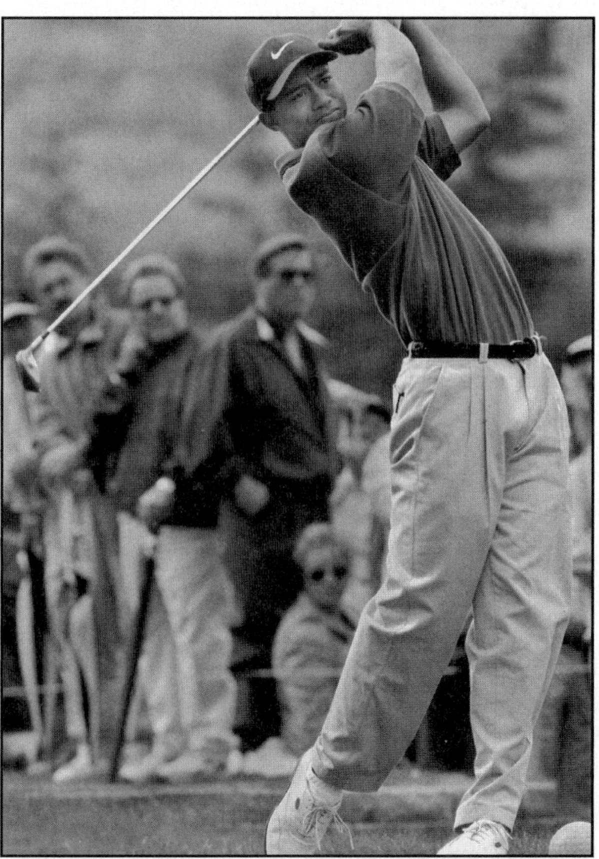

Golf star Tiger Woods hits his tee shot at a 1996 tournament.

Nonetheless, many people in the media and elsewhere have continued to view Woods as a black sports star, and it seems likely that far more Americans see him as African American than as multiracial. After Woods won the Master's tourney, a white golfer, Fuzzy Zoeller, spoke about "that little boy" and joked that he hoped Woods would not pick collard greens and fried chicken for the Master's championship dinner.[25] This white golfer clearly saw Woods as an African American. (He later met with Woods and apologized for his comments.)[26]

In the late 1990s, Congress debated the addition of a "multiracial" category in the U.S. census for the year 2000, a change supported by many Americans of mixed racial and ethnic ancestry. However, some critics suggested that the presence of such a multiracial box for people to check on the census form might reduce the count in other categories, such as "black," which would hurt civil rights enforcement in some areas. Congress decided against the creation of a specific multiracial category for the 2000 census. Instead, individuals were allowed to mark multiple ancestry groups. This political and census debate clearly indicates that racial designations are socially constructed and maintained. Interestingly, in the 2000 census 6.8 million Americans—out of a total of 281 million—indicated by checking multiple categories that they had multiracial ancestry.[27]

Of course, these 2000 census data represent only the tip of the iceberg; additional millions of Americans have multiracial backgrounds. Many Americans' ancestry is some mixture of European, African, Native American, Asian, Middle Eastern, or Latino backgrounds, and today increasing numbers of people are willing to acknowledge this reality and assert their multiracial (and multiethnic) identities. There are today numerous organizations of and periodicals for people of mixed ancestries. Indeed, attention to issues of multiethnic ancestry, interracial dating, intermarriage, and interracial families will likely escalate over the next few decades.

ETHNIC GROUPS

What Is an Ethnic Group?

The term *ethnic group* has been used by social scientists in two different senses, one narrow and one broad. Some definitions of the term are broad enough to include socially defined racial groups. For example, in Milton Gordon's broad definition, an ethnic group is a social group distinguished "by race, religion, or national origin."[28] Like the definition of racial group, this definition contains the notion of set-apartness. But here the distinctive characteristics can be physical or cultural, and language and religion are seen as critical markers or signs of ethnicity even where there is no physical distinctiveness. Today, a number of scholars, such as Werner Sollors in an introduction to *The Invention of Ethnicity*, still view religious, national-origin, and racial groups as falling under the umbrella term *ethnic group*.[29]

Other scholars prefer a narrower definition of ethnic group, one that omits groups defined substantially in terms of physical characteristics (those called racial groups) and is limited to groups distinguished primarily on the basis of cultural or national-origin characteristics. *Cultural characteristics* include language; *national origin* refers to the country (and national culture) from which the person or her or his ancestors came.

The English word *ethnic* comes from the Greek word *ethnos*, originally meaning "nation." In its earliest English usage, in the fifteenth century, the word referred to culturally different "heathen" countries, that is, those not Christian or Jewish. The first usage of "ethnic group" to denote national origin developed in the period of heavy immigration from southern and eastern European countries to the United States in the early twentieth century. Since the 1930s and 1940s, a number of prominent social scientists have suggested that the narrower definition of ethnic group, more in line with the original Greek meaning of nationality, makes the term more useful.[30]

Social scientist W. Lloyd Warner, who was perhaps the first to use the term *ethnicity*, distinguished between ethnic groups—which he saw as characterized by cultural differences—and racial groups, characterized substantially by physical differences.[31] More recent scholars have also preferred the narrower usage. In van den Berghe's view, for example, ethnic groups are "socially defined but on the basis of cultural criteria."[32]

In this book, the usual meaning of *ethnic group* will be the narrower one—*a group socially distinguished or set apart, by others or by itself, primarily on the basis of cultural or national-origin characteristics.*

Such set-apart groups, such as Irish Americans or German Americans, usually develop a sense of a common cultural heritage and ancestry. Some broad social categories, such as the religious category of "Baptists," have been considered by some to be ethnic groups, but in the sense we use the term here they are not. Religious groups that are open to relatively easy conversion are not, strictly speaking, ethnic because ethnicity says something about socially accepted lines of common descent or national origin as well as current cultural characteristics.

Many social analysts who use the broader definition of ethnic group (that is, the one that includes racial groups) argue that the historical experiences of people defined as "nonwhite" are essentially similar to the experiences of white groups. Some social scientists have argued that in the United States the situations and experiences of non-European groups such as African or Asian Americans are in broad ways similar to those of white immigrants from Europe, especially in regard to the process of gradual integration into the Anglo-Protestant core society. Some analysts further assume that the experiences of both European and non-European groups are adequately explained by the same theoretical framework—typically some type of assimilationist framework (see Chapter 2).[33]

In contrast, many analysts who prefer the narrower definition of *ethnic group* as a socially constructed category that differs in important ways from the term *racial group* view the experiences of subordinated racial groups as distinctively different from those of white European ethnic groups.[34] Moreover, the public and scholarly use of the umbrella term *ethnic group* for all groups, including racial groups, in the past two decades has had political and racial overtones: "Indeed, the substitution of 'ethnicity' for 'race' as a basis of categorization is accompanied by increasing unwillingness among the dominant group to accept responsibility for the problems of racism."[35] While this criticism is accurate for much popular and scholarly writing that views such groups as African Americans and Mexican Americans as ethnic groups that are no different in their experiences from groups like Italian Americans and Irish Americans, it does not apply to those scholars who prefer the term *ethnic group* because they feel its use indicates that all groups have genuine and significant cultural histories.[36]

In addition, many scholars emphasize the point that all socially constructed racial groups contain subgroups that can be seen as ethnic groups because they have distinctive cultural identities. Examples of this include Italian Americans within the white racial group and Jamaican Americans within the black racial group.

Definitions of *racial group* and *ethnic group* that emphasize their social meaning and construction directly reject the biological determinism that views such groups as self-evident with unchanging physical or intellectual characteristics. People themselves, both outside and inside racial and ethnic groups, determine when certain physical or cultural characteristics are important enough to single out a group for social purposes, whether for good or for ill.

A given group may be viewed by different outsiders or at different times as a racial or an ethnic group. Indeed, some groups have been defined by the same outsiders on the basis of both physical and cultural criteria. During the 1930s, Jewish Germans, for example, were identified as a "race" in Nazi Germany, in part because of physical characteristics that were alleged to be different from those of other Germans. However, the actual identification of Jewish Germans for persecution and killing by Nazi bureaucrats and soldiers was based more on ethnic characteristics—cultural characteristics such as religion or language—and genealogical ties to known Jewish ancestors than on physical characteristics.

Interestingly, in their first contacts with European societies, black Africans were viewed in ethnic rather than racial terms. St. Clair Drake's research on early black African contacts with Europeans and lighter-skinned North Africans has shown that in the first centuries of contact—during the Egyptian, Greek, and Roman periods—European outsiders generally attached far greater significance to Africans' culture and nationality than to their physical characteristics. Before the sixteenth century "neither White Racism nor *racial slavery* existed."[37] Similarly, Frank Snowden has demonstrated that the early encounters between African "blacks" and Mediterranean "whites" led to a generally favorable image of the Africans among Europeans and to friendships and intermarriage—much different from the black–white relations in modern race-conscious societies. While some Europeans in these periods did express negative views of Africans' color, these views never developed into an acute color consciousness linked to an ideological view of Africans as an inferior species with intellectual deficits. Virulent color prejudice in the form of ideological racism emerged only in the modern world, primarily in the imperial expansion into Africa and the Americas by European nations seeking colonies between the 1400s and the 1700s.[38] Historical conditions have shaped whether and how skin color becomes a marker in the processes of exploitation and oppression.

Ancestry is important to the concept of ethnic group whether it is defined in a narrow or a broad sense. Perception of a common ancestry, real or mythical, has been part of outsiders' definitions and of ethnic groups' self-definitions. Sociologist Max Weber saw ethnic groups broadly as "human groups that entertain a subjective belief in their common descent."[39] In addition to a sense of common ancestry, a consciousness of shared experiences and of shared cultural patterns is important in shaping a group's identity.

Recently, a number of social scientists have focused on the ways in which people's constructions and conceptions of their own and others' ethnic identities change over time and from one situation to another. These social constructionists emphasize the importance of studying the "ways in which ethnic boundaries, identities, and cultures are negotiated, defined, and produced through social interaction inside and outside ethnic communities."[40] Drawing on her field research, Mary Waters has shown the options white Americans have with regard to their ethnic identity. A white person of both English and Irish ancestry may choose either ethnic identity, both, or none, preferring in the latter case to identify only as "American."[41] Waters has also documented how Afro-Caribbean immigrants sometimes view themselves as African Americans and sometimes as an ethnic group distinct from native-born blacks within the African American racial group.[42] Nonetheless, Afro-Caribbean Americans generally have no choice in how they are viewed—as black Americans—by the dominant white group. This fact of American life again reveals the central role that power inequalities play in the social definition of certain human groups as racial groups.

We should note that *racial group* and *ethnic group* are only two of the terms used in research on racial and ethnic relations. Among the other terms are *majority group* and *minority group*.[43] Louis Wirth explicitly defined a minority group in terms of its subordinate position: "A group of people

The United States is a racially and ethnically diverse society.

who, because of their physical or cultural characteristics, are singled out from others in the society in which they live for differential and unequal treatment and who therefore regard themselves as objects of collective discrimination."[44]

However, many scholars today consider it more accurate to use the term *dominant group* for the majority group and the term *subordinate group* for a minority group. This usage is appropriate because a majority group in this sense can be numerically a minority, as was once the case with white Europeans in a number of colonial societies. Indeed, if current trends continue, the white majority, in population terms, is likely to become a statistical minority in the United States by the middle of the twenty-first century.

THE MATTER OF CULTURE

Cultural differences between groups are usually at the heart of racial and ethnic relations and conflict. Sociologists and anthropologists generally define *culture* as the shared values, understandings, symbols, and practices of a group of people. The shared symbols are the means by which people "communicate, perpetuate, and develop their knowledge about and attitudes toward life."[45] There are cultural objects (the symbols and practices) as well as cultural creators and cultural receivers (the people who create and use the cultural objects).[46]

In Chapter 2 we will observe the importance of culture in the process by which one group adapts to another. We will examine the concept of *dominant culture*, the understandings and symbols created and controlled by a powerful group, as well as the concept of an *immigrant culture*, the understandings and symbols of an immigrant group entering the sphere of the dominant culture. Milton Gordon, a prominent assimilation theorist, has argued that new immigrant groups coming into North America after the English have tended to give up much of their own cultural heritage to conform to the dominant Anglo-Protestant core culture: "If there is anything in American life which can be described as an overall American culture which serves as a reference point for immigrants and their children, it can best be described, it seems to us, as the middle-class cultural patterns of, largely, white Protestant, Anglo-Saxon origins, leaving aside for the moment the question of minor reciprocal influences on this culture exercised by the cultures of later entry into the United States."[47]

In subsequent chapters we will also see how some subordinated racial and ethnic groups have drawn on their well-developed cultures to resist discrimination and slavish assimilation to the dominant Anglo-Protestant culture. Some analysts describe these as *cultures of resistance*.[48]

The cultural heritage and present cultural understandings of subordinated groups, such as Native Americans or African Americans, have positive historical and current significance. They not only foster a sense of identity and pride but also facilitate the group's survival and enhance its ability to resist oppression. For example, the strong family and kinship values of various Native American societies enabled them to survive in the face of Euro-American invasions of their lands. Contrary to prevailing white stereotypes about African American families, the strong family ties of African Americans have fostered a sense of pride and identity and have provided crucial support for coping with widespread discrimination.

PREJUDICE AND STEREOTYPES

Another important term in the study of intergroup relations is *prejudice*, which in popular discourse is associated mostly with negative attitudes about members of selected racial and ethnic groups. An understanding of how and why negative attitudes develop is best achieved by first defining *ethnocentrism*, which was long ago described by William G. Sumner as the "view of things in which one's own group is the center of everything, and all others are scaled and rated with reference to it."[49] Individuals who develop *positive ethnocentrism* are characterized by a loyalty to the values, beliefs, and members of their own group. Ethnocentrism often prompts negative views of outgroups through a constant evaluation of outgroups in terms of ingroup values and ways. Such negative views are manifested in prejudices and stereotypes that influence the social, economic, and political interaction among groups.[50]

Prejudice has been defined by Gordon Allport as "thinking ill of others without sufficient warrant."[51] The term prejudice comes from the Latin word *praejudicium*, or a judgment made prior to knowledge or experience. In English the word evolved from meaning "hasty judgment" to the present connotation of unfavorable bias based on an unsupported judgment. Although prejudice can theoretically apply to favorable prejudgments, its current usage in both popular speech and social science analysis is almost exclusively negative. Defined more precisely, *prejudice* is, to closely paraphrase Allport, *an antipathy based on a faulty generalization. It may be felt or expressed. It may be directed toward a group as a whole, or toward an individual because she or he is a member of that group.*[52] As used in this text, *prejudice* has both an emotional and a cognitive aspect; it involves a negative feeling or attitude toward the outgroup as well as an inaccurate belief or image. An example might be "I as a white person hate black and Latino people because black and Latino people always smell worse than whites." The first part of the sentence expresses the negative emotion (the hatred); the last part, an inaccurate generalization. This latter cognitive aspect has been termed a *stereotype*—that is, *an overgeneralization associated with a racial or ethnic category that goes beyond existing evidence.*

Why do some people stereotype others? Why have Irish Americans been stereotyped as lazy drunkards, African Americans and Latinos as indolent, Italian Americans as criminals with "Mafia" ties, Asian Americans as "treacherous Orientals"? Such questions encourage us to examine the role that prejudices and stereotypes play in the history and daily lives of individuals and groups.

Stereotyped images take many different forms. For example, anthropologist Jane Hill has researched the widespread use of mock Spanish as part of the negative images for Latinos in the United States. Many non-Latinos, especially European Americans, sprinkle their language and commentaries with made-up mock-Spanish terms such as "no problemo," "el cheapo," and "hasty banana," and phrases like "hasta la vista, baby." These and similar mock-Spanish terms appear on billboards and in movies, in cartoons, on cards and other items in gift shops, and in elite board rooms—often in association with racial caricatures of Mexican Americans or other Latino groups. This widespread mocking of the Spanish language, Hill argues, indicates a stereotyping of Latinos, especially Mexican Americans.[53] Ridicule of Mexican American language or speech is racist because it has meaning mainly in relation to underlying racial stereotypes. Hill suggests that this mocking enables its (Anglo) perpetrators to support traditional hierarchies of racial privilege without seeming to be racist in the blatant sense.

Moreover, white attacks on variants of English spoken by many Latinos and black Americans are not just concerned with language. Instead, they show a "general unwillingness to accept the speakers of that language and social choices they have made as viable and functional.... We are ashamed of them, and because they are part of us, we are ashamed of ourselves."[54] Language mocking and language subordination are not about standards for speaking as much as they are about determining that some people are not worth listening to and treating as equals. Such mocking blends attitudes and actions; it is part of the "hundreds of taken-for-granted commonplace utterances that function to 'racialize' their targets, constructing them as members of a human group represented as essentially inferior."[55]

Sociological analysts of stereotyping tend to emphasize group pressures on individuals for conformity or rationalization, while psychological analysts tend to stress individual irrationality or personality defects. Much research has highlighted the expressive function of prejudice for the individual. Frustration–aggression theories, psychoanalytic theories, and authoritarian personality perspectives focus on the *externalization* function of prejudice—the transfer of an individual's internal psychological problem onto an external object as a solution to that problem. Psychologically oriented interpretations often attribute racial or ethnic prejudice to special emotional problems of "sick" or "abnormal" individuals, such as a deep hatred of their own fathers.[56]

In a classic study of prejudice and personality, *The Authoritarian Personality*, T. W. Adorno and his colleagues argued that people who hate such groups as Jewish Americans typically differ from tolerant people in regard to central personality traits—specifically, that they tend to exhibit "authoritarian personalities."[57] Those with authoritarian personalities differ from others in their greater submission to authority, tendency to stereotype, superstition, and great concern for social status. They often see the world as sinister and threatening, a view that easily leads to intolerance of outgroups that occupy subordinate positions in the social world around them.

Some scholars have raised questions about this stress on the expressive function of prejudice. They have suggested that social *conformity* may be a much more important factor for most prejudiced people.[58] Most people accept their own social situations as given and hold the prejudices taught at home and at school. Conformity to the prejudices of relatives and friends is a major source of individual prejudice. In this view, most prejudices are not the result of deep psychological pathologies, but rather reflect shared social definitions of outgroups. In such cases prejudice functions as a means of social adjustment. Most of us can think of situations in which we or our acquaintances have adjusted to new racial beliefs while moving from one region or setting to another. As Schermerhorn notes, "prejudice is a product of *situations*," not "a little demon that emerges in people simply because they are depraved."[59]

An additional function of prejudice is to rationalize a subordinate group's powerless position. Herbert Blumer suggested that prejudice is more than a matter of negative feelings possessed by members of one group for another; it is also "rooted in a sense of group position."[60] The dominant group comes to defend and rationalize its privileged position. Prejudice is deeply rooted in the history of human contacts, but modern prejudices can often be found grouped together in some type of ideological racism. Fully developed racist ideologies, as we have noted, appear to have arisen with European imperialism and colonization of people of color around the world. Modern prejudice, Oliver C. Cox argues, "is a divisive attitude seeking to alienate dominant group sympathy from an 'inferior' race, a whole people, for the purpose of facilitating its exploitation."[61] When peoples are subordinated, as in the cases of the white enslavement of Africans in the American colonies and the restrictive quotas for Jewish Americans in some colleges in the 1920s and 1930s, those in power—here, Anglo-Protestant whites—gradually develop views that rationalize the exploitation and oppression of others.

This tendency to develop a racial ideology that defends privilege persists. Scholars in several disciplines have suggested that many whites possess a racial consciousness that consists of not just a few prejudices but a broader structure of racialized thought, a way of processing information about themselves and people of color. A sense of superiority, overt or unconscious, grows out of a process in which whites grow up with power over and separated from racially oppressed people. Many racist ideas are formed by the informal lessons whites learn as children at home and school and as adults as they absorb messages from the media and socialize with relatives, co-workers, and friends.[62]

Some members of dominant groups who discriminate are mainly motivated by a desire for economic or political gain. Such people strive to maintain their undeserved privileges, whether or not they rationalize the striving in terms of racial prejudices and stereotypes.[63] Such striving involves a system of inequality in which the dominant group benefits economically, politically, and psychologically—and acts to maintain its benefits. In the everyday world of discrimination, it is likely that the desire to protect privileges will be accompanied by negative views of the group targeted for discrimination.

Images of people of color that are held by whites today have many similarities with stereotypes of the past, although some significant changes have occurred since the 1950s and 1960s. Researchers David Sears and John McConahay have identified what they term *symbolic* or *modern racism*—that is, white beliefs that serious anti-black discrimination does not exist today and that African Americans are making illegitimate demands for social changes. These social psychologists have found that among whites "old-fashioned racism" favoring rigid segregation and extreme stereotypes has largely been replaced by this modern racism whose proponents accept modest desegregation but resist the large-scale changes necessary for full racial integration of the society.[64] Similarly, Lawrence Bobo has suggested that whites have an "ideology of bounded racial change." That is, whites' support for changes in discrimination ends when such changes seriously endanger their standard of living. In addition, many whites display "a loosely coherent set of attitudes and beliefs that, among other things, attributes patterns of black–white inequality to the dispositional shortcomings of black Americans."[65]

Thomas Pettigrew has noted white reactions to the achievements of African Americans in recent decades and has suggested that what he calls the "ultimate attribution error" on the part of whites includes not only blaming black victims for their failures but also discounting black successes by attributing the latter to luck or unfair advantages rather than to intelligence and hard work.[66] While this research on modern racism has mostly examined white attitudes toward black Americans, some of these new concepts can be used to interpret white prejudices and stereotypes directed at other people of color.

DISCRIMINATION

Distinguishing Dimensions

Public discussions of discrimination and of government programs to eradicate it (for example, affirmative action) are often confusing because the important dimensions of racial or ethnic discrimination are not fully distinguished. As a first step in sorting out the confusion, we suggest the diagram in Figure 1.1. Key dimensions of discrimination include (a) motivation, (b) discriminatory actions, (c) effects, (d) the relation between motivation and actions, (e) the relation between actions and effects, (f) the immediate institutional context, and (g) the larger societal context.[67] A given set of discriminatory acts—such as the exclusion of Jewish American applicants from Ivy League colleges in the 1920s or the exclusion of many children of color from all-white public schools until the 1960s—can be looked at in terms of these dimensions. One can ask what the motivation was for this discrimination. Was it prejudice, stereotyping, or another motive? One can also ask what form the exclusionary practices actually took. For example, in the case of segregated public schools in the South or Southwest, white school administrators refused black or Latino children entrance into their buildings. Also of importance are the long-term effects and costs of these discriminatory practices. One effect was the poorer school facilities many black and Latino children encountered. Yet these practices were not the actions of isolated white administrators. Rather, they were part of an institutionalized pattern of segregated education, the effects of which are still present in U.S. society. Finally, such patterns of school segregation were part of a larger social context of general subordination of black and Latino Americans across various institutional areas. Today, as in the past, racial discrimination remains a multidimensional problem encompassing most institutional areas of U.S. society.

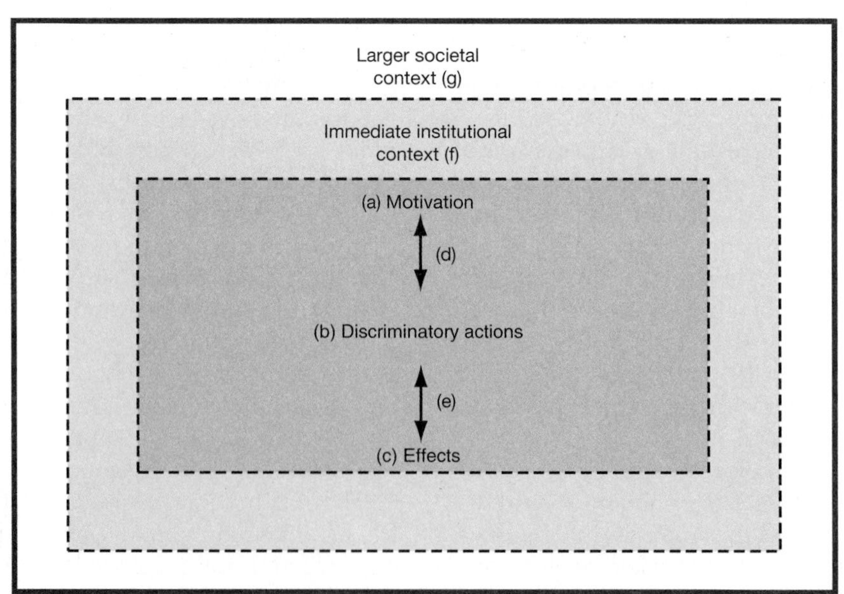

FIGURE 1.1 THE DIMENSION OF DISCRIMINATION

Source: Adapted from Joe R. Feagin, "Affirmative Action in an Era of Reaction," *Consultations on the Affirmative Action Statement of the U.S. Commission on Civil Rights* (Washington, D.C.: U.S. Government Printing Office, 1982), pp. 44–48.

Research on Prejudice and Discrimination

Much research on discrimination has focused on one type of motivation—prejudice [see (a) in Figure 1.1]. Many analysts also emphasize the relation between prejudice and discrimination [see (d) in Figure 1.1], viewing prejudice as the critical cause of discriminatory treatment of a singled-out group. Gordon Allport suggested that few prejudiced people keep their prejudices entirely to themselves; instead they act out their feelings in various ways.[68] In his classic study *An American Dilemma* (1944), Gunnar Myrdal saw racial prejudice as "the whole complex of valuations and beliefs which are behind discriminatory behavior on the part of white Americans."[69] A few years later Robert K. Merton suggested that for some people discrimination is motivated not by their own prejudices, but by fear of the prejudices of others in the dominant group.[70]

Some experimental studies by social psychologists have focused on the relationship between prejudice and expressed discrimination. These researchers have examined whether prejudiced people do, in fact, discriminate, and, if so, how that prejudice is linked to discrimination. Such studies have generally found a weak positive correlation between expressed prejudice (for example, on questionnaires) and the measured discriminatory behavior. Knowing how prejudiced a subject is does not necessarily help predict the character of his or her actions.

In addition, some experimenters have tried to develop nonobvious measures of discrimination. One such measure involved setting up an experimental situation in which whites encountered a black person (a confederate of the researcher) who needed help making a phone call at a public telephone. In this case the researcher found that the racial identity of the person needing help often affected the type of white response. Opinion surveys of white attitudes toward black Americans have shown a significant decline in certain old-fashioned racist attitudes since the 1940s. However, some experimental researchers have asked whether the whites responding to such surveys are now just concealing many of their prejudices. Reviewing laboratory studies that used less obvious measures of discrimination, such as the phone call experiment just mentioned, Faye Crosby and her associates have shown that overt discrimination by whites varies with the situation. It is more likely in anonymous situations than in face-to-face encounters that whites have with blacks they know. These researchers noted that experimental studies have found *much more* anti-black discrimination than they should have uncovered if the unprejudiced views that many whites express in surveys were their real views. Many people seem to hide their actual racial views when responding to opinion pollsters.[71]

Recently surveying college students on three major campuses, Eduardo Bonilla-Silva and Tyrone Forman discovered that racial attitudes expressed on short-answer survey items were frequently different from those expressed to questions requiring some commentary. On a brief survey item, 80 percent of the 451 students said they approved of marriages between blacks and whites. However, when a smaller but similar group of students was interviewed in depth, this figure dropped to only 30 percent. Given time to explain, the majority in the in-depth interviews expressed some reservations about marriage across the color line. This study suggests that a majority of well-educated whites still hold more or less traditionally racist attitudes on issues like interracial marriage.[72]

Defining Institutional and Individual Discrimination

The emphasis on individual prejudice and on bigoted individuals in many traditional assessments of discrimination has led some scholars to accent the institutionalization of discrimination. For example, Stokely Carmichael (Kwame Ture) and Charles Hamilton have distinguished between the concepts of *individual racism*, exemplified by the actions of white terrorists bombing a black church, and of *institutional racism*, illustrated by accumulating institutional practices that lead to large numbers of black children suffering because of seriously inadequate nutrition and medical facilities in most U.S. cities.[73] Carmichael and Hamilton introduced the concept of institutional racism to the discussion of U.S. racial relations. They moved beyond a focus on individual bigots. Institutional racism can involve actions in which dominant group members have "no intention of subordinating others because of color, or are totally unaware of doing so."[74] We should note that the term *racism* is used here for patterns of discrimination that target *racially* subordinated groups, such as African, Asian, or Latino Americans.

In his analysis of racial discrimination and mental health, Pettigrew has distinguished between *direct* and *indirect* racial discrimination, applying the latter term to restrictions in one area (such as screening out job applicants because they do not have a college degree) that are shaped by racial discrimination in another area (the historical exclusion of many black Americans from many first-rate educational facilities, including universities, prior to the 1960s).[75]

Recent conceptual work on discrimination emphasizes the close relationship between its individual ("micro") and institutional ("macro") dimensions, which must be viewed as two aspects of the same phenomenon. Social psychologist Essed has underscored the "mutual interdependence of the macro and micro dimensions" of racial discrimination. From the macro perspective, racism is "a system of structural inequalities and a historical process." From a micro perspective, racism involves individual discriminators whose specific actions are racist "only when they activate existing structural racial inequalities in the system."[76] The routine actions of discriminators reinforce, and are shaped by, a hierarchical system of racial dominance and inequality.

The group context of discriminatory actions is very important. The working definition of *discrimination* we emphasize in this book is as follows: *actions carried out by members of dominant groups, or their representatives, that have a differential and harmful impact on members of subordinate groups.* The dominant and subordinate groups we focus on here are socially constructed racial and ethnic groups. From this perspective, the most serious discrimination involves harmful practices taken by members of powerful racial and ethnic groups against those with much less power and fewer resources. Discrimination involves *actions* as well as one or more *discriminators* and one or more *victims*. A further distinction between *intentional* (motivated by prejudice or intent to harm) and *unintentional* (not motivated by prejudice or intent to harm) is useful for identifying different types of discrimination.[77]

Drawing on the two dimensions of scale and intention, we suggest four major types of discrimination. Type A, *isolate discrimination*, is harmful action taken intentionally by a member of a dominant racial or ethnic group against members of a subordinate group, without the support of other members of the dominant group in the immediate social or community context. An example would be a white Anglo police officer who implements anti-Latino hostility by beating up Mexican American prisoners at every opportunity, even though the majority of Anglo officers and department regulations specifically oppose such actions. (If the majority of Anglo officers in that department behaved in this fashion, the beatings would fall under the heading of type C discrimination.) The term *isolate* should not be taken to mean that type A discrimination is rare, for it is indeed commonplace.

Type B, *small-group discrimination*, is harmful action taken intentionally by a small number of dominant-group individuals acting in concert against members of subordinate racial and ethnic groups, without the direct support of the norms and of most other dominant group members in the immediate social or community context. The bombing of Irish Catholic churches in the 1800s by small groups of British Americans and the burning of crosses at the homes of people of color in several U.S. cities in the early 2000s by members of white supremacist groups are likely examples.

Type C, *direct institutionalized discrimination*, is organizationally prescribed or community-prescribed action that by intention has a differential and negative impact on members of subordinate racial and ethnic groups. Typically, these actions are not sporadic but are carried out routinely by a large number of dominant-group individuals guided by the legal or informal norms of the immediate organizational or community context. Historical examples include the intentional exclusion, by law, of African Americans and Jewish Americans from certain residential neighborhoods and jobs. Type C discrimination can be seen today in the actions of those white real estate agents and owners who regularly create barriers for people of color seeking homes in white neighborhoods. These discriminating whites are acting in accord with informal norms shared by many whites in their communities.[78]

Type D, *indirect institutionalized discrimination*, consists of dominant-group practices having a harmful impact on members of subordinate racial and ethnic groups even though the organizationally or community-prescribed norms or regulations guiding those actions have been established with no intent to harm. For example, intentional discrimination institutionalized in the inadequate school facilities provided for subordinate group members such as black, Latino, and Native Americans—resulting in inadequate educations for many of them—has often handicapped their attempts to compete with dominant-group members in the employment sphere, where hiring and promotion standards usually include educational credentials. In addition, the impact of *past* discrimination lingers on in the *present*: Current generations of groups once severely and openly subordinated usually have less inherited wealth and other resources than current generations in the dominant white group.

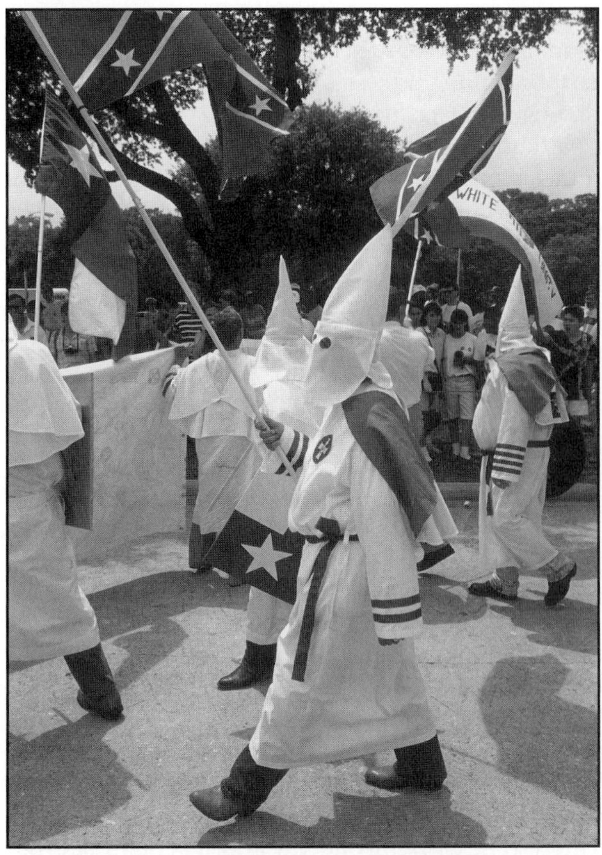

The Ku Klux Klan, created in the nineteenth century as a major terrorist group, marches at a recent rally in Houston.

The Sites and Range of Discrimination

Discrimination includes a spatial dimension. For instance, in a white-dominated society, a racially subordinated person's vulnerability to discrimination can vary from the most private to the most public sites. If the latter is in a relatively protected site, such as with friends at home, then the probability of experiencing racial hostility and discrimination from dominant-group members is low. In contrast, if that same person—for example, a professor—is in a moderately protected site, such as in a departmental setting within a predominantly white university, the probability of experiencing hostility and discrimination increases, although the professional status of the professor may offer some protection there. The probability of hostility and discrimination may increase further as this person moves from work and school settings into such public accommodations as hotels, restaurants, and stores, or into public spaces such as city streets, because the social constraints on discriminatory behavior are usually weaker there. As we will see in the chapters that follow, those members of subordinate racial and ethnic groups who have ventured the most into settings once reserved for members of dominant white groups, either in the past or in the present, are the most likely to face substantial discrimination and hostility.[79]

In his classic book *The Nature of Prejudice*, Gordon Allport notes that discrimination by members of a dominant group against those in a subordinate group ranges from antilocution (speaking against), to avoidance, to exclusion, to physical attack, and finally, to extermination.[80] For example, a dominant-group member, such as an English American, may try to exclude a Jewish American from his or her university or club. Or a non-Asian American may hurl a racist epithet at a Chinese or Korean American walking nearby.

One can also distinguish subtle and covert categories of discrimination from the more blatant forms. *Subtle discrimination* can be defined as unequal and harmful treatment of members of subordinate racial and ethnic groups that is obvious to the victim but not as overt as traditional, "door-slamming" varieties of discrimination. In modern bureaucratic settings such as corporate workplaces, many white employers and managerial employees have internalized inclinations to subtle discriminatory behavior that they consider normal and acceptable. This type of discrimination often goes unnoticed by nondiscriminating members of the dominant group.[81]

For instance, in research on African American managers who have secured entry-level positions in corporations, Ed Jones found a predisposition among whites, both coworkers and senior managers, to assume the best about persons of their own color and the worst about (black) people different from themselves in evaluating job performance. Like Pettigrew's "ultimate attribution error," this critical predisposition, which can be conscious or subconscious, can result in discrimination in promotions and other areas that is more subtle than the blatant discrimination of exclusion. The black managers interviewed by Jones and other researchers report that their achievements are often given less attention than their failures, while the failures of comparable white managers are more likely to be excused in terms of situational factors or just overlooked. This negative feedback on a black worker's performance makes it more difficult for her or him to perform successfully in the future.[82]

Covert discrimination, in contrast, is harmful treatment of members of subordinate racial and ethnic groups that is hidden and difficult to document. Covert discrimination includes acts of sabotage and tokenism. For example, in one research study, a black female mail carrier reported that white male coworkers were hiding some of her mail, so that when she returned from her route, there was still mail waiting to be delivered. Because of this sabotage, her white manager blamed her and gave her a less desirable route.[83] Asian, African, and Latino Americans are sometimes hired as "tokens" or "window dressing": They are placed in conspicuous positions just to make an organization look good instead of being evaluated honestly in terms of their abilities for higher-level employment. Some employers hire a few for "front" positions in order to reduce pressures to expand the number of employees from racially or ethnically subordinated groups to more representative proportions. Tokenism can thereby become a serious barrier to individual and group advancement.

Cumulative and Systemic Discrimination

Various combinations of blatant, covert, and subtle forms of discrimination usually coexist in a given organization or community. The patterns of discrimination cutting across political, economic, and social organizations in our society can be termed *systemic discrimination*. One National Council of Churches group portrayed systemic racial discrimination this way: "Both consciously and unconsciously, racism is enforced and maintained by the legal, cultural, religious, educational, economic, political, environmental and military institutions of societies. Racism is more than just a personal attitude; it is the institutionalized form of that attitude."[84] Central to this systemic discrimination is the *cumulative* impact of much discrimination on its targets. Particular instances of racial or ethnic discrimination may seem minor to outside observers if considered in isolation. But when blatant actions, such as verbal harassment or physical attack, combine with subtle and covert slights, such as veiled sabotage, the cumulative impact of all this discrimination over months, years, and lifetimes is usually *far* more than the sum of the individual instances. Racial and ethnic oppression is typically both systemic and cumulative, and its targets often pay a heavy cost.

Responding to Discrimination

The responses of subordinate-group members to discrimination can range from deference or withdrawal to verbal and physical confrontation to legal action. Even where dominant-group members expect acquiescence in discrimination, some subordinate-group members may not oblige. The targets of discrimination often fight back, sometimes in organized ways, as was exemplified by the civil rights movement of the 1950s and 1960s, and sometimes by individuals in everyday settings, especially if they are among those subordinate group members with some monetary or legal resources. Discrimination that begins as one-way action may become two-way negotiation, often to the surprise of the discriminators.

Consider this example from research by Joe Feagin and Melvin Sikes, in which a black woman manager in a U.S. corporation describes a meeting with her white boss about her job performance:

> We had a five scale rating, starting with outstanding, then very good, then good, then fair, and then less than satisfactory. I had gone into my evaluation interview anticipating that he would give me a "VG" (very good), feeling that I deserved an "outstanding" and prepared to fight for my outstanding rating. Knowing, you know, my past experience

> with him, and more his way toward females. But even beyond female, I happened to be the only black in my position within my branch. So the racial issue would also come into play. And he and I had had some very frank discussions about race specifically. About females, but more about race when he and I talked. So I certainly knew that he had a lot of prejudices in terms of blacks. And [he] had some very strong feelings based on his upbringing about the abilities of blacks. He said to me on numerous occasions that he considered me to be an exception, that I certainly was not what he felt the abilities of an average black person [were]. While I was of course appalled and made it perfectly clear to him.... But, when I went into the evaluation interview, he gave me glowing comments that cited numerous achievements and accomplishments for me during the year, and then concluded it with, "so I've given you a G." You know, which of course just floored me.... [I] maintained my emotions and basically just said, as unemotionally as I possibly could, that I found that unacceptable, I thought it was inconsistent with his remarks in terms of my performance, and I would not accept it. I think I kind of shocked him, because he sort of said, "well I don't know what that means," you know, when I said I wouldn't accept it. I said, I'm not signing the evaluation. And at that point, here again knowing that the best way to deal with most issues is with facts and specifics, I had already come in prepared.... I had my list of objectives for the year where I was able to show him that I had achieved every objective and I exceeded all of them. I also had ... my sales performance: the dollar amount, the products ... both in total dollar sales and also a product mix. I sold every product in the line that we offered to our customers. I had exceeded all of my sales objectives. You know, as far as I was concerned, it was outstanding performance.

Then she noted the final result:

> So he basically said, "Well, we don't have to agree to agree," and that was the end of the session. I got up and left. Fifteen minutes later he called me back in and said, "I've thought about what you said, and you're right, you do have an O." So it's interesting how in fifteen minutes I went from a G to an O. But the interesting point is had I not fought it, had I just accepted it, I would have gotten a G rating for that year, which has many implications.[85]

This example of employment discrimination is a common one and illustrates a number of points made in this chapter. Because of certain physical characteristics, this woman was viewed by her white supervisor as a member of a racial group he stereotypes as generally incapable. He discriminated against her by downplaying her accomplishments with a low evaluation. In this case she did not accept his negative rating. Because of prior experience with his negative attitudes, this woman came to the interaction with some expectation of having to counter his actions. The one-way action that was probably expected by the boss soon became two-way negotiation. This black woman made tactical use of her resources to win a concession and a changed evaluation.

Over the past two decades, there has been an increase in the number of middle-class people of color who have the resources to contest blatant discrimination more directly and, sometimes, successfully. Microlevel discrimination may be the first stage in a two-way encounter. The initial discrimination, the counter, and the discriminator's response, as well as the resources and perceptions of those involved, are important aspects of everyday racism.

Does "Reverse Discrimination" Exist?

Many neoconservative analysts, both scholars and popular commentators, have written about "reverse discrimination" and "reverse racism" in recent decades. Most of these discussions argue that white Americans suffer seriously from the implementation of affirmative action programs that attempt to redress discrimination against those in other subordinate racial groups. During the Republican administrations since the Ronald Reagan administration in the 1980s, the idea of reverse discrimination has been used to legitimate a restructuring of the U.S. Commission on Civil Rights and the U.S. Department of Justice, so that formerly pro-affirmative action agencies have been pressed to become opponents of affirmative action.

Much of the neoconservative discussion uses the phrase *reverse discrimination* in order to deflect attention from the serious problem of large-scale patterns of institutionalized discrimination still directed by whites against racially oppressed people. Discrimination, as conceptualized by most scholars of racial and ethnic relations, emphasizes the dominant group–subordinate group context of discrimination.

Racial discrimination usually refers to actions of members of dominant groups—for example, white Americans—that are taken to harm members of subordinate groups, such as blacks, Latinos, or Native Americans. Historically and today, systemic white discrimination, often called *white racism* when it targets racial groups, is not just a matter of occasional white bigotry but involves the dominant white group's power and resources to enforce white prejudices in discriminatory practices in all major social institutions.

Certainly, individual members of subordinated racial groups can be motivated by their prejudices to take action to harm those in the dominant white group. There is some anti-white prejudice among people of color. There is also some anti-white discrimination, but it is relatively uncommon compared with discrimination against people of color. With scattered exceptions, members of racially subordinate groups usually do not have the power or institutional position to express the prejudices they may hold about whites in the form of substantial everyday discrimination. As a rule, African Americans and other people of color do not have the institutional support to inflict substantial and recurring discrimination on large numbers of whites in such areas as employment, business contracts, college classrooms, department stores, and housing. Indeed, not one member of these racially subordinated groups participates in systemic, society-wide discrimination against white Americans, because the possibility does not exist in the United States. Indeed, there is no indication that any currently oppressed group would want to turn the tables and oppress white Americans on a large scale if they could do so.

Think for a moment about the historical and contemporary patterns of racial discrimination directed by large numbers of whites against just one major group, African Americans. That mistreatment has meant, and still means, widespread blatant and subtle discrimination by whites against blacks in most organizations in all major institutions in U.S. society—in housing, employment, business, education, health services, and the legal system (see Chapter 7). For nearly four centuries now, many millions of white Americans have participated directly in discrimination against many millions of African Americans. Judging from opinion polls, at least 80 million whites currently hold some negative stereotypes of African Americans and millions of these whites will discriminate under certain circumstances. In addition, most whites still observe the anti-black discrimination that takes place around them without actively working to stop it. This widespread and systemic discrimination has brought extraordinarily heavy social and economic losses (the latter estimated to be in the trillions of dollars over nearly 400 years) for African Americans in many institutional sectors of this society.[86]

What would the *reverse* of this centuries-old anti-black discrimination really look like? The reverse of the institutionalized discrimination by whites against blacks would mean reversing the power and resource inequalities for several hundred years. In the past and today, most organizations in major institutional areas such as housing, education, and employment would be run at the top and middle-levels by a disproportionate number of powerful black managers and officials. These powerful black officials would have aimed much racial discrimination at whites, including many years of slavery and legal segregation. As a result, millions of whites would have suffered—and would still suffer—hundreds of billions of dollars in economic losses and lower wages, as well as high rates of unemployment and political disenfranchisement for long periods, widespread housing segregation, inferior school facilities, and violent lynchings. That societal condition would be something one could reasonably call a condition that "reversed the discrimination" against African Americans. It does not now exist, nor has it ever existed.

What is usually termed *reverse discrimination* is something much different from this anti-white scenario. The usual reference is to affirmative action programs that, for a limited time or in certain places, have used racial screening criteria to overcome a small part of the past and present discrimination that targets racially oppressed people. Whatever costs a few years of affirmative action have meant for whites (or white men), those costs do not add up to anything close to the total cost that inverting the historical and contemporary patterns of discrimination against people of color would involve. Affirmative action plans, as currently set up—and there are far fewer effective plans than most critics suggest—do not make concrete and devastating a widespread anti-white prejudice on the part of people of color.[87] As established and implemented, affirmative action plans have mostly involved modest remedial efforts (typically designed some years back *by white men*) to bring token-to-modest numbers of people of color and white women into certain areas of our economic, social, and political institutions where these groups have historically been excluded.

A modest number of white men have indeed paid a price for some affirmative action programs. If affirmative action is successful, it will entail some cost to be paid by those who have benefited most from centuries of racial and gender discrimination. Yet, to compare the scale of white male suffering to the scale of the suffering of people of color or white women from institutionalized discrimination is quite inappropriate and very unrealistic.

A white man who suffers as an individual from remedial programs such as affirmative action in employment or education typically suffers in but one area of life (and often only once) and because he is an *exception* to his privileged racial group. A person of color who suffers from racial discrimination usually suffers *in all areas* of his or her life and primarily because the whole group has been and still is subordinated, not because he or she is an exception.[88]

SUMMARY

In this chapter we have examined the key terms *race, racial group, racism, ethnic group, minority (subordinate) group, majority (dominant) group, prejudice, stereotyping, discrimination, individual* and *institutional discrimination, subtle* and *covert discrimination, systemic* and *cumulative discrimination*, and *reverse discrimination*. These critical concepts loom large in discussions of racial and ethnic issues. More than a century of discussion of these concepts lies behind the voyage we have set out on here and in the following chapters. We must carefully think through the meaning of such terms as *race* and *racial group*, because such concepts have themselves been used in the shaping of racial relations, especially racial oppression, as they still are today.

Ideas about "race" and racial groups have been dangerous for human beings, because they have played an active role in the triggering, or the convenient rationalizing, of societal processes costing many millions of lives. Ideas can and do have an impact. The sharp cutting edge of "race," in the context of theorizing about "racial inferiority," can be seen in the enslavement by white Europeans of millions of Africans between the seventeenth and nineteenth centuries and in German Nazi actions taken against European Jews and Gypsies in the 1930s and 1940s. Sometimes it is easy to consider words and concepts as harmless abstractions. However, some reflection on both recent and distant Western history exposes the error in this naive view. The concept may not be "mightier than the sword," to adapt an old cliché, but it is indeed mighty.

2 Adaptation and Conflict

Racial and Ethnic Relations in Theoretical Perspective

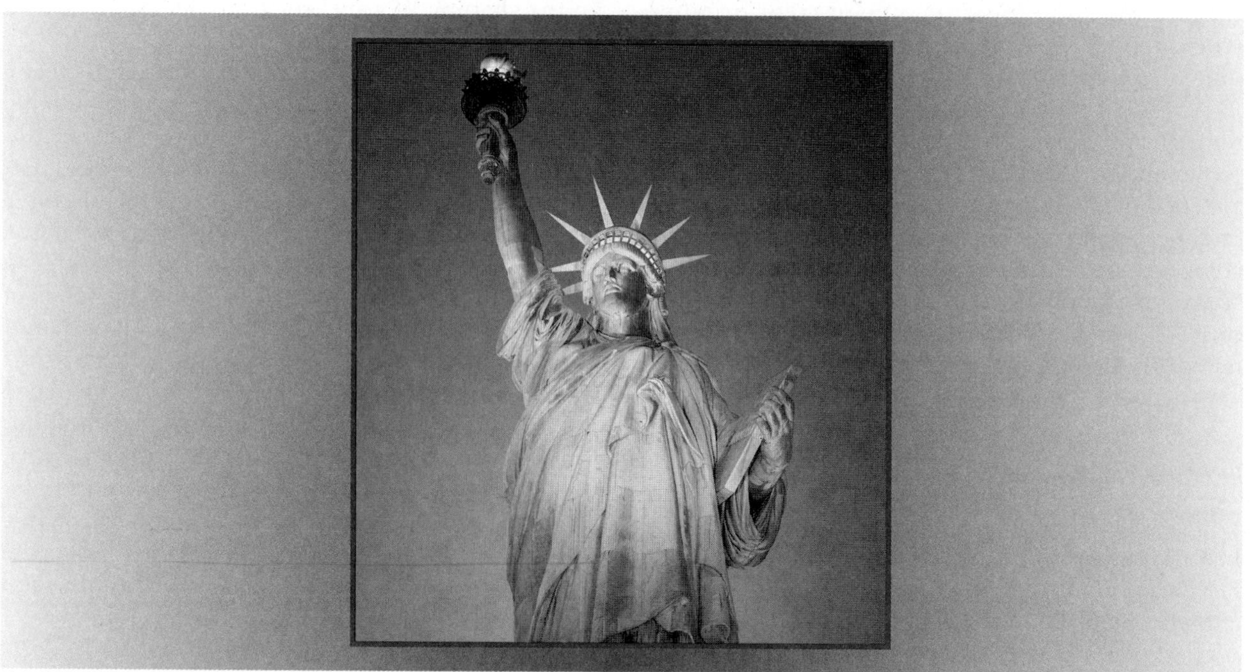

HOW DO GROUPS THAT ARE TERMED RACIAL GROUPS OR ETHNIC GROUPS DEVELOP? How do groups come into contact with one another in the first place? How do they adjust to one another beyond the initial contact? A number of social science theories analyze how intergroup contact leads to initial patterns of racial and ethnic interaction and stratification. Various other theories explore the persistence of racial and ethnic patterns. Group domination and stratification, as well as intergroup conflict, are critical issues in these racial and ethnic theories.

RACIAL AND ETHNIC HIERARCHIES

Like many other societies, U.S. society is made up of a diversity of racial and ethnic groups. As in the 1790s, so in the present the number of racial and ethnic groups in North America remains impressive, although the exact mix of groups is different. Racial and ethnic diversity is basic in the history of this society.

Yet, diversity, as the previously discussed terms *dominant group* and *subordinate group* suggest, has often been linked to a racial and ethnic *hierarchy*, to stratification, domination, and substantial inequality among groups. Human beings organize themselves for a number of different reasons—for example, for earning a living, for conducting religious rituals, and for governing. Among the important features of social organization are ranking systems. Such systems rank categories of people, not just individuals.

In this and in other societies, several social ranking systems coexist. Some systems classify people by their racial or ethnic group, while others rank people by their gender, age, disability, sexuality, or class position. Each ranking system has distinct social categories; rewards, privileges, and power vary with a group's position within the system. Some categories, such as English Americans in the U.S. racial and ethnic system, have generally had much greater power and resources than other categories, such as Native Americans, African Americans, or Latinos. Such power and resource inequality tends to persist from one generation to the next. In racial and ethnic ranking systems, certain ascribed (that is, attributed not achieved) characteristics—such as one group's racial characteristics as perceived by another group—become the criteria for unequal social positions, privileges, and rewards.[1]

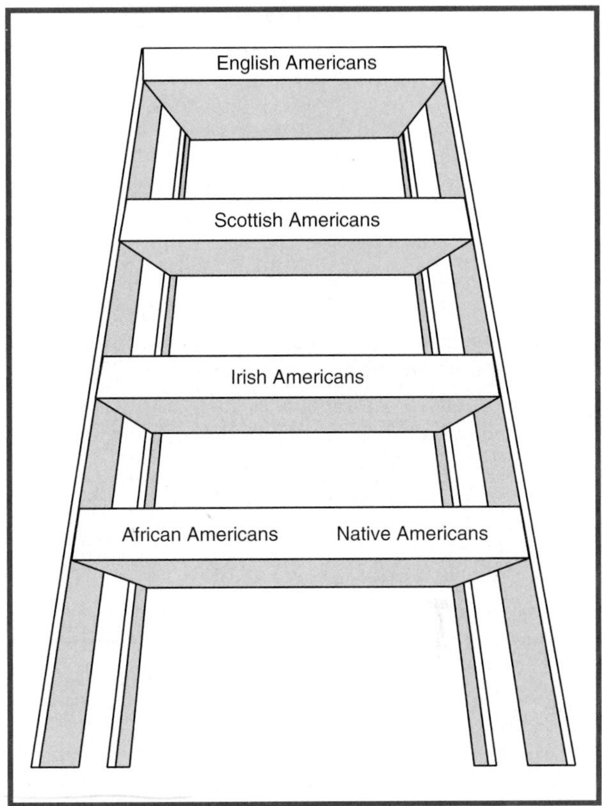

FIGURE 2.1 A LADDER OF DOMINANCE: THE UNITED STATES AS OF 1790

The image of a ladder will make the concept of racial and ethnic stratification clearer. In Figure 2.1 the positions of five selected racial and ethnic groups at a specific time in U.S. history are diagramed on a hierarchical ladder. Some groups are higher than others, suggesting that they have greater privileges—social, economic, and political—than the lower groups. A group substantially higher than another on an important dimension is viewed as a dominant group; one substantially lower than another is seen as a subordinate group. The more groups there are in a society, the more complex is the image, with middle groups possibly standing in a relation of dominance to some groups and in a relation of subordination to others.

Consider the United States in 1790, about the time of its founding. For that year one might roughly diagram the five groups in Figure 2.1 in terms of such factors as overall economic or political power, so that the top group would be English Americans, with Scottish Americans a little down the ladder. Farther down are the Irish immigrants, a group composed at the time mostly of poor farmers and indentured servants. At the bottom in terms of power and resources would be African Americans, most of whom were in slavery in the South. Those Native American ("Indian") groups and individuals within the boundaries of the new nation—most were still outside it—were also at the bottom of the racial and ethnic hierarchy in terms of economic and political power and resources. The new nation encompassed a racial and ethnic hierarchy from its beginning.[2]

Some Basic Questions

A number of social science theories have been developed to explain this diversity, domination, and stratification and the related intergroup adaptation. In some contexts *theory* means vague speculation; but in the social sciences the term refers to a conceptual framework used to interpret or explain some aspect of our everyday existence. The social theorists Ernest Barth and Donald Noel have summarized some major questions raised in the analysis of racial and ethnic relations:

1. How does one explain the origin and emergence of racial and ethnic diversity and stratification?
2. How does one explain the continuation of racial and ethnic diversity and stratification?
3. How does one interpret internal adaptive changes within systems of racial and ethnic diversity and stratification?
4. How does one explain major changes in systems of racial and ethnic diversity and stratification?[3]

MIGRATION AND GROUP CONTACT

Racial and ethnic relations and stratification systems originate with intergroup contact as different groups, often with no common ancestry, come into each other's spheres of influence. Contact can be between an established or indigenous people and a migrating people (group A → land of group B) or between migrating groups moving into a previously uninhabited area (group A → new land ← group B). The movement of the English colonists into the lands of Native Americans in the 1600s is an example of the first case.

Migration has been viewed by Charles Tilly in terms of the following:

1. The actual migrating units (e.g., individuals or families)
2. The situation at the point of origin (e.g., the home country)
3. The situation at the destination (e.g., a U.S. city)
4. The socioeconomic and political framework within which the migration occurs (e.g., modern capitalism)[4]

Certain precontact factors shape both the migration and the outcome of the contact that results from migration. *Push* factors include what is happening in the immigrants' home country—high unemployment or intergroup hostilities, for example. Depressed economies or painful religious or political conflicts in sending countries have generated major migrations to the United States. *Pull* factors also generate migration. Immigrants may be attracted by the portrayal, accurate or inaccurate, of better conditions—such as abundant jobs—at the destination. The outcome of the initial contact is influenced by the resources and characteristics of the migrating group (such as its wealth or language) and of the receiving group (such as its receptiveness to newcomers). Technological assets, such as industrial skills or firepower, have proven an advantage to certain groups. Some argue, for example, that European settlers were able to conquer Native Americans largely because of the latter's less developed weaponry.[5]

Types of Migration

In his pioneering book *Comparative Ethnic Relations*, R. A. Schermerhorn suggested four major types of migration that generate racial and ethnic relations. These can be seen as a continuum that ranges from involuntary to completely voluntary migration:

1. Movements of forced labor
2. Contract-labor movement
3. Movement of displaced persons and refugees
4. Voluntary migration[6]

Movements of *forced labor* would include the forcible removal of enslaved Africans to North America; *contract-labor* transfer includes the migration of indentured Irish servants to the English colonies and of Chinese laborers to western North America. *Political refugees* include the streams of refugees produced by war, such as Jewish immigrants from Europe in the 1930s and Vietnamese refugees in the 1970s. *Voluntary migration* covers the great migration of southern and eastern European groups to the United States in the early twentieth century and of several Asian groups in the late twentieth century.

The voluntary migration of powerful colonizers, sometimes termed *colonization migration*, often precedes the types just listed. Colonization migration can be seen in the English trading companies whose employees founded the first North American colonies, a development that led to the dispersal or brutal destruction of Native American societies already inhabiting the continent.[7] We will return to this issue of colonialism later.

Patterns of Racial and Ethnic Adaptation

The Initial Contact

What happens once different human groups come into contact as the result of migration? Outcomes vary. In the initial stage, outcomes will include the following:

1. Exclusion or genocidal destruction
2. Egalitarian symbiosis
3. An exploitive hierarchy or stratification system

Genocide is the extermination of one group by another—one outcome of contacts between European settlers and several Native American groups on the Atlantic coast of North America. *Egalitarian symbiosis* refers to peaceful coexistence and a rough economic and political equality between two groups. Occasional examples of this outcome can be found in the history of world migrations, but they are rare, especially in North America. Some authors argue that by the early nineteenth century, Scottish Americans were approaching equality with English Americans in many areas. A more common result of migration and contact is hierarchy and stratification. Stanley Lieberson has listed two hierarchies that can result from intergroup contact. *Migrant superordination* occurs when the migrating group imposes its will on indigenous groups, usually through better weapons and political or military organization. The Native American populations of the United States and Canada were subordinated in this fashion. *Indigenous superordination* occurs when groups immigrating into a new society become subordinate to groups already there, as was the case for Africans forcibly brought to North and South America by European colonists.[8]

Later Adaptation Patterns

Beyond the initial period of contact between two groups, the range of possible outcomes of intergroup contact includes the following:

1. Continuing genocide
2. Continuing egalitarian symbiosis
3. Replacement or modification of stratification by inclusion along conformity lines
4. Replacement or modification of stratification by inclusion along cultural pluralism lines
5. Continuing subordination, ranging from moderate to extreme, of a racial or ethnic group

One type of outcome can be a continuing thrust by the dominant group to exterminate the subordinate group. Attempts by European Americans to kill off Native American groups continued until the early twentieth century. Alternatively, an egalitarian symbiosis can continue beyond initial peaceful interaction. Another outcome is for an initial hierarchy, characterized by a sharp inequality of power and resources, to be modified by extensive assimilation of the incoming group into the dominant culture and society. This can take two forms. In the first, inclusion of the new group occurs by means of conformity to the dominant group's culture. By surrendering much of its cultural heritage and conforming to the dominant group, the incoming group gains increased acceptance and resource equality. Some have argued that many non-English European immigrant groups, such as Scots and Scandinavians, eventually gained rough equality with the English Americans in this way.

Another possibility is *cultural pluralism*—substantial economic and political assimilation and greater equality along with substantial persistence of subcultural (for example, religious) distinctiveness. In this outcome, substantial assimilation of the immigrant group to the host group is primarily economic and political, with cultural distinctiveness continuing in certain major respects. The interaction of certain white immigrant groups, such as Irish-Catholic Americans, with the host group English Americans offers a possible example of this outcome.

A fifth outcome of continuing intergroup contact is persisting and substantial racial or ethnic subordination and stratification. The extent and inequality of the stratification can vary, but for many non-European groups, such as Native Americans and Mexican Americans, political and economic inequality has remained so great as to constitute what some term a condition of *internal colonialism*. Even in this case, however, partial acculturation usually occurs in terms of adaptation to the dominant group's culture (for instance, to the English language).

Types of Theories

In the United States, explanatory theories of racial and ethnic relations have been concerned with migration, adaptation, exploitation, oppression, stratification, and conflict. Most such theories can be roughly classified as either order theories or power-conflict theories, depending on their principal concerns. *Order theories* tend to accent patterns of inclusion—the orderly integration and assimilation of particular racial and ethnic groups to a dominant culture and society, as in the third and fourth outcomes just described. The central focus is on progressive adaptation to the dominant culture and on stability in intergroup relations. *Power-conflict* theories give more attention to the first and fifth outcomes—genocide and continuing hierarchy—and to the persisting and substantial inequality of the power and resource distribution typically associated with racial or ethnic subordination. Most assimilation theories are social-order theories. In contrast, internal colonialism theories and class-oriented neo-Marxist viewpoints are examples of power-conflict theories. Moreover, some theorists accent elements from both theoretical traditions.

Assimilation and Other Order Perspectives

In the United States, much social theorizing has emphasized assimilation, the more or less orderly adaptation of a migrating group to the ways and institutions of an established host group. Charles Hirschman has noted that "the assimilation perspective, broadly defined, continues to be the primary theoretical framework for sociological research on racial and ethnic inequality." The reason for this dominance, he suggests, is the "lack of convincing alternatives."[9] The English word *assimilate* comes from the Latin word *assimulare*, meaning to make similar.

Robert E. Park

Robert E. Park, a major sociological analyst, argued that European out-migration was a major catalyst for societal reorganization around the globe. In his view intergroup contacts regularly go through stages of a *race relations cycle*. Fundamental social forces, such as out-migration, lead to recurring cycles in intergroup history: "The race relations cycle which takes the form, to state it abstractly, of *contacts, competition, accommodation* and *eventual assimilation*, is apparently progressive and irreversible."[10] In the contact stage, migration and exploration bring peoples together, which in turn leads to economic competition and thus to new social organization. Competition and conflict flow from the contacts between host peoples and the migrating groups. Accommodation, a critical condition in the race relations cycle, often takes place rapidly. It involves a migrating group's forced adjustment to a new social situation.

Park seems to have viewed accommodation as involving a stabilization of relations, including the possibility of permanent caste systems. Sometimes he spoke of the race relations cycle as inevitably leading from contact to assimilation. At other times, however, he recognized that the assimilation of a migrant group might involve major barriers and take a substantial period of time to complete.

Nonetheless, Park and most scholars working in this tradition have argued that there is a long-term trend toward assimilation of subordinated racial and ethnic groups in modern societies. "Assimilation is a process of interpenetration and fusion in which persons and groups acquire the memories, sentiments, and attitudes of other persons or groups, and, by sharing their experience and history, are incorporated with them in a common cultural life."[11] Even racially subordinate groups are expected to eventually assimilate into the "common culture" and institutions of the society.[12]

Stages of Assimilation: Milton Gordon

Since Park's pioneering analysis in the 1920s, many U.S. racial and ethnic relations theorists and numerous textbook writers have adopted some type of assimilationist perspective, although most have departed from Park's framework in a number of important ways. Milton Gordon, author of the influential *Assimilation in American Life*, offers a multidimensional perspective on assimilation. There is a variety of initial encounters between racial and ethnic groups and an array of possible assimilation outcomes. While Gordon presents three

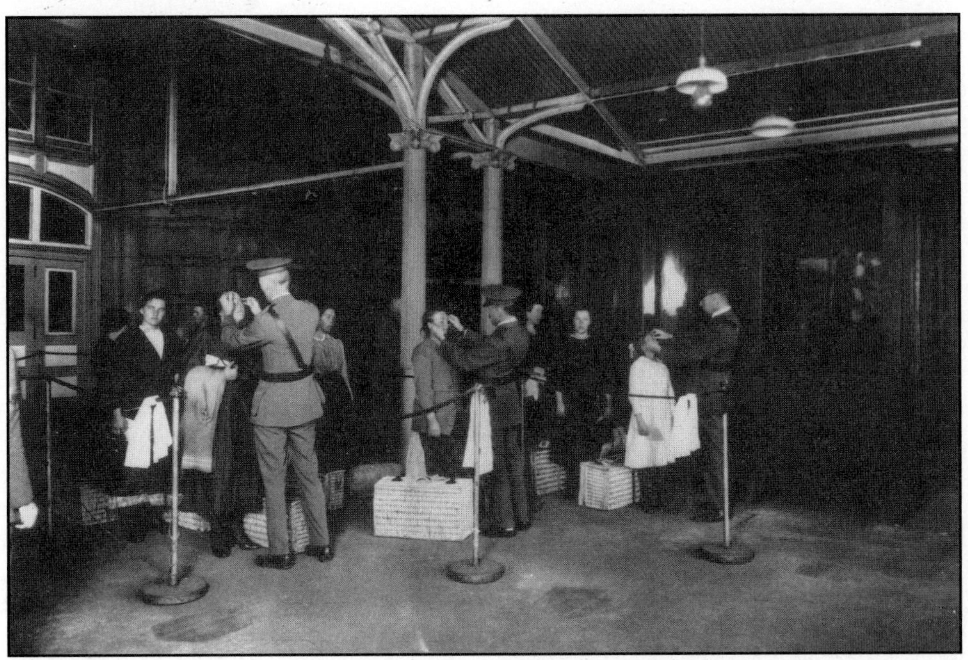

U.S. immigration officials inspect European immigrants at Ellis Island, New York (1923).

competing images of assimilation—the melting pot, cultural pluralism, and Anglo-conformity—he focuses on Anglo-conformity as having been the historical reality for the United States. In Gordon's view immigrant groups entering the United States have given up much of their cultural heritage and conformed substantially to an Anglo-Protestant core culture.[13] Cultural assimilation (also called acculturation) is a very important dimension of intergroup adaptation. Gordon's view emphasizes the way in which new groups must conform to the preexisting Anglo-Protestant culture that they face as they enter the society.

Gordon notes that Anglo-conformity has been substantially achieved for numerous immigrant groups to North America, especially in regard to cultural assimilation (acculturation). Most groups following the early English migration have adapted to the Anglo core culture. Gordon distinguishes seven dimensions of adaptation:

1. *Cultural Assimilation*: change of cultural patterns to those of the core society

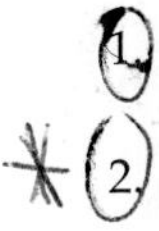

2. *Structural Assimilation*: penetration of cliques and associations of the core society at the primary-group level

3. *Marital Assimilation*: significant intermarriage
4. *Identification Assimilation*: development of a sense of identity linked to the core society
5. *Attitude-Receptional Assimilation*: absence of prejudice and stereotyping
6. *Behavior-Receptional Assimilation*: absence of intentional discrimination
7. *Civic Assimilation*: absence of value and power conflict

Whereas Park believed structural assimilation, including new primary-group ties such as intergroup friendships, flowed from cultural assimilation, Gordon stresses that these are separate stages of assimilation and may take place at different rates.

For Gordon, structural assimilation only relates to families and other primary-group relations. (Primary groups are small groups that are characterized by personal closeness, such as family groups and groups of close friends; secondary groups are specialized and impersonal groups such as corporations.) In his view, the movement of a new immigrant group into the *secondary groups* of the host society—that is, into the employing organizations, such as corporations or government bureaucracies, and educational and political institutions—is not a separate type of structural assimilation. The omission of a thorough discussion of this secondary-structural assimilation is a flaw in Gordon's typology. Looking at U.S. history, one would conclude that admission into the dominant group's secondary groups does not necessarily mean entering the dominant group's friendship cliques or families. Also missing in Gordon's analysis is attention to residential integration and assimilation—to the movement of an incoming group away from segregated immigrant communities into the residential areas of the dominant group, a pattern that has received much attention in recent demographic analyses. Moreover, the dimension Gordon calls *civic assimilation* is somewhat confusing, since he includes in it "values," which are really part of cultural assimilation, and "power," which is a central aspect of structural assimilation at the secondary-group level.[14]

Still, this assimilation theory is useful and continues to influence researchers. For example, Silvia Pedraza has made significant use of Gordon's conceptual framework in her research on Cuban and Mexican immigration, and Richard Alba has contrasted his view of the loss of strong ethnic identities among white ethnic Americans with Gordon's idea of identificational assimilation. Alba and Victor Lee have also pointed out that Gordon's concept of the core culture needs to be modified to take account of the fact that the cultures of new immigrants have sometimes had an impact on that core, particularly in areas such as family ideals and religion. The influence is not simply one way. Moreover, in an examination of Gordon's seven dimensions of assimilation, J. Allen Williams and Suzanne Ortega examined interviews with a midwestern sample and found that cultural assimilation was not necessarily the first type of assimilation to occur. For example, the Mexican Americans in the sample were less culturally assimilated than African Americans, yet more assimilated structurally. Those of Swiss and Swedish backgrounds ranked about the same on the study's measure of cultural assimilation, but the Swedish Americans were less assimilated structurally. Williams and Ortega concluded that assimilation varies considerably from one group to another and that Gordon's seven types can be grouped into three more general categories of structural, cultural, and receptional assimilation.[15]

In a 1978 book, *Human Nature, Class, and Ethnicity*, Gordon did note that his assimilation theory neglects power issues, and he mentions the different resources available to competing racial groups, but gives little attention to the impact of economic power, material resource inequalities, or capitalistic economic history on U.S. racial and ethnic relations.[16]

Focused on the millions of white European immigrants and their adjustments, Gordon's model emphasizes *generational* changes within immigrant groups over time. Substantial *acculturation* (cultural assimilation) to the Anglo-Protestant culture has often been completed by the second or third generation for European immigrant groups. The partially acculturated first generation formed protective communities and associations, but the children of those immigrants were considerably more exposed to Anglo-conformity pressures in the mass media and in schools.[17] Gordon suggests that substantial assimilation along civic, behavior-receptional, and attitude-receptional dimensions has occurred for numerous European immigrant groups. Most have also made considerable progress toward equality at the secondary-structural levels of employment and politics, although the dimensions of this assimilation are not discussed in any detail by Gordon.

For many white, particularly non-Protestant, groups, substantial structural assimilation at the primary-group level is now accomplished, yet still incomplete. Gordon suggests that substantially complete cultural assimilation (for example, adoption of the English language) along with substantial structural (primary-group) separation form a characteristic pattern of adaptation for many white ethnic groups. Still, even these relatively acculturated groups tend to concentrate their informal friendships and marriage ties either in their immediate ethnic groups or in their general socioreligious community. Following Will Herberg, who argued that there are three great community "melting pots" in the United States—Jews, Protestants, and Catholics—Gordon suggests that primary-group ties beyond one's own group are often developed within one's broad socioreligious community.[18]

Gordon recognizes that racial prejudice and discrimination have retarded structural assimilation, but he seems to suggest that non-European Americans, including African Americans, particularly those in the middle class, will eventually be fully absorbed into the dominant culture and institutions.

In regard to black Americans, he argues, optimistically, that the United States has "moved decisively down the road toward implementing the implications of the American creed [of equality and justice] for race relations"—such as in employment and housing. The tremendous progress that he perceives black Americans have made has, in his view, created a policy dilemma for the government: Should it adopt a traditional political liberalism that ignores racial groups or a "corporate liberalism" that recognizes group rights along racial lines? Gordon includes under corporate liberalism government programs of affirmative action, which he generally rejects.[19] The optimism of many assimilation analysts about the eventual implementation of the American creed of equality for African Americans and certain other non-European Americans is problematical, as we will see in Chapter 7.

Some assimilation analysts have argued that certain once-prominent ethnic identities, especially of European Americans, are fading. An advocate of the continuing usefulness of the concept of assimilation is sociologist Richard Alba. He has argued persuasively that, while ethnic identity is still of some consequence for non-Latino whites, a new ethnic group "is forming—one based on a vague *ancestry* from anywhere on the European continent." In other words, such distinct ethnic identities as English American and Irish American are gradually giving way to identification simply as "European American." Similarly, Herbert Gans has suggested that increasingly, especially for white Americans, ethnicity is only "symbolic" and weakening greatly in social significance. Symbolic ethnicity involves little more than a desire to maintain some feeling for ethnic background without strong commitments to traditional ethnic behavior or networks and social ties.[20]

Interestingly, research on intermarriages linking white ethnic groups reveals that large proportions of the children of such marriages see themselves as having multiple ethnic identities, while others choose one of their heritages, or simply "American," as their identity. Moreover, some scholars, such as Alba and Lee, have argued that in the near future skin color may not be the barrier to structural assimilation that it once was. In their view perceptions of racial difference can change over time, and it may be possible in the future that some immigrant groups composed of people of color may, like earlier white ethnic groups, be allowed to integrate fully into the core society. They see signs of this in the favorable situation of many dark-skinned Asian-Indian Americans today (see Chapter 11). However, other analysts, such as Mia Tuan, have examined the situations of third and later generation Chinese and Japanese Americans and found that, although they are substantially assimilated to the core culture, most have a strong sense of their racial and ethnic identity because whites constantly impose the identity of "Asian foreigner" on them. Many whites view them in racialized "Asian" terms—as somehow not "real Americans." From this vantage point it seems unlikely that most Asian Americans will soon be absorbed fully into white middle-class society.[21]

Ethnogenesis and Ethnic Pluralism

Some theorists working in the assimilation tradition reject the argument that most European American groups have become substantially assimilated to a generic Anglo-Protestant or Euro-American identity and way of life. A few have explored models of adjustment that depart from Anglo-conformity in the direction of ethnic or cultural pluralism. It was a Jewish American of Polish and Latvian origin who early formulated a perspective called cultural pluralism. Horace Kallen (1882–1974) argued that membership in ethnic-cultural groups was not a membership one could readily abandon. Writing in *The Nation* in 1915, he argued that ethnic groups had a right to exist on their own terms; that is, democracy applied to ethnic groups. He argued against the ruthless Americanization advocated by many white Anglo-Protestant nativists at the time. By the 1920s he had given the name *cultural pluralism* to the view that each ethnic group has the democratic right to retain its own heritage.[22] Kallen's pioneering analysis set early precedents for the perspective now called *multiculturalism* (see Chapter 13).

More recent analysts adopting a cultural pluralism perspective accept some Anglo-conformity adjustment as inevitable, if not desirable. In *Beyond the Melting Pot*, Nathan Glazer and Daniel Moynihan agree that the original customs and home-country ways of European immigrants were mostly lost by the third generation. But this did not mean the decline of ethnicity. The European immigrant groups usually remained distinct in terms of name, identity, and, for the most part, primary-group ties.[23]

Andrew Greeley has developed the interesting concept of *ethnogenesis* and applied it to white immigrant groups set off by nationality and religion. Greeley is critical of the traditional assimilation perspective because it assumes "that the strain toward homogenization in a modern industrial society is so great as to be virtually irresistible."[24] Traditionally, the direction of this assimilation is assumed to be toward the dominant Anglo-Protestant culture. But, from this ethnogenesis perspective, adaptation has meant more than one-way conformity. The traditional assimilation model does not explain the persistence of ethnicity in the United States—the emphasis among immigrants on ethnicity as a way of becoming American and, in recent decades, the self-conscious attempts to create ethnic identity and manipulate ethnic symbols.

The complex ethnogenesis model of intergroup adaptation proposed by Greeley is illustrated in Figure 2.2. Greeley suggests, as shown in the left-hand box (host/common/immigrant), that in many cases host and immigrant groups had a somewhat similar *cultural* inheritance. For example, some later European immigrant groups had a cultural background initially similar to that of earlier English settlers. As a result of the interaction of subsequent generations with each other and with descendants of earlier immigrants, in schools and through the influence of the media (symbolized by the long arrows in the center of the figure), the number of cultural traits common to the host and immigrant groups often increased. Yet, as is illustrated in the right-hand boxes, late in the adaptive process certain aspects of the heritage of the home country have remained very important to the character of the immigrant-ethnic group. From this perspective, ethnic groups share traits with the host group and retain major characteristics of their nationalities as well. A modern ethnic group is one part home-country heritage and one part common culture, mixed together in a distinctive way because of a unique history of development within the North American crucible.[25]

As we noted previously in discussing the research assessing Milton Gordon's ideas about assimilation, some researchers argue that white-ethnic cultures are blending and white-ethnic identities are fading. They, thus, do not see a persistence of strong ethnic identities like Greeley. Still, a number of research studies have documented the presence today of distinctive white ethnic groups such as Italian Americans and Jewish Americans in several U.S. cities, not only in New York and Chicago but in San Francisco,

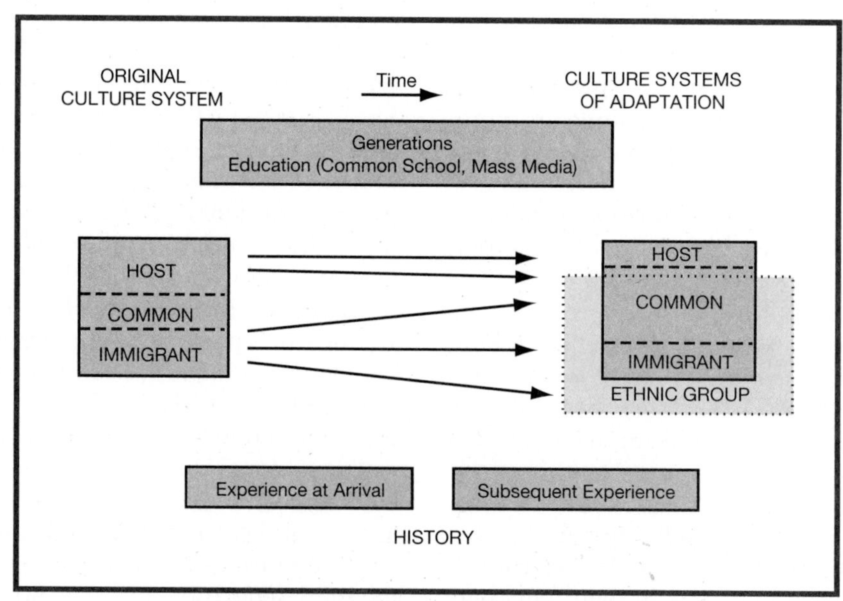

FIGURE 2.2 THE ETHNOGENESIS PERSPECTIVE

Source: Andrew M. Greeley, *Ethnicity in the United States* (New York: John Wiley, 1974), p. 309. Reprinted with permission.

New Orleans, and Tucson as well. William Yancey and his associates have suggested that ethnicity is an "emergent phenomenon"—that its importance varies in cities and that its character and strength depend on the specific historical conditions in which it emerges and grows.[26]

Some Problems with Assimilation Theories

Assimilation theorists usually take as their typical examples of adaptation the European groups migrating more or less voluntarily to the United States. But what of the adaptation and assimilation of non-European groups beyond the stage of initial contact? Some analysts of assimilation include people of color in their theories, despite the problems that arise from such an inclusion. Some have argued that traditional assimilation, cultural and structural, is the necessary, if long-term, answer to the racial problem in the United States. One prominent analyst, Gunnar Myrdal, argued some time ago that as a practical matter it is "to the advantage of American Negroes as individuals and as a group to become assimilated into American culture, to acquire the traits held in esteem by the dominant white Americans."[27] In Myrdal's view there is an ethical contradiction between the democratic principles of the Declaration of Independence and the institutionalized discrimination against black Americans. For Myrdal this represents a "lag of public morals," a problem solved in principle but still being worked out in an ongoing, one-way assimilation process that may or may not be completed.

Optimistic analysts have emphasized *progressive inclusion*, which will eventually provide black Americans and other racially subordinate groups with full citizenship in fact as well as in principle. For that reason, they expect ethnic and racial conflict to disappear as various groups become fully assimilated into the dominant culture and society. Scholars such as Nathan Glazer, Milton Gordon, and Talcott Parsons have stressed what they see as the egalitarianism of U.S. institutions and what they view as the ongoing emancipation of non-European groups. They have underscored the gradual assimilation of (middle-class) black Americans over several decades. Full membership for black Americans seems inevitable, notes Parsons, for "the only tolerable solution to the enormous [racial] tensions lies in constituting a single societal community with full membership for all."[28] The importance of racial, as well as ethnic, hierarchy and stratification is expected to decline as powerful, universalistic societal forces wipe out the vestiges of earlier ethnocentric value systems. As they see it, white immigrants have desired substantial assimilation and have been absorbed. The same is expected to happen eventually for non-European groups.

Assimilation theories have been criticized for having an "establishment" bias. A number of Asian American scholars and leaders have reacted vigorously to the application of the concept of assimilation to Asian Americans, arguing that the very concept originated in a period (1870–1925) of intense attacks by white Americans on Asian immigrants. The term was thus tainted from the beginning by its association with the notion that the only "good groups" were those that could assimilate rapidly and in Anglo-conformity fashion.

Since the 1990s several researchers have explored another assumption of traditional assimilationist thinking—the idea that new immigrants both should and do assimilate to the core culture in a linear, one-directional manner. The old view is that immigrants must gradually "become American" in order to overcome the "inferiority" of their old languages, cultures, and societies. However, this ethnocentric view ignores the fact that the assimilation process can have a significant negative impact. Some research indicates that in certain ways the physical or mental health of immigrant groups *declines* as they become better off economically and more assimilated to the core culture. Over a period of time, immigrants gradually adopt the unhealthy diet of many native-born Americans (and many become overweight) and also experience certain family and social stresses (for example, teenagers become depressed or suicidal) associated with mainstream American life. The shift from the culture of origin to the core culture is not necessarily a shift from an inferior to a superior culture, as many native-born Americans might assume.[29]

Assimilation theorists often do not analyze sufficiently the historical development of a particular racial or ethnic group within a larger national or international context. Recently, a few researchers have developed a perspective called "transnationalism." Like traditional assimilation analyses, transnationalism emphasizes the fact that individual migrants tend to migrate along family and friendship networks. But, as Steven Gold states in an analysis of Israeli immigrants to the United States, transnationalism also emphasizes the "large scale economic, political, and legal structures within which immigrants develop their communities and lives." Transnationalism also sees immigration as an "on-going process through which ideas, resources, and people change locations and develop meanings in multiple settings."[30] Immigrants often maintain their interest in the home country, and their attachments may be strong to two or more "homes" at once. Their motivation for immigration can be complex and multifaceted. They seek opportunities in a new country, but maintain strong ties to the old country. This is the case for the Israeli immigrants that Gold studied; even for most of the second generation, their self-identity is still Israeli, not American.

Biosocial Perspectives

Some U.S. theorists, including some assimilationists, now hold a biosocial perspective on racial and ethnic relations. The old European and American notion that racial and ethnic groups are deeply rooted in human beings' biological makeup has received renewed attention from a few social scientists and biologists in the United States since the 1970s. In *Human Nature, Class, and Ethnicity*, for example, Gordon suggests that ethnic ties are rooted in the "biological organism of man." Ethnicity is a fundamental part of the physiological as well as the psychological self. Ethnicity "cannot be shed by social mobility, as for instance social class background can, since society insists on its inalienable ascription from cradle to grave." Gordon seems to have in mind the rootedness of intergroup relations, including racial and ethnic relations, in the everyday realities of kinship and other socially constructed group boundaries, not the old racist notion of the unchanging biological character and separateness of racial groups. He goes further, however, emphasizing that human beings tend to be "selfish, narcissistic and perpetually poised on the edge of aggression." And it is these selfish tendencies that lie behind racial and ethnic tensions.[31] Gordon is here adopting a Hobbesian ("dog-eat-dog") view of human nature.

Critics of this biosocial view have suggested that it attributes to fundamental "human nature" what are in reality only modern capitalism's highly individualistic values. That is, under modern capitalism, selfishness and narcissism are *learned* rather than inherent in the human biological makeup. Although decidedly different from the earlier biological theories, the modern biosocial analysis remains problematical. The exact linkages between the deep genetic underpinnings of human nature and concrete racial or ethnic behavior are not spelled out beyond some vague analysis of kin selection and selfish behavior. A more convincing sociobiological analysis might attempt to show more precisely how the "desires" of the human genes are changed, through several specified levels or techniques, into social phenomena such as slavery or language assimilation. As yet, this has not been done.

Another difficulty with the biosocial approach is that in the everyday world, racial and ethnic relations are *immediately social* rather than biological. As Edna Bonacich has pointed out, many racial and ethnic groups have mixed biological ancestry. Jewish Americans, for example, have a very mixed ancestry: As a group, they share no distinctive biological characteristics. Biologically diverse Italian immigrants from different regions of Italy gained a sense of being Italian American (even Italian) in the United States. The bonds holding Jewish Americans and Italian Americans together were not genetically based or biologically primordial, but rather the result of real *historical* experiences as these social groups became firmly established in the United States. If ethnicity is primordial in a biological sense, it should always be a prominent force in human affairs. Sometimes ethnicity leads to recurring conflict, as in the case of Jews and Gentiles in the United States; in other cases, as with Scottish and English Americans, it quietly disappears in the ongoing assimilation process. Sentiments based on common ancestry are important, but they are activated primarily in the concrete experiences and histories of specific migrating and host groups.[32]

Emphasizing Migration: Competition Theory

Competition theory is a contemporary example of the exploration of migration issues in the tradition of Robert Park. Park emphasized that ethnic and racial relations stem from the migration of peoples, which in turn leads to competition for scarce resources.

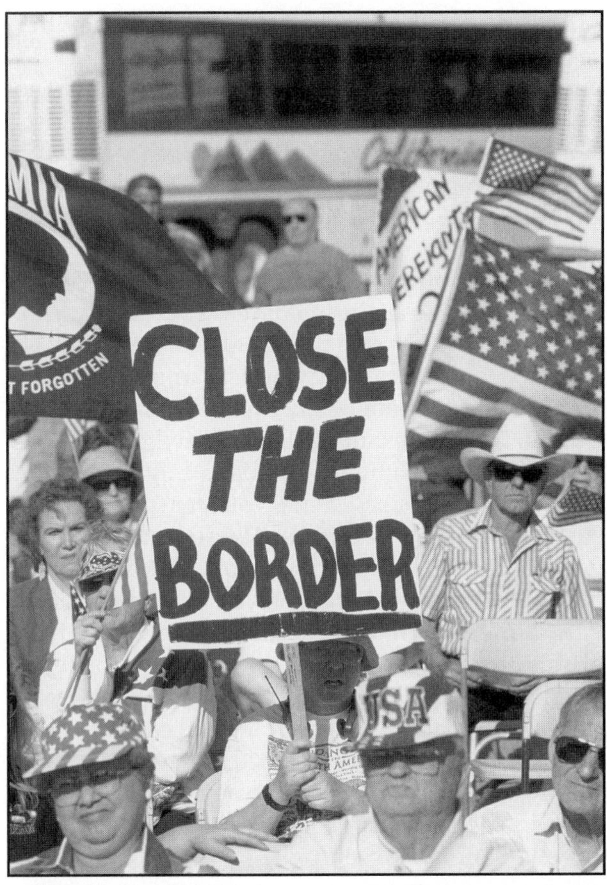

Protests against legal and undocumented immigration have increased in recent years.

Competition theorists have explored the contact and competition parts of the "race relations cycle." Unlike some order-oriented theorists, they do address questions of protest and conflict, although they do not give much attention to power, exploitation, or wealth inequality issues.[33]

Competition theorists view ethnicity broadly as a social phenomenon distinguished by boundaries of language, skin color, and culture. They emphasize the stability of ethnic population boundaries over time, as well as the impact of shifts in these boundaries resulting from migration; ethnic group membership often coincides with the creation of a distinctive group niche in the labor force. Competition occurs when two or more ethnic groups attempt to secure the same resources, such as jobs or housing.[34]

According to competition theorists, intergroup tensions and conflict are fostered by immigration across geographical borders and by the expansion of once-segregated ethnic groups into the same labor and housing markets to which other groups have access. Attacks on immigrant workers or native-born workers of color, for example, increase at the city level when a group moves out of traditionally segregated jobs and thus challenges other groups and not, as one might expect, in cities where ethnic groups are locked into segregation and poverty. Susan Olzak uses empirical data on ethnic and racial violence in the nineteenth century to show that collective action, such as Anglo-Protestant crowds attacking new European immigrants entering the United States, increases when immigration expands and economic recessions occur. The ethnic boundary of the native-born was mobilized against immigrant and black workers "when ethnic competition was activated by a rising supply of low-wage labor and tight labor markets. In this case the ethnic groups that mobilized were not fully assimilated, but had retained aspects of their traditional identity and drew on that for mobilization against other groups."[35] Olzak suggests a distinction between social situations of economic decline, which can increase interethnic competition for jobs and other economic goals, and situations of new ethnic integration, in which the social integration of once-segregated societies brings ethnic groups into new job competition and other economic competition.[36]

Competition theorists have emphasized that economic struggles often accompany political competition, which includes competition among ethnic groups for government positions and tax dollars. Joane Nagel has shown how contenders for political power often organize along ethnic lines and argues that "ethnicity is a convenient basis for political organizers due to the commonality of language and culture and the availability of ethnic organizations with ready-made leadership and membership."[37]

A power-conflict theorist might criticize the competition theorists for studying markets and interethnic competition in cities without a clear sense of the substantial racial discrimination and resource inequality that has undergirded urban job and housing markets in the United States for several centuries. Missing from competition theory is a systematic concern with the issues of inequality, power, exploitation, and institutional discrimination that are accented by power-conflict theories.

POWER-CONFLICT THEORIES

The past few decades have witnessed the development of major *power-conflict* frameworks explaining U.S. racial and ethnic relations, perspectives that place much greater emphasis on economic stratification and power issues than one finds in most assimilation and competition theories. Within this broad category of power-conflict theories are a number of subcategories, including the caste perspective, the internal colonialism viewpoint, and a variety of class-based and neo-Marxist theories.

The Caste School

One early exception to the assimilation perspective was the *caste school of racial relations*, which developed in the 1940s under W. Lloyd Warner and Allison Davis.[38] Focusing on white-on-black oppression in the South, these researchers viewed the position of African Americans as distinctively different from that of other racial and ethnic groups. After the Civil War, a new social system, a caste system, replaced the slavery system of the South. The white and black castes were separated by a total prohibition of intermarriage as well as by great economic and social inequality. Warner and his associates were critical of the emphasis in most social science analysis on prejudiced attitudes and feelings. Instead, they emphasized institutionalized discrimination as the foundation of a castelike system of U.S. apartheid.[39]

Early Class Theories of Racial Relations

W. E. B. Du Bois, one of the first sociological analysts in the United States, was a black civil rights activist who had experienced the brutality of white racism firsthand. Drawing on Marxist class analysis in many of his later writings, Du Bois was perhaps the first major theorist to emphasize that racial oppression and class oppression are inextricably tied together. In his view the interplay of racism and capitalism explained why there has never been true democracy and freedom for people in all racial groups in the United States. In a 1948 article titled "Is Man Free?," he argued that both black workers and white workers were prevented from exercising full democratic rights because of the control of a small capitalist class (for example, the owners of workplaces) over the U.S. economy and U.S. politics. He believed that a democratic society must include not only equality for Americans of color but also decision-making control of workplaces by workers. Du Bois's sociological ideas are still fresh and provocative, but to this point in time only a modest number of scholars have used them to analyze U.S. society.[40]

An early power-conflict analyst who drew on Du Bois and on class analysis was Oliver C. Cox, a scholar whose work has also been neglected, in part probably because of its Marxist approach. Cox emphasized the role of the capitalist class in racial exploitation. For example, he analyzed the economic dimensions of the forced slave migration from Africa and the oppressiveness of later conditions for enslaved African Americans. The slave trade was "a way of recruiting labor for the purpose of exploiting the great natural resources of America." The color of Africans was not important. They were chosen "simply because they were the best workers to be found for the heavy labor in the mines and plantations across the Atlantic."[41] A search for cheap labor by a profit-oriented capitalist class led to a system of racial subordination. Racial prejudice developed only later as an ideology rationalizing this economic subordination of African Americans.

Internal Colonialism and "Coloniality"

Analysts of internal colonialism view racial stratification and class stratification under U.S. capitalism as separate but related systems of oppression. In theorizing, neither should be reduced to the other. An emphasis on power and resource inequalities across racial lines is at the heart of the internal colonialism theory and its recent descendant "coloniality" theory.

Internal Colonialism The conceptual framework of internal colonialism is built in part on the work of analysts of *external colonialism*—the worldwide imperialism of certain capitalist nations, including the United States and European nations.[42] Balandier has noted that Europe's capitalistic expansion has affected non-European peoples across the globe since the fifteenth century: "Until very recently the greater part of the world's population, not belonging to the white race (if we exclude China and Japan), knew only a status of dependency on one or another of the European colonial powers."[43] External colonialism involves the running of a country's economy and politics by an outside colonial power. Many European colonies eventually became independent of their colonizers, such as Britain or France, but continued to have their economies directed by the capitalists and corporations of the former colonial powers. This system of continuing economic dependency has been called *neocolonialism*. Neocolonialism is common today where there were once few white colonists in the colonized country. In contrast, European colonies that experienced a large in-migration of white settlers show a different pattern. In such cases external colonialism becomes *internal colonialism* when the control and exploitation of non-European groups in the colonized country passes from whites in the home country to white immigrant groups within the newly independent country.[44]

Non-European groups in the United States can be viewed in terms of this internal colonialism. Internal colonialism here emerged out of classical European colonialism and imperialism and took on a life of its own. The origin and initial stabilization of internal colonialism in North America predate the Revolutionary War. The systematic subordination of non-Europeans began with "genocidal attempts by colonizing settlers to uproot native populations and force them into other regions."[45] Native Americans were killed or driven off desirable lands. Enslaved Africans were a cheap source of labor for plantation owners and other farmers before and after the American Revolution. Later, Asians and Pacific peoples were imported as contract workers or annexed in the expansionist period of U.S. development. Robert Blauner, an internal colonialism theorist, notes that agriculture in the South often depended on black labor; in the Southwest, Mexican agricultural development was forcibly taken over by European settlers after the Mexican American War in the 1840s. Later agricultural development was based substantially on low-wage immigrant labor coming into what was once northern Mexico.[46]

In exploiting the labor of non-European peoples, who were enslaved or paid low wages, white agricultural and industrial capitalists often reaped enormous profits. From the internal colonialism perspective, contemporary racial and ethnic inequality is grounded in the economic interests of whites in low-wage labor—the underpinning of capitalistic economic exploitation. Non-European groups were subordinated because of European American desires for labor and land. Internal colonialism theorists have also emphasized the central role of government support for the exploitation of groups such as Native, African, Latino, and Asian Americans.

"Coloniality": Racial Colonialism Today In the past few years, colonialism theory has been reinvigorated by research showing how the global colonialism of the past created social structures of oppression that persist into the present. Drawing on the work of Aníbal Quijano, Ramón Grosfoguel and Chloe Georas have shown that the current situation for key racial and ethnic groups in the United States is still one of "coloniality"—a situation of cultural, political, and economic oppression for subordinated racial and ethnic groups without the existence of an overt colonial administration and its trappings of legal segregation. Official decolonization does not mean an end to coloniality, for the colonial hierarchies of racial and ethnic oppression often remain. Indeed, seen from this perspective, most mainstream analyses of racial relations underestimate the major continuities between the overtly colonial past and the racial and ethnic hierarchies of the present.[47]

Grosfoguel and Georas cite the examples of Puerto Ricans and African Americans in the United States. Both were early colonial-racial subjects of a global U.S. empire, and their situations today show many aspects of that overt colonialism. Today, European Americans remain at the top of, and in control of, the racial hierarchy, and African Americans and Puerto Ricans remain as racially subordinated groups at the bottom.

A Neo-Marxist Emphasis on Class

Analysts of racial and ethnic relations have sometimes combined an internal colonialism perspective with an emphasis on class stratification that draws on the Marxist research pioneered by Du Bois and Cox. Thus, Mario Barrera suggests that the heart of internal colonialism is an interactive structure of class *and* racial stratification that divides U.S. society. Class, in the economic-exploitation sense of that term, is central in this perspective. Basic to current internal colonialism are four classes that have developed in U.S. capitalism:

1. *Capitalists*: that small group of people who control capital investments and the means of production and who buy the labor of many others
2. *Managers*: that modest-sized group of people who work as administrators for the capitalists and have been granted control over the work of others
3. *Petit Bourgeoisie*: that group of small-scale merchants who control their own businesses and do most of their work themselves, buying little labor power from others
4. *Working Class*: that very large group of blue-collar and white-collar workers who sell their labor to employers in return for wages and salaries

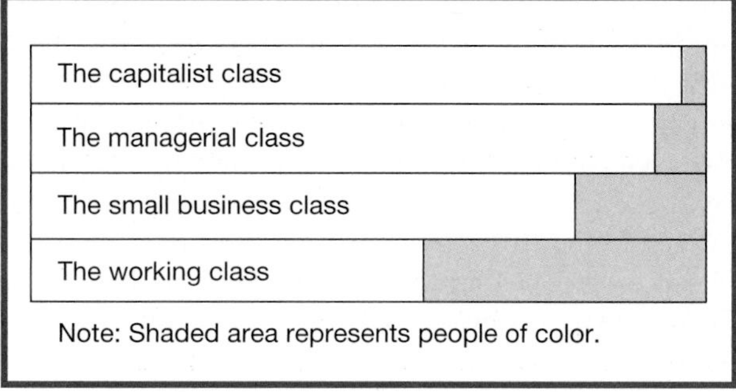

FIGURE 2.3 THE CLASS AND RACIAL STRUCTURE OF INTERNAL COLONIALISM

The dominant class in the U.S. political-economic system is the capitalist class, which in the workplace subordinates working people in all racial and ethnic groups to its profit and investment needs. It is the capitalists who decide whether and where to create jobs. They are responsible for the flight of U.S. capital and jobs from central cities to the suburbs and to other countries.

Barrera argues that each class contains segments that are set off in terms of racial group and ethnicity. Figure 2.3 suggests how this works. Each class is crosscut by a line of racial segmentation separating those who suffer from institutionalized discrimination, such as black Americans and Mexican Americans, from those who do not. Take the example of the working class. Although black, Latino, Asian, and Native American workers may share the same *class* position with white workers in that they are struggling against capitalists for better wages and working conditions, many (or most) are also in a subordinate position because of structural discrimination along racial lines within that working class. Barrera notes that the dimensions of this discrimination often include lower wages for many subordinate-group workers, as well as their concentration in lower-status occupations. These Americans suffer from both class exploitation (as wage workers) and racial exploitation (as workers of color).[48]

Cultural Resistance and Oppositional Culture

Internal colonialism theorists accent the role of the cultural stereotyping and racist ideologies of dominant groups seeking to subordinate people of color. A racist ideology dominates an internal colonialist society, intellectually dehumanizing the colonized. Stereotyping and prejudice, seen in many traditional theories as more or less temporary problems, are viewed by colonialism analysts as a way of rationalizing exploitation over a very long period. Attempts are made by the dominant group to envelop subordinate groups in dominant cultural values, traditions, and language—in the case of people of color, to "whiten" their cultures. In a system of internal colonialism, cultural as well as racial markers are used to set off subordinate groups such as Native Americans, Latinos, Asian Americans, and African Americans from the white European American group.[49]

A number of power-conflict scholars have honed the idea of *oppositional culture* as a basis for understanding the resistance of non-European groups to this dominant Euro-American culture. For example, Bonnie Mitchell and Joe Feagin argue that the oppositional cultures of Americans of color are "distinct from the dominant Euro-American culture, while also reflecting or reacting to elements of the larger society.... In the colonies and later the United States the pressures on non-Europeans for conformity to the Euro-American culture forced minority Americans to become bicultural, to know both the dominant Euro-American culture and their own oppositional culture as well."[50]

In the centuries of intergroup contact before the creation of what is now called the United States, Mexico, and Canada, the area of North America was populated by a diverse mixture of European, African, and Native American cultures. The nation of the United States created in the late 1700s encompassed African enslavement and the genocide of Native Americans. Faced with oppression, these and other victims of white colonialism have long drawn on their own cultural resources, as well as their distinctive knowledge of Euro-American culture and society, to resist oppression in every way possible. The cultures of those oppressed by European Americans have not only provided a source of individual, family, and community resistance to racial oppression and colonialism, but have also infused, often in unrecognized ways, some significant elements into the evolving cultural mix that constitutes the core culture of the United States. The cultures of racially colonized groups such as African, Latino, and Native Americans have also helped preserve key aspects of U.S. ideals, including the tradition of civil rights and social justice.[51]

Looking back over U.S. history, several researchers have researched the cultural strategies developed by subordinated groups to resist oppression. James Scott has shown that intentional deception is central to much interaction between the powerless and the powerful.[52] Enslaved African Americans were not free to speak their minds to their masters, so they spoke or sang among themselves in ways (for example, in spirituals) that disguised their criticism of racial oppression. The backstage discourse of oppressed groups includes openly expressed ideological critiques that cannot be discussed publicly. Early Afro-Christianity was an example of how enslaved African Americans resisted the "ideological hegemony" (attempts to brainwash) of white slavemasters. In public religious services, enslaved African Americans pretended to accept Christian preaching about obedience. However, when and where no whites were present, Afro-Christianity often emphasized "themes of deliverance and redemption, Moses and the Promised Land, the Egyptian captivity, and emancipation."[53] For many of these Americans, the Promised Land meant the North and freedom, and the afterlife was often viewed as a place where their white oppressors would be punished.[54] Surviving elements of African culture and religion were also major sources of the inclination to resistance and rebellion.

Anti-Colonial Nationalism

Ideological resistance takes different forms. For example, anti-colonial *nationalism* has developed as part of the cultural resistance to European colonialism and its racist ideology. Pan-Africanism and cultural nationalism are two examples of this resistance to both internal colonialism and liberal solutions for that colonialism.

From the early 1900s to the 1960s, for example, W. E. B. Du Bois was a major advocate of cultural nationalism. He saw pan-African nationalism as a partial solution for the colonized conditions in which people of African descent around the world (in the diaspora) found themselves; he argued that the pan-African movement "means to us what the Zionist movement must mean to the Jews."[55] Over objections from the U.S. State Department, Du Bois succeeded in putting together the first Pan-African Congress in 1919, which was attended by delegates from fifteen countries. The Congress did not ask for immediate decolonization of Africans and their descendants around the globe, but for more democratic treatment. The Congress called for abolition of slavery and for curtailment of colonial exploitation. The Pan-African Congress was an important step toward uniting people of African descent and was perceived as *radical* by most white European and American leaders.[56]

The 1920 Harlem Renaissance was a dramatic flowering of writing and arts focused on African American values and traditions. This form of cultural nationalism accented not so much political and economic resistance strategies but resistance in the form of an enhanced cultural identity and a strong sense of peoplehood.[57] Since at least the 1920s, a series of African American leaders and organizations, including Marcus Garvey, Malcolm X, and the Nation of Islam, have rejected assimilation and integration philosophies and accented African values, traditions, languages, and cultures.[58]

Other racially oppressed people have also drawn on cultural nationalism as a means of resisting Euro-American culture and discrimination. For example, in Chapter 8 we will examine protests by Mexican Americans in New Mexico. The Alianza Federal de Mercedes, founded in the 1960s by

Reies Lopez Tijerina, sought to recover lands in New Mexico that had been taken by Anglo-American invaders and to establish a stronger Mexican American identity with links to the Mexican heritage. A militant *Chicano* movement, which emphasized Mexican culture and national pride, also emerged among Mexican Americans in a dramatic way in the 1960s and 1970s.

Afrocentric Theories

Several social scientists have developed a comprehensive Afrocentric perspective that includes a strong critique of the cultural imperialism of Euro-Americans and the Eurocentric character of the dominant culture. In several books since 1980, sociologist Molefi Kete Asante has broken new ground in the development of this perspective, arguing for the use of the term *Afrocentricity*. Asante underscores and analyzes the fundamental Eurocentric bias in the dominant culture, particularly the elements of that culture that have been absorbed by African Americans. He is critical of the language of much ethnic analysis: "The use of the terms *ethnicity*, *disadvantaged*, *minority*, and *ghetto* are antithetical to our political consciousness which is indivisible from the international political struggle against racism. Our American situation has never been defined as 'ethnic' until now when it is beneficial for the oppressor."[59]

Similarly, anthropologist Marimba Ani writes: "European cultural imperialism is the attempt to proselytize, encourage, and project European ideology.... European nationalism implies European expansion, that, in turn, mandates European imperialism."[60] Beginning in the 1400s, this imperialism came to encompass most of the globe. This physical invasion was supported by a well-developed theory of white European supremacy, a worldview that attempted to destroy the cultures and self-conceptions of African and African American peoples.

Seen from this perspective, the Euro-American worldview includes the myth of European cultural and national superiority, a celebration of materialism over cooperative and spiritual values, and a belief in the superiority of the Judeo-Christian religious tradition over other religious traditions. Colonial invaders from Europe have sought to convert all

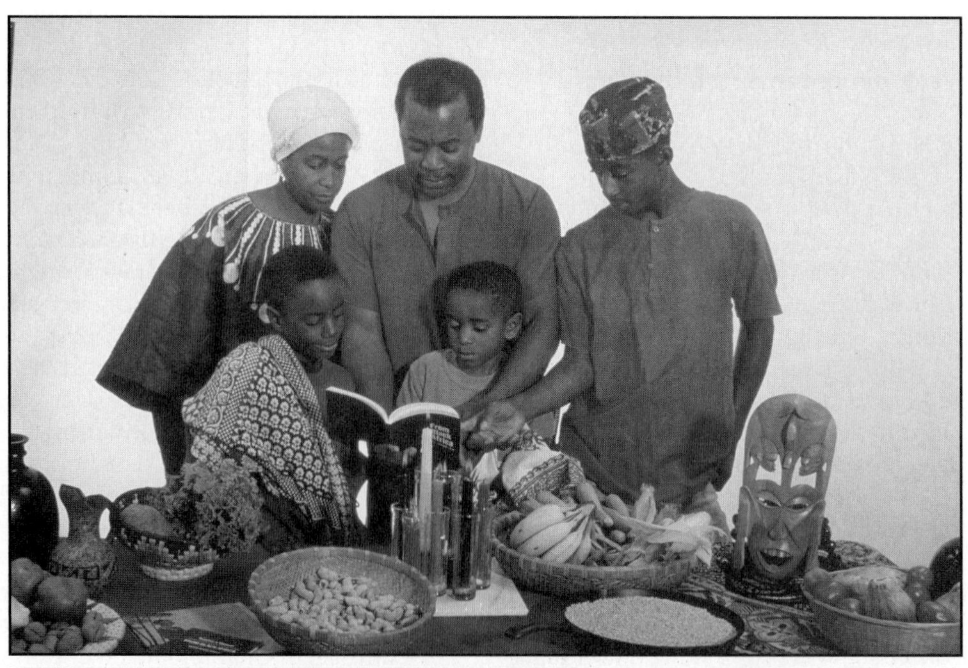

An African American family in African garb celebrates Kwanzaa.

conquered peoples to these myths and conceptions. Because of the profound effect this Euro-American view has had on the subordinated peoples, Afrocentric theorists argue that African Americans must direct their "energies toward the recreation of cultural alternatives informed by ancestral visions of a future that celebrates ... Africaness."[61] The central focus of this is to develop a cultural viewpoint that is rooted in African values and philosophies.

Criticism of Internal Colonialism Theories

A neocolonial situation is one in which a postcolonial country (for example, an African country) has separated politically from a European colonial power but continues to be economically and politically dependent on that country. The former colony uses indigenous leaders to help the former colonial power exploit the local population economically. It has a distinct territorial boundary. Joan Moore suggests that this neocolonialism model does not apply very well to subordinate racial groups in the United States because these groups are not generally confined to a specific bounded territory nor do they contain the exploitative intermediary elite of overseas neocolonialism.[62]

However, most internal colonialism researchers do recognize that the situations of groups like Mexican Americans or African Americans in the United States are different from the situations of racially subordinate groups in a newly independent (once colonized) nation overseas that is still economically dependent on a distant European country. Those internal colonialism analysts would argue that there are still many aspects of colonialism evident in racial and ethnic relations in the United States. They might emphasize that major non-European groups still (1) are residentially segregated, (2) are exploited and underpaid in their workplaces and lacking in material resources when compared with whites, (3) are culturally stigmatized, and (4) have had some leaders co-opted and used by white elites.

The Split Labor Market View

The internal-colonialism analysts are sometimes unclear about whether all classes of whites benefit from the colonization of people of color or just the dominant class of capitalist employers. A power-conflict perspective that helps in assessing this question is the *split labor market* view, which treats class in the sense of position in the "means of production." This viewpoint has been explored by sociologist Edna Bonacich. She argues that in U.S. society, dominant-group (white) workers do not share the interests of the top economic class, the capitalists. Yet both the employer class and the white part of the working class discriminate against the racially subordinated part of the working class.[63]

Developing a class analysis of racial subordination, Oliver Cox argued that the capitalist class, motivated by a desire for profit and cheap labor, sought African labor for the slave system in the United States. Ever since, this employer class has helped keep African Americans in a subordinate economic position in U.S. society. Similarly, Al Szymanski argued that since employers have not created enough jobs for all those wishing to work, black and white workers are pitted against each other for too few jobs, often to the broad advantage of employers as a class.[64]

In contrast, Bonacich emphasizes that discrimination against black workers by white workers seeking to protect their own privileges, however limited these may be, is very important. Capitalists bring in black and other racially subordinated workers to decrease labor costs, but white workers resist because they fear job displacement or lower wages. For example, over the past century white workers' unions have restricted the access of black workers to many job ladders, thus splitting the labor market and reducing black incomes. Research on unions provides historical evidence for this argument. Stanley Greenberg concludes that from the 1880s to the 1960s the industrial unions in Alabama "helped forge a labor framework" that created and perpetuated rigidly segregated white and black jobs.[65] In some areas informal segregation maintained by white workers persists to the present day. White workers gain and lose from this structural racism. They gain in the short run, because there is less competition for better-paying job categories from those who are racially excluded. But white workers lose in the long run because employers can use a cordoned-off sector of lower-wage workers of color to undercut them.[66]

In the 1930s, interestingly, W. E. B. Du Bois explained how both of these class perspectives might be brought together. Du Bois examined the "public and psychological wage" that white workers have received in the U.S. system of racial oppression.[67] Most working-class whites—those with far fewer resources than whites in the higher classes—have come to accept less in the way of economic and political resources and power because of their access to the racial privileges of whiteness. And it is the white elite that has historically convinced and pressured white workers to accept an ideology celebrating whiteness. When white working people, viewing themselves as racially superior, have refused to organize effectively with workers of color against stubborn white employers in order to secure better wages, they have usually received fewer economic resources than might have been the case had they organized with workers of color. White workers often accept this lesser economic situation because they have come to prize the privileges of whiteness.

Ordinary whites suffer in the class-stratified society that is the United States, and the dominant racial ideology—with its racist stereotypes of Americans of color—makes it harder for most of these whites to understand not only the situation of the racialized "others" but also their own oppressed economic situation. Most whites do not feel powerful or privileged, especially relative to the white elite, but they are generally unable to see the real sources of class and racial inequality in the society. Indeed, many whites target Americans of color as bearing primary responsibility for their, or the nation's, economic difficulties. Some even join white supremacist groups, which sometimes engage in terrorism against Americans of color. Whites, thus, pay some price for their racial privilege, and this privilege prevents them from realizing in U.S. society the full meaning of concepts that many of them consider important: fairness, freedom, and economic justice.

Middleman Minorities, Ethnic Enclaves, and Segmented Assimilation

Drawing on insights of earlier scholars, Edna Bonacich has also explored the in-between position, in terms of power and resources, that certain racial and ethnic groups have occupied in many stratified societies. These groups find their economic niche as small-business people positioned between other producers and consumers. Some ethnic and racial groups become small-scale traders and merchants doing jobs that dominant groups are not eager to do. For example, many first-generation Jewish and Japanese Americans, excluded from mainstream employment by white Protestants, became small-scale merchants, tailors, restaurant operators, or gardeners. These groups have held "a distinctive class position that is of special use to the ruling class." They "act as a go-between to this society's more subordinate groups."[68]

Bonacich and John Modell found that Japanese Americans fit what has been termed the "middleman minority" model. Before World War II, Japanese Americans resided in highly organized communities. Their local economies were based on self-employment, including gardening and truck farming, and on other nonindustrial family businesses. The social solidarity of the first generation of Japanese Americans helped them establish successful small businesses. However, they faced hostility from the surrounding society, and in fact were driven into the businesses they developed because they were denied other employment opportunities.[69]

Some middleman groups, such as Jewish and Korean American merchants in certain central cities today, have become targets of hostility from groups that are less well off, such as poor Latino and African Americans. In addition, strong ingroup bonds can make the middleman group an effective competitor, and even Anglo-Protestant capitalists may become hostile toward an immigrant group that competes too effectively. In some cities Jewish business people have been viewed negatively by some better-off Anglo-Protestant merchants, who have the power to discriminate against them, as well as by the poor renters and customers with whom they deal as landlords and merchants. Some scholars of racial and ethnic relations have criticized the application of "middleman minority" theory to Asian Americans, arguing that Korean Americans and Chinese Americans, although substantially involved in trade, have rarely been a *middle* group of entrepreneurs situated between a poor racial or ethnic group and a richer racial or ethnic group. More generally, this middleman perspective also does not deal adequately with the movement of large numbers of the middleman group into the dominant group, as has happened for Jewish Americans.

A somewhat similar perspective, *enclave theory*, examines secondary-structural incorporation into the economy, especially the ways in which certain non-European immigrant groups have created social and economic enclaves in cities. Both the middleman and the enclave perspectives give more emphasis to economic inequality and discrimination than assimilation perspectives. Enclave theorists stress the incorporation of certain groups, such as Asians and Cubans, into the United States through the means of small businesses and specialized "ethnic economies." The major differences between the two viewpoints seem to stem from the examples emphasized. Groups studied by enclave theorists, such as Cuban Americans, have created enclaves that are more than merchant or trading economies; they often include manufacturing enterprises, for example. These economic enclaves may compete directly with established Anglo-Protestant business elites. In contrast, the middleman groups develop trading economies and are likely to fill an economic niche that complements that of established white businesses.

Alejandro Portes and Robert Manning examined the communities of Cubans in Miami and Koreans in Los Angeles, groups that have developed many small businesses that cater to customers inside and outside their communities. Enclave economies require an immigrant group with entrepreneurial talents, business experience, capital, and a pool of low-wage labor. These characteristics enabled Cuban Americans in Miami to build a strong enclave economy. These enclaves, unlike the "colonies" of internal colonialism, typically do not relegate newcomers to a permanent position of inferiority. Enclave scholars sometimes criticize the internal colonialism and split labor market viewpoints for trying to encompass all subordinated groups, although they agree that the situations of African Americans, Mexican Americans, and Native Americans can be explained as internal colonialism. Enclave analysts have so far paid insufficient attention to the exploitation that goes on in the enclave economy, such as the exploitation of low-wage immigrant workers by the immigrant (for example, Cuban American) employers. They also tend to neglect the impact of the surrounding political and economic system—in the Cuban and Korean cases, multinational capitalism—which shapes the initial migration as well as the character of the specific enclave economies. In some ways, then, these enclave theorists straddle the fence between the order and power-conflict theories.[70]

Some immigration analysts who are concerned with structural barriers that prevent some immigrant groups from assimilating in the manner that might be predicted from a traditional assimilation perspective suggest the concept of *segmented* assimilation. Ruben Rumbaut has underscored the diversity of adaptation experiences of various immigrant groups, calling on immigration researchers to spell out what is "being 'assimilated,' by whom, under what circumstances, and in reference to what sector of American society." Reviewing the immigration literature, Alejandro Portes and Min Zhou have argued that the outcomes of adaptation by immigrants to U.S. society vary greatly, with some confined to the lower economic rungs of the societal ladder and others experiencing rapid economic development while maintaining much of their traditional culture. An example of segmented assimilation is the situation of many second-generation Mexican Americans today. Unlike the children of earlier white immigrants from Europe, who soon moved into better economic circumstances and living conditions, many second-generation Mexican Americans continue to face very difficult economic circumstances, with low-paying jobs and inadequate housing (see Chapter 8). The experiences of immigrants include both upward and downward mobility, and thus reflect a variable and segmented assimilation. The arguments about segmented assimilation parallel to some degree the ideas of the ethnogenesis theory. The main difference lies in the greater attention given by segmentation theorists to major structural barriers such as the discrimination and entrenched segregation that have faced many people of color.[71]

Women and Gendered Racism

Most theories of racial and ethnic relations have neglected gender stratification, the hierarchy in which men as a group dominate women as a group in terms of power and resources. In recent years a number of scholars have researched the situations of women within racial and ethnic groups in the United States. Their analyses assess the ways in which male supremacy, or a *patriarchal system*, interacts with and operates within a system of racial and ethnic stratification. Discussing racial and ethnic cultures around the globe, Adrienne Rich has defined a patriarchal system as "a familial-social, ideological, political system in which men—by force, direct pressure, or through ritual, tradition, law and language, customs, etiquette, education, and the division of labor—determine what part women shall or shall not play, and in which the female is everywhere subsumed under the male."[72]

Asking whether racism or patriarchy has been the primary source of oppression, social psychologist Philomena Essed examined black women in the United States and the Netherlands. She found racism and sexism interacting regularly. The social oppression of women of color is often a *gendered racism*.[73] For example, under slavery African American women were exploited not only for labor but also often as sex objects for some white men, such as slaveholders. After slavery they were excluded from most job categories available to white men and white women; major employment changes came only with the civil rights movement of the 1960s (see Chapter 7). Today, racism has many gendered forms. In the mass media, the white woman is usually the standard for female beauty. Women of color are often stereotyped as exotic sex objects, matriarchs in female-headed families, or "welfare queens." In the economy they are found disproportionately in lower-paid "female jobs," such as typists or nurse's aides. Some women of color are closely bound in their social relations with those who oppress them in such areas as domestic employment (maids) and other low-paid service work.

Sociologist Patricia Hill Collins has argued that a black-feminist theoretical framework can highlight and analyze critically the negative stereotypes of black women in white society—the historical and contemporary stereotypes of the docile mammy, the domineering matriarch, the promiscuous whore, and the irresponsible welfare mother. These severely negative images persist among many whites because they are fostered by the mass media and because they undergird white discrimination against black women in the United States.[74]

Scholars assessing the situations of other women of color, including Native Americans, Asian Americans, and Latinas, have similarly emphasized the cumulative and interactive character of racial and gender oppression and the necessity of liberating these women from white stereotypes and discrimination. For example, Denise Segura has examined labor-force data on Mexican American women and developed the concept of *triple oppression*, the mutually reinforcing and interactive set of racial, class, and gender forces the cumulative effects of which "place women of color in a subordinate social and economic position relative to men of color and the white population."[75] Indeed, an increasing number of social scientists are today calling for much more research that explores the character, interaction, and consequences of the triple oppressions of "race," class, and gender.

It is also important to note that men in certain racial or ethnic groups also face a type of gendered racism. For example, gender-specific stereotypes are often directed at certain men of color. While African American women are often stereotyped as "welfare queens," African American men are often stereotyped as oversexed criminals. Asian American women are sometimes stereotyped as exotic sex objects, while Asian American men are sometimes stereotyped as impotent or unmasculine.

The State and Racial Formation

Looking at the important role of governments in creating racial and ethnic designations and institutionalizing discrimination, Michael Omi and Howard Winant have developed an innovative theory of *racial formation*. Racial tensions and oppression, in their view, cannot be explained solely in terms of class or nationalism. Racial and ethnic relations are substantially defined by the actions of governments, which range from the passing of legislation, such as restrictive immigration laws, to the imprisonment of groups defined as a threat (for example, Japanese Americans during World War II).

The U.S. government has greatly shaped the contours and politics of racial relations: The U.S. Constitution and a lengthy series of laws openly defined racial groups and interracial relationships (for example, slavery) in racist terms. The U.S. Constitution counted each enslaved African American as three-fifths of a person, and the Naturalization Law of 1790 explicitly declared that only white immigrants could qualify for naturalization. Many non-Europeans, including Africans and Asians, were prevented from becoming citizens. Japanese and other Asian immigrants, for example, were banned by law until the 1950s from becoming citizens. In 1854 the California Supreme Court even ruled that Chinese immigrants should be classified as "Indians"(!), thereby denying them the political rights available to white Americans.[76]

For centuries, the U.S. government officially favored northern European immigrant groups over southern Europeans, such as Italians, and over people from other continents. For example, the Immigration Act of 1924 was used to exclude Asian immigrants and most immigrants from southern and eastern Europe, those whom the Anglo-Protestant political leaders in Congress saw as racially inferior and a threat to their control of the society. Northern European Americans working through the government thereby greatly shaped the subsequent racial and ethnic mix of the United States.

Toward a More Comprehensive Theory of Racial Oppression

All the authors reviewed in the last section are grappling with important dimensions of racial oppression in the United States. Drawing on these authors, particularly Du Bois, Cox, and Blauner, and on our own recent work, we here suggest a more comprehensive power-conflict theory, one we can call a *theory of racial oppression*. We accent six major themes in the development of racial oppression:

1. *Initiation of Oppression*: At an early point in time, the European colonists established hierarchical group relations with the people of color they oppressed and exploited for their land and labor. Later, descendants of these white colonists would add yet other people of color into the system of racial oppression. Typically, the subordinated groups were viewed as culturally inferior or, by the late-1700s, as biologically inferior "races."
2. *Mechanisms of Oppression*: In the past and in the present, racial hierarchies are supported by a range of dominant-group feelings and attitudes, including hostility, contempt, and fear. Although stereotypes and prejudices are important, racial hierarchies are perpetuated centrally by the discriminatory practices carried out by members of the dominant racial group (in this case, white Americans) against those in subordinate racial groups.
3. *Privileges of Oppression*: Great material and symbolic privileges come to those in the dominant racial group. Much misery and serious social and economic burdens come to those in subordinate racial groups. Critical to the maintenance of hierarchical group relations is the ongoing societal reproduction of this unjust enrichment and unjust impoverishment over many generations.
4. *Elite Maintenance of Oppression*: The actions of the white economic and political elites have created or shaped the institutions and ideologies that reflect the elites' interest in racial and class hierarchies. Most non-elite whites have more or less accepted the society's racial hierarchy, along with fewer material resources than elites, because of their access to certain privileges and advantages associated with "whiteness."
5. *Rationalization of Oppression*: Once a system of racial oppression and privilege is put in place, it is thoroughly defended and rationalized by an ideology. Since the 1700s a racist ideology accenting superior and inferior racial groups has been created and circulated by those whites in power. It has been accepted and further circulated by rank-and-file whites.
6. *Resistance to Oppression*: Opposition to oppression is a constant in North American history. Americans of color have a long history of individual and group protest against the reality and burdens of racial oppression by white Americans. Some anti-racist whites have periodically joined in this struggle against racial oppression.

To varying degrees, these dimensions are relevant to understanding the situations of most non-European Americans, including Native Americans, African Americans, Latinos, Asian Americans, and Middle Eastern Americans. While we will examine these dimensions in detail in later chapters, let us illustrate them briefly here, with particular reference to white oppression of African Americans over nearly four centuries.

W. E. B. Du Bois, in *The World and Africa* (1946), showed how the great misery and poverty then evident in Europe's African colonies were "a main cause of wealth and luxury in Europe. The results of this poverty were disease, ignorance, and crime. Yet these had to be represented as natural characteristics of backward peoples."[77] Du Bois argued that the history of African colonization has been omitted from mainstream histories of European development, wealth, and affluence. He further argued that any serious understanding of European wealth must *center* on the history of African colonialism, for the economic resources of Africans were taken to help create that wealth.

Similarly, the first step in developing a comprehensive theory of racial oppression in the United States is to put the four-centuries-long white domination of people of color at the center of the analysis. From the beginning, colonialism in North America involved racialized oppression and exploitation: The European colonists built up wealth by unjustly taking for themselves the economic and human resources of Native Americans and Africans. Today, a major educational task is to forget the falsified past often taught in U.S. school books and to learn instead about our actual past.

Together with Du Bois, Oliver Cox was one of the first to examine the colonial origins of oppression in North America. He showed how capitalism, which was involved in the movement of Europeans overseas, created a situation "favorable for the development of white race prejudice."[78] Modern racial prejudice and racial ideology developed as these colonizers moved from viewing colonized populations as "heathens" to seeing them as racially inferior. Colonialism, with its theft of land and labor, created modern racial relations. The racial oppression of recent centuries did not arise out of some "abstract, natural, immemorial feeling of mutual antipathy between groups" but rather grew out of "a practical exploitative relationship" that was combined with a rudimentary form of racial prejudice.[79]

Examining the origins of *racial hierarchies* in the colonialism and exploitation of particular historical periods, rather than in innate intergroup hostilities, is a second major theme for a comprehensive theory of oppression. "Race" is not an inborn human trait but rather a *way of relating* between individuals and groups. A comprehensive theory of oppression must begin with the real world of everyday experience and the historical relationships between groups of human beings.

This conceptual framework recognizes the centrality of the history of economic exploitation in North America, which began with the seizure of Native American lands (see Chapter 6) and the enslavement of Africans (see Chapter 7) by violent means. Land and labor obtained by theft formed the economic and social foundation of what became the United States. Most Native Americans were killed or driven out of white areas, while enslaved Africans were forced to become a central part of the economy of new white communities. This genocidal action against Native Americans and the importation, subordination, and exploitation of enslaved Africans set in place the foundation for nearly 400 years of racialized oppression in North America.

By the mid-1600s, the liberty and lives of Americans of African heritage were controlled by a system of racial oppression. For most, this took the form of legalized slavery. Transplanted and enslaved Africans became a major point of reference for the construction of the colonial economy, polity, legal system, and values, and even "white" selves. Their subjugation became the model for the treatment of other Americans of color in later periods. The white-male elite among the colonizers reinforced this economy of oppression by legalizing it in the founding laws of the new republic. The enslavement of African Americans was upheld in key provisions of the U.S. Constitution. Wealthy slaveholders such as George Washington and Thomas Jefferson led in the creation of the legal system of the new nation; Americans of color had *no* representation whatsoever in the process. From the beginning, local, state, and federal governments were used to create and enforce racial exploitation and oppression.

A third theme in this comprehensive theory is the importance of the power and privilege of whites and the related burdens of the racial "others." Oppression operates from a socially organized set of ideas and practices that deny African Americans and other people of color the privileges, power, opportunities, and rewards that society offers whites. The racial hierarchy stipulates different resources and life chances for the dominant and subordinate groups.[80] Black Americans and white Americans have different group interests because they have had unequal access to "life, liberty, and the pursuit of happiness" and to the material and other resources that shape everyday life.

For systemic racism to persist across generations, it must reproduce all the necessary socioeconomic conditions. These conditions include a greatly disproportionate control by whites of major economic resources and of the political, police, and ideological power to control subordinate racial groups. This *social reproduction process* is often hard to see because it is so much a part of everyday existence. Every new generation of whites has inherited an array of social, economic, and political privileges. Earlier structures of racial oppression were reinforced by legal segregation and legal discrimination in most areas of life. Yet, once legal slavery and segregation were eliminated, this did not eliminate the racial hierarchy with privileged whites at the top and impoverished people of color toward the bottom. Over centuries now, the majority of whites have inherited some economic resources—often in the form of a farm, some house equity, or family savings—or other valuable resources such as job training or the ability to get a good education from their white ancestors, who themselves usually benefitted significantly from legal slavery, legal segregation, or other legalized discrimination. For example, under the Homestead Act, from the 1860s to the 1930s, the federal government gave some 246 million acres of land for some 1.5 million homesteads, almost entirely for white families. Research by Trina Williams estimates that perhaps some 46 million (mostly white) people today are the descendants and heirs of those who received just this one major "welfare" benefit from the government.[81] The ancestors of contemporary African Americans were mostly excluded from this farm land, and many other economic resources, by blatant discrimination.

In addition, many whites still discriminate today against African Americans and other people of color in order to protect their interests and privileges (see Chapter 7). For example, frequent discriminatory actions by whites still restrict the access of African Americans and other Americans of color to better-paying jobs or to certain residential areas. This discrimination outweighs their commitment to the values of racial equality.[82] Today, the majority of low-wage service and unskilled menial jobs in numerous employment sectors are held by African Americans and other people of color; workers in these jobs often service better-off whites, such as employers, managers, and skilled workers. As a result, "these jobs entail a transfer of energies whereby the servers enhance the status of those served."[83]

The other side of white privilege is the set of material and psychological burdens that bear down on African Americans and other people of color. In its everyday operation the racial system often tries to dehumanize those in a subordinated group. The most precious asset of the racial "other," the control over life and liberty, is that which is most taken away. Institutionalized discrimination and inequality constitute the social structure of racial oppression, and part of its psychological dynamic is individual dehumanization. Our conceptual framework recognizes some degree of variation in these discriminatory burdens depending on the social position and gender of the oppressed individual. For example, women of color often face gendered racism—the double burden of suffering discrimination because they are not white and because they are female. Historically and in the present, institutionalized oppression has prevented most Americans of color from developing to their full potential.

A fourth aspect of our theory of oppression recognizes the differential role of different class and gender groups among white Americans. The actions of the white elite—originally centrally composed of slaveholding planters and merchants, but later of industrialists and other major entrepreneurs—are critical in the creation and maintenance of the racist system at the foundation of U.S. society. As Du Bois and Cox made clear early on, in the process of protecting its top position, this mostly white male elite has worked to create organizations, institutions, and ideologies that substantially incorporate its interests. The elite holds disproportionate power and wealth. When its interests conflict with those of other racial or class groups, the elite works hard to deflect challenges to its dominance.

Racial domination has affected a number of subordinated racial groups because early on the white elite made racial exploitation and domination a central organizing principle of intergroup life in the United States.[84] The exploitative and discriminatory treatment of racially subordinated groups has varied, but in every case it is the dominant white group—and within it the ruling elite—that has set the basic terms for this treatment and, thus, for group development.

In the economic arena, the ruling elite has been substantially interested in the exploitation of the land and labor of Americans of color, while the white working and middle classes have been more concerned about job and housing competition with Americans of color. Ordinary whites are important in enforcing discrimination in everyday life, since they constitute the majority of whites. Middle-class and working-class whites are responsible for much of the everyday discrimination against people of color, as recent studies of employment and housing discrimination show (see Chapters 7 and 8).

A fifth theme in our theory is that once racial oppression is in place, it is defended and rationalized.

The taking of the land and labor of Americans of color is rooted not only in the laws and founding documents of U.S. society but also in a strong ideology accenting the alleged cultural, intellectual, or biological inferiority of those at the bottom of the racial ladder. This ideology is structured by certain intellectuals and other elite leaders and communicated to the public in overt and subtle forms, often through schooling, churches, or the mass media.

Since the 1700s, white intellectuals and other leaders have tried to hide the actual sources of racial and class inequalities. The dominant group has regularly generated images of itself as racially superior and explained inequality in racist terms. A comprehensive theory of oppression must include this rationalization process. From the 1600s, religious, economic, political, intellectual, and media elites have perpetuated negative images of racialized outgroups in order to legitimate oppression. The often unseen power of the white elite still works through the racist beliefs and images (for example, the woman of color as a lazy "welfare queen") perpetuated in the media, schools, workplaces, and churches of the nation.

A sixth aspect of a complete theory of racial oppression emphasizes the many countering and resistance strategies developed by members of racially oppressed groups, both individually and collectively. Protest against racial oppression includes not only overt confrontation with members of the dominant group but also the development of an alternative perspective on the everyday world one must live in, a perspective generated over a long period of time by those fighting discrimination and other domination. Americans of color are theorists of their own experience, as they have frequently made clear in the long history of anti-discrimination protest and civil rights movements. Out of their everyday experiences with the white-generated system of racism, Americans of color have created countercultures of resistance that are the foundation for individual and group strategies to counter or destroy oppression.

Evidence of a counterculture of resistance, for example, can be seen in the black and Mexican American protest movements that were so powerful in the 1950s and 1960s. Organized protest against discrimination during this period included economic and bus boycotts, sit-ins, and demonstrations. African American resistance to segregation spurred the creation of civil rights organizations such as the Southern Christian Leadership Conference (SCLC). Many demonstrations included large-scale participation by Americans from all class backgrounds. This organized activism was often rooted in a strong local base of churches, clubs, and other organizations that provided money and mobilized people to enable civil rights organizations to achieve success in fighting racism and segregation.[85]

In summary, then, a racially oppressive society can best be comprehended in its totality. These six dimensions are important to a fully developed framework for understanding past and present oppression in the United States.

A Final Note: Dissecting the "Black–White Binary Paradigm"

Recently, some academic researchers and other commentators have criticized what they see as a "binary black-white paradigm," which is said to dominate too much analysis of U.S. racial and ethnic relations. For example, Angela Oh, a perceptive Asian American member of President Bill Clinton's Advisory Board on Race, called on social policy analysts to reject the black-white paradigm for a broader view. Similarly, Juan Perea has argued that the binary black-white paradigm assumes "race in America consists ... of only two constituent racial groups, the Black and the White."[86] These analysts feel that government, social science, and the media give (1) far too much attention to black and white issues and (2) far too little attention to the situations of other groups such as Asian Americans, Latinos, and Middle Eastern Americans. As we will see in later chapters, the view that non-black non-European groups lack adequate attention and research has substantial merit, although the oppressive racial situation faced by African Americans also receives too little research attention. However, many of these commentators suggest or imply, incorrectly, that the various U.S. racial and ethnic groups have played similar or equivalent roles in the development of the basic foundation of racial and ethnic relations in the United States.

In contrast, advocates of a more critical power-conflict perspective on racial oppression, such as Lewis Gordon and Joe Feagin,[87] argue that a thorough understanding of the current and historical situations of all non-European groups requires a recognition that the economic and social foundation of the colonies, and later the United States, was created with the enslavement of Africans and the destruction of many Native American societies. As we have seen previously, once the white-on-black oppression became an institutionalized foundation of the new society, it was rationalized in a thoroughgoing racist ideology that has endured to the present day.

From this power-conflict perspective, U.S. society is not an array of disconnected racisms affecting peoples of color, but instead this society has a central racialized core that asserts and maintains substantial white (European American) superiority over all groups of color—a core of racial domination that whites first developed for African Americans (and, to some extent, Native Americans) within the new society and then extended to other non-European groups. Since the mid-nineteenth century, other groups of non-European workers—for example, Japanese, Chinese, Filipino, Puerto Rican, and Mexican Americans—have been brought into the racialized system to be exploited as low-wage labor. The more powerful white group exploited, evaluated, and imaged later non-European immigrants and their descendants within the preexisting framework of white-on-black oppression.

The dominant white group has typically placed new non-European groups somewhere on a white-to-black continuum of status and privilege—with white as the highly favored end. For nearly four centuries white minds and practices have constructed and maintained this continuum of racial privilege. As we will see later, at some points in U.S. history, white Americans have come to view certain groups among Americans of color as more socially acceptable than African Americans or than the darker-skinned, or less acculturated, members of those same groups. For example, whites have come to grant some Asian and Latino Americans an intermediate status between the white and black ends on the socioracial ladder and continuum. The "model minority" stereotype that white commentators have applied to some Asian American groups (see Chapters 10 and 11) provides evidence of this strategy. Asian Americans themselves did not create this "model minority" perspective; elite white commentators did. Indeed, at earlier points in U.S. history, Asian immigrants' character, values, and social position were very negatively stereotyped by whites—even as "black" or "near-black." In recent years, powerful whites have constructed certain groups within the Asian American category, such as middle-class Japanese Americans, as "model minorities" and as "nearer-to-white" on the status continuum. They then criticize African Americans or Mexican Americans for not possessing the work ethic, and for not achieving the economic successes, of such "model minorities." As Gary Okihiro has expressed it, historically whites have "upheld Asians as 'near-whites' or 'whiter than whites' in the model minority stereotype, and yet Asians have experienced and continue to face white racism 'like blacks' in educational and occupational barriers and ceilings and in anti-Asian abuse and physical violence.... This marginalization of Asians, in fact, within a black and white racial formation, 'disciplines' both Africans and Asians and constitutes the essential site of Asian American oppression."[88] By placing certain groups of color in an intermediate status on the socioracial ladder and continuum, white Americans as a group can effectively maintain and perpetuate the age-old racial hierarchy.

SUMMARY

This chapter has reviewed major theories of migration and subsequent patterns of intergroup adaptation. Migration—varying from the movement of conquerors to slave importation to voluntary immigration—creates intergroup contact and thus racial and ethnic relations and conflicts. Adaptation can have different outcomes in the period of initial contact, ranging from genocide to peaceful symbiosis to some type of societal hierarchy and large-scale inequality. Further adaptation may lead to further genocide, to egalitarian symbiosis, to full assimilation to the core culture and institutions, to some type of cultural pluralism, or to continuing large-scale inequality and a continuing hierarchy.

Most theories discussed in this chapter fall under the two broad categories of order theories and power-conflict theories. Both types of theories offer insights into the character and development of racial and ethnic relations. Assimilation theories tend to focus on voluntary immigrant groups and emphasize inclusion along conformity lines or pluralism outcomes. Assimilation analysts have pointed out the different dimensions of intergroup adaptation, such as acculturation and marital assimilation, and have often accented the role of value consensus in holding a racial and ethnic system together.

In contrast, power-conflict theories typically focus on involuntary immigration or colonial-type oppression and thus examine the substantial inequality and hierarchy in society. Power-conflict theories have certain recurring themes:

1. A central concern for major racial and ethnic inequalities in economic position, power, and resources
2. An emphasis on the interrelationship of racial oppression, the economic institutions of capitalism, and the subordination of women under patriarchal systems
3. An emphasis on the role of the government in legalizing and maintaining exploitation and segregation and in defining racial and ethnic relations
4. An emphasis on resistance to racial or ethnic domination by those who are oppressed

In analyzing U.S. history, power-conflict analysts have emphasized the forced character of much cultural and economic adaptation, particularly for non-European groups, and the role of coercion, segregation, exploitation, colonization, and institutionalized discrimination in keeping groups such as African, Latino, and Native Americans on the bottom rungs of the societal racial and ethnic ladder. Power-conflict perspectives have examined the role of government in racial oppression and have stressed the importance of oppositional cultures in providing the foundations for subordinate group resistance to racial oppression.

Power-conflict theorists have often emphasized the importance of examining racial and ethnic relations in the context of the historical and global development of capitalism and patriarchy. In the introduction to Part II we will explore the utility of such an approach in evaluating the broad contours of racial and ethnic relations over more than three-and-one-half centuries of North American and world history.

PART II

A Nation of Immigrants

An Overview of the Economic and Political Conditions of Selected Racial and Ethnic Groups

IN THE CHAPTERS THAT FOLLOW, we examine a number of important racial and ethnic groups in U.S. society. For each we look at aspects of its history and analyze its current situation in terms of the theories of racial and ethnic relations reviewed in Chapter 2. Before examining these groups in detail, we will set them in the historical context of nearly four centuries of North American economic and political development. We accent two important dimensions of this society in our brief overview: the changing capitalistic economy and the expanding political and governmental framework. Within these broad frameworks, each group has worked out its own cultural and social patterns in the complex nation we call the United States.

Immigration, the Economy, and Government

North American economic development has seen several stages: mercantilism and early commercial capitalism, coupled with a plantation-slave economy, competitive industrial capitalism, and advanced multinational capitalism. Economic institutions and developments and related government actions have shaped the character of all periods of immigration and immigrant adjustment.

Native Americans were the original inhabitants of the land to which the English and subsequent immigrants migrated; many in the indigenous societies lost their lives and lands as a result of the often brutal European invasion and conquest.

The table on pages 50–51 briefly lists most of the immigrant groups discussed in this book. Each group entered North America under particular historical circumstances. Many started in slavery, low-wage jobs, small-scale farming, or small businesses. Political and economic conditions at the time of entry were very important. Some groups entered when low-wage jobs were plentiful on farms or in cities; others entered when fewer jobs were available. The extent of racial and ethnic discrimination and oppression has varied considerably. Also important were the economic and other resources brought by the immigrant groups. Those immigrants who came voluntarily and with a little economic capital, some education, or entrepreneurial experience frequently had access to better jobs or developed small businesses—opportunities not available to immigrants with less in the way of economic or cultural resources.

Commercial Capitalism and the Slave Society: 1607–1865

Colonial Society and Slave Labor

The colonial society that grew up on the east coast of North America during the 1600s was tied closely to England and the expansionist policies of the English political and economic elites. The early economic system in these colonies was a combination of state enterprises under the English king and enterprises

Selected Immigrant Groups: An Overview

Immigrant Group	Time of Entry	Economic Conditions in North America	Government Conditions and Actions
		Phase One: Commercial Capitalism and the Slave Society: Early 1600s–1860s	
1. English	1600s–1800s	Mercantilism; land taken from Native Americans; English entrepreneurs and yeoman farmers; commercial capitalism emerges.	English state creates land companies; colonial governments define individualized property and protect property.
2. Africans	1600s–1800s	Enslaved as property; became major source of labor for plantation capitalism.	Colonial governments establish slave codes; U.S. Constitution legitimates slave trade; U.S. government substantially controlled by southern oligarchy.
3. Irish Catholics	1830s–1860s	Driven out of Ireland by oppression and famine; labor recruited for low-wage jobs in transport, construction.	U.S. government opens up western lands; Irish take urban political machines from English Americans.
		Phase Two: Industrial Capitalism: 1860s–1910s	
4. Chinese	1850s–1870s	Contract labor and low-wage work in mining, railroads, construction; menial service work for whites.	Local governments recruit Chinese labor; anti-Chinese laws passed in California; 1882 Exclusion Act.
5. Italians	1880s–1910s	Moved as European peasants into U.S. industrial capitalism; overseas recruitment for low-wage industrial and construction jobs in the cities.	Government backing for labor recruitment; U.S. treaties with Europe; intervention in European affairs (World War I); incoming numbers reduced by 1924 Immigration Act.
6. Eastern European Jews	1880s–1910s	Industrial capitalism utilized their skilled and unskilled labor; small entrepreneurs reestablished themselves; much anti-Semitism.	Government backing for labor recruitment; U.S. treaties with Europe; incoming numbers reduced by 1924 Immigration Act.

developed by independent entrepreneurs, including, by the eighteenth century, the slave plantation owners in the South and the merchants in the North. As was the case with other European colonial powers, the objective of English colonization was to secure raw materials and markets for English goods. The first joint-stock companies were formed by merchants under the auspices of James I of England. Employees of the Southern Company settled Jamestown; this was the English colony that bought the first Africans from a Dutch ship in 1619.

English merchants and entrepreneurs invested capital in the extraction of raw materials for home industries. The colonies served the empire as a source of raw materials and agricultural products and as a dumping ground for the surplus workers and peasants displaced by the expansion of capitalism and other economic changes in Europe. Production for profit was not the only important economic dimension, for the colonies also became home to many English and other northern European immigrants—people displaced from the land

SELECTED IMMIGRANT GROUPS: AN OVERVIEW (CONTINUED)

IMMIGRANT GROUP	TIME OF ENTRY	ECONOMIC CONDITIONS IN NORTH AMERICA	GOVERNMENT CONDITIONS AND ACTIONS
	PHASE TWO: INDUSTRIAL CAPITALISM: 1860S–1910S (CONTINUED)		
7. Japanese	1880s–1900s	Recruited as agricultural laborers for Hawaii; later migrated to West Coast as laborers; served in domestic work; created small farms and businesses.	Government backing for labor recruiting; U.S. imperialism in Asia; conquest of Philippines and Hawaii; government laws exclude Asians.
	PHASE THREE: ADVANCED INDUSTRIAL (MULTINATIONAL) CAPITALISM: 1910S–EARLY 2000S		
8. Mexicans	1910s–2000s	With Asian/European labor cut off, Mexicans recruited for farms and industry; low-wage jobs in urban industries.	U.S. government provides labor recruitment programs and fosters U.S. agribusiness in Mexico, stimulating out-migration; U.S. Border Patrol monitors immigration; new laws regulate immigration.
9. Puerto Ricans	1940s–2000s	Early farm labor migration; U.S. corporations recruit labor; blue-collar work in service economy.	Conquest of Puerto Rico in 1898; U.S. government-supported agribusiness takes over economy, creates surplus labor, stimulates migration to United States.
10. Recent Asian, Caribbean, Latin American, and Middle Eastern Groups	1960s–2000s	Many political and economic refugees; create economic niches, small businesses; make use of expanding service economy.	U.S. intervention in Asia from 1853 to 2000s; government action in South Korea, Vietnam, Taiwan, Philippines stimulates out-migration; Cubans, Haitians, Middle Easterners (Arabs) flee political repression and societal turmoil.

in Europe and seeking to become small farmers. In the colonies there were two major modes of production, the household (small-farm) mode and the capitalist (slave plantation and merchant) mode.[1] The North American colonies had so much available land that it was difficult for English entrepreneurs to secure enough European labor, particularly for large-scale agriculture. They tried using white indentured servants, but these immigrants worked off their terms of servitude and went into farming for themselves.

From the 1600s to the mid-1800s, people of African descent were a major source of (slave) labor for the white merchant and agricultural capitalists in the British colonies. In the late eighteenth century, the emergence of cotton and sugar as international commodities created a strong demand for enslaved workers on the southern plantations. The number of enslaved African Americans increased from 59,000 in 1714 to 3.9 million in 1860. This forced labor generated great wealth; it built up profits (capital) not only for further investments in expanding plantations and related business enterprises, but also for depositing in banks, where it could be used or borrowed by the white merchants, shippers, and industrialists of the North and South.

Civil War: The Southern Plantation Oligarchy versus Northern Entrepreneurs

By the late 1700s the slave mode of production was generally profitable. The South was the most prosperous and powerful region in the country from the late 1700s to about the 1850s. White southerners owned much of the productive land, much of the agricultural produce for export, many processing mills and other valuable equipment, and the millions of enslaved African American laborers. These African American laborers generated much of the wealth of the (white) nation, including capital invested in other (for example, industrial) enterprises. White southerners dominated U.S. politics, as most presidents between Washington and Lincoln were either slaveholders or sympathetic to slavery; for decades few major decisions made by the federal legislative and judicial branches went against the interests of the slaveholding oligarchy. The U.S. Civil War was to a substantial degree a struggle for economic and political power between northern industrialists and small farmers on the one hand and the southern plantation oligarchy on the other. The victory of the North in that war marked the arrival of northern industrialists as the dominant force in the U.S. economy and government.[2]

Immigrant Laborers in the North

During the 1800s in the northern states, the growing industrial working class and the class of small farmers were increasingly peopled with immigrants from Ireland, Germany, and Scandinavia. Immigrant labor often became the labor for the growing number of industrial enterprises—the textile mills, railroad shops, and foundries. The pull factors motivating millions of Irish Catholic immigrants to cross the Atlantic after 1820 were the same as those that have attracted immigrants for centuries to a country portrayed by industrial labor recruiters and others as the land of opportunity. There were major push factors as well. In Ireland a potato disease created severe food shortages; this crisis plus the continuing political and economic oppression of Ireland by England generated the migration of 1.6 million Irish to the United States over several decades. Many small farmers and artisans from Ireland sold their labor to U.S. employers; they became domestic servants, railroad laborers, miners, and industrial workers in cities.

The arrival of large numbers of white immigrants from northern Europe laid the foundation for new patterns of racial conflict. African Americans became a smaller percentage of urbanites in the North. Free black workers were used by industrial entrepreneurs in the North mostly as low-wage labor, sometimes as strikebreakers. Using them against white strikers increased the hostility of these workers toward African Americans. By the 1840s free black workers in the North were being forcibly displaced from jobs by white immigrants, including Irish American workers. While the Irish immigrants arrived from a country where the English oppressed and stereotyped them as an "inferior race," within a generation in the United States the majority of the Irish had come to see themselves as part of a "superior white race."

Western and Global Expansion

In the early decades of the nineteenth century, the new nation of the United States began to expand its own empire well beyond that envisioned by its former British overlords. Since that time, the U.S. empire has gradually and continually expanded—first into Mexican and other lands to its West, later into Latin America, and eventually to Asia and around the globe.

Fostered by U.S. governmental decrees and military protection, the great westward expansion across North America in the nineteenth century brought not only Native Americans but also a new group—the Mexicans—into the orbit of exploitation by white entrepreneurs, soldiers, and settlers. The racist ideology of the "white man's civilizing responsibility" for non-European groups guided white expansionists and justified for them the taking of Mexican and Native American lands in the West. Expansionists believed the "Mexican race" and the "Indian race" should become subordinate to the "Anglo-Saxon race." The first Mexican citizens, long residents of the Southwest, did not migrate; they and their land were brought into the United States by force as the result of the imperialistic Mexican-American War in the 1840s.

In 1822, President James Monroe announced in what came to be called the Monroe Doctrine that the Americas were now the U.S. sphere of influence and that no more European colonization would be tolerated. Soon, the United States replaced the European colonial powers as the dominant colonial nation in the Americas. Since the middle of the nineteenth century, the U.S. government and U.S. businesses have expanded their involvement not only to western North America but also to Latin America and all other continents. Over the course of two centuries, U.S. economic and political ties have gradually become more extensive and complex than those of any other modern empire. They have included not only myriads of business linkages and economic exploitations but also numerous military adventures, government aid of many kinds, and far-reaching mass media and other cultural linkages. Over the past century and a half, U.S. involvement in most other countries has had far-reaching consequences, not only for these countries but also for the United States itself. As we will see, the history of immigration to the United States often parallels the development of economic exploitation and political or military involvement in other nations. Some have called this large-scale and continuing immigration "the harvest of the U.S. empire."

INDUSTRIAL CAPITALISM: 1865–1920

Industrial Capitalism and Government Expansion Overseas

The Civil War was followed not only by westward expansion but also by an industrial boom. An economy dominated by competitive capitalism, by small and medium-sized businesses, gradually became one that was dominated by large enterprises. The growth of these enterprises was dramatic, and the United States soon surpassed Great Britain in numerous industrial production categories. The proportion of workers engaged in agriculture declined between the 1860s and the 1920s, while the proportion in manufacturing doubled. By the last two decades of the nineteenth century, many corporations were growing dramatically through mergers and acquisitions.

Leading U.S. industrialists expanded corporate investments and activities in numerous countries overseas, often backed by a U.S. government growing in military power. The movement of U.S. Navy ships, as well as merchants and missionaries, into countries such as China, Japan, and the Philippines often disrupted the economies and other social institutions in these countries, thereby increasing the surplus of farm workers and shaping out-migration. U.S. military and economic power pressured Asian countries to submit to U.S. influence. Given the often difficult economic conditions in these nations, U.S. labor recruiters enticed many Asian workers to Hawaii and the west coast of the United States. More than 200,000 Chinese laborers came to the United States between 1848 and 1882 to do the hard work in West Coast mining, railroad, and service businesses. After the Chinese were excluded by a racist immigration law, Japanese immigrants were recruited for similar low-wage jobs. Japan sent many thousands of emigrants to Hawaii and to the United States, a migration triggered by U.S. political influence and by labor recruiting by U.S. employers.[3]

The U.S. victory in the Spanish-American War of the 1890s resulted in the annexation of Puerto Rico and the Philippines by the expansionist U.S. government and the effective domination of Cuba. When the United States took over Puerto Rico, much of that island was owned by small local farmers, but soon U.S. companies were controlling much of the production. Puerto Rico, the Philippines, and Cuba would later send large numbers of emigrants to the U.S. mainland.[4]

African Americans: Exclusion from Western Lands

The second half of the nineteenth century was a period of major governmental growth and bureaucratization in the United States. Government action had a major influence on racial and ethnic relations. One of the first actions of Abraham Lincoln and the new Republican legislators in the early 1860s was to pass the Homestead Act, a major wealth-building program for the many white immigrant families seeking land, including the Germans, Scandinavians, and Irish. A European American family wishing to farm was often given 160 to 320 acres of land if they would develop it. After the Civil War, the U.S. Land Office ruled that most black Americans were ineligible for these land grants because they were not citizens when the act was passed. For the most part, black families did not have the opportunity that many white families had to build up landed wealth through farming, wealth passed down to millions of their descendants.[5]

In the late 1800s and early 1900s, southern black workers were one possible source of labor for northern industries, but the white oligarchy in the South, after a brief postwar Reconstruction period, took back control of the South's economy and state governments and made certain that most of the newly freed African Americans remained in the South as low-wage laborers, tenant farmers, or sharecroppers. In addition, there was little distribution of plantation land to the black men and women who had made that land so fruitful for whites. They did not receive the "forty acres and a mule" that some government leaders promised them.

Southern and Eastern European Immigrants

Unable to use southern black labor, or preferring not to use it, northern industrialists turned to Europe. The majority of the 20.7 million immigrants to the United States between 1881 and 1920 were from southern and eastern Europe. Labor shortages and increasing wages for native-born white workers encouraged U.S. industrialists to seek immigrant labor. A 1910 survey of twenty major manufacturing and mining industries found that six out of every ten workers were foreign-born. Without this immigrant labor, the great industrial expansion of the United States would not have been possible.[6] In some cases these new workers displaced native-born white workers. Anti-immigrant hostility (nativism) among the workers in older European American groups increased as a result.[7]

European Immigrants and Black Americans

The intellectual Irving Kristol once argued that "The Negro Today Is Like the Immigrant of Yesterday." In this view the experience of black Americans moving to the industrial cities is not significantly different from that of white immigrant groups: African Americans should eventually move up economically and socially just as those immigrants did.[8] However, this argument overlooks important differences between the experiences of white and black immigrants to the industrial cities. Group mobility was possible for European immigrants because of the following:

1. Most arrived at a time when urban jobs were generally available; U.S. industrial capitalism was expanding, and opportunities were relatively abundant.
2. Many had some technical or other skills or a little capital—resources available to few African Americans.
3. Most faced far less severe employment and housing discrimination than black workers in the cities.
4. Most found housing, however inadequate, reasonably near their workplaces.
5. In key cities, the political system was changing from Anglo-Protestant business dominance to shared power between business elites and political machines oriented to white immigrant voters.[9]

In the critical periods of large-scale European immigration, cities such as New York, Philadelphia, Boston, and Chicago were expanding centers of manufacturing. Blue-collar jobs were frequently available, if not plentiful. In the mid-nineteenth century, Irish and German immigrants were attracted to rural areas and to cities, where most found industrial, service, or government jobs. From 1890 to 1930, southern and eastern Europeans came in large numbers to the cities. One study notes that "the Italian concentration in construction and the Polish in steel were related to the expansion of these industries as the groups arrived."[10] Many migrated as a result of labor recruiting by U.S. employers in Europe.

Among the European immigrants who arrived in the period between 1880 and 1920 were large numbers of Jewish immigrants fleeing oppression in Europe. Although often poverty-stricken, many Jewish immigrants were part of an urban industrial proletariat and came with some experience in skilled trades. One study found that two-thirds of the Jewish immigrants were skilled workers, whereas other southern and eastern European immigrants were primarily peasant farmers or farm workers. When Jewish immigrants entered in large numbers around 1900, the clothing industry was moving to mass production and offered jobs for tailors and seamstresses, as well as unskilled jobs, and there were also chances for small-scale entrepreneurs in a number of cities.

The situation for the African Americans who began to move to the northern cities from the South after 1910 was quite different. Black workers who migrated from the South had little access to good government jobs and were regularly displaced by the white immigrant groups, who forced them out of job after job, such as construction and transport jobs, and into marginal, low-paying jobs or unemployment. Stanley Lieberson has explored why southern and eastern European immigrants have done well in northern cities, compared with black Americans. Among his conclusions are that (1) black migrants were the victims of more severe discrimination over a longer period than were white immigrant groups, and (2) economic competition between whites and the growing group of black workers in the urban North led to extensive hostility and institutionalized discrimination by whites.[11]

Advanced Industrial (Multinational) Capitalism: 1910s–2000s

Mexican Immigrants

With the industrialization accompanying World War I came a sharp decline in the number of laborers available for agricultural work. The need was filled in part by Mexican labor, recruited with substantial help from the federal government. Mexican laborer and family migrations increased significantly in the 1920s. Agencies in cities such as Los Angeles and San Antonio recruited Mexican workers for agriculture and for some low-skilled jobs in the steel, auto, and other urban industries. Robert Blauner has captured the contrast between the non-European and the European immigrants of this period and later: "America has used African, Asian, Mexican, and, to a lesser degree, Indian workers for the cheapest labor, concentrating people of color in the most unskilled jobs, the least advanced sectors of the economy, and the most industrially backward regions of the nation."[12]

Large Corporations and the U.S. Business Cycle

Since 1900, large corporations, many with an international orientation, have come to dominate the U.S. economy and politics. By the 1920s, a large number of Americans, including recent immigrant workers, were working in the auto industry or in related industries such as steel. Aggressive competition among auto firms in the 1920s resulted in the production of more cars than were needed in the economy. This overproduction, a chronic problem in a capitalist economy, resulted in major cutbacks in employment in the auto-related industries, thus helping to trigger the 1930s' Great Depression, which hit especially hard among black and Latino migrants to cities. Unemployed whites, including recent immigrants, took over many of the lower-paying jobs previously held by workers of color. The latter had very high unemployment rates. The federal government grew as political and business leaders tried to develop economic and social programs to save the foundering capitalist system. Still, racial discrimination was perpetuated in the New Deal relief programs of the 1930s; typically, workers of color received lower wages than whites, were employed mainly as unskilled laborers, and were often employed only after whites.[13]

The Postwar Era: The United States and the World

For three decades after World War II, the U.S. government, the U.S. military, and U.S. multinational corporations substantially dominated the world economy, in large part because major industrial societies elsewhere, such as Germany and Japan, had been destroyed by the war. Since World War II, it has become easier for U.S. multinational corporations to move capital investments from the central city to the suburbs, from northern to southern cities, and from U.S. cities to cities overseas. Much of this "capital flight" has resulted in economically abandoned central cities. The federal government has facilitated this outward expansion of investment and jobs by funding home mortgage programs and highway systems built in accord with the needs of companies developing plants and of middle-class (disproportionately white) workers living outside central cities. As a result, after World War II many white Americans—often the children and grandchildren of European immigrants—followed the new industrial plants and allied workplaces to the suburbs.

Into the central cities came other workers and their families—African Americans, Puerto Ricans, Mexicans and Mexican Americans, Native Americans, Asian Americans, and Middle Eastern Americans. After World War II these immigrants to northern and western cities inhabited residential areas increasingly abandoned by industry and by the children and grandchildren of earlier European immigrants. Among these were Puerto Ricans, many of whom were recruited for low-wage city jobs in the 1950s and 1960s. U.S. industrial and agribusiness development in Puerto Rico helped to stimulate a large out-migration. Many older cities have thus seen an increase in black, Latino, and Asian American political influence in recent years.

Government Involvement Overseas and Asian Immigration

Until the mid-1960s, U.S. immigration legislation was so restrictive that most Asians desiring to emigrate could not enter. By the mid-1960s, the discriminatory quotas for Asians had been lifted, and since then there has been an increase in immigrants, especially Chinese, Korean, Filipino, Asian Indian, and Vietnamese immigrants. U.S. support for South Korea during and after its war with North Korea built strong ties between the two countries. A succession of dictators in South Korea drove out some dissenters, who migrated to the United States; other Koreans came for economic or educational reasons. The immigration of the Chinese, the Filipinos, and the Vietnamese is generally related to the involvement of the U.S. government and corporations overseas. The U.S. arming and political support of the Philippine government and of the Chinese government on Taiwan, and U.S. participation in the wars in Korea and South Vietnam, have played an important role in creating large groups of Filipinos, Koreans, Chinese, and Vietnamese oriented to the United States. More recently, increasing corporate and political ties between the United States and mainland China have facilitated the immigration of mainland Chinese. As with earlier immigrants, Asians have generally migrated to the United States seeking better economic opportunities or greater political freedom.

Latin American Immigration

Caribbean immigrants to the United States since the 1960s have included Cubans and Haitians moving to Florida. The U.S. government long supported a dictatorship in Cuba, which was overthrown by a guerrilla movement led by Fidel Castro. Many Cuban businesspeople and professionals fled in the first period of emigration after Castro took power. Often having economic and educational resources, these Cubans established a major economic niche and political influence in south Florida. After 1980, a significant number of poorer Cubans migrated to the United States, some of them expelled as alleged "undesirables" by the Castro government. Most Cuban immigrants have been welcomed by the U.S. government as political refugees from a Communist government, and hundreds of millions of dollars in federal subsidies have been provided to facilitate their adjustment to a new country. In contrast, Haitians who fled politically repressive governments on their Caribbean island were for the most part not welcomed by the U.S. government. Many were forced to return, and most of those allowed to stay were not provided the same level of government support as the Cuban immigrants. A major reason for this seems to be that the Communist government in Cuba is seen as a political opponent of the United States, whereas the repressive governments in Haiti were long viewed as political allies of the U.S. government.

In recent decades much investment capital and federal aid have shifted from northern to Sunbelt cities. The growing economy of the Sunbelt has created a demand for low-wage workers in sectors such as construction, manufacturing, and agriculture. Many people have migrated there from Mexico and Central America for economic reasons. Others, like earlier European groups, have come fleeing political oppression. Mexican immigrants still make up a significant portion of the undocumented immigrants. They are attracted by the possibility of jobs, and many are pushed by economic problems in their home country. U.S. corporations operating in Mexico have played a significant and continuing role in generating Mexican out-migration. For example, some U.S. agribusiness firms have stimulated the development of export-oriented agriculture in Mexico, taking over large amounts of land for that purpose and driving off many Mexican peasants who had farmed the land to feed their families. Many of these farmers have become migrants to Mexican cities and to the United States.

Middle Eastern Immigration

Immigrants from the Middle East have come to the United States for more than a century. Arab immigrants from more than twenty countries comprise the largest group among these. Immigration from Arab areas has occurred in two major segments—the first from about 1880 to 1945, and the second, much larger immigration from 1946 to the present day. Between 1880 and World War II, Arab immigrants came in modest numbers. They were working-class and middle-class people who came mostly seeking economic opportunity. They were usually from what was then Greater Syria, an area that included what would later be known as Lebanon, Syria, and Palestine/Israel. By the mid-1920s, Arab Americans numbered an estimated 200,000; most were Christians. These early immigrants and their descendants make up about half of the approximately three million Arab Americans in the United States today. The discriminatory 1924 Immigration Act sharply reduced immigration from the Middle East.

With the abolition of this racist immigration law in the 1960s, immigration to United States was opened to people of all nationalities, and the number of Arab immigrants increased. The 1970s' Lebanese civil war and the 1980s' Israeli military invasion of Lebanon generated numerous immigrants; others have fled wars been Iraq and Iran and between Iraq and Kuwait. The largest numbers have come from Lebanon, Syria, Egypt, and Palestine. Whether Muslim or Christian, most have a strong sense of their Arab origins. Most have settled in large metropolitan areas.

While those in the earliest period of immigration were generally poor, many who have immigrated since the 1960s have been educated professionals or businesspeople. Today Arab Americans as a group are disproportionately self-employed in their own businesses.

Early Arab immigrants were frequently catalogued with southern and eastern European immigrants as "inferior races" by leading white intellectuals in the United States. In more recent decades Arab peoples, including Arab Americans, have continued to face widespread stereotyping. The U.S. mass media (including movies) have often portrayed Arabs or Arab Americans in negative and stereotyped terms.

Immigration Restrictions

European immigrants made up more than half of all those coming to the United States during the decade of the 1950s. Their proportion dropped to one-third by the 1960s and to less than one-fifth by the early 2000s. The change is substantially the result of the abolition of the discriminatory national-origin quotas in the 1965 Immigration Act. Since the 1960s many Asian, Middle Eastern, and Latino immigrants have been viewed as a "problem" by native-born Americans. Congress has passed immigration legislation with provisions limiting the recent, mostly non-European, immigration to the United States. Many native-born workers and leading politicians are concerned that the United States cannot absorb so many new immigrants, even though the ratio of immigrants to the native-born population was *higher* in the early twentieth century than it is in the early twenty-first century. The percentage of foreign-born in the U.S. population today is smaller than that of many other nations, including several in Europe. Implicit in many European American discussions of the new immigrants is a concern that most are from Asia and Latin America—that is, they are not white and not European.[14]

Significantly, the new Asian and Latino immigrants, and their children and grandchildren, are part of a growing population of Americans of color. In many areas of the United States, including nearly half of the nation's 100 largest cities and the states of Hawaii, New Mexico, and California, Americans of color are now a majority of the population. They soon will be the majority in Texas (about 2004) and will become a majority in several other states a decade or two from now. As their numbers increase, Americans of color will likely press even harder for more equitable treatment in social, economic, and political institutions across U.S. society. Moreover, they will likely achieve increased representation in our society's major decision-making positions, including those in the U.S. Congress.

SUMMARY

In this introduction we have briefly reviewed the economic and governmental contexts within which particular groups have immigrated and adjusted. We have suggested that the time of entry for particular groups and the resources they bring affect their economic and political success. A complete understanding of the streams of migration to the United States requires an analysis of immigration in light of the economic and political contexts of entry and adaptation. Capitalist development and expansion, as well as U.S. political involvement overseas and domestic governmental expansion and legislative action, have not only shaped the context and character of U.S. immigration and the patterns of racial and ethnic relations in North America for several centuries, but have also provided crucibles within which the family patterns, the distinctive cultures, and the political resistance to discrimination of specific immigrant groups have developed.

3 English Americans and the Anglo-Protestant Culture

Cleveland Amory tells a story about prominent English American families in Massachusetts. A Chicago banking firm wrote a Boston investment company for a letter of recommendation for a young Bostonian. Eloquently praising the young man's virtues, the company's letter pointed out that his mother was a member of the Lowell family, his father a member of the Cabot family, and his other relatives members of other prominent New England families. The bank wrote back, thanking the company but noting that this was not the type of letter of recommendation they had in mind: "We were not contemplating using Mr. _______ for breeding purposes."[1] Apocryphal or not, this story illustrates the elite status of the "proper Bostonians" and suggests their prominence in New England's history.

The story underscores the importance of inbreeding, descent, and interlocking family ties over generations. Ethnicity involves cultural or nationality characteristics that are distinguished by the group itself or by important outgroups, but lines of descent are major channels for passing along these ethnic characteristics to later generations.

English Americans are the third largest ethnic group in the United States, after the Germans and the Irish. Approximately 28.3 million Americans are estimated to have significant English ancestry according to a census 2000 survey report.[2] The phrase *English Americans* itself may sound a bit strange. More often other labels are used. Most common are the inaccurate terms *Anglo-Saxon* and *white Anglo-Saxon Protestant*. Although in-depth analyses of this ethnic group are rare, numerous authors have commented on its central importance: "Our American culture, our speech, our laws are basically Anglo-Saxon in origin."[3]

Milton Gordon's view of the shaping impact this first large group of European immigrants had on the dominant culture of the United States has already been noted: "If there is anything in American life which can be described as an overall American culture which serves as a reference point for immigrants and their children, it can best be described ... as the middle-class cultural patterns of, largely, white Protestant, Anglo-Saxon origins."[4] This comment suggests the importance of this dominant culture in the adaptation process faced by later immigrant groups.

Note that the term *Anglo-Saxon* is an inadequate designation for the immigrants from England and their descendants. The term derives from the names for two Germanic tribes, the Angles and the Saxons, that came to the area now called England in the fifth and sixth centuries A.D. But other people were there already—the Celts—and the Germanic tribes were followed by the Normans from France. The English settlers of the American colonies already embodied several centuries of the blending and fusion of several nationality types and cultures.[5]

Some authors have used *Anglo-Saxon* and related terms such as the ethnocentric "old-stock Americans" in even broader senses. These terms are sometimes used in a loose way to also include British groups other than the English—the Scots and the Welsh. Certain other north European groups that have substantially assimilated to the Anglo culture—particularly Scandinavian and German Protestants—are sometimes included in the terms *Anglo-Saxon* and *Anglo-Protestant*. In any event, when the terms *Anglo-Saxon*, *Anglo-Protestant*, and *British Americans* are used by authors, English Americans and the dominant culture they generated are at the heart of the discussion.

Early on, Americans of British descent expressed a sense of superiority and prominence in the nation. In the late 1780s, John Jay, the first chief justice of the U.S. Supreme Court, wrote in *The Federalist*, "Providence has been pleased to give this one connected country to one united people—a people descended from the same ancestors, speaking the same language, professing the same religion, attached to the same principles of government, very similar in their manners and customs."[6] This ethnocentric perspective—inaccurate at the time—has been a central problem for non-English groups ever since.

THE ENGLISH MIGRATIONS

Some Basic Data

Although the English were not the first Europeans to come to North America (the Spanish came earlier, for example), they were the first to colonize it in large numbers. By the early eighteenth century, there were approximately 350,000 English and Welsh colonists in North America. At the time of the Revolution, this number had increased to between 1 and 2 million.[7]

Migration to the American colonies was heavily English until 1700. Then the English migration generally receded to modest levels, until well into the nineteenth century.[8] Nearly 3 million English migrated to the United States between 1820 and 1950; the majority came between 1880 and 1900. The English migration to the colonies, and later to the United States in the nineteenth century, was one of the largest population flows in this period. The English were the first sizable European group in what was to become the United States and continued to be an important segment of the European migration until World War I.[9]

The First Colonial Settlements

The English settlers' seventeenth century migration, together with their pattern of settlement, was different from later European migration streams. This movement can be viewed as *colonization migration*, a concept explored in Chapter 2. Unlike other types of migration, colonization involves the subordination of indigenous people. As we will show in detail in Chapter 6, the first victims of English and other European colonialism on this continent were many Native American societies. English settlers participated actively in killing Native Americans and otherwise driving them off their lands.[10]

Pilgrims aboard the Mayflower sign the Mayflower Compact.

Why did the English Crown become interested in establishing North American colonies? English advocates in the colonial period put forth various explanations for colonial development. The need for trading posts and for new sources of raw materials, as well as for new markets for English goods, received much attention.[11] Other colonial advocates emphasized Protestant missionary objectives, the search for a passage to Asia, the need to stop Spanish and French expansion, and the need for a place for England's surplus population. "What England primarily looked for in colonies was neither expansion of territory *per se* nor overseas aggregations of Englishmen, but goods and markets."[12]

The English colonization was a case of Lieberson's migrant superordination (see Chapter 2). It had dire consequences for the preexisting Native American societies. Geographical expansion proceeded rapidly. At first, some Native American groups were treated in a friendly fashion, if mainly because the colonists depended on Native American food and advice for survival. As the colonists gained numerical superiority over the native population, they forced Native Americans back into frontier areas or slaughtered them.[13] Few European settlers seemed concerned over the genocidal consequences of their colonialism. Most of the European invaders viewed the Native Americans as "savages" who should be driven off the valuable land.

The English established large settlements in North America. The first joint-stock companies were formed by merchants under the auspices of James I of England in the early 1600s. Employees of the Southern Company settled Jamestown, a colony where the primary goal was economic. Initially planning to develop the colony with poor-white labor, the leaders at Jamestown soon perceived a labor shortage and bought Africans from a Dutch ship in 1619, laying the foundation for the brutal institution of human slavery in North America. The northern colony of Plymouth was settled in 1620 under the auspices of another royal company. Many of these settlers—later called "Pilgrims"—were Puritans who had broken with the Anglican church.[14] Both settlements nearly expired in their early years because of disease and starvation. The Plymouth colony managed to survive only with the aid of supportive Native Americans.[15]

According to historian David Fischer, there were four distinctive groups of English-speaking immigrants to North America. First came the aforementioned Puritans from England's eastern counties, who entered the Massachusetts area primarily between 1629 and 1640. They brought to New England "nucleated settlements, congregational churches, town meetings, and a tradition of ordered liberty."[16] A second group of immigrants came to the Virginia area between 1642 and 1675. This group consisted of a small number of Royalists from the south of England and numerous indentured servants. Their culture was characterized by "extreme hierarchies of rank, strong oligarchies, Anglican churches, a highly developed sense of honor, and an idea of hegemonic liberty."[17] A third group—Quakers from the North Midlands of England and Wales who came to the Delaware Valley between 1675 and 1725—established a "pluralistic system of reciprocal liberty" based on spiritual and social equality, austerity, and an intense work ethic.[18] A fourth group of immigrants came to the Appalachian backcountry from the borderlands of northern Great Britain and northern Ireland between 1718 and 1775. This group represented a variety of ethnic ancestries (English, Scottish, and "Scotch-Irish") and had extreme socioeconomic inequalities, but its members shared the ideal of natural liberty.[19] Each of these four groups had a distinctive type of culture—distinctive speech patterns, architecture, family ways and child-rearing customs, dress and food ways, religious orientation, and organization of public life. These cultural patterns interacted with each other and eventually fused together to create the dominant Anglo-Protestant culture of the colonies.

The American Historical Association has developed rough estimates of the "national stocks" of the white population in 1790 based on a surname analysis (see Table 3.1).[20]

TABLE 3.1 "NATIONAL STOCKS" AS PERCENTAGE OF THE WHITE POPULATION (1790)

SURNAMES	WHITE POPULATION
English	60.1%
Scottish, "Scotch-Irish"	14.0
German	8.6
Irish (Free State)	3.6
Dutch	3.1
French, Swedish	3.0
Other	7.6
Total	100.0%

These estimates give the English the primary position among whites, with other British groups accounting for significant proportions. In addition, it is important to note that African Americans, then mostly enslaved, made up about *one-fifth* of the total population at that time.[21]

Later Migration

A modest flow of British and other European immigrants entered the United States between the American Revolution and 1820, but the century following 1820 saw the greatest Atlantic migration in history. The English and other British contributions to this nineteenth-century migration have been neglected. English immigrants moved in large numbers from manufacturing and mining industries at home to comparable positions in U.S. industry; their skills helped spur the dramatic industrialization of the nineteenth century.[22] When English American workers were eventually displaced by machines or later immigrant groups, they often moved up into managerial, professional, and technical positions. With their help, U.S. industrial productivity soon surpassed that of the home country.[23]

The ease with which many English immigrants moved into industry indicates the swiftness of their assimilation at the level of secondary organizations. Their skills kept most from the poverty that other immigrants usually faced. Larger numbers moved into clerical and professional jobs than was the case with most other white immigrant groups in this period. Acculturation was easy for the English immigrants. They were more readily hired where the ability to speak English was important. These immigrants also avoided most of the anti-immigrant agitation others faced. Indeed, new English immigrants often shared the ethnocentric or racist views held by previous English settlers, including the stereotyping of Jews, hostility toward African Americans, and dislike of southern Europeans. Structural assimilation in the primary-relations sphere, to use the concept developed by the assimilation theorist Milton Gordon, was usually rapid for them. English immigrants never faced enforced residential segregation, and marriage with English American citizens was common.[24]

Smaller numbers of English immigrants have come to the United States since 1910, generally fewer than a few thousand each year. In the 1930s, more people returned to England than came in as immigrants. The modest English migration since 1910, coupled with dramatic increases in immigration from other areas, has had a significant demographic effect. Since 1910 British Americans as a group have declined as a proportion of the total U.S. population.[25]

Other Protestant Immigrants

The terms *Anglo-Saxon* and *Anglo-Protestant* have sometimes been used by researchers to include not only the English but also the Scots, the Welsh, and even Scandinavians and Germans. The Welsh entered the colonies in relatively small numbers, beginning in the early 1600s. The total number who came has been estimated at just over 100,000. Many found employment in industrial jobs or farming. The first generations retained their customs, language, and distinctive communities, but most were soon substantially assimilated to the white Anglo-Protestant mainstream.[26]

In terms of political and economic power, the Scots were perhaps the closest to the dominant English group from the 1700s onward, although they too were subject to Anglo-conformity pressures. By the late eighteenth century, there were perhaps 250,000 Scots in the United States, a number that was supplemented over the next century by three-fourths of a million migrants. In the colonial period, some Scots were prosperous merchants, clerks, soldiers, and middle-income farmers, although the majority probably were servants, laborers, and poor farmers. Many settled in rural and frontier areas. Scots experienced hostility from some English Americans in the early period. Assimilation to the English core culture gradually accompanied inclusion in the economic system; by the early 1800s many if not most Scots had achieved parity with their English American neighbors. They, too, were becoming an important segment of the white Anglo-Protestant mainstream.

German immigrants made up the largest non-British group during the eighteenth century. Germans constituted nearly one-tenth of the colonists, and in the century after 1820 several million more came to the United States. Some were Catholics and Jews, but the largest proportion was Protestant. Many became farmers, merchants, and, later, industrial workers. Over several generations much, but by no means all, of the German culture was reshaped or displaced by the well-established Anglo-American patterns. Cultural assimilation, together with substantial mobility in the economic and political spheres, came in a few generations for German Protestants. Yet for years some distinctiveness persisted in the form of certain German customs, festivals, and residential concentrations. Jewish Germans (see Chapter 5), who immigrated in the middle decades of the nineteenth century, remained somewhat distinctive, in part because of the often vicious anti-Semitism directed against them (and later Jewish immigrants) by many other Americans.

Scandinavian immigrants, such as Swedes and Norwegians, did not enter in large numbers until the 1870s and 1880s. In all, perhaps 2 million came. Many immigrants entered as farmers and laborers, but the second and third generations moved into skilled blue-collar and white-collar positions. Here, too, substantial assimilation to the British American core culture came in just a few generations. Still, some distinctiveness in family customs and residential location, especially in midwestern areas, persists even today.

These white Protestant groups from northern Europe assimilated relatively rapidly in the cultural, economic, and political spheres, although this process was not always peaceful. In the period of early contact, even some of these white northern European groups suffered physical attacks and extreme cultural conformity pressures from English Americans. However, this did not last long. Within a generation or so, English Americans were intermarrying with Scottish, Welsh, and "Scotch-Irish" Americans, and sometimes with Scandinavians and Germans. By the early twentieth century, the designations *white Anglo-Saxon Protestant* and *white Anglo-Protestant* increasingly came to blur the distinction between the English and the later northern European immigrant groups.

The Invention of the "White Race"

The eighteenth and nineteenth centuries saw the emergence of the "white race" as a deliberately constructed social group for the first time in North

American or, for that matter, world history. From the beginning, English settlers and their descendants saw themselves as quite different from Native Americans and African Americans, whom they initially stereotyped as "uncivilized," "idolaters," and "savages." English Americans saw themselves as "republicans" of great virtue; they were concerned with protecting the new nation and reserving it, as some explicitly stated in the 1790s, for the "worthy part of mankind."[27] By the early 1800s, the growing importance of southern cotton plantations for the U.S. economy as a whole (northern entrepreneurs and bankers were often linked to the southern cotton economy) increased the demand for Native American land and for African and African American slaves. At the same time, slavery was being abolished, sometimes slowly, in the northern states.

As a result of these developments, a white Anglo-Protestant elite developed and circulated the idea of an advantaged "white race," in part as a way to provide racial privileges for propertyless British and other European American immigrants and to prevent the latter from bonding with Americans of color. As sociologist W. E. B. Du Bois suggested, these white workers came to accept a lesser economic position and lower wages in return for the "public and psychological wage" that went with "whiteness." In return for acceptance of their subordinate class position, white workers, including new immigrant workers from Britain, were allowed or encouraged by the white elite to be part of a racial hierarchy in which all whites enforced deference from African Americans and other Americans of color.[28]

Moreover, David Roediger's research shows how many nineteenth-century European immigrants, who did not define themselves initially as "white" but rather as Irish, German, or Italian, gradually came to construct themselves as "white" as they moved up economically and politically in U.S. society. The development of a racial ideology and of white nationalism was accelerated during Andrew Jackson's presidency (1829–1837). By the late nineteenth century or early twentieth century not only the later English immigrants but also immigrants from Scotland, Scandinavia, Ireland, and Germany had come to accept a place in the "white race." Their racial privileges generally included the right to substantial personal liberty, the right to travel and immigrate, and the right to vote. Similarly, the white elite's response to eighteenth- and nineteenth-century farmer protests and union organization among white immigrants often included efforts to convince white farmers and workers to embrace racial solidarity within a socially invented "white race."[29]

NATIVIST REACTIONS TO LATER EUROPEAN IMMIGRANTS

Nonetheless, in the 1700s and 1800s, some native-born white Americans, themselves descendants of earlier immigrants, were hostile to new European immigrant groups. Anti-immigration agitation, or *nativism*, goes far back in American history, but the term appears to have been first used in the 1840s and 1850s. Nativists were nationalists who saw themselves as the *only* true Americans.[30]

Before the American revolution, nativists focused on the religious and moral desirability of new immigrants. Certain religious groups (such as Catholics), "paupers," and convicts were discouraged by English Americans from entering the colonies. Anti-foreign sentiment was directed primarily at non-English immigrant groups, of which the French Huguenot refugees were one example. At least one Huguenot community was violently attacked by nativists.[31] "In the early years Englishmen treated the increasingly numerous settlers from other European countries, especially Scottish and Irish servants, with much condescension and frequently with exploitative brutality."[32] In Virginia and Maryland discriminatory duties were placed on non-English servants coming into the colonies. Catholics among the Irish were "doubly damned as foreign and Papist."[33]

Established colonists felt ambivalence about the new immigrants. On the one hand, immigrants provided needed labor for employers, ship captains profited from immigration, and new immigrants were encouraged to settle in frontier areas to increase colonial security. On the other hand, immigrants were sometimes seen as a threat, and English American mobs occasionally tried to prevent their landing.[34]

More Fear of Immigrants

Anti-foreign sentiment took legal form in the late 1700s after the Federalist party became concerned about political radicalism among certain new immigrants and about non-English immigrants' growing support for Jeffersonian Republicans. The 1798 Alien Act empowered the English American president (John Adams) to deport immigrants considered a threat to the new nation. The period of residence required for citizenship was raised from two to five years in 1795 and to fourteen years in 1798. Attempts were also made to set an exorbitant fee for naturalization. These strategies were designed to limit the political power of the new non-English immigrants.[35] Numerous attempts were made to reduce the influence of new immigrants by pressuring them to assimilate to English-dominated institutions.

Concern about the many non-English immigrants who did not know the language and customs led Benjamin Franklin to establish a Pennsylvania school in the 1740s.[36] Franklin held strong ethnic prejudices and stereotypes about the German immigrants in his region; he feared they would "shortly be so numerous as to Germanize us instead of us Anglifying them."[37]

Anti-Catholic sentiment fueled much nativist agitation, especially in the nineteenth century. Irish and German immigrants entering during the 1840s and 1850s were periodically targeted by bursts of nativist agitation; a variety of secret societies, sometimes termed the Know-Nothing movement, fought both immigration and Catholicism. (When questioned, members of these societies are reported to have said, "I don't know nothing.") During the 1850s ethnocentric Know-Nothings were elected to state legislatures, Congress, and state executive offices. They also precipitated numerous violent attacks against new immigrants and Roman Catholics.[38]

Nativism was often coupled with racist ideologies in the nineteenth century; other northern Europeans joined English Americans in this perspective. U.S. development was seen as the perfect example of what could be accomplished by the "Anglo-Saxon race." Anglo-Saxonism was picked up by expansionists who lusted after Mexican land in California and Texas. European Americans legitimated their vigorous thrust into those areas by a perceived mandate to colonize "inferior races." One European American expansionist commented that "the Mexican race now see in the fate of the aborigines of the North, their own inevitable destiny. They must amalgamate or be lost in the superior vigor of the Anglo-Saxon race, or they must utterly perish."[39] This Anglo-Saxonism was to play an important role in racist thought after the Civil War. It provided the rationalization for U.S. imperialist military and business expansion overseas, in places such as the Philippines.

After the Civil War the upper classes became a stronghold of Anglo-Saxonism. Some U.S. intellectuals came under the influence of social Darwinism, which extended Charles Darwin's evolutionary thinking into the societal realm. This perspective contained notions of Anglo-Saxon racial superiority that were based on a theory of the social "survival of the fittest." One prominent advocate of biological evolution, John Fiske, celebrated the superiority of English civilization and claimed it was the destiny of the English people to populate *all* the world's empty spaces.[40] Even more influential were popular writers such as Josiah Strong, a Congregationalist minister whose book *Our Country* (1885) sold thousands of copies in the United States. Strong was a vigorous advocate of Anglo-Saxon superiority myths, in combination with attacks on Catholics and non-British immigrants as undesirable aliens in the United States. The English peoples were rapidly multiplying, he argued, and the United States was destined to be the seat of an "Anglo-Saxon race" whose numbers would approach (by the 1980s, he predicted) a billion strong![41]

Nativism and Racism since 1890

Increased immigration from southern and eastern Europe and from Asia around the turn of the twentieth century focused anti-immigration sentiment on these groups. For example, Henry Cabot Lodge, an English American aristocrat from New England and a powerful political figure, was fiercely determined to defend the United States against immigrant "threats" in the 1890s and early 1900s. English Americans formed the Immigration League to halt southern and eastern European immigration. The League worked diligently for a literacy test, which passed Congress, and associated itself with the eugenics movement started by Sir Francis Galton, a prominent English Darwinist. The early U.S. eugenicists feared that allowing so-called "unfit" southern and eastern European (especially Catholic and Jewish) immigrants to enter would destroy the "superior race" of north Europeans. In their view, the unfit should be sterilized, excluded, or even eliminated.[42]

Perhaps the most prominent American to contribute to the development of racial nativism was

Madison Grant, an American of English extraction who fused various racist ideas in his influential book *The Passing of the Great Race* (1916). Worried about the influence of newer groups from southern and eastern Europe, Grant claimed that interbreeding with the inferior European "races" would lead to mongrelization. Northern Europeans—the "Nordic race"—were the superior "race."[43] By the 1920s this "scientific" racism helped fuel pressures for immigration legislation that discriminated against non-British white groups. Various national origin quotas were set to restrict immigration from southern and eastern Europe.

The 1920s and 1930s saw an outpouring of racial nativism on many fronts. Nativist organizations such as the revived Ku Klux Klan, an old U.S. terrorist group, provided a social outlet for those who wished to subordinate African, Catholic, and Jewish Americans and preserve the "Anglo-Saxon race." Opposition to foreign immigration resurfaced again after World War II, when various members of Congress and (northern) European American organizations opposed legislation that would permit political refugees, such as European Jews and Catholics, to migrate to the United States.

In recent decades some nativism has continued to take the form of stereotyping and harassing those not of northern European ancestry. For example, Democratic party presidential and vice-presidential candidates have sometimes been targeted because of their Catholic or southern European ancestry. In the 1984 national election, attacks were leveled at the Italian ancestry of Democratic vice-presidential candidate Geraldine Ferraro. Among other things, Republicans (many of northern European ancestry) alleged that she and her Italian American husband had connections to organized crime. Since the 1990s a number of Italian Americans involved in politics, such as former Governor Mario Cuomo of New York, have suffered similar "mafia" stereotypes.[44]

Another recent form of nativism can be seen in the various anti-immigration organizations that have flourished in the past decade or two. Like their predecessors in the early twentieth century, these organizations have opposed and stereotyped recent immigrants, particularly those coming from Asia and Latin America since the late 1960s. Immigrants' languages and cultures have often been the focus of this nativist opposition. White supremacy groups,

In a Denver demonstration, right-wing skinheads give the Nazi salute.

including the Klan, have held rallies across the United States and published racist literature and Web sites attacking non-European immigrant groups (sometimes called, with African Americans, the "mud people") as a threat to "American jobs" and to the Anglo-Protestant culture. These contemporary nativist groups include not only significant representations of northern European Americans but also, ironically, many whites with southern and eastern European ancestries, those whose parents or grandparents were targets of earlier nativist organizations.

THE DOMINANT CULTURE AND MAJOR U.S. INSTITUTIONS

Most analysts of the U.S. racial and ethnic scene have assumed that the dominant culture and major institutions are substantially English or Anglo-Protestant. During the first century of colonial settlement along the east coast, an English heritage integrated most of the colonies. Political, legal, and economic institutions were generally based on English models. However, the major U.S. institutions were not identical to those in England. The dominance of the Anglican church in some colonies soon gave way to religious diversity, and the colonies had no hereditary ruling class. The availability of land for (white) immigrants—the basis of much U.S. wealth—often fostered more democratic institutions. Traditional English ways were often modified under the new colonial conditions.[45]

Language

The United States has no official language, but the continuing dominance of the English language signals the huge social impact of early English settlers and their descendants. When Europeans first came, perhaps a thousand Native American languages were spoken; several hundred of these are still spoken. Today, however, the number of Americans speaking these original languages is far smaller than those speaking the languages of the European conquerors.

The principal U.S. language over the past two centuries has not been a thorough blend of Native American and early immigrant languages, but an English language that has incorporated words from both European and U.S. sources. W. Lloyd Warner and Leo Srole have argued that "our customary way of life is most like the English, and our language is but one of the several English dialects."[46] Historically, assimilation pressures on non-English-speaking immigrants have first taken the form of language pressure. As early as the 1740s, native-born Americans of British background attacked new immigrants (such as Germans) for their alleged threats to the English language and Anglo-American culture. From then to the present, the dominance of the English language has been a major concern of nativists.[47]

Today, millions of Americans live in homes in which a language other than English is spoken. In recent decades this group of non-English-speakers has been attacked as un-American by organized nativists, who worry that many newcomers, especially Latin American and Asian immigrants, will not accept English as their primary language. They are especially concerned that Spanish, spoken by 7–8 percent of Americans at home, is challenging the dominance of English. One result of lobbying by nativist organizations has been the introduction of legislation to make English the official language of the United States. In 1986, for example, California passed a ballot proposition that declared English to be the official language of this most populous state in the Union. In recent years numerous other states have passed this type of nativist legislation. In 1981 an English Language Amendment to the U.S. Constitution was introduced in Congress; it has been reintroduced in subsequent sessions of Congress but has not yet been passed.[48]

In 1997 a group called National English Campaign announced that its goals were to (1) replace ethnic group identification and "hyphenated ethnicity" with an "American identity" based on individual citizenship and (2) establish English as the official language of government, schools, and elections.[49] Such goals suggest fear of a pluralism of racial and ethnic groups and cultures and an emphasis on an English-oriented American identity.

Contemporary organizations with nativist undertones, such as the California English Campaign (said to have 200,000 supporters) and the National English Campaign, have fought bilingual programs across the nation. In 1997 they pressed for a California ballot initiative to limit instruction of immigrant children to one year in their native language before they moved into classes taught in English.[50]

Such groups often argue that they are not trying to discriminate against immigrants but wish immigrants to quickly become part of the mainstream by adopting English as their primary language. However, one such group, called U.S. English, was a project of a nonprofit organization that also supports immigration restrictions. A member of the U.S. Commission on Civil Rights resigned as president of U.S. English when she learned that its founder held anti-Latino views; among other things the founder had apparently forecast a political takeover of the United States by Latino Americans.[51]

Civil rights leaders have pointed out the discriminatory nature of several actions advocated by pro-English groups, in particular the prohibition of Spanish usage in government agencies, the elimination of bilingual programs in public schools, and the elimination of bilingual ballots in states with numerous Latino voters. A number of research studies have shown that children who are "denied the right to view the world through their language and culture are made to feel inferior" and may react in such negative ways as dropping out of school or engaging in drugs or crime—outcomes that cost not only themselves but the greater society dearly.[52] The implementation of English-only laws can have other negative effects, including the banning of testimony by non-English-speakers in court and the removal of language interpreters in government agencies.

Nativist campaigns to promote the English language underscore the traditional dominance of that language—and the uneasiness that descendants of earlier immigrants still feel in the presence of languages and cultures brought by relative newcomers to this "nation of immigrants."[53] As one legal scholar notes, their "first myth is that our national unity somehow depends solely on the English language, ergo we must protect the language through constitutional amendment or legislation. A corollary is that the only language of true American identity is the English language."[54]

What is ironic about these English-only movements is that most of the attacked immigrants not only recognize that English is the language of social and economic discourse in the United States, but also strive hard to learn the language. In a recent year, for example, some 40,000 immigrants were turned away or placed on waiting lists for adult English classes in the city of Los Angeles alone. Significantly, three-fourths of Latino immigrants speak English *every day*.[55] In addition, English-only nativism serves to further segregate English Americans from the rest of the world. Lack of knowledge of languages other than English cripples many Americans who conduct business abroad or deal politically with people in other nations across the globe.

Religion and Basic Values

The English religious influence on the United States has been of great importance. The various English denominations represented a variety of beliefs and practices. Anglicans in Virginia were characterized by a hierarchy of priests and a liturgical form of worship. This group favored a state church supported by compulsory church taxes. Presbyterian churches in the Appalachian backcountry favored a national church governed by strong ministers. Congregationalists and Separatists in New England favored moderate separation of church and state and more democratic church governance. Baptists (Rhode Island) and Quakers (New Jersey and Pennsylvania) both advocated strict separation between church and state. The communally organized Baptists favored a fellowship-centered form of worship. The spirit-centered worship of Quakers followed from a belief in an Inner Light that dwells in all people.[56] It was these latter groups who set the principle of separation of church and state at the heart of the U.S. political system.

For the first two hundred years, English churches, or descendants thereof, dominated the American scene. The Anglican church received some early government support but lost its privileged position during the Revolution. Anglican and Congregational churches were in the majority at the time of the Revolution, although Baptist and Presbyterian churches and Quaker groups were by then becoming more numerous. In the century after 1776, English dominance of U.S. religious institutions decreased as Catholic, Jewish, and other religious groups grew with the new immigration.[57]

Nonetheless, the Catholic and Jewish faiths, as well as non-British Protestantism, have been greatly shaped by the "American way of life," a phrase Will Herberg applies to the dominant Anglo-Protestant culture.[58] One important study of Judaism has shown the substantial impact of Protestant institutions on eastern European Judaism. Immigrant synagogues made major changes over time in response to the dominant culture. For example, Jewish religious schools adapted to Protestant American scheduling and Sunday school formats. Reform Jews adopted English as the language of worship and introduced Friday-night services.[59] Yet the Anglo-Protestant culture's impact on the non-Protestant religions of later immigrants has been uneven and incomplete. Although new immigrants have been expected to adapt in many areas, some religious heritages from the home countries have been preserved. Contemporary U.S. religious patterns can be described as a type of cultural pluralism.

Certain Anglo-Protestant values have also had a significant impact on later immigrants. The importance of the ascetic (austere and self-denying) Protestantism that early English settlers brought to the colonies cannot be underestimated. "American condemnation of British sexual and political impurities focused on the King. Idleness, wealth, and power had corrupted him."[60] Puritanism helped to establish the so-called "Protestant work ethic" at the center of the U.S. value system—the idea of hard work as a duty of every individual, originally of an individual who seeks to please God. This work ethic was linked by many to the pursuit of personal profit. The emerging capitalistic system in the late 1700s and the 1800s was pervaded by the "pursuit of profit, and forever *renewed* profit, by means of continuous, rational, capitalistic enterprise."[61]

The influence of English religious traditions on music and the arts in the earliest period is further evidence of the extensive English impact on early American culture. The first book published in the New England colonies was the *Bay Psalm Book* (1640), which drew heavily on the English religious music tradition. "Yankee Doodle" was probably an English tune whose original lyrics satirized ragtag colonial soldiers. Only when the Revolution began did American soldiers take it over from the British. Before, during, and after the Revolution, English melodies were the basis of most popular and political songs.[62] The national anthem, "The Star-Spangled Banner," took its melody from an English drinking song.

Interestingly, however, over the next two centuries English influence on U.S. popular music receded dramatically before the pervasive influence of African American music (jazz and rock and roll, for example), "Scotch-Irish" country music, and the Mexican American music of the Southwest. Today, popular music is one major area of U.S. culture from which the English influence has almost disappeared.

Education

English and other British Americans took advantage of what few educational opportunities were available in the colonial period; more affluent parents sent their children to the private schools established before 1800. With the public school movement, which began in earnest in the first decades of the nineteenth century, British dominance of public schools became a fact of life. British Americans saw the urban public schools as a means of socializing non-British immigrants into Anglo-Protestant and U.S. industrial value systems. In the nineteenth century, most public school systems were established by British American industrialists and educators who shaped curricula and instruction and supervised schools. Although some—for example, John Dewey—believed education should bring greater opportunities for poor immigrants, many educators emphasized the social-control aspects of schools. Americanization pressures on immigrant children were often intense. Whether children were Irish, Jewish, or Italian, Anglicization was designed to ferret out non-Anglo-Protestant ways and assimilate the children to Anglo-Protestant manners, work habits, and values.[63]

Public schools' social-control function and the British American influence on their structure and operation remain evident today. More recent immigrants, such as Asians and Latinos, have faced Anglo-conformity pressures similar to those experienced by earlier Irish and Italian immigrants. Indeed, the public schools are still a major battleground for those concerned with making English the official language of the United States.

Political and Legal Institutions

The political and legal institutions that affect all Americans have been shaped, and are still being shaped, by the English political heritage in at least two basic ways: laws and traditions inherited from the English and their concrete application by English immigrants and their descendants. Given the early majority of English settlers in east coast colonial society, English legal institutions became dominant. Concern for the rule of law and insistence on the "rights of Englishmen" were central. The famous Mayflower Compact (1620), a political framework theoretically providing for equality under the law, was part of this English political tradition. New England, with its Puritan institutions, often provided the model for later U.S. political and legal developments.[64]

The North American colonies developed a distinctive set of political institutions—often those characteristic of sixteenth-century England. The basic ideas included unity of government and society, subordination of government to law, a balance of power between the legislature (Parliament in England) and the executive (the king in England), and heavy reliance on local governments.[65] American political and legal institutions, including the U.S. Constitution, have reflected these ideas ever since. Authority and power were being centralized in England, but here they were separated into three branches—executive, judicial, and legislative. The position of the U.S. president is unusual: The United States, unlike almost every other modern political system, does not distinguish between the head of government and the chief of state. Indeed, the Watergate scandal of the Richard Nixon presidential administration in the 1970s and the "Contragate" scandal of the Ronald Reagan White House in the 1980s show just how powerful the U.S. executive branch is relative to Congress. The United States is a new society, but it is an "old" political state.

Representative government in the colonies and, later, the United States is another example of English influence. Using Parliament as its model, the British Crown established representative colonial assemblies almost from the start.[66] Gradually these assemblies grew in power vis-à-vis the London government. Indeed, Crown infringements on them helped generate the Revolution.

The U.S. legal framework also reflects English influence. Prior to the Revolution, English common law was asserted to be "the measure of rights of Americans."[67] Tension between the new nation and mother England caused some objections to the continuation of English-based laws in the new nation. Some Americans wanted a new U.S. legal code, but for the most part U.S. lawyers only "sought to reshape or add to the existing stock of authoritative legal materials."[68] Although there was variation in how English statutes were brought into the U.S. legal system, their implementation was thoroughgoing: "The use of English statutes was provided for at an early stage in twenty-six of the twenty-eight jurisdictions organized between 1776 and 1836."[69] Although the U.S. legal system has been patched many times, the basic cloth today is still English common law.[70]

Officeholding

In addition to their fundamental impact on U.S. political institutions, English Americans have had a major impact on the operation of those institutions. The first president of the United States, George Washington, was of English ancestry, as was the forty-third president, George W. Bush, more than two centuries later. English Americans have filled a disproportionate number of major offices at various political levels throughout U.S. history.

Maurice Davie notes that "the colonial assemblies were almost exclusively English in makeup."[71] The Declaration of Independence was signed by fifty-six European American men, thirty-eight of whom were English by background or birth; nine were Scottish or "Scotch-Irish," three Irish, five Welsh, and one Swedish.[72] A majority of the members of the Constitutional Convention were also English, and the Constitution was framed around their concerns not only for democratic institutions reminiscent of English institutions but also for the protection of their own property and wealth. As a result, most people of wealth in the new nation—merchants, slaveholders, financiers, shippers, wealthy farmers, and their allies—supported the new U.S. Constitution out of economic self-interest. Slaves, indentured servants, poor farmers, laborers, and women had no say in the framing of the U.S. Constitution. Not surprisingly, the framers of the Constitution perpetuated social class lines similar to those in England.[73]

Studies of U.S. presidents, Supreme Court justices, and members of Congress have revealed a distinctive pattern persisting to the present. Presidents and presidential candidates have been informally "required" to possess ancestry qualifications, preferably British American or other northern European ancestry. Of the U.S. presidents from Washington to Bush, about two-thirds had English ancestry and *all* the rest had other northern European backgrounds.[74]

No southern Europeans, Jewish Americans, Latino Americans, Asian Americans, Middle Eastern Americans, or African Americans have been president. A study of the origins of Supreme Court justices from 1789 to 1957 found that more than half were of English or Welsh extraction. In all periods, including the present, northern Europeans have dominated the nation's highest court.[75] Moreover, an analysis of 162 prominent political leaders (including presidents, representatives, senators, and Supreme Court justices) of the period between 1901 and 1910 found that more than half were of English or Welsh origin.[76]

Even when new immigrant groups have managed to break into U.S. politics, as in the case of Irish and Italian Americans, they have often been subservient to Anglo-Protestant leaders who have continued to hold the highest political offices. Newer immigrants and their children did gain significant electoral and political power in the first decades of the twentieth century in some U.S. cities, but not as elected officials at the national level. Only one Catholic American has *ever* been president, Irish American John F. Kennedy (1961–1963). His brief presidency marked only a temporary shift from a more or less homogeneous political establishment at the very top, for Kennedy was followed by more men of northern European Protestant stock.[77]

While the domination of northern European Americans at the very top of national politics persists today, some challenges to this dominance can be seen at political levels below the top. For example, in the early 2000s the cabinet of President George W. Bush included a number of Americans whose ancestral background was not northern European. Bush's cabinet included people of Asian, Latino, and African American backgrounds, perhaps signaling the growing racial and ethnic diversity in national politics.

What of the English American impact on local governments? A study of New Haven up to 1960 illustrates English political dominance in New England. For many decades a patrician elite there "completely dominated the political system. They were of one common stock and one religion, cohesive in their uniformly conservative outlook on all matters, substantially unchallenged in their authority, successful in pushing through their own policies, and in full control of such critical institutions as the established religion, the educational system (including not only all the schools but Yale as well), and even business enterprise."[78] A study of the mayors of Cleveland in the period between 1836 and 1901 found that most were part of an Anglo-Protestant elite with strong ties to New England. Their political framework was guided by what was termed the "New England creed," one proposition of which was "The good society is white and Protestant."[79]

In recent decades Americans of British ancestry have had to compete with non-British immigrants and their descendants for power in local and state politics, and today the racial and ethnic mix in local and state political institutions varies considerably across the nation. Irish, Italian, and, most recently, African, Asian, and Latino Americans have risen to political power in the large cities of the Midwest, East, South, and West. Still, English and other British Americans continue to exercise great influence in local politics, especially in suburban politics, although they and their ethnicity receive little mass media attention.

Economic Institutions

The English heritage is reflected in U.S. economic institutions—in the values that shape those institutions and in the actual dominance of English American individuals. Just as the U.S. legal system incorporated portions of the English legal system, the early forms of capitalism that dominated much of northern Europe during colonial times shaped the colonies' economic system. The British Crown wished to increase the raw materials and the markets available to the home country. To this end, the first English colonies were established by state-chartered trading companies or were proprietary colonies established by men of wealth.

Mercantile capitalism, which still existed in the colonies at the time of the Revolution, was a state-directed capitalism linked to English nationalism. The American Revolution was in part a clash between English and British American commercial interests, a clash that unified the colonies and brought a political break between two similar economic systems.[80]

Industrial capitalism developed in the United States after 1830, again with intimate connections to the English system. The basic ideas and many technologies for U.S. industrial development came from

England; English capitalists and skilled workers provided much of the know-how for U.S. economic development. After the Revolution, as before, Britain and the United States formed a single north Atlantic economy.[81]

Direct Participation in the Economy

English and other British Americans have influenced the operation of the U.S. economy through direct control of critical positions. In the beginning they established most of the colonies and controlled much of the land and wealth. In the early period control of the colonies lay primarily in the hands of English and other British American landowners and merchants.[82] In the late prerevolutionary period, small and medium-sized farmers with their own land came to have more influence in many colonies.[83] Whatever their background, English Americans with land and wealth often needed labor. Because they had no surplus population, the colonies imported labor from Europe and Africa. By the 1730s a substantial Irish migration had begun, and a large proportion of these immigrants were indentured servants. The brutal African slave trade eventually supplanted the trade in white servants.[84]

As we move toward the Civil War period and then into the twentieth century, we find few studies on the English or British American dominance of the economy. A study of the wealth of men living in 1860 concluded only that the wealth of "native-born males," doubtless mostly British Americans, was about twice that of "foreign-born males."[85] U.S. industrialization in the nineteenth century was partially fueled by English and Dutch capital. U.S. business elites have long been dominated by Americans of British or other northern European descent. In the nineteenth century, the most famous of these were industrialists and financiers, many of whom have been regarded as "robber barons." They included John D. Rockefeller, Leland Stanford, J. P. Morgan, Jay Gould, and Jim Fisk, all men of great wealth and power. Their ethnic heritages were typically English, with a few other northern European heritages mixed in. Many of their associates or family members became senators, representatives, and governors.[86]

A study of top executives and entrepreneurs in the late-nineteenth-century iron and steel industry found that few came from recent immigrant families; most were native-born and had fathers with capitalist or professional backgrounds. Most did not fit the image of a poor immigrant "making good," as did the steel magnate Andrew Carnegie, who came to America as a poor boy. More than half were of English or Welsh ancestry; most of the rest were either Scottish or Irish.[87] A survey of two hundred major executives serving the largest companies from 1901 to 1910 found that 53 percent were of English or Welsh origin, 7 percent were Scottish, 14 percent were Irish, and 8 percent were Canadian or British (unspecified).[88]

A few studies have made clear the extent of British American dominance in local economies. For instance, in the 1930s Burlington, Vermont was dominated by "Old Americans"—those who had been in the United States for four generations, probably heavily English and English Canadian. They controlled banking and manufacturing, and they constituted a disproportionate number of professionals and political officials.[89]

A few studies of the economically influential have been done since the 1930s. The "proper Philadelphians" about whom Baltzell has written typically had English or British backgrounds. This is suggested by the dominance of Episcopalians and Presbyterians in the Philadelphia *Social Register* for the year 1940.[90] In an analysis of the 1950s and 1960s, Baltzell further underscored the continuing dominance of British Americans at the national level.[91]

Contemporary Elites

Thomas Dye's 1970s study of major decision makers in the United States identified four thousand people in the top positions in corporations, government, and the public sector. Dye concluded that "great power in America is concentrated in a tiny handful of men. A few thousand individuals out of 200 million Americans decide about war and peace, wages and prices, consumption and investment, employment and production, law and justice, taxes and benefits, education and learning, health and welfare, advertising and communication, life and leisure."[92] Decisions of importance are reached at the middle and lower levels of the society, but it is the few thousand people in the top positions who make the most critical decisions—those affecting the lives of many millions of Americans in all racial and ethnic groups. Dye's research revealed that the social origins of the top four thousand were not representative of the U.S. population as a whole. Indeed, most were affluent, white, Anglo-Protestant men. This group contained only a few African Americans and virtually no Mexican Americans, Native Americans, or Asian Americans. Dye has estimated that these elites were "at least 90 percent Anglo-Protestant" and noted that "there were very few recognizable Irish, Italian, or Jewish names" in the group.[93]

Since the late 1980s, magazines such as *U.S. News & World Report* have proclaimed that those in the media, politics, and the universities who most influence American life are now a more diverse and representative group. Elites "today represent a real break with their predecessors. Almost none of them are WASP's; fewer still are in the *Social Register*."[94] This view of an integrated top elite has increased since the 1980s as much political commentary has moved in a more conservative direction. But this view was and is largely inaccurate. One must be careful to distinguish social and economic realities from rags-to-riches myths. By the early 2000s the upper reaches of U.S. economic (and other) institutions had broadened to include not only British Americans but also those with other northern European ancestry, particularly German, "Scotch-Irish," and Scandinavian Americans, and a handful of Catholic and Jewish Americans were beginning to penetrate elite bastions of economic power. Yet, as we begin the twenty-first century, Catholic and Jewish Americans are still not proportionately represented at the top of the economic pyramid. And very few non-Europeans can be found at or near the very top of the largest (Fortune 500) corporations.

Several research studies since the 1980s have found a continuing pattern of disproportionately white and north European Protestant dominance at the top levels of U.S. industrial, public interest, and governmental organizations. One study found that 57 percent of business leaders were Anglo-Protestants, much higher than their proportion in the population. When other white Protestants were added in, the proportion rose to 79 percent.[95]

In recent decades the acronym *WASP*, originally shorthand for *white Anglo-Saxon Protestant*, has been widely used, often with derogatory and stereotypical implications, as English and other British Americans have increasingly been challenged for political and economic dominance by Americans from southern and eastern Europe.

English Americans as a Group: Economic and Educational Data

In the 1990 census, approximately 23 million Americans listed English as their first ancestry, just over 9 percent of the total population; some 97 percent of these were native-born. A 1999–2000 census survey estimated that 28.3 million Americans had some English ancestry.[96]

The only detailed data available are for 1990. In 1990 the educational attainment of English Americans as a group was higher than that of either the total population or the total (non-Latino) white population. (In census tabulations, many Latinos are counted as white, but some are counted as black.) A slightly larger percentage of English American youth was enrolled in school than in either of the larger groups, as Table 3.2 illustrates.[97]

TABLE 3.2 EDUCATIONAL ATTAINMENT

	ENGLISH ANCESTRY	NON-LATINO WHITE	TOTAL POPULATION
15–19-year-olds in school	85.0%	82.0%	81.0%
Those 25 years and over with less than fifth grade	0.7	1.3	2.7
Those 25 years and over with high school or more	84.0	79.0	75.0
Those 25 years and over with college degree or more	28.0	22.0	20.0

TABLE 3.3 INCOME AND POVERTY

	ENGLISH ANCESTRY	NON-LATINO WHITE	TOTAL POPULATION
Median family income	$40,875	$37,628	$35,225
Per capita income	$18,594	$16,074	$14,420
Family poverty rate	4.5%	7.0%	10.0%

Taken as a group, English Americans were also economically better off than the total population or the total (non-Latino) white population (see Table 3.3).[98]

The median income for families of English ancestry was about 16 percent greater than that of all American families and almost 9 percent greater than that of all (non-Latino) white families. The poverty rate for families of English ancestry was less than half that of all families.

Occupational distribution data show broad similarities between English Americans and the general population, although a somewhat larger proportion of Americans of English ancestry hold white-collar jobs and a somewhat smaller proportion hold blue-collar jobs than in the general population, as can be seen in Table 3.4.[99]

In addition, English Americans are more likely to be self-employed and less likely to be unemployed than either the general population or the total (non-Latino) white population, as can be seen in Table 3.5.[100]

Still, it is important to note that not all those with English ancestry are well-off in terms of education, income, and occupational position.

ENGLISH AMERICANS TODAY

Although they constitute the group whose culture and institutions have usually been the standard against which other groups' degree of assimilation is measured, English Americans are rarely researched. One analysis by the first author of a large data bank

TABLE 3.4 OCCUPATIONAL DISTRIBUTIONS

	ENGLISH ANCESTRY	NON-LATINO WHITE	TOTAL POPULATION
Managerial and professional	34%	29%	27%
Technical, sales, administrative	33	33	32
Service	10	12	13
Farming, forestry, fishing	2	2	2
Precision production, craft, repair	10	12	11
Operators, fabricators, laborers	11	13	15
Total	100%	101%	100%

TABLE 3.5 EMPLOYMENT AND UNEMPLOYMENT

	ENGLISH ANCESTRY	NON-LATINO WHITE	TOTAL POPULATION
Unemployed	4.3%	5.0%	6.30%
Self-employed	8.7	8.0	6.97

of thousands of articles and stories in hundreds of U.S. magazines, newspapers, newsletters, journals, and other publications that appeared between 1978 and 1997 found not one serious article focusing on Americans of English ancestry. In this sixteen-year period, it was very rare for journalists or editors even to mention English Americans in any context. This neglect of such a powerful ethnic group suggests just how much the English have blended into, or become, the sociocultural background of this society.[101]

As we have seen, some 28 million or so Americans today claim partial or total English ancestry. Those of English descent still have some tendency to marry others with the same or similar backgrounds. One analysis found that just over half the women with English ancestry had mates who were partly or wholly of English ancestry.[102]

Residential dispersal has been characteristic of English Americans and other north European Americans. One study by Richard Alba in New York found that respondents with English ancestry had dispersed throughout the New York region. Their early ancestors had immigrated to the area in the seventeenth and eighteenth centuries, and later descendants had much time to move around. In this study, 95 percent of those with English or Dutch ancestry reported mixed ethnic backgrounds; many had ancestors from two or three countries. In addition, 40 to 50 percent of those with British backgrounds said that their ethnic identity had no importance to them. Alba cautions that this latter response may mean that many have come to see their English or British American identity as synonymous with a "truly American" identity. They may have so completely integrated their English or British identity with their definition of what is American that they see no need to identify assertively with their country of origin. In contrast, more recent immigrant groups (for example, southern European Catholics) were much more likely to identify strongly with their national heritage.[103]

While English Americans can be viewed for many purposes as a cohesive ethnic group, regional variations in certain aspects of English American culture are still evident today. As Fischer has pointed out, the concepts of liberty brought by the four groups of English immigrants in the 1600s and 1700s evolved in somewhat different ways in the colonies. In New England, the Puritans' concept of ordered freedom, which was codified into written laws, "became an instrument of savage persecution." Ordered freedom involved the liberty to impose individual restraints on the Puritans themselves without interference by outsiders, to grant certain exemptions from these restraints to particular individuals, and to practice the "true" religion and persecute dissenters. In Virginia, the idea of hegemonic freedom—the belief that liberty was the birthright of the free-born English and gave those with high status the right to rule people of lower ranks—"permitted and even required the growth of race slavery for its support." In the Delaware Valley, the Quakers' belief in reciprocal freedom, which recognized each individual's right to dissent, caused them to withdraw from the world. In contrast, "the [Appalachian] backcountry belief in natural freedom, which favored minimal government and the supremacy of private interests, sometimes dissolved into cultural anarchy."[104] All those of English descent, however, emphasized the importance of individual freedom as they saw it. All these interpretations can still be found today as different regional variations on the theme of freedom.

Fischer has also analyzed the relationship between present-day regional diversity in the United States and the distinctive colonial cultures of the four groups of English immigrants. Regional differences in homicide rates provide an interesting example. Homicide rates today are low in the areas of New England in which the early Puritans established a tradition of order and nonviolence, and high in the southern areas that were first settled by immigrants from northern Great Britain's borderlands, whose culture was somewhat violence-prone before emigration. Other social indicators examined by Fischer include education, attitudes toward gender equality, and patterns of local government and public life. Those areas with high rates of high-school and college graduation today are generally the ones whose colonial culture valued education highly. Those states that failed to ratify the Woman's Suffrage Amendment (1918–1921) and the Equal Rights Amendment (1972–1978) were those in whose colonial culture women had a comparatively low status. Many New England communities today continue the colonial practice of governance by town meetings. Current regional differences in the levels of taxation and public spending are broadly similar to what they were in the colonial period. Significantly, "each of the four cultural regions of British America ... [has] kept its own customs of enculturation for many generations."[105]

One distinctive region is the South, which was settled substantially by English from the borderlands. The largest white ethnic group in the South today is still Americans of English descent.[106] Sociologist Lewis Killian notes that one part of the southern white population is descended from early Irish immigrants, those often called "Scotch-Irish" (see Chapter 4). There are also large proportions of French, Spanish, or German descent. Killian argues that English and other British Americans have become mostly submerged in a larger, ethnically diverse white population that has emphasized whiteness above all else: "For a southerner, the salient fact was and is whether he was white or black; all else was secondary."[107]

The theoretical frameworks of assimilation analysts generally take the English (or British) Americans and their culture and institutions as the starting point for the analysis of assimilation in the United States. Gordon's important seven-stage framework (Chapter 2) generally assumes Anglo-conformity as the general trend of adaptation by subsequent immigrant groups in the North American colonies and, later, in the United States. Typically, assimilation theorists assume that later immigrant groups will eventually be included in the dominant society.

Looking at the history of English Americans, however, power-conflict theorists would emphasize the ways in which the English colonization process initiated racial and ethnic stratification in the United States. The violent subordination or extermination of Native Americans by English settlers is a clear example of *migrant superordination*, which takes place when a migrating group imposes its will on an indigenous group. The entry of later groups of immigrants and their relegation to a subordinate position in the stratification system dominated by English Americans, as was the case for enslaved Africans, is an example of *indigenous superordination*. Such concepts acknowledge the social hierarchy, with its unequal power and resources, that developed over the course of U.S. racial and ethnic history.

SUMMARY

This chapter examines one of the most neglected of U.S. ethnic groups, English Americans. The degree to which they now blend into the background of U.S. culture and society makes it difficult to assess the power, location, and achievements of these early immigrants and their millions of descendants. Americans of English ancestry still make up a substantial proportion of the U.S. population, and they still tend to share certain values and customs and to marry others of northern European ancestry.

The English were the first to establish major colonies in the area that became the eastern United States. *Dominance* is the appropriate term for English influence on U.S. religious, economic, and political institutions. The colonization migration of the English created a dominant culture and hierarchical social structure to which subsequent immigrant groups were required to adapt. The study of group assimilation in the United States begins with the English. For centuries, English migrants and their millions of descendants have been disproportionately represented in key social, economic, and political positions in this society.

Between the mid-1800s and the present, English Americans have been joined in their dominant position by certain other European American groups. The result is a more diverse Anglo-Protestant group, but one that still holds disproportionately great power.

The tremendous impact of Anglo-Protestant Americans on U.S. culture and institutions does not mean that substantial segments have not remained working-class or poor. There have long been significant regional and denominational differences within English and British American groups. Indeed, Episcopalians differ from Congregationalists, and southerners differ from New Englanders.

In recent decades, English and British Protestant dominance has been challenged by Catholic Americans and Jewish Americans with European ancestry as well as by non-European groups. Some analysts have argued that Anglo-Protestant influence is on the wane. Schrag, for instance, argues that "Anglo-Saxon Protestants" are on the road to cultural decline and offers as evidence the increasing non-Anglo-Saxon dominance of music, literature, and art. But even Schrag presents a different conclusion for the economic sphere: The Anglo-Protestant "elite still controls its own corporate offices, its board rooms, its banks and foundations."[108] Analyses declaring the significant decline of whites of English and British ancestry as a force in this society are, as the data in this chapter suggest, somewhat premature.

4 Irish and Italian Americans

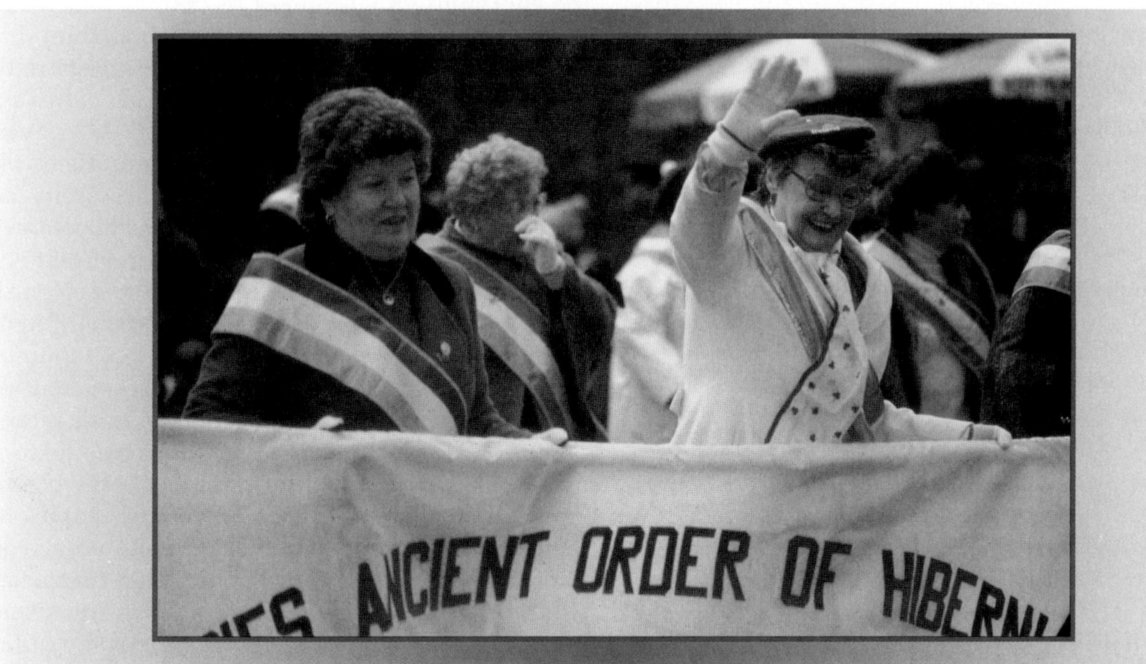

NUMEROUS DISCUSSIONS OF ETHNICITY HAVE FOCUSED ON *WHITE ETHNICS*, A TERM sometimes used for white Catholic and Jewish Americans. White Anglo-Protestant Americans have, on occasion, blamed these groups for major societal problems, such as political machines or anti-black racism in U.S. cities. They have sometimes spoken of white ethnic "hardhats" as though they were uneducated buffoons with a corrupt or authoritarian bent. Not surprisingly, white ethnics have counterattacked, arguing that hypocritical Anglo-Protestants have little awareness of the historical experiences of Catholic and Jewish Americans.

IRISH AMERICANS

The purpose of this chapter on the Irish and Italian Americans, and the next on Jewish Americans, is to analyze the neglected experiences of some of the non-English white Americans who helped build the United States. Irish Americans are one of the major groups, especially among those in the large cities, that come to mind when white ethnic groups are mentioned.

IRISH IMMIGRATION: AN OVERVIEW

Placed on the migration continuum from slave importation to voluntary immigration, the Irish migration to North America falls toward the voluntary end. Even so, this movement was less voluntary than the migrations of some other European groups, for economic and political pressures to leave Ireland were often great. Perhaps 200,000 to 400,000 Irish left for the colonies prior to 1787; between 1787 and the 1820s, approximately 100,000 migrated.[1] The heaviest period was between 1841 and 1860, when 1.6 million Irish entered the United States. Migration peaked again in the 1880s and 1890s, then dropped sharply in subsequent decades.[2] For example, in the period 1961–1992, only about 107,000 Irish immigrants entered the United States.[3]

In the 1990 census more than 22.7 million Americans listed "Irish" as their primary ancestry, and more than 4.3 million listed "Scotch-Irish." Almost all in both groups were born in the United States. A census 2000 supplementary survey estimated the number of Irish and Scotch-Irish Americans (first and second ancestry) at 38.3 million.[4] Together, these two groups now make up about 14 percent of the U.S. population.[5]

The Eighteenth-Century Migration

The Irish first came to the United States in the 1650s, when Captain John Vernon supplied 550 persons from southern Ireland as servants and workers for the English colonists and entrepreneurs in New England.[6] However, large numbers of Irish did not arrive on North American shores until the 1700s.

Both push and pull factors influenced Irish immigration. The image of North America as a land of opportunity was a major pull factor, but domestic pressures were also important. In the 1100s the English conquered Ireland and imposed a repressive and often bloody rule. By the 1600s, large numbers of Scots were being encouraged to migrate across the channel to Ireland to develop and manage the lands given to English and Scottish landowners by the king of England.[7]

As a result of England's colonization of Ireland, the Ulster (northern) Irish who migrated to North America included a significant number of persons of Scottish ancestry. Traditional scholars have held that virtually all Irish immigrants before 1800 were "Scotch-Irish" Protestants from northern Ireland.[8] However, Michael O'Brien has cited "unquestionable proof that every part of Ireland contributed to the enormous emigration of its people, and while there are no official statistics now available—for none were kept—to indicate the numerical strength of those Irish immigrants, abundant proof of this assertion is found in authentic records."[9] Moreover, many southern Irish immigrants gave up their traditional Catholicism because of the scarcity of Catholic churches in the North American colonies and because of the extremely hostile Protestant environment in many areas of Ireland and the colonies that made the open practice of Catholicism difficult if not dangerous.[10]

Because the northern Irish in the first streams of immigration regarded themselves as Irish rather than Scotch-Irish, the term *Scotch-Irish* was seldom used in the first two centuries of Irish presence in America. The new migrants gave Irish names to their settlements and joined organizations such as the Friendly Sons of Saint Patrick rather than Scottish American societies.[11] The term *Scotch-Irish* came into heavy use only after 1850, when some older Irish Protestant immigrants (and their English friends) sought to distinguish themselves from the more recent Irish Catholic immigrants who were, at that time, the focus of intense stereotyping and discrimination.[12] By the late nineteenth century, the issue of the "Scotch-Irish race" and its impact was being widely discussed. Prominent politicians engaged in overtly racial stereotyping when they praised the members of the "Scotch-Irish race" as exemplary pioneers and democrats while damning the "Catholic Irish race as inferior and lazy."[13]

Early Life

What was life like for the early Irish settlers in an English-dominated society? In North America, perhaps half became indentured servants; others became subsistence farmers or farm workers, often in frontier areas. English Americans often treated their

Irish Protestant and Catholic servants and other workers as lowly subordinates, even to the point of physical brutality.[14] Faced with anti-Catholic hostility, significant numbers of the Irish immigrants gave up Catholicism. Not all converted, however. Pressing for religious tolerance, several prominent Irish Catholics wrote the new President George Washington in the late 1700s asking that the full religious rights of Catholics be protected.[15]

The pull factors motivating millions of Irish Catholics to cross the Atlantic after 1830 were the same as those that attracted European immigrants for centuries to North America, which was portrayed, often in exaggerated terms, as the land of golden opportunity. Push factors loomed even larger. The famine that came to Ireland in the 1840s spurred emigration to the United States. Irish peasants relied heavily on potatoes for food. A potato blight caused a massive failure of that crop, and many people starved to death or died from hunger-related diseases. Ireland actually produced more than twice enough food to feed its population, but the English landlords saw to it that most of these foodstuffs were exported to England and elsewhere or consumed by those in Ireland with money. English leaders advocated emigration to the United States and elsewhere as the proper solution for the poor Irish.[16]

The Atlantic crossing was often dangerous. Few ships arrived that had not lost a number of their poorly accommodated passengers to starvation or disease. The survivors usually chose urban destinations in the United States. New York became a major center, eventually housing more Irish than the Irish city of Dublin. Like most urban migrants, the new immigrants went where relatives or fellow villagers had settled. The early Irish immigrants often clustered in small, dispersed settlements within cities, unlike the huge segregated communities that were characteristic of later immigrant groups.[17]

These early Irish settlements were reinforced by a second large stream of immigrants from Ireland between 1870 and 1900 and by significant but declining numbers of immigrants from 1900 to 1925. These later immigrants were forced out not by famine, but primarily by poverty and the hope for a better life.[18]

From the beginning, women have been crucial to the establishment of strong Irish American communities. One distinctive aspect of the Irish immigration was the presence of large numbers of young single women. Because they had no hope of inheritance and little hope of marriage in poverty-stricken Ireland, they saw the United States as a land of opportunity. Once in the United States, these women did not subscribe to the cult of womanhood that emphasized that the woman's place was only in the home. Most did not live lives of sheltered domesticity but rather became self-sufficient individuals with distinctive work histories. They made important social and economic contributions to the upward mobility of Irish Americans into the middle class.

For six decades young, unmarried women came to the United States to avoid the terrible life usually awaiting them in Ireland. In contrast with male Irish immigrants and female immigrants from many other countries, these women were willing to postpone or forego marriage and to work as domestic servants. Many supported their families in the old country. The decisions they made about work were an expression of fundamental life-choice values that persist among Irish Americans today. Interestingly, the daughters of these women often became schoolteachers or clerical workers.[19]

STEREOTYPES

Both Protestant and Catholic Irish Americans suffered from nativistic concern over their presence and political persuasions. Yet it was the nineteenth-century Irish, the poor Catholics from the famine-ridden Emerald Isle, who were attacked the most.

From the 1820s to the mid-1840s, the Anglo-American stereotype of the Catholic Irish emphasized their alleged character faults, such as ingratitude, wickedness, and ignorance. With the increase in Irish migration in the late 1840s, words like *temperamental*, *dangerous*, *quarrelsome*, *idle*, and *reckless*—characteristics emphasizing conduct as much as character—came into use to characterize and stereotype the Irish. The Anglo-American image of the Irish hardened and became less tolerant as the number of Irish immigrants grew.[20]

The Ape Image

Irish Catholics were stereotyped in cartoons that used outrageous and hostile symbols—an apelike face, a fighting stance, a jug of whisky, a shillelagh.

Caricatures of Roman Catholic bishops as crocodiles supposedly threaten Protestant children on American shores.

The influential caricaturist Thomas Nast published cartoons of this type in *Harper's Weekly* and other magazines. One of his caricatures shows a stereotyped southern black man and an apelike Irishman, both portrayed as ignorant voters and a threat to orderly politics. The apelike image of the Irish was imported from England to the United States. With the rise of debates over human evolution in England, the Irish poor came to be regarded by many in England and the United States as the "missing link" between the gorilla and the human race. With the constant threat of Irish rebellion on the one hand and the press of evolutionary Darwinism on the other, "it was comforting for some Englishmen to believe—on the basis of the best scientific authority in the Anthropological Society of London—that their own facial angles and orthognathous features were as far removed from those of apes, Irishmen, and Negroes as was humanly possible."[21] In rationalizing the exploitation of the Irish and Africans, racist theorists and commentators on both sides of the Atlantic developed dehumanizing animal stereotypes. Notice the comparable position of black and Irish Americans in this mythology.

Sociologist Andrew Greeley has underscored the parallels in prejudice and stereotyping:

> Practically every accusation that has been made against the American blacks was also made against the Irish: Their family life was inferior, they had no ambition, they did not keep up their homes, they drank too much, they were not responsible, they had no morals, it was not safe to walk through their neighborhoods at night, they voted the way crooked politicians told them to vote, they were not willing to pull themselves up by their bootstraps, they were not capable of education, they could not think for themselves, and they would always remain social problems for the rest of the country.[22]

Changing Attitudes

In the early decades of the twentieth century, the harsh attitudes toward Irish Americans gradually gave way to acceptance as nativist hostilities were transferred to newer immigrant groups. However, not all negative attitudes toward Irish Americans disappeared. As late as 1932 white students at

Princeton University were given a list of eighty-four positive and negative traits and asked to identify those they associated with ten racial and ethnic groups, including Irish Americans. Five of the ten traits most frequently assigned to Irish Americans—"pugnacious," "quick-tempered," "quarrelsome," "aggressive," and "stubborn"—comprise a traditional stereotype of Irish aggressiveness. Significantly, fifty years later, a similar questionnaire given to a predominantly white sample of Arizona State University students found a significant decrease in the negative imagery. Only "quick-tempered" and "stubborn" remained among the top ten traits assigned to the Irish.[23]

In a 1980s nationwide opinion poll that asked respondents whether various immigrant groups had, on balance, been good or bad for this country, Irish Americans received the second-highest percentage of positive answers, only slightly less than English Americans.[24] The reduction in the racial and ethnic stereotyping of Irish Americans that appears to have taken place since the 1930s indicates substantial *attitude-receptional assimilation,* to use Gordon's conceptual term. Yet, even today, stereotypes of Irish Americans still exist. In a study of white ethnic groups in a metropolitan area in New York, about one-fifth of those with Irish ancestry reported encountering stereotypes of Irish Americans as politicians and police officers, heavy drinkers, or poets. They also encountered the traditional image of Irish women as "long-suffering."[25]

PROTEST AND CONFLICT

From their first decades in North America, Irish Americans suffered not only verbal abuse and stereotyping but also intentional discrimination and violent attacks from Anglo-Protestant Americans. On occasion, Irish Americans have retaliated, even to the point of violence. Irish Americans have also been responsible for starting racial or ethnic conflict. As we noted in Chapter 2, intergroup conflict often involves a struggle over resources and can be generated by substantial group inequality.

Assimilation theorists have usually neglected the conflict that has characterized interethnic and interracial relations. Indeed, some social science and popular views of U.S. history embody a myth of peaceful progress. According to this assimilationist view, the members of each white ethnic group have ascended the socioeconomic ladder by pulling themselves up by their own bootstraps—by hard work, not by active protest and collective violence. This image is incorrect. To secure their "place in the sun" Irish Americans have had to struggle with many other groups, from established Anglo-Protestants to Native Americans. They have been involved in open conflict with groups above and below them in power and social position.

Early Conflict

Irish immigrants' first major conflict was with the established groups that controlled the major institutions in the North American colonies at the time of the initial Irish immigration. A few eighteenth-century Irish settlements were damaged or destroyed by Anglo-Protestant attacks. For example, British Americans attacked and destroyed an Irish community in Worcester, Massachusetts in the eighteenth century. Both Catholic and Protestant Irish migrants faced widespread and bitter opposition from the already established groups.[26]

In the colonial period, many English Americans considered the backcountry Irish Americans to be crude frontier people. Settling in frontier areas, the Irish sometimes defied laws or regulations made by English American officials and engaged in aggressive protest against them, such as in the Whisky Rebellion and the Regulation movement, in order to relieve domination and expand their own political power.[27] The Irish were often encouraged to settle in the frontier areas of the colonies to protect and shield the dominant Anglo-Protestant interests from Native Americans to the west. The bloody practice of scalping was institutionalized by English and Irish settlers determined to exterminate Native Americans. Placing bounties on the scalps of Native American men and women became common in New England and the middle colonies.[28]

By 1850 most large cities had seen anti-Catholic demonstrations and riots carried out by Protestants. Philadelphia became a center for anti-Irish Catholic violence. There, in 1844, two major riots "resulted in the burning of two Catholic churches ... the destruction of dozens of Catholic homes; and sixteen deaths."[29] In the 1850s Anglo-Protestant nativist groups such as the Know-Nothings played a major role in attacks on Irish Americans.[30]

Conflict with Other Groups

Conflict in mining areas was a major feature of the Irish American experience in the latter half of the nineteenth century. A major coal strike in 1875, called the Long Strike, forced many Irish American miners to the brink of starvation. The British American mine owners broke the strike and crushed attempts at unionization.[31] In response, secret Irish organizations linked to the Ancient Order of the Hibernians (AOH) sometimes resorted to assassination and sabotage. The owners reacted with violence against the AOH groups. The Anglo-Protestant establishment engineered the shooting deaths of numerous Irish workers, and the miners replied with armed defense and guerrilla warfare.[32]

In addition to conflict with British Americans, Irish Americans found themselves contending with other groups for land and other economic resources. Irish American Protestant farmers seized Native American lands on the frontier. As early as the 1840s, Irish competition with and discrimination against black workers in northern cities engendered substantial hostility between the two groups. Between the 1840s and the 1860s, Irish workers attacked black workers in several northern cities. During the Civil War, Irish American hostility toward African Americans increased; the two groups competed for many low-wage jobs in northern cities. Irish opposition to black workers was partially economic—the fear of job competition from black Americans moving North.[33] Excluded from discriminatory all-white unions, black workers sometimes were used by white employers as strikebreakers. The use of black strikebreakers on the waterfront, combined with Irish opposition to the Civil War military draft, helped to spur the 1863 Irish riot, usually termed the Draft Riot—the most serious riot in U.S. history. An estimated four hundred white rioters were killed in the streets, together with some free blacks and some white police officers and soldiers. Irish American rioters attacked "Yankees," the police, and blacks.[34]

Within a generation or two, Irish Americans had come to see themselves as members of a distinctive "white race." As we noted previously, one Anglo-American ruling class response to unrest among white immigrant farmers and laborers in the nineteenth century was to emphasize racial solidarity with the immigrants in a "superior white race."[35]

Between 1850 and 1890, the majority of Irish Americans came to see themselves as "white" and, as a rule, began to develop the negative prejudices toward African Americans shared by most other whites. Historical analysis has shown that, among Irish Americans, the psychological movement from a likely sympathy for the oppression of African Americans to their own version of white-racist thinking was intentionally fostered by some in the Anglo-American press, by some Anglo-Protestant and many Roman Catholic religious and community leaders, and especially by Democratic Party organizations such as Tammany Hall.[36]

English Americans increasingly, if grudgingly, accepted this change in the racial status of Irish Americans, in part because the Irish had growing political power in cities across the nation. David Roediger has underscored this politics-makes-strange-bedfellows argument: "The emphasis on a common whiteness smoothed over divisions in the Democratic ranks within mainly northern cities by emphasizing that immigrants from Europe, and particularly from Ireland, were white and thus unequivocally entitled to equal rights." Some Irish Americans opposed the racist thinking directed at black Americans, but they were not able to stem the tide.[37]

Irish–black conflict has now persisted for more than a century and a half, especially in large cities. In recent decades, Irish American and other white ethnic groups' concern over certain black gains from governmental anti-discrimination programs has been a recurring topic in the media. Many white ethnic Americans have felt that African Americans have received a disproportionate share of government attention and benefits, compared with what urban white ethnics have received.

Politics and Political Institutions

When the Irish began arriving in the seventeenth century, much of the general political framework of the colonies had already been fashioned by the English. Yet those Irish immigrants who came in the eighteenth century did play a role in shaping the nation's initial institutions. Eight of the fifty-six signers of the Declaration of Independence were Irish immigrants. Seven Irish Americans were members of the Constitutional Convention, and at least four were members of the first U.S. Congress.[38]

Political Organization in the Cities

Most of the Irish who immigrated after the Revolutionary War settled in eastern cities, where they often became involved in urban politics. Discussions of Irish Americans in politics have often focused on Irish Catholics and their so-called "political bosses and machines." Indeed, the theme of corrupt urban machines has been tied to hostile views of Catholic immigrants. Many such analyses have characterized Irish Americans as more corrupt in their political activities than other groups. In fact, the Irish immigrants entered an urban political system that already had weaknesses, including corruption and the absence of a secret ballot. Anglo-Protestant political machines—by which those in power secured for their poor constituents jobs, housing, and food—already ruled in numerous cities before there were sizeable Irish American communities.

Politics was one means to social mobility for Irish Americans, a way to achieve power in the face of intense Anglo-Protestant opposition. In the nineteenth and early twentieth centuries, the dominant perspective on government tended toward a hands-off view, with government staying out of economic affairs as much as possible. It was against this do-nothing background that desperate urban residents, plagued with unemployment, low incomes, and poor housing, joined large political organizations. Taking control of local party organizations, immigrant leaders shaped government programs to benefit the poor. Providing jobs was one of these political machines' critical functions.[39]

One of the first political machines was New York City's Tammany Society. In 1817, a group of Irish Americans, incensed at discrimination at the hands of this Anglo-Protestant machine, broke into one of its meetings and demanded the nomination of an Irish American for Congress. Although they were driven away this time, a few decades later Irish Americans were able to take over two New York political organizations, including Tammany Hall.

One Tammany Hall figure, William M. "Boss" Tweed, has long been singled out by critics who have claimed that he was uniquely greedy and politically corrupt. In reality, Tweed was an urban leader who represented the underdog, including Irish and Jewish Americans, in nineteenth-century New York. He was tolerant of various religious beliefs, family-oriented, and ambitious. He identified with New York's poor immigrants and worked to build schools and hospitals. He was attacked by the Anglo-Protestant elite because of his identification with the poor. Tweed's own ethnic background remains unclear; he was apparently of Scottish or Irish descent. Because of growing Irish political power, Tweed became a powerful leader and rewarded Irish and other immigrant constituents with jobs, schools, and social services. Interestingly, Tweed may well have been less politically corrupt than many Anglo-Protestant politicians who dominated urban politics before and after his era.[40]

With the election of New York City's first Irish American mayor in the 1880s, Irish Americans began to play a major role in city politics. They held many elective posts and gained heavy representation in appointed positions. In vigorous competition with English and other British Americans, the Irish gradually won a place in the political sun in Boston, Brooklyn, Philadelphia, New Haven, and Chicago.[41]

By the 1960s these Irish political organizations were gone except in Chicago, where the paramount Irish American boss, Mayor Richard J. Daley, maintained enormous power into the 1970s. By the 1980s, Daley was dead, and Chicago's Irish-dominated political machine was weakened to the extent that a black mayor, Harold Washington, was elected against the machine's wishes. Soon, however, the Irish were back. In 1989 Richard M. Daley, son of the former mayor, was elected mayor and has held that office now for more than a decade. Today, Irish Americans hold many major Chicago-area political offices. In contrast, the number of Irish Americans in political office in New York City has declined steadily over the past few decades. Still, one study found that Irish Catholic politicians continue to exercise significant influence in certain areas of metropolitan Albany, the New York state capital.[42]

Pragmatism in Politics

For most Irish Americans, politics is an honorable profession. Family and friends provide the important networks for entry into political positions. In local politics Irish Americans have developed a pragmatic political style based on concern for individuals and loyalty to leaders. Indeed, pragmatic politics, with its themes of coalition and compromise, is a major Irish contribution to U.S. politics. In this framework, the political machine functions as a broker to balance the interests of the city's mosaic of racial and ethnic groups so that a coalition can hang together. Irish American political leaders have often pressed for racially and ethnically balanced tickets, which have contributed to urban coalition building.[43] Irish American political organizations have also made a major contribution to the bricks-and-mortar development of cities. Without the Irish American contractors associated with the earlier political machines, who would have met the need for public buildings, streets, and subways in many cities?[44]

With suburbanization and intermarriage, this Irish political style has begun to fade, but has by no means disappeared. One study of fifty-one cities found that those with large Irish American populations were more likely than other cities to have a government (often Irish-dominated) that provided a high level of public services for residents. These Irish-populated cities were more responsive to poor groups, including poor black residents, than other cities. Some analysts have attempted to link the upward mobility of Irish Americans to a growing "conservatism," noting that in the 1960s and 1970s Irish American electorates in areas like New York and Connecticut preferred the more conservative political candidates in mayoral, gubernatorial, and senatorial races. Elsewhere, however, Irish Americans have continued to vote for liberal and moderate Democrats in many local and state races.[45] Irish Americans, especially Irish Catholics, are as a group more liberal than most other white groups.

National and International Politics

One study of the period between 1901 and 1910 found that 13 percent of 162 prominent political leaders, including presidents, senators, representatives, and Supreme Court justices, were Irish American (generally Protestants), compared with 56 percent who were of English or Welsh descent.[46] Irish Catholic influence at the national level was weak. Andrew Jackson, a Presbyterian slaveholder from Tennessee who served as president from 1829 to 1837, was the nation's first Irish American president and the only one both of whose parents were immigrants. Woodrow Wilson, a "Scotch-Irish" Protestant from New Jersey, was president from 1913 to 1921. Although this was a crucial time in the history of Ireland, Wilson was not sympathetic to Irish Catholic causes and did not support the Irish struggle against English domination. More recently, at a precedent-setting 1994 Saint Patrick's Day White House dinner, which was attended by prominent Irish American industrialists, academics, politicians, and entertainers, Ireland's prime minister presented then President Bill Clinton a genealogy of Clinton's Irish ancestors.[47] Clinton had shown much concern with the political conflict in Northern Ireland.

In recent decades the issue of an independent, united Ireland has generated substantial financial and political support among Irish Americans. In the 1980s, IRA (Irish Republican Army) fugitive Joe Doherty became a rallying point for Irish American opposition to British rule of Northern Ireland. He was convicted in absentia in Belfast, Ireland, for his part in the killing of a British military officer and held in U.S. prisons from 1983 until he was extradited to Britain in 1992. During the years he was held in prison, Doherty wrote a popular column in the New York newspaper *Irish People* supporting the IRA's cause and received visits from more than one hundred members of Congress, as well as from New York's Cardinal O'Connor, in support of his request for political asylum. In 1992, following the U.S. Supreme Court's decision to deny Doherty political refugee status, his Irish American supporters protested on a Manhattan street corner named in his honor.[48]

Irish American support for the Catholic Irish cause in Northern Ireland has created political tensions in the United States. Some non-Irish politicians have criticized Irish American support of the Catholic struggle in Northern Ireland and U.S. efforts to broker peace between the British government and Sinn Fein, the political arm of the IRA. Several times in the 1990s, Gerry Adams, the head of Sinn Fein, was granted a visa to visit the United States—first to participate in a conference on Northern Ireland, then to meet with U.S. government officials following his announcement of an IRA cease-fire in Northern Ireland, and in 1995 to meet with President Bill Clinton. In 1997 Adams came to the United States again to raise funds and to meet with White House officials, although the president did not meet with him—reportedly to put pressure on Sinn Fein for concessions in negotiations over the future of Northern Ireland.[49]

Many observers feel that Irish American political leaders' peace negotiation efforts and President Clinton's decision to lift a twenty-year ban on official U.S. contacts with Sinn Fein have played a significant and positive role in encouraging the peace process in Northern Ireland. In the early 2000s Sinn Fein has continued its efforts in the United States and has raised substantial funds from Irish Americans. As of mid-2002, the various parties contending over Northern Ireland continue to debate conditions for resolving the conflict. The controversy over Northern Ireland's future and possible independence from Britain not only illustrates an interethnic struggle (between Catholics and Protestants in Ireland) that continues to the present but also demonstrates how events in the country of origin of one U.S. population group can long affect ethnic relations within the United States. This theme will reappear regularly in the chapters that follow, as, for example, in the effects of events in Italy on Italian Americans and in Japan on Japanese Americans. World politics remains the larger context for interethnic and interracial relations in the United States.

The Only Irish Catholic President

Alfred E. Smith, the Democratic candidate for president in 1928, was the first Irish Catholic to carve out an important role in presidential politics. Yet his Catholic religion, along with his calls for modification of Prohibition and his lack of knowledge about regions of the United States other than the East, counted against him in this first Irish Catholic presidential campaign.[50]

Not until 1960, more than three hundred years after the first few Irish Catholics had come to the United States and more than a century after sizable Irish American Catholic communities had been established, was the first and only Irish Catholic president elected. Six of the thirty-six presidents, from Washington to Nixon, had Irish American backgrounds, but except for John Kennedy all of these were Protestant Irish, as were the more recent presidents, Ronald Reagan and Bill Clinton.

In the 1960 presidential election, Irish Catholic votes in New England, New York, and Pennsylvania helped to create John Kennedy's narrow victory. Nationwide, he received an estimated 75 percent of the Irish vote but only 50.1 percent of the total vote. As president, Kennedy acted not only on behalf of Irish Americans but also, to some extent, on behalf of America's other emergent urban ethnic groups. Thus, Kennedy appointed the first Italian American and the first Polish American to a presidential cabinet and the first African American to head an independent government agency.[51]

The only Catholic (Irish) president in U.S. history, John F. Kennedy, is given the oath of office.

THE IRISH IN THE ECONOMY

One type of structural assimilation involves large-scale movement by members of an immigrant group into the secondary-organization levels of a society, such as into positions in government agencies and private economic organizations, including farms and factories. The majority of Irish immigrants started out at the bottom of the economic pyramid, filling the hard, often dirty, low-wage jobs in rural areas and cities. As with other immigrant groups, most Irish immigrants found jobs through preexisting ethnic networks. "The process was cloaked in favoritism and operated quite independently of qualifications. The result can be called 'ethnic mobility, collective style.'"[52]

Irish labor was critical to industrial and commercial development in the United States. Irish immigrants after 1830 typically became urban workers, miners, or transportation workers. They migrated looking for work—Irish men found it in unskilled jobs, on the docks and in the factories of large cities; Irish women found it as servants, usually in Anglo-Protestant homes. Many Irish immigrants were single females unattached to family groups. Impoverished in an alien land, these women frequently moved into domestic work where they could live with a family. Jewish and Italian women generally came with their families. Irish women who came alone did so not by choice but because of adverse economic conditions in Ireland.[53]

Male immigrants became farm laborers, railroad laborers, miners, and textile workers. Many died helping to build transportation systems, as the old saying "There's an Irishman buried under every railroad tie" indicates. Irish Catholics encountered direct institutionalized discrimination in employment. Stereotyped as dumb, unskilled, or rowdy, Irish American men and women were often denied well-paid jobs by employers. Few would hire them except for unskilled positions. By the 1840s, Boston newspapers were carrying anti-Irish advertisements with the phrase "None need apply but Americans."[54]

Upward Mobility

Significant numbers of Irish Catholics became upwardly mobile near the turn of the twentieth century. They entered the urban economy when expanding industries needed large numbers of low-wage workers. Major cities grew and developed as capitalists centered new types of manufacturing in the industrial heartland, from Pittsburgh to Chicago to Detroit. Powerful urban political machines facilitated mobility by providing jobs and other economic resources for the upward trek. Urban political machines channeled money into building projects, facilitating the emergence of a business class. Irish Americans were important in a few labor organizations in Massachusetts and New York as early as the 1850s. By the early 1900s unions had become important for Irish dockworkers, construction workers, and miners, among others. To the present day, Irish Americans have been prominent in labor organizations, including the AFL-CIO.[55]

Information available on mobility among Irish Americans after 1900 suggests increasing economic security for a growing segment. The mostly Protestant descendants of pre-1830 immigrants were still disproportionately concentrated in farming areas, in towns, and in southern and border states. In the late nineteenth and early twentieth centuries, and probably in later decades as well, a significant proportion became relatively prosperous farmers, owners of small businesses, and skilled blue-collar workers, as well as part of the growing white-collar categories. Over time, many more or less blended into the Anglo-Protestant mainstream, although some remained poor and forgotten in rural areas. Moreover, by the 1930s, Irish Catholics had not blended fully into the Anglo-Protestant mainstream. In a study of Newburyport in the 1930s, Lloyd Warner and Leo Srole found Irish Americans moving closer to native-born Yankee residents in socioeconomic status. No Irish, however, could be found at the top. The Depression hit Irish Americans hard, postponing for a decade the major economic breakthrough just within their reach.[56]

Recent Successes

In recent decades many Irish Catholics have been employed in government jobs, such as in police, fire, and public works departments; in the courts; and in schools and colleges. In seeking government jobs, like other groups after them (for example, African Americans), they often faced less discrimination there than they did in the business sector. By the 1970s, two-thirds of younger-generation Irish

Catholic men held white-collar positions, compared with 38 percent of their fathers. Both generations were more likely to be found in better-paid, white-collar jobs than their counterparts in most other ethnic Catholic groups.[57] By the 1990s, the occupational distribution for Irish Americans paralleled that of all whites in the United States. Although Scotch-Irish Americans fared substantially better than other Irish Americans on all economic indicators, both groups had a higher median family income and a lower rate of poverty than whites as a group. The median income of Irish Americans is now only a little lower than that of English Americans.[58]

Today, Irish Americans hold positions of leadership in all areas of American life. Mass media symbols of Irish American success have typically been athletes, entertainers, politicians, or, less often, entrepreneurs such as Joseph Kennedy, John Kennedy's influential father. Another group of Irish American heroes has received little notice—the growing group of Ph.D.s and academics. Catholics make up about one-fourth of faculty members in top state colleges and universities, and about half of these are Irish. Irish American Catholics are heavily represented in humanities departments. In addition, many graduate-trained Irish Catholics have moved into local, state, and federal government as lawyers, administrators, researchers, and elected officials.[59]

EDUCATION

Organized education on a significant scale for Irish Protestants began after the Civil War. In the South, public schools spread during the often progressive Reconstruction period, and by the early twentieth century many of the Protestant Irish had taken advantage of them. The Catholic Irish, in contrast, relied on parochial and public schools in urban areas of the North for organized education. In part, because of the often severe anti-Catholicism, parochial schools did not become numerous until the period between 1820 and 1840. By the late 1800s and early 1900s a parish and parochial school system had become the center of the Irish Catholic community in numerous cities.[60]

By the 1960s the nearly 13,000 elementary and secondary Catholic schools had an enrollment of 5 million children. Irish Catholic Americans were at the center of this immense network. Gradually too, these parochial schools have come to receive some governmental aid, bringing opposition from some Protestant and Jewish American groups and not a few court cases on the issue of separation of church and state.[61]

By 1910, Irish Catholics were enrolled in college in large numbers, indeed above the national average for all whites. The educational achievements of Irish Catholic Americans were increasingly impressive. Significant numbers of Catholic colleges were established, and college attendance continued to increase.[62]

Today, Irish Americans continue to place great emphasis on education; the most recent available (1990) census data show that the educational attainment of Irish Americans as a group is now equal to that of whites as a group. Other data indicate that the educational attainments of both Irish American Catholics and Protestants are increasing relative to the general white population.[63]

In the past decade a number of Irish American leaders have pressed for more coverage of Irish and Irish American history in U.S. schools and colleges. In 1997, Tom Hayden, a California State Senator of Irish heritage, proposed a bill that would reshape the educational curriculum so that children in the racially and ethnically diverse state of California could learn about the dramatic potato famines discussed earlier. Similar efforts to change the educational curriculum to include more Irish history have been made in New Jersey and New York.[64]

RELIGION

In the political and economic spheres, Irish Americans were pressured early to assimilate to the established Anglo-Protestant culture. In the religious sphere, the earliest Irish immigrants, whether Catholic or Presbyterian, mostly blended into various American Protestant denominations. However, later groups of Irish Catholic immigrants played a major role in firmly establishing what may well be the most influential non-Protestant institution in the United States—the Roman Catholic church. Although the Catholic church has had to adapt to some extent to the preexisting Protestant religious system, its growing strength has served to accent the constitutional issue of the separation of church and state and to reinforce the right of all Americans to choose any faith.

Initially, as we have seen, Irish Catholics had to fight intense anti-Catholic prejudice and sometimes violent discrimination designed to prevent the Catholic church from taking root in Anglo-Protestant soil. Still, new churches sprang up wherever Catholic workers went.[65] The Catholic church's hierarchy in the United States has long been disproportionately composed of Irish Americans. One analysis of Catholic bishops from 1789 to 1935 revealed that 58 percent were of Irish extraction. In the early 2000s Irish Americans still account for a disproportionate number of Catholic priests but no longer generate a disproportionate number of Catholic bishops.[66]

In northern cities, many Irish neighborhoods were built around a parish church, and local politics was often blended with church and school. Moreover, over the past few decades, many central city churches have been closed or merged, as Irish Americans have moved to the suburbs. Today, in the suburbs of many cities the Irish Catholic parish survives. Loyalty to the church remains strong; one 1990s survey found that more than half of Irish Catholics go to services every week, a much higher proportion than for other whites in the survey.[67]

Irish American priests have shaped the U.S. Catholic church in a number of distinctive ways, some conservative and some progressive. Irish American archbishops and cardinals have often been politically and socially conservative, while many local Catholic priests have helped to lead progressive struggles, such as the struggle for expanded civil rights. For example, the former president of Notre Dame University, Father Theodore M. Hesburgh, symbolizes the liberalism in Irish Catholicism. For many years, including those he spent on the U.S. Commission on Civil Rights, Father Hesburgh was outspoken in his support for civil rights laws, anti-segregation action, and affirmative action to benefit Americans of color.[68]

ASSIMILATION THEORIES AND THE IRISH

Now we will examine how the theories and concepts discussed in Chapter 2 help illuminate the experiences of Irish Americans. Some power-conflict analysts specifically omit immigrant groups such as the "white ethnics" from their analyses, preferring to focus on racially subordinated groups because these have generally endured much greater violence and repression in North America. The assimilation theories of Milton Gordon and Andrew Greeley seem the most relevant for analysis of groups such as Irish and Italian Americans. Yet, we should keep in mind something many assimilationists tend to forget—the substantial conflict and social stratification that has characterized the experiences of Irish and Italian Americans.

Each generation of Irish Americans has become ever more incorporated into the core institutions than prior generations. The eighteenth-century Irish moved up the social and economic ladders slowly; the immigrants were typically Protestants. Substantial assimilation came by the late nineteenth century for many of their descendants. By the early 1900s the successful assimilation of "Scotch Irish" Protestants was considered a standard for subsequent immigrant groups to emulate.[69]

Cultural assimilation came relatively rapidly for the early Irish immigrants and their descendants. Assimilation came slowly but surely at the level of structural integration into the economy and the polity and gradually at the level of primary social ties. Sometime in the past century, many Scotch-Irish became a difficult-to-distinguish part of the Anglo-Protestant mainstream.

Assimilation came more slowly for large numbers of Irish Catholics who immigrated after 1830. Some adaptation to the dominant Anglo-Protestant culture, particularly learning the English language and the core culture's basic views and values, is necessary to successful achievements within mainstream institutions. Significantly, Ireland's customs and American customs often had similarities. The English language was familiar to many immigrants. While assimilation at other levels took several generations, significant cultural assimilation took place in the first decade.[70]

Religion was an exception. Most of these Irish Catholic immigrants did not become Protestants. Conflict with the Anglo-Protestant American nativists intensified Irish American commitment to the Catholic church. Still, the Catholic churches made adjustments to the English-dominated milieu in such areas as language and restructured church organizations. Such adaptations made the U.S. Catholic church and school system an important medium within which new Catholic immigrants began their acculturation and even some structural assimilation (for example, priests helped immigrants secure employment).[71]

Has commitment to the Catholic religion declined in later generations of Irish American Catholics? Some analysts have claimed this, arguing that cultural assimilation will thus soon be complete. However, some recent studies have not found this to be the case. As a group, Irish Americans are among the most likely to attend mass of all Catholic groups.[72]

Since the mid-nineteenth century the Catholic Irish have experienced substantial changes in the dimensions of assimilation that Gordon calls *behavior-receptional assimilation* and *attitude-receptional assimilation*—in effect, discrimination and prejudice. Stereotyping has declined substantially since the days of the commonplace apelike image, although negative feelings directed against Irish Catholicism have persisted among some Protestant Americans. Anti-Catholic discrimination has also declined significantly, although it still can sometimes be seen at the very highest levels of the U.S. economy and government.

Patterns of Structural Assimilation

At the structural-assimilation (secondary-group) level, Irish Americans made slow but significant movement, over several generations, into Anglo-Protestant organizations and institutions. We have seen the steady movement of the Irish from unskilled work into white-collar occupations—and the relatively high occupational levels of Irish American Catholics in recent decades. Residential dispersal, often to suburban areas, has paralleled these developments, although some residential self-segregation persists in some cities in the East and Midwest. After a century of struggle in the political sphere, Irish Catholics are now substantially integrated at the local and state government levels; in the past few decades, they have moved significantly into the judicial, legislative, and executive branches of the federal government, although they are not yet present in representative numbers at the very top of the political system.

Some have argued that the higher status that accompanies economic assimilation is causing many Irish Americans to move away from the Democratic party. Urban politicians, particularly Democrats, have long given great attention to the Irish American community, and numerous Democratic party leaders are still Irish. One research analysis found that 61 percent of Irish Catholics and 54 percent of Irish Protestants identified themselves as Democrats. These percentages question the accuracy of one assimilation theory of ethnic politics—that economic mobility destroys traditional ethnic voting patterns. As of the early 2000s, absorption into a Republican party dominated by white Protestants has not happened for the majority of Irish American Catholics.[73]

As for structural incorporation at the level of primary-group ties, data on informal groups and voluntary associations point to some interesting trends. Since World War II, if not before, ethnic clubs and organizations have declined in importance for the Irish Catholics. This probably indicates increasing integration into the voluntary associations of the larger white society. Irish American attendance at Catholic parochial schools has also declined.[74]

Intermarriage is a major indicator of substantial assimilation at the primary-group level. One national survey in the 1960s reported substantial endogamy (within-group marriage) for Irish Catholics; 65 percent of respondents with Irish fathers also had Irish mothers, and 43 percent of Irish married men had a wife with an Irish father. Yet more than half the respondents to that national survey had a non-Irish spouse. One more recent survey of a large metropolitan area in New York found 82 percent of Irish Americans there had mixed ethnic ancestry. And in the late 1990s, one commentator estimated that at least two-thirds of Irish Americans are now marrying outside the group.[75]

Is There an Irish American Identity Today?

The intermarriage rate poses challenges to continuing Irish American identity. Among the final stages of assimilation is what Milton Gordon and Andrew Greeley have seen as "identificational" adaptation. Ultimately, this type of assimilation would mean a loss of a sense of Irishness and the development of a sense of peoplehood that is solely American or Anglo-Protestant American. One's sense of identity would no longer be Irish. This may have happened for many Irish Protestants, but the majority of Irish Catholics still have some sense of Irishness, however vague.

Some analysts argue that Irish Americans are losing their ethnic identity because of the decline in immigration from Ireland. For example, Marjorie Fallows has argued that the American Irish are fully acculturated to the Anglo-Protestant culture. In her view, distinctive ethnic traits that are culturally significant are rare among the American Irish today. Even though there are still a few ethnically distinct Irish Catholic communities in northern cities, most Irish Catholics do not live there. From this viewpoint, cultural and structural (primary-group) assimilation are all but complete for those Irish Catholics living outside ethnic neighborhoods.[76]

Richard Alba interviewed respondents in eight white ethnic groups in a metropolitan area in upper New York State. He found a decline in the significance of ethnic identity among Irish Americans, especially in the fourth and later generations. However, those with pure Irish ancestry had a stronger sense of their ethnic identity than most of the other groups examined. Those with mixed Irish ancestry were also loyal to their Irish heritage. They were three times as likely to identify solely as Irish as they were to choose another ethnicity from their mixed background.[77]

Certainly, the Irish Catholic group has changed over generations of contact with the public school system and the mass media, but it has retained enough distinctiveness to persist as an ethnic group into the first decade of the twenty-first century. The theory of ethnogenesis discussed in Chapter 2 seems appropriate to Irish Catholic Americans. Over several generations, the large numbers of Irish who came after 1830 and their descendants forged a distinctive U.S. ethnic group. Ethnicity was an important way for the Irish Catholics to assert their own identity in a buzzing confusion of diverse nationality groups. Because of nativistic attacks and discrimination, ethnic identity was less voluntary for Irish Catholics in the first few decades than it was to become later. The Irish immigrants' cultural heritage was distinctly different from that of the British American host culture. Over several generations of sometimes hostile interaction with Anglo-Protestants, the Irish immigrants and their descendants adapted substantially to the host society. This process created a distinctive Irish American ethnic group that reflects elements of its nationality background but also much of the host culture.

In an analysis of opinion poll data, Greeley examined survey questions that tap what he views as traditional Irish Catholic sociocultural traits: gregariousness, gathering in a public house, religious intensity, and activity in religious organizations. Greeley concluded that Irish Catholic distinctiveness persists, particularly in certain northern cities. He even found some evidence of a return to higher levels of self-conscious identification among young Irish Americans.[78] Other reports have also indicated a resurgence of interest in things Irish. One late 1990s survey reported a growing interest in studying the original Irish language (Gaelic), Irish dance, and Irish music among Irish Americans. And we have noted the pressures being placed on public schools to include more Irish and Irish American history. In addition, there has been some interest in having a Gaelic mass at some Irish American celebrations. Whether this trend will continue remains to be seen. Whatever happens, however, it is clear that the impact of the Irish background on Irish American thought and behavior remains strong.[79]

ITALIAN AMERICANS

For many decades Italian Americans have been targets of hostility from other racial and ethnic groups, especially Anglo Protestants. This mostly Catholic group has been attacked for being unsophisticated, superpatriotic "hardhats" with connections to the "Mafia." By the 1960s, a counterattack developed. Many white ethnic leaders, including Italian Americans, came to view Anglo-Protestant intellectuals and officials critically and spoke out against such stereotyping.

The strong defense of things Italian and the achievements of Italian Americans had, by the 1990s and early 2000s, brought this group greater acceptance among other Americans. The rising prominence of Italian Americans in the United States can be seen in the selection of Geraldine Ferraro, an Italian American member of Congress, as the Democratic party's first female vice-presidential candidate (in 1984) and the substantial national support for New York governor Mario Cuomo as a possible Democratic presidential nominee during the 1990s.

ITALIAN IMMIGRATION

Italian explorers, including Cristoforo Colombo (Christopher Columbus), played a major role in opening the Americas to European colonization and exploitation. An Italian navigator, Amerigo Vespucci, made a number of voyages to the Americas shortly after Colombo's voyages. Because of his early maps, the continents came to be named after him.[80]

Numbers of Immigrants

Since 1820, more than 5 million Italians have migrated to the United States. Very small numbers migrated to the North American colonies and the United States prior to the mid-1880s. Between 1880 and 1920, Italian immigration was heavy, with more than 4 million recorded immigrants. Prior to 1880, most immigrants were from northern Italy; after 1880 very large numbers came from southern Italy.[81]

As we saw in Chapter 2, certain factors are relevant to the study of migration: the point of origin, the destination, the migrating units, and the larger context. As with the Irish, land and agricultural problems triggered much of the Italian out-migration. National unification under a government controlled by northern Italians had brought heavy taxes to southern Italy. Low income, poor soil, a feudal land system, unreasonable taxes, and government corruption were important push factors at the point of origin.[82] The often exaggerated image of the United States as a place of expanding opportunity was a major pull factor. Some came to stay, but the majority of the early immigrants saw the United States as a temporary workplace.[83]

Migration along kinship networks, typical for poor and working-class migrants from European countries, lessened the pain of resettlement. Italians often came in groups from the same villages. Industrialized East Coast cities were popular destinations. In the larger cities immigrants often went to "Little Italies," where fellow villagers resided.[84] Remigration for Italians was well above that of other groups. In some years in the early 1900s, returnees to Italy equalled 60 to 70 percent of new immigrants.[85]

Nativist agitation by Anglo-Protestant groups resulted in legislative attempts to restrict this southern European immigration. Between 1924 and 1965, nativist-motivated immigration quotas sharply curtailed Italian immigration. The Immigration Act of 1924 established a small discriminatory quota for Italians. By 1929, the annual quota for Italians was only 5,802, compared with 65,721 for Great Britain. The quota system was based on nativists' belief that those countries that had furnished the most "good American citizens"—that is, Protestant immigrants prior to 1890—should receive the largest quotas. The British, Germans, Irish, and Scandinavians were given three-fourths of the total, although the demand from those countries had slackened considerably by that time.[86]

Pressure on Italy's small quota produced a backlog of 250,000 applicants by the time the 1965 Immigration Act replaced the discriminatory national-origin quota system. Gradually, by the late 1970s, that backlog was exhausted, and since that time the annual number of Italian immigrants has dropped sharply.[87] More than 11 million Americans listed Italian as their first ancestry in the 1990 census; most of these were U.S. born.[88] Counting both the first and second ancestries listed by respondents in the census 2000 supplementary survey, the census bureau estimated there were 15.9 million Italian Americans in 2000, making them one of the largest ancestry groups in the United States.[89]

Life for the Immigrants

What was life like for the large numbers of Italians who immigrated in the peak period between 1880 and 1920? Most worked as unskilled laborers, often on transportation systems such as canals and railroads and on water and sewer systems. Pay was low, and individuals as well as families were usually poor. Segregated in "Little Italy ghettos" within cities, Italian immigrants and their children frequently faced economic, political, and social discrimination. There is irony here, since *ghetto* is thought to be a Venetian word first applied to the practice of segregating Jews in the sixteenth century. In the United States it was the Italian Catholics who found themselves in ghettos. In inner city areas of large cities Italian Americans often replaced earlier immigrant groups as part of a residential invasion-succession process. Yet other immigrant groups would follow on their heels.[90]

Some analysts have viewed working-class communities in cities as disorganized "slum" areas with little positive social life. This was not true for Italian American communities. As with the Irish before them, Italians developed their own extensive friendship and kinship circles, numerous political clubs, important avenues for upward mobility, and commonplace community celebrations. Festivals and indigenous organizations, including mutual-benefit societies whose members made monthly payments to ensure a proper funeral upon their demise, were central to Italian American communities.[91]

STEREOTYPES

By the end of the nineteenth century, nativist stereotypes of the "apelike" Irish were giving way to negative stereotypes of southern and eastern European immigrants, especially those who were Catholics and Jews. The Italian stereotypes were harsh.[92] Italian immigrants were scorned by nativists as "dangerous, contemptible, inferior, and disloyal"—the "off-scourings of the world."[93]

Popular writers, scholars, and members of Congress warned of the peril of allowing these "inferior" stocks from Europe into the United States. Thus, Kenneth Roberts, a prominent journalist, expressed a fear that the newer immigrants would make Americans a mongrel race: "The American nation was founded and developed by the Nordic race, but if a few more million members of the Alpine, Mediterranean and Semitic races are poured among us, the result must inevitably be a hybrid race of people as worthless and futile as the good-for-nothing mongrels of Central America and southeastern Europe."[94] Nativist writers included Italians and European Jews when they spoke of "Alpine, Mediterranean, and Semitic races."

Stereotypes of Inferiority in Intelligence

In the first three decades of the twentieth century, Anglo-Protestant stereotypes of southern and eastern European immigrants' intellectual inferiority were based in part on misreadings of the results of the new psychological tests that were often inaccurately labeled intelligence (IQ) tests. The term *intelligence test* is inaccurate because the tests measured only selected, learned verbal and quantitative skills, not a broad or basic intelligence. In 1912 the American analyst Henry Goddard gave the European researcher Alfred Binet's diagnostic test and related tests to a large number of immigrants from southern and eastern Europe. His data supposedly showed that 83 percent of Jewish and 79 percent of Italian immigrants were "feeble-minded," a category naively defined in terms of low scores on the new English-language tests.[95]

During World War I prominent U.S. psychologists developed verbal and performance tests for large-scale testing of wartime draftees. Although the results were not used for military purposes, detailed analyses were published in the 1920s and gained public and congressional attention because of the racial-inferiority interpretation many Anglo-American psychologists placed on the test scores of the southern and eastern European immigrants among the draftees.[96]

In 1923 Carl Brigham, a Princeton psychologist who would later play a role in developing college entrance tests, argued for the intellectual inferiority of white immigrant groups, including Italian Americans, drawing on data from the army tests. The average scores for foreign-born draftees ranged from highs of 14.87 for English and 14.34 for Scottish draftees, to an average of 13.77 for all white draftees, to lows of 10.74 for Polish and 11.01 for Italian draftees. The low test scores for groups such as Italian Americans were boldly explained in aggressively *racial* terms; those low-scoring groups were considered not only unintelligent but also "inferior racial stocks." Psychologists such as Brigham even used these results to support the ideology of "Nordic" superiority that was being espoused by overtly racist theorists such as Madison Grant. Expressing great concern for the country's future, Brigham also argued that the sharp increase in southern and eastern European immigration had lowered the general level of American intelligence.[97]

The political implications of Brigham's analysis were proclaimed: Immigration limits were necessary, and political means (for example, government-ordered sterilization) should be developed to prevent the continued propagation of these "defective strains" in the U.S. population.[98] Here was pseudoscientific support for such government action as passage of the 1924 Immigration Act, which would soon severely restrict southern European immigration.

The U.S. government played an important role in the stereotyping of Italian immigrants, a point that Omi and Winant underscore in their racial formation theory (see Chapter 2). Psychologists working with government agencies helped to generate the official view of these immigrants as undesirable racial or ethnic groups, and Congress used their research to support racist arguments against immigration.

The "intelligence" differences measured by the usually brief psychological tests were assumed to reflect the inferior or superior genetic background of the undesirable European "racial" stocks. In the early decades of the twentieth century, few analysts and political leaders seriously considered the possibility that the linguistic (English), cultural (northern European–American), and educational bias in the tests and in the psychologists' interpretive procedures could account for the so-called "racial" differences.[99]

Some immigrant leaders developed strategies for dealing with concern over "blood" lineage. One prominent Italian American leader, Fiorello La Guardia, suffered personal attacks that incorporated stereotypes. For his criticism of officials such as President Herbert Hoover he received letters such as the following: "You should go back where you belong and advise Mussolini how to make good honest citizens in Italy. The Italians are preponderantly our murderers and boot-leggers."[100] La Guardia's countertactic was sometimes a biting humor.[101]

Ethnic slurs and epithets, including *dago*, *wop*, and *guinea*, that have often been hurled at Italian Americans reveal the intensity of anti-Italian hostility. *Dago*, a corruption of the Spanish name Diego, was originally used for Spaniards or Mexicans. After 1880, however, it was applied by northern European Americans to Italian immigrants. Similarly, the term *guinea* was an early term for African Americans, whose ancestors had come from the Guinea coast of Africa. After 1880 northern European Americans used *guinea* to classify Italians as "no better than blacks."[102] The ease with which racist epithets were transferred to later racial and ethnic groups reveals not only the fear that established groups often have of newcomers but also the way in which certain European newcomers have come to be classified, as in the case of the Italian immigrants for a time, as somehow *not white*.

The Mafia Myth

The most persistent Italian American stereotype has been the image of serious criminality. As early as the 1870s, Italians were depicted as lawless, knife-wielding thugs looking for a fight. Even a report of the influential U.S. Immigration Commission, issued in the early 1900s, argued that certain types of criminality were "inherent in the Italian race."[103] Yet the validity of the criminality stereotype is disputed by government data. For example, in 1910 the imprisonment rate for Italian immigrants was much lower than public stereotypes would suggest: 527 prisoners per 100,000 for the Italian-born, compared with 727 for the English and Welsh foreign-born.[104]

Small-scale crime, fostered by poverty and discrimination, was a problem in most central city communities, but it usually did not involve a criminal conspiracy. Prohibition catapulted some Italian Americans into organized crime, which at the time was controlled mostly by Irish and Jewish Americans. By 1940 two dozen Italian American "crime families" were operating in major cities. For many immigrant groups, including Italian Americans, such crime has been one of the only avenues for economic mobility. Unfortunately, the Sicilian word *Mafia* has been used to describe organized crime, although many of these gangsters have been neither Sicilian nor Italian. Significantly, Italian Americans had *low* crime rates in the 1920s and 1930s.[105]

The image of Italian criminality has taken on a widespread mythological character; the stereotype of the Italian American male as a Mafia hoodlum committed to crime and violence persists. Into the early 2000s, Italian names for criminals in various TV programs and movies have implied ties to the so-called "Mafia." Without exception, every non-Italian respondent in Waters's study of white ethnics in California and Pennsylvania used the Mafia and gangsters to characterize Italian Americans; most said their ideas were based on mass media images.[106]

In the fall of 1997, the CBS television network aired a miniseries, "Bella Mafia," about several Italian American wives linked to organized crime. Some Italian Americans, including the National Italian American News Bureau, protested the gangster stereotypes of Italian Americans there and encouraged viewers to protest by not watching the program. In the late 1990s, other Italian Americans have fought against stereotypes on labels and trademarks. One lawyer working with the Commission for Social Justice of the Order of the Sons of Italy in America—a group with half a million members—has successfully stopped the federal government from issuing label trademarks that are insulting to Italian Americans, such as product labels with terms like "Mafia Mob" or "Cosa Nostra."[107]

Significantly, FBI statistics show that *only 4 percent* of the 500,000 Americans estimated to be involved in organized crime belong to Italian American crime networks. In addition, reports in the 1990s indicated that, except in a few New York City and Chicago areas, the power of Italian American "crime families" had declined significantly. More recent immigrant groups, including some from Asia and Latin America, had taken over much of the organized crime in U.S. cities.[108]

Stereotypes and Discrimination

One study of the portrayal of Italian Americans on prime-time television that examined a sample of 263 programs for one 1980s season found that negative images of Italian Americans outnumbered positive images by two to one. Most of the ninety-six Italian characters in the shows studied were men with low-status jobs.[109]

One Italian American in California described his experience with ethnic slurs: "When I joined the office in the new location I became a member of the Rotary Club, and of course there were very few Italian members. So the minute I came on board, they started referring to me as the Godfather of the country." He went on to say that he found this humor very degrading, since he had to explain that he had no ties to the so-called Mafia. Numerous other Italian Americans have reported similar experiences, including barbed Mafia jokes and discrimination in corporate workplaces.[110]

The Mafia myth appeared in the 1984 presidential election when a smear campaign aimed at Democratic vice-presidential candidate Geraldine Ferraro, an Italian American, insinuated that *she* had important "mob connections" because her husband had inherited a real estate business founded by his father and the brother of a New York crime figure. Recalling the first time her son had been called a "wop," when he was six or seven years old, Ferraro indicated that her family's encounters with anti-Italian attitudes were common. The problem of the Mafia myth has also plagued the presidential aspirations of New York governor Mario Cuomo since the mid-1980s. A mid-1990s national survey by the Joint Civic Committee found that three-fourths of Americans still viewed Italians as somehow linked to crime.[111]

The Mafia image is not the only negative stereotype to which Italian Americans are subjected. Among all the European ancestry groups included in Alba's study of white ethnics in a large metropolitan area of upper New York State, the Italian American respondents reported encountering the greatest number of stereotypes. The stereotyped images referred to physical appearance (big noses), mannerisms (talking with hands), family life (being especially family-oriented), as well as alleged Mafia connections. Similarly, Waters's non-Italian white respondents in a California and Pennsylvania study held both negative and positive stereotypes of Italian Americans. Some described Italians as dirty, loud, temperamental, selfish, unambitious, combative, and not very bright; others listed characteristics such as having excellent food, doing well in business, being affectionate, being family-oriented, and being clean housekeepers.[112]

CONFLICT

The myth of peaceful progress is again dispelled by the history of Italian Americans' struggles with Anglo-Protestant nativists, Irish Catholics, and African Americans. Irish and Italian Americans fought on the streets of Boston by the 1860s, and Italian parents sometimes accompanied their children to school for protection. In the 1870s striking Irish American workers in New York attacked Italian American strikebreakers.

By the 1880s Anglo-Protestant nativist attempts to control immigrants from southern Italy sometimes took the form of vigilante action. In the 1880s in Buffalo, New York, more than three hundred Italians—most of the local Italian population—were detained by police after an incident in which one Italian had killed another; only two of the three hundred were found to be holding weapons. Replying to the governor of New York, the police chief of Buffalo explained that he thought Italian Americans as a rule carried concealed weapons and were a threat to social order.[113]

Legalized Killings

In the South during this early period, several dozen Italian immigrants were killed by mobs motivated by economic competition and a desire to maintain racial lines. Italian immigrants were viewed as a threat to white solidarity in the South because they were more likely than other whites to support black political rights. They often worked as laborers alongside blacks or sold to them as small shopkeepers. In one town, five Sicilian shopkeepers were lynched for this reason.[114] One well-publicized attack occurred in New Orleans after the 1891 murder of a white police superintendent who was investigating crime among Italian immigrants. A number of immigrants were jailed for the murder, and the police refused to intervene when a large group led by prominent citizens stormed the jail and killed eleven of them. Newspapers and major political figures praised the deed, using the vigilante incident to advance the continuing stereotype of Italian criminality.[115]

One of the most famous murder trials of all time was that of Nicola Sacco and Bartolomeo Vanzetti, Italian-born workers who were tried for robbery and murder in Massachusetts. Numerous witnesses testified that the defendants were elsewhere at the time of the crime, but the judge ignored the testimony of the Italian-born witnesses. Anti-Italian prejudice was very evident at the trial and in the views of the presiding judge. While their guilt or innocence is still debated, the two men clearly did not receive a fair trial. As suspected "radicals," they were executed in 1927 in the midst of public hysteria over left-wing, "un-American" activities.[116]

Conflict with African Americans

Since the 1930s, conflict has arisen between Italian Americans and groups lower on the socioeconomic ladder. "Law and order," school desegregation, and busing have been major issues in northern metropolitan areas. In the 1960s and 1970s, Italian American leaders sometimes complained that black Americans were the "darlings" of white Protestant liberals and received disproportionate press coverage and federal aid. Italian Americans in some areas of such cities as Newark and Philadelphia found themselves surrounded by large numbers of African American immigrants from other regions who were often poor. Realistic fears about urban crime were coupled with exaggerated views of the black role in such crime, much as Anglo-Protestant fears earlier had exaggerated the Italian role in urban crime.[117]

In the spring of 1990, a group of Italian American youths attacked and killed a black youth, Yusuf Hawkins, in the predominantly Italian Bensonhurst area of New York City. The attackers believed that the victim was on his way to date a young Italian American woman. Actually, Hawkins had gone to Bensonhurst to inquire about buying a used car. Members of the Federation of Italian American Organizations actively sought to calm racial tensions, calling Italian residents' attention to their own history of discrimination.[118]

Opinion surveys of Italian Americans in the 1960s and 1970s showed significant anti-black prejudice and strong opposition to neighborhood desegregation.[119] By the 1990s, Italian American attitudes expressed in opinion surveys, like those of many other whites, had liberalized on some matters. Sixty percent of Italian Americans, compared with 55 percent of all whites, said they would work for improved racial relations, and 85 percent of Italian Americans, compared with 79 percent of all whites, said they would vote for a black presidential candidate.[120] On the whole, Italian Americans seem to hold less negative views of African Americans than in the past. Yet among Italian Americans, as among other white groups, a sizeable proportion remain openly racist in their attitudes toward black Americans, a situation that has on occasion fueled anti-black discrimination and violence, such as the Bensonhurst attacks.

POLITICS

The first major Italian influence on U.S. politics was that of Filippo Mazzei, a friend of Thomas Jefferson who came to the colonies to help with agricultural development. Mazzei helped Jefferson bring legal reforms to Virginia. Mazzei's writings speak vigorously of freedom and equality and include phrases similar to those Jefferson later used in the Declaration of Independence—for example, Mazzei's phrase "All men are by nature created free and independent."[121]

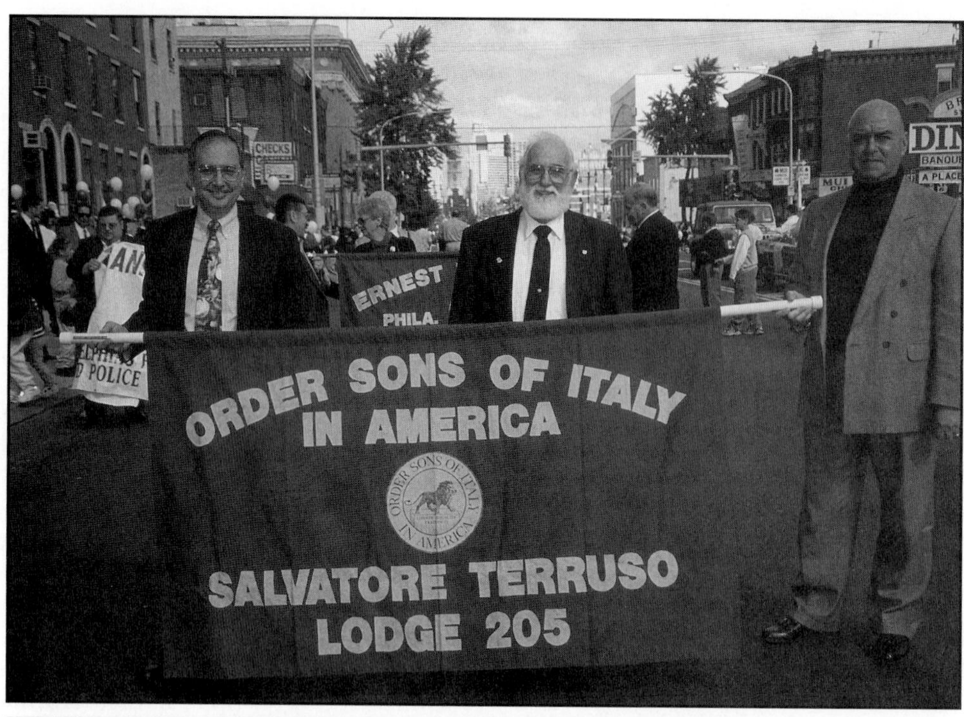

Italian Americans march in a Philadelphia parade.

City Politics

During and after the great migration of 1880–1920, Irish American political leaders often recruited Italian Americans into the Democratic party. In Chicago, Italian Americans benefited from the political patronage system; many were employed by the city in the 1890s, mostly in menial positions, such as street sweeping. By 1892, Italian Americans elected a Chicago alderman, and by the mid-1890s they had a few representatives in the Illinois legislature. Italians had begun to enter elected offices in New York City by 1900, and by 1920 they held enough power in city politics to enable them to distribute life-sustaining job favors.[122]

By the late 1930s, Italian mayors were elected in a few large cities, such as New York, San Francisco, and New Orleans, and also in a number of smaller cities. Prominent Italian American mayors in recent decades have included Anthony Celebrezze (Cleveland), Joseph Alioto (San Francisco), George Moscone (San Francisco), and Frank Rizzo (Philadelphia). Most of those who have served as chief executives in major cities have been Democrats.

State and National Politics

Very few Italians served in state and national legislatures prior to 1900. Indeed, prior to 1950, New York had sent only six Italian American representatives to Congress. The most famous was Fiorello La Guardia. In Congress he vigorously supported Italian immigration and attacked nativism and the anti-Italian quota system it fostered. He was the first Italian American to rise through ethnic politics in New York City, where he was elected mayor in 1934. La Guardia demonstrated that Italian Americans supported movements to reform urban machines and promote honest government.[123]

International politics has affected Italian American political activities, just as the Ireland–Britain struggle has affected Irish Americans. During the Great Depression, the Italian dictator Mussolini became a hero for many Italian (as well as non-Italian) Americans—although anti-fascist activity was also a significant force in Italian American communities.

During World War II, Italian Americans suffered some discrimination. Italian American subversion was widely alleged, but not proven, and the use of the Italian language on the radio was prohibited in New York and Boston. Several hundred Italian Americans, legal residents of the United States, were imprisoned at a Montana concentration camp where Japanese Americans were also interned. More than a half million Americans of Italian American ancestry were officially seen as "enemy aliens," and some had their rights curtailed. The property of some was confiscated; restrictions were placed on travel; nighttime curfews were imposed; and some living in coastal areas were forced to move. The justification for ignoring the civil rights of hundreds of thousands of Italian Americans was similar to the rationalizations for the internment of Japanese Americans. They were *alleged* to represent a security threat. Recently, legislation has been introduced in Congress to require the government to openly acknowledge these violations of the civil rights of Italian Americans.[124] It is significant, however, that the government action taken against Italian Americans was far less severe than that against Japanese Americans, perhaps because Italian Americans were by that time considered to be "white" by most of the government officials who were involved.[125]

World War II contributed to Italian American mobility and assimilation, particularly after 1945. The solidarity with other Americans that was generated by the struggle against fascism in Germany and Japan helped Italian immigrants and their children assimilate more rapidly to Anglo-Protestant culture and institutions. Italian Americans enlisted in the armed forces in significant numbers and served in ethnically integrated units. (In contrast, African Americans and Japanese Americans served in *segregated* units.) The war contributed to "a different vision of America, which included ethnic Americans, or more precisely those who were white, in the magic circle of full citizenship."[126]

Between the 1970s and the early 2000s, the number of Italian American cabinet members, governors, and state legislators has grown. This signals substantial political advances for this ethnic group. Today, some areas of the country, such as Long Island, have large numbers of Italian American officials, including state legislators. Local officials have gained national attention. Mario Cuomo, former governor of New York, was a contender for the Democratic party's presidential nomination in 1990s. He was also a keynote speaker at the 1984 Democratic party convention that nominated Geraldine Ferraro as its vice-presidential candidate. Ferraro, an Italian American, was the first woman ever to be nominated for vice-president. In the late 1990s, New York City's mayor and one of the state's U.S. senators were of Italian ancestry. In the 1990s New York's mayor, Rudolph Giuliani, a Republican, was heralded as a likely presidential candidate, and in the early 2000s he was internationally celebrated for his role in providing personal and governmental support for the families of victims of the World Trade Center attacks. By the late 1990s, thirty-two Italian Americans, representing numerous states, were members of the U.S. House of Representatives.

In the 1960s Republican strategists began a concerted effort to win the white ethnic vote, including the Italian American vote, away from the Democratic party. Fears of black civil rights demands and protests among white ethnics were used, in part, for this purpose. By 1990, poll data indicated that 49 percent of Italian Americans called themselves Republicans, compared with 39 percent who called themselves Democrats.[127] Analysis of opinion data on Italian Americans by the National Opinion Research Center indicates that over the past two decades they have moved to the political right on major issues such as capital punishment and the restriction of immigration. Still, the data indicate continuing political liberalism among Italian Americans on such matters as support for the United Nations and increased government spending to help the poor and the central cities.[128]

Italian Americans, like other U.S. ethnic groups, have lobbied politically on behalf of their home country. In the late 1990s, the United Nations was considering a U.S. proposal to add Germany and Japan, but not Italy, as permanent members of the Security Council. Italian American citizen groups organized protests against what they called a "blatant insult" and argued that Italy should be placed on the Security Council because of its great importance in past and current UN activities.[129]

THE ECONOMY

Structural adaptation by immigrant groups includes their movement into secondary-organization levels of the host society—into economic as well as political and educational organizations.

Economic mobility means attaining higher levels of employment and the attendant economic benefits. Italian Americans started near the bottom of the ladder. The small number of immigrants prior to 1880 were mostly artisans, street merchants, and political exiles, primarily from northern Italy. The southern Italian immigrants, who came after 1880, were economically oppressed. They responded to the tremendous U.S. demand for unskilled labor in the late nineteenth century.[130]

Early Poverty and Discrimination

Urban poverty coupled with dangerous working conditions was the lot of most immigrants: "The Italian immigrant may be maimed and killed in his industrial occupation without a cry and without indemnity. He may die from the 'bends' working in the caissons under the river, without protest; he can be slowly asphyxiated in crowded tenements, smothered in dangerous trades and occupations (which only the ignorant immigrant pursues, not the native American); he can contract tuberculosis in unsanitary factories and sweatshops."[131] Some among the first generation of the post-1880 Italian immigrants were skilled workers, but most suffered from a lack of skills. Overall this group had the highest percentage of unskilled laborers among major immigrant groups in this period. Few were clerical workers or professionals. Women were employed primarily in trade occupations.[132]

Isolate, small-group, and institutionalized discrimination (see Chapter 1) held Italian Americans back. From the first years of heavy migration, the new Italian residents were "abused in public and isolated in private, cuffed in the works and pelted on the streets, fined and imprisoned on the smallest pretext, cheated of their wages, and crowded by the score into converted barns and tumble-down shanties that served as boarding houses."[133] Discrimination in wages was often blatant. For example, an ad for laborers to build a New York City reservoir listed daily wages as $1.30 to $1.50 for "whites" and $1.15 to $1.25 for "Italians."[134] Institutionalized discrimination was equally problematic. For example, recruitment practices often had a built-in bias. Then, as now, informal social networks were the major means of circulating job information. In most urban job networks, Anglo-Protestant and Irish American sponsors functioned to protect their own kind and often discriminated against Italian American workers.[135]

Upward Mobility

Economic progress came slowly but steadily. The proportion of Italian American workers who were laborers dropped from 50 percent in 1916 to only 31 percent fifteen years later. Small-business and skilled blue-collar positions were more common by 1931.[136] Mobility was evident, but so was the persisting economic differential between Italian Americans and other whites. An early 1930s study in Newburyport, Massachusetts revealed that Italians there were lower than other whites on the "prestige" ladder and somewhat lower on the occupational ladder. The Great Depression slowed advancement, but did not stop it. By 1939 Italian Americans had begun to supplant Jewish Americans as the major group in a number of important unions of skilled workers.[137]

By the 1920s, organized crime was providing some better-paying jobs for Italian Americans in northern cities, although the so-called "good citizens" of the cities, both non-Italians and Italians, were the ones who supported the bootlegging, prostitution, and gambling operations with their active patronage.[138] Later, money from organized crime would flow to legitimate enterprises, just as it had earlier for other ethnic groups. Members of families successful in organized crime would eventually move out of illegitimate enterprises altogether. This trend, according to Ianni, supports "the thesis that for Italian Americans, as for other ethnic groups, organized crime has been a way station on the road to ultimately respectable roles in American society."[139] But only a few Italian Americans achieved upward mobility this way. Moreover, the line between legitimate and illegitimate business has often been fuzzy in this society, and not just in the case of white ethnics in organized crime. During the late nineteenth and early twentieth century, the Anglo-Protestant "captains of industry" were often involved in a variety of questionable economic and political activities, including illegal activities.[140]

Some Italian Americans became nationally prominent entrepreneurs and scientists. Amadeo Giannini, founder of the Bank of America, made his fortune in California financing generations of small businesses and ranches; he permitted his depositors a voice in bank management. Italian Americans such

In 1912, textile laborers and armed soldiers face off during the strike by the International Workers of the World at Lawrence, Massachusetts.

as Di Giorgio and Gallo began to play major roles in restaurant, agricultural, wine, and contracting businesses. Scientists Enrico Fermi and Salvador Luria won Nobel Prizes. As with groups before and after them, Italian Americans also found upward mobility in sports. Two notable examples are Rocky Marciano and Joe DiMaggio.[141]

Recent Decades

By the 1950s Italian Americans had advanced further, although not to the level of major white Protestant groups. One urban study in the 1950s suggested that second-generation Italian Catholics had yet to equal white Protestants in the proportion holding higher-level white-collar jobs.[142] The 1990 census showed significant mobility in the occupational distribution for Americans of Italian ancestry. Compared with the total white population, Italian Americans now had a greater proportion in professional, managerial, technical, and other white-collar jobs and a smaller proportion in blue-collar jobs.[143] Although Italian Americans are still underrepresented among top corporate officials, the National Italian American Foundation reported that in the early 1990s some 150 Italian Americans held top- or second-ranking positions in large American companies.[144]

By the 1990 census, the median family income for Italian Americans ($42,242) was substantially higher than that of all whites ($37,628), and poverty rates for Italian Americans were substantially below those of the larger group. The unemployment rate for Italian Americans was slightly below that of all whites and well below that of the total population.[145]

Some Persisting Problems

Over the past few decades, discrimination against Italian Americans has sometimes been a problem at the highest levels of this society. The failure to hire Italian Americans at the City University of New York (CUNY) was documented in a 1970s study of CUNY's higher-level positions that concluded: "In decision-making positions of Dean, Director and Chairman of the system's 18 colleges, there are only 20 Italian Americans out of a total of 504 positions."[146] Only a small percentage of the faculty were Italian Americans, and these tended to be at the lowest ranks.

In 1975 an affirmative action program for Italian American faculty was put into place, but fifteen years later the percentage of Italian American faculty had not increased. Little change occurred between the 1970s and the 1990s. At the beginning of the 1990s, Italian Americans still constituted less than 6 percent of CUNY's faculty, in contrast with the larger percentages of Italian Americans on the faculties at private universities in New York City. At that time CUNY's student body was about 17 percent Italian American.[147]

In the early 1990s, CUNY professors protested discrimination in the hiring of Italian Americans in a class action complaint against the university. In 1994 CUNY settled a lawsuit brought by the director of the university's Italian-American Institute; CUNY's administration agreed to make the Institute a permanent part of Queens College and to hire a distinguished senior professor in Italian American studies. At the beginning of the twenty-first century, litigation and dispute over the implementation of the settlement have continued.[148]

Over the past decade, some private clubs have barred Italian Americans, and Italian Americans are still underrepresented in the very top positions of major corporations. Still, the overall picture of recent occupational and income mobility for Italian Americans, a white ethnic group oppressed on a large scale only a few decades ago, is impressive. At least two among them, Mario Cuomo and Lee Iacocca, have been touted as presidential candidates. Italian American men are prominent among movie directors. Women of Italian American ancestry have moved into important positions in the mass media, including the writer Anna Quindlen. The majority of Italian Americans have made strides up the socioeconomic ladder and on many socioeconomic indexes they have surpassed Anglo-Protestants.

EDUCATION

Many Italian immigrants came from areas in Italy where the poor received little schooling. Like many immigrants to the United States, they often adopted a pragmatic approach to education, valuing it but asking, "What is the practical value of this for jobs, for later life?" Many poor families made sacrifices to put their first child through elementary school, and then expected this child to get a job to put later children through school.

As they had been with the Irish, Protestant educators were very concerned over the alleged corruption and cultural inferiority of Italian Americans. Many schools became pressure cookers of Americanization in which these educators sought to teach Italian immigrants Anglo-Protestant ways as quickly as possible. Anglo-Protestant norms about health, dress, work, and language were pressed hard on the immigrants and their children. Ethnic discrimination was often a fact of school life. These pressures were especially strong for second-generation children, most of whom attended public schools. Public schools were Procrustean beds shaped in Anglo-centric form. Rather than give in to hostile pressures, some Italian American children left school.[149]

Despite such obstacles, Italian Americans made dramatic progress in educational attainment. By 1970, Italian Americans' median level of educational attainment was higher than that of the total population of the United States and only slightly lower than that of the white population as a whole.[150] By 1990, native-born Italian Americans had achieved educational parity with the larger white group.[151]

RELIGION

The Roman Catholic church has been important in the lives of Italian Americans. The pre-existing Irish Catholic churches were often overwhelmed by the numbers of Italian immigrants. For many Italians, Irish Catholicism was too orthodox. Religion was not an intimate part of political identity for the Italian immigrant, as it was for the Irish immigrant, whose religious expression was tied to a nationalist heritage of anti-English agitation. Saints were important to Italian Catholics, as were the religious festivals that played an important role in cementing the Italian community.[152]

Irish American priests often held negative views of the new Italian parishioners, who were not considered to be as serious as Irish American worshippers. Tension sometimes escalated, and when ethnic parishes for Italian Americans developed, the latter were warned away, on occasion forcefully, from Irish American parishes. Italian Americans reciprocated. Many first-generation Italian Americans preferred to send their children to public schools rather than to Irish-dominated parochial schools.[153] Gradually, Italian Catholicism, with its festivals and ceremonies, took its place alongside Irish Catholicism.[154]

A 1960s study of Italian and Irish Catholics in New York City suggested the controversial conclusion that third-generation Italians were becoming more "Irishized" in their religious practices; the data showed less emphasis on the Virgin Mary, fewer masses for deceased relatives, and more emphasis on generous contributions to the church when this generation was compared with earlier generations. In national surveys between 1988 and 1991, only 70 percent of Italian Americans classified themselves as Catholics, and many of those were nonpracticing. Catholicism today seems less central for Italian Americans than for Irish Americans. Still, in the early 2000s some Italian American communities, such as that on New York's Long Island, still have parades, feasts, and church bazaars honoring traditional saints or the Virgin Mary.[155]

Assimilation or Ethnogenesis?

Acculturation pressures came early for southern and eastern European immigrants. Unlike British immigrants before them, they spoke no English, nor were they familiar with the customs of Anglo-Protestant society. Often concentrated in so-called "Little Italies," Italian immigrants often learned Italian dialects other than their own, although most picked up some English. In addition to language and community factors, cultural adaptation was also slowed by poverty, the intention of some to return home, and anti-immigrant hostility and discrimination in the new environment.[156]

The first-generation family was in transition, cross-pressured between the old Italian and the new American ways. Families became less patriarchal and kin solidarity often weakened somewhat, as did ties to religion. Children were more on their own. Speaking Italian at home was sometimes a point of intergenerational conflict, since the younger members felt school pressures to speak only English.[157]

Marriage was a second point of intergenerational conflict. First-generation parents saw it as a family matter, while many children and grandchildren tended to see it as an individual matter. Given this tension, it is not surprising that second-generation families adapted in different ways. One type substantially abandoned the old ways, changing the Italian name and moving out of an Italian residential area. This was rare. A second type rejected the old ways in part, perhaps by moving out of concentrated Italian American communities but remaining near enough to maintain close ties to the first generation. This was the largest group. A third type stayed in the old community and retained many of the old ways.[158] At the beginning of the 1990s, Italian Americans were still concentrated in the Northeast; they constituted about one-sixth of the population in several northeastern states such as New York. No longer a predominantly central-city group, they were about as likely to reside in suburbs as the average white American.

Structural Assimilation

Structural assimilation involves the movement of a group into the secondary organizations—the businesses and bureaucracies—of the larger society, as well as into its primary social networks: social clubs, neighborhoods, and friendship circles. Structural movement by Italian Americans over the first several decades came with considerable resistance from earlier groups. Positioning at the lower economic levels was a fact of life for a time.

In recent decades Italian Americans have made impressive gains in employment, income, and education and advances in politics. This upward educational and occupational mobility has contributed to assimilation in other areas. Increasing equal-status contact with members of other white groups in the workplace, the suburbs, and colleges has in turn created cross-ethnic friendship networks and marriages.[159]

The economic success of Italian Americans and other white ethnic groups is sometimes compared with the relative lack of success of other groups, such as African Americans. Why were Italian Americans so successful in assimilating over time to Anglo-Protestant institutions and organizations? The answer to this question lies not only in the hard work and sacrifice of several generations of Italian Americans, for those factors are also characteristic of African Americans. It lies also in the timing of Italian immigrants' entry into the United States. Jobs and housing near jobs were available to the masses of Italians who arrived in the last decades of the nineteenth century and the first decades of the twentieth century. The second and third generations emerged with enough economic support from their parents to obtain the education they needed for the better-paying jobs that opened up during and after World War II.[160] Expansion of jobs on the middle rungs of the occupational ladder made upward mobility possible for many white ethnic Americans. Of even greater importance is the fact that the poverty and ethnic discrimination that Italian immigrants faced, although serious, were never as thoroughgoing as the extreme poverty and the severe and institutionalized racial discrimination faced by African Americans and other non-European Americans.

By the World War II period, the earlier view of Italian Americans as an "inferior race" held by Anglo-Protestant officials and commentators had been replaced by a conception of Italian Americans as part of the "white race." This change reduced anti-Italian discrimination in many settings. Wartime solidarity had hastened the assimilation of white ethnics, including Italian Americans, into Anglo-Protestant institutions, including the regular units of the armed forces. In contrast, African Americans and Japanese Americans were kept in segregated units. After the war many Italian Americans took advantage of GI grant programs to get a college education at colleges and universities across the United States.

Residential patterns have contributed to a continuing ethnic identity for Italian Americans. Alba's 1980s study in a large New York metropolitan area found that Italian Americans there were still one of the most residentially concentrated of white ethnic groups. They were more likely than other ethnic groups to name a relative as a close friend and had one of the highest rates of intraethnic friendships. Among three generations of Italian Americans in Tardi's late-1980s New Jersey study, sharing problems and needs with family members was the daily norm. Her respondents defined their Italian American ethnicity in terms of a warm and cohesive family structure that they perceived as distinctive among white ethnic groups.[161]

While kinship and primary-group ties often remain strong among Italian Americans, suburbanization has shrunk formerly large ethnic enclaves.[162] Alba and his associates have reported that in both 1980 and 1990, *most* of the nearly 3 million Italian Americans in the Greater New York area lived outside of Italian American neighborhoods (defined as census tracts in which at least 35 percent of the population was of Italian ancestry).[163] In the early 2000s, New York's Italian Americans are much less concentrated in primarily Italian neighborhoods than in previous decades. The majority now live in the suburbs.

Studies of marriages in New Haven (1870) and Chicago (1920) found high rates of in-marriage for Italians: 94 to 98 percent of all marriages were endogamous. In-marriage decreased in subsequent decades. While 84 percent of the respondents in Bridgeport's 1970s study reported that both of their parents were of Italian ancestry, only 44 percent were themselves married to Italian Americans. Still, the rate of *religious* endogamy was high: Most marriages outside the Italian group were with persons raised as Catholics. Exogamous marriages were more likely for those with higher-status educational and occupational achievements. More recently, one 1997 analysis estimated that 73 percent of Italian Americans in their 30s were now marrying outside their ethnic group.[164]

Alba argues that while ethnicity is still important for the first and second generations, a transition is underway for later generations. He sees ethnicity receding for the third and fourth generations, as Italian Americans become more structurally integrated into the mainstream of white America: 54 percent of all Italian American respondents in his upper New York State study reported ethnically unmixed ancestry. Yet, for those born after 1940, the proportion dropped to only one-third. National survey data also suggest high levels of mixed ancestry for Italian Americans. It seems likely that a much more assimilated Italian American group will emerge as the younger generations replace the earlier ones.[165]

Across-the-board assimilation of Italian Americans is progressing, although this group still encounters significant stereotyping and some discrimination. Italian Americans remain underrepresented at the very highest economic and political levels of U.S. society.

An Italian Identity?

Identificational assimilation involves giving up one's ethnic identity for that of the dominant Anglo-Protestant culture. For many Italian Americans, this is happening slowly. Ethnic ties and accents are still found in older generations and among all generations in certain ethnic enclaves. In a number of substantially Italian American neighborhoods in northern cities, older Italian Americans and new Italian immigrants of the past few decades are helping to keep some cultural characteristics alive. One 1980s study of Belmont, a community in the Bronx with a substantial Italian American flavor, found some persisting ethnic neighborhoods and traditions.[166] And a 1980s study of Italian Americans in Scottsdale, Arizona found that rather than losing their cultural identity, these respondents had preserved some Italian American subculture. Sixty percent maintained daily or weekly contact with relatives locally, and a large percentage of friendships were with other Italian Americans. In the New York State study cited earlier, Italian Americans were the most likely of the various white ethnic groups to feel a sense of ethnic identity and to consider their ethnic identity as very important. Among those of mixed ancestry who identified ethnically, almost three-fourths described themselves solely as Italian American.[167]

Marcus Lee Hansen once argued there is often an increase in ethnic awareness in the third generation of an immigrant group; this substantially assimilated generation vigorously searches out its ethnic roots. Younger Italian Americans have faced less discrimination and stereotyping than older generations. This has enabled younger generations to express their ethnicity openly. However, in her New Jersey study, Tardi found a strong pride in ethnic identity among Italian Americans of the first, second, *and* third generations. The structural factors associated with greater freedom to express ethnic pride, such as diminishing overt discrimination and increasing numbers of highly visible Italian Americans in public life, have apparently affected all generations.[168]

One study of Italian Americans in California found a relationship between the strength of ethnic networks and identity and the work an individual does. Most working-class Italian Americans no longer worked with large numbers of other Italian Americans and therefore expressed their ethnic identity differently from shopkeepers and independent professionals, who were better able to express their ethnicity in their work, such as by serving a partially ethnic clientele. Participation in the economy may or may not work to destroy ethnic identity, depending on the character of one's participation and on where one works.[169]

Andrew Greeley's ethnogenesis model seems to fit the Italian experience. Italians came to the United States with significant differences from the dominant British American group, but they shared some historical background and a Christian religious tradition with that group. Interaction in public schools and media influence served to narrow the gap substantially. Italian Americans assimilated in major ways to the Anglo-Protestant host culture, but in other ways they retained some distinctiveness. Because of their strong national heritage, residential segregation, and strong community and kinship networks, a distinctive U.S. ethnic group developed over time. Today, Italian Americans are no longer dominated by their national heritage. But most have not yet become just like British Protestant Americans. For the most part, they remain Italian *and* American. As a group Italian Americans have experienced very substantial adaptation without complete assimilation, at least at the level of identity.

Some scholars see structural forces such as increasing intermarriage, increasing levels of education, loss of the Italian language, and residential mixing in the suburbs as further diminishing, if not eradicating, this sense of ethnic identity among most Italian Americans over the next decade or two. Membership in Italian American organizations is declining. The remaining sense of Italian American identity has not retarded the increasing rates of intermarriage.[170] Yet the continuing presence of significant numbers of foreign-born Italian Americans fosters some connection to the old ethnic identity.

A NOTE ON ETHNIC DIVERSITY AMONG WHITE AMERICANS

There are numerous white ethnic groups other than the Italian, Irish, and English American groups that we have considered at some length. For reasons of space, we cannot assess in detail the many other groups that make up the white population of the United States. We can, however, pause briefly to note how diverse and extensive this population is. A recent (November 1999–December 2000) U.S. Census Bureau sample survey interviewed respondents at

TABLE 4.1 ANCESTRY GROUPS

ESTIMATED TO BE LARGER THAN 2,000,000	
Dutch	5,221,803
English	28,264,856
French	9,775,761
German	46,488,992
Irish and Scotch-Irish	38,293,533
Italian	15,942,683
Norwegian	4,541,254
Polish	9,053,660
Russian	2,980,776
Scottish	5,423,030
Swedish	4,339,357
ESTIMATED TO BE IN THE 300,000–2,000,000 RANGE	
Austrian	795,131
Belgian	377,451
Canadian	635,400
Croatian	392,121
Czech	1,396,279
Danish	1,502,600
Finnish	797,642
Greek	1,179,064
Hungarian	1,519,788
Lithuanian	714,097
Portuguese	1,321,155
Romanian	397,576
Slovak	821,325
Swiss	998,009
Ukrainian	862,762
Welsh	1,898,279

about 58,000 residential addresses in all fifty states.[171] They asked about the ancestry of the respondents and recorded the first and second ancestries that were given. The reports from that survey estimate the numbers for certain national-origin populations for the entire country. In Table 4.1 we list from these reports those national-origin groups with more than 300,000 people giving first and second ancestry responses (combined).

Those Americans in the eleven largest ethnic groups mostly have ancestries linked to northern and central European areas. The very largest groups list German, Irish, English, Italian, French, and Polish ancestries, in that order. Russia and the Netherlands, as well as the Scandinavian countries of Sweden and Norway, also have many representatives in the U.S. population. The second list refers to sixteen countries or areas that have generally supplied fewer immigrants than the first list, but which still constitute major points of origin for many of the ancestors of contemporary white Americans. Distinctive in the second list of ancestral origins are numerous countries or areas in central, southern, and eastern Europe, with a few north European countries or areas sprinkled in. Leading this list are those with Welsh, Hungarian, Danish, Czech, Portuguese, and Greek as their first or second ancestries. One county in the Americas, Canada, is also represented in this list, a country with large populations that also have English, Irish, Scottish, and French ancestries.

While these data do not include vague choices made by some respondents, such as "American" or "British American," and are estimates based on a large sample survey (not a population census), they do give us some insight into just how diverse the white population is at the beginning of the twenty-first century. The data also suggest how the early immigrations from Europe were actually limited to just a few countries, for the English, Irish, and German ancestries are by far the largest categories in the list. These data are yet one more indicator of the complex ethnic and racial mosaic that is the contemporary United States.

SUMMARY

Irish immigration to North America began with the arrival of indentured servants and farmers in the 1700s. This early immigration included more southern, or Celtic, Irish than the often exaggerated accounts of the "Scotch-Irish" have suggested. The majority of the descendants of these early migrants were, or became, Protestants. They settled disproportionately in the South and in frontier areas. Over the next several generations many of the descendants of these early settlers became part of the white-Protestant mainstream. However, a significant proportion remained poor. The Protestant Irish in particular have received little attention from scholars.

After the 1830s, large numbers of Irish Catholic immigrants settled in the cities of the North, where many suffered violence at the hands of Catholic-hating nativists and discrimination by Anglo-American employers. Movement toward economic equality with older groups was slow for the poverty-stricken Irish Catholics. Conflict, sometimes violent, marked their climb. Frequently political innovators, the Irish Catholics shaped the political organizations of major cities in order to facilitate their integration into the dominant political and economic institutions. They diversified U.S. religious institutions by bringing in a strong Catholic church and school complex.

Economic mobility has been so dramatic that by the 1990s Irish Americans ranked at or above the national average for all whites on a number of important socioeconomic indicators, including educational level, occupational distribution, and income. At the beginning of the twenty-first century, Irish Americans are a major segment of Middle America.

Today, a significant portion of the descendants of the Italian immigrants who entered the United States over the past century are still clustered in certain northern cities and states. However, increasing numbers are now scattered across suburban areas with other white groups. The majority of Italian Americans remain Catholic, although many are not active. Italian Americans have played and continue to play an important role in the culture, politics, and economy of the United States. Poverty and difficult working conditions greeted the hardworking Italian immigrants. They were not prepared for the intense nativist attacks from Anglo-Protestants, who falsely stereotyped Italian Americans as an inferior, immoral, and criminal people and sought to prove Italian American "racial inferiority." Italian American communities have been stigmatized by a widespread Mafia myth and have sometimes endured violent attacks by other white Americans.

Political avenues were closed for a time; the economy often consigned Italian Americans to low-paid jobs; public schools sought to transform them into carbon-copy Anglo-Protestants. Yet, despite these problems, the immigrants and their descendants persevered and prospered. Particularly after World War II, they began to succeed more conspicuously in politics, the economy, and education. Their economic and political mobility has made them another U.S. success story, although a considerable cultural-conformity price was often exacted for that success.

Today, Italian Americans are one of the major groups in the great American drama of blending and pluralism. As a group they have so far retained a significant degree of ethnic distinctiveness that seems likely to persist for some time to come. Yet some researchers predict that in the next few decades social forces such as suburbanization and intermarriage will diminish the Italian American ethnic identity and accelerate Italian Americans' identification with a general "European American" or "white American" identity. They too are now an important segment of Middle America.

5 Jewish Americans

JEWS HAVE BEEN SCAPEGOATS FOR THE HATREDS OF THE DOMINANT PEOPLES IN various nations around the globe for thousands of years. From the Egyptian and Roman persecutions in ancient times to the massacres and expulsions in Spain in the late 1400s to the brutal pogroms of the Russian czar in the 1880s to the German Nazi massacres, Jews might be regarded as the most widely persecuted racial–ethnic group in world history. Residing in many lands, the continually harassed ancestors of Jewish Americans forged strong and distinctive cultural traditions. Indeed, some of the intellectual pillars of modern Western civilization—Karl Marx, Sigmund Freud, and Albert Einstein—were Jews.

Jewish Americans have made enormous contributions to the success of the United States—as pioneers in trade and commerce, industrial workers, professionals, scholars, government officials, and entertainers. They have benefited from a political structure that separates church and state and prohibits religious qualifications for holding public office. Jewish immigrants have often come from countries in which they were clearly outsiders constantly struggling to survive. They were prohibited from owning land, and subjected to government-sponsored persecutions and mass murder. In the

United States, Alan Dershowitz points out in his book, *Chutzpah,* "the Jews did not have to evaluate every single event by reference to their own survival."[1] For the most part, U.S. law never became the enemy of Jewish Americans. Still, more than any other white ethnic group, they have often been treated as outsiders in the United States.

By tradition, Jewish ethnicity is based on matrilineal ancestry: A Jew is a person whose mother is Jewish. In the contemporary United States, many Jewish writers define Jews as those who identify themselves as Jews.[2] Some Jewish Americans focus their identity primarily on their religion; others define their Jewishness primarily in terms of group membership.*

MIGRATION

From 1500 to World War II

Most of the earliest Jewish immigrants came as individuals to the Atlantic Coast colonies in the 1600s seeking economic opportunities denied to them in Europe. The first Jewish community dates from the arrival in 1654 of twenty-three Jews who fled the Catholic Inquisition in Portuguese-controlled Brazil. Most were *Sephardic Jews,* whose background was the Jewish subculture of Spain. These refugees had been refused entry into the Spanish-controlled Caribbean islands. They also faced resistance in New Amsterdam before they were grudgingly allowed to settle there.[3]

Over the next hundred years, small numbers of descendants of *Marranos*—Jews who had been forced to publicly convert to Christianity during the Spanish Inquisition under threat of death but who privately maintained allegiance to Judaism—came to the North American colonies. The immigration of the *Ashkenazi Jews* (those from England, Germany, and Poland) began slowly in the early 1700s, and this group soon outnumbered the Sephardic Jews. Many of these immigrants were attracted by reports of U.S. prosperity. Most integrated into the Sephardic communities and adopted their acculturated practices.[4]

After 1820, central European Jews came in dramatically increased numbers in response to declining economic conditions and increased anti-Semitism in Europe, as well as to U.S. economic expansion. These immigrants have often been called "German Jews," although they came from Bohemia and Moravia as well as Germany. The typical immigrant of the 1830s and later was a single man. This stream of immigrants included peddlers, merchants, and craft workers from small towns, and many settled in the Midwest, Far West, and South. By 1860, Jewish American communities and synagogues had been established in many cities. Geographic mobility facilitated acculturation.[5]

Eastern European Jews, the largest group of Jewish immigrants, began to arrive in the 1870s. The overwhelming majority came from Russian-controlled areas where anti-Semitism, overpopulation, and lack of economic opportunities were major push factors. In Russia in the 1880s, government-sponsored massacres, called *pogroms,* affected all Jews and contributed to an increase in out-migration.[6]

Jewish immigration from 1881 to the 1920s totaled 2.5 million. By the mid-1920s, Jewish Americans composed 3.5 percent of the U.S. population. Eastern European Jews constituted a large proportion of all immigrants. Unlike some non-Jewish immigrants of this period, few returned home. Most settled in East Coast cities and worked as peddlers, street vendors, and unskilled workers. These immigrants brought with them a distinctive language and culture (Yiddish), a strong sense of Jewish identity, Orthodox religious observances, and a determination to succeed.[7]

After the 1924 Immigration Act, a discriminatory law aimed at limiting eastern and southern European immigration, the number of Jewish newcomers declined. Between 1921 and 1936, fewer than 400,000 immigrants entered the country. During the Great Depression, the number of immigrants from all parts of the globe was sharply reduced. President Franklin Roosevelt's administration did permit some modest increase in Jewish refugees from Germany because of the Nazi persecution. However, Roosevelt, and particularly his State Department, did much less than they could have to allow Jews to flee persecution. The obstacles to Jewish immigration were callous if

*In this chapter we will use the term "Jewish American" as shorthand for Jewish Americans of European descent. However, we should keep in mind that there are a few very small religious groups of African Americans who adhere to Judaism, as well as small groups of Latino and Asian Jews.

not hostile: The U.S. State Department adopted the policy of requiring affidavits of financial solvency and good character and used visa regulations to slow the flow of refugees fleeing Hitler's death camps. In June 1940, the State Department put an end to most immigration from Germany and central Europe. More than 400,000 slots within U.S. immigration quotas for refugees from countries under Nazi control were left unused between 1933 and 1943. Some of these unfilled slots may represent lives lost to extermination by the Nazis because of U.S. immigration policy.[8] The 150,000 refugees who did manage to enter between 1935 and the early 1940s included many highly talented people, including the brilliant physicist Albert Einstein.

World War II to the Present

After the arrival of thousands of postwar refugees, Jewish migration again tapered off to an estimated 8,000 annually in the 1950s and 1960s. New sources of immigrants replaced the old. By the 1970s, a significant number of Israelis—estimated at 100,000 or more—had come to the United States. Large numbers were undocumented immigrants. The past two decades have again seen an increase in Israeli immigrants to the United States. By the late 1990s, there were about 200,000 Israeli immigrants in the United States.[9]

Between the late 1960s and the early 2000s, a new group of eastern European Jews, this time from the Soviet Union (later, the former Soviet Union), came to the United States. By 2000, this immigration totaled more than 400,000; most came after the fall of the Communist state in 1991. Most are proud of their Jewish heritage. They emigrated because of Russian anti-Semitism and because of economic and political chaos in their homeland.[10] One recent analysis of this immigration notes that since the end of Communism "old ethnic and religious hatreds have reentered political discourse, appearing now as a resurgent nationalism."[11]

Since World War II, internal migration has shifted the Jewish population from cities to suburbs. The proportion living in the East has declined, while the proportions in the South and West have doubled. Thus, a late-1980s survey in Rhode Island revealed that the Jewish population of Greater Providence had dropped about one-fifth since the 1960s, and the state's total Jewish population had also declined.[12]

The 1999 *American Jewish Yearbook* estimated the Jewish American population at about 6 million—nearly half the world's Jewish population. A very high percentage (91 percent) of Jewish Americans were born in the United States, and about half live in three large metropolitan areas—New York–northern New Jersey, Los Angeles–Riverside–Orange counties, and Miami–Ft. Lauderdale. Since the peak year of 1937, Jewish Americans have declined as a percentage of the total U.S. population—to about 2.1 percent today.[13]

Prejudice and Stereotypes

Jewish Americans have been socially defined by outsiders on the basis of both (real and alleged) physical and cultural characteristics. From the early 1900s onward, varying numbers of non-Jews have considered Jews to be a biologically inferior "race."[14] No group in history has suffered a broader range of stereotypes for a longer period than have the Jews. For centuries, Jews have been targets of hostile attitudes and discriminatory behavior, collectively known as *anti-Semitism*. For two thousand years, the writings of Christendom have been rife with anti-Semitism. Jews have been cursed and killed as "Christ killers," a view Christian immigrants brought with them to North America. Many Christian ministers and priests have passed along anti-Semitic views to each new generation, to the present day.[15]

Anti-Semitism has involved a number of other negative themes. Unlike African, Native, and Latino Americans who are frequently stereotyped as unintelligent, Jewish Americans have often been seen as too intelligent and crafty. This "devious" stereotype likely developed to rationalize the American Jews' relative success as "middleman" merchants in U.S. society.[16]

After the Civil War, a crude stereotype of Jewish Americans as social climbers was frequently circulated in the media, including then-popular vaudeville shows. Clumsy Jewish figures speaking inflected English were depicted as out of place in high-society positions. By the 1880s, newspaper and magazine cartoons were caricaturing Jewish Americans as long-nosed, garishly dressed merchants speaking broken English. During this period, Jewish Americans were also excluded from many areas of life. For example, in 1877 a prominent banker was denied accommodation in a major New York hotel. The following year a Jewish American was excluded from the New York City Bar Association, and New York's City College banned Jewish Americans from Greek-letter fraternities. In many contexts Jewish Americans were still classified as outsiders.[17]

One of the most vicious attacks on Jews was the fictional book called *The Protocols of the Elders of Zion*. This highly stereotypical tract was originally created by the Russian secret police and attempted to show that Jews, as anti-Christian agents, were taking covert control of the world and destroying Western civilization. Automobile pioneer Henry Ford worked to spread these and other vicious stereotypes. In May 1920, a summary of *The Protocols* appeared on the front page of Ford's newspaper in Dearborn, boosting the paper's circulation. By the 1920s this book was widely circulated in the United States. Ford's paper and *The Protocols* played an important role in a new burst of malicious anti-Semitic stereotypes and agitation.[18] Anti-Semitic groups still circulate *The Protocols* today.

In subsequent decades, numerous mass media cartoons stereotyped Jewish Americans as "Communist" sympathizers and alleged that "Jews were taking over the government." At the beginning of World War II, members of Congress, the press, and prominent U.S. citizens falsely accused Jewish Americans of bringing the United States into war with Germany. One 1940s social science study found substantial support among samples of non-Jewish Californians for stereotypes of Jews as revolutionary, clannish, and parasitic. After World War II, a *Fortune* magazine poll found that three-fourths of non-Jewish Americans who felt some U.S. groups had more power than was good for the country expressly cited the Jews.[19]

Anti-Semitism has persisted to the present day. For example, the president of a major Baptist organization publicly stated that God does not hear the prayers of Jews, and a leader of a conservative group repeated the old stereotype that Jews had a "supernatural" talent for moneymaking. Jewish Americans in a number of metropolitan areas who were interviewed in the 1980s reported a significant incidence of anti-Semitism, typically encounters with negative remarks. Between 17 and 28 percent of the respondents reported such experiences during the previous year; the rate was highest for young adults.[20]

Some older Jewish Americans who experienced hostility, discrimination, and exclusion during the early decades of the twentieth century feel that the relatively better current situation is proof that anti-Semitism is no longer a significant problem. Others, particularly members of the younger generation, are more skeptical. Dershowitz discusses a number of social phenomena that constitute a new variety of anti-Semitism. The "new strains of the old virus" include virulent anti-Zionism and the application of higher standards of moral and political conduct for Israel and Jews in general than for other nations or ethnic groups.[21] In a 2000 national survey of Jewish respondents, 32 percent said that anti-Semitism is still a very serious problem, and another 63 percent said it is somewhat of a problem. Only five percent said it is no longer a problem. Most respondents in that survey felt that the most anti-Semitic U.S. group was the "religious right." Twenty-three percent of the respondents thought most members of this group were anti-Semitic; another 30 percent felt that many were.[22]

Recent surveys have found that non-Jewish Americans tend to seriously overestimate the Jewish American presence in the United States, placing that group at about 25 percent of the U.S. population instead of the actual 2.1 percent. This population estimate may indicate the negative view that Jews are too dominant in the country.[23]

In the past decade a number of research studies have examined the stereotyped images of American Jews in popular culture. One recent report by the American Jewish Committee noted that stereotypical Jewish characters in television are only one of the problems: "The prevalence of interdating and intermarriage plots (to a point where they have become the paradigm for any romance involving a Jewish character); the virtual disappearance of Jewish families; the artificial limits on the number of Jewish characters on a single show, which might stigmatize it as 'too Jewish'; and finally, the often tasteless representation of religious themes and characters are related issues."[24]

Joyce Antler has documented the critical roles Jewish women have played in their communities. Through their contributions to drama, literature, cinema, radio, and television, Jewish women have "helped to shape the main currents of modern and postmodern life." Yet popular culture continues to perpetuate many of the stereotypes of Jewish women that have shaped societal understandings, such as images of the "yiddish Mama," the assertive "Jewish Mother," and the "Jewish American Princess" (JAP).[25] Negative images of Jewish American women are still commonplace in jokes and on greeting cards. Numerous women scholars and media personalities have worked to reduce or destroy these negative images of Jewish women, as well as of Jews in general. In a series of major films, Barbra Streisand, an influential Jewish American actor and singer, has portrayed "feisty Jews and feisty women," creating positive images that have staying power.[26]

OPPRESSION AND CONFLICT

During the 1880s, Jewish American merchants in the South suffered violent attacks from farmers who blamed them for economic crises, and in the 1890s the farms and homes of Jewish American merchants were burned in Mississippi. In the early 1900s, riots erupted against Jewish factory workers in New Jersey. Just before World War I, Leo Frank, the Jewish part-owner of a Georgia pencil factory, was convicted of killing a female employee, although evidence pointed elsewhere. After being beaten up in prison, he was taken from the prison hospital and lynched by an angry mob.[27]

About this time the Ku Klux Klan was revived, and these white terrorists proceeded to wage violence against black, Jewish, and Catholic Americans. During the 1920s and 1930s, crosses were burned on Jewish property; synagogues were vandalized. On occasion, the victims fought back. In the 1920s, Jewish and Catholic immigrants protested and attacked parades and gatherings of the Ku Klux Klan in Ohio and New Jersey.[28]

Organized Anti-Semitism and Hate Crimes

Between 1932 and 1941, the number of openly anti-Semitic organizations in the United States grew from one to more than one hundred. Two dozen were large-scale operations that held numerous anti-Semitic rallies, some drawing thousands. Millions of anti-Semitic leaflets and newspapers were distributed. The German-American Bund and the Silver Shirts were two of several prominent anti-Semitic groups. Father Charles Coughlin's organizations—the National Union for Social Justice and the Christian Front—became active in anti-Jewish agitation in the 1930s.[29] In 1940 the FBI arrested more than a dozen members of a Christian Front terrorist group that reportedly intended to kill "Jews and Communists, 'to knock off about a dozen Congressmen,' and to seize post offices, the Customs House, and armories in New York. In the homes of the group were found 18 cans of cordite, 18 rifles, and 5,000 rounds of ammunition."[30] Coughlin did not openly advocate anti-Semitic violence but defended those who did.

Increased anti-Semitism in Germany was an important factor in the rising number of neo-Nazi attacks against Jewish Americans in the United States. German gentiles had long applied negative stereotypes to their Jewish neighbors. The Nazi Holocaust began with restrictions on Jewish communities, which were soon followed by deportation to forced-labor camps and extermination by starvation and mass killings. An estimated 6 million European Jews (as well as millions of other "undesirable" Europeans, such as Gypsies and homosexuals) were killed by the Nazis. Extermination and forced migration reduced the Jewish populations in countries such as Poland and Germany to 10 percent of their former numbers. In the United States, the sense of oppression among Jewish Americans was reinforced not only by newspaper reports of European refugees but also by the growing knowledge that the U.S. government was aiding Nazi actions in Germany—at first by continuing economic and diplomatic relations (until 1941) and later by turning its back on thousands of Jewish refugees.[31]

Violent attacks on Jewish Americans, their property, and their synagogues have been common since World War II. More than forty major incidents were reported in 1945 and 1946 in the United States. The Anti-Defamation League (ADL), established in 1913 as a branch of the fraternal organization B'nai B'rith, publishes an annual report on anti-Semitic incidents. Generally, only blatant instances of anti-Semitism are reported to the ADL; subtle discrimination is usually not reported. The ADL's first survey (1979) counted 129 reported cases of vandalism, such as attempted arson and the painting of swastikas on synagogues. Between 1979 and 1984, some 3,694 anti-Jewish incidents were reported,

Anti-Semitic vandalism remains common in many areas of the United States.

and the annual figures have continued at high levels. Reported incidents include threatening phone calls, attacks on individuals, and acts of vandalism against property. For example, in 1996 a bomb was exploded at a Jewish Center in New York City, and, in Wisconsin, Jews praying inside a synagogue were shot by two men with a BB-gun.[32]

The ADL has reported an increase in the number of anti-Semitic groups participating in the development of a global network of anti-Semites by spreading racist propaganda via numerous Internet Web sites.[33] Moreover, attacks on Jewish Americans by white supremacy organizations have continued in recent decades. Members of one neo-Nazi group, The Order, which was formed in Idaho to conduct a war against the "Zionist Occupation Government," machine-gunned a Jewish American talk-show host in Denver, committed armed robberies, counterfeited money, set fire to a synagogue, and killed police officers trying to capture them. The number of hate crimes by certain groups of actively racist skinheads (white neo-Nazis who shave their heads) has also grown in recent years.[34]

It was not until 1990 that the U.S. Congress passed the Hate Crime Statistics Act requiring the Justice Department to collect hate crime data from local police departments. "Hate crimes" have been defined in congressional legislation as crimes against people and their property generated by prejudice against racial, ethnic, religious, disability, or sexual orientation groups. The most recent FBI figures report 7,876 crimes motivated by these types of bias, including 17 murders, during 1999. Some 1,289, or 16 percent, of these incidents were directed at Jewish Americans. (Not all local police departments submitted a report to the FBI.)[35]

In recent years more than forty state legislatures have passed hate crimes laws, most of which make religious desecrations special crimes. A number of state legislatures have increased the penalties for crimes clearly involving racial and ethnic hatred. Late in 2000 the first two men accused of a hate crime, an attack on a Bronx synagogue, were being prosecuted under New York state's hate crime law.[36] A more comprehensive federal approach to dealing with anti-Jewish and other hate crimes (the Hate Crimes Prevention Act introduced in Congress in 1999) has been strongly supported by Jewish organizations but has been stalled by conservative white members of the U.S. Congress.

Religious Discrimination and Conflict

A number of federal court cases have involved religious discrimination. During the 1950s and 1960s, Orthodox Jewish business owners contested local "blue laws" that required businesses to close on Sunday, the Christian holy day; they argued that such laws violated their First Amendment right not to be penalized for their religious practices. The Supreme Court upheld the blue laws. Specifically Christian religious observances, such as reciting the Lord's Prayer, were once standard in public schools. The imposition of these practices on Jewish children was contested in courts from New York to California. In the 1960s, the Supreme Court ruled against officially sanctioned religious practices in public schools.[37] Although in the 1980s a more conservative Supreme Court upheld the practice of prayers in state legislatures and the local government practice of constructing Christian nativity scenes on public property as part of an official Christmas celebration, the Court reaffirmed the principle of the separation of church and state in a 1992 decision, *Lee v. Weisman*, by not allowing public prayer at high school graduations.[38]

In a five-to-four decision, the Court ruled in 1986 that the U.S. Air Force could require an Orthodox rabbi employed as a chaplain to remove his small religious cap, the yarmulke, when working indoors. Since childhood, Rabbi S. Simcha Goldman, an Orthodox Jew, had observed the Orthodox tradition of keeping his head covered, a tradition designed to remind individuals of God's omnipresence. The Pentagon decided to spend a large amount of money defending its position of preventing Orthodox Jews from wearing the yarmulke. Several dissenting justices asked why military authorities had the right to limit religious freedom when civil authorities did not. The impact of these recent cases is to give high court sanction to the official government decisions that decide which religious expressions are permissible within the government sphere, and which are not.[39]

Jewish Americans Fight Back

Fear of street crime and anti-Semitism led to the formation of self-protective associations beginning in the late 1960s. In 1968, Rabbi Meir Kahane organized the Jewish Defense League (JDL) in New York City, in part to deal with threats against Jewish American communities. The JDL's goals included the reinvigoration of ethnic pride and also the use of armed citizen patrols to protect communities from street crime. During the 1980s, JDL members protesting the treatment of Jews in the Soviet Union disrupted Soviet diplomatic activities, and some even tried to assassinate high-level diplomats. Strober has argued that the JDL touched a "middle-class nerve" and that for many Jewish Americans the traditional organizations had appeared unwilling to vigorously defend Jewish interests.[40] Although most Jewish Americans have strongly disapproved of the JDL's violent tactics, many supported some of its defensive aims, at least in the beginning. In 1990, Rabbi Kahane was assassinated, but the organization has continued its aggressive efforts to defend Jewish American issues and communities. It has been associated with terrorism in the United States and overseas. The FBI has reported that the JDL and related groups such as Kahane Chai, founded after Kahane's death, were responsible for a dozen terrorist acts across the United States. The Anti-Defamation League issued a report that condemned the "Kahanists' reckless violence against Jews [who do not agree with the group] and non-Jews" and described these extremists as a "cult of violence and racism who speak only for themselves."[41] The overwhelming majority of Jewish Americans do not support such groups.

Jewish-Black Relations

African Americans and Jewish Americans share a long history of mutual support and assistance. For example, three Jewish immigrants participated in John Brown's armed struggle against slavery in the 1850s. In 1917 a Jewish newspaper condemned antiblack violence in the East St. Louis riot. Joel Springarn, a Jew, was chairperson of the NAACP during most of the period between 1914 and 1939. Moreover, at the end of World War II, the 761st Tank Battalion, an all-black unit in the segregated armed forces, led General George Patton's Third Army and was the first unit to liberate the Jews in the Nazi concentration camps at Dachau and Buchenwald. Although they were denied equality at home, these black troops risked their lives for the American cause and helped to free Jewish and other victims of Nazism. Then, during the 1960s civil rights movement, Jewish Americans made up more than half of the white students who went to the South to register black voters and of the white lawyers who defended imprisoned civil rights protesters. Some Jewish Americans were murdered by white southerners for this effort. Jewish Americans also provided substantial financial support for civil rights.[42]

Conflict has also erupted between Jewish Americans and African Americans, especially since the 1960s. In the 1960s riots and rebellions—and again in similar 1980s and 1990s rebellions—black rioters have sometimes attacked local Jewish (and other white and Asian) businesses that they considered to be exploitative in their communities. This and other developments generated a backlash among many Jewish Americans. In some areas, black street criminals have been blamed for destroying the peace of Jewish neighborhoods. Controversies between Jewish and African Americans in certain areas of New York City have gained media attention. In the 1990s, for example, tension escalated between Hasidic Jews and blacks in Brooklyn after crime patrols, which were set up by the Williamsburg area Hasidic community to police the area, harassed and beat some black and Latino residents from nearby areas who ventured into the Hasidic community. In the nearby area of Crown Heights, a Hasidic driver accidentally ran over a black child, setting off anti-Jewish rioting by angry groups of black residents in which a rabbinical student was murdered. The traffic death, rioting, and murder greatly increased tensions between the black and Jewish residents of New York City.[43]

Since the 1960s, black anti-Semitism and criticism of Zionism have alienated a significant number of Jewish Americans from active participation in intergroup coalitions. Anti-black sentiments have also been found among Jewish Americans.[44] Jewish Americans' greater access to economic advancement compared with African Americans is a source of antagonism. In recent decades a few black leaders have aimed anti-Semitic remarks at Jewish merchants and landlords whom they believed were exploiting their poorer brothers and sisters in black communities.[45] Some black leaders have been unwilling to disavow the comments of Louis Farrakhan, a leader of the Nation of Islam, whose anti-Semitic utterances included a reference to Judaism as a "gutter religion."[46] Into the early 2000s the negative statements about Judaism by a few Nation of Islam ministers have continued to create tensions between the Jewish and black communities.

Letty Pogrebin has discussed some reasons for current tensions between these two groups: "The differences between blacks and Jews are rarely more obvious than when each group speaks about its own 'survival,' a word that both use frequently but with quite dissimilar meanings.... Blacks worry about their actual conditions and fear for the present; Jews worry about their history and fear for the future." Some members of each group fear the other group, but for different reasons: Some Jewish Americans fear the greater numbers of urban blacks and a few leaders such as Farrakhan who have made anti-Semitic remarks. Some African Americans, in contrast, fear Jewish Americans primarily because they are part of the dominant white group.[47]

Still, the tensions between Jewish and African Americans that have arisen in some urban communities have not substantially affected Jewish American commitments to civil rights and anti-discrimination legislation. Among the major white groups in the United States, Jewish Americans remain the most liberal on racial issues. National Opinion Research Center polls have found that Jewish American views on racial matters are closer to those of the African American respondents than to those of white Protestants and Catholics.[48] A nationwide survey conducted for the Anti-Defamation League of B'nai B'rith found that Jewish Americans were among the least likely of all white Americans to hold negative views about African Americans. Compared with all white Americans, Jewish Americans were more likely to believe that black Americans do not receive equal treatment in the economic, educational, or judicial arenas. Their beliefs on racial matters were generally much closer to those of black Americans than to those of other whites.[49]

Many Jewish American individuals and organizations continue to support black civil rights causes and black communities. For example, even though some Jewish businesses were burned during the 1992 Los Angeles riot, thirty synagogues and Hillel centers (campus organizations for Jewish students), as well as the anti-hunger organization Mazon, provided large amounts of clothing and food to the black churches that provided relief to families in riot areas.[50]

The pattern of mutual support has also been evident in the national political arena in the 1990s and early 2000s. One study by the American Jewish Congress of the votes of the thirty-nine black and thirty-two Jewish members of the U.S. Congress found that much of the time the two groups voted *alike* on matters of interest to their communities, including issues of separation of church and state and important government social programs.[51]

It is also important to note that there is actually some overlap in the membership of the groups called African American and Jewish American. A few small groups of African Americans adhere to Judaism, and some of these religious adherents have created the Alliance of Black Jews.

In the late 1990s, black and Jewish citizens in numerous dialogue groups have sought ways to ease tensions between these two traditional allies in the civil rights struggle. For example, in January 1997 some seventy black and Jewish teenagers joined in celebrating Martin Luther King, Jr.'s birthday by volunteering in eight local soup kitchens. Operation Understanding, a cooperative group created by an African American member of Congress and a Jewish executive, is sponsored by the Urban League and the American Jewish Committee. Each year the group has brought together groups of Jewish and black students to visit sites of importance to each group, such as Ellis Island, where large numbers of eastern European immigrants entered the United States, or the Mississippi location of the murder of black and Jewish civil rights workers. These groups also work together on projects such as rebuilding recently burned black churches in the South.[52]

POLITICS

From their first arrival in the colonies, Jewish Americans were treated as outsiders to the political system. Members of the first Jewish community in New Amsterdam were specifically barred from holding public office, and, in general, voting and officeholding in the colonies were limited to Christians. Still, Jewish Americans made substantial contributions to the American Revolution, and the new government to which the Revolution gave birth brought important benefits to Jewish citizens by establishing the separation of church and state. The U.S. Constitution's prohibition of religious qualifications for public office and the Bill of Rights' protection of speech and religious choice granted political freedom at the federal level. However, political enfranchisement was slower to come at the state level. By 1790 only five states had removed voting and officeholding restrictions; six others carried Christians-only provisions for political participation as late as 1876. Still, "anti-Semitism never became rooted in the political tradition of American society," as it had in the European political systems.[53]

In the first years of the U.S. republic, anti-Jewish practices by some Federalist party officials, combined with Federalist support for the Alien and Sedition Laws, guaranteed that most Jewish Americans would support the liberal Jeffersonian political party, later to become the Democratic party. Although Jewish Americans supported Democrats for decades, some gravitated to the anti-slavery Republican party in the 1850s.[54]

The voting power of Jewish Americans increased as they became more concentrated in northern cities at the beginning of the twentieth century. While some Socialist party candidates received strong support, many Jewish Americans remained Republicans or supported the Irish-dominated Democratic machines, which provided jobs and shelter to needy immigrants.[55] Eastern European Jews became known for exercising the franchise and for undertaking volunteer political activity. Whereas in the early twentieth century, Irish Americans used ethnic politics to advance their immediate economic and family interests—to create jobs and patronage—Jewish Americans, although concerned with the same bread-and-butter matters, were more political-issue-oriented, particularly in regard to expanding civil rights.[56]

Jewish Americans and Political Parties

By 1910, few Jewish Americans had won electoral office, but few had been appointed to high-level positions. An occasional city-council member, one or two state legislators, a judge—this was the extent of their success. Jewish political representation at the national level was modest as well. The appearance of an internationalist Democratic candidate, Woodrow Wilson, brought a majority of Jewish voters to the Democrats for the first time in decades. Wilson appointed a few Jewish Americans to important positions, including the legal genius Louis Brandeis to the Supreme Court.[57]

Franklin Roosevelt brought Jewish Americans firmly into the Democratic fold in 1932. Roosevelt's anti-Nazi rhetoric and his support of government programs such as social security and of the right to organize unions won many Jewish voters. Until Roosevelt, only a few Jewish Americans had served in the executive or judicial branches of the federal government. Roosevelt brought numerous Jewish Americans into the federal government. Benjamin Cohen, Felix Frankfurter, and Louis Brandeis served as advisers to Roosevelt, and Roosevelt appointed Henry Morgenthau, Jr., secretary of the Treasury.[58]

Nonetheless, Roosevelt's strong regard among Jewish Americans did not lead him to take dynamic action on behalf of refugees from Nazi-dominated Europe. One reason was his fear of the intense anti-Semitism prevailing in the United States during the 1930s and 1940s, especially among white gentile members of Congress. Anti-Jewish discrimination was common in politics, social affairs, education, employment, jury selection in certain states, and real estate decisions.[59]

Since Roosevelt, a substantial proportion of the Jewish American vote has generally gone to Democratic presidential candidates. Thus, in the 2000 Annual Survey of American Jewish Opinion (ASAJO), 59 percent of those Jewish Americans surveyed identified with the Democratic Party and only 9 percent with the Republican Party. In this same survey, 45 percent spoke of themselves as liberal, 36 percent as middle of the road, and only 18 percent as conservative.[60]

Historically, Jewish Americans have been underrepresented among elected and appointed officials. It was not until 1974 that a Jewish American (Abraham Beame) became mayor of New York City. Also in the 1970s, Dianne Feinstein became the first Jewish woman to be elected mayor of a major city, San Francisco.[61] Only somewhat more than one hundred Jewish Americans have held the office of state governor, U.S. senator, or House member. The only American of Jewish ancestry to be considered for president was Barry Goldwater (a convert to the Episcopal religion), who was defeated in his bid for the presidency in 1964. So far, only a half-dozen Jewish Americans have ever served on the U.S. Supreme Court, although perhaps one-fifth of the nation's lawyers in recent decades have been Jewish. In 1993 President Bill Clinton appointed the first Jewish American woman (the second woman ever) to the Supreme Court—Ruth Bader Ginsburg. By the early 2000s there were two Jews on the U.S. Supreme Court. And, as of the late 1990s, eleven others served in the U.S. Senate. Jewish Americans also served the country as secretaries of the treasury and agriculture as well as chair of the Federal Reserve, U.S. trade representative, and budget director under the Democratic president Bill Clinton. In 2000 the Democratic Party, for the first time in major party history, chose a Jewish American, U.S. Senator Joseph Lieberman, for its vice-presidential candidate. (The Democratic candidates for president and vice president in 2000 won the popular vote, but lost that election in the electoral college).[62]

Senator Joseph Lieberman (D-Ct.), here campaigning in 2000 with his wife Haddassah, was the first Jewish American to be nominated for vice-president by a major political party.

Discrimination still plays a role in limiting the number of Jewish Americans who occupy the political front lines. The proportion of Jewish Americans in elected office is low given their high proportion among political activists and contributors. Although there are more Jews than Presbyterians or Episcopalians in the United States, in recent years Jewish Americans have not held nearly as many congressional offices as have the more powerful Protestant groups.[63]

Unions and Community Organizations

Eastern European immigrants actively protested oppressive working conditions in the 1890s, organizing to fight long hours, low pay, and unsafe conditions. New York City data for the 1930s show large numbers of Jewish Americans in food, entertainment, clothing, and jewelry unions. Jewish union leaders often went beyond the problems of wages and working conditions to grapple with broader issues, developing health, pension, and educational programs that would be imitated by all unions. Jewish Americans also played an important role in the growth of the American Socialist party and other subsequent labor–liberal parties.[64]

Jewish Americans have long been well organized. By the 1930s, several important civic and civil rights organizations had been established: the Anti-Defamation League, the American Jewish Congress, the American Jewish Committee, and the United Jewish Appeal. Since 1906 the American Jewish Committee has vigorously fought anti-Semitic prejudice and discrimination. The American Jewish Congress, established early in the 1900s, has also fought for civil rights. The Anti-Defamation League has carried out a vigorous campaign to root out anti-Semitism. The United Jewish Appeal, established in 1939, has been a successful fund-raising organization that has aided a variety of causes, including refugees and the state of Israel.[65] The North American Jewish federation movement, now made up of nearly two hundred social and educational agencies representing and serving Jewish Americans, has been an important agent of "civic Judaism." The federation movement originally emphasized philanthropy and immigrant adjustment but more recently has stressed social activism and political issues.[66]

The founding and survival of Israel have been concerns of major Jewish American organizations in recent decades. During the 1950s, political pressure for U.S. government support for Israel was largely unheeded, but by the 1960s such support had sharply increased. Since the 1960s, Jewish American political pressure has been mobilized for numerous other causes, such as support for Jews in the (former) Soviet Union and opposition to political candidates who support Middle Eastern leaders and groups viewed as hostile to Israel.[67]

In addition to combating anti-Semitism, some organizations have worked to eliminate all racial prejudice and discrimination and to ensure the continued separation of church and state. For example, early in his term as president (2001), George W. Bush proposed what was termed a "faith-based initiative" to involve private religious organizations in providing social services with federal government aid. Apparently, the initial proposal permitted religious content in those social services. At a meeting between a Bush representative and the Jewish Council for Public Affairs, a coalition of 10 national and 113 local Jewish American organizations working on public policy and social service issues, Jewish concerns about the separation of church and state were strongly articulated. Jewish American leaders feared that government support might go to specifically religious activities, which would violate the principle of government neutrality.[68]

In recent years, some Jewish Americans have accused the well-off board members of the American Jewish Committee, the American Jewish Congress, the United Jewish Appeal, and the Anti-Defamation League of being more sympathetic to the needs of employers than to traditional concerns for workers, the poor, and racial discrimination. This criticism may be unfair to some degree, but it does highlight a dilemma faced by Jewish Americans today. As perhaps the most affluent of the white ethnic groups, Jewish Americans might be expected to develop the generally conservative orientation of other high-income white groups.[69] Some have become politically and economically conservative. Yet, given their past experiences with discrimination and the periodic recurrence of anti-Semitism, the majority of Jewish Americans still remain more liberal, politically and economically, than non-Jewish whites.

The Economy

Jewish immigrants have contributed to the prosperity of America from their earliest presence in colonial communities. One Jewish immigrant from Poland, Haym Salomon, played a critical role in financing the American Revolution with a loan to the struggling revolutionary government.[70] The opening of commerce in the Americas presented opportunities for some European Jews, especially those who had centuries of experience as a "middleman" trading minority in Europe, where they were excluded from land ownership and skilled-worker guilds. However, their success in commercial pursuits in Europe had made them an accessible scapegoat for the non-Jewish poor, who saw them as exploiters, and for the non-Jewish rich, who viewed them as an economic threat. In North America, as in Europe, the often marginal nature of their businesses, as well as anti-Semitic discrimination, fostered the growth of an ethnic economy in which Jews relied on economic aid from one another in order to maintain their businesses and communities.[71]

Establishing an Economic Niche: A "Middleman Minority"?

The rate of penetration of a new immigrant group into the core economy and society depends on its economic background as well as conditions at the point of destination. Most German and other central European Jews were poor when they came. They arrived when frontier development and industrial growth were exploding, and they found that their experience as merchants was in demand. As street vendors, they roamed city streets and the countryside. Many eventually became prosperous shopkeepers.[72] By the 1890s, a majority of the German and other central European Jews seemed to be moving up the economic ladder.

The next wave of Jewish immigrants, those from eastern Europe, entered the expanding industrial economy at an opportune time. Most were poor and poorly educated, but their experience in coping with oppression in Europe provided them a cultural heritage replete with strategies for finding economic niches in which to survive. Men, women, and children—whole families—engaged in low-wage manufacturing work. The long hours and poor conditions of industrial capitalism's factories, often miserable sweatshops, led to participation in reform and union movements on the part of these immigrants and their children.[73] In the early 1900s, more than one-third of the eastern European immigrants were employed in the garment industry, one-fourth were in building trades, and one-fifth were in retail trade. Members of the second generation were encouraged to seek clerical and sales work. A number went into law, medicine, and dentistry.[74]

Jewish women often contributed significantly to family incomes. A Philadelphia study in this early period found that one in three Jewish American households had a woman working outside the home. Most unmarried women worked outside the home. Because of the low wages of both male and female workers, families needed the wages women earned outside the home or from taking in sewing or laundry in the home. Wives often joined their husbands in the small retail shops that supplied many Jewish neighborhoods. Many women were left to raise their children alone when their husbands died or deserted the family.[75]

From the Depression to 1950

As in the case of Japanese Americans, the solidarity of the Jewish American community and its heavy involvement in small and medium-sized businesses were sources of community survival during the Great Depression. Whenever possible, Jewish American businesses dealt with one another and hired unemployed relatives. Organized crime also provided a way out of poverty for a small proportion in the early decades, but participation in organized crime declined significantly as large numbers of Jewish Americans moved out of the working class and into the middle class, and suburban areas, following World War II.[76]

The ethnic economy provided a fallback position for those who faced anti-Jewish discrimination. One goal of anti-Semitic organizations was to reduce the number of Jewish Americans in private and public employment. Non-Jewish whites in the teaching, banking, medical, legal, and engineering professions sought to prohibit Jewish Americans from employment in their sectors. In many cities Jewish Americans found it difficult to secure skilled blue-collar jobs and clerical jobs. The Great Depression increased this problem. Signs proclaiming "no Jews need apply" were commonplace. Jews faced discrimination in the teaching profession, particularly in smaller cities and at colleges. From 1900 to the 1950s, discrimination was rife in housing, in large cities from Philadelphia to Boston and Chicago, as well as in smaller cities and towns. Even for the significant numbers who managed to move into the suburbs, Protestant-oriented organizations and recreational facilities were often off limits.[77]

One obsession of anti-Semites, to the present day, has been the alleged Jewish dominance of banking. This fear increased in the Great Depression. Yet a 1936 *Fortune* magazine survey found very few Jewish Americans in banking and finance. A later survey found that *only 600* of the 93,000 banking officials were Jewish. Jewish Americans were rare in heavy industries, public utilities, the press, and radio. The only sectors in which Jewish Americans dominated were clothing, textiles, and the movies. Even in law and medicine, Jews held few powerful positions. The author of the 1936 *Fortune* article seemed puzzled by the clusters of Jews found in certain industrial and business areas and explained the situation in the stereotypical terms of Jewish clannishness.[78]

Such clustering patterns were by no means mysterious; they reflected the extent to which Jewish Americans were forced to work outside mainstream industries and businesses because of blatant and well institutionalized anti-Semitic discrimination. They were channeled by this discrimination into higher-risk economic spheres marginal to the mainstream economy.[79]

After World War II, extensive employment discrimination continued to be directed at Jewish Americans. Job advertisements included restrictions, and many employment agencies discriminated. Even so, many Jewish Americans were able to share in postwar prosperity, particularly in new and riskier industries, such as television and plastics. Jewish Americans remained concentrated primarily in trade, clothing, and jewelry manufacturing; commerce; merchandising; certain light industries; mass communications; and certain professions.[80] The 1957 Current Population Survey found that three-fourths of Jewish American men were employed in white-collar jobs, compared with 38 percent of white Protestants.[81] In 1950 no more than 3 percent of corporate executives, presidents, and board chairpersons were Jews. Given the preponderance of Jewish Americans in commercial and business employment, this proportion was much lower than it would have been if there had been no discrimination. Indeed, a large proportion of Jewish executives made it to the top only in Jewish businesses.[82]

Family Success: Income

The 1990 National Jewish Population Survey (NJPS) estimated the 1989 median annual income for all Jewish American households (families and individuals) to be $39,000. In the same year, the median income for all U.S. households was $28,906 and for all white households $30,406.[83] In the 2000 Annual Survey of American Jewish Opinion, involving 1,010 Jewish respondents, some 57 percent reported household incomes above $50,000, and a third reported household incomes above $75,000, figures well above those for all white households.[84]

Occupational Mobility: Achievements and Problems

Continuing occupational mobility has characterized Jewish Americans since the 1960s. In the 1960s occupational data for New York, Providence, Milwaukee, Detroit, and Boston showed that 20 to 32 percent of Jewish American males were in professional positions and another 28 to 54 percent were in managerial positions. More than half of all Jewish American workers in each city were in these two categories, while most of the rest held either clerical or sales positions. In comparison, the majority of the total employed population in each of those cities held blue-collar positions. More recent research has confirmed this trend toward white-collar employment. One 1990 survey revealed that most Jewish American workers held salaried white-collar positions or were self-employed.[85]

Contrary to the old stereotype, in recent decades Jewish American executives have not controlled banking. Excluding one New York bank (31 percent of whose top managers were Jewish), in 1976 only 2.5 percent of the executives in commercial banks nationwide were Jewish. A decade later, another analysis found that only 3.4 percent of the executives in ten of the nation's largest corporate banks were Jewish.[86] A 1980s study of Jewish Americans in the corporate elite found that most were in Jewish-founded corporations or occupied lower managerial positions in other corporations. Those who have cracked the top of the corporate establishment, such as Irving Shapiro, formerly chief executive officer of DuPont, have usually been brought in from the outside (Shapiro was formerly in government). They have rarely been given the chance to start at the bottom of the corporate hierarchy and work their way to the top.[87]

In the mid-1980s, an estimated 6 to 8 percent of senior executives in U.S. corporations were Jewish Americans. However, Abraham Korman's 1988 study of the distribution of Jewish American executives in corporate America found that they constituted less than 5 percent of senior executives (below the overall corporate percentage of Jewish executives) in many of the largest and most powerful corporations in terms of annual sales and number of employees.[88]

Korman's interviews with management consultants and corporate managers documented that the "outsider" status of Jewish managers was taken for granted. These interviewees agreed that to succeed in the corporate hierarchy, Jewish Americans must divest themselves of *all visible Jewish identity*. This suggests the oppressiveness of one-way assimilation pressures in this society. Some Jewish respondents cited specific anti-Jewish actions that had blocked their career advancement; some were even denied job titles appropriate to their actual duties. Like Asian Americans (see Chapters 10 and 11), many found they could hold professional or staff positions but would never be seriously considered for the higher executive positions.[89]

Until the past two decades, higher-level government positions have rarely been open to Jewish Americans. One Jewish American noted that when he began his career in the early 1960s, "the State Department (and the CIA and FBI) was virtually closed to Jews."[90] Interestingly, in the late 1990s the mass media made much of the fact that a dozen or so top people in the U.S. State Department were of Jewish background, including then Secretary of State Madeleine Albright. This did mark a change in Jewish representation. However, some Jewish Americans found such media attention offensive, since similar attention was not given to the prevalence of Presbyterian or Catholic government officials.

Perhaps because the academic sphere offers greater freedom to excel than other employment spheres, many of the nation's writers, scholars, and professors have been Jewish. Jewish Americans are well represented among distinguished scholars at major universities and among top literary figures. They include Nobel laureate Saul Bellow and prominent intellectuals such as Noam Chomsky, Stephen Jay Gould, Irving Howe, and Seymour Martin Lipset.

The effects of anti-Semitism keep many Jewish Americans from the full social recognition and political power that economic success brings to others. In 1983, for example, New York City finally introduced a law banning discrimination, including anti-Jewish discrimination, in private clubs; the law did not pass until 1985, and then only after the minimum club membership covered was increased from one hundred to four hundred. In May 1992, a bill banning racial and gender discrimination in large private country clubs made its way to the floor of the New York State senate after being blocked for ten years by its white Protestant opponents. In March of the same year, a similar bill banning discrimination in private clubs finally passed the Florida legislature. The American Jewish Congress headed a coalition of civil rights groups that worked together to get the bill passed. Still, by the late 1990s, Florida was one of the few states with strong laws prohibiting discrimination in private clubs. In the 1990s some experts estimated that three-fourths of the nation's private golf and country clubs had no black members, and many had either no female or Jewish members or only token numbers. Much discrimination has been hidden by secrecy at the higher socioeconomic levels of this society.[91]

In the 2000 ASAJO, 95 percent of the respondents thought anti-Semitism was still a problem in the United States; only 13 percent believed it would decrease in the future. In addition, 47 percent of those interviewed disagreed with the following statement: "Virtually all positions of influence in the United States are open to Jews."[92] Reports of discrimination still appear periodically in the mass media. In the late 1990s, an employee at a major rental car company reported that he was told by supervisors that Hasidic Jews were "the worst people to rent to." Two employees reported that supervisors rejected business accounts from Jewish applicants. While the company denied the allegations, the complaints raised the question of whether this overt type of economic discrimination against Jewish Americans has yet disappeared.[93]

EDUCATION

Education, secular or religious, was not as high a priority for the earliest groups of Jewish immigrants as it was for later groups; the earlier arrivals focused on success in business rather than on entering a profession or preserving the European tradition of religious scholarship. Significant participation in public schools came in the nineteenth century with the surge of eastern European immigrants, for whom secular education was a means of becoming "American." Parents often pushed their children to succeed in school so that they could prosper economically and socially. College was especially valued as a door to a career for the young. Eastern European immigrants established numerous schools that taught

Hebrew and Jewish religious practices to ensure that their U.S.-born children would retain their ethnic and religious identity.[94]

Educational mobility for the second- and third-generation Jewish Americans came swiftly. Large numbers graduated from high school, and a significant number pursued college educations. By 1920 the proportion of Jewish students in New York City colleges and universities was estimated to be greater than the Jewish proportion of the population. By the late 1930s, about 9 percent of the nation's 1.1 million college students were Jewish Americans.[95]

Discriminatory Quotas for Jewish Students

Jewish progress in higher education was countered in part by discrimination on the part of Anglo-Protestant whites. Restrictive quotas for Jewish American students were imposed at numerous colleges and universities from the 1920s to the 1950s. In 1918, Dean Frederick Jones of Yale University called for a ban on Jewish students because they were winning most of Yale's scholarships; in 1922, Harvard University president A. L. Lowell called for discriminatory quotas. Covert methods to limit Jewish admissions, such as "character" tests and requirements for "geographic balance" in an entering class, were employed by many schools. Various states restricted Jewish admissions to law schools and to the bar.[96]

Jewish Americans were also excluded from teaching positions in higher education. Between the 1920s and the 1940s, Jewish Ph.D.s, even the most distinguished, found it difficult to secure appointments at Anglo-Protestant-dominated universities. However, the sudden increase in college enrollments following World War II created a demand for college teachers; by the end of the 1960s the proportion of Jewish faculty members in U.S. institutions of higher education had risen to 9 percent.[97]

Affirmative Action Programs

Affirmative action programs, which seek to improve educational opportunities and job chances for black and other non-European groups, have become a political issue for some Jewish Americans. Jewish Americans have long been among the most vigorous supporters of the principle of merit because of the quota restrictions that denied them access to higher education and jobs from the 1920s to the 1950s. Some have opposed contemporary affirmative action programs, such as those in college admissions, because of Jewish Americans' heavy commitment to higher education, a commitment that reflects the past exclusion of Jewish Americans from many sectors of the academic world. College admissions preferences for non-Jewish groups can disproportionately affect Jewish Americans' access to college degrees and perpetuate the effects of anti-Jewish discrimination in the past.[98]

However, voicing support for affirmative action, Harvard law professor Alan Dershowitz, a Jewish American professor and scholar, notes the "real difference between the institutional impact and intensity of the hurt suffered as part of an invidious pattern of racial *subordination* and as part of a benevolent pattern of racial *equalization*." He points out the bias of admission programs, such as those in Ivy League colleges, that hold fairly constant the number of students admitted from certain white Anglo-Protestant pools (descendants and relatives of alumni and those admitted to achieve "geographic balance"), yet at the same time make room for certain affirmative action applicants (Latinos and blacks) by reducing the number of other groups (Jewish and Asian Americans) who are admitted. He argues that it would be much more equitable for those white Anglo-Protestant groups that have long benefited from the exclusion of all subordinate racial and ethnic groups to bear a *heavier share* of the costs of equalization through affirmative action.[99]

Continuing Achievements in Education

Severe discrimination declined after World War II, and since that time the educational attainment of Jewish Americans has reached ever higher levels. The aforementioned 1990 NJPS estimated that only about 6 percent of Jewish adults twenty-five and older had less than a high-school education, compared with almost one-fourth of all white adults.[100] In the 2000 ASAJO, which involved 1,010 Jewish respondents, 86 percent reported some college education, 60 percent reported at least a college degree, and 37 percent reported some graduate work. These figures are much higher than the U.S. white population taken as a whole. It is estimated that 5 percent of all college students now are Jewish.[101]

Schooling in Jewish religion and culture also persists. Surveys of Jewish Americans in recent decades have found strong support among parents for some Jewish education for children, and large percentages of adults and children have reported receiving such education. In 2000 there were about 212,000 pupils in Jewish day schools. The 1990 NJPS estimated that approximately half of all Jewish adults nationwide had received some Jewish education. The emphasis on formal learning of one's heritage and religion in the lower grades has carried over to colleges and universities. By the 1990s, there were more than three hundred faculty positions in Jewish studies.[102]

RELIGION AND ZIONISM

Religious freedom was variable in the British colonies, but most restricted Jewish American participation in colonial life. Anti-Jewish bias sustained a vigorous oppositional culture that formed the base for Jewish protest against religious and political oppression from colonial days to the present. While the new nation remained fundamentally Christian after 1790, religious freedom gradually became law in each of the new states.

As the numbers of German and other central European Jews increased, some broke away from Sephardic congregations and founded their own synagogues. Communities often had multiple synagogues representing different traditions. During the 1850s and 1860s, most Jewish congregations Americanized their religious practices, in part to achieve greater respectability in the eyes of non-Jews. The Reform movement became organized in the Union of American Hebrew Congregations in the 1870s. The Reform temples had shorter services, organ music, and English prayers.[103]

The role of *Judaism* (the Jewish religion) in Jewish identity was a point of conflict between the established German Jews and the later eastern European immigrants. German Jews saw themselves as Americans whose religion happened to be Judaism. They generally endeavored to be inconspicuous. In contrast, the new immigrants from eastern Europe had a strong desire to maintain their old ethnic identity. Most were Orthodox, observing the Sabbath and kosher dietary laws insofar as immigrant life would permit. Theirs was a grass-roots adaptation of Orthodoxy that focused on family and group feeling and stressed charitable acts and the observance of rituals.[104]

A Jewish elder shows youngsters how to blow a shofar, the ram's horn used in religious observances.

Conservative Judaism, which began in the 1880s as a modified traditionalism in reaction to Reform groups, appealed to the second generation of eastern European Jews. The Conservative synagogues observed many Orthodox rituals and traditions, although they discontinued strict dress codes and the separation of men and women at worship services.[105] By 1935, Orthodox synagogues had about 1 million members, Conservative synagogues about 300,000, and Reform temples about 200,000. The authority of the rabbi, as well as the traditional ritual and theology, became less important as one moved from Orthodox to Conservative to Reform congregations. Many synagogues built in the new middle-class neighborhoods after the 1920s were designed as community centers as well as religious centers. The Jewish atmosphere in concentrated neighborhoods provided a strong sense of group solidarity. During this period some second-generation eastern European Jews turned away from all branches of Judaism. Secularism, socialism, labor radicalism, and Zionism became the new "religions" of many younger Jewish Americans during the Great Depression and World War II.[106]

Trends in Religious Practice and Identity

Expanding suburbanization for Jewish families after World War II brought an increase in the number of congregations in suburbia. As a small minority in the new suburbs, Jewish families sought a way to ensure the Jewishness of their children. Synagogue membership and ritual observances saw marked increases.[107]

Jewish American religion currently reflects a substantial interest in the traditional Jewish heritage, maintenance of the synagogue as a community center, and home religious practices. Rituals remain important for many. In the 2000 ASAJO, some 59 percent of the Jewish respondents reported belonging to a synagogue or temple. Moreover, 10 percent identified as Orthodox, 31 percent as Conservative, 31 percent as Reform, and 25 percent stated that they were "just Jewish" or listed other commitments. Three-fourths reported that they always lighted candles for Hanukkah. Seventy-one percent said they always attended a Passover Seder, and 45 percent celebrated Purim usually or always.[108]

Judaism has become one of the major U.S. religious traditions. Modern Judaism is a voluntary faith: Jewish Americans can reject it or accept it to varying degrees. Some call much Judaism a "cardiac" religion, emphasizing the heart or ethics rather than traditional ritual and doctrine. The tolerance that has developed for different denominations within Judaism is similar to that of Protestantism.[109] Orthodox Judaism, which bases Jewish identity on descent from a Jewish mother, still involves ritual observance with fewer adaptations to the secular world. In contrast, Reform Judaism accepts Jewish heredity through either a Jewish father or mother and emphasizes humanitarian Jewish principles rather than traditional ritual. Conservative Judaism represents a middle path between Orthodoxy's traditionalism and Reform's strong humanitarianism.[110]

Israel and Zionism

Concern for the survival and prosperity of the Middle-Eastern nation of Israel occupies a place near the center of modern Jewish consciousness. For many Jewish Americans, "Israel represents Jewry's positive response to centuries of anti-Semitism in general and to Hitler's attempted genocide in particular."[111] Whether active in religious Judaism or not, many Jewish Americans share the commitment to *Zionism*—the right of Jews everywhere to have a secure national homeland free of anti-Jewish discrimination. This commitment to Israel has affected not only Jewish voting patterns and Jewish–black relations (because of pro-Arab sentiments among some black leaders) but also Jewish American philanthropy. Jewish American financial support has been critical to Israel's survival in the face of opposition from nearby Middle Eastern governments.

In the 2000 ASAJO, three-fourths of the Jewish respondents said they felt fairly or very close to Israel, and 42 percent reported having gone to Israel at least once.[112] Yet, many Jewish Americans have periodically raised questions about the direction of Israel's development. One-fourth of the respondents and numerous leaders in an American Jewish Committee survey agreed that Israel's continued occupation of territories it has captured by force would "erode Israel's democratic and humanitarian character." Most favored "territorial compromise for credible guarantees of peace" and peace negotiations between Israel and the Palestine Liberation Organization (PLO) if the latter organization recognized the state of Israel and renounced terrorism.[113]

Since 1990 there have been ongoing negotiations between the Israeli government and the PLO over the future of the Palestinian population. An agreement was reached giving the PLO some political authority over the Palestinian population in certain of the occupied areas, and Israeli troops were withdrawn. A new U.S. organization, Builders for Peace, was created jointly by some Jewish and Arab Americans to funnel new investment capital into the Palestinian areas.[114]

A majority of Jewish Americans have backed peace negotiations between the PLO and the Israeli government, although many remain skeptical or cautious in their assessments of the possibility of a lasting peace. A late 1990s survey of American Jews found that 82 percent supported the creation of a Palestinian state if Israel's security and control over east Jerusalem could be guaranteed.[115] However, in the 2000 ASAJO, more than half (57 percent) were opposed to Israel compromising on the status of Jerusalem as a united city under Israeli jurisdiction in order to secure peace. And in that recent survey 69 percent of the respondents agreed with the pessimistic view that the "goal of the Arabs is not the return of occupied territories but rather the destruction of Israel."[116]

ASSIMILATION OR PLURALISM?

Two different theoretical perspectives have been used to explain the experiences of Jewish Americans—Anglo-conformity perspectives or cultural pluralism approaches. Most scholarly analyses of Jewish Americans have reflected some type of assimilation viewpoint. The dominant perspective among Jewish Americans themselves has been at least partially assimilationist: the view that substantial adaptation to the surrounding culture is critical to achieving economic success and avoiding anti-Semitic prejudice and discrimination.[117]

Since the early 1800s, certain Jewish leaders have favored cultural pluralism as an alternative to Anglo-conformity assimilation. It was Horace Kallen, a Jewish American, who best formulated this perspective (see Chapter 2). Kallen argued that for most people, ethnic-cultural group membership was not easily abandoned and that ethnic groups had a right to exist on their own terms; that is, democracy should be fully applied to ethnic groups. He argued against the ruthless Americanization long advocated for European immigrants by many white Anglo-Protestant Americans. By the 1920s, Kallen had given the name *cultural pluralism* to this view. However, some scholars have argued that Kallen's cultural pluralism is not a useful perspective for understanding the adaptive history of Jewish Americans, since massive acculturation and substantial assimilation in other areas have been facts of life for most.[118]

Patterns of Assimilation

Partial cultural assimilation came relatively quickly for each of the three major streams of Jewish immigrants and their children. Most Sephardic and German Jews rapidly adapted to their environment, picking up English and certain North American folkways, but they maintained a strong commitment to Judaism. Then came large numbers of eastern Europeans. German Jews pressed these new immigrants to Americanize rapidly. For the most part the two groups remained separate. Most new arrivals were committed to retaining their distinctiveness and their sense of Jewish peoplehood. Their eastern European Yiddish culture, which in the United States became in part an oppositional culture, played a crucial role in perpetuating the Jewish heritage. These immigrants had no illusions that they would cease to be outsiders in a predominantly non-Jewish society, yet they embraced the opportunities for jobs, citizenship, and education.[119]

Second-generation (and later) eastern European Jews were more affected by assimilation pressures and rapidly picked up the language and values pressed on them in the media and the public school system. Like the young Italian Americans discussed in Chapter 4, they were caught between the culture of their parents and the dominant Anglo-Protestant culture, a situation almost guaranteed to create family tensions. Their Judaism, particularly the Reform and Conservative variants, was substantially Americanized. Many members of the third eastern European generation moved out of predominantly Jewish neighborhoods. Still, they too were usually eager to accent their Jewishness in a combination of religious and secular practices.[120]

Israeli Prime Minister Ehud Barak addresses the Conference of Presidents of Major American Jewish Organizations in 1999.

Recent research by Riv-Ellen Prell has documented the dilemmas faced by young Jewish women in the second and third generations. Many second-generation women were pressured to reject their mothers' poverty and strong-woman reality and adopt instead the more servile "lady-like" virtues of the Anglo-Protestant core culture, which included devotion solely to home and family. "My mother's task growing up was to become simultaneously an American and a woman, and her mother could be of little help in either pursuit.... Power was the last thing she needed: Propriety and normality were her paths."[121] In their turn, third-generation women often struggled against their mothers for a liberated woman's life less constrained by gender expectations and limitations.

The central and eastern Europeans advanced relatively quickly in the sphere of structural assimilation at the secondary level of the economy and, sometimes, politics. A large portion achieved substantial economic success in the first generation. As a group, the eastern Europeans moved from a blue-collar concentration to a white-collar concentration in three generations. The ethnic niche economy was critical for many. Hard work and mastery of the educational system facilitated upward movement.

We should note, however, that even today Jewish Americans' occupational distribution underscores the point that many of the prosperous among them are not yet fully integrated into the upper reaches of the U.S. economy and society. The underrepresentation or absence of Jewish Americans at the very top in many spheres of the economy and politics is indicative of continuing, if now subtle, discrimination.

Why were Jewish Americans generally able to move up the economic ladder so successfully? Some have explained this in terms of certain values and religious traditions. Nathan Glazer has argued that "Judaism emphasizes the traits that businessmen and intellectuals require, and has done so at least 1,500 years before Calvinism.... The strong emphasis on learning and study can be traced that far back, too. The Jewish habits of foresight, care, moderation probably arose early."[122]

Others have argued that this relative success has had less to do with religious factors than with historical and structural conditions. Although eastern

Europeans were among the poorest, least-educated European Jews, most were not illiterate peasants lacking urban experience. Most who came between 1880 and 1920 were from urban areas of Europe where they had worked in a variety of urban occupations, such as manufacturing, craftwork, and small-scale commerce. Their literacy level was relatively high compared with most other immigrants at this time. European Jews migrated at a time of expanding manufacturing and trade. Their urban backgrounds and skills fit well with the needs of U.S. industry. Stephen Steinberg concludes that, contrary to what Glazer has argued, Jewish immigrants did not need to rely only on their religious values; they came in with "occupational skills that gave them a decisive advantage over other immigrants."[123] The fit between Jewish skills and economic circumstances at this critical time in U.S. history was better than it would be for later migrants (such as African Americans and Puerto Ricans) to the big cities.

Arthur Hertzberg attributes these immigrants' success largely to their "'Jewish head' ... the heritage of siege mentality, of centuries of being an embattled bastion in a hostile 'exile,' and of having only one tool for survival, the use of one's wits." This interpretation suggests a type of oppositional culture that facilitates survival under anti-Semitic oppression.[124]

Moreover, in recent decades the decreasing residential concentration of Jewish Americans has not eliminated their informal social cohesion and strong voluntary organizations. Their geographic mobility is based on the same factors as that of other Americans: housing markets, family life cycle, and economic constraints. "It is no longer the case," Calvin Goldscheider suggests, "that the greater the residential dispersal and integration, the weaker the informal ties to the Jewish community.... The evidence from Jewish communities ... shows that there are few long-term effects of migration on ethnic cohesion."[125] Informal social ties remain relatively strong among Jewish Americans in many U.S. towns and cities. For example, the large Jewish community in Los Angeles is substantially interconnected in terms of Jewish organizations and family ties despite a dispersed housing pattern.[126] Still, the pattern of having Jewish friends and related community connections seems to be strongest for those who are most religious. In the NJPS, 45 percent of religious Jews, but only 12 percent of secular Jews, reported that most or all of their friends were Jewish.[127]

Despite the affluence of current generations, some economic and social discrimination against Jewish Americans persists. Some time ago, the leading assimilation theorist, Milton Gordon, argued that while Jewish Americans have experienced partial assimilation at the behavior-receptional level (that is, discrimination has declined), less assimilation has occurred at the attitude-receptional level because of the persistence of anti-Semitic ideas and views.[128] This is still the case, for anti-Semitic prejudice and white supremacist propaganda can still be found in communities across the United States. Indeed, the development of white nationalist Web sites on the Internet in recent years has kept many anti-Jewish images—and thus, organizations—very much alive.

Intermarriage

Opposed by some on the grounds that it threatens the solidarity and survival of the Jewish American community, intermarriage has generally increased with each successive generation, reflecting the decline of negative images, desires to assimilate, and greater acceptance of ethnic diversity in the United States. Out-marriage has been more common for those Jews who are geographically separated from large Jewish communities. Since the 1960s, the proportion of interfaith marriages has risen steadily—from 11 percent for those who married prior to 1965 to 31 percent during the period between 1965 and 1974 to 57 percent for those who married in the late 1980s. In the 2000 ASAJO, 85 percent of those Jewish respondents who were married had a Jewish spouse. However, 64 percent reported that one or more of their children had a non-Jewish spouse.[129]

The younger generations' apparent trend to intermarriage has led some observers to predict that the American Jewish community will disappear within a few decades. However, as a result of Judaism's increasing acceptance of mixed marriages, some intermarried couples, along with their children, have embraced Judaism and identify themselves as Jewish. One late 1990s' analysis estimated that one-fourth of all intermarried couples had taken this step.[130]

Reviewing the 2000 ASAJO, the American Jewish Committee concluded that among Jewish Americans the traditional "taboo on mixed marriage has clearly collapsed." According to that national survey more than half (56 percent) of the respondents disagreed with the assertion that "It would pain me if my child married a gentile." In addition, some 40 percent said they were "neutral" regarding marriages between Jews and gentiles, and 16 percent viewed such marriages as a "positive good." In addition, 78 percent said that they would support a rabbi officiating at such marriage ceremonies under some circumstances. And, contrary to the views of some religious leaders, more than two-thirds of these respondents did *not* agree with a statement that "the best response to intermarriage is to encourage the gentile to convert to Judaism." Only one-fourth favored an attempt to convert the gentile partner to Judaism.[131]

Goldscheider argues against the view that intermarriage can be regarded as an unambiguous measure of assimilation because "strong communal bonds and networks link the intermarried to the community.... There is evidence as well that an increasing proportion of American Jews are accepting the intermarried within the community."[132] However, in *The Vanishing American Jew* (1997) Alan Dershowitz has argued that the Jewish American group will disappear if the intermarriage rate remains high and the birth rate low. Indeed, he has called for a renewal of Judaism and a reinvigorated system of Jewish education.[133]

Does the Jewish American community generally share this concern that intermarriage is now destroying Jewish identity and solidarity? The 2000 ASAJO project suggests that a bare majority may not. Asked whether anti-Semitism or intermarriage was the greater threat to the continuing Jewish presence in the United States, 50 percent of those respondents picked anti-Semitism; 41 percent cited intermarriage; and 7 percent cited both equally. This survey found a bit more concern over external threats than over internal threats of intermarriage, although concern over the latter seems to be growing.

Recent Immigrants: Strong Jewish Identity

The social and economic adjustment of recent Jewish immigrants raises some interesting issues concerning assimilation and U.S. culture. The close ties between Israel and the United States make this trek westward easy for Israeli immigrants, who generally are more economically successful than most other immigrants. Many come with professional or managerial experience. Still, Israeli immigrants often maintain some distance from native-born American Jews in their language and values.[134]

Many Jewish immigrants from the former Soviet Union report difficulty assimilating to U.S. culture. Most left their homeland because of anti-Semitism. While most respondents in one survey of émigrés rated their lives as Jews, as well as their housing, income, and overall standard of living, better in the United States than in the former Soviet Union, most also reported having trouble with English and with finding a job. This was true even though a large percentage (like those in other post-1965 immigrant groups) had been well-educated urban professionals. Most considered their cultural environment worse in the United States, and large percentages felt their friendships, social status, and workplace atmospheres were worse here. They liked the freedom, but disliked the vulgarity and "low" cultural tastes here. This mostly well-educated group of immigrants appears to be assimilating satisfactorily to the U.S. economy and to material conditions but is having trouble with certain social and cultural adjustments.[135] One 1999 study notes that "depression, anxiety, high blood pressure, and psychosomatic illnesses are common among this and other recent immigrant groups."[136]

Steven Gold has examined adaptation among a diverse group of refugees from the former Soviet Union in two immigrant communities in Los Angeles and San Francisco. In both cities the Jewish population was geographically concentrated; residents of the full-faceted Los Angeles community could lead an active life without any knowledge of English. Some, particularly younger, well-educated émigrés, found desirable jobs and moved into the middle class. Many middle-aged émigrés who had no transferable job skills or who were unwilling to take a lower-prestige job than they had held in their native country had more difficulty adapting and often remained isolated from fellow émigrés. Few voluntary support organizations had been formed in either California city. Most support came from their extended families. The strong sense of Jewish identity of these relatively recent immigrants is yet another factor reinforcing Jewish ethnicity in the United States.[137]

Although many of these Jewish immigrants aligned themselves with the Republican party in the 1980s, by the 1990s most were concerned over Republican attempts to limit immigration and social service programs. In the past decade many of these new immigrants from the former Soviet Union have allied themselves with Latino, Asian, and Caribbean American groups to fight attempts to restrict legal immigration and support programs for immigrants in the United States.[138] Interestingly, in a 2000 survey of all Jewish American groups, one-fifth of the respondents supported increased immigration to the United States from countries overseas, and 46 percent were satisfied with the current (substantial) level of immigration. Only a minority (27 percent) favored a decrease in immigrants.[139]

Contemporary Jewish Identity and the Future of the Jewish American Community

What does it mean to be Jewish American today? Many scholars now stress that in U.S. society all Jews are "Jews by choice."[140] While this may exaggerate the current reality, it does indicate the degree of change that has occurred since the intense, highly racialized anti-Semitism of the first five decades of the 20th century. In that era, many white gentiles insisted on targeting and singling out Jews for discrimination and persecution. Today, most people of Jewish ancestry can make their identity choices in an atmosphere of less discrimination and greater acceptance and freedom.

For many religion alone seems to be less important as a basis for identity than a composite of factors. Asked to specify the basis of Jewish identity, 90 percent of the respondents to the NJPS cited cultural or ethnic group membership; this was true for both religious and secular Jews. Fewer than 5 percent of all respondents defined Jewishness only as religious group membership.[141] Significantly, Israel has been a major focus of this Jewish American identity and consciousness. This focus has helped to reduce the possibility of identificational assimilation. The Jewish American population in 1970 was estimated to be about 5.4 million; by 2001 it had risen to approximately 6 million. On the average, Jewish American families have fewer children than the population as a whole, and the core population has almost one-third more elderly persons than the total U.S. population. The 1990 NJPS found that virtually all children of Jewish parents were being raised Jewish. Even though only a modest percentage of non-Jewish-born spouses in mixed marriages have converted to Judaism, an estimated 28 percent of their children were being raised Jewish.[142]

The *ethnogenesis* perspective (Chapter 2) recognizes the reality of cultural differences among contemporary ethnic groups and seems to fit the Jewish experience. Jewish Americans are a composite group mostly of Sephardic, central European, and eastern European origin. In the United States, the Jewish immigrants and their descendants have forged a distinctive ethnic group, shaped partially by their Jewish and European cultural heritage and partially by the long history of adaptation to the Anglo-Protestant core culture. Despite substantial adaptation, ethnic distinctiveness remains. Persisting anti-Semitism, respect for an ancient heritage, a commitment to the state of Israel, and parents' desire to socialize their children in the Jewish heritage continue to shape the behavior and beliefs of many Americans of Jewish ancestry.

Sociologist Sylvia Barack Fishman has recently described Jewish Americans' pattern of adaptation to the core culture as "coalescence." The liberal social and political values held by most American Jews have come to be seen as "Jewish" values. Through the critical adaptive process of coalescence, Jewish Americans have merged their ideas with American ideas, incorporating "American liberal values such as free choice, universalism, individualism, and pluralism into their understanding of Jewish identity."[143]

How strong is Jewish identity today? Is it, as Herbert Gans argues, only a "symbolic ethnicity" without lasting significance? In this view ethnicity for many white ethnic Americans is today little more than a desire to maintain some feeling for ethnic background without strong commitments to ethnic behavior or strong social ties.[144] We have previously noted concern for a vanishing Jewish identity. Some scholars have argued that the weakening of religious ties among Jewish Americans indicates that Jewish ethnicity is "well on its way to becoming memory."[145] Some Jewish American leaders have expressed concern over changes at the organization level. For example, the 189 agencies that make up the Jewish Federation movement have recently faced a decline in private and governmental support. Jewish organization leaders are worried that assimilated Jewish Americans with a weak sense of identity may not support such organizations to the extent that their parents and grandparents did.[146]

One recent study of Jewish American youth suggests that parents today face enormous problems: The "all-pervasive consumer society that surrounds us increasingly affects the environment of American children. The sophisticated marketing of fashion in clothing, toys, foods, films, etc., uses peer pressure to help produce a highly materialistic, present-oriented youth culture which is at odds with Jewish values of spirituality, learning, tzedakah [charity], and self-discipline as exemplified by Sabbath observance."[147] This study concludes with a call for an expanded role for Jewish community organizations in helping families socialize new generations of children in Jewish religion and these traditional values. Recently, the Board of Governors of the American Jewish Committee called on Jewish Americans to give high priority to Jewish education as a way to foster Jewish identity and continuity.[148]

Even scholars such as Hertzberg who advocate a revival of true Judaism among Jewish Americans to ensure the survival of ethnic identity recognize that what he views as declining Jewish ethnicity will probably last at least a few more generations. Richard Alba has pointed out that certain distinguishing features of Jewish culture and history—in particular, their extensive social networks, especially those rooted in religious congregations and schools, and their long tradition of survival as a minority in non-Jewish societies—support the survival of their ethnic identity.[149]

Silberman suggests that the greater acceptance of Jewish Americans in a largely non-Jewish society today, compared with sixty years ago, makes Jewish Americans less likely to abandon their Jewishness, since their identity has ceased to be the focal point of widespread discrimination and instead has become a badge of pride linked to a worldwide Jewish struggle such as that of Israel.[150] From this perspective, a sense of Jewishness is likely to remain strong for the majority of Jewish Americans for the foreseeable future. Indeed, in the 2000 ASAJO, 59 percent of the Jewish respondents ranked "being Jewish" as "very important" in their own life; another 33 percent ranked it as "fairly important." The three factors rated as most important to their Jewish identity were "being part of the Jewish people" (chosen by 45 percent of the respondents), "commitment to social justice" (21 percent), and "religious observance" (16 percent).[151]

Accepting and Challenging White Privilege

Jewish Americans remain significantly differentiated in identity, history, and experience from other white Americans, yet for the most part they are now accepted as "white" Americans. As recently as the World War I period, most of the white Anglo-Protestant majority regarded Jewish Americans as an "inferior race" that was not fully part of the "white race." Then after World War II, in part because of German Nazism and its anti-Semitic Holocaust, the dominant white gentile group granted Jewish Americans, albeit slowly, access to many institutionalized white privileges, especially occupational and residential mobility. The racist construction of Jewish Americans as "not white" has increasingly been limited to extremist groups.

In addition, as Jewish American social scientist Karen Brodkin has shown, many American Jews worked hard to become accepted as "white." Many moved to suburban areas, changed their names, or underwent cosmetic surgery in order to assimilate better to the image of successful Euro-American whiteness. Brodkin describes the way that after World War II many Jewish intellectuals and other prominent Jewish Americans (especially writers and entertainers) successfully embraced white gentile values and institutions and perpetuated images of Jewish Americans as a "model minority." She also documents how many ordinary Jewish Americans came to accept a range of pre-existing Anglo-Protestant values and views as part of becoming white.[152]

Nonetheless, Brodkin notes many American Jews are uncomfortable with this move to embracing or accepting white privilege, given their long history of fighting racial and ethnic oppression. Looking to the future, she suggests that "the challenge for American Jews today is to confront that whiteness as part of developing an American Jewishness that helps build an explicitly multiracial democracy in the United States."[153]

SUMMARY

Jewish Americans, most of whom are descendants of central and eastern Europeans, have become substantially assimilated in the cultural arena. An economically prosperous ethnic group that has made dramatic progress up the socioeconomic mobility ladder, Jewish Americans have constantly struggled against widespread prejudice and discrimination. Theirs is substantially a success story. But they paid a price for their success. Significant anti-Semitism persists today and often limits movement to the very top in the economy and especially in politics. Coupled with substantial vertical progress over the decades has been horizontal mobility in the form of suburbanization.

Central to an adequate understanding of Jewish Americans today is an understanding of their ties to Israel. The creation of Israel and periodic Arab–Israeli conflicts have generated a strong commitment to Israel, philosophically and financially. Jewish Americans continue to see Israel as an essential place of refuge for a people that has survived the Roman persecution, the Spanish Inquisition, Russian pogroms, and the Nazi Holocaust. This commitment has motivated thousands of Jewish Americans to immigrate to the work camps, towns, and cities of Israel. Yet, in recent decades a significant number of Israeli immigrants have come to the United States seeking to escape the threat and reality of war in the Middle East. And many Russian Jews have come seeking better economic and political opportunities. These immigrants provide a contemporary reminder of the sojourner nature of much of the Jewish experience.

In this chapter we have demonstrated how diverse the United States still is—a diversity that fosters vitality and creativity. Jewish American participation in U.S. institutions means that this nation is *not* by definition a Christian country; it is a nation of many religious groups, including Protestants, Catholics, Jews, and Muslims. One contribution of Jewish Americans has been their stand for the Jewish religious and cultural heritage despite nativist discrimination and other opposition—and thereby for the expansion of liberty for all residents of the United States.

Jewish Americans have contributed substantially to the emphasis on education in the United States, to high achievement in the arts and sciences, and to the values of justice, tolerance, and fairness. Jewish Americans have not been passive victims of anti-Semitic prejudice and discrimination; they and their organizations have often occupied the forefront of the fight against the racial-ethnic prejudice and behavioral racism that continue to plague U.S. society.

6 Native Americans

In spring 2001, an Italian American leader in Denver, Colorado, tried to bring back the Columbus Day Parade, which he and others viewed as a celebration of the heritage of Italian Americans. This proposal was opposed by local Native Americans on the grounds that Christopher Columbus was a brutal conqueror who with his men had slaughtered and enslaved indigenous peoples. The U.S. Justice Department worked out a modification whereby the march would be renamed The March for Italian Pride, and it took place under police protection. Still, Native American, African American, and Latino protesters objected to the celebration of Columbus under any name and sat down in the street to block the parade, and 139 people were arrested for protesting. This event is but one in a long series of protests by Native Americans and other racially oppressed Americans against the genocidal conquests of indigenous peoples by European colonizers in the Americas.[1]

In the early 1990s, Native American groups across the nation held protests against the celebration of the 500th anniversary of Columbus's 1492 voyage to the Americas. In Washington, D.C., protesters spray-painted "500 years of genocide" on a statue of

Columbus and read a list of human rights violations while pouring blood onto the statue.[2] Suzane Shown Harjo explained the Native American position regarding the Columbus Quincentenary: "As Native American peoples ... we have no reason to celebrate an invasion that caused the demise of so many of our people and is still causing destruction today. The Europeans stole our land and killed our people."[3]

With this chapter we begin to consider several non-European groups that were racially subordinated in the process of European colonization and expansion. The term *white* as a self-designation for Europeans developed in the context of contact with the darker-skinned peoples of Africa and the Americas, whom Europeans came to call *black* and *red*, respectively.[4] Many of the latter were subordinated economically, politically, and culturally. In this and subsequent chapters, we will see critical differences in the past and present experiences of European and non-European Americans. We will also examine the relevance of assimilation and power-conflict theories for interpreting the past and present of the subordinated racial groups.

The first victims of European colonization of this continent were the Native Americans—the members of the hundreds of indigenous groups present at the time of the European invasion. Called collectively (and erroneously) "Indians" by their conquerors, the indigenous peoples have long suffered at the hands of the white intruders. Reflect for a moment on the notion of Europeans "discovering" America. In fact, the fifteenth-century European explorers were *latecomers*, for the continent they happened upon was already peopled by millions of people. The ancestors of these peoples discovered the continent at least twenty thousand years earlier—when, most scholars believe, they migrated across the land bridge from Asia to Alaska.

CONQUEST BY EUROPEANS AND EUROPEAN AMERICANS

Human migration varies from voluntary movement to forced slave importation. Migration often involves the incorporation of a new immigrant group into the social framework of a dominant racial or ethnic group that is already established within certain geographical boundaries. In the case of Native Americans, however, it is the dominant group itself that migrated; that is, the Europeans moved into the territories of the indigenous groups. This process can be termed *colonization migration*. Unlike other types of migration, colonization migration involves the conquest and domination of a preexisting geographical group by outsiders. Such migration also illustrates *classical colonialism*.

How many Native Americans were there when Europeans came into North America? Early on, some analysts estimated the native population in the year 1500 at about one million people. In recent decades this estimate has been sharply revised upward. A considered estimate by Kirkpatrick Sale puts the number in North America at 15 million at the time of conquest, with tens of millions in Central and South America as well. Thorough assessments by Henry Dobyns and Russell Thornton also support a figure larger than earlier estimates, whose low figures have been used to legitimate the European conquest of an allegedly unoccupied land.[5]

By 1890, the combined effects of European diseases and violence had sharply reduced the number of Native Americans in North America to approximately 250,000 people. This indigenous population remained below 400,000 until the 1950s, when it began to grow. The 1990 census counted more than 1.9 million people as American Indian. In the 2000 census 2,475,956 people identified themselves as American Indians (including Alaskan Natives). Another 1,082,683 people identified themselves as white and Indian, while 182,494 identified themselves as black and Indian. (The 2000 census was the first to allow people to indicate a multiracial identity.) The total of these three groups and other (Indian-other) groups is more than 4.1 million, which marks a substantial increase in the Indian population since 1990.[6]

Today most of the 558 federally recognized Indian tribes have fewer than 10,000 members each; only four have populations of more than 100,000. The two largest groups are the Cherokee and the Navajo. Today most Indians do not live on reservations; only a minority live on more than 300 reservations and trust lands, most of which are in rural areas. About half live west of the Mississippi. The states with the largest Native American populations are California, Oklahoma, and Arizona.[7]

In the past few decades, the number of Americans claiming Indian ancestry has increased dramatically.

For example, the tribal enrollment officer of the Cherokee Nation receives one thousand applications a month from people who wish to enroll on the basis of claimed Cherokee ancestry.[8] Drawing on archival and interview data, sociologist Joane Nagel has suggested that one major reason for the large increase reported in recent censuses is the result of identity switching—the change in self-identification from non-Indian to Indian in response to Native American activism promoting pride in being Native American.[9] The tendency for white and other Americans with Indian ancestry to more openly assert this ancestry also appears to be increasing, however modest their ancestral claim may be. One reason is that in many areas of the country the stigma of being part-Indian has declined significantly. Some analysts have also suggested that economic and government benefits available to some tribal members may have accelerated the willingness to claim Indian ancestry.[10]

The term *Indian* and most names of major Native American groups are terms of convenience applied by white Americans. In most history books, not one of the major Native American groups is recorded under its own name. For example, the "Navaho" call themselves *Dine*, meaning "The People."[11] The renaming of Native American nations by outsiders is a result of their subordination and suggests one major difference between colonized groups and European immigrants: Colonized peoples have had little control over the naming process.

Although many non-Indians today think of Indians as a single category, the latter have for centuries been a diverse and complex array of nations and societies, with major differences in population, economies, polities, language, and other customs. Native American groups have ranged from small nomadic bands to complex, hierarchically organized nations with large territories. The diversity is important to keep in mind, as the image of the typical Indian in the non-Indian mind is of a plains Indian living in a tipi, hunting bison, and dressed with a feathered headdress.

Most have never fit this image. As one researcher has noted, "Lumping Indians together into one group presumed to have the same cultural and physiological characteristics is the same as assuming that all Europeans are alike, that they speak the same language, have the same heritage, and share the same values. Historic tribes differed substantially in regard to religious beliefs and practices, language, dress, hairstyles, physiology, political organization, social structures, gender roles, world view and living conditions in response to the environment, which varied from forests, deserts, mountains, plains and coasts to subarctic and arctic areas."[12]

Early Cultural Borrowing

The cultures of the Native American societies encountered by European colonizers in the Western Hemisphere were often more highly developed than those of European societies. Some nations built great cities and roads, developed advanced agricultural systems, and created calendars and numerical systems superior to those of Europeans. In what came to be called the "Americas," most Native American societies had complex and "sophisticated systems of government, community organizations, economy, means of communication, gender roles, arts, and elaborate clothing and hairstyles. Indians were and are extremely religious."[13] The European invaders borrowed heavily from Native American agriculture and pharmacology. An estimated *60 percent* of the foods (for example, potatoes, corn, peanuts, and many grains) eaten by people around the globe today were first developed by Native Americans in the Western Hemisphere. Many medicinal plants and their derivatives (for example, quinine) were taken from Native Americans.[14]

In the first decade of English settlement, a significant number of English colonists deserted to Indian communities, often in search of food or better living and working conditions. In the winter of 1609–1610, one in seven of the Jamestown colonists deserted to Algonquian communities, a loose alliance of about 14,000 people in thirty communities led by a paramount chief named Wahunsonacock. Generally better nourished than the whites, the Algonquians hunted, fished, gathered food, and cultivated beans, squash, and maize. Their matrilineal society had no social classes, no bureaucracy or state, and little economic specialization. The chiefs, who were not called by their titles, worked alongside other members of the groups. So many English workers were leaving the colony that English authorities established severe punishments to prevent desertion to Native American settlements. Not surprisingly, the reality of societies without property holding, kings, classes, and states provoked much worry and discussion among European elites.[15]

Geographical Location and Relocation

There were several hundred Native American groups in North America at the time of the European invasions. In this chapter, we will sometimes be speaking of these many groups as though they were one Native American group; at other times we will be speaking of one specific group within this larger category. Initially, many moved westward as whites advanced. Most Native American groups have faced substantial pressure to migrate. *Forced migration* at gunpoint was the lot of some native groups after their defeat by whites. Groups in the West, such as the Navaho, were rounded up after military engagements and forced to migrate to barren reservations. Perhaps the most famous forced march was the "Trail of Tears," in which thousands of Cherokees, Creeks, Chickasaws, Choctaws, and Seminoles were relocated from their eastern lands to "Indian Territory" in present-day Oklahoma.

Internal migration over the past century has involved relocation from reservations and other rural areas to the cities. During the 1950s and 1960s, an urban relocation program was expanded by the federal government to cover many Native American groups and numerous cities; a Bureau of Indian Affairs (BIA) branch was set up to oversee relocation services.[16] The scale of internal migration can be seen in the more than 200,000 Native Americans who moved to the cities between the 1950s and 1980s. By 2000 more than half resided in cities.[17]

The Colonial Period

Many white historians have asserted that white "settlers" encountered roving bands of Indians with whom they often came into conflict. Yet in reality it was the *Native Americans who were the settlers*, those who had long settled the land, used it, and developed it. European colonists developed various strategies for dealing with those whose land they coveted. These ranged from honest treaty making with equals, to deceptive treaty making, to attempts at extermination, to enslavement like that of Africans, to confinement in the often barren, prison-like areas called reservations.[18]

European colonists slowly gained dominance over Indian groups, usually forcing them into frontier areas or killing them.[19] Few whites seemed concerned about the genocidal consequences of this expansion. Some English colonists relied on friendly Native Americans to survive the first devastating years, yet the colonists soon turned on their neighbors. In New England, for example, a war with the Pequots in 1637 ended when whites massacred several hundred inhabitants of a Pequot village and sent the survivors into slavery.[20] The English defeat of the French after a ten-year war resulted in the French withdrawal from the continent in the mid-1700s. This move brought more Native American societies into contact with the often less sophisticated and generally more brutal policy of the English.[21]

Treaties, Reservations, and Genocide

With the founding of the new United States, the indigenous peoples found themselves in a strange position. They were viciously stereotyped and attacked in the Declaration of Independence, where Jefferson accused the British king of working "to bring on the [white] inhabitants of our frontiers, the merciless Indian Savages, whose known rule of warfare is an undistinguished destruction of all ages, sexes and conditions." Later, the U.S. Constitution only briefly mentioned Indians in giving Congress the power to regulate commerce with them.

By action or inaction, federal officials supported the recurring theft of Indian lands. A French observer of the 1830s noted the hypocrisy of high-sounding treaties: "This virtuous and high-minded policy [of treaty making] has not been followed. The rapacity of the settlers is usually backed by the tyranny of the government."[22] The procedure was often not one of immediate expropriation of land but rather of constant encroachment by whites, a gradual land-taking process sanctioned after the fact by the government and legitimated by treaties.

The subordination of Native Americans was encouraged by Andrew Jackson, a slaveholding president who was critical of treaty making. Jackson encouraged the states to defy Supreme Court rulings concerning Indians. Gradual displacement gave way to brutally oppressive marches over hundreds of miles at gunpoint, a near-genocidal policy explicitly designed to rid entire regions of those falsely stereotyped by whites as "savages." Congress passed the Indian Removal Act in 1830, and within a decade many Indian groups in the East had migrated "voluntarily" or at gunpoint to lands west of

Here is an etching of a meeting between U.S. army generals and Sioux and other Native American leaders at North Platte, Nebraska.

the Mississippi under the auspices of "negotiated" treaties. Atlantic and Gulf Coast groups, as well as midwestern groups, were forcibly removed to the Indian Territory in the infamous "Trail of Tears." Large numbers died, and the relocated peoples faced serious survival problems in the new lands.[23]

Westward-moving whites also precipitated struggles with the Plains societies, many of which had by that time abandoned farming for a nomadic lifestyle. The often genocidal actions of federal troops and white farmers were a new experience. The nomadic, horse-oriented Plains peoples came to symbolize "the Indian" in white imaginations. Media presentations have severely distorted the reality of the Plains wars, which, unlike Hollywood's version, usually did *not* involve warriors in war bonnets on stallions facing a brave collection of U.S. Army officers backed by heroic soldiers on a sunswept plain.[24]

Myths about Conflict

Movies and television have portrayed the years between 1840 and 1860 as an era of large-scale and constant conflict between white overlanders and Indians. Movies and television have created unforgettable, often racist images of the West—wagon trains moving across the West, wagons in a circle, whooping Indians on ponies, thousands of dead whites and Indians, and treacherous "red savages." However, research studies by John Unruh and others have made clear that these images are largely mythological. Between 1840 and 1860, approximately 250,000 whites made the journey across the plains to the West Coast; far fewer than 1 percent died at the hands of the native inhabitants. Between 1840 and 1860, a total of *only 362 whites and 426 Native Americans* died in *all* the recorded battles between the two groups along wagon train routes. There is only *one* documented attack by Indians on a wagon train in which there were as many as two dozen casualties for the white settler-invaders. Most white accounts of massacres by Indians are either fictions or great exaggerations of minor encounters.[25] Instead, Native Americans often provided food, horses, or guidance for weary white travelers.

A recurring pattern emerged in the growing conflict between whites and the indigenous inhabitants. White farmers would move onto Indian lands to farm. The U.S. government, by means of a treaty involving threat or coercion, would provide land for the resettlement of the Indians affected. More white farmers, prospectors, and hunters moving along migratory paths from the East would intrude on these new Native American lands. This new land theft would be legitimated by yet another treaty, and the process would begin again. Or perhaps a U.S. government treaty promise of supplies or money to those Native Americans living in a restricted area would be broken, and some would leave the area seeking food or revenge. The U.S. Army would then take repressive action, sometimes intentionally punishing an innocent group and precipitating armed uprisings.

Many treaties, still part of U.S. law, were masterpieces of fraud; consent was gained by deception or threat. More than three hundred treaties with Indian groups were made between 1790 and the Civil War. Most were *not* honored in full by the U.S. government. As time passed, treaties established regulations governing Indian behavior and provided for restricted areas called reservations. This treaty process was abandoned altogether by the U.S. government by 1871. Still, hundreds of ratified treaties between the United States and many Native American groups remain in effect.[26]

White Massacres of Native Americans

Serious treaty violations by whites often led to conflict. For example, in an 1862 uprising in Minnesota, the eastern Sioux killed some farmers after losing much of their land to the invading whites and suffering at the hands of government agents. Delays in supplies promised by the government resulted in the Sioux burning and killing throughout the Minnesota Valley, and massive white retaliation followed. About the same time, conflict occurred in Colorado between Native American groups and a state militia left in charge when the U.S. Army was withdrawn. Indian guerrilla warfare was met with savage retaliation. In 1864, Colonel John Chivington, a minister, and his Colorado volunteers massacred nearly two hundred Cheyennes in a peace-seeking band at Sand Creek.[27] The massacre was one of the most savage in western history: "Children carrying white flags were slaughtered and pregnant women were cut open. The slaughter and mutilation continued into the late afternoon over many miles of the bleak prairie."[28]

After the Civil War, with federal government support, large railroad corporations gobbled up millions of acres in the West. Buffalo were slaughtered by the millions, and the hunting economy of the Plains was destroyed. Farmers, miners, and the army repeatedly violated treaties with Indian tribes. One example was the Dakota Territory of the Sioux. Conflict over the illegal white invasion escalated; troops were sent in to force Sioux bands onto a smaller reservation, even though the Sioux were already on what the government regarded as "unceded Indian territory." In this force was the infamous Colonel George A. Custer. The most widely known battle of the Plains struggle occurred at the Little Big Horn in 1876 when Custer and his soldiers were wiped out by a group of Sioux and allied groups that had refused to settle on the reservation.

One of the last engagements took place at Wounded Knee Creek fourteen years later. Attempting to round up the last few Sioux bands, the Army intercepted one group and forced them to camp. A white colonel ordered a disarming, which was carried out in ruthless fashion. One young Sioux shot into a line of soldiers; the troops replied by shooting at close range with rifles and machine guns. Approximately three hundred unarmed Indians, many of them old men, women, and children, were killed on the spot or while running from the camp.[29]

In the Southwest, Indian resistance was, on occasion, substantial. Military expeditions against the scattered Navaho and Apache communities in the Southwest attempted to destroy them or hem them in. Colonel Kit Carson convinced the Mescalero Apaches to agree to reside on a reservation. Establishing headquarters in Navaho territory, Carson began a scorched-earth program, destroying Navaho fields and herds. He then herded his captives three hundred miles to a reservation—the infamous "Long Walk" that is central to the Navaho collective memory of oppression. By 1890 most of the remnants of the Native American groups had been forced onto reservations.[30] Still, even on the reservations, most groups maintained their historic cultures, including language and religion, and drew on their cultures to resist pressures of acculturation to white culture.

RACIST IMAGES AND STEREOTYPES

Soon after the arrival of European colonizers in the Americas, stereotypes of Native Americans as lazy and wild and of Europeans as hardworking and steady, along with classification by physical characteristics, served to distinguish colonizers from colonized. Another early European myth, that of the "child of nature" or "noble savage," was a mixture of appreciation and racial prejudice.[31]

European Americans were often shocked at the strength of Indian societies and cultures and at the unwillingness of the indigenous residents to submit to the "civilizing" pressures of white missionaries and landseeking farmers. Violent resistance reinforced the stereotype of the "savage." This racialized image became common after the first battles in which Indians resisted the seizure of their lands. By the mid-1600s, Europeans were writing that the Indians were "wild beasts" who should be hunted down like other animals.[32]

The era of westward expansion imprinted on the white mind, in popular novels and later in films and TV programs, the image of "cruel" Indian "warriors" attacking "helpless" white families. Yet the media have seldom focused on the much more significant savagery of attacks on Indian families, farms, and communities by white soldiers, hunters, and farmers. Ironically, however, a staggering number of fictional Indians have been killed in the mass media, especially in pulp fiction: "The Indian, who had been all but eliminated with real bullets, now had to be resurrected to be killed off again with printer's ink."[33] Cowboy-and-Indian movies added to false images of Indian "savagery." Distorted images of Indians can still be found in textbooks in U.S. schools.

One erroneous image is that of the "primitive hunter" who made little use of the land. Most groups that were killed off or forced off their lands were composed *not* of nomadic hunters but of part-time or full-time farmers. Groups such as the Cherokee had, by the time of the forced removal in the 1830s, significantly developed their farms and other agricultural enterprises.[34]

Two paradoxical stereotypes have long been applied to Indian women, both based on the women's relationship with white men: a "Princess" who may save a white man from her own people, and a "Squaw" (a derogatory term) who becomes the white man's sexual partner. Rayna Green documents how the image of the esteemed Princess, portrayed as only slightly darker-skinned than Europeans and often with distinctly European features, became a symbol of the New World in Europe, a many-faceted "Mother figure—exotic, powerful, dangerous, and beautiful."[35] In contrast, the "Squaw" was portrayed negatively by white racists as darker, fatter, and cruder than the "Princess." She shared the negative traits of drunkenness, stupidity, and thievery attributed by whites to Indian men, and her destruction by whites was thereby justified as necessary to the progress of European colonialism.

Studies of elementary, high-school, and college social science (for example, history) textbooks have found a number of negative stereotypes about Native Americans. Most history texts deal briefly with Native Americans, if only in the past tense. Some children's books today portray Indians as Pocahontas-type "princesses," "squaws," or "warriors." In an analysis of Houghton Mifflin's history and social science series for kindergarten through eighth grade, Communities United, a group that seeks to find and remove stereotypes of racially oppressed people from school textbooks, found "justifications and trivializations of some of the most vicious social practices in our history."[36] James Loewen's study of high school textbooks found significant improvements in recent years, with more attention to the diversity of early Indian societies and some recognition of their important cultures and contributions. Still, the high school books are riddled with conventional and erroneous assumptions about Indians and whites, and many authors "still write history to comfort the descendants of the 'settlers.'"[37]

Studies of the media, including popular films (both older and contemporary ones) have revealed substantially exaggerated stereotypes of Indians, including the continuing use of "Indian warrior" and "Indian princess" images.[38] Some scholars have also criticized the tendency of many white observers to define Native Americans and their ancient traditions in terms of eighteenth- and nineteenth-century white observations. This limited basis for definition has influenced North American art, literature, the media, and the mainstream view in general and has contributed to the invisibility of contemporary Indians.[39] The Academy Award–winning film *Dances with Wolves* (1990) is an example of the focus on the past. Although this film presents a more sensitive treatment of white–Indian history than its predecessors, it views the historical Indian experience, while regrettable, as proceeding to an inevitable and negative conclusion. The film diverts attention from the present reality of Native Americans, perpetuating the notion that the latter are a relic of the past. As the Indian sociologist Ward Churchill has stated, "native people are forced to live, right now, today, in abject squalor under the heel of what may be history's most seamlessly perfected system of internal colonization, out of sight, out of mind, their rights and resources relentlessly consumed by the dominant society."[40]

Note, too, that *Dances with Wolves*, *Geronimo* (1993), *Last of the Mohicans* (1993), and other recent Hollywood films feature *white* actors in order to attract white audiences and thus to be profitable. Even the popular animated Disney film *Pocahontas* (1995) perpetuates backward stereotypes of Native Americans. What appears to be a fun children's movie about a real-life character is actual pseudo-history that distorts the history of Native Americans. Jacquelyn Kilpatrick, in *Celluloid Indians* (1999), notes that the Disney producer said he sought to dramatize the "essence" of the real Pocahontas story. However, "the logic of that reasoning may be difficult to follow, but evidently to depict her 'essence' they needed to change her age and her body, and give her a motive for her actions that boils down to falling desperately in love with the first white man she sees."[41] The historical Pocahontas was actually a 10–12-year-old child when she was involved with John Smith, not the much older Barbie look-alike of the Disney movie. As a child and a woman, she was an Indian living at a time when white colonizers were invading Indian lands—and soon would decimate her society and other Indian societies by violence and disease. Her own life included kidnaping and rape at the hands of whites, a major trip to England, a marriage to a white planter named John Rolfe, and an early death from disease in England. This is not the story whites like to hear, and not the one told in the movies and other mass media.[42] The mainstream film industry has yet to make a fully honest film about the oppression and destruction of Native American societies, one told substantially from the perspective of Native Americans and dominated by Native American actors.

There are only a few studies of white attitudes toward Native Americans. One 1970s study updated earlier research by E. S. Bogardus on social-distance attitudes. In Bogardus's 1920s research study, white college students were asked how close, on a scale from 1 ("would marry") to 7 ("would not allow them in nation"), they would allow a given racial or ethnic group to themselves. Bogardus found that white students rejected all close contact (such as friendships) with Native Americans. Using the same social-distance scale, the 1970s study found that white respondents still rejected Native Americans in primary-group relations, such as marriage and club membership. This study also found that white views of Native Americans mixed romantic stereotypes with traditional negative stereotypes.[43]

Today, stereotypes of Native Americans are commonplace and can have serious social consequences. Stereotyped views of Indians in the minds of white law enforcement officials can lead to discrimination in policing, arrests, and sentencing. For example, recent reports on state prisons and juvenile facilities have shown that Indians are overrepresented relative to their percentage in the population and tend to receive harsher sentences compared with whites. One review of Montana State Prisons suggests that "Socially sanctioned racism can and does seep into every level of the criminal justice system from the numbers of police arrests, severity of charges, sentencing, treatment by correction officers, and parole board decisions."[44] One reason for this bias is that many whites, including some law enforcement personnel, view Native Americans as trespassers and outsiders or hold images of them as lazy, drunken troublemakers. In addition, members of white supremacist groups have been active in carrying out hate crimes and developing Web sites that circulate negative stereotypes of Native Americans.

Suzane Shown Harjo, a founding trustee of the National Museum of the American Indian, has noted that whether a stereotypical image is hostile or benevolent, "There is no such thing as a good stereotype.... It reduces people or a person to a consumable, easily digestible, prejudged image or word. It sets up a system or prejudice either for or against a person or a people and, in that way, denies the humanity of that person or people ... or it wrongly characterizes people."[45] In the mid-1990s, the Cable News Network (CNN) aired "Native Americans: The Invisible People," a rare series that presented the historical circumstances surrounding several contemporary Native American issues, including land-use treaty violations, federal recognition of Native American nations as legal entities, and the protection of Native American sacred sites.[46] It is interesting that CNN should be the first major television network to present in some detail such historical and contemporary realities; CNN's founder, Ted Turner, also owned the Atlanta Braves baseball team, whose supporters have helped perpetuate negative Native American stereotypes through their constant use of the team's name and of the famous "tomahawk chop." Indeed, the team's name and fans' behavior have generated recurring protests by Native American organizations.

The CNN program and some changes in the accuracy of school textbooks may signal a slow trend toward more honesty in dealing with U.S. history in regard to Native Americans. Interestingly, 57 percent of the respondents in a recent (2000) nationwide poll of registered voters reported that they believed public schools do not teach enough about Native American history, and three-fourths thought that U.S. colleges and universities should provide more courses on Native Americans.[47]

POLITICS

Native American Cultures and Societies: Before European Influence

Many European Americans have viewed Native Americans as not having had "civilization" until it was brought to them by the European colonizers. Yet, at the time of initial contact most Native American societies were at least as old as European societies and had cultures and civilizations that were at least as developed as those in Europe. Indeed, many Native American societies were more egalitarian than European societies. Generally, both men and women had respect and social status. Women often played as important a role as men. Some groups, such as the Cherokees and the Iroquois, were matrilineal and matrilocal; "the husband-father role was to sire children, who belonged to their mother's clan, lived in their mother's family's home and inherited her property. Chiefs were from the women's side of the family."[48] Among the Iroquois tribes, women elders even chose the tribal leadership. In many other societies, women also had significant political input. Democratic political institutions were commonplace in Indian societies. Indeed, Benjamin Franklin, Thomas Jefferson, and other colonial leaders admired and learned from the democratic institutions of Indian nations such as the Iroquois. Interestingly too, a prominent symbol of the United States, the eagle clutching a bundle of arrows, was taken from Iroquois eagle and arrow symbols.[49]

The fact that most of Native American history has been written by whites is perhaps one reason why the political and social roles of Indian women have been downplayed. Indeed, contact with Europeans frequently forced Indian groups to alter these gender roles; white leaders usually refused to deal with Indian women as leaders or spokespersons. Efforts of white officials, including political officials and missionaries, to convince Indian groups of the inferiority of women and the superiority of men resulted in some decline in social and political power for women in numerous Native American communities.[50]

The Politics of the European Invasion

At first, the European colonizers dealt with Native Americans as independent nations. As European communities gained strength, they began to treat these nations as groups to be exterminated or as dependent wards. Many eastern groups were destroyed or decimated. Those remaining in the East were militarily weak enough by the 1830s for the government to force them westward. About the same time, the Bureau of Indian Affairs (BIA) was established to coordinate federal relations with Indians; its work ranged from supervision of reservations to provision of some supplies. Until the 1880s, the BIA's role of attempting to protect Native Americans put it in conflict with a military policy that often sought genocidal extermination.

Under BIA domination, indigenous Indians leaders were often set aside and replaced by white-controlled leaders. Indigenous religions were suppressed, and large numbers of Christian missionaries were imported. With the end of treaty making in 1871 and the reduction of major Indian groups to life on reservations by the 1890s, Indians entered into a unique relationship with white America: They were (and are) the only subordinate racial or ethnic group whose life was to be (and is) routinely administered directly by a specific bureaucratic arm of the U.S. government. The action of the BIA is a clear example of the role of government in defining and controlling racial and ethnic groups, a point underscored by Omi and Winant in their theory of racial formation (see Chapter 2).[51]

From the Dawes Act to the New Deal

A major federal policy shift regarding land took place in the late nineteenth century. Indians, white reformers argued, should be taught new rules of land use and ownership. The 1887 Dawes Act provided that reservation lands be divided among individual families—even though the European tradition of private ownership and individual development of land was an alien value system for most Native Americans. Advocates of the new policy hoped that individual land allotments would convert Indians into individual entrepreneurs. Unallotted lands could then be sold to white outsiders. This new federal policy soon resulted in a large-scale land sale to whites; through means fair and foul the remaining 140 million acres of Indian lands were further reduced to 50 million acres by the mid-1930s.[52]

In 1884 a Native American named John Elk moved to the city (Omaha, Nebraska), adapted to white ways, and attempted to vote. Denied this citizenship right, Elk took his case to a federal court, where he argued that the Fourteenth Amendment made him a citizen and that the Fifteenth Amendment guaranteed his right to vote.[53] The court ruled that he was not an American citizen—that he was in effect a citizen of a *foreign* nation and thus not entitled to vote. However, under the Dawes Act, the "wards" of the government could become citizens if they showed themselves competent in managing their land allotments. Belatedly, in 1924, the U.S. Congress passed the Indian Citizenship Act, granting citizenship, including voting rights, to all Native Americans.

The 1934 Indian Reorganization Act (IRA) established yet another federal policy to deal with Native Americans. Designed by commissioner of Indian affairs John Collier, the law was intended to establish Indian civil and cultural rights, allow for semiautonomous tribal governments similar in legal status to counties and municipalities, and foster economic development on reservations. The IRA would end land allotment, require careful BIA supervision of the sale of lands, and provide for federal credit and preferential hiring of Indians in the BIA. Native American groups were supposed to vote on whether they wanted to come under the act.[54]

Yet this apparently progressive new law had serious defects. It ignored fundamental economic problems and maintained the subordinate ward relationship of Native Americans to the federal government. The law, which excluded Oklahoma tribes, gave the secretary of the interior what many Indians saw as excessive power. The secretary, whom some called the "dictator of the Indians," made rules for elections, could veto constitutions, supervised expenditures, and made regulations for land management on the reservations.[55] One analyst has noted that "the expressed purpose of this law was finally and completely to usurp the traditional mechanisms of American Indian governance (e.g., the traditional chiefs, council of elders, etc.), replacing them with a system of federally approved and regulated 'tribal councils' ... structured more along the lines of corporate boards than of government entities."[56]

Many Native Americans saw the IRA as a violation of the sovereignty guaranteed them by treaties, and the law was ratified only by manipulation of the voting process. After four years, 189 Native American nations were reorganized. Many of these groups incorporated themselves. Many also developed central councils with constitutions reflecting certain values of the surrounding white culture. The seventy-seven groups that succeeded in voting down the act still operated under their traditional cultures and customs. Numerous groups began some self-government, managing their own property and governing their own affairs under federal supervision.[57]

More Fluctuations in Federal Policies

In the 1950s, House Concurrent Resolution 108, which called for the *termination* of federal supervision of Indian groups, brought yet another major shift in federal policy. The intent was to reject the

Indian Reorganization Act and return to the policy of forced conformity to white values in regard to land ownership. Termination was supported by land-hungry whites and political conservatives seeking to cut government costs, as well as by some acculturated Indians living off the reservations. Between 1954 and 1960, federal guardianship of several dozen Indian groups was "terminated." Because of its negative effects, including the problems of dealing with unfriendly local white officials and land entrepreneurs, this termination policy soon came to be viewed as a failure. For example, in the case of the Menominee, who became a new political unit under Wisconsin state law, distribution payments to individual members exhausted the group's funds and development capital, the local hospital had to be closed because it did not meet state standards, and local power plants were sold to an outside company. Termination was costly for many groups unprepared to deal with the intrusions and treachery of the outside white world.[58]

From the 1960s to the 1980s, federal policy shifted yet again. President Richard Nixon called on Congress to maintain Native Americans' tie to the federal government and to prohibit termination without consent. Congress passed legislation that made credit available for business purposes and established a self-determination procedure whereby Indian nations would assume some administration of certain federal programs. In the 1970s, some groups began to run their schools and social-service programs.[59]

The powers of the Bureau of Indian Affairs have been far-reaching. The BIA defines who is an "Indian" by determining which tribes are officially acknowledged by the federal government. The bureau keeps records of fractions of "blood" lines in order to identify who is eligible for tribal membership. Official status usually brings a number of benefits to a group, including economic development aid and health, education, and housing benefits. To obtain federal recognition, a group must document a continuous history and prove that its members are Indians. Several groups have been denied official recognition by the BIA, an action that amounts to administrative death unless the group can successfully appeal its case to the courts or Congress. For example, in 1992 the six-hundred-member Shinnecock group in New York State debated the merits of applying for recognition; it estimated the cost of doing so would be $250,000.[60] In this government-controlled process of defining who is an Indian and what is a tribe, we again see evidence of the racial formation theory suggested by Omi and Winant.

Governments often intrude into the process by which racial and ethnic groups are defined. Today, the BIA continues to supervise tribal government, banking, utilities, and highways, as well as millions of dollars in tribal trust funds. The BIA supervises leasing and selling of Indians lands, and, until recently, all control of social services was in the hands of federal agencies. Some Indians regard the BIA as the lesser of two evils, noting that in recent decades it has to some extent protected them against predatory exploitation from whites and has periodically expanded self-determination. From this perspective, to terminate the BIA would be to end what protection it does provide.[61]

Growing numbers of Indians have called for an end to BIA control and have worked for recognition of their groups as sovereign nations. The Indian Self-Determination and Education Assistance Act was amended to enable several Indian nations to plan for autonomous governance. Federal government support for self-government was furthered when a U.S. Senate investigation revealed BIA mismanagement. A Senate committee recommended an end to the government's paternalistic control over Indian affairs. One Native American leader pointed out that federal actions "still retain the legally groundless presumption that Indian nations are somehow inherently subordinate to the United States," and that the Senate committee's call for negotiated agreements instead of treaties "denies Indian peoples the formal recognition of their national sovereignty implied by treaties."[62]

In 1996 several Indian leaders filed a lawsuit on behalf of the half million Indians who sought a financial accounting and general reform of the government's Indian trust account system, which had been mismanaged for more than a century. To this point in time, the U.S. government has fought the lawsuit. Soon after the lawsuit was filed, a federal judge ordered the departments of Interior and Treasury to produce records for the trust accounts for the five named plaintiffs. These trust accounts stem from land allotments made to individual Indians in the late nineteenth century. Profits from the land—such as leasing fees and royalties for oil and gas, logging, and other land uses—should have been held in trust by the federal government. Yet the government has not yet produced the records, in part because they have not kept records or have lost those that they once had. The federal judge referred to this as "fiscal and government irresponsibility in its purest form." As of early 2002, the trust fund mismanagement case has not yet been resolved.[63]

Growing Pressures for Political Participation

For those on reservations, political participation has often been directed at reservation elections and service in tribal governments. With some exceptions, the reservations have been exempt from state control and taxation; subject to BIA approval, Native American groups have made their own laws and regulations. Tribal governments have often combined legislative and executive functions in one elected council, and voter turnout for elections has often been substantial. Political conflict has periodically occurred on reservations between those leaders who prefer to work closely with the BIA and those who support sovereignty for Indian nations.[64]

Native Americans did not have the right to vote in all states in elections outside reservations before the 1924 Indian Citizenship Act. States such as Utah, Arizona, and New Mexico even barred reservation Indians from voting until the 1940s; as late as the 1960s and 1970s, some states made voting and jury participation difficult. State literacy tests and gerrymandered voting district lines have also reduced Native Americans' voting power in western states. The number of potential Indian voters has risen to substantial proportions in nonreservation areas since the 1960s. In a few urban areas, Indian voting strength is great enough to function as a *swing vote* (a bloc that can affect close elections).

The number of Indians running for political office has increased since the 1990s, although few have been elected. Only a handful have served in state and federal legislatures, most since the 1950s. About two dozen have served in state legislatures since 1900. The New Mexico legislature had its first Indian representatives in 1964. Very few Indians have ever served in Congress—perhaps a half-dozen representatives and two senators have had some Native American ancestry. The most famous, Charles Curtis, was born on the Kaw reservation in 1860. Said to be one-fourth Indian, Curtis was a representative for fourteen years, a senator for twenty, and vice-president under Herbert Hoover.[65]

Since 1935 only four Native Americans have served in Congress; there has rarely been more than one Native American representative at any one time. Ben Reifel, a Sioux, was a representative from South Dakota from 1961 to 1971. In 1992, Congress's only Native American member at the time, Representative Ben Nighthorse Campbell from Colorado, was elected senator from that state. In 2000 Campbell was joined by Brad Carson, who was elected in Oklahoma with the help of an organized campaign to get out Indian voters. Carson was elected in the congressional district with the largest Indian population in the country and is the only Native American (Cherokee) now in the House of Representatives. In addition, in the 2000 elections, Winona LaDuke, an Indian activist from Minnesota's White Earth Reservation, ran with Ralph Nader as the Green Party's vice-presidential candidate. The number of Indian voters has grown significantly over the past few decades. As of election day 2000, an estimated 1.6 million Indians were of voting age.[66]

The slight Indian representation in state legislatures and Congress is paralleled in town and city governments. Even in metropolitan areas with substantial Indian populations, few have been elected to city councils, school boards, and county governments. Police harassment of Indians in towns near reservations is sometimes a problem, in part revealing discrimination by local authorities. Complaints by Native American leaders in several cities have focused on the lack of efforts to recruit Native Americans as police, parole officers, and government attorneys, as well as on unnecessarily high arrest rates.[67]

The recent economic improvements that have come from gambling operations, which we will examine later, have enabled a few Indian groups to contribute significant amounts of money to local and national political campaigns and to fund lobbying in Washington, D.C., thereby expanding political influence. This political influence has already helped to stop the passage of legislation detrimental to Indian interests. Nonetheless, the large majority of Native American groups have not yet been able to prosper economically or politically in the United States.[68]

PROTEST AND CONFLICT

Organized Native American protest against subordination has perhaps been the most sustained of any group in the history of North America. Violent resistance to white oppression between 1500 and 1900 produced some of the greatest protest leaders the continent has seen. The end of armed conflict did not end protest. By the late nineteenth century, a number of new protest organizations had sprung up. One was the Indian Rights Association, founded by whites concerned with protecting and "civilizing" Native Americans. By exposing the corruption and oppression on reservations, such progressive groups did lay the basis for reforms in federal government policy. The Society of American Indians, established in the early 1900s, was one of the first organizations formed by Native Americans. The goals of this self-help-oriented organization included developing pride and a national leadership and improving educational and job opportunities.[69]

In the 1920s, John Collier organized the American Indian Defense Association to fight attempts by government officials to establish "executive order reservations" not covered by treaty and thus made more accessible to exploitation by whites who wished to extract minerals. The National Congress of American Indians (NCAI) was formed in the 1940s and pressed for education, legal aid, and progressive legislation. The NCAI vigorously opposed the termination policy of the 1950s and 1960s and campaigned for a strong self-determination policy. NCAI is the oldest and largest advocacy group. The group has campaigned against anti-Indian stereotyping, including sports teams' use of Indian symbols. The National Indian Youth Council, created in 1961, has fought vigorously for civil rights, sometimes organizing civil disobedience. The Youth Council has been active in education and has taken up causes critical to the protection of Native American lands.[70]

Confrontation with the Federal Government

The term "Red Power" appeared during the expanded activism of the 1960s. Protest actions and civil disobedience movements during the 1960s continued a long tradition of pressuring white-controlled institutions into concessions. Civil disobedience involved such activities as delaying dam construction, occupying government facilities, picketing, and sit-ins.[71] Some of these protest actions have brought significant changes benefiting Native Americans.

In 1968 the American Indian Movement (AIM) was organized to address problems ranging from police brutality to housing and employment discrimination. An Indian Patrol, established by the organization to supervise contacts between Indians and the police, pressed for improvements in police behavior. In spring 1973, AIM organized a large-scale occupation of Wounded Knee, South Dakota, a hamlet on the Pine Ridge reservation. Several hundred AIM members participated in a seventy-one-day armed protest directed against the U.S. Justice Department's decision to send agents to Pine Ridge to support a Sioux leader who was being challenged by activists who wanted to replace him with a traditional Council of Elders.[72]

In its attempts to convict AIM protesters, the government behaved like a police state and used illegal wiretaps, altered evidence, and paid witnesses—which led a federal judge to dismiss the case. Afterward, U.S. government agents participated in a campaign to destroy the AIM movement and were thought by some knowledgeable observers to have been involved in several suspicious accidents and murders involving AIM members. Two hundred AIM members were harassed and arrested, but only a dozen or so were ever convicted. This political struggle was a major example of an open confrontation between militant Native Americans and a Native American establishment supported by the BIA and other white officials.[73]

The Case of Leonard Peltier

In recent years a number of Native American protest efforts have sought to free Leonard Peltier, a Lakota/Ojibwa. Seen by many, including the international civil rights group Amnesty International, as a political prisoner, Peltier has been in a federal penal institution for two decades. He is accused of shooting two FBI agents in the confrontation between Indians and government agents at the Pine Ridge Reservation in 1975. Initially, several men were accused, but only Peltier was tried and sentenced. Even federal officials admit that it is unclear who shot the federal agents, and numerous members of Congress have supported a new trial. Recent revelations that the FBI has withheld documents (including a critical ballistics test) from the defense attorneys in this case, as well as evidence that the FBI has withheld evidence in other major cases, have added support for the international calls for freeing Peltier. Millions of people around the globe have signed petitions or joined groups protesting Peltier's confinement as a political prisoner.[74]

Anti-Indian Racism and Sports Mascots

In recent decades AIM and other Indian organizations have protested the use of Indian names, sacred symbols, and "tomahawk chop" gestures by white-oriented sports teams. Some protest efforts have focused on the World Series and the Super Bowl. Before one 1990s Super Bowl, AIM sponsored a two-day conference on racism in sports. These nationally televised sports events brought degrading caricatures into the homes of Native Americans who otherwise have little contact with white fans' and teams' behavior. "We couldn't ignore it anymore," one Indian woman stated. "People started coming up to me at work and going, 'chop-chop' and 'woo-woo.'" Some prominent team names like *Redskins* are openly derogatory and racist, yet many whites refuse to acknowledge this fact. Most names, such as *Redskins*, *Chiefs*, and *Braves*, together with the associated caricatures used by many sports teams, involve offensive anti-Indian stereotypes. The white parodies of sacred chants, face paint, headdresses, and drums for entertainment purposes are taken by many Native Americans as assaults on their cultures, because most of these have spiritual significance.[75]

Since 1997, members of the National Coalition on Racism in Sports and the Media have joined local protesters in Cleveland in demonstrations against the Cleveland baseball team's use of the "Chief Wahoo" symbol. Called the *Indians*, Cleveland's team has come under intensive criticism for this caricatured image, which is seen by many Native Americans as extremely negative and racist.[76] Images and mascots like Chief Wahoo are "invented Indians," as a recent book *Team Spirits* (2001) puts it. They are not real but "perpetuate inappropriate, inaccurate, and harmful understandings of living people, their cultures, and their histories.... Through fragments thought to be Indian—a headdress, tomahawk, war paint, or buckskin—Native American mascots reduce them to a series of well-worn clichés, sideshow props, and racist stereotypes."[77]

Today, an estimated 80 colleges and universities still use Indian logos, primarily in connection with sports. Debates similar to those in Cleveland have taken place around Chief Illiniwek, the dancing Indian present at sports events, who has been a symbol for the University of Illinois for 75 years. In spring 2001 most of that university's trustees expressed support for this symbol for the university, but appointed a committee to study the matter.[78] University of Illinois scholar David Prochaska argues that these mascots catch on because of "imperialist nostalgia," a mutated celebrating by whites of those whom their ancestors killed or put on reservations. The fictional Chief Illiniwek is *not* dressed like the Woodlands Illiniwek after whom he was named. Instead, whites "playing Indian" at sports events dress up in a pseudo-Sioux costume with a war bonnet like a Plains Indian. Such actions are clearly *not* attempts to celebrate authentically the nation's indigenous inhabitants.[79]

As Laurel Davis explains, such mascots and related fan actions are often based on myths and stereotypes of Native Americans as wild savages or bloodthirsty warriors and ignore the historical reality of the European takeover of Native American lands and the genocidal policies toward native nations. "The holocaust and oppression of Native Americans [are rendered] invisible, justified, or even glorious."[80] The symbolism chosen by college and other sports teams stereotypes Indians as historical people rather than as contemporary people. Indians are portrayed as a generic "Indian" group rather than as diverse nations and are thus robbed of control over their public image. Use of these symbols often mocks the religious significance of Native American sacred symbols. Vigorous opposition among some white men to the elimination of Indian sports symbolism may even suggest that the protest movement threatens a particular version of white male identity that is rooted in the mythology of the American West. Note the following statement made by a prominent pro-football player: "The reason there's so much violence in football is we can't kill Indians anymore."[81]

Recently, the U.S. Census Bureau decided not to include pictures of sports teams that still use these stereotyped Indian symbols in the Bureau's promotional materials. In spring 2001 the U.S. Commission on Civil Rights issued a statement condemning the use of stereotyped Native American images for sports symbols and noting that such images are especially insensitive in view of the history of forced assimilation and oppression of American Indians.

Recent Gains and Continuing Protests

The Indian civil rights movement has achieved some gains in raising public consciousness. Films portraying Native Americans as savages and white people as heroes have been less common since the 1990s. Films such as *Powwow Highway* and *Dances with Wolves* have portrayed Native Americans in a more sympathetic, if often paternalistic, light. In the 1970s some colleges and universities, including Dartmouth and Stanford, dropped the name *Indians* for their sports teams. In 1992, in direct response to AIM protests, the *Oregonian* became the first newspaper to discontinue using names that stereotype Native Americans.[82]

In the 1990s a coalition of petitioners sued to force the Washington Redskins football team to change its name. In April 1999 a federal government agency voided the trademark rights of the team because its logo was derogatory and violated the law. Recently a number of colleges and universities have given up their Native American logos, while numerous local governments, especially school boards, have had to face the issue. A number of high schools across the nation have changed team names from such terms as *Indians* and *Redskins* and removed offensive mascots. The Minnesota Board of Education and the Los Angeles and Dallas School Districts have forced their local schools to give up Indian mascots. In Los Angeles, money has been provided to schools to paint over images and purchase new uniforms. Some white alumni have protested the ban as injurious to school spirit and too costly.[83]

Other recent protests have focused on a variety of issues. Indian protests in Oklahoma led the state legislature to pass a unanimous resolution that requires local governments to delete the derogatory word "squaw" from the names of geographic places. In January 2001, in Austin, Texas, several hundred Native Americans and their supporters rallied at the State Capitol to press for a proposed repatriation and grave protection law. This legislation would protect unmarked Indian graves and their contents on both public and private lands in Texas. However, the Texas state government continued its anti-Indian reputation by opposing this law and also tribal desires to develop gaming enterprises. At the Austin rally, which was organized by a Native American student group at Texas A & M University, a Texas Indian leader spoke effectively of her tribe's long oppressed history in Texas.[84]

Honoring Treaties: Fishing Rights and Land Claims

Fishing rights and land claims have often provoked conflict between Indians and whites. For more than a century, Indian nations have struggled with whites over fishing rights in the Pacific Northwest and the Great Lakes region. Shootings and court battles have occurred in the state of Washington over Indian rights to catch fish, particularly salmon and trout—rights guaranteed by treaties between the Indian nations and the U.S. government. White anglers and commercial fishing companies object because their fishing opportunities are reduced when Native Americans exercise treaty rights. A court decision, *U.S. v. State of Washington* (1974), ruled that Native American fishing rights reserved by the treaties are different from those allowed whites. The court ordered the state to protect Indian anglers.[85]

White anglers defied the court's decision, protesting that it discriminated against them, and the state appealed the decision. Native American fishers were harassed and assaulted, and protests were directed at the judge. The federal government spent millions to increase the fish available and to compensate whites who suffered economic hardship. In 1979 the Supreme Court upheld the lower-court ruling, and government enforcement gradually reduced illegal fishing by whites. This decision helped to revitalize reservation economies in the state of Washington. In the words of one Indian leader, "the opportunities created directly or indirectly from the legally secured right to fish are the difference between staying and leaving" for many families in more than two dozen communities.[86]

Historically, Native American lands were taken without adequate compensation. The cause of East

Coast land-claims conflict was stated simply in a report by the U.S. Commission on Civil Rights:

> The basic Eastern Indian land claim is that Indian land in the East was invalidly transferred from Indians to non-Indians in the 18th and 19th centuries because the Federal Government, although required to do so, did not supervise or approve the transactions.[87]

In recent decades many indigenous groups, such as the Oneida and Mohawks in New York and the Passamaquoddy in Maine, have pressed their land claims in court. For example, the Mohawks have pressed a claim for the return of thousands of acres in upstate New York. A number of groups have won their cases, and some illegally taken lands have been restored. Prior to 1960 the U.S. Indian Claims Commission denied most claims for compensation for land taken. However, Native American and other pressures on the federal government since then have resulted in increases in the compensation paid by the commission.[88]

In recent years, the Sioux have pursued the return of land both in U.S. courts and in the United Nations. In 1980, after a lengthy court battle, the U.S. Supreme Court awarded the Lakota Sioux $122.5 million for more than 7 million acres taken illegally in the 1870s. Although the land (including the Black Hills) had been *guaranteed* to the Sioux nation by an 1868 treaty made by the U.S. government, it was stolen by whites a few years later when gold was discovered on the reservation. Following a war between the Sioux and the U.S. army, the Lakota and others lost control of a large area. In 1987, U.S. Senator Bill Bradley (D-New Jersey) introduced a bill to return substantial land and to offer money as damages for stolen land. The bill gained considerable support from the Lakotas before it was withdrawn by its sponsor in 1990. From 1981 to 1987, Native Americans staged an occupation of Camp Yellow Thunder in the Black Hills to protest the government's failure to live up to its treaty.[89]

Sioux leaders have taken their case to the United Nations, where some have been part of the U.N. committee that has written a Declaration on the Rights of Indigenous Peoples. The declaration provides for the "restitution of the lands, territories and resources" and the "enforcement of treaties." The U.S. government pressed for changes in the draft declaration.[90]

White backlash against Native American land claims, fishing claims, and other militant protests led to the creation of a national organization called the Interstate Congress for Equal Rights and Responsibilities and a variety of other anti-treaty organizations. Senator Mark Hatfield of Oregon publicly noted that this "very significant backlash ... by any other name comes out as racism in all its ugly manifestations." Some white members of Congress introduced bills to break treaties, overturn court decisions, and extinguish native land claims, arguing that the demands by Native Americans had soured "friendly relations." Native American groups responded that they were seeking what was *legally* theirs under official agreements with the U.S. government. Whites had become hostile because of the expense of living up to U.S. law and, as one Indian leader noted, "because of the lack of educational systems to teach anything about Indians, about treaties."[91] White stereotypes about Native Americans and white ignorance of treaties have played a critical role in opposition to Indian struggles for justice.

The Native American Rights Fund (NARF), a nonprofit national legal defense firm, has represented various tribes in lawsuits and negotiations for treaty-guaranteed land and natural resource rights and for restoration of the status of tribes as sovereign nations. NARF has won hundreds of victories. The organization has secured the return of land to the Passamaquoddy and Penobscot nations in Maine; Native American control over taxation, local courts, and educational programs; and economic enterprises on reservations.[92]

Reports from some human rights groups have documented an increase in harassment and violence perpetrated by whites against Native Americans over the past decade. Native Americans have been the victims of property crimes as well as beatings and murder. Many hate crimes against Native Americans have occurred in rural white communities that border reservations. Indians in urban areas have also been targeted. Hate crime incidents seldom receive media coverage. Rodney Barker, author of *The Broken Circle* (1993), the story of a series of hate crimes against Native Americans in New Mexico, reported that numerous Native Americans had personally told him about hate incidents they or their families had experienced, "but the newspaper was refusing to carry those reports.... Everyone tries to dissociate themselves from the historical pattern and say, 'Well, this is an aberration, it's not representative of what's going on here.' And yet, how many of those (crimes) does it take before you see the pattern is still in evidence?"[93]

Fighting for Fairness: Suing the Department of Agriculture

Native Americans are the oldest farmers in North America, yet most have had to struggle to maintain a living at this occupation. The U.S. government has a uneven record regarding fairness to farmers who are not white. In early 2000 more than 700 Native American families joined a class action suit against the Department of Agriculture (USDA) charging that government agency with discrimination.[94]

The lawsuit cites several types of discrimination. First, Indian farmers are often discouraged from applying for the USDA disaster assistance or farm support loans, while this is not the case for comparable white applicants. Second, Indian applicants are often asked to fill out more complicated forms or to fill out the forms with less assistance from USDA employees than is offered to comparable whites. Third, USDA guidelines are interpreted more advantageously for white than Indian farmers. The latter also tend to receive smaller amounts when they do manage to secure loans. In addition, the USDA's locations favor white farmers and make it difficult for many Indian farmers to get to the offices. The USDA has denied the lawsuit's charges of systemic discrimination, contending that there is only a problem with a few employees. However, the history of U.S. government treatment of African American and Native American farmers suggests that a deeper investigation of USDA racial policies is in order. Indeed, black farmers recently won a $1 billion judgment against the USDA for similar discrimination against thousands of black farmers over many decades.[95]

Activism and Self-Determination

As we have seen, since the 1970s many Indian groups have renewed pressure on the U.S. government to accept the terms of long neglected treaties made with Indian nations. Native American protests of various kinds, including lawsuits, have not only led to restoration of lands and other resources, they have been important to the passage of congressional laws that increase the self-determination of Indian nations. Tribal control of lands and resources has been increased by such laws as the 1975 Indian Self-Determination and Education Assistance Act, the 1979 Archaeological Resources Protection Act, the 1983 Land Consolidation Act, and the 1988 Indian Gaming Regulatory Act. Numerous other legislative acts are linked to this trend, including the 1978 American Indian Religious Freedom Act, the 1990 Native American Languages Act, and the 1990 Indian Arts and Crafts Act. This legislation indicates that the earlier federal policy of termination of tribal groups has ended. Coupled with these legislative changes are many changes on reservations, where "communities are developing tribal court systems, establishing tribal education systems including tribal colleges, extending tribal sovereignty and control over resources and taxation, securing and enforcing tribal hunting, fishing, and water rights, and building tribal economic development programs."[96]

The resurgence of Indian self-determination has been accompanied by a renewed emphasis on Indian culture and spirituality. The 1989 National Museum of the American Indian Act authorized construction of a new museum on the mall in Washington, D.C., to bring together in one place the Smithsonian's dispersed collection of Indian sacred objects. The museum is to be mostly under Native American control. Equally important, the Act requires that extensive government holdings of Indian funerary objects and burial remains be returned to their tribes. This Act provides federal recognition of the long struggle of Native Americans for respect for their burial sites and sacred objects. In addition, the recent Native American Graves Protection and Repatriation Act (1990) requires museums to notify Native American groups of their holdings of Native American objects and to facilitate their return.[97]

The greatly increased Native American activism since the 1960s is now bearing fruit in a strong resurgence of Native American cultures and societies and a strong insistence on indigenous rights across the United States.

THE ECONOMY

Before being forced onto reservations, most indigenous groups, which ranged from the Pueblo agriculturalists of the Southwest to hunting societies on the Plains to mixed agricultural-hunting societies elsewhere across the continent, had self-sufficient, land-based economies.

The loss of land to whites destroyed traditional economies. Melissa Fawcett Sayet, a Mohegan elder, has explained how she cried in anguish when her high-school teacher taught the concept of *manifest destiny*, which stated that the United States had a *right* to expand from the Atlantic Ocean to the Pacific and would inevitably do so. By the 1880s, Native American nations had lost millions of acres as whites proceeded westward; millions more acres were lost with the breakup of the remaining lands under the 1887 Dawes Act. Native American lands were usually reduced to areas considered at the time to be the least valuable to white farmers and entrepreneurs, although in recent years some of that land has been found to be rich in natural resources. Today Native Americans control only about 3 percent of the land in the continental United States, although indigenous peoples "still retain unassailable legal title to about ten times the area now left them."[98]

Economic exploitation accompanied the growth of industrial capitalism and urbanization in the late nineteenth century. The encroachment on Indian lands by white lumbering, ranching, and railroad interests redirected resources from rural Indian lands to fuel growth in urban centers. Bison and other game were killed for skins to be sold in Eastern cities, and white ranchers and farmers took lands for cattle raising and agriculture, hastening the impoverishment of Native Americans. Rural poverty increased as corporations reached out from metropolitan areas to develop more and more land; this in turn pressured many Native Americans to migrate to the cities. Joseph Jorgensen has argued that the poverty of rural Native Americans is "not due to rural isolation [or] a tenacious hold on aboriginal ways, but results from the way in which U.S. urban centers of finance, political influence, and power have grown at the expense of rural areas."[99] Indian wealth and resources were unjustly transferred to the white population.

Poverty and Land Theft

The poverty of many reservations is also rooted in the destruction of local economies and often in mismanagement by BIA officials. Testifying before a congressional committee on the food situation in the winter of 1883, a member of the Assiniboine nation pointed out that its members were healthy until the buffalo were destroyed, and that the substitute BIA rations were not adequate:

> They gave us rations once a week, just enough to last one day, and the Indians they started to eat their pet dogs. After they ate all their dogs up they started to eat their ponies. All this time the Indian Bureau had a warehouse full of grub.... Early [the next] spring, in 1884, I saw the dead bodies of the Indians wrapped in blankets and piled up like cordwood in the village of Wolf Point, and the other Indians were so weak they could not bury their dead; what were left were nothing but skeletons.[100]

Government agents were responsible for supplies, instruction in farming, and supervision of lands. Yet many agents were notorious for their corruption or incompetence.[101]

The reorganization policy of the 1930s, which provided for some Indian self-government, put a partial brake on corruption and blatant land theft, but serious problems persisted. As we have seen, federal policy fluctuated between tribal self-determination and the forced individualism of "termination." Some Indian lands were sold to pay taxes, and many Indians fell deeper into poverty as land resources were depleted. For many years, Indian lands have also been taken for dams, national parks, and rights-of-way for roads. The sale of lands to white lumbering and mineral interests continues. Much of the substantial money made in agriculture or ranching on the reservations has actually flowed to whites. Facing local and USDA discrimination and often having limited technical schooling, technical assistance, and capital to buy seeds, livestock, or machinery, the Indian farmer has frequently been faced with suffering a low yield or else leasing to outsiders.[102]

Land, Minerals, and Industrial Development

Native American reservations encompass about one-third of all low-sulphur coal, 6 percent of oil and gas reserves, and half of all known uranium reserves. Yet, historically it is whites who have benefited most from these natural resources. White corporate executives have eagerly eyed these resources, and a few have even called for the abolition of the reservations and the Bureau of Indian

Affairs so that these resources can be better exploited.[103] Historically, when desirable mineral resources have been found on Indian land, the land has often been taken over by white entrepreneurs and corporations. An example is the 1952 mineral extraction agreement between the Navaho Tribal Council and Kerr-McGee Nuclear Corporation. Over a period of eighteen years, Kerr-McGee employed 150 Navaho men to mine uranium on Navaho land, paying them only two-thirds of the prevailing off-reservation wage. Once the easy-to-reach deposits were mined, the company closed the facility, leaving radioactive debris that threatened the water supplies of downstream communities. Many Indian miners contracted cancers related to their mining of uranium.[104]

Three dozen tribes made national headlines in the 1970s when they announced the creation of the Council of Energy Resources Tribes (CERT) and hired a former Iranian oil minister to help them get better contracts with white-owned companies. Many whites worried that tribes were going to behave like OPEC and seek to be completely independent in making contracts with energy corporations.[105] By the early 2000s, CERT's membership had expanded to 47 U.S. tribes and four Canadian groups. By providing technical and financial assistance to help member groups control their own energy resources, the organization has brought new jobs and increased income to some Indian groups.[106]

Persisting Economic Problems

Before 1940 most Indian men were poor farmers or unskilled workers. With increasing urban migration, the proportion in farm occupations has dropped dramatically—from 68 percent in 1940 to about 5 percent today.[107] Indian workers in cities have usually been concentrated in the secondary labor market—that sector of urban economies that is characterized by job instability, low wages, and little mobility. This sector is disproportionately composed of racially oppressed workers. The primary labor market—that sector characterized by skilled jobs, higher wages, and greater mobility—is predominantly composed of white workers. The census figures in Table 6.1 (the most recent data) compare the occupational distributions of Native Americans with those of whites.[108]

Today, Native Americans are far less likely than white Americans to hold managerial or professional positions. Native American men are concentrated in blue-collar and service-sector jobs. The majority of Native American women hold clerical, sales, or service-sector jobs. In some white-collar occupational categories, Native Americans are very rare. For example, as of spring 2001, there were, in the United States and Canada together, only seven Native American broadcast reporters.[109]

Through the years, unemployment rates for Native Americans, both on and off reservations, have been far higher than for most other groups. In 1940 one-third of all Native American men were unemployed, compared with fewer than one-tenth of white men. By 1960 the rate had risen to 38 percent, compared with just 5 percent for all men. This increase reflected in part the move from agriculture to the less certain work opportunities in urban areas. By 1970 the rate had dropped to 12 percent for Native American men, still three times the national figure.[110] The 1990 unemployment rate for all Native American men (15 percent) was also three times that of white men, and the rate for all Native American

TABLE 6.1 OCCUPATIONAL DISTRIBUTIONS (1990)

	MEN		WOMEN	
	NATIVE AMERICAN	*WHITE*	*NATIVE AMERICAN*	*WHITE*
Managerial and professional	15%	27%	22%	30%
Technical, sales, and clerical	16	22	40	45
Service	14	8	23	15
Farming, forestry, and fishing	5	4	1	1
Precision production	23	20	3	2
Operators, fabricators, laborers	27	19	11	7
Total	100%	100%	100%	100%

TABLE 6.2 CIVILIAN EMPLOYEES IN EXECUTIVE BRANCH AGENCIES, SEPTEMBER 2000 (PERCENTAGE OF EMPLOYEES BY CATEGORY AND RACIAL GROUP)

Native American civilian employees in the executive branch of the federal government are most heavily represented in clerical, technical, and blue-collar job categories. Their percentage is lowest for professional positions. The percentage of Native American workers is highest at the lower pay levels and lowest at the highest pay levels.

	NATIVE AMERICAN	WHITE
All white-collar workers	2.0%	70.4%
Professional workers	1.4	78.2
Clerical workers	2.7	56.4
Blue-collar workers	3.0	65.4
Pay Plans		
General Schedule	2.0	69.7
GS1	2.2	46.6
GS2	3.3	53.6
GS3	4.1	54.5
GS4	4.5	55.8
GS15	0.7	84.2
Senior Pay Levels	0.8	86.5

Source: Office of Personnel Management, <http://www.opm.gov>.

women (13.1 percent) was almost three times that of white women.[111] In that year the unemployment rate for Native Americans living on reservations was 25.6 percent; on some reservations the rate exceeded 50 percent.[112] (These rates do not include the large proportion of Native American workers who have given up looking for work.) Native Americans have endured the longest Depression-like economic situation of any U.S. racial or ethnic group.

For decades Native Americans also had the lowest median family income and the lowest per capita income of any racial or ethnic group in the United States. The income of Native Americans on reservations has been lower than that of those living in nonreservation areas. In 1939 the median income of men on reservations was less than one-fourth of the median income for all U.S. men. Some improvement has occurred in the decades leading up to the present, and by the late 1990s the median household income for all American Indian (and Alaska Native) families ($30,784) had reached approximately 71 percent of the median income of white households ($43,287). The median income of Indian families on rural reservations was much lower than that of those in urban areas. In addition, approximately 26 percent of all Native Americans had incomes below the official poverty line. This was well above the white figure of 8 percent.[113]

Part of Native Americans' economic improvement in recent decades may be an effect of the large increase of people who now identify themselves as Native American. That is, people of mixed ancestry now reclaiming their heritage are frequently more affluent than those of unmixed ancestry.[114] Still, at the beginning of the twenty-first century, many Native Americans remain among the poorest of all Americans.

Poverty and unemployment are usually accompanied by inferior living conditions. Generally speaking, Native Americans face the worst housing conditions of any U.S. group. Today, Native Americans are much more likely than whites to have inadequate nutrition, to die of tuberculosis or diabetes, to live in small apartments or houses, and to have inadequate water or other facilities. Mortality rates are higher than for the nation as a whole. Although life expectancy for Native Americans has increased in recent years, it is still below the national average. Inadequate medical facilities, coupled with poor nutrition resulting from low incomes, constitute a major part of the problem. Cutbacks in federal health programs since the 1980s have reduced access to medical care for many Native Americans.[115]

Recent Economic Developments

With the growing self-determination movement and the recognition of tribal sovereignty in the courts, dozens of Indian nations have developed gambling and other enterprises in attempts to improve local economies. As of mid-2000 there were 310 Indian gaming operations under 198 tribe–state government gaming compacts in 28 states. Annual revenues of these operations totalled approximately $7.4 billion. While this economic development is significant, one should keep in mind that Indian gaming constitutes only about 10 percent of the U.S. gaming industry.[116] Some mass media reports have greatly exaggerated the economic return from these operations. Most Native American groups have *not* benefited from gaming; most are still struggling to overcome serious poverty and other economic problems. The

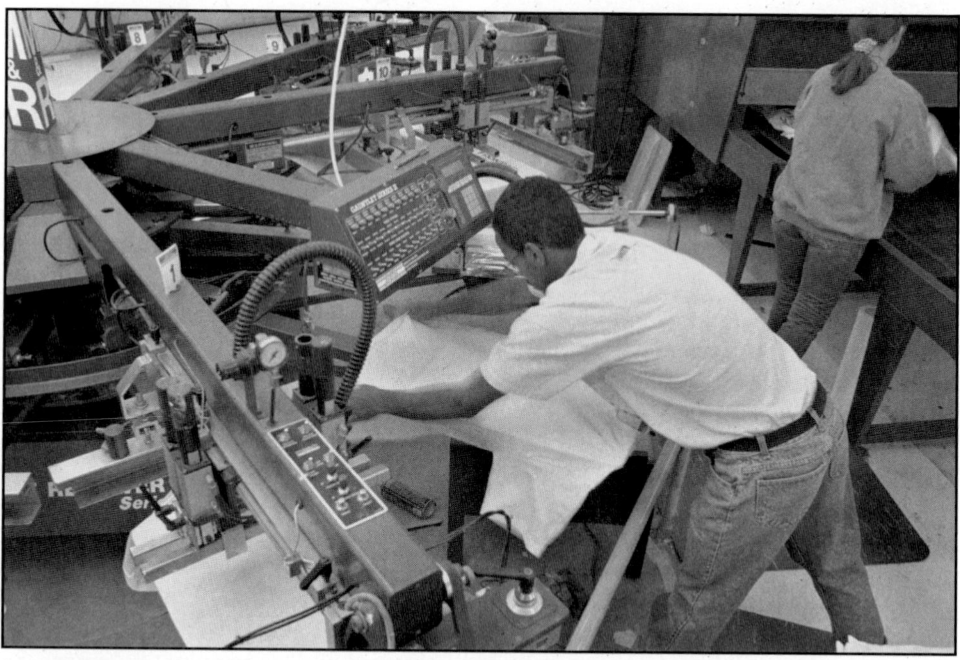

Workers print designs on t-shirts at a factory owned by the Oneida Nation.

majority of the nation's 558 federally recognized Indian groups have no gaming operations, and just 20 of the tribal gaming operations receive 55 percent of all Indian gaming revenues.[117]

Profits from gaming enterprises constitute the first regular income for some Indian groups. Federal law requires that gaming profits be used for such things as education, economic development, courts and policing, and physical infrastructure. Where gaming revenues are significant, they have paid for educational and health-care facilities, water treatment plants, job training, roads, and housing, and have reduced unemployment for Indians. Gaming revenues have also helped to create new businesses. For example, profits from the Choctaw Nation's bingo hall in Durant, Oklahoma have helped create truck stops, a motel, and a restaurant. These enterprises employ numerous Choctaws. Tourist dollars generated by Indian gaming operations also provide substantial benefits to nearby white businesses.[118]

In Oklahoma the Cherokee Nation Industries has used some of its gaming profits to build a plant that manufactures fiber-optic cable boxes and another plant that manufactures steel cables, some of which have been used on the international space station. Profits from these industries have been reinvested. Some Indian groups are investing current gaming profits into more diversified businesses.[119]

Interestingly, a 2000 poll of registered voters nationwide found that three-fourths felt that Indian nations should be permitted to use reservation lands to develop such enterprises as casinos, gas stations, and golf courses.[120] Still, white investors, lenders, and management firms have claimed a large share of the revenues from many of the gambling operations. One federal government investigation found that many tribes had been victims of economic exploitation, theft, and embezzlement by white management firms.[121]

Other economic opportunities have been rejected by Indian leaders. For example, in recent years many reservation leaders have been approached to provide landfill space for out-of-state garbage or nuclear waste. Reservations are attractive to waste management companies because of their low population density and because they are not generally subject to state environmental regulations or state taxes. In addition, enforcement of federal pollution regulations has often been lax on reservations. Most tribes have rejected the offers. One Rosebud Sioux leader stated, "Here it is, almost the twenty-first century, and we're still fighting the invaders, only now they're trying to make us take their trash."[122] The widespread problem of government and private dumping in communities populated by Americans of color is documented by a growing body of research. Such dumping is often a type of "environmental racism."

EDUCATION

The first extended experiences of subordinated Native Americans with white-dominated education came early in the reservation period. Influential whites supported education as the channel of forced acculturation to white culture. In white-controlled schools, the "wild Indians"—as whites stereotyped them—could be "civilized." By 1887, 14,300 children were enrolled in 227 schools, most operated by the BIA or by religious groups.[123]

Still, by 1900, a modest percentage of Indian children were receiving any schooling in white-oriented schools. In the Southwest, perhaps one-fourth of the school-age children in the four decades after 1890 had experience with BIA and other boarding schools; a small percentage of the rest attended public schools. From the beginning, the BIA and mission schools were run according to an Anglo-conformity assimilationist approach. Intensive efforts were made to destroy Indian ways; students were punished for speaking their native languages. By the 1930s, some boarding schools were being replaced by day schools closer to home, and a bilingual policy was being discussed. Yet, even by 1945, large proportions of Indians were still not enrolled in formal schools.[124]

Enforced acculturation has been a recurring issue in BIA and local public schools, where white administrators and teachers have blamed educational problems on cultural differences and emphasized the contrast between the collective values of Indians and the individualism of white Americans. Many white teachers have attempted to make their pupils "less Indian." To this day, many school textbooks provide little to help Native American children identify with their own cultures.[125]

Partly because of organized protest since the 1960s, government aid for primary, adult, and vocational education has expanded substantially. Government attention has been refocused on local public and BIA schools, and many federal schools have developed Native American advisory boards, added Native Americans to their staffs, and added classes in native art, dance, and language. However, in the words of one AIM member, the central "curriculum taught in Indian schools [has] remained exactly the same, reaching exactly the same conclusions, indoctrinating children with exactly the same values as when the schools were staffed entirely by white people."[126]

The movement of many Native Americans to the cities has resulted in a decline in the proportion of children in BIA schools. By the late 1990s fewer than 10 percent of Indian children attended BIA schools. Most now attend local public schools. One Department of Education task force, most of whose members were Native Americans, concluded that local and federal educational systems have failed to meet the needs of Indian students. Their report cited the absence of an Indian perspective in the curricula, the loss of Indian language ability, the shift away from Indian spiritual values, and the racism of many white teachers and administrators. The report called for implementation of multicultural curricula that embody respect for Native American history and culture and for programs that guarantee that Native American students learn English well.[127]

As of the late 1990s, more than 134,000 Native Americans were enrolled in colleges nationwide.[128] While most of these students attended mostly white public colleges and universities, several thousand attended two dozen Native American–controlled community colleges, where greater efforts are made to integrate Indian history and culture into courses and where more attention is given to students' cultures. In addition, since the 1960s more than one hundred colleges and universities have begun to provide facilities for the study of Native American issues, such as by establishing American Indian Studies centers.[129]

Native Americans' educational attainment levels have remained below those of the general population. Some educational gains have been made since the 1960s. Nonetheless, by 1990 less than two-thirds of Native Americans over the age of twenty-five were high-school graduates, compared with three-fourths of all Americans in that age range.[130]

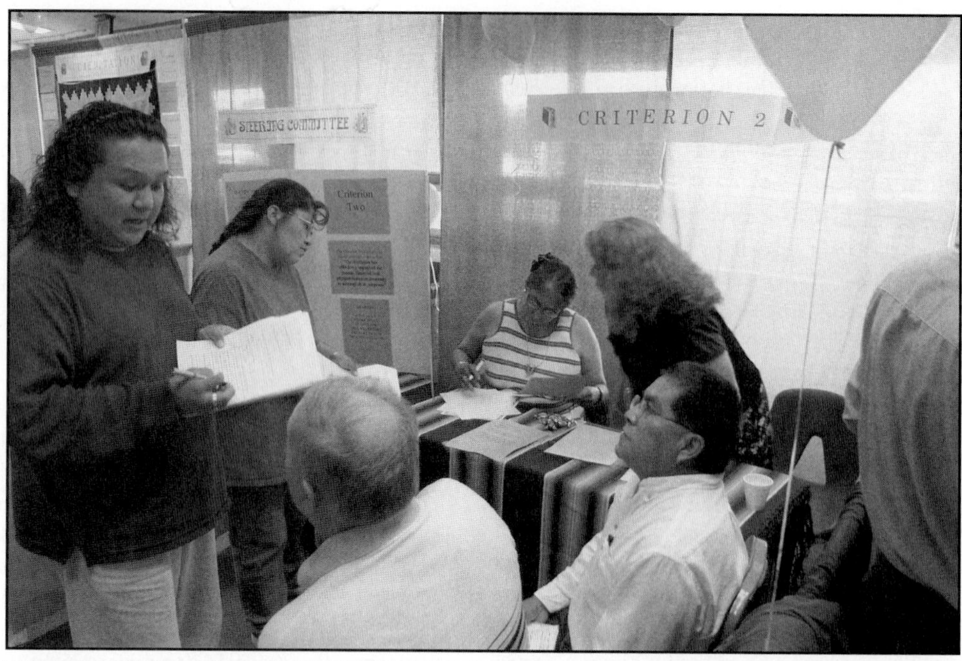

Students register at a Navaho college in the Southwest.

Moreover, Indian students in historically white public school systems have often been disproportionately placed in special education classes. The Department of Education task force report mentioned earlier put the proportion of Native American students who drop out after tenth grade at 36 percent, the highest of any racial or ethnic group and more than twice that of whites.[131]

RELIGION

As we have seen, Indian groups have periodically pressured museums and other facilities to return religious and art objects, particularly those that were illegally acquired. Many Indians have protested the display of Indian skeletal remains in museums and have called for the return of the remains for proper burial ceremonies. Following enactment of the Indian Arts and Crafts Act (1988) and Native American Graves Protection and Repatriation Act (1990), the U.S. government has required white-controlled museums to consult with the relevant Indian groups about returning these holdings.

In 1989 the Omaha tribe in Nebraska celebrated the return of their 400-year-old sacred pole, which had been in the possession of a Boston museum. However, as of spring 2001, the tribe was unable to raise funds for a facility to protect the sacred pole, which they regard as a living person, as Umon'hon'ti ("venerable man").[132] Problems of storage and maintenance are becoming common as more historical documents and sacred objects are returned to Native American groups that lack the economic and other resources to adequately house these highly valued objects.

Pressures for acculturation to European American culture have been clear in the case of religion. The early white conquerors often attempted to convert those they stereotyped as "heathen Indians" to Christianity. With the reservation period came a jockeying among Christian denominations for control; reservations were often divided up among the Christian denominations. For a number of reasons, including fear of whites, many Native Americans became loosely affiliated with a Christian denomination.[133] Today, however, only a minority of Native Americans still identity themselves with Christian denominations.

Revitalization Movements as Protest

Colonized peoples have often lashed out at European oppressors by joining millenarian movements, often led by visionaries and oriented to a "golden age" in which supernatural events will change their oppressive conditions. Among the most famous Native American millenarian movements were the Ghost Dance groups that emerged on the Great Plains. In the 1870s the prophet Wodziwob told of a vision in which the ancestors of Native America came on a train to Earth with explosive force, after which the Earth swallowed up the whites. A number of Native American groups joined in the movement in the hope of salvation from white oppression. The movement declined when the cataclysm failed to occur. It experienced a resurgence in the late 1880s when the new prophet Wovoka told of a vision that ordered him to found another Ghost Dance religion. Religious fervor spread through the Plains tribes. The cooperation among all Native Americans that Wovoka advocated did increase solidarity, but the movement was suppressed by white officials who were disturbed by the resurgence of millenarianism.[134]

Long used by individual Indian practitioners to treat sickness, peyote rituals became a group religion in the 1880s and spread throughout the Plains between 1880 and 1900. This new religion reflected an ambivalence toward Christianity. Rituals involved singing and praying but were distinctive in the visionary experiences induced by eating peyote (a hallucinogenic cactus plant).[135] Attacks by Christian missionaries and government officials on the religious movement welded believers together, and in 1918 the Native American Church was formally incorporated as an association of Christian groups protecting the Sacrament of Peyote. By the 1920s white legislators in seven states had passed anti-peyote laws, and the BIA had issued proclamations banning its use. In the 1930s the commissioner of Indian affairs finally came to the defense of indigenous religions and allowed the resurgence of the old ways.[136] By the 1960s, 40 percent of Native Americans on some reservations were Native American Church members.[137] Today, the Native American Church has about 250,000 members in two dozen states, in many tribal groups, and many other adherents in Mexico and Canada. The legality of the sacred peyote sacrament was not assured until the Religious Freedom Restoration Act was passed in the mid-1990s.

In contrast to Christianity, most traditional religious beliefs and practices of Native Americans are not exclusive; a person can be a Christian and a traditional believer. Because of this, a great variety of traditional and Christian religious practices now coexist among Indian groups.

Questioning Christianity

Using the standard of their own religious beliefs, numerous Native Americans have criticized Christianity as a crude religion stressing blood, crucifixion, and bureaucratized charity rather than practicing true sharing and compassion. Native American leaders often stress that Europeans are newcomers who sharply accelerated war and conflict in North America and mostly betrayed the Indians who aided them in becoming established. In addition, Europeans and their cultural ways have greatly polluted the surrounding environment.[138]

Today, many Native Americans argue that remedies for environmental damage lie in recognizing the superiority of Native American religious values, including a respect for the environment and a strong sense of community. This is an example of the role of oppositional cultures in U.S. society (see Chapter 2). Indian respect for land and ecology is strongly rooted in ancient cultures and has long been a basis for opposition to the dominant European American culture's land-use values. In recent years many whites have come to recognize the validity and importance of the Native American approach to respecting and protecting the natural environment.

Assimilation and Colonialism

Theoretical analysis in the field of racial and ethnic relations has long neglected the condition and experiences of Native Americans. The classical external colonialism model applies to Native Americans' encounters with Europeans, making this group distinct among U.S. racial and ethnic groups. In the earliest period, Native American societies on the Atlantic Coast saw their lands seized and their members driven off or killed by outsiders. The primary

European strategy was to remove or destroy the indigenous peoples who stood in the way of settlement. This process prevailed as European Americans moved westward from the Atlantic over the next several centuries. A policy of genocide often preceded, or coexisted with, a reservation policy.

Assimilation Perspectives

Some white observers have argued that the opportunity to assimilate is more open for Native Americans than for other people of color.[139] In the 1920s and 1930s, even a few Native American professionals argued that Native Americans should voluntarily follow the lead of the white immigrant groups and blend quietly into the European American culture.

Applying an assimilation model to Native Americans, one might focus on the extent to which traditional Indian cultures have undergone Europeanization. Schools and missions in the nineteenth century brought changes in religion, language, and dress styles to many groups. Other changes, such as land-ownership orientations, have also been substantial. Assimilationists cite the cultural adaptations of many Indians as evidence of movement toward gradual inclusion in the dominant culture but argue that Indian cultural traditions are major barriers to further acculturation.[140]

Living patterns and the sense of Native American identity today vary widely. For example, the Sioux and Navaho have a strong group identity, whereas certain other groups have for the most part lost their old ways and identities. Some reservation groups, such as the western Pueblos, the Navaho, and the Sioux, confine their social contacts substantially to people of their group; others, such as a significant segment of the Blackfeet in Montana, have intermarried with whites and substantially acculturated to European American ways. Some small California tribes, such as the Nomlaki and the Yuki, have "forgotten ancient customs, abandoned the native language, and look upon themselves more as extended families than as members of any particular tribe."[141]

The intensive, often forced, acculturation of Native Americans has failed to destroy Native American cultures. Cultural survival despite extremely unfavorable conditions is evident in the persistence of traditional Native American languages, which has been significant. An estimated 155 Native American languages are still spoken in the United States today, although many are spoken by only a few people. In 1990 the U.S. Congress finally passed the Native American Languages Act, which commits the government to working with Native Americans to "ensure the survival of these unique cultures and languages."[142] This marked a clear reversal of earlier government programs that openly sought to destroy Indian languages.

Structural assimilation at other than low-paid job levels in the economy has come slowly for Native Americans. Movement into the economic mainstream did not begin until the urban migration of the past few decades. Still, urban integration has often involved less-well-paid blue-collar positions and inadequate housing conditions. Some political integration has also taken place in towns and cities.

Structural integration at the primary-group level with white families has come slowly, although it is greater in urban areas than on reservations. One study in Spokane, Washington found little social integration of Native Americans into white voluntary associations in that area. Some shift can be seen in urban family patterns, which today often involve less emphasis on extended families than in the past. In numerous areas intermarriage with whites is on the rise. One Los Angeles study found that one-third of the married Native American respondents had white spouses. Census data have shown a similar pattern among urban Native Americans nationwide, although the rural rate of intermarriage is about half that in urban areas. Intermarriages between members of different Native American groups have also become common in the cities.[143]

An assimilationist theorist might argue that adaptation has occurred on Milton Gordon's other dimensions of assimilation (attitude-receptional, behavior-receptional, and identificational assimilation). Some movement can be glimpsed in the area of white attitudes; the traditional stereotyping of Native Americans by whites appears to have declined somewhat on some dimensions. Blatant discrimination appears to have decreased in certain sectors of the society. Still, as we have seen in the sections on economy, education, and politics, many types of direct and indirect discrimination continue to restrict Native Americans today. And the stereotypical use of Indian logos and mascots by sports teams persists.

Native Americans dance at a recent Pow Wow in New York.

Attachment to ancestral identity seems particularly strong among those who have predominantly Native American ancestry. A number of organizations, including the National Congress of American Indians and the National Indian Education Association, have tried to build a "pan-Indian identity" and promote unity across many tribes. Since the 1980s, regular pan-Indian conferences and Pow Wows have been held in all regions of the United States. Still, local group membership remains very important for many Native Americans, and most on reservation lands identify themselves in local terms, such as Navaho or Sioux, rather than in pan-Indian terms.[144] The strongest pan-Indian identity has developed in urban areas, where intergroup contacts and intermarriage are common.

One study found that Native Americans in Los Angeles have experienced a degree of spatial assimilation as evidenced by some residential dispersion within predominantly white neighborhoods. Yet many urban Native Americans are scattered among low-income neighborhoods populated by poor whites and other people of color.[145] Historically, when Indians have moved from reservations to cities, their ties to traditional tribal cultures have weakened in the urbanization process. However, increased self-determination on reservations has sparked a degree of "retraditionalization." Many city dwellers have thus returned to their home reservations to participate in traditional ceremonies and gatherings, thereby countering some of the urban pressures for assimilation to the dominant culture. Two countervailing trends can thus be seen, one decreasing ties to traditional cultures and another increasing ties. These trends are accentuated by the growing numbers of people who are now willing to recognize and assert their Native American ancestry.[146]

Power-Conflict Perspectives

Because of the colonial history of Native Americans, some theorists have persuasively argued that power-conflict models are particularly relevant to the Native American experience. Analysts such as Robert Blauner cite Native Americans as a clear case of an externally colonized minority.[147]

Power-conflict analysis accents the deception, genocide, and land theft that were part of the subordination process. Much assimilation rhetoric—"civilizing the Indians"—was a cover for aggressive exploitation by land-hungry whites. Treaties and laws that allowed individual Native Americans to become "citizens" only after meeting such criteria as accepting individual land allotments involved great pressure, even coercion and force. Unlike assimilation analysts, power-conflict analysts look at the broad sweep of the acculturation process and see the *force* behind much of it. This theme is evident, for example, in the statement by the commissioner of Indian affairs in 1879:

> Indians are essentially conservative, and cling tenaciously to old customs and hate all changes: Therefore the government should *force* them to scatter out on farms, break up their tribal organizations,

> dances, ceremonies, and tomfoolery; take from them their hundreds of useless ponies, which afford the means of indulging in their wandering, nomadic habits, and give them cattle in exchange, and compel them to labor or to *accept the alternative of starvation*.[148]

On the reservations, forced acculturation was often the rule in missions and boarding schools, where children were isolated from their families.

Since the 1970s some Native American children have even been removed from their homes to white foster homes or institutions. White social workers have sometimes argued that the homes of poor Native Americans are not "fit" places for these children. Anthropologist Shirley Hill Witt has written of one Mormon child-placement program that aggressively sought the placement of Native American children. A former president of the Mormon church reportedly stated the following:

> When you go down on the reservations and see these hundreds of thousands of Indians living in the dirt and without culture or refinement of any kind, you can hardly believe it. Then you see these boys and girls [placed in Mormon homes] playing the flute, the piano. All these things bring about a normal culture.[149]

It is ironic that white culture should be held up as the "normal culture" against which poor Native Americans are judged, because the poverty in the lives of Native Americans is substantially the result of whites' destruction of Native American resources, theft of land, and discrimination. The Indian Child Welfare Act, passed in 1978, has gradually achieved a significant reduction in the number of Native American children removed from their parents and placed in non–Native American homes.

Power-conflict analysts accent the one-way character of assimilation pressures. A study of Native American college students at the University of Oklahoma found that success in college was linked with two different sets of factors. Those who had done well in high school and on college entrance tests tended to do well at the university. Significantly, those with a strong Native American identity were more likely than assimilated Native Americans to fail and drop out, regardless of their academic ability. The white-oriented university context is particularly problematic. The changes that are expected are typically unidirectional: The Native American student (like other students of color) is expected to conform to the Eurocentric college environment. As a rule, historically white institutions do not change significantly to reflect the cultures and needs of Native American students.[150]

At all educational levels, Native American children often face great acculturation pressures; many capitulate to some degree, adopting some white stereotypes of themselves or behaving in Anglo-preferred ways. This behavior can damage the inner self and create great stress. Caught between their native culture and Anglo pressures, some even commit suicide.[151]

A colonialism analyst would likely stress that many Native Americans remain isolated politically and geographically—on the reservations, in rural areas, or in segregated urban areas. Many remain colonized on their own lands. This is reminiscent of external colonialism. Whites are often ignorant of Native American conditions. In Oklahoma there has been a prevalent white misconception that the reservation Cherokee group is dying out. Yet the group is one of the largest in the nation, holding strongly to its language and traditional values.[152] By denying the existence of viable and enduring Native American communities, whites can ignore their Native American neighbors and the persisting problems rooted in colonialism.

Perhaps the strongest argument for the continuing relevance of a colonialism model can be found in the data we examined on Native American income, employment, housing, education, and political participation. Although there have been some important gains, many Native Americans remain on the lower rungs of the socioeconomic ladder. Many in rural areas and central cities live in poverty; reservations have long had high unemployment rates. To a disproportionate degree, Native Americans in urban areas have had to face low-wage jobs, absentee landlords, and racial discrimination.

Many Native Americans are fighting back aggressively against the vestiges of colonialism, such as the racist symbols used by many sports teams and the waste dumping that constitutes environmental racism. A renaissance of Native American cultures can be seen in the many protest movements and Pow Wows in recent decades. We also see a resurgence in the strong self-determination efforts of many Indian nations and in the gaming and other economic development projects on and near reservations. We see growing numbers of Americans reclaiming their Native American identities publicly and returning to reservations for group celebrations and rituals.

Power-conflict analysts are the most likely to emphasize the importance of this struggle against white pressures and oppression. Resistance and resurgence are rooted in the historical cultures of Native American tribes, the ancient traditional cultures that have often emphasized harmony with the natural world and the foolishness of a self-indulgent individualism and hyper-materialism. Native American groups' traditional cultures provide a valuable source of the fundamentally humanitarian, earth-centered values that may be declining in the larger U.S. society.

In a recent commentary, Richard Williams, a historian and executive director of the American Indian College Fund, has argued that over the past several decades American Indians have "made their return from near annihilation to revival and renaissance in one of the greatest survival stories in all of human history." Since the 1960s, efforts to organize Native Americans nationwide to force the government to uphold treaties and respect Indian rights have brought a dramatic revival of Native Americans as a group. "For the first time," Williams notes, the government is "being held accountable to its own laws and treaties with Indian nations under its own legal system."[153] As we noted previously, various federal laws passed since 1970 have indeed facilitated self-determination for Indian tribes and have helped to improve education, health, and other programs on and off reservations. Growing numbers of Native Americans have reasserted their rights and their identities as part of the evolving mix in this increasingly multiracial and multiethnic nation.

SUMMARY

Native Americans today remain highly diverse. There are many different rural and urban groups, but most are still subordinated in numerous ways to whites who have greater economic, political, and bureaucratic (BIA) power. Native Americans are the descendants of the only groups that did *not* immigrate to North America in the past five hundred years. They were brought into the European American sphere over a long period, during which many Native Americans fought fierce battles with the invaders. Genocide, the destruction of all Native Americans, was often the goal of the white invaders. The many battles with whites were followed by the present reservation era, with its long line of white bureaucrats and officials seeking to dominate or exploit Native Americans.

Often stereotyped by whites as culturally or intellectually inferior, Native Americans have long suffered and still face exploitation and discrimination in the economic, political, religious, and educational spheres. In the economic sphere, they have had their lands taken, they have been forced by job circumstances to relocate to often inhospitable cities, and their mobility has been limited by continuing racial discrimination. While significant economic gains have occurred in recent decades, for many Native Americans on and off reservations this progress has been slow and has yet to be matched by substantial political progress. The BIA remains an intrusive federal bureaucracy, although it has become more progressive and now employs many more Native American officials than in earlier years. Recently, the U.S. government has been investigated for serious mismanagement of Indian trust accounts.

For decades, protest organizations have underscored the strengths and discontent of Native Americans. In recent years, activists have emphasized the cultural uniqueness of Native American respect for the human community and for all aspects of the natural environment. Many Indian groups have organized to regain fishing rights and lands that were stolen by whites. Calls for maintaining cultural distinctiveness and recognizing the many virtues of Native American cultures have been heard. Vigorously opposing celebrations of Columbus's "discovery of America," Native Americans have called attention to the brutality of past and continuing colonization. Native Americans inhabited America prior to any European settlement or government and thus have a unique position in regard to citizenship. Indeed, some Indians argue that they are *not* citizens of the United States nor do they want to be. Because they predate the European invasions, they are citizens of their own long-established nations.

The desire for full recognition of their sovereignty is strong for most Native American nations. While the U.S. government has made moderate progress in returning land and control of various aspects of life to many Native American groups, most still have a neocolonial relationship to the federal government. In recent years many Native American nations have pressed for a government-to-government relationship that would replace this current neocolonial relationship with the government of the United States.[154]

7 African Americans

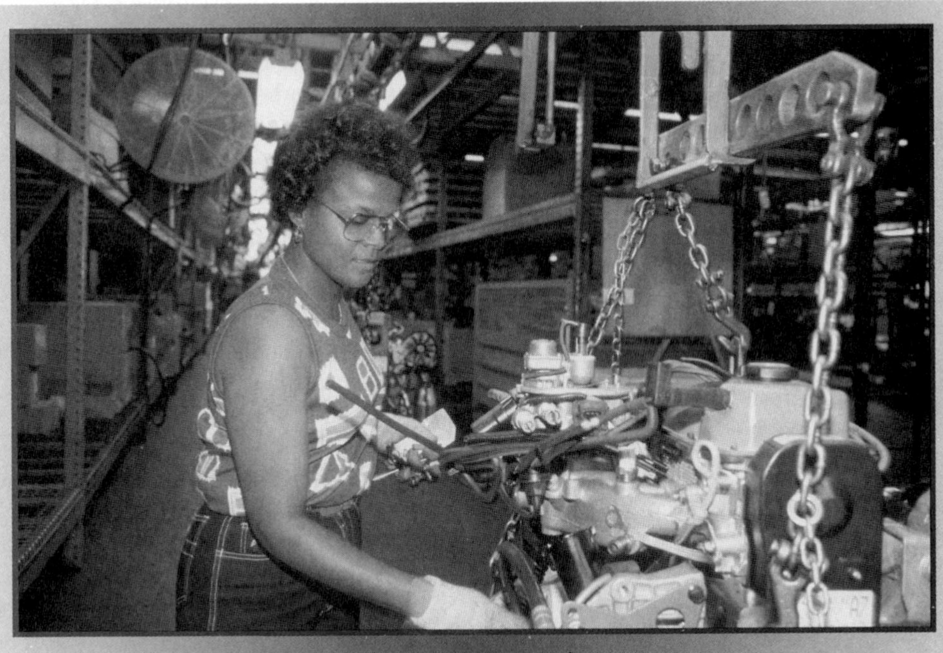

A few years ago one of the nation's talented African American journalists, Leanita McClain, committed suicide. Just thirty-two years old, she had won major awards and was the first African American to serve on the *Chicago Tribune*'s editorial board. Why did such a talented person commit suicide? The answer is doubtless complex, but one factor looms large: the problem of coping with an often discriminatory white world. Reviewing her life, one writer notes the conformity to white ways that is faced by black female employees in historically white workplaces: "Black women consciously choose their speech, their laughter, their walk, their mode of dress and car. They trim and straighten their hair.... They learn to wear a mask."[1] Black Americans in the corporate world not only face subtle and blatant discrimination but also suffer from the intense pressure to adapt to the values and ways of that overwhelmingly white world.

Many African Americans have family trees in North America that extend back to the 1600s and 1700s, well before the American Revolution. They were among the first immigrants to North America, and they are far older as a group than many white immigrant groups. That a people who have been here almost as long as the first

European settlers should still find themselves so discriminated against, so unwelcome in many traditionally white institutions and places, is a problematical dilemma for the present day and also for the future of this nation.

FORCED MIGRATION AND SLAVERY

The African American experience is an example of the slave-importation end of the migration continuum (Chapter 2). Unlike white immigrants who, for the most part, came to North America voluntarily, most Africans had no choice; they came enslaved and in chains. Their destinations were generally determined by European and European American slave traders and buyers. Many whites saw this enslavement as a solution to the demand for cheap agricultural labor on farms and plantations throughout the Americas.

The European Trade in Human Beings

Dutch and French companies early dominated the forcible importation of Africans; England entered the trade in the 1600s. Some Africans were enslaved directly by Europeans raiding local societies. In other cases, African coastal rulers, motivated by greed or fear of European firepower, succumbed to slave-trade pressure and became go-betweens serving European slave traders. Still, the Atlantic slave trade was invented and dominated by Europeans and, later, European Americans.[2]

Once captured, those enslaved were often chained in corrals called barracoons, where they were branded and held for transportation. The voyage was a living hell. Enslaved Africans were chained together with little room for movement. The horror was summed up by one young African:

> I was soon put down under the decks, and there I received such a salutation in my nostrils as I had never experienced in my life: so that with the loathsomeness of the stench, and crying together, I became so sick and low that I was not able to eat, nor had I the least desire to taste any thing.... On my refusing to eat, one of them held me fast by the hands, and laid me across, I think the windlass, and tied my feet, while the other flogged me severely.[3]

Suicides were common among enslaved Africans, and uprisings brought death to Africans and white sailors alike. The widely believed white myth that Africans only passively endured their fate is contradicted by 155 recorded shipboard uprisings by Africans between 1699 and 1845; many other violent attacks on slavers doubtless went unrecorded.[4]

In 1619, twenty Africans were brought to Jamestown by a Dutch ship, and by the mid-1600s the slave status of Africans had been fully institutionalized in North American colonial laws. From the mid-1600s to the 1860s, virtually all Africans were imported for involuntary servitude. Estimates of the number brought alive into the Western Hemisphere range from 10 to 15 million. Most were brought to the West Indies and South America; only 5 percent were brought directly to North America. From the 1600s to the Civil War, an estimated half million Africans were brought into the colonies and, later, the United States.[5] In addition to those who arrived alive in the Americas, millions more died in the process of enslavement and transportation across the Atlantic.

A number of prominent European Americans in the early period of this nation were wealthy because they *owned* other human beings. These included George Washington, James Madison, and Thomas Jefferson. In an early draft of the Declaration of Independence, the young Jefferson actually attacked slavery, but he was careful to blame it on England's King George. However, as a result of other slave owners' opposition, this anti-slavery language was not included in the final version of the Declaration. One of the greatest democratic manifestos in world history was severely compromised by the unwillingness of whites to include African Americans within its powerful framework.[6]

Slaveholding interests forced the full recognition of slavery in several sections of the U.S. Constitution. These included a provision that each slave be counted as three-fifths of a person for the calculation of congressional representation (for whites); a fugitive-slave provision; and the postponement of prohibition of slave importation to 1808. Although the slave trade was officially abolished as of 1808, the ban was not seriously enforced. Thousands of Africans were still forcibly imported.[7]

Most white families did not own enslaved African Americans. In 1860, only one-fourth of the 1.6 million white families in the South owned 3.8 million

African Americans. A majority of those enslaved were held on larger farms and plantations, where they performed most of the labor and produced agricultural products to be marketed for the profit of slaveholders and their many descendants. Most plantation owners were agricultural capitalists attuned to trade for profit. The wealth and power of the slaveholding gentry rose dramatically as a result of this slave-based agriculture. This white plantation gentry dominated the U.S. economy and the federal government from the late 1700s to the 1850s.[8] Power-conflict theorists emphasize the government's role in the creation of oppressive racial arrangements (Chapter 2). For centuries the U.S. government and southern and border state governments passed laws to benefit the powerful slaveholding gentry and reinforce the racialized definition of and oppression of black Americans.

The Lives of Africans under Slavery

There has long been a magnolias-and-mint-julep mystique about the slave system, which lingers on, particularly in racist Hollywood movies such as the ever popular *Gone with the Wind*. According to this fictional white imagery, residing in a big plantation house with multiple columns surrounded by magnolia trees, a paternalistic white master "cared kindly" for the "contented, happy slaves."

However, slave autobiographies describe the brutality and oppressiveness of living conditions. Most rose before dawn, then worked in the house or the fields until dark. Food, clothing, and housing were crude and often inadequate. The whip and chains were the common and brutal mechanisms of control. Numerous white masters were extremely brutal and violent, such as the owner of one African American who told about moving from Georgia: "Then he chains all the slaves round the necks and fastens the chains to the hosses and makes them walk all the way to Texas. My mother and my sister had to walk. Emma was my sister. Somewhere on the road it went to snowing, and Massa wouldn't let us wrap anything round our feet. We had to sleep on the ground, too, in all that snow."[9] African Americans could not legally protest such extreme brutality, for slaveholders controlled the state militias and the courts.[10]

Although many analyses of slavery do not discuss the role of enslaved women, it is important to note that the U.S. slave system included African American women and children as well as men. Most women, as one put it, "worked in the fields every day from 'fore daylight to almost plumb dark."[11] The brutality of many slaveholders was not tempered when it came to the women: "Beat women! Why sure he [master] beat women. Beat women just like men. Beat women naked and wash them down in brine."[12] African American women were often the victims of coercion and violence, including rape by white overseers and slaveholders.

Whites, including many social scientists, have long been preoccupied with black families; contemporary problems of poverty and so-called "broken" families have been traced back to the conditions of slavery. Until recently, supportive family life was viewed as nonexistent for the majority of enslaved African Americans.

Yet there is historical evidence that paternalistic slave owners fostered families—if often in their own self interest—and, most significantly, that enslaved African Americans worked hard to preserve their families to the extent possible under the extreme conditions. Typical families were protective, supportive environments that helped enslaved African Americans to survive. Those enslaved frequently deserted masters in family units; the desire to find lost loved ones was a common cause of desertion. In an extensive analysis of enslaved black families on plantations, Herbert Gutman found that enslaved women were expected to have children by one man; that the names of fathers were given to sons; that adoption was commonly used to ease disruption caused by death and the breakup of families; and that many families managed to persist over generations. Of course, the threat to the black family was great. Marriages were likely to be disrupted at some point, by death or sale of a spouse by the slaveholder. An accurate picture of the slave family must include the strong African American attempts to maintain family stability and the frequent disruption of families by callous slaveholders.[13]

Faced with physical torture and white attempts to eradicate their cultures, the many peoples of Africa among those enslaved—the Yorubas, Akans, Ibos, Angolans, and dozens of other groups—became a single African American people and forged a distinctive African American culture.[14] Drawing on deep African spiritual roots, these new Americans shaped their own religion, their own art and music, and their own philosophical and political thinking about racial oppression, liberation, and social justice. In the colonies and later in the United States, pressures on African Americans to conform to the dominant Eurocentric culture forced them to become *bicultural*, to know the dominant culture as well as their own. Since the days of slavery, African Americans have struggled to maintain what Mitchell and Feagin, among others, have termed an "oppositional culture," a culture part African and part an African American adaptation to the concrete history of white oppression.[15] This culture has provided the foundation for active black resistance to white oppression since the seventeenth century.

Active Resistance

Enslaved African Americans often had to be submissive, but this was only one response to domination. An assertive reaction grounded in African American culture was common. Many observed the servile etiquette when necessary, but many also rebelled in dozens of small and large ways.

Antislavery action took several forms, including passive and violent resistance, flight to the North, and psychological withdrawal. Those fleeing slavery became a problem for slave owners that was serious enough to generate the fugitive-slave provision in the U.S. Constitution and subsequent fugitive-slave laws. The most famous route to freedom was the Underground Railroad, the network of those formerly enslaved and other anti-slavery Americans, black and white, who passed along tens of thousands to the North between the 1830s and the Civil War. One famous "conductor" on this railroad was a former slave, Harriet Tubman, one of the greatest of U.S. heroes. She went south nineteen times, risking her life to deliver more than three hundred people to freedom. Southerners committed to the "happy Sambo" view of black workers sometimes went to absurd lengths to explain the fugitive-slave problem. White physician Samuel Cartwright, incredibly, attributed the problem to a strange disease, "drapetomania," by which he meant the unhealthy tendency to flee one's owner![16]

Nonviolent resistance sometimes took the form of a slow working pace, feigned illness, and strikes. Violent resistance was directed at the property and persons of slave owners or overseers. Tools, livestock, fields, and farmhouses were destroyed; white slavemasters and overseers were killed. In addition to mutinies aboard slave ships, there is evidence of 250 slave revolts or conspiracies to revolt during the slavery period. Newspapers of the day provide considerable evidence that whites feared uprisings.[17]

In 1800 a group of enslaved African Americans led by Gabriel Prosser gathered weapons and planned to march on Richmond. The Virginia governor took action to protect the state capital from the rebels. One thousand armed African Americans rendezvoused, but a heavy rain cut them off from the city, and they disbanded. Betrayed, the leaders were arrested; at least thirty-five, including Prosser, were put to death.[18]

In 1831, Nat Turner, a self-taught, religious man, led a rebellion in Southampton County, Virginia. Seventy enslaved people recruited by Turner attacked, and dozens of whites were killed. The freedom fighters were eventually defeated by hundreds of white soldiers. Turner escaped but was later captured and executed.[19] These leaders of slave revolts took seriously the principle of "liberty and justice for all" and could be included among U.S. revolutionary heroes. Sterling Stuckey has shown that African culture and religion were a major source of the black revolutionaries' resistance-oriented philosophy and inclination to rebellion.[20]

These revolts contradicted the white apologists' notion of "happy slaves"; given the opportunity, those enslaved sometimes did resist violently. Slavery wasted the lives and energies of millions of African Americans and denied most any opportunity to create wealth for their descendants. Slavery also brought major costs for whites and their descendants. In the southern and border states, whites lost much of their own humanity and morality, as well as much of their own freedom of speech and press, because of the legal controls and requirements of the totalitarian slave system. The nation as a whole lost as well from its failure to live up to its egalitarian ideals.

Many African Americans joined abolitionist organizations to work for the liberation of their brothers and sisters. Frederick Douglass, formerly enslaved himself, was an important leader among the abolitionists. In a July 4, 1852 speech in Rochester, New York, Douglass spoke eloquently: "What, to the American slave, is your Fourth of July?

I answer: A day that reveals to him, more than all other days of the year, the gross injustices and cruelty to which he is the constant victim. To him your celebration is a sham."[21] Another influential African American abolitionist was the former slave Isabella Van Wagener, better known as Sojourner Truth, who was enslaved in New York in the 1790s; in the mid-1800s she became an influential anti-slavery lecturer and an early advocate of women's rights. Black women played a key role in the anti-slavery movement.

Outside the Rural South

Between the 1600s and the early 1800s, many northern whites either owned African Americans or considered the U.S. slavery system to be legitimate. Significant numbers of enslaved African Americans could be found in northern states. Indeed, the wealth of many northern whites was built up with forced black labor, as well as the labor of European immigrants. Benjamin Ringer notes that "despite the early emancipation of slaves in the North, [racialized colonialism] remained there, not merely as fossilized remains but as a deeply ingrained coding for the future."[22] Consider Massachusetts, where slavery was legalized in 1641, right after Africans were brought in. Massachusetts merchants played a central role in the American slave trade. Not until the 1780s did public opinion and some court cases come together to abolish slavery in New England. Even then, it was not a recognition of the rights of African Americans that ended slavery, but pressure from white working people who objected to competition from enslaved labor. In New York, enslaved African Americans made up some 7 percent of the population by 1786. A statute of emancipation was not passed there until 1799, and it provided for only partial emancipation. A realization that slavery was long entrenched in the North's economic and legal system is essential for an understanding of the racial oppression (see Chapter 2) that African Americans still face today in the urban North.[23]

Before the Civil War, "Jim Crow" laws in the North enforced the segregation of ostensibly "free" African Americans in public transportation, hospitals, jails, schools, churches, and cemeteries. Racially segregated railroad cars were established first in Massachusetts. In northern cities, many whites enforced severe housing discrimination and segregated housing areas at a time when most southern cities had no comparable segregation because most southern African Americans lived in or near the residential areas of slavemasters.

Racist Ideologies and Stereotypes

Over time the dominant group in a racial hierarchy, such as white Americans in the United States, develops strong beliefs to rationalize their economic, social, and political position. For nearly four centuries—in pamphlets, books, and articles—white intellectuals, theologians, and politicians have devised theories of the biological, mental, and moral inferiority of African Americans in order to rationalize their exploitation of the latter.

Negative views of African peoples existed in Europe before the founding of the colonies, but until the 1700s these did not develop into a systematic racist ideology. Recall from Chapter 1 the eighteenth-century notions of a racist hierarchy that included a social construction of an "African race" as inferior to "Caucasians." Thomas Jefferson took up these European notions and developed a racist ideology that personified the moral dilemmas of whites in the eighteenth century: He wrote an indictment of slavery in the original draft of the Declaration of Independence, yet was the owner of two hundred human beings. Jefferson wrote of his strong opposition to interracial sex, yet he enslaved a black teenager, Sally Hemings, who, according to DNA evidence, probably bore him at least one child, whom he also enslaved.[24] (Until the DNA evidence revealed this likely relationship, most white commentators denied that he could have had children with Hemings.) Jefferson wrote of the inferiority of African Americans, and held many in slavery, yet he foresaw that they would ultimately have to be freed from slavery if the nation was to make progress. Still, he freed few of those he himself had enslaved, even at his death.[25]

Seeing African Americans as Inferior: White Stereotypes

At an early date, many whites considered the dark color of enslaved African Americans to be unusual and ugly. By the mid-1800s, racist defenders of slavery were portraying African Americans as an inferior, "apelike" human group. This was the same stereotyped image that Anglo-Protestants had applied earlier to Irish immigrants.[26] Many negative stereotypes have become widespread since the days of slavery. Black men and women have been alleged to have an offensive odor. Black women have been stereotyped as immoral; black men, as oversexed and potential rapists. Extreme white images of black sexuality may reflect deep white psychological problems with the idea and reality of "racial mixing." Much white guilt and anger may ultimately be linked to the historical fact that much interracial mixing before and after 1865 involved the forcible rape of black women by white men, particularly overseers and slave owners.

Patricia Williams, a distinguished law professor and author, has illustrated this point by relating the story of Austin Miller, her great-great-grandfather. Miller, a thirty-five-year-old white lawyer, bought Williams's eleven-year-old black great-great-grandmother Sophie and her parents. Soon Miller forced the child Sophie to become the mother of Williams's great-grandmother Mary. Like many African Americans, Williams must deal with the reality that her prominent white ancestor was not only a prominent lawyer but also a rapist and child molester.[27]

The Pseudoscience of "Intelligence" Testing

The theme of intellectual inferiority along racial lines has received much public attention since World War II. Earlier in the twentieth century, this theme was applied to white immigrants, who were considered to be very inferior in intelligence to native-born Anglo-Protestants, but in the past few decades the focus has been on Americans of color. For example, Arthur Jensen and Richard Herrnstein, along with a few other white social scientists, have alleged that differences in "intelligence test" (IQ) scores are not determined primarily by environmental factors such as education, socialization, racial discrimination, and socioeconomic circumstances, but reflect real genetic differences between black and white groups. They argue naively that differences in intelligence can be reliably measured by relatively brief paper-and-pencil and object (or symbol) manipulation tests that are inaccurately labeled "IQ tests." Groups with low social status or income are argued to be, on the average, intellectually and genetically inferior to groups with greater status and income levels simply because the former average lower scores on the so-called IQ tests. Some of these academics and writers argue that poor and rich Americans, or black and white Americans, have such different types of intelligence that they require different educational techniques. They also express concern about high black birthrates, which they believe will lower the collective national intelligence.[28] Richard Herrnstein and Charles Murray's best-selling book *The Bell Curve*, published in 1994, argued for the discredited theory that there are significant genetically determined differences in intelligence between black Americans and white Americans.[29]

Although the reactionary views of Jensen, Herrnstein, and Murray have been successfully refuted by many social scientists—especially their denial of environmental effects on test results—their notions about intelligence have spread to other academics and journalists and to politicians around the globe. For example, Michael Levin, a philosophy professor at a New York college, has cited Jensen's research on white and black intelligence to support his arguments against affirmative action.[30] In 1971, Patrick Buchanan, then an adviser to president Richard Nixon who was himself to become a Republican presidential candidate from 1992 to 2000, picked up on Herrnstein's arguments. In a memo to Nixon, Buchanan alleged that "every study" showed black groups had lower IQs than white groups and that Herrnstein's views about race and IQ provided "an intellectual basis" for considering cuts in certain government social programs.[31]

In the 1930s a number of social psychologists began seriously questioning whether IQ test results could be used as evidence of genetically determined differentials. They showed how white–black differences in IQ test scores reflected major differences in education, income, and living conditions. A number of studies showed that test scores of black children improved with better economic and educational environments. Strikingly, results from large-scale IQ testing revealed that black children and adults in some northern states scored higher than whites in some southern states.[32] Using the logic of Jensen, Herrnstein, and Murray, one would be forced to conclude that white southerners were mentally and "racially" inferior to black Northerners. Most such white analysts would doubtless avoid this interpretation; obviously they, as defenders of a theory of black IQ inferiority, do not wish to argue that data on IQ might actually show black intellectual superiority. Rather, they would accept an environmental explanation for uncomplimentary regional IQ-score differentials for whites. Differentials favoring whites are also most reasonably interpreted as reflecting environmental conditions, not genetic factors.

Some analysts have focused on the cultural bias—specifically, the white middle-class bias—inherent in traditional U.S. achievement and other psychometric tests (including IQ, SAT, and GRE tests), which measure only certain types of learned skills and certain acquired knowledge—skills and knowledge that are not equally available to all racial and ethnic groups because of centuries of discrimination and inadequate family incomes and educational facilities. Researchers have also found that achievement-test taking itself is a skill white middle-class children are more likely to possess because they and their parents are most familiar and experienced with such testing.[33]

The most fundamental problem for those who insist on racial differences is the equation of these test results with general intelligence. From the beginning, the so-called intelligence (IQ) tests have been intentionally misnamed. These tests measure only selected verbal, mathematical, or manipulative *skills*. Clearly, they do not measure many aspects of human abilities, such as creativity and imagination. They do not measure musical, artistic, farming, fishing, and many other skills that reflect human intelligence. They penalize those who do not spend their lives enmeshed in the culture of the test makers. Intelligence is much broader than what relatively short paper-and-pencil or symbol-manipulation tests can measure. Intelligence is more accurately defined as a complex ability to deal creatively with one's environment, whatever that environment may be. At best, only a very small portion of human intellectual ability can be revealed on any short test. Given this problem of what social scientists call the "validity" of a measure, the modest and brief IQ tests by no means reveal what the defenders of racial inequality claim that they do.[34]

Contemporary Anti-Black Prejudices and Stereotypes

To what extent does the white public still accept negative stereotypes of African Americans? In one 1990s nationwide opinion survey, 38 percent of the white respondents felt blacks were "more prone to violence than people of other races"; 35 percent felt that blacks preferred welfare over work; 13 percent felt that blacks were less intelligent "than people of other races." Three-fourths of the national sample of whites accepted at least one of eight stereotyped images of African Americans. The survey also found that the most prejudiced whites (those who accepted four or more anti-black stereotypes) tended to be older and less well educated than the population as a whole. However, education does not eradicate stereotyping and prejudice; two-thirds of white college graduates accepted some of the anti-black stereotypes. Recent surveys of whites continue to show that a majority still think in stereotypical terms about African Americans. An early 2000s survey of whites by Harvard researchers found that 58 percent agreed that one or more of these traits characterized African Americans: lazy, aggressive or violent, prefer to live on welfare, or complaining. One-third agreed with two or more of these negative traits.[35]

These negative, often hostile white stereotypes are harmful for African Americans across the spectrum of life experiences. For example, negative stereotypes can affect the health care they receive. In a survey of practicing psychiatrists, Doris Wilkinson found that "cultural conditioning to racial beliefs and attitudes ... pervades therapeutic contexts in which minority women are clients."[36] Another recent study used actors to portray black and white patients with certain coronary disease symptoms. Several hundred physicians were asked to view recorded interviews and patient data to assess the probability of coronary artery disease and suggest treatment. Blacks were less likely to be recommended for cardiac catheterization than were whites with the same dress, occupations, and medical histories. A 1999 study of lung cancer patients found that blacks were less likely to receive the best surgical treatment than whites.[37] Such studies suggest that doctors' stereotyped images of black patients—such as the views that they are not as intelligent or will not take as good care of themselves as white patients—may affect the kind of medical treatment they receive.

Most white Americans admit to pollsters that they hold some anti-black attitudes. In one National Opinion Research Center (NORC) survey, 59 percent of white respondents took an anti-black position on at least one of the following items: (1) Do you think there should be laws against marriages between blacks and whites?; (2) White people have a right to keep blacks out of their neighborhoods if they want to, and blacks should respect that right; (3) Blacks shouldn't push themselves where they are not wanted; (4) A law says that a homeowner can decide for himself whom to sell his house to, even if he prefers not to sell to blacks; (5) Do you think blacks get more attention from government than they deserve?[38] Education has some effect on these anti-black attitudes, but not as much as one might expect. While three-fourths of those whites with less than a high-school education took an anti-black position on one or more of the statements, about 58 percent of high-school and junior-college graduates, and 50 percent of college graduates, showed a similar pattern of anti-black responses. Only among those whites with some graduate education did a majority reject the anti-black position on all of these items.

Examining white views on social change, John McConahay has described what he calls "modern racism": the white view that black Americans have illegitimately challenged cherished white values and are making illegitimate demands for changes in racial relations. This white hostility is reflected in negative views of certain black actions and achievements. McConahay and his associates argue that the most extreme anti-black stereotypes and white opposition to all desegregation have to some extent been replaced by new prejudices and stereotypes.[39]

Unlike the racists of the 1950s who espoused segregation, many whites today publicly state their support for equality of opportunity. Most whites believe that serious racism is no longer widespread and that African Americans today have fully equal opportunities. Only one-third of whites in one recent NORC survey agreed that "blacks have worse jobs, income, and housing than white people ... mainly due to discrimination." Sixty percent disagreed with this statement. A survey for the National Conference found that a large majority of whites felt that blacks have an equal opportunity for a quality education and equal opportunities for skilled jobs.[40] Clearly, black and white Americans hold dramatically different views about the continuing reality of discrimination in the United States. In a survey in Pennsylvania, researchers found that "Eight of 10 blacks said they felt the differences in jobs, housing, and income were primarily due to discrimination. Most white people, on the other hand, said they thought the differences were due to a lack of will power or motivation."[41] Three-fourths of the black respondents thought the justice system was racially biased, compared with only one-fourth of the whites. Indeed, the majority of whites thought that discrimination against whites was now a serious problem.

A majority of whites also feel that black Americans are too demanding, paranoid, and pushy. A *Times-Mirror* national survey found that 51 percent of whites agreed that equal rights have been pushed too far in the United States, a proportion up from 42 percent only two years earlier.[42] In national surveys a majority of white Americans indicate opposition to government programs that would aggressively attack racial discrimination in employment, housing, or other areas of society. A majority of whites accept desegregation if it is defined as a few black employees at work, a few black students in the schoolroom, or a few black families in a large residential community. But more substantial desegregation achieved by vigorous government action is unacceptable to the majority.[43]

Do racial prejudices and stereotypes generate racial discrimination? One review of twenty-three research studies found that whites who express prejudice tend to be more likely to discriminate than those who do not and that whites "systematically alter their expressed racial attitudes and behaviors to appear in a more socially desirable—unprejudiced and egalitarian—light." The experimental research suggests that the increase in positive white racial attitudes during and since the 1960s–1970s has represented conformity to a more liberal climate rather than a basic change in racial attitudes.[44] Today, many whites continue to conceal their anti-black views in order to appear socially acceptable.

Recent research on white university students has found that attitudes expressed on short-answer survey items are often different from those expressed in reply to questions requiring detailed commentary. Recall that in one study cited in Chapter 1, some 80 percent of 451 students said they approved of marriages between blacks and whites when the issue was presented in a brief survey item. However, when a similar but smaller group was interviewed in depth, the proportion that unequivocally approved of racial intermarriage dropped to just 30 percent. Given time to explain, the majority expressed reservations about marriages across the color line.[45] Seen from this perspective, the apparent decrease in anti-black prejudices and stereotyping among whites over the past several decades may reflect, for many whites at least, increased concern for public or social acceptability rather than abandonment of racial prejudices and stereotypes.

Levels of anti-black discrimination also remain high. One recent study asked 2,000 black respondents about several settings, such as the workplace, where they might face discrimination. Seventy percent of the female and 84 percent of the male respondents reported encountering discrimination in at least one setting. The majority reported discrimination in at least three settings.[46] In a 1997 Gallup survey of black respondents, 45 percent of the total sample, and 70 percent of black men under the age of 35, reported that they had experienced discrimination in one or more of five areas just *within the past month*.[47]

INTERRACIAL CONFLICT

Antiblack Violence

Lynching is one of the most brutal forms of collective violence that human beings engage in. It is a group killing carried out by vigilantes seeking revenge for an actual or imagined crime by the victim. Before the Civil War, most lynchings in the United States were carried out by white mobs against whites. After the Civil War, lynching became a means of keeping African Americans subordinated, "in their place" as white southerners often said. Table 7.1 shows the racialized pattern of recorded lynchings.[48]

TABLE 7.1 RECORDED LYNCHINGS, 1882–1956

YEARS	WHITE VICTIMS	BLACK VICTIMS
1882–1891	751	732
1892–1901	381	1,124
1902–1911	76	707
1912–1921	53	533
1922–1931	23	201
1932–1941	10	95
1942–1951	2	25
1952–1956	0	3

There have been other lynchings since the 1950s. In 1981, in Mobile, Alabama, Klan members hung a black man, and in 1998, white supremacists dragged James Byrd, Jr., to death near Jasper, Texas. Experts estimate that, from the end of the Civil War to the present, at least half of all lynchings of African Americans have gone unrecorded. The actual number has been estimated to be at least 6,000 for the decades since the Civil War. In many periods there was an "inclination to abandon such relatively mild and decent ways of dispatching the [lynch] mob's victim as hanging and shooting in favor of burning, often roasting over slow fires, after preliminary mutilations and tortures ... a disposition to revel in the infliction of the most devilish and prolonged agonies."[49]

Lynchings are a show of force by whites, who may be fearful of black assertiveness. White lynchers expect that brutal lynchings will discourage black challenges of racist practices such as segregation. Until recently, white lynchers have seldom been punished for these terrible crimes, and many lynchings have taken place with the acquiescence or participation of the police. Some lynchings have been public; others are carried out in secret. Hundreds of black citizens—and some white civil rights workers—in the South were killed by whites in secret attacks between the 1940s and the 1960s.[50]

Beginning in the World War I period, many Black southerners moved to northern cities to escape oppressive conditions, but in the North they often met more violence. In a white riot in 1900 in New York City, for example, a substantially Irish American police force encouraged working-class whites to attack black residents. One of the most serious white-dominated race riots occurred in 1917 in East St. Louis. White workers, who saw new black workers as a job threat, attacked a black community. Thirty-nine black residents and nine of the white attackers were killed. This riot was followed in 1919 by a string of white riots from Chicago to Charleston.[51]

Opposition to black workers searching for better jobs has long been a cause of white violence. Black workers often become scapegoats whenever a serious economic downturn threatens white livelihoods.

African Americans, as well as Asian, Latino, and Jewish Americans, have been inaccurately blamed for economic troubles by white workers who have little understanding of how a capitalistic system works. For example, many do not recognize that job cutbacks and job displacement are often the result of decisions by white employers and investors to export jobs to low-wage labor areas outside the United States in pursuit of higher profits.

White supremacy groups have long been in the forefront of those who blame black, Latino, Asian, and Jewish Americans for problems rooted elsewhere. The Ku Klux Klan, a leading white supremacy group for most of the past century, gained strength in the 1920s and again since the 1970s. Other racist groups, such as the White Aryan Resistance (WAR), have emerged in recent decades. One 2000 count found that more than 602 Klan, neo-Nazi, racist-skinhead, and other hate groups, involving at least 25,000 white Americans, were active in 50 states. Some groups make extensive use of white supremacist Web sites (at least 366 Internet sites in 2002), thereby increasing the potential readers of their racist literature. They often augment their supremacist ideologies with white-power music or neo-pagan religious doctrines and rituals. In addition to the activists, some 200,000 more whites are thought to be passive supporters, including those who buy supremacist publications.[52] White supremacy groups have been involved in numerous attacks on and murders of blacks and other minorities, although until 1987 no supremacist group had been found guilty of such violence. In that year a court awarded $7 million to the family of Michael Donald, the 1981 victim of a Klan lynching.[53]

In recent years, there have been numerous hate-motivated murders and hate-inspired assaults, including many against African Americans. The Southern Poverty Law Center's Klanwatch, which conducts a comprehensive hate crime survey, estimates that fewer than half of all hate crimes are reported to police and that many hate crimes that are reported are not classified as such.[54] In one Iowa incident, a black doctor was awakened in the night when a firebomb was thrown through his bedroom window. He later found the word "nigger" scraped on his car door. In a Texas incident, the home of a black family was pelted with eggs and their car was set ablaze in the street outside their home.[55] In June 1998, a black man, James Byrd, Jr., was killed near Jasper, Texas by white men whose tattoos and racial views strongly suggested ties to white-supremacist ideas. They dragged him along a road until his body was dismembered. After this lynching, a Klan group held a rally nearby for the white-supremacist cause. This Jasper lynching triggered copycat crimes in at least two other cities.[56] Given the increase in hate groups and hate crimes, many people have called for increased penalties for perpetrators of hate crimes, and some state legislatures have passed such legislation.[57]

Black Protest against Oppression

As with other groups we have examined, it is important to distinguish violence used to oppress black Americans from violence used by black victims to *resist* oppression. Since the 1930s, black urbanites have, on occasion, violently rebelled against oppressive conditions. Historically, white violence to enforce discrimination and oppression has preceded black attacks on that oppression.

A few riots involving pitched battles between black residents and white police officers, often sparked by a police incident, occurred in the 1930s and 1940s, particularly in New York City. The underlying causes involved job discrimination and restrictions on political participation, issues that have periodically prompted black Americans to lash out in nonviolent resistance movements as well as in violent riots. In the 1960s and 1970s, many U.S. cities experienced black uprisings against local symbols of oppression, especially white police officers, businesses, and landlords. Large-scale black rebellions occurred in Los Angeles in 1965, in Detroit and Newark in 1967, and in Washington, D.C. in 1968. An angry generation of African Americans showed their willingness to engage in violent protest against racism and related economic problems, and the impact was felt across the nation.[58]

Rebellions against oppressive conditions have continued over the past two decades or so. In the spring of 1980, black anger over local economic and political conditions exploded in a major riot in Miami. Black residents lashed out at white and Cuban American police officers and the larger white society. The rioting cost sixteen lives, caused 400 injuries, and resulted in $100 million in property damage. Following the riot, 27 percent of a nationwide sample of African Americans said they felt the rioting was justified. Another 25 percent were unsure.[59] More uprisings occurred in Miami between 1982 and 1991, all triggered by incidents involving white or Latino police officers shooting to death an African American or being acquitted for such a killing. In Los Angeles in the spring of 1992, the acquittal of police officers who were videotaped beating an unarmed black man triggered the most costly uprising so far in U.S. history. During days of rioting in central Los Angeles, more than 10,000 blacks and Latinos were arrested, and more than 50 people were killed. Property damage exceeded $1 billion. At one point, 20,000 police officers and soldiers patrolled the area.[60] Rioting also broke out in other cities. As in the 1960s riots, the underlying conditions fuelling the uprising included racial discrimination, poverty, unemployment, and poor housing.

In spring 2001, the killing of a black man by white officers in Cincinnati sparked a large-scale rebellion by many black residents there. Numerous local and national organizations had warned that police practices, as well as underlying employment and housing problems, could trigger rioting in major U.S. cities, including Cincinnati, 43 percent of whose population is African American. At least four suspicious killings of black citizens by police officers had occurred in Cincinnati since 1995, and no officer has ever been convicted for such killings in the city's history. Several days of rioting resulted in 800 arrests, dozens of injuries, and extensive property damage. In March 2001 the ACLU and local black citizens filed a lawsuit against the city for racial profiling, a practice used by some police departments that unfairly singles out citizens of color as potential criminals and results in extensive harassment.[61]

The role of white officials and police officers in generating or accelerating nonviolent protests and rioting by African Americans, while overlooked by many white Americans, has been very significant. Police malpractice that targets people of color remains a major problem in most U.S. cities. A recent Gallup survey asked black respondents if they had faced discrimination from the police. Strikingly, 15 percent of all the respondents, and 34 percent of young men, reported that they had been treated unfairly by the police in just the past month.[62] In a search of major newspaper articles from a several-year period in the 1990s, one researcher found reports of 130 incidents of serious police brutality.

In Cincinnati in June 2001, African Americans engage in a nonviolent protest against the killing of a young unarmed black man by the police.

White officers were involved in more than nine in every ten of these cases; black or Latino citizens were the victims in 97 percent of the police incidents. An officer was actually punished in *only 13 percent* of the incidents, and the punishment was typically slight. Police brutality is usually a racial crime in the United States.[63]

Occasionally, hidden police violence becomes public. In 1991 a white photographer in Los Angeles captured on videotape the beating of Rodney King by white police officers while more than a dozen other officers watched. Initially, the white Los Angeles police chief did not condemn the officers, saying only that the beating was an "aberration." In a nationwide poll, three-fourths of black respondents said that the police in most cities treat black citizens less fairly than white citizens of the same income and educational level; two-thirds felt that blacks were treated less fairly than whites by judges and the courts.[64] Numerous recent state and national polls have revealed the same critique of the justice system by Americans of color.

THE ECONOMY

According to the assimilation perspective, most members of an immigrant group coming into the society will gradually experience secondary-structural assimilation into the U.S. economy (Chapter 2). Over several generations most members of a particular racial or ethnic group are expected to move into ever higher levels of employment. However, this assimilation view of economic mobility does not apply very well to African Americans. Although they have been here since 1619, they have still not been incorporated, in representative numbers, in the nation's better-paying jobs.

White Enrichment, Black Losses

Over the course of U.S. history, whites at most class levels have benefitted greatly from the racial oppression that has targeted African Americans. White privilege includes the array of material benefits and advantages inherited by each generation of whites. This white privilege began in early white gains from slavery and has persisted under legal segregation and contemporary patterns of discrimination.

For nearly four centuries, African Americans have been critical to the building of U.S. wealth and prosperity. From the 1600s to the early 2000s, they have provided much of the hard labor necessary for economic development. From the early 1600s until the 1860s, the labor of most African Americans was stolen as they toiled for white slaveholders. Much of the surplus capital and wealth of the nation's white families and communities came directly, or by means of economic multiplier effects, from the African slave trade and the slave plantations or related commercial trade and banking enterprises. Much of British, French, and American industry, shipping, and banking depended on enslaved labor. From the 1600s to the 1800s, most major agricultural exports in the Atlantic trade were produced by enslaved Africans. Without this enslaved labor, it seems unlikely that the successful British and U.S. textile industries would have developed when they did. Without that first major industry (textiles) it is unclear how or when Britain and the United States would have become industrial powers. Indeed, even James Watt's improved steam engine, which greatly accelerated Western industrialization, was financed by British investors with capital accumulated in the Atlantic trade in enslaved human beings and slave-produced products.[65]

Since the 1600s, over the course of some fifteen generations now, the exploitation of black Americans has redistributed material rewards and wealth earned by black labor to generations of whites, leaving the former relatively impoverished as a group and the latter relatively privileged as a group. Consider the value of the African American labor that was stolen. One researcher has calculated that the value (as of 1983) of the slave labor expropriated by whites from 1620 to 1865 was somewhere between $1 and $97 trillion, depending on the rate of (lost) interest chosen.[66] Yet more labor was stolen under legal segregation in the form of discriminatory wages. One research study estimated the cost of this labor market discrimination for just the years 1929–1969 (in 1983 dollars) at $1.6 trillion.[67] Calculating the cost of anti-black discrimination from the end of slavery (1865) to the end of legal segregation (1969), and putting that calculation into current dollars would likely increase the wage-loss estimate under segregation to several trillion dollars. Since the end of official segregation, black Americans have suffered additional economic losses from continuing racial discrimination in employment. The sum total for the current worth of all the black labor stolen by whites through slavery, segregation, and contemporary discrimination is staggering—at least a few trillion dollars.

Whites also benefited from numerous federal government programs that gave away critical resources that could be used to accumulate individual and family wealth over several generations. In the late 1800s and early 1900s, the government distributed land, mineral rights, airline routes, radio and television frequencies, and other resources. During this period black Americans were generally excluded from such benefits because of racial segregation and other discrimination. Under the Homestead Act, from the 1860s to the 1930s, the federal government provided some 246 million acres at minimal cost to 1.5 million homesteads. Research by

Trina Williams estimates that some 46 million Americans *today* are the likely beneficiaries, to varying degrees, of this huge wealth-generating program.[68] Almost all these beneficiaries are white, for black families were largely excluded from this huge land giveaway. Stephen DeCanio's research suggests that much of the long-term racial gap in income and wealth is a direct result of this racial gap in access to arable land.[69]

After the Civil War, some Republican party proposals sought to give formerly enslaved African Americans some arable land—the famous 40 acres and a mule. Yet, this did not happen. With no major land distribution to accompany their emancipation, many formerly enslaved workers were forced to sell their labor to the former slave masters and other whites because they continued to control the agricultural system. Exploitative, semi-slave farm labor became the lot of many. Black sharecroppers and tenant farmers were often tied to one farm or rural area by mounting debts owed to the usually exploitative and discriminatory, white-controlled provisions and lending system. With less money and much less legal protection than whites and faced with discrimination in land and consumer-product transactions, most freed blacks who remained in the South were unable to become independent farmers of means. Those who went to the cities fared little better. Most black men there were confined to service sector jobs, and unemployment was common. Few manufacturing jobs, including those that employed white women, were open to black women or men.[70] Reflecting on the high rate of stillbirths among black mothers in this period, a black physician commented: "Why should we be surprised at the great number of still-births among our women? ... They do heavy washing, make beds, turn heavy mattresses, and climb the stairs several times during the day, while their more favored white sister is seated in her big armchair, and not allowed to move, even if she wanted to."[71]

The Migration North

In 1900, nine black Americans in ten still lived in the South. Soon, however, the bustling economy in northern and border cities, the declining significance of "King Cotton" in the South, and the cruelty of southern segregation stimulated increasing numbers to move North. After the 1920s' anti-immigrant legislation and the subsequent decline in overseas immigration, demand for black laborers in northern industries increased. Thousands of poor farmers, unable to finance the technological innovations necessary to circumvent the pestilence of the boll weevil and crop diseases, were driven, often with their families, from farms to cities. The major push factors were racial segregation and the declining viability of cotton farming; the major pull factor was service and industrial employment.[72]

The migration North accelerated during World War II. By the mid-twentieth century, millions of African Americans had migrated to what many saw as an economic "promised land." They went to the large cities in the Northeast, Midwest, and West. These migrants generally were forced to settle in low-income areas already occupied by black families, swelling their size. Some assimilation theorists argue that this northern migration brought great opportunities for economic mobility to African Americans, whom they see as just another in a line of urban immigrant groups (such as the Irish and the Italians) successfully seeking their fortunes in the city. However, if we accept this view, we would expect that black economic gains between 1900 and the early 2000s would have closed the black–white gap. The reality, however, has been quite different.[73]

The racial division of labor in the cities was enforced by discriminatory laws, violence, or informal discrimination. The urban economy can be divided into a primary and a secondary employment sector—the split labor market described in Chapter 2. The primary labor market, composed disproportionately of privileged white workers, is characterized by skilled jobs, high wages, and job ladders that offer significant upward mobility. The secondary labor market, composed disproportionately of workers of color, is characterized by instability, low wages, and little mobility.[74] The dramatic rise of corporate capitalism after 1900 that created employment for large numbers of workers also resulted in union organizing to expand workers' wages and rights. However, to counter the white workers' increasing demands, white employers offered certain concessions, including separating white workers from less-privileged workers of color in the workplace. In this way, white workers got what W. E. B. Du Bois called a "psychological wage" (that is, the sense of white superiority and privilege) in return for accepting lower monetary wages than they would have gotten by organizing more aggressively with black workers.[75]

Increasing numbers of black men and women moving out of farm occupations found themselves channeled into relatively unskilled jobs in urban industrial and service sectors. The principal occupations of black men became truck driver, porter, janitor, and cook. Black women served as maids, restaurant workers, and dressmakers as white women began to move into clerical and professional jobs.[76] Census figures for 1930 revealed the continuing dominance of agricultural and domestic service jobs. Of every 1,000 black workers, 648 were in agricultural or domestic service jobs compared with 280 of every 1,000 whites. Most of the remainder held other unskilled blue-collar positions.[77] Highly educated black men and women were frequently forced to do menial jobs. Most of the few black professionals were teachers, ministers, and physicians serving the black community; likewise, black business people usually served a black clientele. As a result of discrimination and segregation, black incomes were sharply lower than those of whites.[78]

Most labor unions had traditionally been segregated. By the late 1930s, black pressure and federal legislation had forced many American Federation of Labor (AFL) unions to begin to reduce discrimination in recruiting black workers. The new Congress of Industrial Organizations (CIO) began with an official nondiscriminatory policy in order to attract black workers in the automobile, steel, and packing industries. In 1930 at least twenty-six major unions *officially* barred black workers from membership; by 1943 the number had dropped to fourteen. Nonetheless, official discrimination was usually replaced by informal exclusion or restriction of black workers in the historically white unions, practices that have persisted in more subtle forms in some unions to the present day.[79]

Economic Changes since the 1940s

The 1940 census revealed a continuing and heavy concentration of black workers in agriculture and the secondary labor market of cities. During World War II, industries with severe labor needs were forced to make concessions to black demands for better job opportunities. Under pressure from civil rights and union leaders, President Franklin Roosevelt issued executive orders that reduced job discrimination in war-related industries. However, at the end of the war this progress came to an abrupt end: Layoffs hit black workers much harder than whites.[80]

During the economic expansion between 1955 and 1972, the proportion of African Americans in professional, managerial, sales, clerical, crafts, and operatives jobs increased and the proportion in unskilled and service jobs decreased. The largest increase was for black women in the clerical category. By the 1980s, growth in the proportion of black employees in better-paid job categories slowed, and, in the early 2000s, black workers are still less likely than white workers to be in the better-paid managerial, professional, technical, sales, and crafts job categories. In 2000, some 22 percent of black workers held managerial and professional jobs compared with 31 percent of white workers. In contrast, black workers were more likely than white workers to hold blue-collar jobs in the service, operative, transportation, and handler-laborer categories (40 percent compared with 25 percent).[81]

Even within the white-collar job categories, black workers tend to be in subcategories with lower pay and less job status. For example, within the professional-technical category, black employees today are most commonly found in social work, kindergarten teaching, vocational counseling, dietetics, and health care. They are less often found among lawyers and judges, dentists, artists, engineers, and professors at historically white universities. In addition, whites are much more likely to be self-employed than blacks.[82]

Persisting Discrimination: A Business Example

Seventy-one percent of white respondents in one 2001 poll thought African Americans had at least the same opportunities as whites. In that national opinion survey six in ten of the white respondents also thought that the average black person got health care access that was equal to or better than that of the comparable white person. Yet the research data show that whites are far more likely to get adequate or better medical care than African Americans. Half the white respondents felt that whites and blacks are about as well off in the jobs they hold, although whites are much more likely than blacks to have professional, managerial, or good-paying blue-collar jobs. About 42 percent also thought that the average black worker earned at least as much as the average white worker, although there is a large gap in actual earnings.[83] Surveys such as this indicate that many whites refuse to accept the experienced testimony of most African Americans to the effect that they still face serious discrimination in the workplace and many other areas of society.

Numerous research studies confirm that racial discrimination today continues to confront black employees working for wages and also those trying to succeed in businesses of their own. In several research studies since 1990, the first author has supervised interviews with several hundred working-class and middle-class African Americans in numerous cities. Many have related concrete stories of discrimination in employment or business settings that document the types of discrimination discussed in Chapter 1. The reader will recall that isolate discrimination involves the actions of an individual acting alone, such as a white manager expressing anti-black views by discriminating against black employees without the support of fellow workers or a discriminatory company policy. Following is a description of the actual experience of the successful owner of a consulting firm:

> I have a contract right now with a southwestern city government; and I practically gave my services away. I had to become very creative, you know. I wanted the contract because I know I could do the work, and I have the background and the track record to do it. However, in negotiating the contract, they wanted to give it to all these other people who never had any experience ... simply because they're a big eight accounting firm, or they're some big-time institution. So, I had to compete against those people. But it was good because it proved that I could be competitive.

She then explained that a professional panel evaluating the bids gave her the highest rating because of her track record. But a barrier was thrown up, because

> the director of their department made a very racial statement, that "they were very sick and tired of these niggers and these other minorities because what they think is that they can come in here and run a business. None of them are qualified to run a business, especially the niggers." (Now, a white person, female, heard this statement, and because they had some confrontational problems—I think the only reason she really told me was because of that.) He was going to use that, not overtly, but in his mind that was going to be his reason for rejection.... Even though they [the panel] all recommended me (I got all five consensus votes), he was going to throw it out.... I had to really, really do some internalizing to keep myself from being very bitter.[84]

This incident involved one white man's blatant attempt to restrict a talented black person's advancement, apparently without the overt support of other whites. Such examples of isolate discrimination motivated by prejudice are still common in the lives of African Americans today. Small-group discrimination is also common. Small-group discrimination, such as that shaped by prejudiced supervisors or union officials wishing to subvert company or union regulations that require the hiring or promotion of skilled black employees, continues to be omnipresent in U.S. workplaces, although these discriminatory practices are often hard to fully document.[85]

Direct institutional discrimination consists of organizationally prescribed actions carried out routinely by whites in companies and businesses. Today, this typically takes an informal, even covert, form in employment settings. Examples include outright exclusion, the relegation of black employees to special jobs or sections, or restricting the mobility of black employees beyond the entry level. One Urban Institute study sent comparable white and black applicants to the same employers to apply for jobs. A significant proportion—more than one-fifth—of the black applicants suffered job discrimination at the entry stage.[86]

Discrimination in Corporations and the Military

Once a person is hired, discrimination does not end. Having reluctantly abandoned the traditional, overt, and exclusionary barriers of earlier decades, many white managers have retreated to a second line of defense: hiring black workers for nontraditional jobs and putting them in conspicuous or powerless positions. Research studies by sociologist Sharon Collins have documented that African Americans moving into professional and management jobs in corporations frequently find themselves tracked into special "job ghettos," such as members or heads of departments of affirmative action, "community affairs," or "special markets."[87] Black professionals and managers "are rarely found in line positions concerned with developing or controlling production, supervising the work of large numbers of whites or competing with their white 'peers' for significant positions."[88] One mid-1990s study of ninety-four large corporations found that only 6 percent of management positions and 2 percent of upper management positions were held by white women or by African Americans, Latinos, or Asian Americans. Early 2000s reports indicate that the pattern of less than 2 percent executives of color is continuing throughout most of the private sector.[89]

An example of racial problems in major corporations came to public attention in 1996 when the *New York Times* quoted from the taped transcript of a 1994 meeting of several top executives at Texaco, an international oil company and then the nation's fourteenth largest corporation, to discuss a lawsuit filed by black employees. According to the transcript, these top corporate officials did not take the black complaints of discrimination seriously and discussed destroying documents requested by the black plaintiffs. Black employees were called "black jelly beans" who all agree with diversity efforts and who "seem to be glued to the bottom of the bag." The federal Equal Employment Opportunity Commission found that Texaco had discriminated against black employees in regard to promotions.[90] In an affidavit filed with the court suit, a white manager in a midwestern office of Texaco reported a black employee's discrimination complaint to his boss, a senior executive in Texas. The boss reportedly replied that he would "fire her black ass." When the manager pointed out that Texaco's official policy protected those who complained of discrimination from dismissal, the senior executive reportedly said: "I guess we treat niggers differently down here."[91] Court documents obtained by the *New York Times* also showed that only six of Texaco's 873 highest-paid executives were black, and that no black person had ever held one of the top 49 jobs in the firm.[92]

The stereotypes of white investors and executives are often a determining factor in the location of new jobs. The spatial mismatch of jobs in many cities is often the result of capitalist investors' intentional movement away from black populations. One 2001 research report on the situation of black workers and other workers of color in Atlanta, Boston, Detroit, and Los Angeles found that in general the movement of jobs from central cities to suburban areas by employers has severely limited employment opportunities for many urban blacks. This study also found that apparently some employers intentionally selected workplace locations inaccessible to black workers. In Boston and Los Angeles, employer surveys found that employers were more likely to express a desire to move away from neighborhoods with increasing numbers of black families than from other neighborhoods. In addition, numerous employers admitted that their hiring decisions involved stereotypes about the personality traits, attitudes, and behaviors of black workers and other workers of color. White employers held stereotyped images that white male and female workers work better than black workers and often rejected skilled black workers even before checking on their abilities.[93]

There is clear evidence of the corporate world's glass ceiling. In fall 2000 there were only two black executives heading Fortune 500 companies. And there were only five black chief executive officers in the next 500 largest firms. According to a report of the federal Glass Ceiling Commission, about 95 percent of top corporate officials (vice presidents and above) are white (non-Latino) men, yet they make up only about 38 percent of the adult population. Despite the controversy over their alleged impact, government and private affirmative action policies have done little to alter white male dominance at the top of U.S. economic (and other major) institutions.[94]

Discrimination occurs in military workplaces as well. A major survey of 40,000 U.S. military personnel—including enlisted members and officers—found that about one-fifth of the black personnel had faced career-related discrimination within the previous year. Three-fourths had faced negative and offensive racial encounters during that year: 52 percent had been told offensive racist stories; 49 percent had suffered unwelcome attempts to draw them into offensive discussions of race; 46 percent had endured acts of racial condescension; 37 percent had encountered hostile racial stares; 28 percent had endured racist comments or epithets; and 20 percent had been confronted with racist periodicals or other materials. In addition, 6 percent had been physically threatened or intimidated because of their race. A large percentage of black enlisted personnel and officers also reported racial harassment from people in the civilian community.[95]

TABLE 7.2 CIVILIAN EMPLOYEES IN EXECUTIVE BRANCH AGENCIES, SEPTEMBER 2000 (PERCENTAGE OF EMPLOYEES BY CATEGORY AND RACIAL GROUP)

Black civilian employees in the executive branch of the federal government are most heavily represented in clerical positions. Their percentage of blue-collar workers is more than twice that of professional workers. The percentage of black workers is highest at low pay levels and lowest at the highest pay levels.

	BLACK	WHITE
All white-collar workers	16.7%	70.4%
Professional	8.7	78.2
Clerical	29.1	56.4
Blue-collar workers	19.1	65.4
Pay Plans		
General Schedule	17.5	69.7
GS1	30.1	46.6
GS2	26.7	53.6
GS15	6.3	84.2
Senior Pay Levels	7.1	86.5

Source: Office of Personnel Management, <http://www.opm.gov>.

We might note that African Americans also face discrimination as consumers. For example, a study of automobile buying experiences that used black and white, male and female testers with similar dress, economic stories, and bargaining scripts revealed both racial and gender discrimination. In more than 180 negotiations at ninety car dealerships, white men were quoted much better prices than were black men, black women, or white women.[96]

Government Action and Inaction on Discrimination

Government action on discrimination has been a hotly debated issue. Some opponents argue it has gone too far, to the point of large-scale "reverse discrimination" that hurts whites and unfairly favors people of color. Other analysts, with much more evidence, argue that federal government anti-discrimination policies have always been modest and, since the early 1980s, have had a declining impact on discrimination in such spheres as employment and housing because of weak civil rights enforcement by most recent presidential administrations.

The 1964 Civil Rights Act and its amendments prohibit discrimination in employment. The Equal Employment Opportunity Commission (EEOC) was created to enforce the act, primarily by investigating complaints, seeking conciliation, and filing suit to end discrimination by labor unions, private employers, state governments, and educational institutions. Until the 1980s the federal courts and the EEOC made some progress in reducing racial barriers in traditionally white employment arenas.

Under the Ronald Reagan and George H. W. Bush administrations in the 1980s and early 1990s, however, EEOC efforts to halt racial discrimination in workplaces declined substantially. The EEOC reduced the number of field investigations of the critical class-action complaints of discrimination as well as other broad, institutionally focused investigations of employment discrimination. The Reagan administration destroyed or weakened other civil rights enforcement agencies, and, for the most part, President George H. W. Bush continued this negative approach. In addition, Presidents Reagan and Bush appointed several conservative justices to the U.S. Supreme Court, who subsequently handed down a number of backtracking decisions on civil rights issues.

In the 1990s the Clinton administration began to enforce civil rights laws more vigorously, but this slow progress was discontinued under the conservative administration of George W. Bush in the early 2000s.

However strong they are, civil rights laws do not guarantee real equality of opportunity in everyday settings. Few of the millions of cases of racial discrimination perpetrated by white Americans each year against African Americans and other Americans of color are countered by effective private or government remedies. Generally speaking, U.S. and state government agencies have neither the resources nor the staff to vigorously enforce anti-discrimination laws. Over the past decade or two, many black victims of discrimination have given up on government's ability or even willingness to deal with this problem. In a 1989 decision, one of the few liberal justices then on the Supreme Court, Harry Blackmun, asked whether the conservative majority on the court, and by implication in the country, "still believes that race discrimination—or, more accurately, race discrimination against nonwhites—is a problem in our society, or even remembers that it ever was."[97]

Unemployment, Income, and Poverty

For decades the black unemployment rate has been more than twice the white unemployment rate (see Table 7.3).[98] In 1989 the black–white unemployment ratio reached a record high of 2.53. Since then it has fluctuated, but it remained at 2.2 at the beginning of the twenty-first century. The fact that in economic recessions black workers tend to lose their jobs at twice the rate of white workers and tend to be recalled at a slower rate contributes to high unemployment for this group. As we noted previously, the movement of capital and jobs to suburbs is an additional contributing factor. The majority of new jobs in recent decades in metropolitan areas have been created outside the central city areas where most African Americans live.

Even higher than the unemployment rate for African Americans is the *underemployment rate*, which includes those with no jobs, those working part-time, and those making poverty wages. Nationwide surveys have found that large numbers of black workers have part-time work even though they want full-time work, receive very low wages, or are discouraged workers (those who have given up looking). An estimated one-third of black workers fall into these subemployment categories, while the proportion for whites is much lower.[99]

Since 1950, black family income has not risen above 62 percent of white family income, as can be seen in Table 7.4.[100] Census data also show that in 1999 black per capita income was less than 60 percent of non-Hispanic white per capita income.[101]

Families headed by single, separated, or divorced mothers tend to be poorer than those with both parents present. The proportion of black families headed by women increased from 18 percent in 1950 to just over 44 percent in 1999.[102] From 1970 until the mid-1990s, the poverty rate for black female-headed families with children under eighteen years old remained well over 50 percent, peaking at almost 64 percent in 1982. In 1999, this poverty rate dropped to just over 46 percent. In contrast, only 25 percent of non-Hispanic white families in this category were below the poverty level in that year.[103] One scholar has noted that "Families headed by black women are primarily poor, not because they do not have husbands, but because they do not have jobs."[104] Like black men, black women face major employment problems in part because of intentional discrimination in the present and in part because of the continuing effects of past discrimination.

Whatever the type of family, African Americans average significantly fewer dollars than whites. In 1999, black families were four times as likely as white families to live in poverty. Almost one-fourth of all blacks, and one-third of black children, fell below the poverty line. Between 1974 and 1993, the number of black Americans living in poverty increased from 7.2 million to more than 10.9 million, and then gradually dropped to just under 8.4 million by 1999. Moreover, a much smaller proportion of black families than non-Hispanic white families owned their own home (47 percent compared with 74 percent), and a substantial majority of black families nationwide could not afford to buy a modestly priced house in their community.[105]

Over the centuries, most African Americans have had little opportunity to build up multigenerational wealth. Today, black households as a group have a much lower net worth than white households. The

TABLE 7.3 UNEMPLOYMENT RATES

YEAR	BLACK (OR NONWHITE)	WHITE	RATIO
1949	8.9%	5.6%	1.6
1959	10.7	4.8	2.2
1969	6.4	3.1	2.1
1979	12.3	5.1	2.4
1989	11.4	4.5	2.5
1999	8.0	3.7	2.2
2000	7.6	3.5	2.2

TABLE 7.4 BLACK (OR NONWHITE) MEDIAN FAMILY INCOME AS A PERCENTAGE OF WHITE AND NON-HISPANIC WHITE FAMILY INCOME

YEAR	WHITE FAMILY INCOME	NON-HISPANIC WHITE FAMILY INCOME
1950	54%	
1960	55	
1970	61	
1980	58	57%
1990	58	56
1999	62	59

median net worth of white households is almost seven times that of black households. In addition, most of the wealth that black families do hold is in cars and houses. White families are far more likely than black families to have interest-bearing bank accounts and to hold stocks. One striking thing about the wealth data is that they show the long term impact of centuries of racial oppression. Some data even indicate that white families with modest incomes—in the $7,500–15,000 range—have *greater* net worth than black families with much higher incomes, in the $45,000–60,000 range. The likely reason for this is the fact that many modest-income white families are more likely than some higher-income black families to have built up some equity in a house—which has often been made possible because the white families have inherited a house or some money from their parents, or because they have not faced discrimination in holding a good job or finding decent housing in the past. Moreover, many middle class African Americans are first-generation middle class, and while their incomes may be good for the present, they have not inherited the wealth that enables them to build up much future wealth. In addition, since they are first generation, many middle class African Americans are likely to be assisting parents or relatives who are poor or working class.[106]

TABLE 7.5 PERCENT DISTRIBUTION OF HOUSEHOLD NET WORTH BY RACIAL GROUP AND AMOUNT OF NET WORTH, 1995

In 1995 more than one-fifth of black households had zero or negative net worth, and the net worth of an additional one-fourth was less than $5,000. One-third of white households had a net worth of $100,000 or more, compared with about 6 percent of black households. Less than 1 percent of black households had a net worth of $250,000 or more, compared with almost 12 percent of white households.

	WHITE	BLACK
negative or $0	8.8%	21.7%
$1–$4,999	12.5	24.7
$5,000–$24,999	17.3	20.7
$25,000–$99,999	28.5	26.6
$100,000–$249,000	21.1	5.5
$250,000 or over	11.9	0.8

Source: U.S. Census Bureau, "Asset Ownership of Households: 1995, Table 4. Percent Distribution of Household Net Worth, by Amount of Net Worth and Selected Characteristics," published April 9, 2001, <http://www.census.gov/hhes/www/wealth/1995.html>.

Is There a Distinctive African American "Underclass"?

Since the 1970s, a number of commentators have contended that the black community is polarized between an affluent middle class and the very poor. Sometimes they also argue that discrimination has mostly been eradicated for middle-class black Americans, thus lessening the need for affirmative action.[107] The plight of the poor is often discussed as though their economic conditions were not the main problem; their values and behavior are said to be the main source of their problems. From this perspective, poor black Americans (called "the underclass") are locked into a lower-class "culture of poverty," with its alleged immorality, broken families, delinquency, and lack of emphasis on work. These stereotype-based arguments about poor Americans are recent versions of largely discredited culture-of-poverty arguments that have been made since the 1960s.[108]

Perhaps the greatest weakness of arguments that focus on the alleged cultural inferiority of poor African Americans (and other poor Americans) is the neglect of structural factors. Many of the problems faced by this group are created by the corporate executives who move U.S. jobs overseas. In addition, discrimination is still commonplace in such areas as employment and housing. If the notion that discrimination is irrelevant were true, poor black Americans should face roughly the same social, economic, political, and housing conditions as comparably poor white Americans. This is not the case. Because of discrimination, poor black families do *not* live in integrated neighborhoods with poor white families. African Americans, including low-income workers, are *more* likely to be laid off in recessions than white Americans. Poor blacks are *less* likely than comparably poor whites to get unemployment compensation when they are laid off. They tend to hold lower-paying and less secure jobs than poor whites, and they face far more discrimination at the hands of white police officers and other whites than do poor whites.

The cumulative effects of past and present discrimination in the socioeconomic problems of poor African Americans must be recognized. Past racial segregation and exploitative discrimination, coupled with blatant, subtle, and covert racial discrimination today, are the likely reasons for much black poverty, unemployment, and underemployment.[109]

Housing Discrimination

The 1968 Civil Rights Act officially banned most housing discrimination in the United States. However, this and subsequent housing laws have been weakly enforced, and discriminatory practices in housing persist widely across the nation. Using white and black testers, recent housing audit studies in New Orleans, Montgomery, Fresno, and San Antonio have found very high (61 percent to 77 percent) discrimination rates for black testers seeking rental housing.[110] This widespread housing discrimination is often covert, such as in the case of a landlord falsely telling a black renter that an apartment has been rented. Major insurance companies also create housing barriers. One recent investigation had black, Latino, and white testers pose as homeowners seeking insurance. They contacted major insurance companies' offices in nine cities. Overall, 53 percent of the black and Latino testers—ranging from 32 percent in Memphis to 83 percent in Chicago—experienced racial discrimination in insurance coverage and price. Whites were often offered more insurance options and lower rates.[111]

The aforementioned movement of capital and jobs to suburbs or to other countries contributes to persisting racial segregation and housing inequality in cities. Racial apartheid is still the reality in U.S. cities. The white population of central cities has decreased, and most suburbs are now predominantly white. Today most whites live in suburbs or nonmetropolitan areas, while the majority of Americans of color live in cities. White fears about the new sociospatial reality of our cities seem to be increasing. Ironically, whites now fear the residential segregation that they themselves have created by more than a century of exclusionary racial practices. Segregation has consequences. One study by several journalists examined two adjacent but largely segregated working-class residential areas of Chicago, one white and one black. According to the field interviews, the whites live in an insulated world where they "live out entire lives without ever getting to know a black person." The study found racial fear and suspicion of the other group in both residential areas. However, the black residents were "fearful because much of their contact with white people was negative," while "whites were fearful because they had little or no contact."[112]

POLITICS AND PROTEST

Before 1865, African Americans, whether enslaved in the South or theoretically "free" in the North, were not allowed to participate as equals with whites in the political system. Most were disenfranchised. Some petitioned legislatures and executive officials for redress of their grievances, but most petitions were ignored. The Civil War brought an end to slavery and increased black participation in electoral politics. The Thirteenth Amendment to the U.S. Constitution abolished slavery, the Fourteenth Amendment asserted that the civil rights of black Americans could not be denied by the states, and the Fifteenth Amendment guaranteed black men (but not women) the right to vote.

From Reconstruction to the 1920s

Following the Civil War, the Reconstruction period came to the South as a breath of fresh air. Federally enforced Reconstruction policies were precipitated by southern unwillingness to make major changes in the treatment of freed blacks or to prevent the unrepentant leaders of the Confederacy from resuming power. A brief period of limited federal military occupation resulted. Reconstruction brought much political progress to black southerners. Black men gained the right to vote. New state constitutional conventions included black delegates, although in most states the majority of all delegates were white.[113] Between 1869 and 1901, twenty black men served in the U.S. House and two in the U.S. Senate. Hiram R. Revels and Blanche K. Bruce, both from Mississippi, were the first African Americans to serve in the U.S. Senate.[114] Indeed, the fact that *only two* African Americans, Edward Brooke (R-Mass.) and Carol Moseley Braun (D-Illinois), have served in the U.S. Senate since Revels and Bruce testifies to the continued pervasiveness of political discrimination in the United States.

During Reconstruction southern state governments were mostly controlled by whites who had not been major supporters of the Confederacy, including farmers of modest means. But conservative forces in the South soon brought an end to Reconstruction. Few Americans know that a major reason for the end of Reconstruction was the development of *white terrorism*. Many in the South's white elite, with the collusion of some U.S. presidents and some in the northern elites, conducted an extensive terrorist campaign against Reconstruction governments and newly freed black southerners. A leading Confederate general, Nathan Bedford Forrest, was the first Grand Dragon of the newly created Ku Klux Klan, and no less a figure than General Robert E. Lee pledged his "invisible" support to the Klan. This white terrorism gradually destroyed the often progressive southern governments, and thousands of men, women, and children were severely beaten, raped, or killed by members of the Klan and similar white supremacist groups. The Confederacy had lost the four-year war, but fought on for "twelve more years—using every weapon at its disposal, including the ultimate one of mass terrorism—until the nation finally acceded to most of the Confederacy's modified war aims."[115] After a few years of this white terrorism, northern interest in the South waned. Most northern leaders were not interested in punishing those Southerners who led the rebellion; few Confederate leaders were imprisoned for war-making activities or for participation in the terrorism.[116]

Although considerable segregation existed during Reconstruction, the racialized system was not nearly as all-encompassing as it would later become. By the early 1900s, enforced segregation became the rule in the South and was legitimated by a major Supreme Court decision. *Plessy v. Ferguson* (1896) upheld racial segregation in Louisiana railroad cars and delivered a major blow by asserting the legality of "separate but equal" facilities for blacks. The all-white Court reasoned that white racist attitudes were natural and that "legislation is powerless to eradicate racial instincts or to abolish distinctions based upon physical differences, and the attempt to do so can only result in accentuating the difficulties of the present situation."[117]

In 1915 the Supreme Court began a slow swing back to the protection of some black civil rights by declaring grandfather clauses for voting unconstitutional. Black voter registration increased very slowly. By the 1920s, black migration to the cities had brought a few black leaders to the political forefront in the North. Independent political organizations were established in a few cities, but the only major success was that of Adam Clayton Powell, Jr., in New York City. In 1945, Powell became a black member of Congress, only the fourth member, and the first from outside the city of Chicago, in the twentieth century. In the North, most black voters supported the Republican party, but by the 1930s they had begun to shift to the Democratic party.[118]

The Limits of Black Progress: Political Discrimination

Southern voter registration increased sharply between the 1940s and the 1970s, raising the number of black voters from 250,000 to 4 million. A big jump in registration occurred after passage of the Voting Rights Act in 1965. Since their re-enfranchisement in 1965, black southerners have developed numerous effective political organizations and campaigns. In 1965 there were approximately seventy black elected officials in the South. Three years later, the figure had climbed to 248. More than three decades later, in 1999, the number was 8,936 for all states. Just over one-third of these officials were women. Still, black officials remained only 1.7 percent of all elected officials across the United States, and there were only 39 black members of Congress. Recent research has demonstrated that the increase in black elected officials that began in the late 1960s was linked to the 1965 voting rights act, "perhaps the single most successful civil rights bill ever passed."[119]

Over the past few decades, black voters have continued to face attempts to reduce the efficacy of their political participation. Research by Chandler Davidson and Frank Parker has demonstrated that electoral discrimination persists in such forms as vote dilution, gerrymandering, the changing of elective offices into appointive offices, and unnecessary revisions in qualifications for office.[120] A major example of vote dilution is the at-large electoral system, whereby candidates are elected citywide rather than from smaller districts. In cities across the nation, this system has been demonstrated to sharply reduce the participation of black candidates and voters in local campaigns. As long as black voters constitute well under half of the voters in a city, black candidates are unlikely to win elected office in an at-large system because many whites will rarely or never vote for a black candidate. Responding to conservative white supporters in the 1980s, the Ronald Reagan administration tried to weaken the Voting Rights Act. However, in 1982, after a long battle, civil rights forces persuaded Congress to pass a twenty-five-year extension of key provisions of the act and to add an amendment allowing the U.S. Justice Department to prosecute local government officials for discrimination in electoral procedures without having to prove racial prejudice on the part of officials.[121]

African American voters also face discrimination in the form of purges of voter-registration rolls, unannounced changes in polling places, intentionally difficult registration procedures, and threats of retaliation. These practices have been documented from Florida to Texas.[122] Indeed, the 2000 election in which George W. Bush became president was marked by continuing discrimination against black voters, more than 90 percent of whom voted for the Democratic party candidate in that election. Protests from civil rights groups focused national attention on this discrimination in major states such as Florida and Illinois. Reports indicated that black voters had sometimes been harassed by the police and turned away by poll officials who claimed, in error, they were not on the voter registration lists. Some black polling places were suddenly moved.[123] The persistence of these and other discriminatory practices has renewed debates over governmental remedies. Since the early 1980s, voting rights issues have been at the center of debates about democracy in the United States. A number of legal scholars have pointed out that, while the enforcement of the Voting Rights Act has helped to increase the number of black-majority voting districts and elected officials, it has not reshaped local and state legislative bodies to give black officials a proportionate influence on their operations.

Law professor Lani Guinier has suggested remedies that might increase black influence on government bodies, one of which is cumulative voting, a procedure in which each voter is given a number of votes equal to the number of positions to be filled in a legislative body. If ten members of a commission are to be elected, each voter has ten votes and may use them to vote for one candidate for each of the positions or cast all ten votes for one candidate. Cumulative voting is currently used in selecting corporate boards of directors. Guinier argues that this strategy would increase the probability that a black candidate will be elected in an area in which the majority of voters are white. Some cities, such as Alamogordo and Peoria, have already experimented with this procedure. Other mechanisms, such as the requirement of legislative "supermajorities" to pass most laws, might be considered if cumulative voting and traditional strategies do not generate significant black political power.[124]

Some analysts argue that increased black votes and elected officials accomplish much for black voters, while others feel that black citizens are unlikely to gain much through an electoral process still mostly controlled by whites. In most jurisdictions, black officials have been unable to dramatically reorder local priorities in employment, housing, and education. Yet they have often been able to bring some expansion of capital-based services for local black residential areas. In Florida, however, James Button found that black elected officials were often more effective in changing employment opportunities for their constituents than in improving capital-based services. Many black officials also have had a positive influence on voter turnout. They have become a "direct and effective conduit for political input from black citizens," and the legitimacy of holding elected office has given them "influence and power in the public realm that other black leaders and organizations [have] rarely had."[125]

African Americans have won mayoral elections in a number of major cities with large black populations—including Philadelphia, Detroit, New York City, and Los Angeles—and also in a few predominantly white cities, such as Seattle and Kansas City. In 1990 the state of Virginia elected L. Douglas Wilder, the grandson of a slave, the first black governor of any state.[126]

The Federal Government

The New Deal era (1933–1940) was the first period since Reconstruction in which the federal government gave attention to the needs of its black citizens. Franklin Roosevelt appointed more than one hundred African Americans to important government positions. New Deal programs helped black Americans survive the Great Depression, even though most economic recovery agencies discriminated substantially in favor of white citizens.[127]

Between 1901 and 1929, Congress had *no* black members, and from 1929 until 1945, only one. In 1945, Adam Clayton Powell, Jr. (New York) joined William Dawson (Illinois) in the House, and ten years later Charles Diggs was elected from Michigan. By 1992, in part thanks to the registration of new black voters after the 1960s civil rights revolution, there were twenty-six black members, including four women, in the U.S. House. The redrawing of election districts following the 1990 census to bring states into compliance with the 1982 amendments to the Voting Rights Act increased the number of black-majority congressional voting districts. By the late 1990s, there were thirty-nine black representatives, including eleven women, in the U.S. House and one black woman (the first ever), Carol Moseley Braun from Illinois, in the Senate. However, Moseley was defeated in her bid for a second term.[128]

The first black person ever to serve in a presidential cabinet was Robert Weaver, appointed Secretary of Housing and Urban Development by President Lyndon Johnson in 1967. Johnson also appointed Thurgood Marshall as the first black Supreme Court justice.[129] From the 1970s to the early 2000s, the pattern of a few token black appointments in presidential cabinet positions and one Supreme Court appointment has persisted under Republican and Democratic presidents. African Americans continue to be significantly underrepresented in federal legislative, executive, and judicial positions.

The black vote has sometimes been very important in federal elections. Black voters played a role in Roosevelt's fourth election in 1944, and they were important to Truman's election in 1948.[130] The black vote in a few key states reportedly decided the 1960 presidential election in favor of the Irish Catholic John Kennedy. Black voters also played a role in electing Lyndon Johnson in 1964 and Jimmy Carter in 1976. They voted overwhelmingly for Albert Gore in 2000 and helped provide him with a popular vote (but not electoral college) majority. During recent elections, African American voters have continued to help elect white and black (usually Democratic) members of Congress who support civil rights issues, to some extent offsetting the impact of conservative white voters. African American voters have been centrally important in pressing the nation in the direction of its stated political ideal of "liberty and justice for all."

The Republican Party's Appeal to White Voters

Black voters have often found themselves voting for losing presidential candidates since the late 1960s, largely because of the barely disguised pro-white strategy of many conservatives in the Republican party. This political strategy, which was used by Richard Nixon in winning the 1968 presidential election, was celebrated in Kevin Phillips's *The Emerging Republican Majority*. Phillips suggested that Republicans did not need "urban Negroes" and other "vested interests" to win national elections.[131] In recent decades, the Republican party has moved from the party of Abraham Lincoln and one that advocated expanded civil rights for black Americans to one opposed to most aggressive government or private action (including affirmative action) to eliminate discrimination against black and other Americans of color in employment and other institutional areas. Once the recipient of a majority of black votes, the Republican party now receives relatively few of those votes. And Republican national conventions since the 1980s have had very few black delegates.[132]

Since 1990, speeches and ads by some conservative Republican candidates for election or reelection (for example, Senator Jesse Helms in North Carolina) have included politically charged code words, such as "racial quotas" and "unqualified minorities," in attempts to win whites votes. Partially as a result of these racial appeals to whites, the overwhelming majority of black voters have continued to support Democratic candidates at the local, state, and national levels. Still, this black allegiance has not always been enthusiastic because in some cases white Democratic candidates have also used barely disguised anti-black tactics to court white voters.

African American Organization and Protest

Certain fundamental values held by most African Americans have long provided a source of strength to cope with and resist discrimination. African Americans' respect for and commitment to civil rights and human liberty is one of the major sources of support for civil liberties in the United States today. Over the centuries, black resistance to white-generated discrimination and oppression has ranged from legal strategies, to the ballot, to nonviolent civil disobedience, to violent attacks on the racist system.[133]

The goals of black protest movements over the past century have included desegregation of public accommodations and schools and the opening up of housing and employment once reserved for whites. In 1905, in reaction to the pro-white accommodationist position of more conservative black leaders such as Booker T. Washington, the pathbreaking black sociologist W. E. B. Du Bois and other black and white leaders formed the Niagara movement to focus on legal and voting rights as well as economic issues. Not long thereafter, some of these leaders helped create the still-influential National Association for the Advancement of Colored People (NAACP).

From the 1900s to the 1950s, Du Bois played a role in the development of pan-African nationalism as a partial solution for the oppression faced by people of African descent across the globe. In 1919, working with other black leaders, Du Bois put together the first Pan-African Congress, to which delegates from fifteen countries came. Speaking for black peoples "of the world," the Congress called for abolition of slavery and for an end to colonial exploitation. Cultural nationalism was also strong in the 1920s Harlem Renaissance, a dramatic flowering of literature and the arts that celebrated black perspectives, traditions, and history.

Black organizations directed at self-help and philanthropic activity, such as the Urban League, were also created in the early twentieth century. These organizations provided aid for the urban poor and worked to end segregation. Legal action became a major strategy. One early NAACP victory was a 1917 Supreme Court decision, *Buchanan v. Warley*, that knocked down a Louisville, Kentucky law requiring residential segregation—one of the first steps in reversing the segregationist position the Court had taken since the late 1800s. Still, most Supreme Court decisions before the 1930s hurt the civil rights cause by reinforcing racial segregation in schools, transportation, and the jury system.[134]

Against fierce resistance the NAACP began a large-scale attack on segregation in schools, voting, transportation, and jury selection. Beginning in the 1930s, NAACP and other lawyers won a series of cases that over the next several decades expanded the legal rights of defendants, eliminated the all-white political primary, protected black citizens' voting rights, reduced discrimination in unions, voided restrictive housing covenants, and desegregated schools and public accommodations. The Supreme Court's separate-but-equal doctrine in *Plessy v. Ferguson* increasingly came under attack. Dramatically reversing its 1896 position, the Supreme Court in *Brown v. Board of Education* (1954) ruled that "in the field of public education the doctrine of 'separate but equal' has no place."[135]

By the 1940s and 1950s, African American communities were generating more militant anti-discrimination efforts. During World War II, a threatened march on Washington, D.C., to be led by A. Philip Randolph and other leaders, helped pressure President Roosevelt to issue an order desegregating wartime employment. After World War II, these black leaders organized against the peacetime draft on the basis that black citizens should not have to serve in a segregated army. President Harry Truman eventually set up an agency to rid federal employment of discrimination and a committee to oversee desegregation of the armed forces. The U.S. military became, and probably still is, the most desegregated of major U.S. institutions.[136]

The 1950s and 1960s brought yet another increase in protests against discrimination. One strategy was the boycott, such as that of segregated buses in Montgomery, Alabama in the mid-1950s, where black seamstress and NAACP member Rosa Parks refused to give up her seat on a segregated bus to a white person. Her arrest triggered a successful boycott by the black community that brought the boycott leader, Dr. Martin Luther King, Jr., into national prominence. King went on to become the leader of the newly created Southern Christian Leadership Conference (SCLC). In 1960, a sit-in by black students at a whites-only lunch counter in Greensboro, North Carolina touched off a long series of sit-ins by thousands of black southerners and their white allies. Freedom Rides on interstate buses came in 1961; blacks and whites tested federal court orders desegregating public transportation. Near Anniston, Alabama, the first bus of Freedom Riders was burned; in Birmingham, the riders were attacked by an angry mob of white segregationists.

In 1963, Dr. King, other black leaders, and many local black citizens launched a series of demonstrations against discrimination in Birmingham, Alabama. The fire hoses and police dogs used against the peaceful demonstrators, many of whom were children, gained national publicity for the movement. An agreement desegregating businesses and employment ended these protests, but another round of demonstrations was touched off when a black home and motel were bombed. Then came the massive 1963 March on Washington in which King dramatized rising aspirations for freedom in

Dr. Martin Luther King, Jr., gives his "I Have a Dream" speech at a large civil rights demonstration in Washington, D.C., in 1963.

his famous "I Have a Dream" speech before thousands of black and white supporters.[137]

Direct action against segregation in the North began in earnest in the 1960s with boycotts in Harlem, sit-ins in Chicago, school sit-ins in New Jersey, and demonstrations in Cairo, Illinois. The Congress of Racial Equality (CORE) accelerated protest against discrimination in housing and employment. School boycotts, picketing at construction sites, and rent strikes became commonplace. In 1964, protesters in New York threatened a stall-in to disrupt the World's Fair. Led by Stokely Carmichael (Kwame Ture), the Student Nonviolent Coordinating Committee (SNCC) helped to germinate a national movement for desegregation and real "black power." The growing number of organizations oriented toward black nationalism and self-help included the Black Panthers, a group of young men and women who started breakfast programs for children and engaged in surveillance of local police officers to reduce police brutality in cities. The Nation of Islam ("Black Muslims") pressed for black pride and established black-controlled social programs and businesses. Pride and consciousness grew in all segments of the black community in the North.[138]

White commentators on the nonviolent civil rights era have suggested that Dr. Martin Luther King's image was largely a media creation and that the civil rights movement was primarily a middle-class movement. Neither is true. Many local demonstrations included large-scale participation by African Americans from all economic backgrounds. Research on the development of these resistance movements has demonstrated they were grounded in organized activism that was in turn rooted in what Aldon Morris has called "a well-developed indigenous base."[139] This broad base included community churches, clubs, and other voluntary organizations that provided money and mobilized people, thus enabling activists in organizations such as the SCLC and SNCC to successfully fight racial discrimination and segregation across the country.

Progress and Retreat

The 1960s civil rights movement played an important role in pressuring Congress to pass major legislation prohibiting discrimination in employment, voting, and housing—the Voting Rights Act of 1965 and the Civil Rights Acts of 1964 and 1968. However, as we have noted previously, many of these advances have been undercut from the 1980s to the early 2000s by conservative presidential administrations. From 1981 to 1993, for example, government civil rights agencies reduced important enforcement activities, such as compliance reviews of government contractors and class-action suits against discriminatory employers. The 1980s Reagan administration tried to cut back the Voting Rights Act and federal programs designed to increase employment among African Americans and other groups.[140] The George H. W. Bush administration (1989–1993) continued the negative approach to African Americans, who responded by pressing their fight to improve civil rights enforcement. Bush appointed conservative Supreme Court justices, whose decisions limited discrimination victims' right to sue. These events convinced many black citizens that the federal government had turned its back on them.

The arrival of Bill Clinton in the White House in 1993 brought renewed hope among African Americans for better enforcement of civil rights laws. Clinton's civil rights record was better than those of Reagan and Bush: He appointed more African Americans (and women) to important government positions, including judgeships, than his predecessors, and his administration put greater emphasis on the enforcement of civil rights laws. For example, class-action suits brought on behalf of black individuals (including a group of secret service agents) who reported discrimination at Denny's restaurants were resolved by a consent decree in which the company agreed to pay $46 million in damages. This more aggressive Department of Justice involvement in anti-discrimination lawsuits was a clear break from the policies of the two previous Republican administrations.[141]

The national election in 2000 brought a conservative president, George W. Bush, to power. His conservative appointments have caused concern about further backtracking on civil rights enforcement. Many Republican party leaders have made clear their desire to eliminate affirmative action that is designed to increase representation of people of color and women in better-paying jobs and in education.

As of the early 2000s, the resurgence of conservative white political power at the national level has begun to generate new organizational activity in support of civil rights enforcement and the expansion of equal opportunity among Americans of color in communities across the nation. Civil rights groups have continued to protest on behalf of expanded opportunities for African Americans and other Americans of color. Washington, D.C. and other cities have seen important demonstrations against discrimination and the weakening of civil rights enforcement. From time to time, the NAACP Legal Defense Fund, the Leadership Conference on Civil Rights, and other civil rights organizations have mounted enough pressure to stop government officials from achieving conservative goals. For example, they have periodically helped block some very conservative appointments to federal judgeships, including Supreme Court positions.

African Americans have repeatedly organized movements for expanded civil and economic rights. For example, in 1983 leaders from several communities of color put together a very important grassroots organization called the Rainbow Coalition, which included black, white, Latino, and Native American activists who supported a progressive political agenda. By 1984, the group had registered 2 million new voters. One of the Coalition's leaders, Jesse Jackson, won nearly 4 million votes in Democratic party primaries—one-fifth of all the votes cast. Jackson was the first African American to reach this level in politics. Still active in the early 2000s, the Coalition has generated multiracial political organizations in many states. New voters registered by this movement have helped elect numerous representatives to the U.S. Congress.[142]

Sociologist Patricia Hill Collins has demonstrated that black women were an integral part of the civil rights movement of the 1960s, even though leadership roles were generally reserved for black men. Since the 1960s a number of such analysts have criticized black male leaders for failing to address certain issues that are relevant to black women, as distinct from the general issue of racial discrimination. In recent years more black women have moved into important positions in groups such as the Rainbow Coalition and have pressed for increased attention to the joint effect of sexism and racism on African American women.[143]

African American author and teacher Toni Morrison is a Nobel Prize winner.

EDUCATION

During the Reconstruction period after the Civil War, black southerners gained their first access to schools, both those sponsored by the federal government and by private organizations. However, by 1900, public schools in southern states were legally segregated under the so-called "separate but equal" rule, and educational facilities for black students were grossly inferior. Little money was spent on these children. In 1900 some southern counties spent ten times as much per capita for the education of white children as for that of black children.[144]

Despite relentless discrimination and segregation, black Americans pressed on toward their dream of a good education. By the early 1900s, a million-and-a-half black children were enrolled in schools. The South had thirty-four black colleges. Influenced by the nationally known leader Booker T. Washington, who advocated vocational education for black youth, black college curricula focused on skills suitable for an agricultural economy, which at that time was declining. Other black leaders, especially W. E. B. Du Bois, felt that Washington was too conservative, and they advocated a full range of educational opportunities for black youth.[145]

African Americans have long taken advantage of educational opportunities wherever these become available. In 1940 more than half of black adults over the age of 24 had less than a sixth-grade education, and fewer than 8 percent were high school graduates, compared with 26 percent of white adults. Forty years later, the proportion of black adults with high school diplomas had risen above 50 percent, and by 2000 almost 80 percent were high school graduates and almost 17 percent had completed four years of college or more (compared with 88 percent and 28 percent, respectively, of non-Hispanic white adults).[146] Although educational opportunities and attainments for blacks today are still not equal to those for whites, the black–white educational attainment gap has narrowed much more than the economic gap between black and white Americans.

The Desegregation Struggle

Movement toward school desegregation began in earnest in the 1930s with an NAACP legal strategy. Lawsuits attacking racial discrimination in graduate schools were the first to expose the "separate-but-equal" doctrine for the sham it was. In the 1930s and 1940s, a series of federal court decisions forced the desegregation of law schools and other graduate programs at several major universities. In 1954, black parents won the famous school decision, *Brown v. Board of Education of Topeka*. This decision forced the desegregation of Topeka schools and other school systems and set in motion government action to desegregate all school systems. This government action met massive resistance. White judges, often fearing violent reactions by whites, generally allowed desegregation to proceed at a snail's pace during the decade after *Brown*. Most white-dominated school systems circumvented *Brown* as long as they could, and most black children remained segregated. Increasingly, whites set up private white schools or resorted to violence. In 1956, President Dwight Eisenhower was forced to federalize the Arkansas National Guard to protect black children braving violent white mobs to desegregate a high school.[147]

The 1960s and early 1970s brought widespread desegregation throughout the South and court orders to desegregate some northern school systems. In *Swann v. Charlotte-Mecklenburg Board of Education* (1971), one of a series of court cases following *Brown* that expanded the attack on segregated schooling, the Supreme Court upheld the use of busing as a means of disestablishing a dual school system. In *Keyes v. Denver School District No. 1* (1973) the Court ruled that evidence of government-imposed segregation in part of a school district is sufficient to require complete district desegregation. Segregated schools now included those created by the deliberate location of new schools to reinforce existing segregation patterns. The following year, however, the Supreme Court began to back off from the implications of school desegregation in a ruling that rejected the inclusion of suburban districts in central-city desegregation plans. In *Milliken v. Bradley* (1974) the Court overturned a lower-court order requiring the integration of the substantially black Detroit city school system with the surrounding white suburban school systems. Since that time, an ever more conservative Supreme Court has gradually backed away from enforcing the desegregation of public school systems in any region of the country.[148]

In its early years, school desegregation reduced the number of black principals and teachers and thus had a negative impact on many black communities. Over several decades, most desegregation occurred at formerly all-white schools, where white teachers and principals predominate, rather than at the all-black schools, where black teachers and principals were common. In such cases, desegregation significantly reduced the number of black teachers with whom many black children come in contact.[149] Fewer black teachers has meant fewer role models for black children.

The Current Public School Situation

Today, decades after the U.S. Supreme Court declared racially segregated public schools inherently unequal, there is ample evidence that local, state, and federal governments have not provided equal educational opportunity for most children of color. Federal judge Robert Carter, one of the NAACP's lawyers in the *Brown* case, has condemned the nation's "dismal progress" toward educational equality: "Thus far, for most black children the constitutional guarantee of equal education opportunity which *Brown* held was secured to them has been an arid abstraction, having no effect whatsoever on the bleak offerings black children are given in the deteriorating schools they attend."[150]

Although national polls show the overwhelming majority of Americans support equal educational opportunities for all racial groups, recent analyses indicate that resegregation has occurred in many of the nation's school systems. According to a study by the Civil Rights Project of Harvard University, the proportion of black students in majority white schools *decreased* from 1988 to 1998. In the 1998–1999 school year, more than 70 percent of black students attended predominantly segregated (more than 50 percent nonwhite) schools, and more than 36 percent attended intensely segregated (90 percent or more nonwhite) schools. This represents significant resegregation compared with the low point of segregation (1980) when 63 percent were in predominantly segregated schools and 33 percent were in intensely segregated schools. In addition, predominantly black schools have a much higher concentration of poverty than do predominantly white schools. The average black student attends a school in which more than 39 percent of the students are poor, compared with fewer than 20 percent in schools attended by the average white student.[151] Harvard researchers conclude that "We may be deciding to bet the future of the country once more on separate but equal. There is no evidence that separate but equal today works any better than it did a century ago."[152]

Resegregation is in part the result of federal government policies that have opposed mandatory school desegregation and supported voluntary desegregation and neighborhood schools. Recent presidential administrations have cut back efforts to desegregate public schools and instead supported vouchers or tax deductions for private-school tuition. Local authorities have also supported these policies. In some school districts, school-choice policies have had an overwhelming effect on racial diversity. For example, one middle school in Winston-Salem, North Carolina went from two-thirds white to 97 percent black over the course of one summer after school choice was offered to parents.[153]

Some social scientists have observed that school desegregation can encourage housing desegregation. Cities with metropolitan-area school desegregation plans have experienced more rapid housing desegregation than cities without such plans. The extent of housing desegregation in cities of similar size and racial mix is directly related to the scope of their school desegregation programs. Cities with school desegregation plans that cover only the central cities have been found to have less housing desegregation than cities that desegregated schools in both central cities and suburban areas.[154]

Racial tracking and other forms of racial discrimination persist within our public school systems. A report by the community organization ACORN on New York City schools found widespread racial steering.[155] Trained testers, posing as parents, were sent to twenty-eight elementary schools in half the city's thirty-two community school districts. The white parent-testers were able to speak with an educator, such as the principal or assistant principal, much more often than the black and Latino parent-testers. Whites were two-and-one-half times more likely to get a school tour than testers of color, and on the average whites were given much more information. School staff members were more likely to mention programs for gifted children to white testers than to the black and Latino testers. The report describes these actions as "institutional racism" that is likely rooted in conscious prejudices, malign neglect by officials, and the "dysfunction that results when a vital public responsibility is managed by people whose racial, class, and cultural reality is totally different from that of the people whom they are supposed to serve."[156]

In the early 2000s, St. Louis was one of a handful of cities with a longstanding court-ordered desegregation plan bringing together poor inner-city children with those in the mostly white suburbs. By the desegregation plan's eleventh year (1994–1995), African American students made up at least 15 percent of the student population in all but two of sixteen suburban school districts. Drawing on interviews with 300 educators, parents, students, and lawyers, an evaluation study of the impact of St. Louis desegregation reported that many black students had achieved academic, and sometimes social, success in integrated suburban schools. Those who had succeeded in the suburban schools tended to have strong parental support or were especially gifted. Although a small percentage had developed a "raceless persona," most struggled "endlessly to maintain their self-esteem and to carry their cultural heritage with them to the other side of the color line so that whites might partake of it and eventually learn to value it."[157] However, each year about one in ten of the black students who transferred to the white schools found the social demands of white suburbia too great or the hostile attitudes of white teachers too intolerable and returned to their central-city neighborhood schools.[158]

As of mid-2001, the St. Louis school system was still struggling with difficulty to meet the needs of its large numbers of poor children. It has had to contend with periodic threats to its accreditation, and it continues to have a large dropout rate and a low high school graduation rate. Clearly, the problems of poverty, inequality, and racism cannot be met by working on public schools alone.

White hostility in desegregated schools has many negative effects on black children. Indeed, since 1980 many local black leaders have shifted their emphasis away from comprehensive school desegregation plans to other educational objectives. For example, black groups in Atlanta, where the school population is predominantly black, settled a desegregation lawsuit without a racial-balance plan in exchange for complete desegregation of the school faculty and administration.[159] Many educators have become more concerned with the survival of black children, especially black males, than with desegregation. Educators in some cities with substantially black school enrollments, such as Atlanta and Washington, have developed a curriculum with more emphasis on the cultural heritage of African American children.

In a growing number of cities, African American educators are creating special schools, or programs within public schools, for poor black males. Spencer Holland, director of Morgan State University's Center for Educating African American Males, has articulated the philosophy behind African American–centered programs: "Integration tactics don't matter to the lives of the children I deal with. We black people have to take care of these black children now."[160] This relatively new thrust adopts a survival strategy to support black children and black community institutions in the face of continuing anti-black discrimination and little government action against that discrimination.

Suburban whites also pay a significant price for continuing school and housing segregation. Gary Orfield has noted that whites who grow up in more or less segregated suburban enclaves will have "no skills in relating to or communicating with minorities."[161] As the United States becomes more diverse and multiracial, this lack of skills will become ever more of a disadvantage in social and political interaction. Such white isolation will also be a major handicap as the United States becomes more involved in international trade and diplomacy in a world where non-European nations are becoming ever more influential and powerful.

College Attendance and College Experiences

In a recent poll, 96 percent of black youths aged 11 to 17 stated that their biggest hope or dream for their future was to go to college.[162] Yet in 2000, only 56 percent of black students entered college immediately after high-school graduation, compared with 66 percent of their white counterparts.[163] The proportion of African Americans between the ages of 25 and 34 who were college graduates (18 percent) was just over half that of whites in this age group (35 percent).[164]

Until the 1960s, black college students in the South were restricted to all-black colleges. Desegregation opened many historically white colleges and universities for black students. By the 1970s, three-fourths of black college students nationwide were in predominantly white schools. Still, many black students today attend historically black colleges, where the campus culture is more hospitable to black students than that of traditionally white schools.[165]

Black students often face serious problems at predominantly white colleges. Murty and Roebuck have noted that "Frequently black students find white universities to be hostile places where they are seen as 'special admits' and beneficiaries of affirmative action. Moreover, adjustment requires adherence to white cultural norms, thereby necessitating the abandonment of black cultural roots."[166] Black students often establish their own networks, in part because of exclusion from white networks. Half the black students questioned in a University of Michigan study said they did not feel part of campus life. Many were disenchanted with their college environments. In the survey 85 percent of the black students reported experiencing discrimination on campus, including comments by professors that "black students aren't very bright" and vandalism such as "KKK" being painted on a house owned by a black organization.[167]

Research conducted by the first author at a major historically white university found a similar pattern. A questionnaire given to a random sample of three dozen black juniors and seniors asked them to assess this statement: "Today the [State University] is a college campus where black students are generally welcomed and nurtured." Only two (6 percent) of the thirty-six agreed, while 89 percent strongly disagreed or tended to disagree and 6 percent answered, "not sure." One young black woman stated the following:

> This university does cater to white students. The commercial strip near the university is for white people. You know, bars everywhere—all white boys in it, no black people. The frat row's white. No black Greeks, nothing. So they're coming from where they're coming from.... Sometimes I'm like, "God, if I was white, I'd have the best time."... They get to have parties at frat houses; they don't have to pay for it. You know, they just have the best time. Everything is geared toward them. Their [campus] paper is geared toward them. Everybody agrees.[168]

A tragic aspect of the barriers at predominantly white colleges is that African American students often identify these colleges not primarily with educational experiences to be savored but rather with an "agonizing struggle" with campus racism just to get a college degree.

Religion and Culture

One of the first major stereotypes of Africans and indigenous people in the Americas involved what Europeans saw as their "savagery." The irony of slave-trading, warring Europeans seeing Africans as "savage" was lost on Europeans at the time and has been lost on most of their descendants. The enslaved Africans brought African religions and music with them. At first, slave owners feared that "Christianizing" African Americans would give them ideas of freedom—as though they did not already have those ideas. Protestant missionaries were instructed that conversion of those enslaved to Christianity did not bring freedom, and laws were passed to support this position. Later, many slave owners encouraged missionaries, particularly Baptists and Methodists, to convert African Americans so they could be better controlled.[169]

Over time, African American religion mixed African and European elements, and the African values often prevailed over the European.[170] As slaveholders had feared, Afro-Christianity developed a strong element of protest. The view of God that many held—for example, the emphasis on God's having led the Israelites out of slavery—was not what slaveholders had hoped for. Hidden by Christian symbolism, slave spirituals sometimes embodied a strong yearning to be free. Regular religious meetings, which whites accepted as a natural aspect of Afro-Christianity, provided opportunities to plan revolts. Those enslaved were permitted to preach, and some preachers became resistance leaders. The freedom discourse African Americans developed in private was different from the discourse used in the presence of white masters.[171]

Because African Americans, whether enslaved or free, were generally excluded from white churches, they developed their own church organizations. In Philadelphia, for example, Absalom Jones and Richard Allen, after being mistreated at a white Methodist church, established the Free African Society in 1787. Later, Jones established the first Negro Episcopal church, and Allen played a role in the emergence of the African Methodist Episcopal church.[172]

The role of black churches became increasingly important after the Civil War. Churches were mutual-aid societies, ministering to those facing sickness and death, and they functioned as centers for the pooling of economic and other resources. Many of the new schools established after the Civil War were under religious auspices. Later, with migration to cities after World War I, many African Americans shifted to a less otherworldly style in their religious organizations. Urban social welfare and civil rights activity increasingly became part of church life. New urban churches became both religious and political forces. One is the Nation of Islam mentioned earlier, a group that broke with the Christian heritage and background. For decades now, Nation of Islam leaders have pressed for a religious approach suffused with much black pride and a strong self-help philosophy. Afrocentric leaders have arisen from this movement, including Malcolm X and, more recently, Louis Farrakhan.[173]

Today, African Americans mostly attend Protestant churches. They are members of a great diversity of groups, from the older Methodist and Baptist denominations to newer evangelical groups. Whatever its form, however, the black church is often, as one minister has explained, "the hub of existence in the black community," a "holistic ministry," and a "social center."[174]

Organizations protesting oppressive conditions have long been rooted in African American religion. Religious gatherings and leaders have played a significant role in spreading protests against antiblack racism since the days of slavery. Since the early 1900s, black ministers have often been political and protest leaders. The nonviolent civil disobedience movement that took place from the 1950s to the 1970s had significant religious underpinnings.[175] The prominent minister-leader Dr. Martin Luther King, Jr., who was raised in a religious family known for its strong support of civil rights, came naturally to his religious view of the legitimacy of nonviolent protest as a way to win concessions while at the same time healing the wounds of oppressed and oppressor. King led black (and white) citizens in effective protests, for which he earned a Nobel Peace Prize, and he died a hero whose example today inspires Americans of all backgrounds.[176]

The effectiveness of churches in providing leadership, as in mobilizing millions of formerly disenfranchised voters, is deeply rooted in African American culture. For example, the call-and-response format of many religious services, which allows the congregation to give the minister feedback on the sermon, has provided a context for response to calls to register to vote and participate in other political activities by black religious and political leaders. Political and protest leaders have harnessed the religious sentiments of an oppressed people to mobilize action against discrimination. In addition, African American music and singing have frequently reflected a strong element of protest against racial prejudice and discrimination from the days of the spirituals to the more recent blues, jazz, gospel, and hip hop traditions.[177]

RECENT IMMIGRANTS

In the mid-1990s and again in the early 2000s, Colin Powell, a retired U.S. Army general and son of Jamaican immigrants, was mentioned as a possible Republican vice-presidential or presidential candidate. For a time, General Powell, formerly head of the Joint Chiefs of Staff, was called by some "the most respected figure in American political life."[178] In 2001 he became the first African American to serve as U.S. secretary of state. Powell is a representative of one of several ethnic groups that today make up the broad group called African Americans.

Approximately 5 percent of the African American population is made up of immigrants from Africa and the Caribbean who have come since 1970.[179] The 1990 census reported more than 200,000 African-born individuals living in the United States, most arriving since 1980, with the largest concentrations in New York, California, Massachusetts, and Texas.[180] This is a highly educated population; this group has a higher median family income and lower unemployment rate than other African Americans. However, despite their educational achievements, they are still less well-off economically than whites.[181]

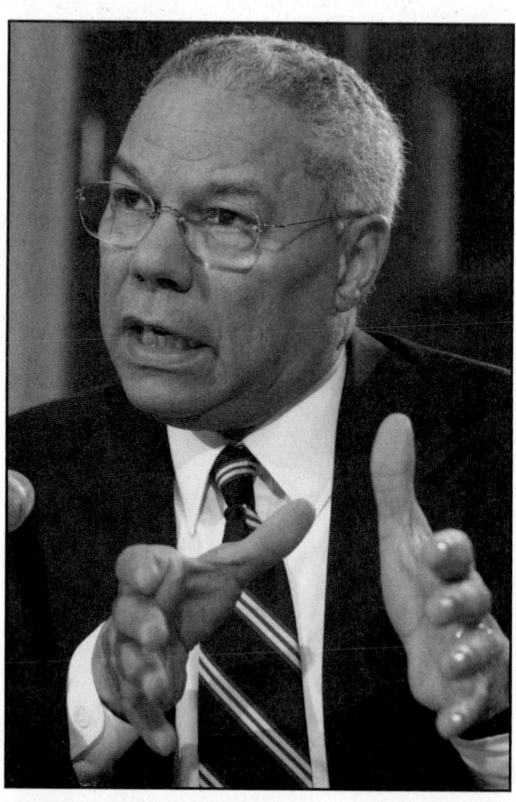

Secretary of State Colin Powell, the son of Jamaican immigrants, is the first African American to hold a major presidential cabinet position.

The 1990 census reported almost 1.1 million black Americans of Caribbean ancestry. One-third have immigrated since 1980, and most live in New York or Florida.[182] Caribbean Americans include a number of different national-origin groups, including Martinicans, Guadeloupeans, Haitians, Trinidadians, and Jamaicans.[183] The members of each group usually do not identify themselves as "Caribbean Americans" but rather expect their particular culture and national-origin identity to be respected by other Americans. These immigrants sometimes view themselves as African Americans and sometimes as an ethnic group distinctive from others in the general black group. Nonetheless, the Afro-Caribbean Americans have no choice about the "black American" designation assigned to them by the dominant white group.[184]

In recent years, Haitian immigrants have received more public attention than other Caribbean newcomers. Since the 1970s, thousands have sought political refuge in the United States. These immigrants, most of whom were fleeing a brutal dictatorship, were permitted to enter the United States until 1981. However, in marked contrast to Cuban refugees who fled political persecution between 1960 and 1994, who automatically qualified for permanent residence under U.S. legislation and were provided with financial support from the U.S. government, Haitians received no significant financial support from the government and were left to cope on their own or with the assistance of private charities. Between 1981 and mid-1994, most Haitians were refused entry; the U.S. Coast Guard intercepted immigrants at sea and returned them to Haiti, where they often faced persecution or death. This U.S. policy drew harsh criticism from U.S. and international human rights organizations. Amnesty International described Haitian prisons as torture and death traps. Beginning in 1981, those reaching the United States were held at detention centers around the country.[185]

The ouster in 1991 of Haiti's democratically elected president by military leaders created another flight of Haitians. As an example to stop attempts to immigrate, the U.S. government repatriated 500 immigrants in late 1991. Finally, in May 1994, President Bill Clinton announced that the United States would no longer send Haitian refugees home without a hearing.[186] Following the U.N.- and U.S.-supported overthrow of Haiti's military government in 1994, large numbers of the Haitian refugees opted to return home.[187]

Economic and Educational Situations

As a group, Caribbean Americans are better off economically than other African Americans as a group, although their situation is closer to that of other African Americans than to that of white Americans.[188] Compared with other African Americans as a group, Caribbean Americans are a bit more likely to hold white-collar jobs, somewhat more likely to hold service-sector jobs, and less likely to hold certain other blue-collar jobs.[189]

Immigrants are often willing to take lower-wage jobs than native-born Americans. In a study of native-born and immigrant black workers at a New York City worksite, Mary Waters found that white managers preferred black immigrants over native-born blacks for food-service jobs because the former were thought to be "more flexible" and "loyal." The immigrants' tendency to separate the hierarchy of the workplace from society's racial hierarchy caused white managers to see them as "nicer to be around most of the time." In some areas such as New York City, whites have singled out West Indian immigrants as a type of "model minority," as somehow "better" than native-born African Americans, who are stereotyped as lazy and criminal. This sometimes results in West Indian immigrants getting better treatment from whites than native-born African Americans. Still, the West Indians, particularly the second- and later generations, often face much racial discrimination, just like other native-born African Americans. In the previous study, white managers also reported that, compared with other African Americans, Caribbean immigrants were "more likely to challenge racial ceilings on the job and institutional racism."[190]

In 1990 the median family income for Caribbean Americans was substantially higher than that of other African Americans as a group but still well below that of whites. Caribbean American families were twice as likely to be in poverty as white families but only half as likely as other black families.[191] The more recent arrivals have much lower family incomes and a much higher poverty rate. In 1990, Caribbean Americans who entered the United States earlier, before 1980, were much nearer the white group in both median family income and poverty rate.[192] In addition, Caribbean Americans have somewhat higher levels of education than other African Americans as a group, but they are below the educational attainment levels of white Americans as a group.[193] Within the Caribbean group, members of the second generation have a higher educational attainment than do the immigrants.[194]

Racial History and Racial Discrimination

The relatively recent Caribbean and African immigrants have had a different racial history than African Americans whose ancestors came to North America generations back and in chains. In most cases neither they nor their recent ancestors have experienced legal segregation in the United States. Most come from countries in which black people are the majority and have a significant role in major institutions, including politics, education, and the economy. In numerous Caribbean nations, many if not most police officers, government officials, and white-collar workers are of African ancestry. Most immigrants have not grown up under recent white domination but only experience it when they immigrate to the United States.

Because they have lived in a black-run society, Caribbean Americans often question the odd system of racial categorization in the United States. For example, a Haitian perspective on racial matters is illustrated by a humorous story about "Papa Doc" Duvalier's reply to a journalist who asked him what percentage of the Haitian population was white:

> "Ninety-eight percent." The startled American journalist was sure he had either misheard or been misunderstood, and put his question again. Duvalier assured him that he had heard and understood the question perfectly well, and had given the correct answer. Struggling to make sense of this incredible piece of information, the American finally asked Duvalier: "How do you define white?" Duvalier answered the question with a question: "How do you

define black in your country?" Receiving the explanation that in the United States anyone with any black blood was considered black, Duvalier nodded and said, "Well, that's the way we define white in my country."[195]

African Americans who have grown up in the United States are constantly dealing with discrimination at the hands of whites and are routinely reminded of the significance of their African origin. In contrast, in the Caribbean immigrants' home countries, racial identity typically has much less significance. When most of the population is black, it is common for a person to not be constantly conscious of racial identity.[196]

Haitian American sociologist Yanick St. Jean has noted that many Caribbean immigrants continue to see themselves as culturally different, as "foreigners" in the United States regardless of their length of residence. For that reason they feel, usually erroneously, that white Americans are more likely to accept them than they are to accept other African Americans and that racial discrimination is mainly directed at other blacks and only indirectly at them.[197] Indeed, Waters' interviews with Caribbean American workers revealed that many shared some white stereotypes of African Americans.[198]

Although they have a strong black or African identity, Caribbean and African immigrants sometimes distance their identity from that of other African Americans. One reason is that there has been friction between immigrants and native-born African Americans, many of whom expect immigrants to reject their island identities and heroes and to speak without a foreign accent. St. Jean has noted that for Caribbean and African immigrants "the level of resistance to assimilation into African American groups is extremely high. As one social scientist correctly said: 'They want to be black; they are proud of being black; they just don't want to be black in the United States'.... The notion of blackness in this country is so different from their own. In the Caribbean, blackness is strength. In the United States it is not. Assimilating means moving from a positive image to a less than positive one."[199]

Initially, many Caribbean immigrants think that native-born African Americans exaggerate the discrimination they face. After they have lived for a substantial time in the United States, however, they usually change this view because they too experience exclusion and other forms of anti-black discrimination. When asked in an interview by the first author, "How do you personally feel being black in a mostly white society?" one Caribbean American professional, Mark R. (a pseudonym) stated the following:

> I usually interact with American whites from a distance. Most are acquaintances, not friends. Co-workers do not know who I am, what I really want. I am not invited to their informal gatherings. Occasional exchanges in hallways are only superficial. I feel I am expected to live in an intellectual ghetto, a very special and preset place which I call "colonization of thinking." From all appearances, I am expected to fail. I am denied even the basic respect due to me as a human being.... Some things I would never admit to. They are just too demeaning.
>
> I feel my differences are neither acknowledged nor respected. I am a Haitian American. I cannot and will not discard my Haitian origins. But in this society everyone must move in the same direction. It simplifies. It unifies. And to the extent that it also inferiorizes, the denial is a perfect tool to keep "others," and blacks in particular, within the boundaries of American cultural definitions. If and when my differences are acknowledged, AIDS, poverty, and religion are quick to surface as if these were synonymous with Haitian.

Why do many whites associate AIDS and "voodoo" religion with Haitian immigrants? Many Americans have erroneously believed that AIDS originated in Haiti or that Haitians have extremely high rates of AIDS. In 1990, acceptance of this stereotype led officials in the U.S. Food and Drug Administration to ban blood donations by Haitians, an action that provoked civil rights protests. Indeed, the evidence contradicts the notion that Haitians had a uniquely high AIDS rate at that time. One report found that San Francisco's rate of new AIDS cases was *ten times* that of Haiti and that other U.S. cities also had rates significantly higher than Haiti's. Yet people in these cities were not generally banned from donating blood. Medical anthropologist Paul Farmer has concluded that stereotypes of and discrimination against Haitian Americans are rooted in racist images of "savage and exotic" African peoples.[200] Haitians are not the only ones who face such stereotypes. Many white Americans also devalue the cultures of other Caribbean Americans and hold prejudices against people with both African and Caribbean backgrounds.

ASSIMILATION FOR AFRICAN AMERICANS?

Assimilation Theories

Assimilation theorists such as Milton Gordon have argued that the theory of assimilation is applicable to all ethnic and racial groups. Gordon has applied his scheme to black Americans, whom he has viewed as assimilated at the cultural level (in language and Protestant religion), with some black–white cultural differences remaining because of a so-called "lower-class subculture." Beyond this acculturation, however, Gordon noted little integration of black Americans into the core (white Anglo-Protestant) society at the structural level, little intermarriage, little erosion of discrimination, no demise of group identity.[201]

As we noted in Chapter 2, Gordon wrote optimistically about the eventual assimilation of African Americans, a trend he and others have seen in the now substantial black middle class. For that reason, assimilation-oriented scholars sometimes call for an end to anti-discrimination programs such as affirmative action. Optimistic assimilation-oriented analysts have often evaluated black progress in terms of cultural, economic, and social integration. The prominent sociologist Talcott Parsons once argued that racial and ethnic inclusion is basic to U.S. society and that this process will eventually encompass black Americans.[202]

Some social scientists and popular analysts have indeed argued that there has been a major collapse in anti-black discrimination in recent decades and that the full integration of black Americans into the core economy and society is well underway. These assimilationist scholars cite what they view as dramatic progress for the black middle class as proof of ongoing assimilation. They often suggest that the major remaining problem is a troubled black "underclass," whose difficulties are not primarily related to current discrimination. While recognizing that some discrimination remains, many assimilationists have in effect blamed black Americans for their slower economic and social mobility. In a famous 1960s report, Daniel P. Moynihan viewed black families headed by women as a serious retardant to progress. These arguments have been regularly resurrected from the 1970s to the early 2000s. Some scholars have pointed to a "poverty subculture" among low-income black Americans as a continuing barrier to group progress. The theme of certain white scholars and media analysts sometimes boils down to "Why can't black people be like us?" This notion suggests that black individuals, like those in white immigrant groups before them, should be able to assimilate—to move up gradually through the various levels of the economy, society, and polity—if they will only work hard and address their own cultural problems.[203]

Power-Conflict Perspectives: The Continuing Significance of Racism

As we noted in Chapter 2, power-conflict analysts reject the optimistic assimilationist view of African American mobility and incorporation into the society. From this perspective, the traditional assimilationist view denies the pervasiveness and persistence of racial oppression and related societal barriers. The current condition of African Americans is much more rigidly constricted and resistant to change than that of white ethnic groups. Once the system of racial subordination was established in the seventeenth century, those whites initially in the superior position, and generations of their descendants, have continued to monopolize the lion's share of the economic, political, and educational capital in the United States. Since the late 1960s, legal segregation in employment, education, and housing—which lasted nearly a century—has been replaced by informal, but still extensive, racial discrimination.

Articulating a theory of internal colonialism, Robert Blauner has argued that major differences exist in the levels of social and economic oppression that black Americans and white ethnic groups have faced over time.[204] Africans were enslaved and brought across the Atlantic Ocean in chains. Incorporated into the economy against their will, they and their descendants provided hard labor to build the wealth of U.S. society—first as enslaved laborers, later as tenant farmers, then as urban laborers. Even with northward migration, their lesser economic position relative to whites was little altered. They faced extensive racial discrimination even as the economic system was rapidly industrializing. This fact reveals a major problem in assimilation theory: Historically, initial incorporation of white immigrants into U.S. society has occurred voluntarily, most often at the lower economic levels, those offering some, if often modest, chances of upward mobility. This was not the case for most Africans. Enslaved Africans suffered attempts to destroy their cultures and were forced to give up many traditional ways as part of their incorporation into the economy of slavery. The Protestant religion and the English language were forced on them. They were generally forced to give up control of their own bodies, which became the property of whites; multiracial children were often the result of the rape of African American women by white slaveholders and overseers. In contrast with the assimilation view, power-conflict theorists emphasize the *forced* acculturation and *forced* secondary-structural incorporation of African Americans.

Power-conflict perspectives thus take a different view of the lack of full assimilation of black Americans into the economy and society in recent decades. They assign little importance to the so-called "subculture of poverty," but instead emphasize persisting racial hostility, stereotyping, and discrimination, both individual and institutionalized. When white ethnic groups such as the Irish began arriving in U.S. cities, mostly northern cities, they did not gain socioeconomic mobility solely on the basis of fair competition. In the process of coming to see themselves as "white," they sometimes displaced and discriminated against free blacks, who were then usually relegated to the lowest-paid jobs or unemployment. By the mid-nineteenth century, white immigrants were crowding black workers out of numerous occupations. Black workers were forbidden by law to enter such crafts as blacksmithing and mechanics, and Irish and German immigrants began to fill jobs once held by black workers.[205]

After the Civil War, most black families in the South remained where they were and became poor tenant farmers and sharecroppers. The new industrial economies of the growing cities mostly drew workers from southern and eastern Europe, not from the U.S. South. Discrimination prevented African Americans' structural assimilation into the economy on an equal-status basis with these European immigrants, who soon came to be defined as white. After 1910, with the trek northward, black southerners moved into low-paid jobs in urban industries; not until World War II did a significant proportion of black workers find some better-paid jobs in industry. The decline in demand for skilled black labor at the end of that war marked the beginning of the growing urban unemployment problem that persists to this day. Black migrants found that the opportunity awaiting them in northern cities was much paler than the promised-land image that had drawn them. For many decades now, racial discrimination in cities has seriously limited opportunities in both jobs and housing. Since World War II, the demand for black workers has been reduced not only by discrimination but also by automation and the export of U.S. jobs, by top corporate executives, to the suburbs and low-wage areas overseas.[206]

In Chapter 2 we noted the development of a renewed Afrocentric perspective that builds in part on earlier pan-African theories such as that of W. E. B. Du Bois. This Afrocentric approach usually emphasizes the role of European imperialism in dispersing Africans around the globe and in damaging and reshaping African societies and cultures. This approach examines the continuing Eurocentric bias in the dominant culture: The Euro-American worldview includes the myth of white (Western) cultural superiority over other cultures and celebrates individualism and materialism more than the cooperative and spiritual values often accented in non-Western civilizations. Because of the Euro-American view's negative impact on African Americans, the latter should direct their efforts to recreate cultural alternatives more fully informed by their African heritage; they should develop a reinvigorated African American or African diaspora culture.[207]

Power-conflict analysts underscore the point that racial oppression is neither dead nor dying. White racist practice handicaps black Americans today in all major institutional arenas, from public accommodations to employment, business, education, and housing. Power-conflict theorists are usually pessimistic about further incorporation of African Americans into these critical institutional arenas without major changes in the racist attitudes and actions of the white majority.

SUMMARY

Clearly, the social, economic, and political progress of African Americans has been severely restricted by slavery and legal segregation. Even during the first great migrations of European immigrants in the early 1900s, African Americans—many of whom were already "old" (tenth-generation) Americans—were still sharply segregated and violently oppressed. Jim Crow segregation greatly hampered the lives, including the economic mobility, of blacks freed from slavery and several generations of their descendants. Later, a northward trek of black Americans reflected protests against southern oppression, protests in this case "by the feet." Other types of protest against subordination, both nonviolent and violent, have punctuated the long course of U.S. racism. The segregation period was followed by a long epoch, still in process today, of widespread and informal discrimination.

In the first decade of the twenty-first century, most African Americans live in cities, North and South. In recent years, the migration pattern of African Americans has changed; more are now moving to the South than are leaving. Wherever they live, African Americans continue to face much discrimination and economic inequality. The Civil Rights Acts of 1964, 1965, 1968, and 1991 have made many acts of discrimination illegal, but they have not ended the millions of cases of blatant, subtle, and covert discrimination in business, jobs, housing, education, and public accommodations that African Americans face each year. Government anti-discrimination programs are too modest and understaffed to remedy this widespread anti-black discrimination.

The specter of "slavery unwilling to die" can be seen today: Informal barriers to voting continue in the South; most black children still attend de facto segregated schools; the majority of black families still live in mostly segregated residential areas; most black workers at all income levels face informal discrimination by banks, real estate agents, landlords, and homeowners; many black defendants are tried by juries in which black citizens are underrepresented if not absent; and most black workers face constant subtle or blatant discrimination in the workplace.

The impact of this racial discrimination remains painful, stifling, and cumulative. Reflecting on the costs of racism, a successful black entrepreneur has commented on what it is like to be black today in a predominantly white society:

> *One step from suicide!* What I'm saying is—the psychological warfare games that we have to play everyday just to survive. We have to be one way in our communities and one way in the [white] workplace or in the business sector. We can never be ourselves all around.[208]

8 Mexican Americans

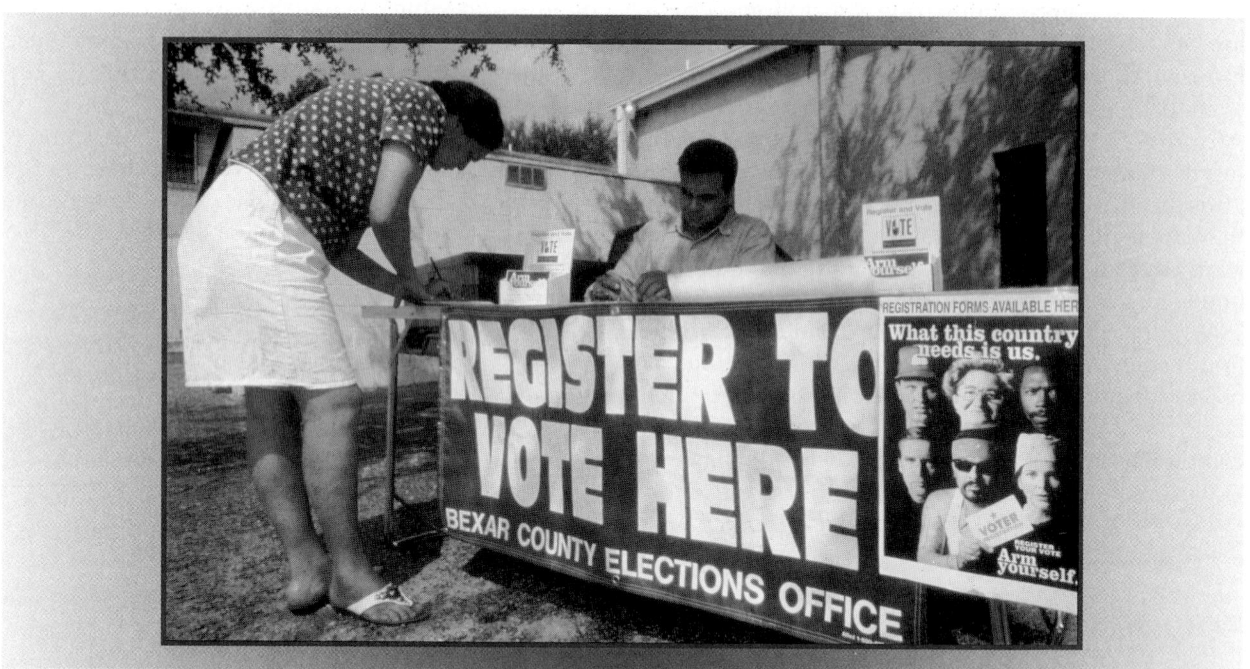

In May 1990, three white men were drinking beer in suburban San Diego. After a while, they decided to go "shoot some aliens" at the U.S.-Mexico border. Using a high-powered rifle, one man killed a twelve-year-old Mexican youngster who was crossing the border. The white man was sentenced to only two years in jail for manslaughter.[1] Clearly, the life of the young immigrant was not considered to be valuable by his killer, and the U.S. court did not place much value on it either. In recent years, white hostility toward Latin American immigrants has sometimes reached violent levels. This hostility has often been fed by stereotyped discussions of immigration in political circles and the mass media.

Many non-Latino Americans hold stereotypical views of Mexicans as sleepy farmers under big sombreros, "wetbacks," or mustachioed banditos eating a diet of tortillas or involved with folk Catholicism. Such popular images are often supplemented by negative treatments of Mexicans and Mexican Americans in schoolbooks that distort the history of the Southwest, as in the myths that glorify heroic white Texans confronting a backward and corrupt Mexican people. In addition, popular and scholarly accounts of U.S. history by European Americans* frequently omit significant references to Mexican American contributions to the past and present development of the United States.

The 2000 census counted just over 35 million Latinos (Hispanics) in the United States, up 58 percent over the 1990 census.[2] Latinos are now one of the two largest groups of Americans of color, along with African Americans. Coined by the U.S. government, the umbrella term *Hispanic* is widely used to designate persons of Mexican, Puerto Rican, Dominican, Cuban, and Central and South American heritage. *Hispanic* is an English-language word derived from *Hispania*, the Roman name for Spain. This term emphasizes the Spanish heritage of these groups while ignoring other (for example, Indian and African) backgrounds. *Latino*, an alternative collective designation, recognizes the complex Latin American origins of these groups. It is a Spanish-language word and is preferred by many Spanish-speaking Americans.[3] Both terms are used to reflect a new collective racial and ethnic consciousness that did not exist until recent decades. The relatively new idea of a Latino group is an example of the "emergent" character of ethnic and racial identities that William Yancey and his associates have suggested in their analysis of adaptation patterns of earlier immigrants from Europe (see Chapter 2).

Note too that combining the various national-origin groups into one Latino or Hispanic category masks their diversity. As we will see in this and the following chapter, Latino groups differ economically, politically, in their histories, and in certain cultural forms—for example, food, religious practices, and music. Although the Latino population is becoming increasingly dispersed, some geographic distinctiveness remains: Mexican Americans are still disproportionately concentrated in the Southwest; Puerto Ricans and other Caribbean Latinos, in the Northeast; and Cuban Americans, in the Southeast.

In this and the following chapter, we examine three large U.S. Latino groups: Mexican Americans, mainland Puerto Ricans, and Cuban Americans—groups with diverse histories and heritages as well as different experiences in U.S. society. Today, 58.5 percent of U.S. Latinos are Mexican Americans; 11.1 percent are of Central and South American origin; 9.6 percent are mainland Puerto Ricans; and 3.5 percent are Cuban Americans.[4] In the census the rest did not give a national origin. This chapter focuses on Mexican Americans.

THE CONQUEST PERIOD, 1500–1853

Beginning in the early 1500s, Spaniards conquered and sought to Catholicize the native population in what is now Mexico and the southwestern United States and to concentrate this population in agricultural and mining communities for economic exploitation. Since modest numbers of Spanish women migrated to the Americas, sexual liaisons, often forced, between Spanish men and indigenous women were common. The offspring of these unions, sometimes called *mestizos* ("mixed peoples"), outnumbered the Spanish colonizers, and they occupied a middle social position in colonial society below the Spanish but above Indians, persons of mixed Indian and African heritage, and enslaved Africans.[5] Mexican American scholar Ilan Stavans has argued, with some exaggeration, that "we are all children of lascivious Iberians and raped Indian and African maidens, and yet, diversity is our flag."[6]

After centuries of exploitation, Mexico finally won its independence from Spain in 1821. Before the 1830s, Mexicans had established numerous communities in what is now the southwestern United States. Several thousand people with a Mexican way of life and a self-sufficient economy lived on Mexican land grants along the Rio Grande in what would become the state of Texas. Soon, however, thousands of European Americans from the United States moved into the area, and in a few years the new migrants outnumbered the indigenous Mexican population.[7]

The Texas Revolt: Myths and Reality

Both the new U.S. immigrants and much of the Mexican population in the Texas province strongly supported a decentralized system of Mexican government. By 1830, some Mexican residents there had

*We use the terms *whites* and *European Americans* interchangeably in this book. Both refer to "non-Hispanic whites," as defined by the U.S. census.

joined the new white immigrants to protest actions by the central government. Certain Mexican government actions, including freeing slaves and placing restrictions on U.S. immigration, particularly angered the white immigrants. The causes of the Texas revolt are complex, including not only government policies in Mexico City but also the racist attitudes of white immigrants toward Mexicans, the resentment of white slaveholders toward Mexican anti-slavery laws, and the growing number of U.S. immigrants coming in illegally from the North. Until relatively recently, few U.S. analysts have been inclined to see the 1836 Texas revolt as territorial aggression by U.S. citizens against another sovereign nation, which in the end it was, but rather have excused the behavior of the Texans and blamed an oppressive Mexican government for the conflict.[8]

Myths about the revolt that praise the white Texans' heroism persist. Perhaps the most widely known is the legend of the Alamo, which portrays some 180 principled native-born white Texans courageously fighting thousands of Mexican troops. Actually, most of the men at the Alamo mission, located in the center of what is now the city of San Antonio, were newcomers, not native Texans. Many, such as James Bowie and Davy Crockett, were adventurers, not men of principle defending their homes. In addition, the Alamo was one of the best-fortified sites in the West; its defenders had twice as many cannons, much better rifles, and much better training in riflery than the poorly equipped Mexican recruits. After the Alamo fell and several further skirmishes took place, General Sam Houston managed a surprise attack that destroyed much of the Mexican army.[9]

The Texas rebellion was a case of U.S. colonists going beyond an existing boundary and intentionally trying to incorporate new territory into the United States. The annexation of Texas in 1845 precipitated a war with Mexico. Provocative U.S. troop actions in a disputed boundary area generated a Mexican attack, which was followed by a declaration of war by the United States. Again, the poorly equipped Mexican army lost. Many historians question the official view of this war as honorable, citing evidence that Mexico fell victim to a U.S. conspiracy to seize territory by force. In 1848 the Mexican government was forced to cede the Southwest area for $15 million. Mexican residents there had the choice of remaining or moving to Mexico; most stayed, assured on paper of protection of their legal rights and their language and cultural heritage by the Treaty of Guadalupe Hidalgo.[10] However, the white immigrants used legal and illegal means to take much of the land still owned by the existing occupants. Eventually most of the original Mexican landowners lost their lands.

California and New Mexico

In the early 1800s the 7,500 non-Indian residents of California mostly lived on Mexican-run ranches. After gold was discovered in 1849, however, U.S. whites poured into California, once again taking lands and political control from Mexicans. The means of takeover ranged from violence, such as lynchings and armed theft, to legal actions.[11]

At the time of U.S. acquisition, the fifty thousand Mexicans in what became New Mexico had long maintained their own cultural traditions. Well-established villages—Sante Fe dates from 1598—provided the organization to withstand some of the European American invasion. Initially, many Mexican American landholders did fairly well under U.S. rule, continuing to play an important role in commerce and politics.[12] Soon, however, many of them also lost their lands to the invading whites. By the mid-nineteenth century, the U.S. system of private land ownership was replacing the Mexican system of communal lands. Despite treaty promises, old land grants were ignored, and communal land was treated as U.S. government land. Everywhere Mexican landholders lost most of their land. The invasion of the Southwest was not a heroic period in which U.S. "settlers" appropriated unused land. It was in fact a period of imperialistic expansion and the colonization of communal peoples who had long resided in the area.[13]

Past and Present Immigration

Estimates of the number of Mexicans within the new territorial limits of the expanding United States range up to 118,000 during the 1850s. In the decades that followed, millions of immigrants entered the United States, pushed by political upheavals and economic conditions in Mexico and pulled by expanding opportunities in fields and factories north of the border.

The peak immigration periods have been 1910–1930, 1942–1954, and 1965 to the present. Immigrants can be divided into several major categories: (1) those with official visas ("legals"); (2) undocumented immigrants ("illegals"); (3) *braceros* (seasonal farm workers on contract); (4) commuters (those with official visas who live in Mexico but work in the United States); and (5) "border crossers" (those with short-term permits, many of whom become domestics).[14] The exclusion of Asian immigrants by federal action (see Chapter 11) and the pull of World War I–era industrialization sharply decreased the number of U.S.-born laborers available for agricultural work. Consequently, Mexican workers were drawn into the Southwest by the demand for labor. Under pressure from U.S. employers, federal government authorities waived immigration restrictions, allowing more than seventy thousand Mexican workers to enter the United States legally during World War I.[15]

This was yet another indication of the globalizing character of capitalism. U.S. employers went beyond the U.S. labor pool to secure low-wage workers outside the United States. As we have seen in previous chapters, recruitment of overseas labor by U.S. employers has for many decades been a major source of racial and ethnic diversity.

Mexican migration further increased after World War I. In the 1920s several hundred thousand Mexicans, workers and their families, entered the United States. Improved canning and shipping technologies opened new markets for agricultural produce. Not surprisingly, many U.S. business interests opposed restrictions on immigration. The 1924 Immigration Act, which barred most southern and eastern Europeans, did not exclude Mexicans. Mexico had become a major source of low-wage labor for U.S. farmers and other employers. Still, white nativists strongly objected to the growing Mexican population in the United States, which they feared would create a "race problem" that was greater than, as they crudely put it, "the negro [sic] problem of the South" and would threaten white racial and cultural "purity" in the United States.[16]

The Border Patrol of the Immigration and Naturalization Service (INS), which was created in the 1920s, has played a major role in the lives of Mexican immigrants and their descendants. In 1929, legislation made illegal entry into the United States a felony. Although given authority to keep out undocumented Mexican workers, the Border Patrol has historically tried only to regulate the number of immigrants, allowing enough to come in to meet the labor needs of U.S. agricultural and other business interests. In times of economic recession and depression, however, the Border Patrol has conducted exclusion and deportation campaigns. Then, in better times, more workers from Mexico have been allowed in, and the de facto restrictions have been less rigorous.[17]

During the Great Depression of the 1930s, federal enforcement of literacy tests and local government hostility in the Southwest greatly reduced the number of Mexican immigrants. In addition, considerable pressure was put on Mexicans already here, whether citizens or not, to leave the country. Many workers were forcibly deported in massive border campaigns; thousands, including some U.S. citizens, were expelled in organized caravans by social service agencies eager to reduce government expenditures for relief during the Depression.[18]

Braceros and Undocumented Workers: Encouraging Immigration

For a time, World War II shifted governmental approaches to Mexican workers. A 1942 Emergency Farm Labor (*Bracero*) agreement between the United States and Mexico again provided Mexican workers for U.S. agriculture. Over two decades, nearly 5 million *braceros* were brought in for low-wage work at the request of U.S. employers. Again we see U.S. employers going beyond U.S. borders in search of labor. Not surprisingly, this government program stimulated the migration of yet more undocumented workers. Since the 1920s, several million undocumented migrants have entered the United States from Mexico.[19]

Mexico, with the largest Spanish-speaking population of any country, has been the major supplier of immigrant workers for U.S. employers for decades. Today, most are not rural migrants but come from urban areas in Mexico. Mexican workers' entry into the United States has periodically met considerable public opposition. Union officials have called for restrictions that will protect the jobs of native-born Americans. Growing concern among nativist whites led to the inclusion of restrictions on legal Mexican immigration in the 1965 Immigration Act, which set an annual limit of 120,000 persons from the Western Hemisphere. This limit was later set at only 20,000 per year for legal Mexican immigrants.[20]

The U.S. economy, however, depends heavily on both documented and undocumented immigrants from Mexico. Undocumented workers are the "financial backbone of Dole, Green Giant, McDonald's, Stouffers, Burger King, the Octopus car wash chain, Del Monte, Chicken of the Sea, Heinz, Hunt's, Rosarito, Campbell's *m-m-m good*, Wendy's, Taco Bell, Lean Cuisine, Dinty Moore, Hormel, midnight shifts, front lawn raking, pool scrubbing, gas station back rooms, blue-jean stitching, TV assembly, athletic-shoe sole gluing" and many other jobs.[21] Mexican workers and U.S. employers are increasingly linked in the very important international labor market.

Migration and U.S. Involvement in Latin America

For more than a century, U.S. involvement in Mexico and the rest of Latin America has involved both the U.S. government and major corporations, and the goals often have been political and economic colonization—the expansion of the U.S. empire to the south. The U.S. military has intervened many times in Latin America to protect U.S. political and economic interests. In addition, the growing U.S. economy has created a nearly constant demand for low-wage workers in sectors such as construction, agriculture, and food services. Many workers have immigrated from Mexico and other parts of Latin America to fill these jobs.

On the one hand, most immigrants are attracted by the jobs in the United States. On the other hand, many are pushed by serious economic problems in their home countries, and the United States is often directly implicated in these economic problems. For many decades, U.S. corporations investing and operating in Mexico have helped generate out-migration. For example, some U.S. agribusiness firms have built large farming operations in Mexico to grow food for export, thereby taking over large amounts of land and driving off many small farmers who have traditionally farmed the land to feed their families. U.S. corporations' expropriation of agricultural land and wealth in Mexico has forced many Mexicans from rural areas to large cities in Mexico, where jobs are scarce. Like most immigrants before them, they seek work in the United States in order to support their families. Indeed, up to one-third of Mexico's total revenues come from the money sent home to Mexico by maids, laborers, restaurant workers, and other immigrant workers.[22]

Moreover, since the 1960s, U.S. manufacturing and industrial corporations have built thousands of factories and plants in Mexico. Many companies have built assembly operations, called *maquiladoras*, in the Mexican border region to take advantage of low-wage labor and weak environmental standards. Recent international trade agreements such as NAFTA have accelerated U.S. investment and manufacturing development in Mexico. One consequence of the border plants is that workers who migrate from southern Mexico to border areas soon learn that wages are far higher across the border, and some leave for the United States. It is important to note that the increased number of low-wage jobs in the border plants has not benefitted most Mexican workers. The era of "free trade," which was supposed to bring economic benefits to the majority of Mexican workers, has mainly benefitted a modest minority of affluent and upper class Mexicans and U.S. capitalists.[23] Not surprisingly, the Mexican government has made little effort to stop undocumented migration, which relieves poverty and population pressures in Mexico.

We should also note that the number of workers entering the United States illegally is less than many press accounts and anti-immigrant groups suggest. One Urban Institute study reported that most Mexican border-crossers apprehended by the INS annually "are temporary labor migrants who are caught more than once by the INS and who do not intend to live in the U.S. in any case.... A large reverse flow into Mexico goes virtually unnoticed and unreported."[24]

The best estimate for the total number of undocumented immigrants living in the United States in 1994 was about 3.5 million, just under one-third of whom were from Mexico. The *majority* were from Europe, Asia, and other Latin American countries. In the early 1990s, an estimated 200,000 to 300,000 undocumented immigrants entered the United States each year. One study of undocumented workers in California, which spanned most of the 1980s, found that most had friends or relatives in the United States through whom they found employment. The low-paid, often impermanent jobs available to most undocumented immigrants offer very limited economic opportunities. They work hard and mostly rely on their own resources.[25] Contrary to some stereotypes, few undocumented workers use welfare and unemployment programs. Typically, they pay more in income and other taxes than they receive in government benefits. Research studies indicate that undocumented immigrant workers have either no impact on, or in some cases increase, the employment rate of native-born workers taken as a whole.[26] The major exception is in urban areas where there are many unemployed workers of color. Native-born workers in the lowest wage job categories in these areas are indeed sometimes displaced by undocumented workers from Mexico.

The 1986 Immigration Act and Undocumented Immigrants

Growing concern over the presence of undocumented immigrants in the United States led to passage of the 1986 Immigration Reform and Control Act (IRCA). It authorized (1) the legalization of undocumented immigrants resident continuously in the United States since 1982; (2) sanctions for employers who hire undocumented aliens; (3) reimbursement of governments for the added costs of legalization; (4) screening of welfare applicants for migration status; and (5) programs to bring in agricultural laborers.[27] Just over 3 million undocumented immigrants applied for legalization by the January 1989 deadline; 1.7 million applications were accepted for adjustment to legal residence, representing two-thirds of the eligible population. Mexican immigrants made up three-fourths of those legalized.[28]

Many analysts feared that IRCA would encourage employers to discriminate against anyone who looked like an immigrant, especially an immigrant of color. One federal government study found that numerous firms were discriminating against U.S. citizens in hiring to ensure that they were not hiring undocumented workers. Other researchers have found a similar response by many employers and "an IRCA-induced decline in job opportunities" for "unauthorized-looking natives."[29] A 1990 Immigration Act was passed to correct some of these problems in the 1986 law. Nonetheless, employer discrimination against "immigrant-looking" native-born workers, particularly Latinos, continues to be reported in the early 2000s.

Congressional and public debates over this regulatory legislation have periodically revived anti-immigration arguments. Many native-born whites have long been concerned that the United States could not absorb so many immigrants, even though the ratio of immigrants to the native-born U.S. population was much higher in the early twentieth century when southern and eastern Europeans were immigrating to the United States in large numbers. In 1910 the foreign-born represented 14.6 percent of the U.S. population; today, that figure is only 10.4 percent, giving the United States a smaller percentage of foreign-born than many other nations.[30] Given its long history of successful absorption of immigrants, it is unlikely that the United States will soon be overwhelmed by the new immigrants. Implicit in many discussions of these new immigrants is a concern that most are from Latin America and Asia—that is, that they are not whites of European origin.

Anti-immigrant stereotypes and political actions have been commonplace over the past decade. Recently, a white Republican legislator in California distributed a racist poem titled "Ode to the New California" to his fellow state legislators. The poem mocked Mexican immigrants with lines such as, "I come for visit, get treated regal. So I stay, who care illegal.... We think America damn good place. Too damn good for white man's race." When the Latino caucus in the legislature complained, the legislator offered no apology and asserted that the poem was "funny."[31] Many newspaper and Web site commentators claim that immigrants cause employment problems for most Americans, increase crime, and overburden government services. Some Republican politicians and predominantly white citizen groups forced the anti-immigrant Proposition 187 onto the California ballot, and it passed with a substantial majority in 1994, although three-fourths of Latino voters opposed it. Proposition 187 sought to restrict undocumented immigrants' access to public services and required public employees to report undocumented immigrants. However, after legal challenges, in 1999 it was overturned in a settlement agreed to by the new governor of California.

Farmworkers harvest grapes in California.

In 1996 the U.S. Congress passed yet another immigration act, the Illegal Immigration Reform and Immigrant Responsibility Act (IIRIRA), which again focused on reducing the number of undocumented immigrants. This law, along with some welfare-reduction legislation, established regulations that restrict legal immigration as well. IIRIRA increased the number of border control agents and imposed an income requirement for families wishing to sponsor immigrant relatives. Sponsoring families must have an income well above the poverty line and must be financially responsible for immigrant relatives they sponsor. These new requirements discriminate against prospective Latino sponsors because Latino family incomes are, on the average, lower than those of white families.[32] The 1996 legislation was motivated in part by a concern that immigrants are likely to become dependent on public welfare programs. Yet research on Mexican and other Latino immigrants contradicts these often stereotyped notions. Generally, Latino immigrants are employed at higher rates, and use welfare programs less often, than other major racial and ethnic groups.[33] Thus, the notion that Mexican immigrants come to the United States just to get on welfare is contradicted by the high proportion (70 percent) of Mexican-born Americans in the labor force. This is significantly higher than the 52 percent of Canadian-born immigrants or the 57 percent of British-born immigrants who are in the labor force. It is also higher than the overall U.S. workforce participation rate of 65 percent.[34]

Population and Location

Today Latinos are currently the fastest-growing major racial-ethnic segment of the U.S. population, numbering more than 35 million, more than 12 percent of the population. The majority are Mexican Americans. The Latino population of just one metropolitan area, Los Angeles, is now larger than the total population of most states. Latinos (mostly Mexican Americans) are now one-third of all the residents of California, the nation's largest state, and the growth in Mexican American and other Latino communities has been substantial in many other states over the past few decades. Primarily because of the recent growth in the Latino and Asian populations, California now has a population *majority* that is not European American, and this will likely be the case in the second most populous state, Texas, by about 2004. In addition, the 2000 census revealed that the

Mexican American population is increasingly dispersed; large numbers are now the neighbors of other Americans in every U.S. region.

STEREOTYPES AND RELATED IMAGES

Early Images

In the 1830s and 1840s, whites migrating to the Southwest generally did not react favorably to the people already living there. Most coming from eastern and southern states applied stereotypes they had developed for black Americans to the indigenous peoples of the Southwest, both Indians and Mexicans. They attributed laziness and backwardness to what they saw as a Mexican "race." Most Mexicans in what would become the U.S. Southwest were of mixed ancestry, the descendants of Spaniards, Indians, and *mestizos* from farther south, and some had African ancestry. The European American immigrants brought with them a well-developed racist ideology rationalizing the subordination of African Americans, one that made it easy for them to stigmatize the generally darker-skinned Mexican Americans as racially inferior.

Existing records indicate that few of the new white immigrants saw the Mexicans as white but frequently compared them to blacks or Indians. In the words of one land agent, Mexicans were "swarthy looking people resembling our mulattos, some of them nearly black." Sam Houston, a prominent leader of white immigrants to Texas, called them inferior "half-Indians." The widespread white view that Mexicans had a "filthy, greasy appearance," as one traveller wrote, probably led to the derogatory term "greaser" for Mexicans.[35]

In the 1850s, John Monroe reported to Washington that the people in the New Mexico area "are thoroughly debased and totally incapable of self-government, and there is no latent quality about them that can ever make them respectable."[36] Ironically, these Mexicans' knowledge of ranching, agriculture, and mining laid the foundation for successful economic development in the Southwest by later white immigrants.

Increased immigration from Mexico after 1900 triggered more verbal and physical attacks. White supremacist groups raided Mexican labor camps and workers were beaten. The 1911 federal Dillingham Commission on immigration argued that Mexicans were undesirable. A "Brown Scare" hysteria developed in California between 1913 and 1918 amid fears that the Mexican Revolution would spread to the United States. Whites characterized Mexican immigrants as a menace to local communities' health and morals, and public pressure for their deportation mounted.[37] In the 1920s a prominent white member of Congress stereotyped Mexicans as a mongrelized mixture of Spanish and "low-grade Indians" plus some African slave "blood." In 1928 an "expert" witness appearing before the House Immigration Committee testified to the racial inferiority of Mexicans, branding the "Mexican race" a threat to the "white race."[38] Nativist scholars and popular writers alike expressed fear of "race mongrelization." In 1925 a Princeton economics professor spoke fearfully of the future elimination of Anglo-Saxons through interbreeding in "favor of the progeny of Mexican peons who will continue to afflict us with an embarrassing race problem."[39] Interestingly, an explicit category of "Mexican race" was used in the 1930 census, the only census ever to include such a category.

Much white commentary since the 1920s has stereotyped the Mexican American male as a crime-oriented villain. For example, a report by a white lieutenant in the Los Angeles Sheriff's Department after the 1943 "Zoot Suit" riots (discussed later) alleged that the Mexicans' desire to spill blood was an "inborn characteristic," a view endorsed by the officer's superior. Then as now, stereotypes linked alleged social or cultural traits to alleged biological inferiority: "The Mexican was 'lawless' and 'violent' because he had Indian blood; he was 'shiftless' and 'improvident' because that was his nature."[40] Since the 1920s, the results of so-called IQ testing have also been used to argue for the intellectual and group inferiority of Mexican Americans and some other Latinos, as well as of black Americans. A version of this view was expressed in the popular 1994 book, *The Bell Curve* (see Chapter 7).[41]

Contemporary Stereotypes and Prejudice

Stereotypes and prejudice targeting Americans of color can be found at all class levels of U.S. society. The tone and agenda of prejudice and stereotypes are typically set by economic and political leaders. For example, George Murphy, former senator from California, once argued that Mexicans were "ideal for 'stoop' labor—after all, they are built close to the ground."[42] In 1965 the famous Texas historian, Walter Prescott Webb, wrote that it is certain "there is a cruel streak in the Mexican nature.... It may and doubtless should be attributed partly to the Indian blood."[43] More recently, the stereotyping of Mexican Americans by middle and upper class whites seems to have changed for the better, but there are still whites who assert strong negative images. For example, speaking at a community meeting on border issues and Mexican immigration in the 1990s, a California state senator argued that public education should not be provided to the children of undocumented immigrants: "It seems rather strange that we go out of our way to take care of the rights of these individuals who are perhaps on the lower scale of our humanity." Latinos who criticized the senator's stereotypical comments were themselves attacked in the mass media.[44]

For more than a century and a half, numerous public commentators and some scholars have stereotyped Mexicans or Mexican Americans as passive and fatalistic. Some social science studies have reinforced the view that Mexican culture is one of passivity, lack of protest, fatalism, *machismo*, and extreme family orientation. Anthropologists such as Oscar Lewis and William Madsen portrayed what they thought was a folk culture of fatalism and familism in Mexican villages. This view has often been extended to Mexican American communities.[45] Other social scientists have pointed out the errors in assuming that life in villages studied decades ago was the same as life in Mexican American communities today. Traditional analysts have often overlooked the diversity of Mexican American culture from Texas to New Mexico to California—and, more recently, to midwestern and southern states. Researcher Lea Ybarra notes that a characteristic such as male domination in Mexican American families varies with class and educational background, just as it does among other racial and ethnic groups.[46]

Drawing their images from the mass media, political speeches, and other sources, many ordinary white Americans stereotype Mexican Americans and other Latinos in similar terms. One 1980s survey found that whites held stereotypes of Mexican Americans and Puerto Ricans as poor, lazy, or aggressive.[47] These images are still commonplace. In a 1990s survey, white Anglo college students expressed the belief that Hispanics were more likely than Anglos to be physically violent, dirty or smelly, uneducated, poor, and criminally inclined. These respondents also felt that, compared with Anglos, Hispanics placed less value on learning, mature love, physical fitness, and economic prosperity.[48] A majority of white respondents in a 1990s National Conference survey regarding interethnic attitudes believed that Latinos "tend to have bigger families than they are able to support." One-fifth of whites felt Latinos lacked "ambition and the drive to succeed."[49] In contrast, an examination of data from 21 surveys of Mexican Americans and European Americans found that Mexican American workers were *not* less work-oriented than European Americans; the former had a strong work ethic and were productive in their workplaces.[50]

Views of Immigration and Immigrants

The negative stereotypes held by non-Latino Americans are not strong enough to create majority opposition to Mexican and other immigration to the United States, although recent surveys have found some concern over Mexican and other immigration among a substantial number of non-Latino Americans. This opposition is not as widespread as many media discussions might suggest. While 41 percent of the respondents in one 2001 national survey favored a decrease in immigration, another 41 percent supported the current level of immigration or thought it should be increased, and the rest didn't know or were uncertain. Although the majority of respondents in this survey did not favor a more open border with Mexico, there was *no* majority support for a reduction in the current level of immigration. (Surveys of Latinos have found that they are much more supportive of the current level of immigration than the general population.)[51]

Still, in some areas that have experienced substantial recent Mexican immigration, anti-immigrant sentiment is significant. Two-thirds of the respondents in a recent survey in North Carolina, where the Latino population has increased significantly in recent years, felt their neighbors would not accept Hispanics into the neighborhood. Just over half said that they themselves were not comfortable around Spanish-speaking people. Fear of job competition appears to fuel these negative attitudes. Respondents with less than a high school education or who were unemployed were much more likely to express negative views of immigrants than those who had more education or were employed.[52]

In some areas, racist-right groups have organized protests against the growing numbers of Mexican and other Latino immigrants. For example, in spring 2001, forty National Alliance supporters held an anti-immigration rally in a city in northern Georgia, a state whose Latino population has increased dramatically in recent years. Today, on numerous Internet Web sites as well as in videos and books, white supremacist groups describe Mexican and other Latino immigrants as a "cultural cancer," a "wildfire," or a "gang of illegals" making the nation "less beautiful." Some even assert that Mexicans or Mexican Americans have a plan to "reconquer" the United States.[53]

Negative Images in the Mass Media

As a result of protests from Mexican American communities, the use of some extreme stereotypical depictions of Mexican Americans in advertising and the media has decreased in recent years. For example, in the early 1990s, community protests forced a taco restaurant chain in Houston to discontinue a television ad that featured a stereotypical Mexican figure. But serious problems remain. A 1990s' study of the portrayal of Mexican Americans and other Latinos in television programming found that most shows ignore Latinos or present them disproportionately as criminals. Latinos made up only 1 percent of television characters during the 1992–1993 season, down from 3 percent in earlier years. Sixteen percent of Latino characters in network series programs committed crimes, compared with only 4 percent of white characters; 45 percent of Latinos appearing in reality-based shows, such as *America's Most Wanted,* were criminals, compared with 10 percent of white characters on these shows.[54]

Hollywood films are problematical as well. Media scholar Charles Ramirez Burke has commented: "The way we are treated in movies represents a way that we are marginalized in the larger society. In that way it is a very accurate portrayal."[55] Numerous Hollywood films in recent decades, such as *Dirty Harry* (1971) and *Falling Down* (1993), have portrayed Mexican Americans or other Latinos as criminals, drug users, and welfare mothers. Hollywood's unwillingness to cast Latino actors in major roles over several decades led one of the most famous of all U.S. actors to hide his identity. The leading Mexican American (and Irish) actor, Anthony Quinn, used his Irish father's name and did not make widely known the fact that his mother was Mexican American or that he grew up in a Mexican American community.[56]

Mass media stereotyping, prejudice, and discrimination are often subtle, as in the absence or infrequency of positive pictures and images of Latinos in many U.S. magazines and newspapers. In a recent book, Marco Portales, a Mexican American scholar and university administrator, has noted that, "Since the 1950s, when I grew up, I have periodically observed that pictures of Hispanic people are not selected for the covers and inside pages of national and regional mainstream magazines, advertisements, and promotional brochures in the United States."[57] By such omissions, members of this subordinate group are made less visible by members of the dominant group.

Newspapers and magazines can also communicate negative images in the language and metaphors they choose. For example, in an analysis of the language used in a major West Coast newspaper, linguistics scholar Otto Santa Ana has shown that editors and reporters often write racialized reports on immigrants. Santa Ana's examination of numerous articles that appeared around the time of the Proposition 187 vote documents the frequent use of metaphors that portrayed Mexican and other Latino immigrants as animals, invaders, or disreputable persons. Numerous articles have characterized public programs as "a lure to immigrants" and have spoken of the electorate's appetite for "the red meat of deportation," INS agents catching "a third of their quarry," Proposition 187 supporters who "devour the weak and helpless," and the need to "ferret out illegal immigrants." The articles' use of metaphorical language—words such as burden, dirt, disease, invasion, or waves flooding the nation—conveyed an image of Latino immigration as dangerous.[58]

As with mock Spanish, such metaphorical language, which non-Latinos often use without thinking, bolsters the general public's negative view of immigrants. It plays down the humanity of immigrants, who are human beings seeking to make better lives for themselves. While the language of the mainstream media is not nearly as blatantly racist or as strident as that of the white supremacist groups, there is still some overlap in the metaphorical representation of immigrants as threatening, dangerous, animal-like, an invasion, or a disease confronting the nation.

Mocking Spanish

Prominent anthropologist Jane Hill has examined the widespread use of a mocking type of Spanish by otherwise monolingual (in English) whites in the Southwest and across the nation. This Mock Spanish includes made-up terms such as "no problemo," "el cheapo," "watcho your backo," and "hasty banana," as well as the seemingly humorous use of phrases such as "numero uno" and "no way, José." On the surface these terms seem light-hearted, but they subtly incorporate "a highly negative image of the Spanish language, its speakers, and the culture and institutions associated with them."[59]

Mock Spanish, which is common in gift shops, in board rooms, at country-club gatherings, and in the mass media, especially in the Southwest, is most often created by middle- and upper-income, college-educated whites. These whites also create greeting-card texts, coffee-cup slogans, children's cartoons, video games, and cartoons that mock Spanish-speaking people. Scenes in movies such as *Terminator 2* use "adios," "hasta la vista, baby," and similar Spanish terms in an insulting way not common among native Spanish speakers. Hill suggests that in a society in which openly racist talk is often frowned upon this Mock Spanish is used to perpetuate negative images of Mexicans and Mexican Americans: "Through this process, such people are endowed with gross sexual appetites, political corruption, laziness, disorders of language, and mental incapacity."[60]

A Racialized Identity: The Contemporary Situation

Historically, as we have seen, Mexican Americans have been socially constructed by most Anglo whites as a distinctive and inferior racial group. Regardless of how they saw, or see, themselves, they have usually been racialized by the dominant group as inferior and not white. As David Lopez and Ricardo Stanton-Salazar explain, "However ambiguous on the individual level for Mexican Americans, on the group level Mexicans have a history of stigmatization, economic exploitation and racial exclusion in California and the Southwest."[61] In recent decades, Mexican Americans, including recent immigrants from Mexico, have inherited this historical burden of being racialized in negative terms by a majority of whites.

Today the terms Mexican or Mexican American, as used by those outside the group so designated (especially by those in the dominant white group), usually involve a view of Mexican Americans as being distinctive in racial and ethnic terms. Recall that a racial group is one that is socially constructed centrally on the basis of physical characteristics considered important by the dominant group, and an ethnic group is one that is socially constructed mainly on the basis of cultural or national-origin characteristics considered important by the dominant group. Today, the majority of Anglo whites appear to view Latino groups such as Mexican Americans as at least quasi-racial, if not as a fully distinct racial group. Common terms for Mexican Americans and other Latinos include "brown" or "tan" Americans. As Rodríguez notes, "the stereotyped image (for both Hispanics and non-Hispanics) of a Hispanic is 'tan'."[62] Such terminology indicates the continuing importance of color coding; physical characteristics are central to the racialization process.

As in the case of African Americans, outsiders' classification of Mexican Americans as a racial group is only one part of the story. Today, outsiders use language, accent, surname, or first name as well as physical characteristics to identify a person as Mexican American or Hispanic. This typically means that most of those who are lighter skinned will also be identified by most Anglo whites as Hispanic—and therefore as *not* European American or white.

The subordinate group's reactions to the historical experience of being racialized and socially constructed by the dominant group adds yet more layers to current social reality for U.S. racial and ethnic groups. Typically, a subordinate group comes to see itself in racial and ethnic terms, yet this view is often not the same as that constructed for the group by dominant whites. Subordinated groups such as Mexican Americans and other Latinos resist the racialization imposed by whites in various ways. Some claim they are "white" like European Americans. This strategy is painful and may involve alienation from relatives and other members of the group, but it does make some psychological and social sense, for "white" status carries with it privileges, power, and no racial subordination. Other Mexican Americans assert their kinship with black Americans, and many others assert a distinctive Mexican American (perhaps mestizo) identity of their own. They may view themselves as part of a proud "la Raza Unida" or identify with a broader Latino (or Hispanic) community.

Recent surveys suggest the diversity of Mexican American and other Latino responses to the U.S. racial situation. A Houston area survey found that the majority of Latino respondents, including nearly two-thirds of the U.S.-born, did not consider Latinos (Hispanics) to be part of the "white race."[63] When forced by the 2000 census to categorize themselves only in terms of this limited spectrum of choices—white, black, Indian, Asian, or other race—some 52 percent of those who self-identified as Hispanic or Latino chose a racial category other than white. The fact that 48 percent of self-identified Hispanics/Latinos did designate themselves on this limited continuum as "white" may indicate the strength of societal pressure to be white as well as the complexity of chosen identities today within the umbrella category of Hispanics or Latinos.[64]

Conflict and Protest

The Early Period

Coercion was a fundamental factor in the establishment of white domination in the Southwest in the nineteenth century. Mexican land and agricultural development were taken over by theft and force. This created a new system of racial inequality. However, many Mexicans and Mexican Americans resisted. Folk ballads along the border have long sung the praises of Mexican "bandits" who were rebels unwilling to bear quietly the burdens imposed on their people. Their resistance actions are regarded as "crimes" by those in the dominant group, but often *not* by people in the subordinated group. Mexican rebels (for example, Pancho Villa) were often protected and praised by the common people on both sides of the U.S.-Mexico border.[65] Moreover, much land theft and other oppression of Mexicans in the Southwest had an official or semiofficial status. Law enforcement officers such as the Texas Rangers often terrorized Mexicans and Mexican Americans. The white (especially white Texan) myth of the heroic Texas Rangers covers up the oppressiveness of a police force that was long used by the dominant white group to repress the Mexican American population.[66]

More Attacks by Whites

In Los Angeles during the summer of 1943, violent attacks by white sailors on Mexican American youths, particularly those dressed in baggy attire called "Zoot suits," marked the beginning of what became known as the "Zoot Suit" riots. Groups of whites roamed Los Angeles beating up young Mexican Americans, and the latter organized retaliatory attacks. The local mass media had long exaggerated Mexican American crime, and police harassment of Mexican Americans was common. For example, the three years leading up to the riots had seen a sharp decline in the *Los Angeles Times*'s use of the term "Mexican" and a corresponding increase in the derogatory use of "zoot suit" to refer to Mexican Americans. Such labeling served to foster white hostility toward the city's Mexican American residents.[67]

Protests since the 1960s

During the 1960s and 1970s, three dozen Mexican American protest-oriented rebellions took place in southwestern cities. Young Mexican Americans, including groups such as the Brown Berets, took to the streets to fight back against oppressive police harassment and other discrimination. The East Los Angeles protests were among the most important group actions. In August 1970, police attacked demonstrators at the end of a National Chicano Moratorium on the Vietnam War march in which twenty thousand Mexican Americans took part. (Activists in the 1960s and 1970s preferred the term *Chicano* rather than *Mexican American*. By the late 1970s, activists were debating its use, and today *Chicano* is used alongside *Mexican American* by many activists and researchers.) Hundreds were arrested. Other protests along the route of a Mexican Independence Day parade resulted in one hundred injuries and sixty-eight arrests.[68]

U.S. towns and cities have sometimes used local police forces, which historically have included few if any Mexican Americans, to counter and try to end legal strikes and protests by Mexican American workers. From the 1960s to the present, the common practice of preventive police patrolling in Mexican American communities, with its "stop and frisk" and "arrest on suspicion" tactics, has periodically led to unfavorable police contacts for Mexican Americans. Two-thirds of Latinos in one Los Angeles poll reported that incidents of police brutality were common in their city; 35 percent of this group said that racist attitudes were very common among law enforcement officers. At public hearings in the early 1990s, an independent citizens' commission investigating the Los Angeles Police Department heard testimony from Mexican Americans that the department "acted like an army of occupation" treating them like the "enemy." Later that year, following the fatal shooting of a Mexican American youth, leaders from a large number of Mexican American organizations called for an independent commission to investigate discrimination by the Los Angeles County Sheriff's Department.[69]

In a 2001 *Los Angeles Times* poll, some 31 percent of Los Angeles Latinos were strongly critical of the local police department and disagreed with the statement that "most Los Angeles police officers are hard-working and honest." Many also supported oversight of the Los Angeles police department by federal government monitors. These responses were likely influenced by a recent police scandal in the city.[70]

Incidents of police brutality often trigger riots. Two 1990s incidents that received extensive media coverage occurred in California. In the major 1992 south central Los Angeles riot—many called it a rebellion—large numbers of Latinos joined black residents in aggressive and violent protest against racism, police brutality, and oppressive living conditions (see Chapter 7). And in 1996, Riverside County (California) sheriff's deputies were videotaped, and condemned for, clubbing a Mexican woman and man, both undocumented immigrants, with batons in the process of arresting them.[71]

Widespread anti-immigrant sentiment and the introduction of Proposition 187 and similar ballot measures have stimulated Mexican Americans across the United States to organize and take action. In some communities Mexican Americans have responded to the new nativism with school walkouts and protests. A large Los Angeles demonstration against Proposition 187 illustrated the broad-based community support for Mexican American political concerns.[72] In fall 1996, thirty thousand Mexican American and other Latino demonstrators in Washington, D.C. denounced restrictions on immigrants and called for an increased minimum wage, better educational programs, and an end to discrimination against Latinos.[73]

THE ECONOMY

Recall that Mexicans were initially incorporated into the U.S. economy by violent conquest and the large-scale takeover of their lands. An estimated 2 million acres of private lands and 1.7 million acres of communal lands were lost between 1854 and 1930 in New Mexico alone.[74] Across the Southwest, those who lost their land often became landless laborers. In the 1850s, one-third of Mexican Americans in the rural south Texas labor force were ranch and farm owners, one-third were skilled laborers or professionals, and one-third were manual laborers. By 1900, the proportion of ranch and farm owners had dropped to 16 percent, while the proportion of manual laborers—many working for large white-owned ranches and farms—climbed to two-thirds.[75]

Mexican Americans were the original *vaqueros* (cowboys) on ranches across the Southwest, and large numbers became agricultural workers there. Working conditions in agriculture were often so severe and the pay was so low that few competed with Mexicans for these jobs. Women were concentrated in agriculture, domestic service, and manufacturing, particularly in the garment industry and in canneries. Regardless of the job, these men and women generally earned less than whites and were usually assigned the more physically demanding tasks.[76]

Stratification and Discrimination in the Workplace

Mexican Americans have long faced individual and institutional discrimination. Beginning in the 1910s, for decades many agricultural firms, mining companies, and other firms openly paid differential rates for "whites" and "nonwhites"; the latter category included Mexican Americans. The constant availability of undocumented workers allowed white employers to keep wages low. Many U.S. unions also discriminated against Mexican Americans from the 1920s to the 1950s. Attempts to create farm labor unions for Latino and other workers date back several decades, but they were not successful until the 1960s.[77]

By the 1940s there was some improvement, but discriminatory barriers kept most Mexican Americans in low-wage positions. In 1943, President Franklin Roosevelt's anti-discrimination order and the tight labor supply temporarily opened some jobs at decent wages to Mexican Americans, but virtually none moved up into skilled or supervisory positions.[78] Poorly paid jobs and housing discrimination restricted most Mexican Americans to segregated urban *barrios*. Restrictive covenants were often used by whites to exclude Mexican Americans from better housing areas.[79] Since the 1950s, many Mexican American workers have occupied secondary-labor-market positions as farm workers, laborers, domestic service workers, or other service workers and earned wages far below those of whites.[80] Some have also worked in the food-processing plants and other industries in the Southwest. For example, a large garment industry developed in the Southwest to take advantage of unemployment in the female labor force.

Beginning in the 1960s, U.S. firms began building labor-intensive manufacturing plants, called *maquiladoras*, in the northern border region of Mexico to take advantage of low-wage labor. By the early 1990s, approximately 1,800 U.S.-owned *maquiladoras* employed half a million people in furniture, electronics, textile, food-processing, metal-refining, and other industries. Today, wages in these *maquiladoras* are far lower than in the United States. Large numbers of Mexican workers in border cities today live in shacks without water, electricity, or sanitation facilities.[81] Many Mexican workers migrate to the border areas to work in the *maquiladoras* just long enough to earn money to migrate to the United States.

Many white Anglo employers in the southwestern, southern, and midwestern states have sought undocumented Mexican workers because they will work for very low wages and can be exploited more easily than U.S.-born workers. If undocumented workers protest oppressive working conditions, an employer can report them to immigration authorities. Employers in agriculture and in the service industries rely on undocumented workers and have found ways to circumvent the immigration laws that officially prohibit hiring them.[82]

In recent years, investigative reporters have discovered a number of Mexican immigrants working under slavery-like conditions. In New York, deaf immigrants were forced to sell trinkets for very low wages and to live in extremely crowded conditions. Yet, the few exploited workers who come to public attention represent only a small portion of those forced to work under extreme conditions. Many restaurant employees work long (for example, fourteen-hour) shifts for less than the minimum wage. In addition, large numbers of domestic workers, housekeepers, and "nannies" from Mexico, Central America, and the Caribbean work in affluent white households. The "maids and servants" category of workers in the United States has long been racialized; many of these workers are drawn from racial groups considered biologically or culturally inferior by the dominant group. In recent years this occupational racialization has developed a global dimension as affluent U.S. families purchase household and other services by workers from poor countries, including Mexico and Central American countries. These workers often work long hours for less than minimum wage. Drawing on interviews with 153 Latina domestic workers in California, Pierrette Hondagneu-Sotelo concludes that these women pay a high price for their employment: "the loss of dignity, respect, and self-esteem; the inability to even live with their [own] children; and the daily hardships of raising families on poverty-level wages." She adds that these immigrant women workers are among the most politically disenfranchised members of U.S. society.[83]

Since the late 1990s, Mexican American and other Latino workers in several Long Island (New York) communities have cited numerous incidents of employment and housing discrimination at the hands of local whites. For example, a "quality of life" group recently formed in Farmingville has been described as a hate group concerned with keeping immigrants out. In spring 2001, Farmingville's county executive and legislative body vetoed a proposal to fund an immigrant laborer hiring site and community center. The recent beating of two immigrant laborers, apparently by white supremacists, was not enough to secure action for improved conditions.[84]

Employment testing has also documented continuing discrimination in U.S. cities. When matching pairs of whites and equally or better qualified Latinos applied for the same job, one-third of the Latino job hunters in Chicago and 29 percent of those in San Diego encountered discrimination.[85] In other mid-1990s research, many urban employers in Atlanta, Los Angeles, Detroit, and Boston admitted that stereotypes about the personality traits and behavior of Latino and black workers influence their hiring decisions. Many employers believe that workers of color are suitable primarily for lower-paying jobs regardless of their skills, and they seldom consider such workers for skilled positions. Even before they have specific knowledge, many employers stereotype Latino and black applicants as less likely than whites to possess skills of interpersonal communication, called "soft skills," and these applicants are thus less likely to be hired.[86]

In a recent San Diego survey, two-thirds of Mexican American youth reported that they had personally faced discrimination. One young woman reported that as a high school senior, despite a good job interview over the phone, she failed to get the job. She noted that "I guess they heard me over the phone, and I guess I sounded kind of white. Once I got to the store, I saw there were only white girls working there. Well, they never called me back."[87] Additional forms of discrimination often await those workers who are hired. A mid-1990s survey of Mexican American and other Latino workers in Los Angeles found that 31 percent had faced racial discrimination in the workplace during the past year. The discrimination included racial slurs at work and being denied a job or promotion because of their racial-ethnic background.[88]

Well-educated Mexican American and other Latino workers report workplace discrimination, even in industries that publicly claim to be meritocratic. In California's Silicon Valley, a number of Latino and black employees have recently filed lawsuits to fight the high level of discrimination reported there. One 1999 study of 250 high tech firms in this area found only 8 percent Latino and 4 percent black employees in a workforce of 142,000. Yet the workforce in the general San Francisco area is at least 22 percent Latino and black. Once hired by high tech firms, Latinos may face yet other discrimination. One veteran Latina manager reported being given very minor tasks, such as sharpening pencils and typing name tags. She also reported being criticized and belittled more than white employees and being treated much less favorably than comparable whites.[89]

TABLE 8.1 CIVILIAN EMPLOYEES IN EXECUTIVE BRANCH AGENCIES, SEPTEMBER 2000 (PERCENTAGE BY JOB CATEGORY AND RACIAL-ETHNIC GROUP)

Latino civilian employees in the executive branch of the federal government are most heavily represented in the "Other White-Collar" category where Latinos make up 40 percent of border patrol agents, 19 percent of nuclear materials couriers, and 12 percent of correctional officers. Few hold professional positions. The percentage of Latino workers is highest at low pay levels and lowest at the highest pay levels.

	LATINO	WHITE
All white-collar workers	6.4%	70.4%
Professional	4.4	78.2
Clerical	7.7	56.4
Other	15.0	62.8
Blue-collar workers	7.6	65.4
Pay Plans		
General Schedule	6.5	69.7
GS1	13.7	46.6
GS2	12.0	53.6
GS15	3.3	84.2
Senior Pay Levels	3.3	86.5

Source: Office of Personnel Management, <www.opm.gov>.

Continuing Language Discrimination

Language discrimination in the workplace involves treating someone unfairly because they speak a language that is not English, or because they speak a dialect of English that is not in favor. Since 1990, the Equal Employment Opportunity Commission (EEOC) has reported an increase in complaints against employers who bar Spanish-speaking employees from speaking Spanish in job-related or private conversations at work. English-only rules are common in job settings. Many legal scholars feel that such practices constitute national-origin discrimination and thus violate Title VII of the 1964 Civil Rights Act. EEOC regulations state that an English-only rule is discriminatory unless the employer can show a strong business necessity for it.[90]

Court decisions have varied. In *Garcia v. Gloor* (1981) the U.S. Supreme Court upheld an employer's right to fire employees for speaking Spanish. A Mexican American employee of a lumber company was fired for answering a fellow employee's question in Spanish. The Court reasoned that Title VII of the 1964 Civil Rights Act did not equate national origin with primary language and that language discrimination was permissible.[91] In a 1988 case, the Court of Appeals for the Ninth Circuit came to the opposite conclusion after evaluating an English-only rule: "The cultural identity of certain minority groups is tied to the use of their primary tongue." Referring to EEOC regulations, the court stated that "English-only rules ... can 'create an atmosphere of inferiority, isolation, and intimidation' [and] can readily mask an intent to discriminate on the basis of national origin." This case was appealed to the U.S. Supreme Court, but the parties reached a settlement before the Court considered it.[92] In 1991 a federal district judge in California ruled that an English-only requirement for employees in a meat-packing plant was discriminatory. Fluency in English had not been a requirement when the employees were hired.[93]

Lawsuits over language discrimination against Mexican Americans and other Latinos have become more common in recent years. In April 2001 a Catholic university in Texas reached a $2.4 million settlement in an EEOC lawsuit brought by eighteen Latino cleaning personnel. The housekeepers reported that they were called "dumb Mexicans" and told by their supervisor to speak only English, even at lunch and at their breaks.[94] The federal law on language discrimination is still developing, but bars to Spanish are clearly viewed as discrimination under EEOC guidelines and several federal court decisions.

Language discrimination has drawn substantial protest from Mexican Americans. In a recent demonstration of intragroup solidarity in La Puente, a Los Angeles suburb, local Mexican American women organized with Mexican immigrants to stop school board attempts to replace their district's bilingual education program with an English-only policy in school programs.[95]

Unemployment, Poverty, and Income

Unemployment rates for Mexican Americans have been high for decades. Mexican Americans' unemployment rate for 2000 (5.9 percent) was far higher than that of non-Latino whites (3.5 percent). In addition, Mexican American workers were more highly concentrated in low-wage job categories than were white workers.[96] Census data treat some Latinos as white and present both a "white" category and a "non-Hispanic white" category. Data labeled "European American" in Table 8.2 represent the latter census category and do not include Hispanics. Notice that Mexican American men are concentrated in the operator, laborer, production, farming, and service worker categories. Mexican American women are located primarily in sales, clerical (e.g., typists), and service (e.g., maids) categories.

TABLE 8.2 EMPLOYMENT DISTRIBUTION (MARCH 2000)

	MEN		WOMEN	
	EUROPEAN AMERICAN	*MEXICAN AMERICAN*	*EUROPEAN AMERICAN*	*MEXICAN AMERICAN*
Managerial and professional specialty	32.0%	9.1%	34.6%	16.2%
Technical, sales, and administrative support	20.6	12.8	41.3	37.5
Precision production, craft, and repair	18.6	23.5	2.1	4.0
Operators, fabricators, and laborers	17.0	28.6	5.4	13.8
Service occupations	8.7	14.7	15.4	25.7
Farming, forestry, and fishing	3.1	11.3	1.3	2.8
Total	100.0%	100.0%	100.1%	100.0%

TABLE 8.3 FAMILY INCOME LEVELS AND POVERTY RATES

	PUERTO RICAN ORIGIN	MEXICAN ORIGIN	CUBAN ORIGIN	EUROPEAN ORIGIN
Median family income (1999)	$30,129	$31,123	$38,312	$54,121
Percentage of:				
Families with incomes of $75,000 or more	10.9	12.3	22.9	31.6
Families below poverty level	23.0	21.2	15.0	5.5
Children less than 18 years old below poverty line	37.2	31.5	20.2	9.4

Although there is a growing Mexican American middle class, many families remain below the poverty line. Mexican American incomes have been consistently low compared with those of white Americans. Researchers have also examined income differences among Mexican American men based on physical appearance. Although intragroup differences in income were not as great as the income gap between Mexican Americans and whites, dark and "Indian-looking" Mexican Americans were found to earn substantially less than their lighter, more "European-looking" counterparts. Most of this earning differential could not be accounted for by variations in employee qualifications but was found to be attributable to discrimination by employers in U.S. labor markets.[97]

Table 8.3 (above) compares family income levels and poverty rates as determined by the U.S. Census Bureau in a March 2000 survey for mainland U.S. Latinos of Mexican, Puerto Rican, and Cuban origin with those of the European-origin population.[98] On family income and poverty measures, mainland Puerto Ricans as a group ranked as the poorest, followed by Mexican Americans. The median income for Mexican-origin families was less than 58 percent of that of European-origin families. Mexican American families were almost four times as likely as European-origin families to be in poverty. In 1999, about 57 percent of Mexican American men and 69 percent of Mexican American women who worked full-time, year-round earned less than $25,000, compared with 22 percent and 42 percent of their white counterparts.[99]

Problems of Economic Adaptation

Some analysts suggest that the processes of assimilation and adaptation for later immigrant groups, such as Mexicans, are broadly similar to those for early twentieth-century immigrant groups, such as Italian and Russian immigrants. However, as we have seen, the first groups of Mexican immigrants and their children—those who came from World War I to the 1950s—did not achieve the same degree of social and economic mobility as the southern and eastern European immigrants because of discrimination, economic exploitation, and segregation. In addition, later groups of Mexican immigrants, those who have come since the 1960s, have faced different circumstances at the time of entry than the southern and eastern European immigrants did. The white ethnic groups did not experience the high levels of job, residential, and school segregation and the racial stereotyping that are still faced by Mexican

TABLE 8.4 PERCENTAGE DISTRIBUTION OF HOUSEHOLD NET WORTH BY RACIAL-ETHNIC GROUP AND AMOUNT OF NET WORTH, 1995

In 1995 almost one-fifth of Hispanic households had zero or negative net worth, and the net worth of an additional 28 percent was less than $5,000. One in three white households had a net worth of $100,000 or more, compared with just over one in ten Hispanic households. Fewer than 3 percent of Hispanic households had a net worth of $250,000 or more, compared with almost 12 percent of white households.

	WHITE	HISPANIC
negative or $0	8.8%	17.8%
$1–$4,999	12.5	28.3
$5,000–$24,999	17.3	21.9
$25,000–$99,999	28.5	20.6
$100,000–$249,000	21.1	8.6
$250,000 or over	11.9	2.9

Source: U.S. Census Bureau, "Asset Ownership of Households: 1995, Table 4. Percent Distribution of Household Net Worth, by Amount of Net Worth and Selected Characteristics," published April 9, 2001, <http://www.census.gov/hhes/www/wealth/1995.html>.

and other Latino immigrants. Most southern and eastern Europeans came during a period of rapid industrialization, and most had access to blue-collar jobs that required little education. Growing numbers were unionized. These jobs enabled the white workers and their children to advance economically.

In contrast, today the United States has a service economy with relatively fewer industrial jobs. Most well-paid jobs require more than a high school education. In recent decades, immigrants with little education can mostly find low-paid or part-time jobs. Segmented assimilation best describes the experience of these Mexican American workers; they have generally adapted in ways that are different from earlier white immigrant groups (see Chapter 2). Lopez and Stanton-Salazar note that second-generation Mexican Americans today "may not serve as a traditional transition between their parents and their fully integrated and assimilated children, but rather represent the transition from a permanently disadvantaged minority to a permanently disadvantaged minority.... This is not a pretty picture; indeed if decent jobs in the middle are not there it could turn out to be positively ugly."[100] Unlike many of the earlier white immigrants, neither most Mexican immigrants nor the majority of their children have so far been able to accumulate the social and economic capital necessary to make the transition into the stable middle class.

Is There a Latino "Underclass"?

As we saw in Chapter 7, the concept of a troubled *underclass*—characterized by multigenerational poverty, high violent-crime rates, a school dropout problem, teenage pregnancy, and long-term drug use—is common in some analyses of African Americans. Many social scientists and media analysts have accepted the concept of underclass to explain racial and ethnic problems in cities. However, the scholarly and journalistic consensus is that this conservative concept often amounts to a version of the old notion of an "undeserving poor."

In the Barrios seems to have been the first scholarly book to take an in-depth look at poverty issues for urban Mexican and other Latino Americans. Assessing Latino communities in cities from Los Angeles to New York, several social scientists examine the communities' cultures, strengths, and humanity—as well as their problems.[101] Even in the face of substantial poverty and political and economic discrimination, the communities maintain strong family and community support structures, community organizations, and enclave economies. For example, Avelardo Valdez points out that the social and economic conditions in Laredo, along with that city's border location, facilitate illegal drug trafficking and associated illicit activities, yet the area's strong Latino extended families and residential stability have created "a strong sense of community structure and identification."[102] Additional case studies demonstrate how small local businesses and off-the-books enterprises such as street vending have promoted the economic vitality of numerous Latino communities.

The movement of large numbers of immigrants into many Latino communities has also buttressed local economies and maintained a demand for businesses providing Latino goods and services. Néstor Rodríguez demonstrates how the concentration of the poor that underclass theorists emphasize as negative can be positive for poor Mexican American communities. For example, the residential concentration of immigrants in Houston has stimulated the development of an enclave economy, reinforced job and housing networks, and provided a supportive cultural setting.[103] Similarly, Joan Moore and James Diego Vigil discuss Mexican American communities in Los Angeles and present a complex portrait: widespread poverty and continuing immigration together with a strong enclave economy, many extended families, and growing political power.[104]

Contrary to conventional underclass theory, these researchers find no one pattern in Latino responses to poverty. The character and shape of poverty varies somewhat from community to community, but each community has used its own oppositional culture and social, economic, and religious resources to work out survival strategies. While many of the characteristics associated with the conventional underclass portrait can be found in Latino communities, such conditions do not fundamentally *define* the character of these communities. Important formal and informal organizations buttress Mexican American and other Latino neighborhoods. Extended family and other social networks, as well as strong Latino cultural frameworks, remain at the core of these communities; these are reinforced by religious organizations and, frequently, additional community organizations.

Immigrant Workers and Housing Discrimination

Although they once resided primarily in the Southwest, Mexican Americans are now the neighbors of other Americans in many towns and cities. As we have seen, many are immigrants who work hard under difficult conditions and for little pay. They perform much of the hard labor shunned by other Americans: harvesting crops, building and cleaning houses, cutting lawns, and washing dishes. However, when it comes to having these workers as neighbors, many other Americans often treat them as unwanted outsiders.

Growing numbers of Mexican Americans and other Latinos report housing and related discrimination at the hands of their white neighbors. For example, a recent lawsuit by landlords in the Babylon area on Long Island accuses town officials of using rental permits and apartment regulations to drive out Latinos and other residents of color. The enforcement of housing codes can also be used to discriminate. Recently an organization representing Mexican American and other Latino farmworkers in Riverside County, California reached a settlement with county officials resolving complaints of discrimination in code enforcement. A U.S. Department of Housing and Urban Development (HUD) investigation confirmed that county officials used discriminatory code enforcement to exclude Latino residents from mobile home parks. Under pressure, local officials agreed to stop the differential code enforcement and seek new government funding to generate better housing for Latino residents.[105]

In a similar case, HUD cited officials in Elgin, Illinois for violating an agreement to end discrimination in code enforcement. In 1999 the city had settled complaints filed by seven Latino families, but officials failed to honor their promises to change code enforcement and accept HUD monitoring.[106] These examples represent only two of many recent cases that involve the use of differential code enforcement to exclude Mexican American and other Latino residents.

Housing discrimination carried out by landlords plagues Latino families in many cities. Recent audit studies using Latino and white testers in San Antonio and Fresno have found high rates of housing discrimination. In both cities Latino testers faced discrimination in more than half of their encounters with landlords.[107] Moreover, in summer 2000, a large apartment management firm in Orange County, California paid $226,000 in damages and penalties to settle a case brought by the county's Fair Housing Council charging the company with discrimination against Latino and black renters in eight apartment complexes. The settlement also required the company to provide fair-housing training for its management employees.[108]

POLITICS AND PROTEST

Before 1910 a few Mexican Americans, usually handpicked by whites, held office in territorial and state legislatures in the Southwest. White ranchers and those who controlled railroads, mining interests, land companies, and other large enterprises dominated local and state politics.[109] By means of a poll tax, an all-white primary, and threats of violence, these interests kept Mexican American voting strength low. Between 1910 and the 1940s, few Mexican Americans voted in southwestern areas. Over subsequent decades, voting strength was expanded by legal victories in the form of the Twenty-fourth Amendment, which banned the poll tax, and a California court case knocking down an English-only literacy requirement for voting.

In some areas the gerrymandering of voting districts has continued to dilute Mexican American voting strength and prevent the election of Latino political candidates. Lawsuits, for example *Garza v. County of Los Angeles* (1990) and *Williams v. City of Dallas* (1990), have challenged the intentional fragmentation of the Latino voting population and the discriminatory effects of at-large city council seats.[110] These lawsuits have forced some white-controlled governments to create single member districts with Latino voting majorities, and these new districts have elected Latino political officials.

Voter registration and voter turnout among Mexican Americans and other Latinos have risen substantially over the past two decades. Latino voter registration increased 164 percent nationally between 1976 and 1996, compared with a 31 percent increase for non-Latinos. Voter turnout grew by 135 percent over this same period, compared with 21 percent for non-Latinos.[111] Large numbers of potential Mexican American and other Latino voters are too young or have not yet become citizens. Thus, Latinos' electoral strength will likely increase even more in the coming decades.

In a 2001 election, former California Assembly speaker Antonio Villaraigosa came close to being elected the first Latino mayor of Los Angeles.

Growing Political Representation

Numerous examples of slowly expanding, sometimes regressing, political participation for Mexican Americans can be seen in the counties and cities of the Southwest and other regions, from the late 1940s to the present. Los Angeles, which has the largest Mexican American population of any U.S. city, elected its first Mexican American city council member in 1949. However, the city had no Mexican Americans on its council between the early 1960s and the early 1970s.[112] In 1991, Gloria Molina, the daughter of a Mexican immigrant laborer and a former city councilmember, became the first Mexican American, and the first woman, elected to the Los Angeles County Board of Supervisors, filling a position created by court-ordered redistricting designed to remedy Latinos' lack of representation.[113]

Today, the National Association of Latino Elected and Appointed Officials Educational Fund has become one of the most important organizations seeking to educate and empower Latinos politically. The organization's 5,000 members come from all government levels, and the organization has played a major role in increasing voter registration and turnout. A recent study of congressional districts carried out by the organization found that one-fourth of the 435 districts have a Latino population percentage of at least 12.5 percent, enough to be politically significant. In 2001 some 40 percent of these congressional districts were represented by Republicans and 60 percent by Democrats. Given that most Latino voters—with the notable exception of Cuban Americans—vote Democratic, the future translation of Latino residents into voters likely bodes well for Democratic candidates.[114]

Mexican Americans moved from no representation on school boards in prior decades to 470 officials among the 4,600 board members in the Southwest in the 1960s. The total number of Mexican Americans serving at all political levels has increased gradually but significantly since that time, to about six thousand today. Gradually, the growing numbers of registered voters have brought the group greater political power. Mexican Americans and other Latinos currently constitute the largest voting bloc in Miami, San Antonio, Los Angeles, and New York.[115] Several cities, small and large, now have Mexican American mayors. In 1981, Henry Cisneros, who later served as Secretary of Housing and Urban Development in the Clinton administration, was elected mayor of San Antonio, the first Mexican American mayor of a large city. His victory was the culmination of ten years of organization. Cisneros was elected by means of a political alignment between a white business elite and the city's new Latino middle class. In spring 2001, a young city councilmember, Ed Garza, was elected as San Antonio's mayor with a similar coalition. Such coalitions of Anglo business elites and the Latino middle class have been successful in several cities, including those along the U.S.-Mexico border. The most successful Latino politicians since the 1980s have tended to be business- or professional-oriented rather than community activists or labor leaders. In 2001, five large cities had Mexican American mayors (San Jose, Santa Ana, El Paso, San Antonio, and Albuquerque); four of these had a business or professional background.[116]

Between 1984 and 2000, the number of Latinos in state legislatures nationwide increased from 113 to 198. Most are Mexican American. In 2000, New Mexico had the largest number (forty-four) of Latino state lawmakers. In Texas, where an increasing proportion of the voting age population is Latino, Latinos hold thirty-five positions in the state legislature. And in California, the number is now twenty-seven, up some twenty legislators since 1990.[117]

Still, the number of Mexican American and other Latino elected and appointed officials at the state and national levels remains low relative to the Latino population percentage. Only a handful have served in top state executive positions, such as governors. In 1988, President Ronald Reagan appointed Lauro Cavazos as Secretary of Education, the first Mexican American (and Latino) ever appointed to a presidential cabinet. President Bill Clinton appointed two more Mexican Americans to Cabinet posts: Henry Cisneros as Secretary of Housing and Urban Development and Federico Peña as Secretary of Transportation. In 2001, President George W. Bush appointed one Latino to his cabinet, Mel Martinez, a Cuban American. In addition, as of mid-2001, there were nineteen Latino members of the U.S. House of Representatives; sixteen of these were Democrats. This marked a significant increase over the past two decades, but this percentage (4.4 percent) of House members was still well below the Latino percentage (12.5 percent) in the U.S. population. As of late 2001, there were no Latinos in the U.S. Senate.

Still, these growing numbers are politically significant in many ways. For example, the international political concerns of many Mexican immigrants have helped to expand the political involvement of Mexican American and other U.S. leaders in the international arena, including placing a greater emphasis on relations between the United States and Mexico.[118]

Support for the Democratic Party

In the 1990, 1992, and 1994 national elections, at least 70 percent of Latino voters nationwide supported Democratic candidates. In the 1996 election, Latino voters, the majority of whom are Mexican American, for the first time voted at a rate greater than the national rate. This Latino turnout had an important impact not only on the presidential election but also on local and state elections from New York to Florida, Texas, and California. On the average, Democratic candidates garnered 65–70 percent of the Latino vote.[119]

In the 2000 presidential election, an estimated 63 percent of Latinos voted for the Democrat.[120] Significantly, both that Democratic candidate, Al Gore, and the Republican victor, George W. Bush, spoke Spanish during the campaign and actively sought Latino voters, a first for presidential elections. In his first year in office, Bush became the *first* U.S. president to give a White House address in Spanish. Clearly, Mexican and other Latin American immigrants and their children (and grandchildren) are beginning to have a significant influence in the political arena.

The Courts and the Police

Underrepresentation in the judicial system—as jurors and judges—has been common. In *Hernandez v. Texas* (1954), the U.S. Supreme Court upheld an appeal of an all-white jury's conviction of a Mexican American defendant on the grounds that Mexican Americans were excluded from jury service. The court noted that the lack of Mexican American representation on any jury over a period of twenty-five years in a county that was 14 percent Mexican American was evidence of discrimination.[121]

Not until the 1960s was the first Mexican American federal judge appointed. Since the 1970s and 1980s, the number of judges has slowly improved, but it is still relatively low today. Mexican Americans are also underrepresented in most historically white police departments. Many Mexican American applicants have been denied police positions by the indirect discrimination of height and weight requirements and by English-language requirements, as well as by too-low scores on conventional English-language examinations. Also, very few Mexican or other Latino Americans have served at the higher levels of the U.S. Department of Justice or other federal law enforcement agencies.[122]

Given this underrepresentation, it is not surprising that discrimination in the criminal justice system has occurred. Arizona, California, and Colorado have required jurors to be able to speak English, screening out many citizens; the pool of jurors in numerous states has until recently been selected by whatever method has suited (usually white) jury commissioners. Mexican Americans charged with crimes have frequently been judged by juries containing few if any of their peers. Courtrooms in which no one understands Spanish present a language problem for some defendants. Besides facing an absence of Spanish interpreters in courtrooms, defendants have been subjected to excessive bail, poor legal counsel, and the stereotyped views that some white judges hold of Mexican American defendants. In some cases, white prosecutors have successfully excluded Latinos from juries on the basis of language.[123]

An early-1990s Supreme Court decision upheld a prosecutor's exclusion of bilingual Latino jurors who had hesitated before agreeing to accept the official English translation of the Spanish-language testimony that they would hear in the trial. In contrast, a judge in San Diego County, California, dismissed fifteen indictments handed down by the county's grand jury because the pool from which the grand jurors were selected did not represent a fair cross-section of the county. The county population was more than 20 percent Latino, yet the grand jury pool was only 3.4 percent Latino.[124]

The Chicano Political Movement

Disenchantment with the accommodationist perspective of some middle-class Mexican American leaders led to the emergence of the Chicano movement in the 1960s, a militant social movement that sought greater political power. Lacking influence in mainstream parties, many Mexican Americans joined the La Raza Unida party (LRUP). The LRUP's goals included significant representation in local governments and pressing the latter to serve community needs and to reduce poverty.[125] The LRUP's major political successes occurred in Crystal City, a south Texas city mostly populated by poor Mexican Americans. During the 1960s, the LRUP became a leading political force in the area, and by 1970 Mexican Americans had won control of the school board and city council.[126] Refusing to tolerate self-government by Mexican Americans, white officials cut off state and federal funding, almost bankrupting the city, and then blamed the Mexican American leadership for the city's difficulties.[127] By the 1980s, Mexican Americans were identified no longer with the LRUP but rather with the state Democratic party. Yet the LRUP had brought about the democratization of some southwestern communities and a substantial increase in political participation.[128]

Mexican American women held a range of important leadership roles within the LRUP. The vast majority of Mexican Americans elected to office in the Crystal City area were women. As Marta Cotera notes, "Feminism has come easily for Chicanas because of the woman's traditional role and strength as center or heart of the family.... The tradition of activism inherited from women's participation in armed rebellions in Mexico and in the political life of Mexico has also strengthened the Chicanas' position."[129] Mexican American feminists have faced major barriers. From the beginning to the present, many issues of greatest concern to them, including poverty and discrimination, have not been central to the mainstream (white) women's movement. They have also encountered sexism from some men in their own communities who resist women moving beyond a more traditional gender role.[130]

Other Organizations and Protest

Union organization has a long history among Mexican Americans. The first permanent organization was the Confederacion de Uniones Obreras Mexicanas (CUOM), organized in California in 1927 with 3,000 members. One CUOM strike was stopped by deportation to Mexico and numerous arrests. Mexican American women participated in early strikes as members of the International Ladies Garment Workers Union. In addition, mutual-benefit associations developed early. These included worker alliances that pooled resources and provided social support as well as religious brotherhoods. The League of United Latin American Citizens (LULAC) was organized in southern Texas in the 1920s. Oriented toward civic activities, LULAC pressed for an end to racial discrimination.[131]

After a Texas cemetery refused to allow the burial of a Mexican American (World War II) veteran, the American GI Forum was established to organize Mexican American veterans and work for expanded civil rights. In Los Angeles the Community Service Organization worked to organize voters. Two groups that formed about 1960—the Mexican American Political Association in California and the Political Association of Spanish-Speaking Organizations in Texas—focused mostly on political goals. Protests intensified in the 1960s. One Denver group worked for school reform and an end to police brutality. Youth organizations including the Mexican American Youth Organization and the Brown Berets worked for better education, employment, and housing. A new ideology of *Chicanismo* that espoused a philosophy of anti-racism and decolonization developed in many circles.[132]

The Alianza Federal de Mercedes was founded in 1963 by Reies Lopez Tijerina after he had spent some years researching old Mexican land grants. In July 1966 a group of Alianza members marched to Santa Fe, New Mexico and presented a statement of grievances about Anglo theft of Mexican land grants in the state. Another group camped on Kit Carson National Forest land, once part of a Mexican communal land grant. Forest rangers who tried to stop them were seized and tried for violating old land-grant boundaries.[133]

Since the 1980s, the Southwest Voter Registration Education Project and similar groups have participated in hundreds of voter-registration campaigns and have joined in filing lawsuits to dismantle discriminatory election systems. The Mexican American Legal Defense and Education Fund (MALDEF), founded in 1968 to address problems of jury discrimination, police brutality, and school segregation, is another active force for change. MALDEF has filed class-action suits targeting discrimination and has worked to increase voting strength and political representation.[134] MALDEF was one of the groups that in the mid-1990s successfully challenged California's Proposition 187 in court.

With the recent growth in Mexican American and other Latino populations in states outside the Southwest, MALDEF has expanded its civil rights efforts and, as of late 2001, was planning to open an office in Atlanta, where another Latino organization, the National Council of La Raza also was planning to open an office. Reports of discrimination against Latinos in the southeast have influenced the expansion plans of these civil rights groups.[135]

Today, Mexican American women remain active in grass-roots organizing. Mothers of East Los Angeles (MELA) is an effective grass-roots organization that works to defend its community's quality of life. For example, at an early 1990s' neighborhood meeting, MELA members confronted the representative of an oil company wishing to build a pipeline through the center of a Latino community in Los Angeles:

> "Is it going through Cielito Lindo [former president Ronald Reagan's ranch]?" The oil representative answered, "No." Another woman stood up and asked, "Why not place it along the coastline?" Without thinking of the implications, the representative responded, "Oh, no! If it burst, it would endanger the marine life." The woman retorted, "You value the marine life more than human beings?"[136]

Unions for Low-Wage Workers

In the 1960s, Jessie Lopez, Dolores Huerta, and César Chávez created the Agricultural Workers Organizing Committee (AWOC) and the National Farm Workers Association (NFWA). By 1964, the NFWA had a thousand members. In 1965, AWOC workers struck the Delano, California growers; the NFWA met in Delano and voted to join the strike, demanding better wages. The growers refused to talk; picket lines went up; and guns were fired at workers. The NFWA remained nonviolent in the face of provocation by white growers and police. A grape boycott was organized and spread across the country. Picket lines formed wherever grapes were sold, and a massive march on Sacramento was organized. In 1966, AWOC and NFWA merged into the United Farm Workers Organizing Committee.[137]

In 1973, the largest California winery, Gallo Brothers, chose not to renew its contract with the United Farm Workers. As other wineries followed suit, many observers argued that the union was dying.

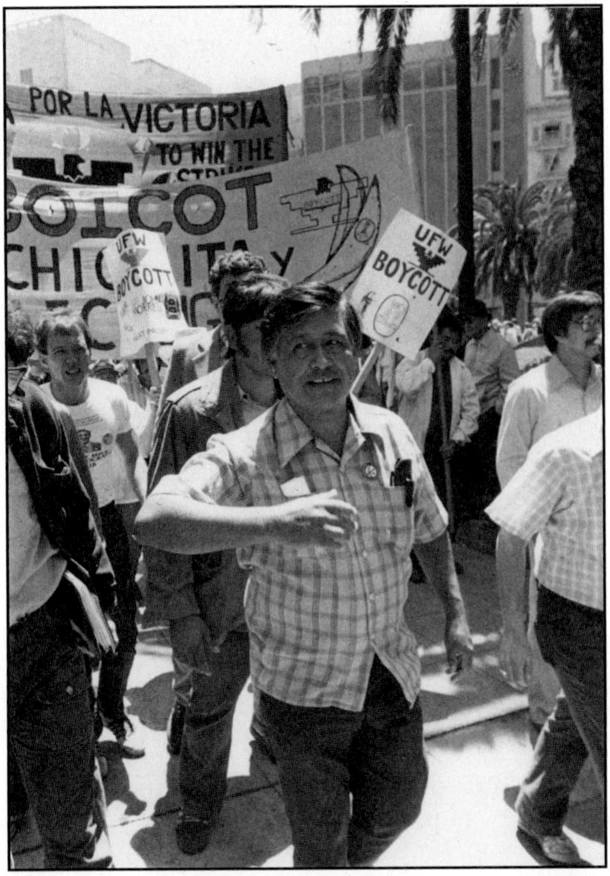

César Chávez marches at the head of United Farm Workers during a 1979 protest.

Yet the struggle continued. Governor Jerry Brown of California worked for legislation to protect workers, and in 1975 signed the Agricultural Labor Relations Act, which provided for protection for union activities and established a labor board to run secret-ballot elections.[138]

The United Farm Workers (UFW), the most successful farm workers' union in U.S. history, altered the structure of power in rural California by using the power of organized numbers to pressure for economic and political change. Among other issues, the UFW addressed the issue of pesticide spraying of farm products in a nationwide campaign to force large farmers to "stop poisoning workers and consumers."[139] In spring 1994, one year after the death of César Chávez, more than eighty current and former farm workers, some of whom had made the first such pilgrimage twenty-eight years earlier, walked the 340 miles from Delano to Sacramento, California, signing up thousands of new UFW members along the way.[140]

Today, many Mexican American and other farm workers still earn low wages and receive few benefits. They often live in very crowded conditions (six to twelve in a tiny apartment or house), and many who favor or join unions are harassed or fired by their employers.[141] In the early 2000s, at least 60 percent of farm worker families remained below the federal poverty line. The UFW, once at 80,000 members, is now down to 27,000. More farm workers are undocumented than in the early days of the UFW. These workers are often afraid to organize. Still, union membership has been growing slowly. Explaining the decline and recent increase, union leaders note that the 1975 Agricultural Labor Relations Act was weakly enforced under sixteen years of rule in the 1980s and 1990s by Republican governors of California. In the early 2000s, however, there is a Democratic governor more sympathetic to workers and labor unions and to enforcement of the act.[142]

Today, an increasing number of Mexican Americans are members of the mainstream unions that represent auto workers, miners, teamsters, dockworkers, and railroad, cannery, garment, steel, and construction workers. Unionizing efforts have recently been successful among undocumented workers, challenging the commonly held assumption that they are willing to tolerate poor working conditions because of the possibility of deportation.[143] In Los Angeles in the late 1990s, Local 11 of the Hotel Employees and Restaurant Employees International Union called for an international boycott of the luxury New Otani Hotel because of its poor treatment of Latino and Asian workers. The workers began large-scale picketing at the hotel and made it clear that the multiethnic composition of the hotel's workforce did not deter union organization and action. Latinas, in particular, were critical to the union and its protest actions. The women activists proved wrong some traditional notions that women would be "unorganizable because of their family responsibilities, marginal commitment to the labor market, and submission to patriarchy."[144] In August 2000, as the boycott and strike continued, a protest against working conditions at the hotel by 400 union workers was met by 200 police officers in riot gear. Forty workers were arrested for blocking the intersection with clothes symbolizing the "dirty laundry" the hotel was unwilling to face.[145] Today, union efforts to improve working conditions continue in numerous cities.

Other Recent Challenges and Conflicts: Latinos and African Americans

The growing Mexican American and other Latino populations in major urban areas have increasingly brought Latinos into situations of both political conflict and cooperation with long-time African Americans residents. Together, the two groups make up a majority of the population in numerous cities. Capitalistic globalization is drawing Mexican and other immigrant workers into the United States, and the shift from an industrial to a service economy is reducing the number of higher-wage, unionized, blue-collar jobs that are available for both groups. Modern capitalism sometimes pits new immigrants against established citizens who also rely substantially on lower-wage blue-collar and service jobs.

Debates in the policy literature periodically focus on whether recent immigration has affected the economic situations of native-born Americans, particularly African Americans. According to available data, employment problems have increased for many African Americans since the 1970s, particularly for those who have not completed high school. Recent National Research Council (NRC) reports indicate that immigration has had a generally positive impact on the U.S. economy as a whole, with a small negative impact on employment opportunities for native-born Americans. Immigration has brought significant benefits to employers and better-off native-born workers, since they are the most likely to use the low-cost labor or services (for example, household work) of immigrants. The negative impact is greatest for less skilled workers, including many African Americans. One recent analysis of immigration's impact concluded that "studies provide compelling documentation that the overall positive economic effects of immigration emphasized by the NRC in the country as a whole do not extend to African Americans.... In general, the economic implications of immigration appear less than benign."[146]

Capitalism-generated competition between immigrants and less skilled black workers has the potential to generate recurring conflict. Indeed, recent conflicts between Latinos and African Americans have occurred in a number of cities. In Dallas, for example, a struggle between the two groups over who should become school superintendent was recently resolved by the appointment of a black Puerto Rican candidate. Tensions between Latino and black groups related to elections in Miami, public housing occupancy in Chicago, and school and hospital hiring in Los Angeles have also been reported in the media. Typically, the issues involve a growing Latino population that has not achieved full representation in public jobs in these cities, jobs that now are often held by black Americans.[147]

The white-controlled media tend to focus on conflict and neglect instances of cooperation, which are more common than conflict. The head of the Los Angeles Human Rights Commission recently reported that at the neighborhood level Latinos and blacks there are generally finding ways to coexist and cooperate. Some black elected officials are working hard to better serve their new Latino constituents, many of whom have recently moved into formerly black areas.[148] Black and Latino communities in Texas have also often shown respect for one another. One 1970s study of Mexican American attitudes in Texas found more positive feelings toward African Americans, more sensitivity to discriminatory barriers, and more support for civil rights protest than were found among whites.[149] More recently, in spring 1995, black leaders and union members marched with Latinos in San Antonio to demonstrate against California's Proposition 187. And in a 1997 election in Houston Latino voters helped elect a black mayor against substantial white opposition. A group of black women from Houston went to Mexico to serve as election observers. Black women also participated in protests against the rape of a representative of Mexico's Zapatista movement. In surveys a majority of Houston's black and Latino leaders report that they interact frequently with leaders of other groups. Programs for Latino children have had the support of black administrators in Houston's public schools, and a black county official in the Houston area has publicly opposed attempts to bar undocumented immigrants from the county hospital. Although incidents of conflict are clearly more likely to receive media coverage than these commonplace instances of cooperation, coalitions between these two communities are significant despite some continuing conflict.[150]

EDUCATION

In the first three decades of the twentieth century, little attention was given to the education of Mexican Americans. Whites who controlled the economy of the Southwest pressed for low-wage labor without the expense of education. Schooling was usually minimal.[151] Before World War II, Mexican American schoolchildren from Texas to California were often segregated. However, as a rule, Mexican Americans were segregated by local laws or by informally gerrymandered school district lines rather than by state law. As with African Americans, discrimination in housing reinforced school segregation.[152]

Recurring Educational Problems

After World War II, many communities began to demand changes in the educational system. A major conference in 1946 called for an end to segregation, the adoption of a Mexican-oriented curriculum, better teacher training, and improved school facilities. In *Mendez v. Westminster* (1946), a federal court ruled that segregation of children in "Mexican" schools in California violated the Fourteenth Amendment because these children were separated on the basis of surnames. The social and educational theory expressed by the judge in the *Mendez* case anticipated the Supreme Court's ruling in *Brown v. Board of Education* almost a decade later. After the *Mendez* decision California laws allowing segregation were repealed.[153]

For decades, some schools with high percentages of Mexican American students prohibited manifestations of Mexican American subculture. Teachers's classroom behavior, which has been shown to have a strong relationship to student achievement, often downgraded children's Spanish heritage. Teachers often anglicized children's names (for instance, Roberto became Bobby). One 1960s study found that the average (white) teacher praised white children more often than Mexican American children, questioned them more often, and used their ideas much more often.[154] In addition, Mexican American children were overrepresented in classes for the mentally retarded. Most Mexican Americans in these classes were "six-hour retarded" children—capable of functioning in the outside world yet mislabeled largely as a result of the cultural discrimination in school testing methods. Tests were (and often still are) usually conducted in English.[155] A 1970s study in Riverside, California found that all of the white children in classes for the mentally retarded showed behavior abnormality, compared with fewer than half of the Mexican American children.[156]

Current Educational Issues: Segregation and Bilingualism

Although certain discriminatory practices, such as disproportionate placement in classes for the "mentally retarded," had been eliminated from most schools by the 1980s, vestiges of bias and discrimination have remained. In the early 2000s, public schools still place too many Mexican American children in learning-disabled classes, school textbooks still neglect Mexican American history, and de facto segregation persists. Recent research by the Civil Rights Project of Harvard University found that intense segregation for Latino students is greater today than at the beginning of the civil rights revolution more than thirty years ago. In 1968 some 23 percent of Latino students attended intensely segregated schools (minority enrollment of 90 percent or more); today more than 36 percent of Latino students attend such schools. On the average, Latino students attend school with approximately 55 percent Latino and 12 percent black students. In addition, the study reports that almost 90 percent of the segregated Latino schools have high concentrations of poverty. The average Latino student attends a school in which 44 percent of the students are poor, compared with fewer than 20 percent in schools attended by the average white student.[157] A spokesperson for the advocacy group called the National Council of La Raza recently explained, "It's now quite obvious that Latinos are highly concentrated in schools that don't have the requirements that research has shown are necessary for a quality education—small schools, small classes, qualified teachers, decent facilities, quality curriculum, high expectations."[158]

In numerous cities, large and growing proportions of the public school children are Latino. For example, at least 70 percent of the children in Los Angeles public schools are now Latino. And many predominantly Latino or Mexican American schools continue to have inferior educational resources. Although MALDEF has challenged school funding inequalities in court, unequal funding persists in school districts across the country. Mexican Americans also remain underrepresented among teachers and administrators in most school systems despite modest increases in their numbers.[159]

From the beginning, the United States has been a land of many languages. In the eighteenth century the Articles of Confederation were officially published in English, German, and French. California's first state constitution (1849), published in both Spanish and English, provided that "all laws, decrees, regulations, and provisions" be printed in both languages. New Mexico's laws were published in both Spanish and English from the time this area became a U.S. territory through the first forty years of statehood until, under nativist pressure, languages other than English were labeled "foreign" and were restricted by law.[160]

When placed in English-only classrooms, children with limited English proficiency frequently become discouraged, develop low self-confidence, and fail to keep pace with their English-speaking peers. Many Latino students today face such a situation. This is the reason bilingual programs remain very important. Although the Elementary and Secondary Education Act (1968) established a mechanism for the federal government to fund bilingual programs in public schools to meet the needs of language-minority children, by 1973 no southwestern state had taken more than a few token steps. The Supreme Court decision in *Lau v. Nichols* (1974), which established a child's ability to understand classroom instruction as a civil right, made it illegal for school systems to ignore the English-language problems of language-minority groups. Since 1968, federal programs have provided substantial funding for local school district programs to increase the English proficiency of children whose primary language is not English. Yet, apart from some stellar programs in schools with sensitive principals in scattered public school systems, the overall picture of bilingual education is still one of snail-like progress—and often of white opposition.[161]

In recent decades, the number of children from non-English speaking homes who have learned English has grown dramatically. (Three-fourths of non-English speaking children are Spanish speakers.) The process of learning English is made more difficult by the fact that many of the latter children attend schools in which most students speak Spanish as their native language. In California, which has the largest number of these Spanish-speaking children, 70 percent of them are not in bilingual programs. Most are in English-only programs, with varying levels of assistance for those who do not speak English. Political attacks on bilingual education in California and elsewhere, often accompanied by anti-immigrant sentiments, have weakened the commitment of many local educators to providing the necessary bilingual instruction.[162]

We should note that one of the numerous myths about bilingual language instruction is the erroneous notion that there is no research evidence that bilingual programs are effective in creating academic success. Yet, numerous research studies show that bilingual programs are often successful if done well. Effective bilingual programs do not create or foster ethnic enclaves. Today, Latino immigrants and their children, including those in bilingual programs, are learning English much faster than earlier European immigrants.[163]

Educational Achievement and Continuing Problems

The education level for Mexican Americans has increased significantly over the past several decades. In 1950 more than half of Mexican American adults had less than a sixth-grade education, and fewer than 8 percent were high school graduates.[164] By 2000 about half were high-school graduates and almost 7 percent had at least a college degree. Yet, the educational attainment of Mexican Americans as a group remains significantly behind the national average. In 2000 more than 84 percent of all U.S. adults were high school graduates, and almost 26 percent had at least a college degree. Table 8.5 compares the educational attainment in 2000 of Mexican-origin, mainland Puerto Rican, Cuban-origin, and European-origin adults over twenty-four years of age.[165]

Mexican Americans' educational attainment is the lowest of the three Latino groups and far lower than that of European Americans. The educational attainment of the Mexican-origin population today shows evidence of decades of limited economic and educational opportunities, including overt and subtle discrimination, as well as of recent immigration of less educated immigrants. In 2000, more than 60 percent of foreign-born Mexican American adults were not high school graduates.[166] Limited education contributes to the wide wage gap between

TABLE 8.5 EDUCATIONAL ATTAINMENT (PERCENTAGES AT SELECTED LEVELS BY RACIAL-ETHNIC GROUP)

	MEXICAN ORIGIN	PUERTO RICAN ORIGIN	CUBAN ORIGIN	EUROPEAN ORIGIN
Less than 9th grade	32.3%	17.5%	18.1%	4.2%
High-school graduate or more	51.0	64.3	73.0	88.4
Bachelor's degree or more	6.9	13.0	23.0	28.1

Mexican American and white workers. As Martha Jimenez of MALDEF has noted, "It's a vicious circle. This wage differential makes it so everyone in the family has to work, which is one of the biggest reasons for the [school] dropout rate."[167]

The dropout rate—some call it the "pushout rate"—for Mexican American students in public schools remains high. Variations in reporting methods for dropout rates and the fact that students drop in and out of school make it impossible to arrive at an exact figure, but estimates of the dropout rate for all Latino groups combined range from two times to three times that of non-Latinos, and Mexican Americans rank at the high end among Latino groups. Poverty and the need to earn money to help support their families are obstacles for these students. Nonetheless, a few schools have increased graduation rates for Mexican American students significantly—in at least one case to 95 percent—by providing programs to address such student concerns as jobs, substance abuse, and teen parenthood.[168]

In the late 1980s, researchers Harriet Romo and Toni Falbo began tracking a group of 100 Mexican American high-school sophomores who were at high risk of dropping out of school. Within two years, 40 percent had dropped out. Only nineteen graduated at the end of their senior year, and only one student remained in school the following year. Many of those who graduated did so with the help of special programs, and their skills were often scarcely better than those of the students who dropped out. Interviews with the students revealed that their school experience had been demeaning and demoralizing. Some expressed the feeling that someone was "always on my back." Many students felt they were better off after they left school. One girl remarked about her job: "At least they care whether I come or not."[169]

Nonetheless, education was *highly* valued by both the students and their families; the anguish of school failure was keenly felt. "School failure involves threats to the self-esteem of the students as well as the status of the family and results in complex intra-family tensions and conflicts.... After a student dropped out, parents felt devastated and angry."[170] In most families, mothers were primarily responsible for children's education. The mothers derived much of their own sense of self from the successes of children and tended to blame themselves, or felt that school personnel blamed them, for their children's failures. These mothers' strategies for helping their children stay in school involved giving encouragement and pointing to individual models of success. Few had the confidence to approach the school for help, and those who did felt themselves at a disadvantage. They reported experiencing frustration over the school's unwillingness or inability to provide help and sometimes encountered hostility from teachers, counselors, or administrators. Yet those with strong parenting skills were able to keep their adolescents in school.

Recent surveys show that Mexican American parents and children value education highly. A survey of Mexican American youth in San Diego found that fully two-thirds of the U.S.-born youth aspired to a college degree, as well as 57 percent of those born in Mexico.[171] Ethnographic research has also shown that immigrant families are very interested in education for their children, although they frequently have little knowledge about how to become involved in U.S. schools. This research shows that public school administrators in the United States typically make little effort to involve immigrant parents with their children's education in a meaningful way.[172]

In a critique of the major explanations offered for the poor school performance by many students of color, including Mexican American students, Catherine Walsh argues that attributing school problems to alleged individual or cultural inadequacies is only blaming the victim. Blaming the incompatibilities arising from the cultural differences between Latino students and the white-dominated educational system on the victims is to overlook the historical and ongoing sociological and ideological significance of these differences. That all culturally different students do not perform equally poorly in school points to the relevance of additional factors. The problem is one of unequal power relationships. To locate the root of school problems, one must look to the character of the school system, not to the student. For example, the mainstream school curriculum is built on the dominant culture and the centrality of the English language and usually equates individual and group success with the adoption of that dominant culture and language. Mexican American history, culture, language, and life experiences are typically ignored. The dominant white group generally controls the structure of public schools and tends to view Latino cultures as negative environments from which students need to escape. Walsh suggests that poor school performance is often a response to alienating and oppressive conditions that have robbed students of identity, dignity, and voice. Learning or not learning can thus be a political statement.[173]

Including the Spanish language and Mexican American culture in the classroom, involving the students' parents in the learning process, and increasing meaningful interaction between students and teachers are important steps toward improving education for Mexican American children. But these steps are inadequate by themselves. From Walsh's perspective, the severe imbalance of power and authority in public school systems must be corrected in order for Mexican American students to be accorded respect and the possibility of establishing a positive identity in public schools.

Since the 1970s, a debate has raged over public school systems' obligation to educate the children of undocumented Mexican residents of the United States. State officials, especially in southwestern states, have complained that educating these children is a burden on their citizens. One Texas court case involved attempts to charge the children of undocumented immigrants a special fee to attend school. After an extended struggle in the lower courts, the Supreme Court ruled in 1982 that schooling must be provided for all children and that children could not be discriminated against on the basis of parental condition, such as immigrant status.[174]

RELIGION

The formal doctrines of the Catholic church are seldom major factors in the lives of Mexican immigrants. However, what has been termed folk Catholicism, a blend of Catholicism and certain non-Catholic beliefs and rituals, has played an important role.[175] Many Mexican immigrants to the United States were, and are, hostile to the established church in Mexico, and most have not been prepared for a U.S. Catholic church dominated by Irish American and other white ethnic priests. In the first decades of Mexican immigration, little provision was made for the religious schooling of Mexican Catholics. Before 1940, the U.S. church also provided little sustenance or aid to a Latino population troubled by poverty and discrimination.[176]

However, in the 1950s and 1960s, some non-Mexican Catholic priests began to take an active role in community protests and union activities benefitting Mexican Americans. For example, in the 1960s, War on Poverty programs were operated in connection with church projects, and a number of groups were formed to protest urban poverty. In some areas, Catholic officials prohibited priests from participating in these programs and protests. The Los Angeles cardinal, for example, refused to provide priests for striking Delano farm workers in the 1960s. In addition, the U.S. Catholic hierarchy has sometimes actively discriminated against Mexican Americans. Very few Mexican Americans achieved positions of responsibility before the 1960s. The first Mexican American bishop was designated, in San Antonio, only in 1970. By the mid-1990s, twenty-two of several hundred bishops in the United States were Mexican American.[177]

The Catholicism of most Mexican Americans has been described as somewhat similar to that of Italian Americans—a general allegiance to the church but less active participation than for Irish Catholics. In recent decades, the church's influence on secular issues appears to be waning in many Mexican American communities; rejection of the church position on issues such as abortion and birth control has been widespread.[178] Nonetheless, in many areas the Catholic church still creates a central place for Sunday mass and Latino holiday celebrations and community gatherings. Celebrations of the feast day of Our Lady of Guadalupe are popular in Latino communities. In response to growing numbers of

Spanish-speaking parishioners, some older parishes in Chicago and a few other cities have re-oriented their services to the needs of Latino members. A number of new churches have been established in Texas and West Coast areas where Mexican immigration is substantial.

A mid-1990s study reported that the proportion of Latinos who identified as Catholic had dropped from 90 percent to about 70 percent over the past several decades.[179] One reason for this is that many Mexican Americans and other Latinos have converted to the Protestant, particularly evangelical, denominations that welcome new immigrants and make them feel, as one person put it, like "part of a family."[180]

ASSIMILATION OR COLONIALISM?

An assimilation perspective is implicit or explicit in many research studies of Mexican Americans. In addition, some media and political commentators have argued that, apart from the recent immigrants, Mexican Americans are gradually becoming assimilated to the U.S. core culture. Assimilationists argue optimistically that Mexican Americans are moving up the mobility ladder just as the European ethnic groups did, and thus are proceeding slowly but surely into the U.S. mainstream at all the assimilation levels described by Milton Gordon. Reviewing the situation of Mexican Americans and other Latinos in the United States today, a spring 2000 article in *The Economist* concludes that "most of the evidence suggests that the latest immigrants are bedding in at least as quickly as their predecessors," and cites Latino rates of home ownership, intermarriage, and gaining citizenship as evidence for its conclusions.[181]

An assimilation theorist looking at U.S. history might emphasize that only 100,000 Mexicans were initially brought in by U.S. military conquest and colonialism. Most Mexicans have arrived later as voluntary immigrants and have been able to improve their economic circumstances relative to their former situation in Mexico. Aspects of traditional culture have begun to decline or disappear as acculturation, a major stage in group assimilation, has proceeded.[182] Cultural assimilation for the first generation, the immigrants, primarily involves adjustment to language and certain norms of everyday work and public settings. Religious and other basic values are less affected; respect for Mexico usually remains strong. Later generations of Mexican Americans have experienced increased cultural adaptation as well as structural assimilation into the economy. The traditional view of the Mexican American family as a large, extended, patriarchal unit is most descriptive of family patterns in agricultural towns in earlier decades. Urbanization and increased incomes have made possible separate residences for nuclear families, and the number of large, extended families in urban areas has declined. Mexican American fertility and family values have increasingly become similar to those of other Americans.[183]

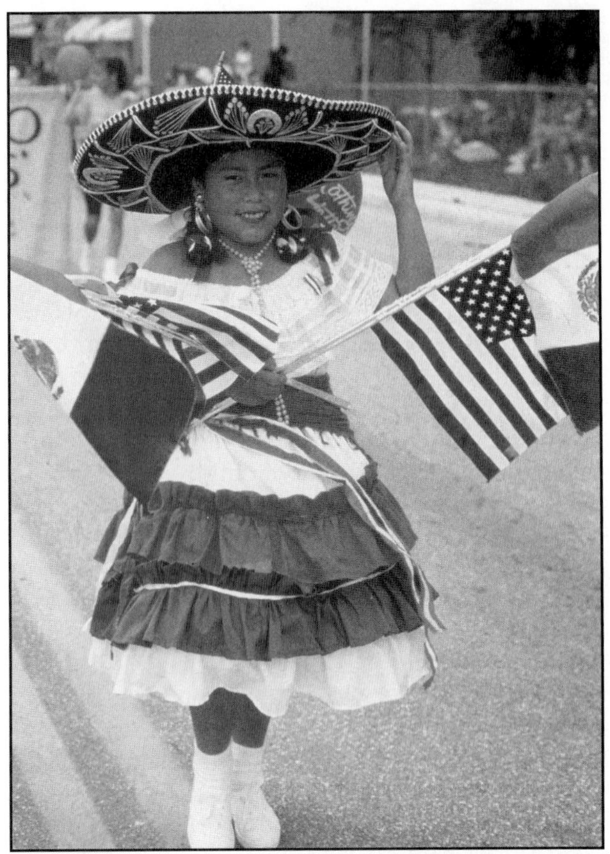

Mexican Americans celebrate Mexican Independence Day.

Yet, a substantial degree of cultural identity persists. The Spanish language remains the primary language or part of a bilingual pattern for a majority of Mexican American families. Closeness to Mexico is an important reason. Surveys in Los Angeles and San Antonio have found that most Mexican Americans wish their children to retain ties to Mexican culture, particularly to language, customs, and religion. One 1990s survey found that most Mexican Americans were bilingual, but a significant minority had little fluency in English.[184] In the 1990 census, half of Los Angeles' Latino (mostly Mexican American) population reported that they did not speak English "very well."[185] Still, most immigrant parents and their children recognize the clear social and economic advantages of learning English. Studies indicate that three-fourths of Latino immigrants are using English every day by the time they have lived in the United States fifteen years, and most of their children come to prefer English. Studies in San Diego and south Florida have found that 66 to 80 percent of immigrant school children prefer English to Spanish.[186]

This widespread use of English among immigrants and their children underscores how wrongheaded the xenophobic calls for English-only laws and school policies are. In general, Latino immigrants are learning English faster than their European predecessors. Indeed, it would be advantageous for all Americans to become at least bilingual. As the outlook and economic ties of the United States become more international, it will be useful for Americans from every background to know well more than one language and culture.

Structural assimilation at the economic level has come slowly even for many in the second and third generations of Mexican Americans. Discrimination and the concentration of many workers at lower wage levels persist. Mexican Americans' limited participation in political institutions has also been problematical, although recent progress can be seen in some areas. Efforts of the Southwest Voter Registration Project and the success of court cases suing for single-member districts have increased Mexican American voter strength.

Behavior-receptional assimilation and attitude-receptional assimilation have varied considerably within the Mexican American group and over time. Widespread prejudice and severe discrimination faced the Mexicans who were conquered during U.S. expansion as well as later immigrants. Over time, however, many lighter-skinned Mexican Americans, especially in larger cities, faced somewhat less prejudice and discrimination. In contrast, darker-skinned Mexican Americans have often been treated the same as African Americans. Today, considerable prejudice and discrimination are directed against Mexican Americans in many parts of the United States. Many whites still view Mexican Americans as an "inferior race" based primarily on the dark skin and other physical features seen as typical of the group. Some research indicates that darker-skinned Mexican Americans do not do as well in occupational, educational, and income attainments as lighter-skinned Mexican Americans, whose physical characteristics are more acceptable to whites.[187]

Today, Mexican Americans still face substantial discrimination. For example, two-thirds of the Mexican American youth in one 1990s survey in California reported that they had personally faced racial discrimination; more than 80 percent said there was racial discrimination against Latinos in the United States.[188]

The Limits of Assimilation

Neither structural assimilation at the primary-group level nor marital assimilation have at this time reached a high level for Mexican Americans as a group. Studies in the 1970s reported some increases in intergroup friendship contacts, particularly for Mexican American children in desegregated environments, although most still had predominantly Mexican American friends. One San Antonio study found that fewer than 5 percent of Mexican American respondents had predominantly white friends; the proportion in Los Angeles was approximately 15 percent. In a 1991 survey, the vast majority of Latinos (mostly Mexican Americans) in the southwest, west, and central United States reported that their close friends (as well as their neighborhoods) were Latino.[189]

The majority of all Mexican American marriages are still within the Mexican American group. In the early decades of the 1900s, fewer than 10 percent of Spanish-surname individuals married outside the group. Mid-1990s data indicate that about 10 percent of first generation Latinos were intermarried, compared with second and third generation percentages in the mid-20s and mid-30s, respectively. For all generations taken together, approximately 17 percent of marriages are outside the Latino group.[190] The current rate of out-marriage appears to be growing and is higher for younger generations. One estimate for native-born Mexican Americans in urban southern California puts the out-marriage figure at 50 percent.[191]

Some assimilation analysts have questioned the extent of Mexican American identification with things Mexican. Nathan Glazer, for example, characterized the militant Chicano movement of the 1960s and 1970s as "one of extreme views espoused by a minority for a short period."[192] This view overlooks the fact that the majority of younger Mexican Americans supported the Chicano movement, even those who did not actively participate, and many in the older generations—that is, families of the activists—were quietly supportive. In addition, the perspectives and actions of Mexican American activists in the 1960s, as well as in more recent years, reflect themes of militancy and change rooted in their historical heritage.

The diversity of self-identification labels sometimes used by persons with ties to Mexico—designations such as *Latino, Hispanic, Chicano, Hispano, Mexican,* and *Mexican American*—indicate a significant diversity of opinion about naming or identity.[193] The San Diego study of second generation Mexican Americans cited earlier found that those who were Mexican-born preferred the term "Mexican;" the U.S.-born preferred "Mexican American" or "Latino/Hispanic." Pride in Mexican identity remains strong among the younger generation.[194] General surveys of Latinos indicate both a desire to fit in and a desire to maintain the traditional culture. In a recent *Washington Post* survey of 2500 Latinos, nine out of ten felt it was important for immigrants to change to fit in, yet the same proportion believed it was important to maintain part of traditional culture as well.[195]

Ethnic identification varies with social class, age, and experience. One research project at the University of California found that many middle-class Mexican American undergraduates had been sheltered by parents and teachers who encouraged them to think of themselves as more or less "white" and to assimilate fully to Anglo-American ways. These students often experienced shock upon arrival at the UC campus, where they were considered to be "Mexican" or "Chicano" and part of a racial group that was a victim of discrimination.[196] The campus experience brought these students out of sheltered families and into a highly racialized society.

Ease of assimilation also varies with social class; upper-middle-class professionals usually face fewer barriers than members of the working class and immigrants.[197] Múrguía has argued that Anglo whites allow lighter-skinned, middle-class Mexican Americans to fit in to some degree and to assimilate more easily. Yet, in his view, group assimilation cannot reach the same level as it has for other Catholics, such as the Irish. Assimilation to the dominant culture and institutions will stop short of complete absorption.[198]

Evidence from a Strategy Research Corporation (SRC) study of Hispanic Americans indicates that assimilation is proceeding slowly. Almost 90 percent of Hispanic adult respondents in the West and Central regions and more than two-thirds of those in the Southwest described themselves as "very Hispanic." (Most Hispanics in the West, Central, and Southwest regions are Mexican American.) When asked how Hispanic-oriented they would like to be in ten years, the percentage replying "very Hispanic" remained virtually unchanged in the Southwest and dropped only a few percentage points in the West and Central regions. Very small percentages in each of these three regions saw themselves as minimally Hispanic. Young people in all regions rated themselves as less Hispanic and projected a lower level of Hispanic identification in the future than did adults. Still, the proportions identifying themselves as minimally Hispanic were extremely low (3–11 percent).[199]

The SRC study ranked respondents' level of assimilation on the basis of identification, language used, and behavioral, attitudinal, and aspirational measures. Only some 13 percent were judged to be fully assimilated in the early 1990s; that is, they appeared to have given up most of their Latino culture. Approximately half were ranked as partially assimilated; although reasonably comfortable in both Spanish and English, their Spanish-language skills predominated and they retained strong ties to Latino culture. The remaining 38 percent, classified as relatively unassimilated, spoke little English. Predominantly recent immigrants, they are the fastest-growing segment of the Mexican American population.[200]

A large majority of the Latino adults in the West and Central regions felt most comfortable speaking Spanish and spoke it more frequently than English at home. The use of Spanish was somewhat less dominant in the Southwest, where the majority of Mexican Americans reside. While a majority of adults in the Southwest felt most comfortable speaking Spanish, fewer than half spoke it more frequently than English at home. More than half of the youth in the West and Central regions felt most comfortable speaking Spanish, whereas a large majority of their counterparts in the Southwest felt most comfortable with English. In all three regions, Spanish was spoken far less frequently at home and on social occasions by the youth than by adults. If the immigration streams from Mexico and other parts of Latin America lessen, linguistic (and probably other cultural) assimilation will likely increase dramatically.[201]

Today, persisting immigration streams from Mexico create problems for a full-assimilation interpretation of the Mexican American experience. The movement of significant numbers of immigrants into established Mexican American communities perpetuates the traditional Mexican culture, supports in-group marriage, and encourages the maintenance of Spanish. Immigrants also create a constant stream of new customers and workers for Mexican American businesses, thereby stimulating the growth of an enclave economy. Immigrants from Mexico, as well as those from Central and South America, have furnished both the means and the reason for the growth of various enterprises, such as authentic Mexican cuisine restaurants, spiritualist healing centers, and Spanish-language media. All of this suggests a clear pattern of partial or segmented assimilation (see Chapter 2).

In addition, Mexican Americans and other Latinos are developing their own mass media. In the early 2000s Latinos are the nation's fastest-growing television audience, and much of this audience is watching Spanish-language networks—Univision Television Network and Telemundo Network Group. In some cities, television stations affiliated with these networks have more viewers than major English-language stations. Spanish-language networks show programs from Latin American countries and provide much more coverage of Latin America and U.S. Latinos than English-language stations. Today, Spanish-language networks are under pressure to increase the presence of darker-skinned Latinos on the air and behind the scenes and to focus more on Latinos in the United States.[202]

The Mexican American impact on the larger society can be seen in a number of areas. Some of the larger society's adaptations to the growing Latino population are relatively superficial, such as the proliferation of Mexican fast food outlets. Other societal adaptations, such as bilingual education and Spanish language ballots and Internal Revenue Service forms, represent a recognition of the reality of a different culture. Advertising directed toward and mass media serving Latino populations have increased. Recognition of the changing character of the consumer market has prompted several corporations, such as large retail chains and phone companies, to recruit bilingual employees. Some observers have even spoken of the "Hispanicizing of America" or used the term "Amexica" for the new diverse nation that is emerging.[203]

Applying a Power-Conflict Perspective

Power-conflict analysts focus on the extent to which many Mexican Americans have *not* moved toward speedy incorporation into the dominant culture and its institutions because of external discrimination and oppression. Economic assimilation and political assimilation at the higher levels are not the reality for the majority of Mexican Americans.

Internal colonialism analysts note that Mexican American history began with Anglo whites' ruthless conquest of northern Mexico in the period between 1836 and 1853. This conquest created a colonial situation for the early Mexican, whose land and person were brought into the United States by force. Some parallels can be seen between this experience and that of externally colonized populations: Land is taken by military force, the native population is subjugated economically and politically, the indigenous culture is suppressed, and the colonizing power often favors a small elite to help maintain the domination.[204]

One problem in applying the colonialism perspective to Mexican Americans is that most entered as voluntary immigrants after the conquest. Internal colonialism analysts focus on the differences between these Mexican immigrants and their European predecessors. Mexican migrants have not come into a new environment; people of their background were already in the southwestern United States. Socially and culturally, they have moved within one geographical area, all of which was originally Mexico. Little time is required to move back and forth across the border—in sharp contrast with the travel time required of most European immigrants.[205]

The most significant difference between the Mexican and European immigrant experience lies in the discrimination and cultural subordination that later Mexican immigrants encountered in the United States. "The colonial pattern of Euro-American domination over the Mexican people was set by 1848 and carried over to those Mexicans who came later to the Southwest."[206] From the beginning to the present, the Mexican American experience has been different from that of European immigrant groups, whose level of segregation has declined sharply with length of residence in the United States. Mexican Americans have been racially and ethnically subordinated to a far greater extent and over a longer period of time than European immigrant groups.

Mexican immigrants have entered an environment in which their progress and mobility have been limited by low wages, inferior schools, and various types of direct discrimination. Pressure and even coercion have been used to acculturate Mexican American school children and adults. John Ogbu has suggested that the rejection of public education by some Mexican American youth is a reaction to their colonized status.[207] Racial stereotyping, especially of darker-skinned Mexican Americans, has helped preserve the racial hierarchy. Land theft and the exploitation of Mexican American labor have been justified by theories of biological and cultural inferiority. Mexican immigrants have been forcefully subordinated by means of rigorous Border Patrol searches and the deportation of those immigrants (and sometimes citizens) whom Anglo-American authorities deemed unworthy. Residential segregation has often reflected racial discrimination. Indeed, much informal racial discrimination in employment and housing persists today. White Americans have gained substantial psychological as well as economic benefits from the discrimination against Mexican Americans.

As we discussed in Chapter 2, Mario Barrera analyzes the Mexican American experience using an internal colonialism model that emphasizes the role of institutionalized racism and exploitative capitalism in past and present inequalities. Each of the major classes of capitalism, the capitalist class and the working class, contains segments defined by racial characteristics. Each class is divided by a racial and ethnic line that separates those who suffer institutionalized discrimination, such as Mexican Americans, from those whites who do not. While Mexican American workers share a similar class position with white workers, in that both are struggling against employers for better wages and working conditions, the former are in a subordinate economic position within the working class because of structural discrimination along racial lines. The dimensions of this discrimination include lower wages for similar work and concentration in lower-wage occupations.[208]

Internal colonialism analysts argue that white employers have intentionally created a split labor market from which the latter have received enormous profits; they have fostered hostility and distrust within the working class by focusing the attention of white workers on Latinos and other racially oppressed workers as a threat to white jobs. Given the dual-market segmentation of the labor force by employers, it is not surprising that white workers often try to solidify their positions and bar workers of color from the better jobs.

Power-conflict analysts emphasize the continuing reality that the majority of white Americans still see Mexican Americans as not white European, as a more or less inferior group distinguishable by physical characteristics and by culture. Given this racialized reality, Mexican Americans could not be fully assimilated into the institutions of U.S. society even if they were to abandon their Spanish language and surnames. Even most of those who are light enough to pass as white are not likely to abandon their families and relatives or give up their cultural heritage, and the latter enables whites to distinguish them for continuing discrimination.[209]

Still, as historian Rodolfo Acuña has recently noted, Mexican Americans and other Latinos feel great pressure to see whiteness, and things white, as best. Mexican American adults sometimes comment unfavorably on the dark skin of a newborn child or play down their Indian background. In an effort to position their group closer to whites, they may also articulate anti-immigrant or anti-black attitudes. As Acuña notes, "the acceptance and internalization of the dominant society's racism by Mexicans and Latinos is irrational and produces a false consciousness. For instance, it is not uncommon for first-year Chicano university students to talk about reverse racism toward whites or express anti-immigrant sentiments."[210] Indeed, some Latino immigrants come to the United States with racist attitudes toward African Americans, even though they have met no (or few) African Americans. Based on interviews with Latino immigrants, one Mexican American scholar recently explained that negative views of black Americans are created by the U.S. media south of the border: "I have traveled to Guatemala and have seen theaters showing the same violent, racist movies we show here. When I asked one migrant in Houston why some migrants have anti-black attitudes, he responded that they first learn about blacks from U.S. movies."[211] Similarly, a research study of foreign-born and U.S.-born Latinas in Houston found that the former had *more* negative attitudes toward black Americans than did the latter.[212] The foreign-born often arrive with negative views of African Americans gleaned from the white-controlled U.S. mass media, which now have a global circulation and influence. Such views make cooperation and coalitions with African Americans more difficult. Clearly, all immigrants to the United States feel enormous pressure to conform to white views and values. We have seen how earlier European immigrants faced similar pressures to adapt to Anglo-American views and values as they sought to be defined as white Americans.

A Pan-Latino Identity

Continuing anti-Latino discrimination has led many Mexican Americans and others to adopt a broader Hispanic or Latino identity in an effort to be "real authentic Americans with dignity. They are beginning to embrace the new and less precise categories of Hispanic or Latino so that they can be part of a larger and more influential group and thereby negotiate better terms of assimilation."[213] Some power-conflict analysts see the possibility of decreasing oppression and of an improved economic, political, and cultural situation in the growing number of pan-Latino organizations and periodic protests.

Several researchers have tracked the growth of the new collective Latino/Hispanic consciousness that has developed in recent decades. This collective consciousness often unites people with such national-origin identities as Mexican American, Cuban American, Puerto Rican, Salvadoran, Nicaraguan, and Dominican. A pan-Latino identity began to develop in the 1960s. Felix Padilla has shown how many Mexican Americans and Puerto Ricans in Chicago, beginning in the 1960s, have to a significant degree transcended old identities and adopted the collective identity of Latino/Hispanic, at the same time holding on in some ways to their national-origin identities. In numerous towns and cities, this pan-Latino process has emerged as part of a political strategy to articulate and accomplish political goals shared by the component groups.[214] The discrimination, imposed inequalities, and political opposition that Latino groups have faced at the hands of whites have contributed to the formation of this collective consciousness. As Padilla has stated, "at the heart of Latino or Hispanic ethnic identity are the circumstantial conditions of structural or institutional inequality.... [S]ome Mexican Americans and Puerto Ricans seek to redress their disadvantaged situation through a collective or large-scale Latino boundary."[215]

This pan-Latino consciousness is facilitated by the language, religion, and similar cultures shared by most groups. On a national level, and in numerous large cities where Latino populations contain more than one national-origin group, a Latino consciousness contributes to a broader sense of community and political solidarity and helps subgroups achieve the collective strength to address local problems of education, bilingualism, jobs, and discrimination. What some observers call a "dual ethnicity" based on both national origin and a collective identity forged in the context of broader Latino concerns appears to be emerging.[216]

Summary

Mexican Americans have an ancient and proud ancestry, substantially Indian with significant Spanish and African infusions. Their vital cultural background is partly Native American but heavily Spanish in language and Catholic in religion. After the European American conquest in what is now the U.S. Southwest, Mexican Americans became part of the complex mosaic of racial and ethnic groups in the United States. They have suffered much stereotyping similar to that of other groups of non-European ancestry, and discrimination in the economy, education, and politics has been part of their lot from the beginning.

The literature on racial and ethnic relations has often compared the situations of Mexican Americans and African Americans, now the largest subordinated groups in the United States. Both groups face substantial prejudice and discrimination at the hands of whites even as we move into the twenty-first century, especially in regard to jobs, business, and housing. Today, across the country, we find both competition and cooperation between these two groups of Americans as they try to make a better place for themselves in a historically racist society.

A distinctive aspect of Mexican American communities today is the constant infusion of documented and undocumented workers. This immigration often renews ties to Mexico and reinforces Mexican culture, undergirding Mexican American communities and identity. The Spanish language has a much stronger foundation in the United States than the languages of white ethnic immigrants, and bilingualism is likely to be a facet of an increasing number of U.S. communities in coming decades. A dramatic aspect of continuing Mexican immigration is that many who come to the United States regularly return to their home countries. A growing global economy has facilitated not only the flow of investment but also movement of people across borders.

Close ties to the culture of the home country Mexico—probably the closest for any immigrant group in U.S. history—slow the assimilation process by providing an external and supportive foundation for the home culture and social networks. Today, the dominant European American culture of the United States is under increasingly great pressure to change as ever larger numbers of non-Europeans insist on the importance and validity of their own cultures.

Mexican Americans have helped to generate a new pan-Latino consciousness that ties them to other Latinos and contributes to a stronger sense of social solidarity. This consciousness is reflected in political efforts to address common problems of education, jobs, and discrimination. What some call a "dual ethnicity" based on national origin and on a collective identity forged in the context of broader Latino issues appears to be emerging across the United States.

9 Puerto Rican and Cuban Americans

PUERTO RICO AND CUBA, BOTH SPANISH-SPEAKING ISLANDS IN THE ANTILLES, ARE the points of origin for the second and third largest groups among the 35 million Latinos in the United States. For a century Puerto Rico has been a subordinated part of the U.S. empire. San Juan, Puerto Rico, founded in the 1520s, is the oldest city now under the U.S. flag. All Puerto Ricans are U.S. citizens, yet Puerto Rico is not a state. Puerto Ricans send nonvoting delegates to Congress but cannot vote in federal elections. Today, the future of the island is debated by groups that support independence, statehood, or a continuation of the current commonwealth status. Unlike the Cuban case, these island political debates have been unimportant to Puerto Rican out-migration; migration to the United States is most significantly influenced by the pull of the mainland economy, coupled with the ease of migration for these U.S. citizens. Generally more prosperous than their Caribbean neighbors, island Puerto Ricans are still only "quasi-citizens of the United States. They can give their lives fighting for the country in U.S. forces, but they cannot vote in national elections. They have only observer status in the U.S. Congress, but they can migrate to the mainland freely."[1] Puerto Ricans are unique in that they are U.S. citizens whether they reside on the island or in mainland cities. According to the 2000 census, just over 3.4 million Puerto Ricans now reside on the mainland, up 25 percent over the previous decade.[2] Today the population on the island is just over 3.8 million.[3] If both groups are included, Puerto Ricans make up about 2.5 percent of the U.S. population.

Cuba has, in the words of Cuban American editor Enrique Fernandez, "oscillated between a corrupt democracy and dictatorships of both right and left, accompanied by a humiliating dependence on a superpower."[4] This political oscillation has generated large out-migrations that have significantly increased the populations of the U.S. Latino communities, particularly in the southeastern United States. Many Cubans came to the United States as political refugees fleeing the Communist government on their island, in a number of distinctive periods of migration. Most have settled in large East Coast cities, particularly in Florida, and today they and their descendants number more than 1.2 million. The island of Cuba has a long history of struggle for independence, replete with heroes such as Jose Martí, a nineteenth-century leader whose maxim was "a nation ... but no master." The struggle for independence continues to be an important theme in the present history and politics of Cuban Americans.

Cuban Americans and mainland Puerto Ricans today play a critical role in the expansion of Latino communities and culture in an increasingly multicultural United States. (*Mainland* refers to the U.S. mainland, as distinct from the territory of Puerto Rico.) Both groups express a strong identification with their home countries and cultural traditions, and both groups are also committed to carving out a permanent place in the United States.

PUERTO RICAN AMERICANS

Borinquén, the original native name for Puerto Rico, had a population of about 50,000 Indians in 1493 when Spanish imperialism reached the island. Spain used the native people there as forced labor in mines and fields. Forced labor, disease, killings, and violent suppression of rebellions caused a major decline in the indigenous population, so enslaved Africans were soon imported by the Spanish. Later on, during the nineteenth century, immigrants and refugees from numerous countries, both European and Latin American, made their way to Puerto Rico. The 1827 census found that the proportions of whites and people of color in Puerto Rico were almost equal. By the end of that century, the island's population comprised thirty-four nationalities. The inhabitants of Puerto Rico today are the product of several different racial and ethnic heritages.[5]

FROM SPANISH TO U.S. RULE

In 1897, Puerto Ricans pressured the Spanish government into granting them autonomy. The following year, during the Spanish-American War, U.S. troops occupied the island. In the peace treaty that ended this war (1899), Spain gave Puerto Rico to the United States, whose leaders saw it as a station for warships and a profitable agricultural enclave. After centuries of Spanish colonial rule, Puerto Rico came under U.S. control with no input from its local inhabitants.[6]

As a U.S. possession, Puerto Rico had a governor from the mainland appointed by the U.S. president. Scholar Manuel Maldonado-Denis describes Puerto Rico's early governors:

> The criterion used by the President of the United States to choose the colonial governor and his cabinet was, with very few exceptions, one of compensation for political favors received. Many of these men came to Puerto Rico without knowing the language or, at times, even the location of the island.... The same can be said of many of the bureaucrats sent to Puerto Rico in the colonial free-for-all: They were ignorant and prejudiced, with the feelings of superiority common to all colonizers.[7]

Acts of the local legislature were subject to veto by Congress, the president, or the governor. English became the mandatory language in schools. In 1917, the Jones Act awarded U.S. citizenship to all Puerto Ricans.[8]

In 1948, Puerto Ricans were finally permitted to elect their governor, and in 1952 the Commonwealth of Puerto Rico was created with a constitution approved by the U.S. Congress. Considerable home rule was granted, including the right to elect local officials, make civil and criminal codes, and run schools. These changes came about only with the permission of the U.S. government, the colonial power that still oversees Puerto Rico. Those living in Puerto Rico have no vote in national U.S. elections and no U.S. senators or House members. Their only representative in Congress is a nonvoting commissioner.

When the U.S. government took over Puerto Rico, much of the land was owned by small farmers who raised coffee, sugar, and other foodstuffs. Puerto Ricans owned 93 percent of the farms. Under U.S. control, heavy taxes and restrictions on credit forced many local residents to sell their land to U.S. companies. Independent farmers were also driven out of operation by the U.S.-forced devaluation of the Puerto Rican peso and the closing of European markets that came with U.S. occupation. By 1930, large absentee-owned companies controlled 60 percent of sugar production and monopolized tobacco production and shipping lines. The island had moved from a locally controlled, diversified economy to one dominated by external sugar companies. Many small farmers and their families were thus forced to seek jobs with the absentee-owned companies or leave for the mainland.[9]

In the late 1940s, Operation Bootstrap, a program designed by the Puerto Rican governor to bring economic development by attracting U.S. corporations, was implemented. Lured by low wages and exemption from taxation, 1,700 factories came to the island by 1975. Per capita income increased. However, tax exemptions for most new industries left the burden of financing the public infrastructure on the local population, resulting in a high income tax. Operation Bootstrap's emphasis on industry and its neglect of agriculture tilted the island economy farther away from its heritage of locally owned farms. Today, little of the island's economy is agricultural, and sugar is no longer of importance.

Since the 1970s, high unemployment rates have pressed much of the island's population to migrate to the mainland. Recurring recessions have brought cutbacks in petrochemical and other industrial plants, increasing unemployment. In the mid-1990s the official unemployment rate stood at 16.8 percent, and in the late 1990s the real unemployment rate (including part-time workers) was estimated at 40 percent or higher.[10] In 1996, the U.S. Congress passed legislation gradually ending (by 2006) the tax incentive that encouraged U.S. firms to locate in Puerto Rico. As a result, many of the hundreds of factories on the island may move to cheaper labor and taxation areas around the globe, thereby continuing the economic crisis for the island and perhaps stimulating yet more immigration.[11]

MIGRATION TO THE MAINLAND

Migration Patterns

By 1900 some 2,000 Puerto Ricans lived on the mainland, most in New York City. Significant immigration to the mainland began in the late 1920s, and by 1940 mainland Puerto Ricans numbered almost 70,000. Over the next two decades, the number increased more than tenfold, to 887,000, largely because of Operation Bootstrap, which resulted in a net loss of jobs and encouraged (for example, in radio ads) emigration. Between 1945 and 1970, about one in three Puerto Ricans left the island. Puerto Rican communities were established in New Jersey, Connecticut, and Chicago, although the majority of immigrants settled in New York.[12]

Puerto Rican writer Jack Agueros has described the impact of the surge of new immigration on established communities:

> Into an ancient neighborhood came pouring four to five times more people than it had been designed to hold. Men who came running at the promise of jobs were jobless as [World War II] ended.... The sudden surge in numbers caused new resentments, and prejudice was intensified. Some were forced to live in cellars, and were then characterized as cave dwellers.[13]

Many Puerto Ricans came as laborers, often with little preparation. For example, Puerto Rican workers brought to New Jersey farms in the 1940s were "flown up here to a strange land, in the dark of the night, and by morning some are in the farmers' fields ready to work. There is no time for any sort of adjustment."[14] Corporations sent recruiters to Puerto Rico seeking cheap labor for the booming postwar economy. Workers came to textile sweatshops in New York; steel mills in Pennsylvania, Ohio, and Indiana; foundries in Wisconsin and Illinois; and electronics industries in Illinois.[15]

The decades since 1970 are sometimes called a period of "revolving-door" migration. Many workers fleeing the island's declining industrialization have arrived in U.S. cities that are also plagued with unemployment. A series of recessions along with deteriorating neighborhoods and living conditions on the mainland, combined with family ties and a desire to nurture children in island culture, have prompted many to return. Often these same people come back after a time because of low wages and poor working conditions on the island. In recent years, manufacturing wages on the island have been much less than those on the mainland, and Puerto Rico's per capita income has been about half that of the poorest U.S. state. For many who come to the mainland to work, intending to accumulate enough money to start a business and begin a new life on the island, the cycle of migration and return becomes a familiar pattern. In recent years the number of professional and other well-educated Puerto Rican workers coming to the mainland has also increased, in part because of an absence of appropriate jobs on the island.[16]

In 2000, more than 47 percent of all Puerto Ricans resided in mainland communities across the United States. Puerto Ricans now make up almost 10 percent of all Latinos on the mainland. Increasingly, many Puerto Ricans have settled in areas other than New York, where in the early 2000s about one-third of all Puerto Ricans still resided.[17]

Joined by Other Latinos: Diversity in the New York Area

The 2000 census shows that New York City's population reached 8 million for the first time. During the decade of the 1990s, the city's Anglo white population decreased by 361,000—to just 35 percent of the city's total population. Most of the city's growth came from Latino and Asian immigrants. In the early 2000s, Puerto Ricans (some 789,000) accounted for approximately 37 percent of the city's Latinos, down from 50 percent in 1990. This decrease occurred in part because, like immigrant groups before them, many Puerto Ricans have moved to suburban areas near New York City, such as Nassau, Suffolk, and Westchester counties. In addition, more Mexicans, Dominicans, Salvadorans, and other Central and South Americans have moved to the bustling city.[18]

Over the same period, Long Island's Latino population increased from 165,238 to 282,693 and is now more than 10 percent of the total population. This Latino population is approximately 27 percent Puerto Rican and 8 percent Mexican or Cuban American. The rest are of Caribbean, Central, or South American origin. Since the 1980s, large numbers of people from the Caribbean and Central and South America have joined Long Island's substantial Puerto Rican community. Unlike earlier migrations, many Latino immigrants today are not moving to the large central cities but rather directly to suburban areas near these large cities such as Long Island.[19]

Increasingly, those who work in Long Island's restaurants and homes and on construction sites are Salvadorans, Colombians, and Dominicans. Indeed, on Long Island the Salvadoran population is nearly as large as the Puerto Rican group. Many of the estimated one million Salvadorans in the United States today are refugees from oppression and civil war in El Salvador. Long Island is one of five major areas of Salvadoran settlement, the others being Los Angeles, San Francisco, Washington, D.C., and Houston. Interestingly, Latino diversity on Long Island has encouraged a pan-Latino consciousness (see also Chapter 8). For example, the town of Brentwood has recently renamed its Puerto Rican Day Parade the Hispanic Day Parade.[20]

PREJUDICE AND STEREOTYPES

Puerto Ricans suffer stereotypes similar to those targeting Mexican Americans and African Americans. The first important stereotypes were mostly developed by white military officers and colonial administrators. (The term *white* again refers to those identified by the census as non-Hispanic whites.) In the 1890s one white officer noted that "the people seem willing to work, even at starvation wages, and they seem to be docile and grateful for anything done for them. They are emotional."[21] Other U.S. officials saw the colonized Puerto Ricans as "lazy natives."

Images of lazy, submissive Puerto Ricans persist today, including among white professionals with Puerto Rican clients. For example, some white teachers have held images of Puerto Ricans as lazy and immoral. Alfredo Lopez has reported attending a college meeting in New York at which an experienced teacher from a poor school spoke about instilling "middle-class values" of thrift, morality, and motivation in the children. Lopez confronted the white teacher about her image of Puerto Rican children:

> It was when I asked what morality was and where it was practiced among middle-class people or what motivation was lacking in our people and how she discovered this, or finally, how the hell a person could be thrifty on eighty-four dollars a week that she began to do some thinking.[22]

Criminalizing Puerto Ricans

Often referred to by the derogatory term *spic*, Puerto Ricans have been viewed by many whites, like Italian and Mexican Americans before them, as a criminal lot. An Aspen Institute conference report noted that the English-language news media often exaggerate certain aspects of Puerto Rican and Mexican American life—poverty, gang violence, and illegal immigrants. Crimes by Puerto Ricans have also been sensationalized in the New York City newspapers and other media. J. Edgar Hoover, a former director of the FBI, promulgated the following racist stereotype:

> We cooperate with the Secret Service on presidential trips abroad. You *never* have to bother about a President being shot by Puerto Ricans or Mexicans. They don't shoot very straight. But if they come at you with a knife, beware.[23]

Stereotypes of Puerto Ricans as criminals and drug users influence police actions in Puerto Rican communities, which are often more closely patrolled than affluent white areas. In the words of one Puerto Rican rights activist, "There is this idea that young Hispanics are all drug abusers who come here to terrorize people." Significantly, one New York survey found that Latino teenagers use drugs *less often* than white teenagers.[24] Such data have not yet corrected the racial bias in drug-use stereotypes circulated in many government agencies or the media.

In Chapter 8 we cited data indicating that Latino actors are rarely used in television programs, and when they are shown, they are much more likely than whites to be portrayed as criminals. Recently, Puerto Rican actor Esai Morales was given a major part as the police lieutenant on the popular television program "NYPD Blue." This marked a significant change for him, as he and other Puerto Rican actors have mostly gotten roles as criminals, alcoholics, or drug dealers. The son of a union organizer, Morales is also an activist for minority rights and a co-founder of Washington's National Hispanic Foundation for the Arts. He is an outspoken critic of the stereotyped roles usually offered to Latino actors.[25]

Other Negative Images

In 1972, *New York* magazine ran an article with the following description of Puerto Ricans: "They came in swarms like ants turning the sidewalks brown, and they settled in, multiplied, whole sections of the city fallen to their shiny black raincoats and chewing-gum speech."[26] Negative stereotypes of Puerto Ricans have also been circulated by some social scientists. In their famous 1963 book *Beyond the Melting Pot*, Nathan Glazer and Daniel Moynihan argued that Puerto Rican society was "sadly defective" in its culture and family system. They characterized Puerto Rican families as disorganized and suggested that this allegedly weak family structure was the reason Puerto Ricans did not move into better-paying jobs.[27] Anthropologist Oscar Lewis developed the influential "culture of poverty" concept, which alleges that those in poverty have a defective subculture. Lewis initially developed this stereotyped perspective from research on low-income Puerto Ricans on the island. Then, in the 1960s, he applied the concept to the poor in the United States, arguing that the culture of the poor is "a way of life which is passed down from generation to generation along family lines."[28] The poor, he contends, adapt in distinctive ways to their living conditions, and these adaptations are transmitted through the socialization process.

The popular view of the supposedly pathological traits of poor communities has been heavily influenced by Lewis's negative culture-of-poverty generalizations. However, culture-of-poverty and similar analyses lack a clear recognition of the role widespread structural unemployment and underemployment play in the creation of poverty and related problems for many Americans.

A late 1990s report on the local economy in New Britain, Connecticut revealed some stereotypes similar to the traditional culture-of-poverty notion. The report, issued by whites in the business elite, alleged that Puerto Ricans' "poor" language skills, family values, and work ethic contributed to the city's economic problems and suggested that Puerto Ricans should be encouraged to leave the city. A large group of Puerto Rican residents organized the Puerto Rican Organization for Unity and Dignity to counter this overt anti-Latino stereotyping and related discrimination and to increase their political clout.[29]

In a summer 2001 radio interview, Republican Jim Hansen, a House Armed Services Committee member, expressed concern about the 2001 protests by Puerto Ricans against the Navy bombing range near the island of Puerto Rico: "I don't see where Puerto Rico should get any favorite treatment over the rest of these people. Now what have they done to get it? They sit down there on welfare and very few of them are paying taxes, got a sweetheart deal." The image of lazy Puerto Ricans on welfare is still found at the highest levels of government. Some whites couple these negative images of Puerto Ricans and other Latinos with fearful views of immigrants. Recall from Chapter 8 white supremacist groups' hostile verbal and physical attacks on Latinos. Other whites, in all parts of the country, including those who are not members of supremacist groups, also articulate hostile views. Recently, homeowners in a mostly white Bronx (New York) village received letters warning of a threat to their area by Latino immigrants, who were described in the letters as "forces of evil" and "low-income trash" seeking to convert the area into a Latino outpost.[30]

Color Coding and White Prejudices

Prejudices and stereotyping motivate much discrimination against Puerto Ricans and thereby have a negative impact on their lives and self-images. To better understand the Puerto Rican experience on the mainland, we can look at the situation in Puerto Rico, for, although prejudice and discrimination exist on the island, there is a considerable difference between the two areas. The U.S. phenomenon of "passing" on the mainland, in which a light-skinned individual hides her or his African ancestry in order to pass for white and bypass much discrimination, is unnecessary in Puerto Rico. Puerto Rican society, like other Latin American societies, recognizes a spectrum of racial-ethnic categories based on multiple physical and cultural characteristics and not just skin color. Indeed, one family's members may represent a variety of skin colors. Today, Puerto Rican society is much more racially integrated than mainland U.S. society. An individual's treatment in the areas of housing, political rights, government policy, and other social institutions is less likely to be racially differentiated than on the mainland. In addition, the island's culture represents a complex synthesis of diverse cultural elements (European, Indian, African), whereas acculturation on the mainland is (with a few exceptions such as music) one-way, with Latino groups typically pressured to adopt European American cultural values rather than the reverse.[31]

European Americans tend to see Puerto Ricans as a "nonwhite" group, frequently grouping them mentally with African Americans or Mexican Americans. One reason for this, suggest Ramón Grosfoguel and Chloe Georas, is the long colonial relationship that Puerto Ricans have had with the U.S. government.[32] Whatever their actual skin color, they were associated in the white mind with colonized people of color. Until they come to the mainland, most Puerto Ricans have seldom dealt with blatant racial discrimination on a large scale. Overt discrimination often comes as a shock to most immigrants. Recalling an experience in high school when a girl whom he had asked to dance turned him down, Piri Thomas, a Puerto Rican who grew up in Spanish Harlem and became well known as author of the autobiographical *Down These Mean Streets*, wrote about his anger at whites' denial of his Puerto Rican identity:

> "Who?" someone asked.
>
> "That new colored boy."
>
> I couldn't see them, but I had that for-sure feeling that it was me they had in their mouths....
>
> "Christ, first that Jerry bastard and now him. We're getting invaded by niggers."[33]

The imposition of rigid U.S. categories of black and white on Puerto Ricans, whose home culture sees racial-ethnic diversity on a complex continuum, creates confusion and anger, whether the individual is called "black" or "white." Such racial identifications deny the individual's identity. Statements such as "You don't look Puerto Rican," or "Are you 100 percent Puerto Rican?" commonly confront Puerto Ricans on the mainland. Faced with the task of categorizing Puerto Rican school children as either "Negro" or "Caucasian" in 1954, New York state officials proposed abandoning racial terms and listing these children as Puerto Rican even though this would imply that Puerto Ricans were a distinct racial category. Indeed, it was probably about this time that Puerto Ricans became distinct from African Americans in white New Yorkers' minds.[34]

Research has revealed a substantial difference in the self-perception of young Puerto Ricans and how they think other Americans perceive them. When asked to classify themselves, most chose neither white nor black but a mixed category of brown. Still, most also felt that other Americans saw them as either white (58 percent) or black (42 percent).[35]

The 1980 census was the first to ask individuals if they were "Hispanic"; it included subcategories for Mexicans, Puerto Ricans, Cubans, and other Hispanics. A separate question asked for "race." Fewer than 4 percent of the Puerto Ricans in New York City stated that their "race" was black; 44 percent classified themselves as white. Some 48 percent wrote in "Spanish" in the space labeled "Other—Specify." This indicates, among other things, the conflict between the polarized U.S. racial structure and the island's racial continuum with which most Puerto Ricans are familiar.[36]

ECONOMIC AND RELATED CONDITIONS: THE MAINLAND

Writing about his experiences as an early immigrant, Jesús Colon has explained that Puerto Ricans did the dirty work of the society and that poverty was usually their lot. Jesús and his brother worked different hours, and to save money they even shared their working clothes: "We only had one pair of working pants between the two of us."[37] Discrimination in employment was common for Puerto Rican immigrants; those with darker skin usually suffered the most. In *Down These Mean Streets*, Piri Thomas recounted a 1945 interview for a job as a door-to-door salesperson. He was not hired; a lighter-skinned friend was. Dark-skinned Puerto Ricans, he discovered by asking other applicants, were discriminated against by the white employer.[38]

Occupation and Unemployment

Puerto Rican immigrants have brought with them a wide spectrum of skills. Some are artists and musicians; others are skilled in crafts. Some operated a business on the island; others held positions of responsibility in the educational, medical, legal, or political systems. On the mainland, however, the many immigrants' skills have gone largely unnoticed and unused. Regardless of their background, most have faced a limited range of jobs. They have often done the "dirty work" for whites. Many have had to take low-paying factory or restaurant jobs. They have cleaned up as busboys and janitors and worked in garment industry sweatshops. Many have faced recurring unemployment.[39]

Table 9.1 shows the occupational distribution for employed Puerto Ricans on the mainland in 2000.[40] Puerto Rican men are disproportionately in lower-paid blue-collar and service jobs. Once mostly domestics and less-skilled blue-collar workers, Puerto Rican women are now concentrated in service, sales, and clerical jobs. Today, Puerto Rican men are less

TABLE 9.1 OCCUPATIONAL DISTRIBUTION (MARCH 2000)

	MEN		WOMEN	
	EUROPEAN AMERICAN	*PUERTO RICAN*	*EUROPEAN AMERICAN*	*PUERTO RICAN*
Managerial and professional specialty	32.0%	14.4%	34.6%	19.9%
Technical, sales, and administrative support	20.6	23.9	41.3	46.4
Precision production, craft, and repair	18.6	17.2	2.1	2.6
Operators, fabricators, and laborers	17.0	27.4	5.4	10.4
Service occupations	8.7	15.9	15.4	20.6
Farming, forestry, and fishing	3.1	1.2	1.3	0.1
Total	100.0%	100.0%	100.1%	100.0%

than half as likely to hold managerial or professional positions as European American men and are almost twice as likely to be employed in service jobs. Puerto Ricans in white-collar jobs tend to occupy the lower-paid positions, such as teacher or librarian. In some East Coast areas, Puerto Rican laborers do much of the low-paid field work that puts vegetables on U.S. tables, often working seven days a week and living in substandard housing conditions.[41]

Unemployment at all points has been much higher for mainland Puerto Ricans than for white workers. Unemployment and subemployment rates for Puerto Ricans have been among the highest of any racial or ethnic group in northeastern cities. In 2000, some 6.4 percent of mainland Puerto Ricans were officially unemployed, compared with 3.5 percent of non-Latino whites.[42] Official rates underestimate the problem. To ascertain the total number of unemployed and subemployed Puerto Ricans, we must add the large numbers who are discouraged from looking for work because of long-term unemployment, those who are working part-time but who want full-time work, and those who receive very low wages.

Puerto Rican analyst Juan Gonzalez has argued that since the 1980s the mainland Puerto Rican community has had two distinctive classes, a modest group of professionals at the top of the social structure, many of them employed in government agencies, including educational agencies, and a large group of workers doing mostly semi-skilled or unskilled blue-collar work. Substantially missing are "two critical groups: the private business class whose members provide any ethnic group's capital formation and self-reliant outlook, and the skilled technical workers who provide stability and role models for those on the bottom to emulate."[43]

Employment Discrimination

Institutionalized discrimination against Puerto Ricans is significantly rooted in color coding and linguistic prejudice. This racial discrimination restricts access to many jobs, contributing to the concentration of Puerto Ricans in low-level employment and to a relatively high unemployment rate.

In New York City, Puerto Ricans have been severely underrepresented (relative to their population percentage) in government jobs. This is in part because they are less well integrated into the important white-dominated job information networks. In many cases, job tests that are, unnecessarily, given only in English screen out Puerto Ricans from good jobs. This procedure is discriminatory when Puerto Rican applicants are capable of doing the jobs and the screening tests are not job-related. Even trash collection jobs have sometimes required screening tests on which those who speak English and have a high-school diploma score better. As with other Latinos, Puerto Ricans frequently find themselves unfairly stigmatized as being of "low intelligence" because of a limited command of English.[44]

Institutionalized discrimination can be seen in height and weight requirements that use white men as the standard. Such requirements have sometimes disqualified Puerto Rican applicants for police and fire department jobs. Even Puerto Ricans' status as U.S. citizens has been a source of discrimination. In some cases, mainland government officials, unaware that Puerto Rico is part of the United States, have asked Puerto Ricans to prove their U.S. citizenship. For other jobs, citizenship status has proved to be a handicap. In a Civil Rights Commission interview, a Puerto Rican woman in California said,

> I've had about six or seven jobs since I came here. What happens is that they hire you temporarily and get rid of you as soon as possible because you don't belong to the right race. I'd even say that bosses here prefer Mexicans (particularly illegals) because they know that unions don't represent them, so they can be exploited easier. At least Puerto Ricans have citizenship and can get into unions.[45]

Employment opportunities are heavily shaped by discrimination. Many white employers classify Puerto Ricans as "black" or "nonwhite" and discriminate against them. Historically, many unions, especially those representing skilled workers, have excluded or restricted Puerto Ricans. Government officials have sometimes winked at these discriminatory practices. Thus, "unions did not facilitate the economic integration of Puerto Ricans as they had for other groups."[46]

Industrial Restructuring

A variety of changing structural factors in the U.S. economy have contributed to high unemployment rates. Early Puerto Rican immigrants came to mainland cities, especially to New York, to fill manufacturing jobs. By the time of the migration of 1946–1964, however, the central cities had mostly entered a period of industrial decline. As New York City moved from an industrial economy to a service-oriented economy, production jobs once open to Puerto Ricans began to disappear. Between 1960 and 1980, New York City lost many manufacturing jobs, and this decline has generally continued to the present. The availability of low-paying service jobs has not kept pace with the decline in production jobs. Technological innovations—automation and computerization—further eroded the number of less-skilled production jobs. Many plants moved to the suburbs, the South, or overseas, taking jobs out of the geographical reach of inner-city workers who did not qualify for most white-collar jobs created in the cities.[47]

Among the major reasons for the sharp deterioration in the economic position of Puerto Ricans were the decline of inner-city manufacturing in northeastern cities and the circular migration to Puerto Rico. The most important reason for mainland Puerto Ricans' rising poverty and unemployment between the late 1970s and the late 1980s was "drastically reduced job opportunities in industrial northeastern cities like New York, Newark, and Pittsburgh, as well as in Puerto Rico."[48] In addition, the constant movement of Puerto Rican workers back and forth between Puerto Rico and the mainland in search of jobs has been disruptive for families and for educational attainment.

The presence of employed workers is crucial for any community's survival. For example, in one area of Brooklyn, numerous unemployed Puerto Ricans live in dire straights yet reside next to employed blue-collar workers who help maintain the community's institutions. A community can handle some unemployment as long as this situation does not become dominant.[49]

Income and Poverty

Mainland Puerto Ricans are one of the poorest groups in the United States. In 1999, median family income for mainland Puerto Ricans ($30,129) was only 56 percent of that of non-Latino whites ($54,121).[50] Almost half of mainland Puerto Rican full-time, year-round workers earned less than $25,000 in 1999, compared with 30 percent of their non-Latino white counterparts.[51] In March 2000, the Census Bureau reported that almost 26 percent of mainland Puerto Ricans fell below the federal poverty line, compared with less than one-tenth of non-Latino whites.[52] The desperate nature of some Puerto Ricans' economic situations is evident in their substantial use of public assistance for both couple-headed and single-parent families. This is especially significant in light of the opposition that most have for public aid; "I'd rather starve than go on welfare" is an often stated sentiment among Puerto Ricans regardless of their poverty status.[53]

Housing Problems

Housing discrimination is still significant. At one Civil Rights Commission hearing, a Rutgers University professor contended that Puerto Ricans have suffered more than African Americans from housing discrimination. Puerto Ricans have been excluded from most decent housing markets and get the "housing scraps" no one else wants.[54]

Compared with other groups, Puerto Ricans use a larger percentage of their income for housing and are more likely to live in dilapidated housing. In the mid-1990s, fewer than one-fourth of Puerto Rican households owned their own home, compared with more than 70 percent of white households.[55] As low-income renters, many Puerto Ricans are vulnerable to the impact of urban decay. Overcrowding and deteriorating housing are characteristic of numerous neighborhoods. The South Bronx, home to a large Puerto Rican community, is a grim example. Once composed of stable communities, this area has been gutted by highway construction, redlined by bankers, and abandoned by employers. Since 1970, the South Bronx has lost much of its housing stock and population. In addition to psychic stress and severed community ties, neighborhood decay has had a negative impact on education and has increased the distances residents must travel to shopping and workplaces.[56] Recently, some Puerto Rican neighborhoods, such as New York City's Williamsburg area, have experienced an influx of whites seeking low-rent housing. In this process of white return to the city and housing gentrification, which is also occurring in Chicago, those with more money drive out those with less.[57]

Puerto Rican and other Latino leaders from Long Island have recently met with New York's attorney general to press for action against the housing discrimination increasingly experienced by Latinos in

Long Island communities. For example, numerous Puerto Rican, Dominican, and other Latino residents in Freeport have reported home invasions, illegal searches, and harassment by local building inspectors. They suspect that many local whites prefer a community that segregates whites and "browns" in separate residential areas. In several other Long Island communities, Puerto Ricans, Dominicans, Salvadorans, and others have also reported that their homes are inspected for housing code violations far more frequently than those of white residents, and they also report differential police harassment.[58]

Discrimination and harassment by local officials against Latinos has persisted despite federal measures to stop such actions. Under a consent decree with the federal government in the 1990s, local officials in Mount Kisco in New York's Westchester County agreed to stop using building codes and park regulations to discriminate against Latino laborers, most of whom were from Central America. In 2000 this consent decree had to be extended because of continuing complaints that a housing ordinance was still being used to unfairly target Latino immigrants.[59]

Recent data on housing segregation suggest that Latinos with darker skin are more likely than those with lighter skin to suffer discrimination at the hands of whites. While a few studies show that some Latino groups are *more* segregated from African Americans than they are from whites, recent research on Puerto Ricans and Dominican Americans shows that they are *less* segregated from African Americans than from whites. One likely reason for this greater segregation from whites is the substantial African ancestry of Puerto Ricans and Dominican Americans. Dominican immigrants are more recent and somewhat more skilled and educated than most Puerto Rican immigrants, and they have generally settled in Puerto Rican communities. Grosfoguel and Georas have noted that despite their "higher-class background" Dominican Americans are placed by whites in the same racially subordinate category in the "coloniality of power" that they place Puerto Ricans (see Chapter 2).[60]

For Puerto Ricans and Dominican Americans, racial discrimination is commonplace in institutional arenas other than housing. Thus, in one New York survey, 80 percent of Latinos reported having been mistreated by the police. More than 70 percent also reported mistreatment by landlords, employers, shopkeepers, the courts, and the schools. A majority of the respondents felt there was substantial discrimination in all areas of life.[61]

EDUCATION

In 2000, just over 64 percent of Puerto Ricans over twenty-four years old had completed high school, compared with more than 88 percent of non-Latino whites. Thirteen percent had completed college, less than half the figure for non-Latino whites.[62]

High dropout rates, or perhaps more accurately *pushout* rates, remain a nationwide problem. These rates tend to be highest in central-city school districts. Despite its high position among the states in per-pupil expenditures and teacher salaries, New York ranks near the bottom in student retention. New York City has a dismal record in educating Puerto Rican students, whose retention rates there have been very low. Some have characterized the poor educational opportunities of Puerto Rican youth as "premarket discrimination"—that is, discrimination that inhibits future success in the labor market.[63]

The low college graduation rate for mainland Puerto Ricans restricts upward mobility. As for African and Mexican Americans, the historically white college setting is an alien environment for most Puerto Rican students. Mila Morales-Nadal has noted the determination and struggles of Puerto Rican women, among the poorest of all people of color, to get an education in order to secure a decent job: "It is not uncommon for some mothers to take their children with them to class in some public colleges." She has concluded that, within the context of higher education, intercultural exchanges that respect and value the language, culture, and identity of Puerto Ricans are vital to the empowerment of Puerto Rican youth.[64]

For many years, Puerto Rican parents have struggled against an educational system that has often failed their children. Local community organizations have been formed to examine educational problems and work for change. When school boards have ignored the findings of critical studies, Puerto Rican leaders and organizations have turned to the courts. Yet, the deficient educational system has proved highly resistant even to court-mandated change; white school administrators' attention to the rights and needs of culturally different students has often been halfhearted.[65]

Barriers to Social and Economic Mobility

Few Puerto Ricans have moved into influential positions in education, and Puerto Rican communities usually have little control over the educational policies and curriculum decisions that affect their children. For example, white authorities frequently are insensitive to Puerto Rican history and culture; the standard curriculum is often based on the assumption that Puerto Ricans are culturally or linguistically deficient. Neglect of Puerto Rican history and culture undoubtedly contributes to a lack of self-esteem among students. The schools attended by most students have a high concentration of Puerto Rican and other students of color, yet the number of Puerto Rican teachers and administrators and the ratio of Puerto Rican teachers and administrators to Puerto Rican students are extremely low.[66] Segregated schooling has serious negative implications: low retention rates, a large majority of students who read below grade level, high student–teacher ratios, less-qualified teachers, and low teacher expectations. In educational research a strong correlation has been established between teachers' expectations and students' academic achievement. Those students, in any group, whose teachers respect them and expect them to achieve are more likely to succeed.

Language

Few U.S. schools today are structured to deal with non-English-speaking students. Prior to the American Revolution, bilingual education (in German, for example) was common and continued to be available to many European immigrants and their children in private, and sometimes publicly funded, schools in the eighteenth, nineteenth, and early twentieth centuries. Only in recent decades has bilingual education become "un-American" and the target of anti-immigrant organizations.

In the current atmosphere of hostility to bilingual education, limited English proficiency creates multiple handicaps for Puerto Rican and other Latino students. Without good bilingual programs children who are unable to understand English instruction fall behind native-English-speaking classmates. Puerto Rican students are often inaccurately assigned to low-ability groups, "language-disabled" classes, or lower grades. On the average, Puerto Rican students do less well than non-Latino white students on achievement tests, most of which are given in English. One psychologist has commented on the extreme inaccuracy of English-language test scores:

> In my clinic, the average underestimation of IQ for a Puerto Rican kid is 20 points. We go through this again and again. When we test in Spanish, there is a 20 point leap immediately—20 higher than when he's tested in English.[67]

In addition, many Spanish-language achievement and "IQ" tests are simply translations of the English-language tests and thus maintain the subtle and overt cultural biases of the original English version. The predictive validity (for college performance) of standardized tests used for college entrance (the SAT and GRE) is considerably lower for Latinos than for whites. Such tests are culturally biased.[68]

Puerto Rican educator Herman La Fontaine has noted that "our definition of cultural pluralism must include the concept that our language and our culture will be given equal status to that of the majority population."[69] Many Puerto Rican educators argue that children should be taught to read and write well in Spanish first, taught subjects in that language, and then taught English as a second language. Civil rights groups have pressed for substantial and well-designed bilingual education programs for Latino children. In their struggle against the New York City school system, Puerto Rican organizations have sought a comprehensive educational program that recognizes the strengths of Puerto Rican culture and the Spanish language.[70] Interestingly, some researchers report that students in bilingual programs have higher attendance and completion rates and that such programs contribute to more positive self-concepts for students. Nonetheless, as we noted in Chapter 8, effective bilingual programs have not become part of the public school curriculum for most Latino children.[71]

Official English Policies and Spanish Speakers

Support for English as the official U.S. language has grown in recent years. Much of this movement is openly nativist and has often targeted Spanish and Spanish speakers, from Florida to California. An amendment to the Arizona Constitution went so far as to make English the language "of all government functions and actions," but a federal judge ruled that this law violated the U.S. Constitution.[72]

Xenophobic Americans praise English-only government policies as a means to unify diverse groups within U.S. society and promote traditional (that is, European American) cultural values. Educator Catherine Walsh reports that instead "such efforts toward linguistic cohesion resonate with a kind of colonial domination, a hegemony that threatens to silence the less powerful [and attempts] to render invisible the complex, abstract, psych-ideological nature of language."[73] Language is one way in which people define themselves. Far from simply a set of neutral symbols, language shapes thought and thus is inseparable from personal identity and everyday life. In her years as a teacher and researcher, Walsh documented the daily struggle faced by language-minority students over *whose* language and therefore whose knowledge, perspectives, and experiences are recognized and accepted and whose are omitted or belittled. She quotes one young bilingual student:

> "Sometimes I two-times think," she said. "I think like in my family and in my house. And then I think like in school and other places. Then I talk. They aren't the same, you know."

Realizing that the language context of her home was not only different but less acceptable than that of the school, this child often told her teacher, "It makes me feel funny, all alone ... different."[74]

POLITICS

In Puerto Rico, 60 percent or more of the island's registered voters usually cast their votes on election days. Yet, among mainland Puerto Ricans, voting rates have been as low as 20 percent. Similar to the experiences of other subordinated racial communities, weak electoral support of Puerto Rican candidates by whites, a lack of campaign funds, a lack of representation in political party leadership, a lack of education, and a feeling of hopelessness regarding political change all contribute to this low level of political participation. In one survey of mainland Puerto Ricans who were not registered to vote, the most frequently cited reasons for not voting were "not interested in politics" (29 percent) and "voting makes no difference" (24 percent). More than one in four stated that language barriers kept them from registering.[75] Voter registration and turnout have generally increased for mainland Puerto Ricans since 1990, especially in areas where governments are responsive to community needs. In the 1994 general election, for example, Puerto Rican voters in Pennsylvania played a decisive role in the reelection of one U.S. Representative.[76]

Election to major political office has come slowly for mainland Puerto Ricans. Since the 1930s, Puerto Ricans have participated in Democratic party politics in New York and New Jersey, but until recent years that participation has usually been token. The first Puerto Rican American was elected to the New York state assembly in 1937; it would be fifteen years before another was elected. In 1965, Herman Badillo became the first Puerto Rican elected president of a New York City borough; six years later he became the first voting member of Puerto Rican background in the U.S. House. Robert Garcia, who followed Badillo, played an important role in building political bridges between African Americans and Puerto Ricans in New York.[77] In 1990, Jose Serrano was elected to fill Garcia's seat. Puerto Rican representation in the House tripled in 1992 with the election of Nydia Velazquez (D.-New York) and Luis Gutierrez (D.-Illinois) to fill seats created by redistricting following the 1990 census. The Congressional Hispanic Caucus has slowly grown—to nineteen members in 2001. In 1997, Aida Alvarez became the first Puerto Rican to hold a cabinet-level position when she was appointed by President Bill Clinton to head the Small Business Administration.[78]

Local and State Government

Puerto Ricans have served on a number of city councils and as mayors of small towns and a few cities. Miami, Florida had a Puerto Rican mayor from 1973 until 1985. In mid-2001, Eddie Perez, president of the Southside Institutions Neighborhood Alliance and developer of a successful education complex, was considered the front runner for the mayor's position in Hartford, Connecticut.[79] By the late 1990s, Puerto Ricans had won twenty-one elected positions in New York City. At the state level, Illinois, Connecticut, Kansas, Pennsylvania, and California had Puerto Rican legislators by the mid-1990s.[80]

The long-term effects of institutional discrimination can be seen in state and city government employment, in which Puerto Ricans are still significantly underrepresented. Partly as a result of this lack of representation, many Puerto Ricans report poor treatment by government and private agencies. Government officials serving them seldom speak Spanish. Government services have historically been less accessible to Puerto Ricans, and job training and employment services have been slow in coming to Puerto Rican communities.[81] One exception to this pattern is the city of Paterson, New Jersey, where many are now employed in government jobs. With several Puerto Ricans on the city council in the mid-1990s, Paterson had the highest percentage of Puerto Rican representation in the nation.[82]

Since the 1980s, the Midwest–Northeast Voter Registration Education Project, which operates in states with significant Latino populations, has conducted many voter-registration campaigns and registered more than a million voters, including many Puerto Ricans. In the late 1980s, the governor of Puerto Rico announced a campaign to register mainland Puerto Rican voters. Local leaders welcomed this intervention by a non-mainland Puerto Rican leader, which again demonstrated the close alliances between mainland and island communities. The project registered more than 84,000 new voters in New York City, and Puerto Rican voter turnout in city elections increased, resulting in more Puerto Ricans on the city council.[83]

Politics and Recent Intergroup Conflict

In this and the previous chapter, we have noted the success of political coalitions between black and Latino communities in some cities. However, other cities have been characterized by political competition. Recently, in Providence, Rhode Island, political conflicts between black and Latino residents have surfaced. The city's population is one-fourth Latino, about half of whom are from the Dominican Republic and the rest from Puerto Rico, Mexico, and South America. African Americans make up about 15 percent of the population; whites are a bare majority. In recent years Latino political organizations there have grown in strength. In 2000, two Latino candidates tried to unseat progressive black elected officials. The fall 2000 primary and general elections saw a large turnout of Latino voters, and one Latino candidate successfully displaced a progressive black elected official; a second Latino came close to ousting another black official. Some local observers suggested that the white elite had intentionally backed the local Latino attempt to unseat black elected officials; others argued that the conflict was primarily the result of the growing numbers of Latino voters. Whatever the reason, local activists, particularly African Americans, have expressed much concern about the lack of a progressive coalition between Latino and black residents in the city.[84]

PROTEST

In Puerto Rico, protests against colonial status have periodically punctuated the era of U.S. rule. Contrary to the stereotype of docility, Puerto Ricans have fought hard to retain their language and culture and to end the island's status as the "last major U.S. colony." In the 1930s, large numbers of Puerto Ricans attacked the colonial government buildings in periodic protests. The Nationalist party began pushing for expanded freedom and for independence. In March 1937, at least twenty Nationalist party marchers who had joined a legal march in Ponce were massacred by heavily armed police.[85] In fall 1950, police raided Nationalist party meetings, precipitating an armed revolt. Hundreds of people were killed, and two thousand were arrested for advocating independence. On the mainland, Puerto Rican nationalists seeking independence violently attacked the residence of President Harry Truman and members of the U.S. House while they were in session.

The future of Puerto Rico is still a major political issue on the island and the mainland. Recent platforms of the Republican and Democratic parties have supported statehood for Puerto Rico. Although pro-statehood sentiment on the island has increased over the past few decades, in a 1993 nonbinding plebiscite, island voters narrowly favored continuing the island's commonwealth status (48 percent to

46 percent for statehood). A small percentage voted for independence.[86] Not surprisingly, a U.S. Congress that had long treated Puerto Rico as a colony ignored this popular vote.

In the late 1990s the U.S. House passed a bill permitting an official Puerto Rican plebiscite on the future of the island, but the bill did not pass the Senate. Significantly, the bill's preamble admitted that the U.S. government had never permitted Puerto Ricans to have genuine self-determination. The bill also recognized that commonwealth status was only a temporary status on the way to statehood or "separate sovereignty" for the island. Today, island Puerto Ricans are divided between the options of commonwealth status and statehood.[87] Supporters of statehood argue that commonwealth status is a second-class status. In contrast, opponents fear the economic changes and loss of Puerto Rican culture that statehood might bring. Writing in the elite journal *Foreign Affairs* in 1997, Ruben Berrios Martinez, President of the Puerto Rican Independence Party, stated the following:

> As a state, Puerto Rico is bound to pay the heaviest of prices: cultural assimilation. In the American system the only way out of an ethnic ghetto is through cultural assimilation into the Anglo-American mainstream, which would subordinate the island's Spanish language and distinct culture.... In any case, assimilation is unacceptable to Puerto Ricans, including statehooders.[88]

One sign of the threat of such cultural assimilation is the view held by many mainland whites that Puerto Rico should not become a state unless it adopts English as its official language.[89]

Tensions between island leaders and U.S. politicians increased significantly in the early 2000s. Numerous protest demonstrations targeted the U.S. Navy's 60-year-old bombing range on the small island of Vieques off the main island of Puerto Rico. Puerto Rican demonstrators have regularly protested the negative impact of Navy bombing on the island's inhabitants. Some New Yorkers went to Puerto Rico to protest the bombing. Bronx Democratic Party chair Roberto Ramirez, assembly member Jose Rivera, and borough presidential candidate Adolfo Carrion, Jr., as well as black civil rights leader Al Sharpton, were arrested in protests on the island. Protesters finally secured a promise in 2001 from President George W. Bush to end the bombing by 2003.[90]

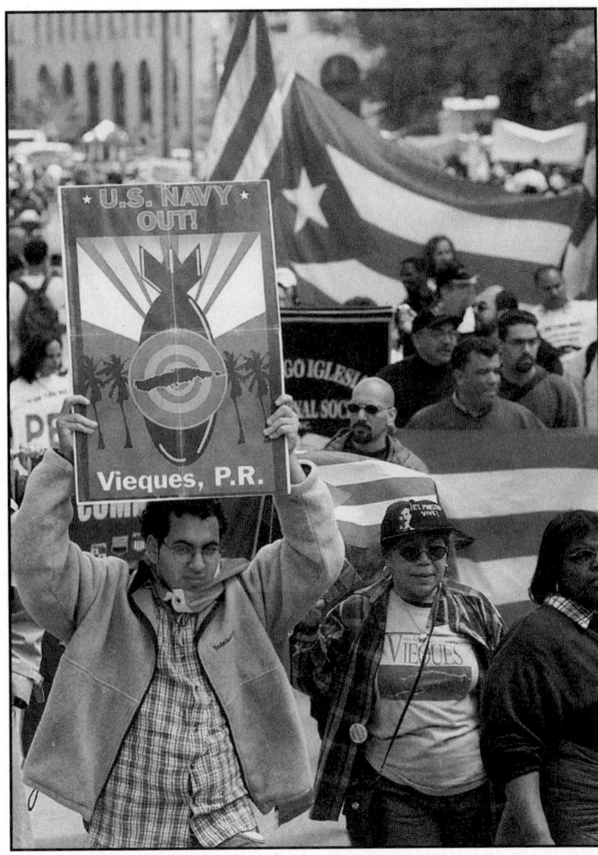

In Washington, D.C., demonstrators protest the U.S. Navy's use of the Puerto Rican island of Vieques for bombing and other military operations.

On the Mainland

Arriving for the most part desperately poor and stigmatized by whites as inferior, Puerto Ricans on the mainland have developed organizations to cope with discrimination and other barriers. Some of the major organizations are the Puerto Rican Legal Project, the Puerto Rican Legal Defense and Education Fund, and the League of Puerto Rican Women. The Puerto Rican Teachers Association has worked to increase representation of Puerto Ricans among teachers and principals and expand bilingual programs. Puerto Ricans have also been active in labor and union organizations on the mainland since the late 1800s.[91]

Protest activity increased in the 1960s and 1970s. In spring 1969 the Young Lords, a militant youth protest group, occupied the administration building of Chicago's McCormick Theological Seminary to publicize poverty there. They opened a community day-care center and school, actively protested the use of urban-renewal land for a tennis club, and set up a people's park on urban-renewal land.[92]

In New York City late in 1969, a Young Lords group occupied the First Spanish Methodist Church for eleven days and organized a day-care center, a breakfast program, and a clothing distribution program. They created a newspaper, *Palante* (Forward), and led a demonstration to protest squalid conditions at a hospital.[93] Children of poor immigrants, the Young Lords articulated a thirteen-point program for a democratic-socialist society. Proudly asserting their Puerto Rican identity, they called for "liberation and power in the hands of the people, not Puerto Rican exploiters." At the peak of their influence, the Young Lords had chapters in twenty cities. The Young Lords, as well as a few other militant groups, were subject to police repression, including infiltration by government agents that sought to create factions. Some leaders were prosecuted, sometimes in rigged trials. Other leaders were more or less co-opted into government anti-poverty programs. The Young Lords had disbanded by the early 1970s. Still, many former members are today influential Puerto Rican professionals and leaders in community organizations.[94]

For several decades numerous Puerto Rican community organizations have worked for a better quality of life and increased participation in the political process. The Puerto Rican Legal Defense and Education Fund has engaged in litigation in support of civil rights; the organization Aspira has worked to improve education; the National Puerto Rican Forum has focused on employment and job training. The National Puerto Rican Coalition, representing more than one hundred local organizations, has served as a liaison between Puerto Rican communities and federal officials and lobbied for educational, health, economic, and civil rights programs.

More Community Protest

Puerto Rican communities have long protested the racial discrimination directed at them by local whites. For example, Chicago community organizations have protested housing discrimination and police brutality. Reports of police injustices targeting Puerto Ricans and other Latinos, including unwarranted arrests and searches, as well as the use of excessive force, are common in several cities that have significant Latino populations. In 1990 a major riot that involved hundreds of Puerto Ricans occurred in Miami after six police officers were acquitted in the fatal police beating of a Puerto Rican drug dealer. Residents of the impoverished Puerto Rican neighborhood said the violent uprisings were directly related to the sense of alienation and powerlessness many felt in the Miami community. They pointed to factors as diverse as the scarcity of Puerto Ricans in powerful government and business positions and the absence of Puerto Rican music on local radio stations. "Cubans get everything; we get nothing," one resident pointedly stated.[95]

Problems with police have persisted. In summer 2001, after a National Puerto Rican Day parade in New York, a milling crowd rioted and protested when police, according to community observers, began arguing with, and then beating and pepper-spraying, people in the crowd. Some community residents were injured, and forty-two people were arrested. New York police authorities defended their violent actions as appropriate, but some in the community questioned what they saw as a pattern of continuing police malpractice.[96]

Some protest movements have brought significant changes for local communities. Thus, pressures from activists led to the founding of a community college in the South Bronx and helped create supportive programs for students at the City University of New York. City and state governments have provided more funds for community projects and hired more Puerto Ricans. Some public schools have added more Puerto Rican studies programs and bilingual programs and hired more Puerto Rican teachers, and some colleges have set up Puerto Rican studies programs.[97]

Coalitions of grass-roots organizations and older established groups, including the National Congress for Puerto Rican Rights, have been created to improve the economic conditions of Puerto Ricans. Since the 1990s, leaders and members of state branches of the National Congress have pressed state and local governments for fair treatment in the courts and better schools for Latino children; they have participated in demonstrations, sometimes with black organizations, against government indifference and police brutality. The National Congress and other Puerto Rican organizations have pressed the media for better reporting on Latino communities and more Puerto Rican and Latino journalists and editors.

In the past few years, a few media outlets have responded to broad community pressures. Some Puerto Ricans like David Gonzalez, the *first* Latino to write the *New York Times'* column "About New York," have begun to articulate a Latino perspective. Also the *Times'* Caribbean and Central America bureau chief, Gonzalez has recently noted that he "took the column's title at face value. I wanted to make sure the groups I knew, my people, were reflected not just in terms of the usual issues—the social issues, which are important—but also the cultural issues in these neighborhoods whose residents exist in New York."[98] Integrating local media outlets not only voices and empowers historically excluded communities but also increases the knowledge available to all citizens and policymakers in an increasingly "rainbow" society. The deepest understandings of this society's distinctive racial-ethnic areas often come from those who are native to the areas' cultures and languages.

Annual parades honoring Puerto Ricans are now held in cities in both New York and New Jersey. One summer 1997 parade in New York City that drew 200,000 people, including elected officials and celebrities, celebrated the strong sense of Puerto Rican identity and asserted concern over discrimination against Puerto Ricans. Significantly, a few days before this Puerto Rican parade, a white businessperson urged area businesses to close their doors and protect their premises during the event, and a former New York columnist writing in a prominent magazine called Puerto Ricans "fat," "dusky," and "semi-savages." These comments, which not surprisingly triggered protest, reveal the continuing stereotypes of Puerto Ricans among some people in the white business and media elites.[99]

RELIGION

Traditionally, most Puerto Ricans have been Catholic, but on the mainland they have generally been led by non–Puerto Rican clergy. The supportive framework that parishes gave to previous European Catholic immigrants has often been missing. One exception to the dependence on non–Puerto Rican clergy is the Bishop of Puerto Rico, who visits mainland parishes.

Religion scholar Joseph Fitzpatrick has argued that Puerto Rican Catholicism is more a religion of the community than of the parish. Community celebrations and processions are important, as is reverence for the Virgin Mary and saints. Formal church worship is less important than communal celebrations and home ceremonies. Still, many Puerto Ricans remain devoutly religious whether or not they attend mass regularly. On the mainland, Puerto Ricans have often shared parishes with black and other Latino parishioners. Latino caucuses have sometimes developed within the Catholic church to press for Spanish-language services and more priests of Latino background. In Fitzpatrick's words, "the principal demand of the Puerto Ricans and other Latinos is for a policy of cultural pluralism in the church that will provide for the continuation of their language and culture in their spiritual life and the appointment of Puerto Ricans and other Latinos to positions of responsibility."[100] Gradually, if too slowly, the U.S. church has moved to integrate Puerto Ricans and other Latinos into parishes and leadership positions.

As is the case for other Latinos, many Puerto Ricans have left the Catholic church for evangelical Protestant churches, which they feel offer a warmer reception and a community feeling. Protestant evangelical groups have made significant inroads into Puerto Rican communities. Many communities now have numerous storefront evangelical churches. New York City alone is said to now have about 1,400 Latino Protestant churches.

ASSIMILATION OR COLONIALISM?

Assimilation Issues

In his influential 1971 book, Joseph Fitzpatrick uses an assimilation model to interpret Puerto Rican experiences. For that time he reported a significant degree of overall assimilation for mainland immigrants and substantial cultural assimilation, particularly for the mainland-born Puerto Ricans who identified with U.S. society and adopted English as their second language.[101] Yet other scholars then and now, such as Walsh, have argued that this cultural adaptation is in fact more limited and gives a "false hope of inclusion in [the dominant] environment."

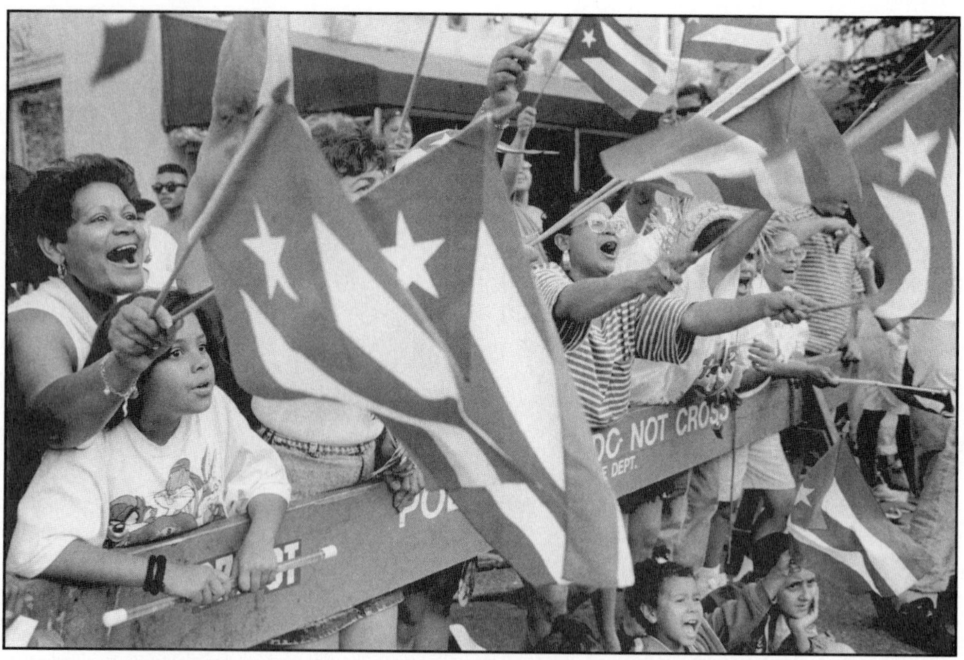

Puerto Ricans wave the flag of Puerto Rico in a New York City parade.

Assimilation may be more apparent than real. Catherine Walsh found that Puerto Rican schoolchildren often deny knowing Spanish when speaking with non-Latinos, even if they use Spanish at home. Earlier, in *Up from Puerto Rico* (1958), Padilla had argued that second-generation Puerto Ricans generally have a different reference group from the first-generation immigrants—that is, the mainland society rather than island society—and as a result many hide their Spanish-language facility in an attempt to assimilate culturally.[102]

The pressure to assimilate culturally has been intense. As Maldonado-Denis notes, the "American ethic is a messianic one, and all ethnic groups are required to assimilate culturally as a condition for achieving a share in the material and spiritual goods of American society."[103] Cultural assimilation pressures begin in Puerto Rico, where for decades the colonial government pressured islanders to assimilate to U.S. culture, such as by requiring the use of English in schools.[104] Today, there is indeed evidence of significant cultural assimilation. In a 1990s survey, Strategy Research Corporation ranked the cultural assimilation level of Latinos on the basis of language use and behavioral, attitudinal, and aspirational measures. The majority (59 percent) of mainland Puerto Rican heads of household were classified as partially assimilated. Fewer than 10 percent were ranked as highly assimilated, while about 32 percent were considered relatively unassimilated. Like other Latino and Asian American groups, the majority of people were biculturally adept, having some ability to operate in two different cultures.[105]

There is significant resistance to complete cultural assimilation. The quest for identity "is taking the form of a strong assertion of the significance of Puerto Rican culture, including language, and also the definition of Puerto Rican interests around militant types of political and community action."[106] Puerto Rican studies programs at a few colleges help to buttress the sense of a distinctive Puerto Rican identity. However, some Puerto Ricans argue that they must assimilate more thoroughly to the dominant culture in order to find better jobs and achieve a higher socioeconomic position. Some argue that this can be done with a minimum of soul selling—that is, with a strong persistence of Puerto Rican culture. Others worry about the heavy cost of thoroughgoing cultural assimilation to Puerto Rican identity; they fear that assimilation pressures will lead to rootlessness.

Many white school teachers are seen to be engaged in an ongoing cultural struggle with their Latino students. The outcome of this struggle varies; students may become culturally assimilated, fully or partially, or they may drop out. Researchers have found that favorable treatment of Latino students in school increases as their "difference," as perceived by the non-Latino teacher, decreases. For earlier white immigrants, acculturation frequently led to some denial of their ethnicity; differences became the source of shame, as noted by the Italian immigrant Leonard Covello:

> We soon got the idea that Italian meant something inferior and a barrier was erected between [children] of Italian origin and their parents. This was the accepted process of Americanization; we were becoming Americans by learning to be ashamed of our parents.[107]

For people of color, however, full cultural assimilation and loss of racial-ethnic identity are impossible; the differences usually are too visible and important in whites' racial judgments. Rather than becoming de-racialized or de-ethnicized "Americans," Puerto Ricans and others of color typically remain distinctive and subordinated.

Today, blatant job discrimination against Puerto Ricans appears to be declining, although substantial discrimination remains. Blatant and subtle forms of mistreatment continue in other areas such as housing rentals and sales. For the most part, the level of behavior-receptional assimilation, to use Milton Gordon's term, is relatively low. Secondary-structural assimilation at the level of higher-paying white-collar jobs has been slow; Puerto Ricans are still disproportionately concentrated in blue-collar, service, and lower-wage white-collar jobs, as well as among the unemployed. The level of Puerto Rican participation in mainland political institutions also remains relatively low, although it seems to be growing somewhat.

Structural assimilation of Puerto Ricans at the primary-group level and marital assimilation have not reached levels comparable to those of white immigrants. One New York study found regular interaction between parents and married children. Despite the wrenching experiences of migration and three decades on the mainland, the first generation remains substantially linked to children and grandchildren. The better jobs and educations of many in the second generation have not ended this integration for most families. However, out-marriage appears more significant for the second generation and may be slowly breaking down intergenerational ties. More than half of U.S.-born Puerto Ricans who are married have a Puerto Rican spouse, compared with more than 80 percent of island-born migrants. Outmarriages, however, are typically to other Latinos or African Americans rather than to whites.[108]

As in other immigrant communities, generational conflict has been a problem. Children who grow up in mainland culture pick up values that conflict with traditional values. For example, the traditional chaperoning of girls has given way to less restrictive mainland dating patterns. Boys' street life is more difficult to supervise. Still, identificational assimilation has come slowly for Puerto Ricans. Most, whether island-born or mainland-born, still see themselves as Puerto Rican. One study of two generations of Puerto Rican families in New York City found that both generations had acculturated to some extent to the mainland culture, "but internally, in the symbolisms linking them to the island, they experienced less change." Even those born on the mainland retained strong symbolic ties to the island of Puerto Rico. Not one of the four hundred persons in the sample identified as purely "North American" in terms of values.[109]

Power-Conflict Perspectives

Power-conflict analysts would agree that Anglo-conformity pressure on Puerto Ricans has been heavy, but they would stress how colonized Puerto Rican Americans as a group remain. Assimilation into the economic and political mainstream has been rather slow, which suggests that non-European migrants such as Puerto Ricans are not, contrary to the views of some assimilation analysts, just like the European immigrants earlier in the twentieth century.

Issues of Puerto Rican identity and history surfaced in a late 1990s debate among some Puerto Ricans about a new Puerto Rican Barbie doll issued by Mattel corporation in its Dolls of the World series. Puerto Rican critics argued that the doll's appearance (skin and hair) was too white European and did not reflect Puerto Ricans' strong Indian and African ancestries. Some also noted that the description of the island on the doll's box neglected this ancestry as well as U.S. colonial oppression of the island.[110]

Other critics of the U.S. treatment of Puerto Ricans worry much more about the negative impact of unemployment and deteriorating central cities on the identities of many Puerto Rican youth. Gonzalez has recently argued that many youth in impoverished areas face such social chaos that they grow up "devoid for the most part, of self-image, national identity, or cultural awareness."[111]

Puerto Ricans are one group that has had the distinctive experience of *external* colonialism. Unemployment in the U.S. "possession" of Puerto Rico is often cited as a reason for out-migration; the prosperity of the mainland economy is cited as a pull factor. But unemployment and mainland prosperity would not have created the great migrations without the long colonial relationship. The economic history of Puerto Ricans is grounded in the history of the colonial relationship between the United States and the island of Puerto Rico. After the war with Spain, the United States took the island by force as an external colony. Since that time the inhabitants have been subject to constant U.S. economic and political intervention. Indeed, it was the creation of a one-crop agricultural society dominated by absentee sugar companies that originally displaced a large group of agricultural workers from the land.

With the later industrialization of Puerto Rico under the auspices of large U.S. firms, many Puerto Rican workers became part of a growing surplus labor population that frequently made its way to the industrialized cities on the mainland. These immigrants from an external colony often became part of the internal colonialism of U.S. central cities where Puerto Ricans often live in significantly segregated communities. Colonialism theorists would also argue that today a co-opted Puerto Rican elite exerts a social control function to keep the Puerto Rican population from rebelling even more against oppressive conditions.[112]

Internal colonialism could be seen in the "urban enterprise zones" created in some central cities in the 1980s and 1990s. These were urban poverty areas that offered significantly reduced taxes and regulations to corporations that opened plants there. Some power-conflict analysts view this program as economic exploitation of Latino and black communities because participating corporations often paid low wages yet received major government benefits. Frank Bonilla and Ricardo Campos have compared this "puertoricanization" of central-city communities to the economic colonialism of Operation Bootstrap on the island of Puerto Rico. Under Operation Bootstrap, Puerto Rico's poverty and low wages were major attractions for multinational corporations. The "puertoricanization" of certain central-city areas can sometimes make them corporate havens of profitability similar to the island of Puerto Rico.[113]

CUBAN AMERICANS

Cuban Americans are the third-largest Latino group in the United States. Like Puerto Ricans, this group has its roots in an important Caribbean island, Cuba, an island with more than a century of close ties to the United States. Indeed, through all the recent decades of political conflict between the U.S. and Cuban governments, the U.S. government has maintained a major symbol of past colonialism on the island—the naval base at Guantánamo Bay.

PATTERNS OF IMMIGRATION

Early Immigration: 1868–1959

Most migrations from Cuba to the United States have stemmed from political upheaval or economic distress on the island. Nineteenth-century wars of independence brought the first immigrants to the United States. Most were from Cuba's middle and working classes. Some went to New York, Philadelphia, and Boston, but most settled in Florida because of its proximity to Cuba and its climate. By 1873, Cubans were the majority of the population in Key West, Florida. After 1885, Ybor City and Tampa in south Florida became home to many Cubans when cigar factories located there. Expecting to return home, these Cuban Americans were committed to the independence of their homeland from Spain and contributed soldiers and financial assistance to the war with Spain. When Cuba finally won its independence, many returned home. Yet, tens of thousands stayed in the United States where they had established homes and held jobs. These early Cuban Americans made major contributions to their adopted homeland; they organized Florida's first labor union and established Key West's first fire department and bilingual school.[114]

These early Cuban exiles lobbied for official U.S. support of Cuba's liberation from Spain. Initially, the U.S. government supported continuing Spanish rule of Cuba. Later, after attempting to purchase the island, the United States sent troops to Cuba. Spain was driven out in 1898, and the United States occupied the island. In 1902, Cuba became a U.S. protectorate. The Platt Amendment to a 1900–1901 U.S. military appropriations bill gave the United States the right to military intervention in Cuba to preserve the island's "independence" and to protect life and liberty. During the first two decades of the twentieth century, U.S. involvement in Cuban politics took the form of military intervention to settle political disputes. After the 1920s, diplomatic interference replaced military intervention. So great was U.S. power in Cuban affairs that no elected president of the island who was opposed by the United States could remain in office long. Cuba was in effect a U.S. colony from 1898 until the Cuban revolution in the late 1950s.[115]

During this long period, U.S. financial domination of Cuba was no less extensive than its political domination. Within fifteen years after Cuba gained independence from Spain, U.S. business investments grew from an estimated $50 million to an estimated $220 million. By the late 1920s, U.S. firms controlled three-fourths of island's sugar industry. By 1959, U.S. businesses controlled 90 percent of Cuba's mines, 80 percent of its utilities, half of its railways, 40 percent of its sugar production, and one-fourth of its bank deposits. Cuba was indeed an economic colony.[116]

The political turbulence that accompanied a succession of repressive dictators in Cuba during the first half of the twentieth century brought political exiles to the United States. Many stayed only briefly before returning to Cuba. They were often replaced in the United States by those Cubans from whose power they had earlier fled. During the corrupt dictatorship of Fulgencio Batista in the 1950s, between 10,000 and 15,000 refugees per year entered the United States.[117]

Recent Immigration: 1959 to the Present

Large numbers of Cubans migrated to the United States after Cuba's 1959 revolution when Fidel Castro, the young rebel leader of the grass-roots insurrection that overthrew the dictator Batista, came to power. To the majority of Cubans, Castro's victory brought hope for economic and political reforms. Land grants to tenant farmers, guaranteed compensation for small sugar growers, and nationalization of utility companies were among Castro's stated goals. However, these reforms were not welcomed by Cuba's business, industrial, and political elites or by U.S. investors. Exaggerated views of the Cuban revolution's threat to U.S. business and political interests, suspicions that Castro was a Communist, and Castro's declarations that he would not tolerate manipulation of Cuba led to open U.S. government and business hostility toward the new Cuba, a break in diplomatic relations, and a U.S. policy that welcomed refugees from Cuba's "Communist oppression."[118] This helped tilt Cuba to supportive Communist regimes in eastern Europe.

The first major immigration after the revolution began with Cuba's monied elite—former government officials, bankers, and industrialists who had done well under the Batista dictatorship and feared Castro's revolutionary orientation. This group's economic position in Cuba was directly related to Cuba's political and economic relationship with the United States. During a second wave of immigration, which began in 1961, large numbers of middle-income and upper-income Cubans chose exile from their native island rather than life under Fidel Castro's increasingly authoritarian government. This group was predominantly composed of professionals, managers, doctors, merchants, and landlords and included more than half of Cuba's teachers and doctors. Many cited loss of jobs, possessions, or sources of income as reasons for their departure. Others reported political persecution, temporary imprisonment, or fear that they would be imprisoned. More than 14,000 children were sent alone by parents who feared having their children educated by a Communist state. These early groups of immigrants were composed primarily of lighter-skinned Cubans. (In 1953 the island's population was at least 27 percent Afro-Cuban.) By 1962, almost 200,000 Cubans had entered the United States. Smaller numbers of Cubans continued to arrive by boat or by way of other countries after air travel between Cuba and the United States was suspended in 1962.[119]

As with earlier Cuban immigrants, south Florida, only 90 miles from Cuba, was the logical destination. Because they were fleeing a Communist government, they found the U.S. government a willing host. Both the immigrants and the government viewed these Cubans as refugees who were forced into temporary exile but who intended to return home when Castro was overthrown. This is a major reason why most chose to stay in south Florida.

To provide for the needs of these refugees, the Eisenhower administration created the Cuban Refugee Emergency Center in Miami and allocated $1 million in federal funds. The Kennedy administration expanded this aid by establishing a Cuban Refugee Program that assisted refugees with resettlement, helped locate employment, and provided for maintenance, health services, education and training programs, and food distribution. Unlike many other Latino and Caribbean immigrants, the Cubans were well treated and welcomed as allies in the struggle against Communism.[120]

A third group of immigrants, totaling more than 250,000, arrived between 1965 and the late 1970s. In late 1965, almost five thousand relatives of refugees already in the United States were allowed to leave Cuba aboard hundreds of boats. This exodus was followed by an airlift negotiated by the U.S. and Cuban governments. Concern with economic scarcities and hope for a higher standard of living in the United States as well as disagreement with Cuba's political regime were the major push factors for this largely lighter-skinned, working-class and small-business group. As with earlier groups, these refugees settled primarily in south Florida, although by the 1970s some were spread among many Cuban communities in other states. A 1968 nationwide study of 300 immigrant families found that relocation patterns reflected family associations: More than three-fourths of new immigrant families had relatives already in the United States. Occupational orientation was also found to be an important criterion in selecting a relocation city. For example, some with a background in government chose Washington, D.C., while some whose background was in business chose New York City.[121]

By the late 1960s, increasing numbers of Cuban immigrants had begun to think of themselves as permanent residents of the United States, more interested in improving their lives and less involved in efforts to bring about the demise of Castro's government. Many owned businesses and homes and had become integrated into the social, economic, and political institutions of their communities. Many also became naturalized citizens.

The Mariel Immigrants

A fourth group of immigrants, the sudden influx of 125,000 Cubans in 1980 often called the "Mariel boatlift" (after the port from which they sailed), gave rise to some popular myths and stereotypes that characterized these refugees as undesirables—poorer and less educated than earlier groups of immigrants and containing a large percentage of criminals and the mentally ill. Some in this group left Cuba voluntarily and some, considered undesirable by the Cuban government, were forced to leave. However, of the entire group, only a few hundred were mentally ill and required institutionalization, and fewer than one in five had been in prison in Cuba. Among this latter group, almost one-fourth had been political prisoners, and the offenses of an additional 70 percent consisted of some form of dissent or other acts that were not crimes in the United States. Fewer than 2 percent were subsequently imprisoned in a U.S. penitentiary. Moreover, the education level of this Mariel group was similar to that of the 1970s' immigrants. More than 11 percent were professionals; 71 percent were blue-collar workers. Unlike earlier immigrants, most of whom were lighter-skinned, approximately 40 percent of the Mariel group were darker-skinned Cubans with more substantial African ancestry. More than half came to waiting families or sponsors, and two-thirds of the rest were easily placed in communities across the nation.[122]

Because their reasons for immigration were substantially economic, most of the Mariel immigrants were ineligible for the financial support available to earlier political refugees. They were allowed to stay by the creation of a special category, "Cuban-Haitian entrant," which included eligibility for emergency assistance, medical services, and supplemental income. On arrival the immigrants were housed in tent cities in the Miami area and flown to military bases in Arkansas, Florida, Pennsylvania, and Wisconsin. Some were held in processing centers for an extended time while the government attempted to identify refugees who were "dangerous." Yet, the vast majority were neither marginal nor criminal. Many of these immigrants became angry at the contrast between their actual socioeconomic conditions

Some of the Cuban refugees not allowed into the United States were held at the Guantánomo naval base in Cuba.

in the United States and the exaggerated reports they had heard in Cuba about the ease of life in the United States. Disillusionment and crowded conditions in the detention centers also led to some inmate riots and scattered violent confrontations between refugees and the police or National Guard troops.[123] Most were eventually integrated into Cuban American communities, yet as a group these later immigrants have not done as well economically as earlier immigrants.[124]

In 1994 the Cuban government again lifted its ban on emigration, and 35,000 Cubans left for Florida, mostly on rafts and small boats. Reversing earlier policy, the U.S. government stopped admitting immigrants, sending them instead to camps at the Guantánamo Bay naval base on Cuba. The U.S. and Cuban governments negotiated an agreement whereby the United States would increase visas for Cubans to at least 20,000 annually, and Cuba would halt the exodus. The U.S. government also agreed to send back Cubans who had not departed legally and were intercepted by the Coast Guard before they reached the mainland. As a result, a large number of immigrants were legally admitted. Still, since the mid-1990s, the number of immigrants has often not reached the allowed quota because of fees and other barriers imposed by the Cuban government. The sometimes heated discussions over immigration issues have continued between the two governments to the present.[125] Most years since the mid-1960s, some 800–1,700 Cubans have tried to reach the mainland using rafts or boats, and the number of smugglers has increased. Under U.S. law, migrants who reach the U.S. shoreline are permitted to stay (at least temporarily). In addition, the Nicaraguan Adjustment and Central American Relief Act, put into effect by the U.S. government since the late 1990s, has given legal resident status to many Cubans and Central Americans who are here illegally.[126]

More than 1.2 million Cuban Americans now live in the United States, and most of these Americans live in urban areas. In the 2000 census, the median age for Cuban Americans was just over 40 years, higher than for the U.S. population as a whole and for other Latino groups.[127] One scholar notes that "the overrepresentation of the elderly among Cubans has clear origins. Dissatisfaction with socialist revolutionary change was likely to be highest among the elderly. In issuing permits, the Cuban government has given preference to the dependent elderly while restricting the emigration, for example, of males of military age."[128]

Intergroup Conflict

One major result of the Cuban migrations is the change in the population mix of Florida. By the late 1980s, Latinos had become a majority of the population in Miami. The 1980 migration swelled public assistance rolls, increased school overcrowding, and created $30 million in expenses for local governments already hurting from federal cutbacks. The millions paid to care for the new Cuban immigrants angered many non-Latinos, and many of the latter unfairly blamed the poor Cuban immigrants for local social problems.

Tensions between Cuban Americans and African Americans

Tensions accelerated between Cuban immigrants and Miami's black residents, many of whom felt that Cuban Americans were getting too much government assistance and were taking jobs away from African Americans. Today, the larger and generally more affluent Cuban American community in south Florida controls many of its own businesses, many of which prefer to hire Cuban Americans. This creates friction with the local black population, which generally faces high unemployment. In one 1980s mayoral election, 95 percent of African American voters voted against the Cuban American candidate. Since 1980, more racial riots have occurred in the Miami area than in any other U.S. city. Miami's 1980 Liberty City riot and 1982 Overtown riot by working class African Americans were precipitated in part by local police involvement in the killing of black men. The Overtown uprising began after a Cuban American police officer shot and killed a black man who was playing a video game. More rioting took place in 1984 when the officer was acquitted of charges in connection with the killing. After the riots some Anglo landlords and businesses that had been damaged were replaced by Latino landlords and businesses. One former black school official complained that "after a generation of being Southern slaves, blacks now face a future as Latin slaves." The 1989 shooting of an unarmed black motorist by a Latino officer precipitated yet another major uprising in predominantly black areas of Miami. After the incident the U.S. attorney for Miami began an inquiry into complaints of police brutality by Anglo and Latino officers toward African Americans. Latino officers themselves asked not to be assigned to black areas of the city where anti-police hostility remained high after the riot.[129]

Cuban American leaders angered the local black community again when they ignored visiting black officials, including South African president Nelson Mandela, who maintained friendly relations with the Cuban government. In addition, black groups have sued Cuban American–controlled local governments for what they see as the obstruction of fair political representation for black voters. In the late 1990s, the head of a new local civil rights group, People United to Lead the Struggle for Equality, commented: "We are very much on edge here, and it's getting worse because of the constant elimination of African Americans from jobs and political offices. They [Cuban Americans] are becoming the oppressor."[130]

Political tensions between African Americans and Cuban Americans in south Florida surfaced again in the 2000 presidential election. Black voters in Florida overwhelmingly supported the Democratic candidate, while Cuban Americans voted in large numbers for the Republican candidate. Black leaders charged that local political and election officials, some of whom were Cuban Americans, played a role in creating discriminatory barriers for black voters in south Florida. Today, intergroup rivalry and competition remain strong in south Florida where a very old immigrant group (African Americans) often loses in a political power struggle with a new immigrant group (Cuban Americans).

Inconsistent U.S. government treatment of the often lighter-skinned Cuban refugees and the darker-skinned Haitian refugees, discussed in Chapter 7, has been another source of intergroup tension in south Florida. Thousands of Haitians, as well as hundreds of thousands of Salvadorans and Guatemalans, have been refused refugee status in the United States since the 1970s; many have been deported to face persecution or death at the hands of their own dictatorial governments. In a clearly political maneuver, the Cuban immigrants were for some years defined as "political refugees" eligible for U.S. citizenship by friendly U.S. officials, while most Haitian and Central American immigrants were classified as "economic refugees" ineligible even for entry into the United States. (However, in 1994 the federal government began to place more restrictions on Cuban immigrants.) This differential government treatment of immigrants has fueled tensions between Miami's Cuban and Haitian communities for two decades.[131]

Racial Division among Cuban Americans

The Cuban American population is diverse in terms of the racial gradient that is central to U.S. society. In Cuba, before the revolution, the society was substantially segregated; lighter-skinned Cubans generally had more residential and economic privileges than darker-skinned Cubans. After the revolution, Castro's government decreed that darker-skinned Cubans should be treated equally with lighter-skinned Cubans, and the former gained greater access to better jobs and housing. Racial status became less important in the lives of most Cubans. However, in the United States, Cuban immigrants suddenly faced a world in which the dominant white group firmly classifies people as black or white and privileges are strongly linked to racial classification. A recent (2000) report in the *New York Times* described the experiences of two men who had been close friends in Cuba, but who had grown apart when they moved to the Miami area.[132] The light-skinned one integrated easily into the predominantly light-skinned Cuban population while the other, who was darker-skinned, was viewed as black by the dominant society and forced to reside in a black community. He soon experienced the discrimination and other costs that come with being defined as "black" in the United States. Although they live only four miles apart, the two friends now inhabit separate and racialized worlds.

Mirta Ojito, the reporter who interviewed the two men, recounted the experiences of the darker-skinned Cuban man named Mr. Ruiz:

> He had seen barrios in Havana with more blacks than others, but he had never lived in a place where everybody was black. Far from feeling comfortable, he yearned for the mixing he had known in Cuba.... [H]e had been taught to see skin color ... as not much more important than, say, the color of his eyes. But this was not Cuba. This was Miami, and in Miami, skin color easily trumps nationality.[133]

In the United States, Ruiz feels that he is constantly under surveillance from whites. Many whites, including many Cubans who identify themselves as white, stereotype African Americans as dangerous, lazy, or criminal. Soon after his arrival, Ruiz faced police harassment, from a light-skinned Cuban American officer, just because he was black. It is clear that the rigid racial division in the United States forces Latin America immigrants into a new world that is hard for most to understand and navigate.

STEREOTYPES AND DISCRIMINATION

Cuban Americans are sometimes stereotyped as being anti-Communist extremists and have been described in some mass media reports, including newspaper editorials, as "crazies" or "nuts" for their nonviolent protests over such incidents as the Elian Gonzalez case. Certainly, some media accounts of this latter case suggested stereotypes of Latinos as overly emotional and irrational. Myriam Marquez, a Cuban American journalist, has recently argued that many other Americans hold this view of Cuban Americans: "We are circling our wagons, hunkering down for battle and waving a foreign flag on American soil. You are sure we will riot because there's no question in your mind that Miami long ago turned into a Banana Republic with a Wild West flair."[134] Yet, while some Cuban Americans have joined far-right, anti-Castro groups, most reject far-right extremism and support participation in U.S. politics using traditional electoral approaches.

Some have also stereotyped Cuban Americans as a predominantly affluent group, sometimes to the extent that they should not be considered a "minority group." As we will see in the following section, Cuban Americans as a group are generally more prosperous than other Latino groups. However, this relative affluence should not be exaggerated, for a large proportion of Cuban Americans live in modest circumstances or poverty. Indeed, a March 2000 census report found that 36 percent of

Cuban American workers earn less than $20,000 a year, compared with 19 percent of non-Latino white workers. Some 17.3 percent were below the poverty line, compared with 9.4 percent of the non-Latino white population.[135]

Non-Latinos, especially in Florida, sometimes express distaste for the Spanish language or other aspects of Cuban American culture. In the late 1980s, Florida voters overwhelmingly (83 percent) approved an "official English" initiative that many of the state's Latinos understandably considered hostile. This initiative mandated that state government business be conducted in English. One Cuban American leader noted that such legislation "opens the way for bigotry and discrimination."[136] The desire of some private clubs in south Florida to provide a place in which their white members do not have to hear Spanish spoken has led them to establish policies that exclude Latinos and other Americans of color. Federal judge Kenneth Ryskamp's connection to a Miami country club with such a policy was one of several actions that apparently led the Senate Judiciary Committee to reject his nomination to a court of appeals seat in the early 1990s. In most regions of the United States, the Spanish that might be heard by middle- and upper-income whites is spoken primarily by working-class Latinos. However, Spanish speakers make up a majority of the Miami population and are to be found in every social class. Judge Ryskamp echoed the sentiments of many whites when he explained that his wife was annoyed because many store clerks spoke mostly Spanish and that it was difficult for her to shop because stores stocked merchandise preferred by Spanish-speaking customers.[137]

Like other Latinos, Cuban Americans have experienced discrimination at the hands of European Americans. In the 1960s, signs outside some Miami apartment buildings proclaimed, "No Dogs, No Kids, No Cubans." Cuban immigrants have also faced employment barriers. One Cuban American FBI agent, Fernando Mata, helped bring a successful class-action lawsuit against the FBI. The court ordered the agency to eradicate employment discrimination against its Latino employees. After the lawsuit Mata, a decorated counterintelligence specialist, lost his security clearance and was suspended by the FBI because of allegations that he was spying for Cuba. However, many FBI agents and civil rights activists outside the agency saw no proof of spying activity and argued that Mata was being harassed because of the anti-discrimination lawsuit. Mata's attempt to sue the FBI for retaliation was rejected by federal courts, including the U.S. Supreme Court in 1996, for "national security" reasons.[138]

Other Cuban Americans have reported discrimination in government agencies. In 2001, a Drug Enforcement Administration (DEA) senior agent, Sandalio Gonzalez, sent materials to Congress indicating that he was being transferred out of the Miami office for what appeared to be discriminatory reasons. The highest-placed Cuban American in the agency, Gonzalez had protested anti-Latino discrimination in the Miami office. He filed a lawsuit seeking to stop the transfer.[139]

THE ECONOMIC SITUATION

Many Cuban immigrants experienced a dramatic decline in occupational status when they entered the U.S. economy. For example, a 1966 survey of Cubans in the Miami metropolitan area found that the percentage of immigrants who were employed as professionals, proprietors, technicians, and managers dropped from about 48 percent to about 13 percent, while the percentage of those employed as unskilled laborers doubled (32 percent in the United States compared with 16 percent in Cuba). Even though many were willing to take jobs far below their previous occupational level, unemployment was widespread. Still, most preferred to remain in south Florida's Cuban communities rather than migrate to other regions.[140]

The increased Cuban presence in south Florida has elevated Miami's importance as a center for Latin American and other international trade. The area's economic growth has expanded the volume of international trade as well as the number of international corporations that have located their headquarters for Latin America in the Miami area. In the eyes of many observers, Miami has become the "capital of Latin America" because of its dominant position in Latin American trade and banking as well as in the underground economy of the drug trade.[141]

A 1968 nationwide survey of Cuban immigrants across the United States found that fewer than half of those who had been employed as professionals in Cuba held professional positions in the United

States; the proportion holding unskilled jobs rose from 5 percent to 25 percent. Interviews with immigrants revealed that as they increased their English proficiency, their educational background and work experience often helped them climb to a position at or near their former level within a few years of resettlement.[142]

Compared with other Latino groups, Cuban Americans have generally enjoyed a greater degree of economic success. There are several interrelated reasons for this. The high-level educational and occupational characteristics and aspirations of many Cuban immigrants, especially earlier arrivals, have helped many attain economic success. In addition, the large numbers of immigrants in one metropolitan area (Miami) make possible the development of an "ethnic enclave" (a concentrated community) with support networks that have greatly facilitated economic adjustment. Discussing the development of the Cuban American enclave in Miami, sociologists Alejandro Portes and Robert Bach suggest that Cubans have done relatively well economically because they migrated not as poor individuals in isolated circumstances but rather as a group that had substantial resources, access to important social networks, and major support from government programs. Silvia Pedraza has underscored this government role. Motivated greatly by government concern to "fight Communism," large-scale federal programs played a major role in advancing the structural assimilation of Cuban immigrants by reinforcing their initial social-class advantage and thereby creating a cumulative advantage for them in the U.S. economy.[143]

The U.S. government assistance provided to Cuban immigrants was unprecedented. The nation's first federally funded bilingual programs were started for Cubans in the 1960s. The very important Cuban Refugee Program lasted until 1974. Over time the U.S. government has provided $1.2 billion in aid to the Cuban refugees, an average of about $63,000 per family (in 2000 dollars). About three-fourths have received some government assistance. Specific government programs to support new businesses, such as loans from the Small Business Administration, were specially targeted to Cuban Americans. As Grosfoguel and Georas note from their data analysis, "In Miami, as well as in Union City, New Jersey, and in New York City, metropolitan areas where large numbers of Cubans settled, the Small Business Administration (SBA) practiced institutionally racist policies against Puerto Ricans and African-Americans while favoring disproportionately the Cubans in the provision of loan programs."[144] In addition, numerous local government programs were also established to benefit the refugees.

For example, more than half of the "minority contracts" on Dade County's new transit system went to Latino contractors. Cuban immigrants are the only large group of Latin American immigrants who have been granted such extensive government aid. This assistance has been critical in helping the Cuban refugees and their children to build their economic infrastructure and in integrating them into the mainstream society and culture.

In addition, the wide range of occupations among the Cuban immigrants has facilitated the development of a large and interdependent local economy capable of providing jobs and incomes for many in Florida's Latino communities, including some immigrants from Central and South America. Once created, the enclave economy has given Cuban American entrepreneurs access to the less skilled workers arriving later on from Cuba. Appeals to group solidarity and Cuban identity have helped some businesspeople exploit their own compatriots as low-wage workers.[145]

While these individual and group factors are important in Cuban Americans' economic adjustment, they do not fully account for this group's mobility. Another factor is the economic organization of the Cuban American family. The Cuban American family is generally "organized around realizing aspirations of economic achievement."[146] Although few women participated in the paid labor force prior to the revolution, gainful employment became an economic necessity for upward mobility in the United States; after immigration, women viewed work outside the home as an opportunity to help the family. Cuban American women, including those who are married with husband present and those with children, are more likely than other Latinas to do paid labor; Cuban American women are also more likely to work full-time and year-round than other Latinas. In addition, three-generation families under one roof are more common among Cuban Americans. Such families provide a major source of child care and additional wage earners.[147]

Among Latino groups, Cuban Americans have relatively high levels of income and education. A comparison of family income and poverty rates and levels of educational attainment for Mexican Americans, Puerto Ricans, and Cuban Americans was presented in Chapter 8. Cuban Americans are nearer the non-Latino white population on most measures than are Mexican Americans or mainland Puerto Ricans. The rate of college completion for Cuban Americans is almost twice that of mainland Puerto Ricans and more than three times that of Mexican Americans.[148] The 1999 median family income for Cuban Americans was 71 percent of that of Anglo whites. In contrast, the median family income for mainland Puerto Ricans was 58 percent that of Anglo whites; for Mexican Americans, it was just 56 percent. The relatively higher economic status of Cuban Americans compared with other Latino groups does not mean that Cuban Americans do not face discrimination. Given this group's relatively high level of education, their median income figure is lower than it is for comparably educated Anglos. Employment discrimination at the hands of whites has been a problem for many Cuban Americans since the 1960s.

As we have already noted, the prosperity of Cuban Americans compared with other Latino groups does not mean that all Cuban Americans are affluent. In 2000, the poverty rate for Cuban American families was almost three times that of whites; one-fifth of Cuban Americans under age 18 and 29 percent of those over age 64 lived in poverty.[149]

POLITICS

The expectation that the Fidel Castro regime would be short-lived led most post-1959 Cuban immigrants to remain politically inactive in the United States for a number of years, although from the time of their arrival they sought to influence U.S. policy toward Cuba. The 1970s saw an increase in the number of naturalized citizens followed by an increase in voter registration and participation in local and state politics. Their political views were shaped by their concern with Cuba. In the 1980s, the Cuban American marketing director of the *Miami News* stated, "Cuban-Americans are definitely super-conservative. Communism for us is the enemy. On domestic issues, we will be more toward the center ... but the Cuban business community is still more in favor of Reaganomics than Mexicans or Puerto Ricans."[150] However, although many Cubans tend to identify with the Republican party, which they consider to be more anti-Castro, they left a legacy of progressive programs in Cuba where social reforms, such as an eight-hour work day, free school lunches, and a minimum wage, instituted in the 1930s, have remained in effect through a succession of Cuban dictators.[151]

Since the 1980s, Cuban Americans have become more politically active. They hold many elective and appointive offices in Florida, including powerful positions in the Florida legislature. In 2001, Miami had a Cuban American mayor, Joe Carollo; Miami-Dade county also had a Cuban American mayor, Alex Penelas. In recent years, the superintendent of the Dade County public schools, the county police chief, two presidents of major local colleges, and many of Dade County's state legislators have been Cuban American. Cuban Americans have also made political advances in urban areas in other states, particularly New Jersey. In 1993, Ileana Ros-Lehtinen, a Cuban American from Miami, became the first Latina ever to serve in the U.S. House of Representatives. In the 1990s two more Cuban Americans, Lincoln Diaz-Balart from Florida and Robert Menendez from New Jersey, joined Ros-Lehtinen in the House.[152] In 2001, President George W. Bush appointed the first Cuban American, Mel Martinez, to a presidential cabinet position, as Secretary of Housing and Urban Development.

Many Cuban Americans remain psychologically and monetarily involved in the politics of Cuba. One major example was the recent case of Elian Gonzalez, a young Cuban boy whose mother drowned while trying to bring him on a boat from Cuba to the United States. Elian's U.S. relatives waged a child custody battle with his Cuban father, who sought to have Elian returned to Cuba. In April 2000, U.S. agents under orders from the Bill Clinton (Democratic) administration seized the boy from his relatives and let him return to Cuba. Both these actions upset many in the Cuban American community and cost the Democratic presidential candidate in November 2000, Al Gore, many Cuban American votes, and perhaps the election. Some in Cuban American communities have called this voter reaction "el voto castigo" (the punishment vote).[153] This case is an example of how

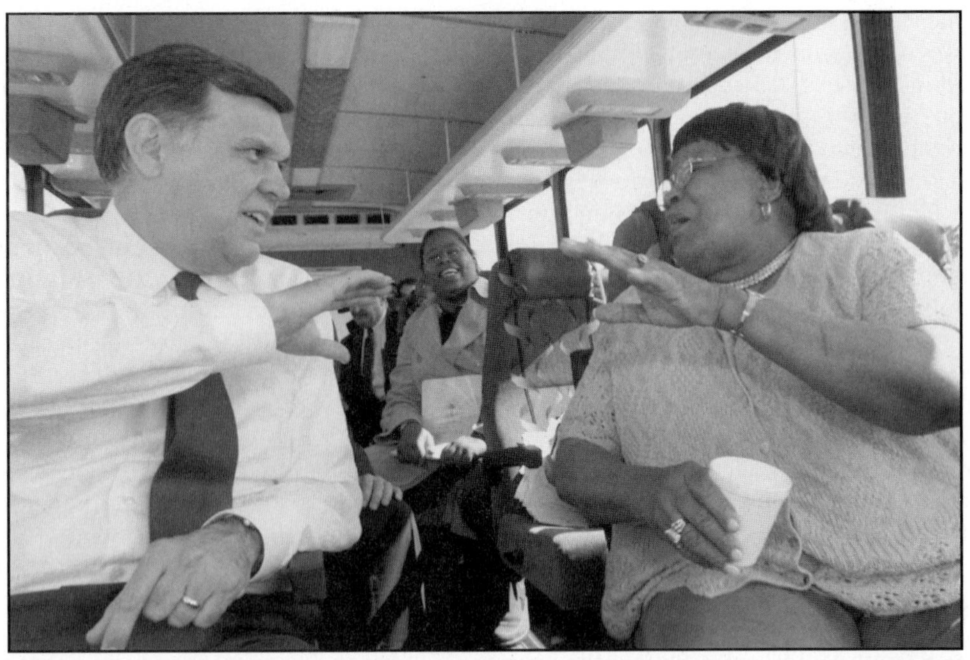

Housing and Urban Development Secretary Mel Martinez talks with Representative Carrie Meek (D-Florida) as they tour Miami's Empowerment Zones.

many U.S. racial and ethnic groups remain actively concerned about the politics of their home countries. Indeed, some U.S. political analysts now worry that U.S. foreign policy is no longer unified but instead has become a balkanized collection of the overseas interests of diverse nationality groups in the United States.[154]

One influential group is the conservative Cuban American National Foundation (CANF), established in 1981 with offices in Miami and Washington. It has been active in lobbying Congress on legislation dealing with Cuba. In an early 2001 speech, Jorge Mas Santos, chair of CANF, indicated that his organization still strongly supported the U.S. embargo on trade with Cuba, which has come under increasing political attack from humanitarian groups since the 1990s. He called on the George W. Bush administration to support and finance "peaceful, pro-democracy activities by local Cuban independent entities, non-governmental organizations and individuals" and to simulate the activity in Cuba of "reputable international NGOs." He also suggested that the United States provide aid to the families of political prisoners, establish a micro-loan program to help small businesses, license U.S. universities to establish business programs in Cuba, and increase the flow of information to Cuba.[155] CANF has worked hard to build close ties with the Bush administration that took office in 2001.

In the recent past, some Cuban exiles have engaged in paramilitary training and plans for terrorist acts against the Cuban government. Exiles recruited by the CIA were involved in the unsuccessful Bay of Pigs invasion in 1961. Members of at least one anti-Castro group in the United States practiced mock invasions well into the 1990s. In 1991, three Miami Cubans entered Cuba by boat with small arms and explosives, but they were captured and tried for sabotage.[156] Cuban Americans have also been active in the operation of Radio Marti, a federally funded station, and its affiliate, TV Marti, which transmit news and public affairs programming from Washington to Cuba via Florida.[157]

In May 2001 a group of prominent Cuban Americans, including three Miami-area Cuban American mayors, met at the elite Big Five Club to hear a presentation from Ramon Saul Sanchez regarding nonviolent action to help the Cuban people and undermine the Castro government. Sanchez heads the Democracy Movement, a major Cuban-exile group created in 1995 that has demonstrated on behalf of Cubans who lost their lives trying to sail from Cuba to the United States. It has sought to sail boats to Cuba on anti-Castro missions. Sanchez proposed the purchase of a ship to carry food, medical supplies, and doctors near the Cuban territorial limit and then request permission to land and unload the supplies. Sanchez explained that the supplies would be designated only for opposition groups on the island.[158]

The collapse of the Soviet Union has brought severe economic hardships to Cuba; the two countries had been linked by trade for decades. The Antonio Maceo Brigade, a progressive Cuban American organization, reported that between 1991 and 1992 fifteen thousand Cuban Americans signed a petition requesting that the United States lift its economic blockade of Cuba to ease the island's economic plight. Yet, at a January 1992 rally against the economic blockade in New York City, five thousand Cuban American counterdemonstrators protested proposals to end the severe sanctions against the Castro government.[159]

The involvement of Cuban Americans in the politics of Cuba is yet another example of the way in which the development and situations of U.S. racial and ethnic groups interact with and are dependent on the world context. As we have shown throughout this book, U.S. racial and ethnic relations are intrinsically international.

ASSIMILATION OR COLONIALISM?

Assimilation Issues

Cuban Americans are a relatively recent addition to the bubbling cauldron that is the United States. Like other Latinos, they have faced prejudice and discrimination, including language discrimination and restriction or exclusion in Anglo-dominated organizations and institutions.

Efforts to maintain the Cuban culture and social order, as well as to bypass country club discrimination by whites, led to the creation in the 1960s of the Big Five Club, a Miami social club originally composed of members of elite Havana yacht and golf clubs. By 2001, the Big Five Club's membership included many of the Cuban American community's most distinguished families. However, as with other immigrant groups, the younger generation seems less interested in joining such social clubs to maintain old ways. According to one Big Five president, "The ones born in this country feel they are more American than Cuban."[160]

Identificational assimilation has come slowly for Cuban Americans. Many still consider themselves exiles rather than immigrants and speak of their "fractured identity." Others—especially those who left Cuba as children and the American-born generations—say they have a "double" rather than a "split" identity. One survey found that only 29 percent of Cuban-born household heads expressed an intention to return to Cuba permanently if the Castro government were to fall.[161]

A recent study compared the identifications of Cuban American and African American women. The African American women felt they were indeed "American," but that they were not seen as such by white Americans, and they felt they were economically and socially excluded. In contrast, Cuban American women did not feel they were American and did not think Anglo whites saw them as American. Yet, their reported feelings of inclusion increased with length of residence. The longer they had been in the United States, the more economically and socially included they felt.[162]

The preservation of Cuban culture and identity in the enclave communities in south Florida provides a crucial foundation for Cuban Americans' economic and political integration into U.S. society. The community solidarity originally created by the first groups of immigrants was rooted in kinship and friendship ties and formed the socioeconomic context into which later immigrants entered. In the mid-1970s, researchers interviewed 590 male immigrant heads of household at the time of their arrival in Miami and again several years later. In the initial interview, 99 percent expressed an intention to remain in the Miami area; at the time of the final interview, 97 percent still resided there. The Miami area's strong enclave community has provided a context in which immigrants and their children adapt to U.S. culture yet continue to carry out routine activities within a Cuban American setting. Six years after these respondents entered the United States, more than one in five were self-employed in the Cuban American community and almost half worked for a Cuban American business. At the economic level most did not assimilate directly to the dominant economic institutions but rather to the enclave economy.[163]

Cuban Americans have made dramatic economic achievements, which increasingly link them into the mainstream economy and society. Recently, UCLA scholars David Hayes-Bautista and Robert Stein have argued that "Latino entrepreneurship has turned Miami into a bustling center of international trade, self-declared gateway to the economies of Latin America and self-appointed music center of Latino USA. Latino politicians run the city and county; Latinos are involved in the fine arts, academia, journalism and broadcasting."[164] While these scholars neglect the continuing problems with discrimination and stereotyping that Cuban Americans face at the hands of Anglo whites and others, they do underscore the important point that of all Latino groups, Cuban Americans are probably the most integrated into mainstream U.S. economic and political life.

Cuban Americans are similar to a few other immigrant groups that achieved a significant degree of economic prosperity and integration during their first generation in the United States. Like Jewish immigrants in the first half of the twentieth century, Cuban immigrants did not follow the model of waiting their turn in the urban economic queue, as did Italian, Polish, and certain other immigrant groups. Instead, in the first generation, many advanced in an economic niche as small-business owners or professionals, often laying a basis for their children's educational mobility and movement into better business and professional jobs. As a result, many of their children are relatively advantaged. Recent reports from south Florida underscore the growing affluence of many in Cuban American communities. For example, children's first communions (receiving the Roman Catholic sacrament) for many Cuban families have become costly celebrations. As Cuban American analyst Daniel Alvarez has noted, "We are a very tight community, and we want to do whatever we can to hold on and keep our kids in touch with their Cuban Catholic heritage."[165] The presence of a large and cohesive group of immigrants in an enclave community provides a context of support for later generations, a situation that exists to a lesser degree for other recent immigrant groups.[166]

Cultural-assimilation pressures on Cuban immigrants have created cross-generational problems similar to those of earlier European immigrants. Language assimilation is significant for the younger generation. One 1980s survey of Miami's Cubans revealed that the young preferred to listen to English-language programs on radio and TV, whereas their parents switched back and forth between English and Spanish programs. Like other immigrant grandparents before them, the grandparents preferred to hear and speak the mother tongue. Parents and grandparents also worried about the excessive freedom and lack of parental respect of teenagers in U.S. cities. Parents and grandparents tended to emphasize Cuban traditions and food; the grandchildren often preferred things American. The older generations were strongly committed to overthrowing Cuba's Communist government and to returning home. The less politically active youth saw the United States as their permanent home. Family and community ties were strong, and the young were proud of their Cuban identities.[167]

Recall, from Chapter 8, Strategy Research Corporation's ranking of the assimilation level of Latinos in the 1990s. The SRC study found Cuban Americans to be the least *culturally* assimilated based on language use and behavioral, attitudinal, and aspirational measures. Fewer than 4 percent of Cuban American heads of household were highly assimilated. Just over 26 percent were partially assimilated, and 70 percent were relatively unassimilated. The high density of Cuban Americans in south Florida and the group's older average age are likely factors in the lower level of assimilation. This survey also reported measures of assimilation by region. The vast majority of Latino adults in the Southeast, most of whom are Cuban American, felt more comfortable speaking Spanish than English and spoke Spanish more often at home. Fewer than one-third reported that they spoke or wrote English well. A large majority considered themselves "very Hispanic" and expected to be "very Hispanic" ten years in the future.[168]

The SRC survey presented a different picture for younger Latinos in the Southeast. Fewer than half of the youth classified themselves as "very Hispanic," and only 40 percent felt they would be "very Hispanic" ten years in the future. Three-fourths spoke English at school and felt more comfortable speaking English than Spanish. A large majority reported that they spoke and wrote English well and that their reading and writing ability in Spanish was poor to fair. About half reported that they used both languages socially, although more than half said they spoke Spanish more frequently at home. They were biculturally adept, with an ability to operate in two languages and cultures. Without exception, the adult respondents felt that it was important for their children to be able to read and write Spanish.

Cuban Americans in south Florida have assimilated selectively. They have developed a vigorous enclave economy and substantial group resources, with increasing links to the larger economic and political institutions. The older generation has attempted to preserve the Spanish language and traditions. However, the younger generation is moving away from many of the old ways and assimilating more rapidly to the dominant Anglo-white culture. This pattern is similar to earlier immigrant groups such as Italian Americans.[169]

Interestingly, the dominant culture does often make modest adjustments to new groups entering the society, as we have seen in earlier chapters. For example, as the Latino population in the United States has grown in recent years, Cuban, Mexican, and other Latino music and foods have become popular. Many restaurants now feature Cuban and Mexican foods, and major store chains, especially in areas with substantial Latino populations, carry foods of interest to Latinos. In south Florida cities, major chain grocery stores carry such things as plantains, guava paste, corn husks, and dried chili peppers. Although smaller Latino-operated stores (*bodegas*) have more goods for Latinos, chain retailers have discovered this group's $350 billion buying power and are striving to discover what products they seek. In this process, non-Latino customers are also exposed to Latino tastes in food and other products.[170]

A Power-Conflict Perspective?

To our knowledge, no one has applied a sustained power-conflict perspective to the case of Cuban Americans. Some might argue that the internal colonialism and other power-conflict perspectives are not useful to interpreting the development of the predominantly light-skinned Cuban American group, which has not been so strongly racialized and victimized as much by long-term economic and political discrimination as other Latino groups. Many of the relatively well-off Cubans who migrated to the United States before 1980 had already been the beneficiaries of U.S. economic and political control over Cuba prior to the 1959 revolution. Instead of becoming low-wage laborers for non-Latino agribusiness and industrialists, as was (and often still is) the case for many Mexican Americans and Puerto Ricans, most Cuban Americans have become part of a south Florida niche economy and enclave society that has helped speed their economic and social mobility.

The opportunities and accomplishments of the U.S.-born generations of Cuban Americans (at least of the lighter-skinned majority), which include growing numbers of businesspeople, professionals, and managerial workers, seem more similar to those of certain white ethnic groups (for example, Italian or Polish Americans) at a comparable point in time than to those of other Latino Americans. Indeed, the adaptive development of lighter-skinned Cuban Americans may best be interpreted as a variation on the ethnogenesis model. This group has experienced substantial cultural adaptation as well as some economic and political integration into the mainstream. Still, the process of ethnogenesis means that major aspects of home-country heritage remain very important to the immigrant-ethnic group character and identity for a long period of time. New U.S. groups like (lighter-skinned) Cuban Americans are, to a substantial degree, increasingly being integrated with the dominant European American group and yet retain major characteristics of their home cultures and nationalities as well. From the ethnogenesis perspective, a new ethnic group is one part home-country heritage and one part common culture mixed together in a distinctive way because of a unique history of social and political development within the U.S. crucible.

Still, substantially greater political and civic integration with the dominant group can occur only if later generations of Cuban Americans disperse residentially from what is now a concentrated and cohesive community in south Florida. Residential dispersion will likely accelerate this assimilation process. Language is a major obstacle to full cultural assimilation of Cuban Americans to the dominant Anglo culture and institutions. Powerful English-speaking Anglos have organized to impose English as the dominant language. Such nativist movements mark a type of cultural colonialism that rejects cultural pluralism if it threatens the core culture. Even though most Anglos probably classify the majority of Cuban Americans as light-skinned, the latter group will not be fully accepted by the dominant group and culture until they reject Spanish and other important aspects of Cuban culture. A significant Cuban sacrifice on the altar of white nativism will be required for the Anglo majority to welcome lighter-skinned Cuban Americans fully into the dominant culture and society. Even then, the many Cuban Americans whose ancestry is substantially and perceptibly African (especially from an Anglo-white point of view) will likely not be admitted into white society. Indeed, given persisting problems of anti-Latino discrimination and language and other cultural domination, it may be time to construct a more developed power-conflict perspective in regard to the case of Cuban Americans.

SUMMARY

The United States now has the fourth largest Spanish-speaking population among all countries, and in the near future that population will likely reach 40 million people. In Chapter 8 we examined Mexican Americans, the largest Latino group in the United States. In this chapter we have examined the second and third largest subgroups.

Puerto Ricans on the mainland are second in population size to Mexican Americans. Puerto Ricans are an important and distinctive American group with an ancient heritage. Like Mexican Americans, they represent a fusion of Native American, Spanish, and African heritages. Today, Puerto Ricans are a divided nation with one foot on the mainland and one foot in the Caribbean island of Puerto Rico. The more or less external-colony situation of the island population complicates the picture.

The island of Puerto Rico is a self-contained society with a variety of classes, including both a local capitalist class and a local working class, as well as a small elite of U.S.-based multinational capitalists. Some argue that social-class problems on the island are different from those on the mainland where most Puerto Ricans are working-class; there are few mainland Puerto Rican capitalists. Other commentators downplay class divisions and stress that there is only one Puerto Rican nation. As one Puerto Rican social scientist has stated, "No matter how we see ourselves internally, the Yanqui always sees us and deals with us as one class and one people with the same problems. Therefore we should band together and not divide ourselves to fight for our nation against the colonizer."[171]

Concentrated in the Northeast, mainland Puerto Ricans have been very important to the social health and economic vitality of the New York City area, especially as whites are leaving the region. Many Puerto Rican workers face hard lives doing difficult, low-wage jobs. Levels of poverty and unemployment remain excessively high.

Like Puerto Ricans, Cuban Americans are rooted in a Caribbean island. The third largest group, they are relatively better off than other Latino groups, with higher levels of education and income. Today they are an urban population mostly concentrated in the southeastern United States. Cuban Americans' relative prosperity stems largely from the fact that most early immigrants migrated as individuals with important personal and group resources, including access to major federal government assistance. Smaller families and a higher level of participation of Cuban American women in the paid labor force have contributed to the upward mobility of this Latino group. Cuban Americans' achievements affirm the advantages of migrating under the auspices of strong family and friendship networks and of receiving government support.

Cuban Americans have developed a powerful urban community centered in Miami. This population's size and resources have allowed Cuban Americans to develop a strong economic and political niche and to maintain their Spanish language as well as many Cuban cultural practices. As is the case with other immigrant groups, members of the younger generation have moved rapidly toward the dominant culture in many areas, including language, much to the disappointment of many in the older generation.

The pride that most Latinos feel in their heritages can be seen in their desire to maintain the Spanish language as well as other cultural patterns. The growing numbers of U.S. Latinos provide support for Spanish-language media, Latino organizations, and the availability of Latino-oriented products and services. Puerto Ricans and Cuban Americans have helped generate the new pan-Latino consciousness we discussed previously. They share with Mexican Americans a common language, a common religion, and similar home cultures. The pan-Latino consciousness contributes to a sense of solidarity that is reflected in efforts to address problems of education, jobs, and discrimination.

In recent years, the now substantial Latino population has had an increasing impact on the larger society. For example, major businesses are now actively recruiting Puerto Rican, Cuban American, and other Latino workers—especially the college educated. Companies as varied as Chevron, PepsiCo, and Pricewaterhouse Coopers operate recruitment programs at high schools and colleges with large Latino student populations, hire Spanish interpreters, and provide mentoring programs to aid Spanish-speaking employees. The executives in these companies seem to be aware of the dramatic increase in the number of Spanish-speaking Latino consumers as well as the growing international trade with Spanish-speaking countries. Growing numbers of Latino voters are also exerting an increasing impact on U.S. politics, as we saw in the Elian Gonzalez case.[172] The United States is now a complex mosaic with growing and very important Latino cultural and social components.

10 Japanese Americans

CHANGES IN U.S. IMMIGRATION LAWS SINCE 1965, ESPECIALLY THE ELIMINATION OF openly racist immigration quotas, have allowed a substantial increase in immigration from Asia and the Pacific Islands. Asian-Pacific Islander Americans are the fastest-growing racial-ethnic group in the United States. However, contrary to the view of many, these Asian-Pacific Americans are not homogeneous. More than a dozen major groups of Americans have roots in Asia or the Pacific Islands. Since their earliest days of immigration, Asian-Pacific groups have sought to maintain their distinctive cultures and identities.

It is important to keep in mind the diversity of groups that are included under the umbrella term Asian American. In 1940, Asian-Pacific Americans were less than half of one percent of the U.S. population. By 2000, they numbered more than 10 million—almost 4 percent of the total population. Table 10.1 (on page 266) shows the number in each of several different groups according to the most recent data.[1]

In the 2000 census, the largest of the Asian-Pacific groups was Chinese Americans. In numbers, Filipino Americans were not far behind. Japanese, Korean, Asian-Indian,

TABLE 10.1 ASIAN-PACIFIC GROUPS

	1980 CENSUS	1990 CENSUS	2000 CENSUS
Japanese	716,331	866,160	796,700
Chinese	812,178	1,648,696	2,432,585
Filipino	781,894	1,419,711	1,850,314
Korean	357,393	797,304	1,076,872
Vietnamese	245,025	593,213	1,122,528
Asian Indian	387,223	786,694	1,678,765
Hawaiian	172,346	205,501	140,652
Cambodian	16,044	149,047	*
Laotian	47,683	147,375	*
Hmong	5,204	94,439	*
Thai	45,279	91,360	*
Samoan	39,520	57,679	91,029
Guamanian or Chamorro	30,695	47,754	58,240

*2000 census data for these groups are not yet available. The total number of Americans identifying as "Other Asian" and mixed Asian ancestry for the 2000 census is 1,285,234.

and Vietnamese Americans constitute the other large Asian American groups. We will examine Japanese Americans in this chapter, then turn to other Asian American groups in Chapter 11.

INTRODUCTION: JAPANESE AMERICANS

Japanese Americans are one of the two oldest Asian American groups. They hold a distinctive place in the racial history of the United States because of their concentration camp experience during World War II. They are the *only* group of Americans to have been forcibly placed in concentration camps on a large scale in the past sixty years. As we will see later in this chapter in the work of Janice Tanaka, Japanese Americans are still paying a personal and economic price for that imprisonment. Today, Japanese Americans are also considered by many non-Asian Americans to be the *most* successful and assimilated of all Asian Americans, and they have been central to the "model minority" stereotype that has been important in the United States since the 1960s. For these reasons, we will devote an extended discussion to their history and experience in North America.

According to the most recent data available, Japanese Americans comprise about 8 percent of Asian Americans. Although the majority of all Asian Americans live in western states, Japanese Americans are the most heavily concentrated there. Among Asian American groups, Japanese Americans have the highest percentage who are U.S.-born, an indication of the group's early entry into the United States and of the small number of recent immigrants.[2] For some non-Asian Americans, Japanese Americans conjure up racial stereotypes of "crafty Orientals," images of militaristic Japanese expansionism in the 1930s and 1940s, or resentment of "unfair" Japanese economic competition today. Even in recent years, movies, political speeches, and vandals' graffiti have included such phrases as "fat Japs" and "little Nips," and Japanese and other Asian Americans have been targets of vandalism and violence. A *Boston Globe* writer summed up some common anti-Japanese incidents:

> A Honda Civic is bashed in Pennsylvania; Japanese-American community centers are vandalized; an American car salesman is fired for saying on national TV that he buys what is best for his money; a Japanese offer to purchase the Seattle Mariners baseball team sets off a national outcry; writers on Japan topics feel required to state they have never been employed by the Japanese. Frighteningly, a Japanese businessman in California is killed, apparently after receiving an anti-Japanese threat.[3]

Many of these verbal and physical attacks seem motivated by whites' fear of Japanese imports and global corporations or by resentment of Japanese competition in world trade. Anti-Asian hostility has especially increased during economic recessions in the United States as non-Asians have sought scapegoats for problems rooted in the faulty economic decisions of non-Asian executives, investors, or workers.

MIGRATION: AN OVERVIEW

Serial and Chain Migration

Asian and Pacific Americans include many immigrant groups: the Chinese, Japanese, Koreans, Filipinos, Vietnamese, and Asian Indians, as well as smaller groups such as Cambodians, Laotians, the

Hmong, the Thai, Samoans, and Guamanians. Historian Ronald Takaki has shown that prominent white historians of immigration have often neglected Asian immigrants in the epic story of U.S. migration. Such a Eurocentric history serves no good purpose, for Americans have "come from many different shores—Europe, the Americas, Africa, and also Asia."[4]

Historically, the immigration of early Asian groups proceeded in serial fashion. This was largely the result of actions of white employers seeking new laborers and white workers who were often motivated by racist prejudices to stop the immigration of a particular Asian group. As we will discuss in detail in Chapter 11, the first significant group of Asian immigrants to the United States were the Chinese. Early Chinese immigrants came to Hawaii, where, by the mid-1800s, U.S. planters were influential. From the 1860s to the 1880s, the Chinese migrated in large numbers to the West Coast to do low-wage work in construction and other industries. After racist agitation and exclusionary legislation stopped most Chinese immigration to the mainland in the 1880s, Japanese workers were aggressively recruited to fill the demand for labor on farms and in construction and mining projects. Similarly, the termination of Japanese immigration in 1908 in its turn spurred employers to recruit Filipinos to fill the labor needs of farms on the mainland and in Hawaii.[5]

Early Immigration

Japan's initial contact with the United States involved "gunboat imperialism." In 1853, U.S. Commodore Matthew Perry sailed his warships into Tokyo Bay, and with this show of force coerced a treaty granting the United States trading rights with Japan. Within a few decades, trade between the two nations had increased dramatically.

Later, the colony of Hawaii became the first destination for Japanese immigrants entering the U.S. sphere. At least 231,000 migrated there between 1868 and 1929. White planters sought low-wage laborers for their fields. At first, Chinese laborers were brought in under labor contracts. After 1884, thousands of Japanese laborers were brought to the Hawaiian plantations, usually under similar contract labor agreements. There were relatively few white laborers in the islands, and Japanese immigrants became part of a racial hierarchy headed by the European American planters. When labor agreements expired in 1894, most immigrants stayed on, laying the basis for Hawaii's present-day Japanese American communities. Propertied European Americans lobbied for annexation by the United States, and in 1898 Hawaii came under U.S. government control.[6]

Japanese workers were numerous on the islands. Dependent on the plantations owned by a few big corporations, they learned they could not "advance themselves through individualism and small business," as they did on the mainland. Rather, as laborers, they adopted a class-based strategy of "unionization, politics, and collective action."[7]

Mainland Migration

Between the 1880s and the so-called Gentlemen's Agreement in 1908, more than 150,000 Japanese entered; between 1909 and the 1920s, another 100,000 came. The immigrants to the mainland moved into a greater diversity of economic positions, from farm labor and mining to shopkeeping and truck farming, than did immigrants to Hawaii. Some came under contract to employers, some under the auspices of relatives, and others on their own. The pre-1908 Issei often had a harder time than those who came afterward, since later immigrants were able to move directly into Japanese American communities.[8] (*Issei*, *Nisei*, *Sansei*, and *Yonsei* are Japanese terms for the first four generations of Japanese Americans. Issei were born in Japan.)

Like the Chinese before them, Japanese immigrants faced serious racial discrimination. Many white employers favored labor immigration; many white workers and unions opposed it. At the turn of the century, one San Francisco mayor campaigned against the Japanese, arguing they were "unassimilable" and a competitive threat. In 1905, California newspapers began a campaign against the so-called "yellow peril," the Asian immigrants whom they saw as a threat. The California legislature passed a resolution calling for exclusion of the Japanese on the grounds that, given their racial differences, they would not assimilate. This racist agitation and other factors led President Theodore Roosevelt to negotiate a prohibition of Japanese immigrants. In 1907–1908, Roosevelt persuaded the Japanese government to agree to an infamous Gentlemen's Agreement whereby no passports would be given by

Japan to any Japanese workers except those already in the United States and their close relatives.[9]

Unlike earlier Chinese immigrants, the Japanese immigrants were able for a time to bring in wives and families. Before 1920, thousands of "picture brides" entered the United States following wedding ceremonies conducted in Japan to husbands they had never met. The large proportion of women and children among Japanese immigrants in the period between 1910 and 1920 led white supremacy groups to allege that a "disloyal alien race" was taking over and would soon overpopulate California.[10]

More Racist Agitation and Restrictions

Many white writers and politicians who proclaimed the threat posed by southern and eastern Europeans to "Anglo-Saxon superiority" often expressed fear of Asian immigrants. The American Legion and the California Farm Bureau Association both pressed for exclusion of the Japanese. By the 1920s, the U.S. Congress succumbed to this agitation by passing the 1924 Immigration Act, which established racist quotas based on a formula that gave preference to "Nordic" nations and excluded Japanese immigration by prohibiting all "aliens ineligible for citizenship" from entry into the United States. In an earlier decision, *Ozawa v. United States* (1922), the Supreme Court had ruled that only immigrants of white or African origin could become U.S. citizens. One striking feature of the new immigration restrictions, which were intended to prevent the development of Asian American families, was that Japanese and other Asian immigrants already in the United States, unlike their European counterparts, were now prohibited from bringing wives they had left behind. The more extreme Cable Act (1922) stipulated that *any* U.S. woman, whether white or Asian American, who married an alien ineligible for citizenship (that is, an Asian) would lose *her own* citizenship. These restrictions served to block many avenues of assimilation into the larger society for Asian immigrants.[11]

Government action against Asians, spurred by white-controlled labor unions and hate groups, persisted. Much of the labor movement supported direct exclusion of Japanese immigrants until after World War II. Not until 1952 did the federal government provide even a small quota for the Japanese and permit first-generation Japanese Americans to become naturalized citizens, and the racist anti-Asian restrictions were not fully removed from U.S. immigration law until 1965.[12]

In 1880, there were only 148 Japanese Americans. By 1920, the number had grown to 111,000. As late as 1965, Asian Americans numbered only about 1 million, and Japanese Americans were the largest group. The 1965 Immigration Act finally permitted significant numbers of new immigrants from Asia, and, since the 1970s, Asian and Pacific peoples have been a major component of U.S. immigration.[13]

Since the end of racist immigration quotas in 1965, large numbers of Japanese immigrants have been allowed to enter the United States, but relatively few have taken advantage of the opportunity to immigrate. Japanese numbers have been lower than those of other Asian groups. In recent years the immigration of a relatively small number of Japanese college students and of professionals and executives of U.S. branches of Japanese corporations and their families has contributed to the revitalization of some Japanese American communities.

STEREOTYPES

Non–Asian Americans have long held a range of stereotypes about Japanese and other Asian Americans. In recent years Japanese and other Asian Americans have often been called "model minorities"—that is, groups of color that are said to be very successful in moving up the socioeconomic ladder by means of hard work. Stereotypes take a variety of forms. Thus, movies about World War II and the Vietnam War have portrayed Asians as devious, corrupt, or evil "gooks." Anti-Asian graffiti such as "Look out for the Asian invasion" and "Stop the Yellow Hordes" have been scrawled on college dorm walls and highway overpasses.[14]

Non-Asians often lump all Asian Americans into one group that is then smeared with stereotypes. Robert Lee lists several racist images that are often applied to those whom non-Asians see as "Orientals" (an offensive term): "Six images—the pollutant, the coolie, the deviant, the yellow peril, the model minority, and the gook—portray the Oriental as an alien body and a threat to the American national family."[15] White Americans, in particular, have often applied the stereotypes used for early Chinese and Japanese immigrants to later Asian immigrants. All Asian groups have suffered from similar stereotypes, such as the "dangerous and wily Oriental" image. In the early years, Chinese immigrants were stereotyped as "docile," "crafty," or "dirty." Initially, whites tended to consider the new Japanese immigrants less threatening and more family-oriented than the Chinese and evaluated them less negatively. Soon, however, white images of the Japanese came to contain the negative notions that the Japanese were also docile, servile, and devious. Immigrants often heard cries of "Jap go home."[16] Since those early days, the word "Jap" has become a derogatory epithet hurled by many non–Asian Americans at Japanese Americans.

Within a short period many of the early Japanese laborers managed to gain some land to farm, usually by contract or lease. Hostile white farmers and workers exaggerated this Japanese American land ownership, which, although growing, never involved more than a small percentage of western farmland. Another widespread myth among whites was that Japanese Americans were incapable of assimilation because of their very different Asian culture. Like other whites, V. S. McClatchy, a Sacramento editor, argued that the Japanese were "for various reasons unassimilable, and a dangerous element."[17] The irony in this was clear to anyone who understood that by state or federal law Japanese immigrants were not allowed to become citizens, directly own land, or marry whites. They were legally prohibited from even trying to assimilate along these social dimensions.

From U.S. presidents and senators to ordinary citizens, many whites exaggerated the differences between themselves and the early Japanese immigrants, often in highly racist terms. James Phelan, U.S. senator from California, argued that Japanese Americans were a great threat to the "future of the white race, American institutions, and Western civilization."[18] Again we see how the construction of "whiteness" in the United States has been based on biased views of the meaning of "civilization" as well as strong negative views of hated outgroups.

The movie industry has played an important role in the circulation of stereotypes of Asian Americans—just as it has for other racially oppressed Americans. Historically, movie images have reinforced stereotypes of Japanese Americans as treacherous and immoral. In the formative period of the movie industry in the early twentieth century, Chinese and Japanese characters were usually pictured as outsiders and villains. Asians and Asian Americans were often crudely stereotyped as "inscrutable," poor at speaking English, and dangerous or treacherous.[19] Between 1900 and the 1920s, the vicious image of the forward, buck-toothed "Jap" exploded in the media. In his widely circulated "Letters of a Japanese Schoolboy," for example, journalist Wallace Irwin stimulated stereotypes about Japanese Americans, including a mode of speech parodied with phrases such as "so sorry, please." White legislators and other leaders frequently spoke of the alleged immorality of Japanese Americans, even using the apelike image that had been applied earlier to Irish and African Americans.[20]

War Propaganda

From the 1890s to the 1930s, anti-Japan sentiment grew among non-Asians. The Japanese people were considered an "inferior race" with the brashness to challenge European and American interests in the Pacific region. Even before the attack on Pearl Harbor, white politicians and labor leaders were already portraying Japanese Americans as disloyal. This image expanded after the bombing of Pearl Harbor, and rumors of spying circulated by the thousands, including such wild stories as Japanese American farmers planting flowers in a pattern to guide attacking airplanes.[21]

California's attorney general (later U.S. chief justice), Earl Warren, depicted Japanese Americans as very dangerous. In 1943, West Coast military commander General John L. DeWitt argued in aggressively racist terms that "A Jap's a Jap.... The Japanese race is an enemy race, and while many second- and third-generation Japanese born on U.S. soil, possessed of U.S. citizenship, have become 'Americanized,' the racial strains are undiluted."[22] With no evidence whatsoever, the national press argued that there were many enemy agents in this "large alien population." Indeed, the main reason for the existence of this alien population was the racist U.S. law that prohibited first-generation Japanese Americans from becoming citizens. Significantly, *no* Japanese American was ever proven to have collaborated with the enemy during World War II.

After the war, the stereotypes slowly began to change. By the 1960s, new stereotypes had developed. Magazines and newspapers frequently praised Japanese Americans for being highly acculturated and successful. However, as Ogawa has noted, the "highly Americanized" and "successful citizens" stereotypes are not entirely positive, for they usually suggest that one must act or think "very white" in order to be a good U.S. citizen. The model minority image was and continues to be used to defend the overall U.S. record on racial relations. This new stereotype implies that because Japanese Americans have become English-speaking, work-ethic models of virtue, they can now be *accepted by whites*. Whites who hold this view often argue that other non–European Americans, particularly African and Latino Americans, can succeed if they too work hard and assimilate culturally like Japanese and certain other Asian Americans have done.[23]

Recent Distortions, Stereotypes, and Omissions

One study of Japanese Americans images in history textbooks found numerous distortions of Japanese American history along with the "successful minority" stereotype. Most textbooks omit the fact that U.S. employers in Hawaii and California actively recruited and economically exploited Japanese laborers. One prominent textbook used in public schools tiptoes around the oppressive circumstances of early Japanese American history by speaking of the Japanese being "added" to the U.S. population. Most textbooks do not deal adequately with the 1924 Immigration Act, which was grounded in the openly racist stereotypes held by leading white lawmakers and which violated the earlier Gentlemen's Agreement. Over objections of the Japanese government, this act stopped Japanese immigration entirely. This was taken as a great humiliation by the Japanese government and played a role in the buildup of animosity that led to World War II.

Many public school textbooks do not adequately cover the internment of Japanese Americans in concentration camps during World War II (to be discussed shortly). Many textbooks see the camp experience as part of the "hysteria of war" and do not discuss the long history of anti-Japanese discrimination that led to the illegal imprisonment. One textbook even suggests that Japanese Americans "have forgiven the government for violating their rights during World War II." The fact is that the imprisonment is well remembered by Japanese Americans today. None has forgotten the experience, and many have not forgiven the U.S. government.[24]

Stereotypes and misperceptions of Japanese Americans are commonplace in many areas of U.S. society. In the mid-1980s, Senator Spark M. Matsunaga of Hawaii, a Japanese American, while assisting the White House in hosting a reception for visiting Japanese officials, was mistaken for one of the officials by U.S. Secretary of State Alexander Haig, who shook Matsunaga's hand and wished him a nice visit! In recent years, U.S. Senator Daniel Inouye, a Japanese American who lost an arm fighting for the United States in World War II, has received hate mail telling him that he should "go home to Japan where he belongs." Other Japanese American officials have reported that white Americans frequently congratulate them on how well they speak English, as though they were foreigners. Many non–Asian Americans seem unaware that the nation has Japanese American elected officials, that such officials' (and their parents' or grandparents') place of birth is the United States, and that their native language is English.[25]

As we noted in earlier chapters, racist imaging sometimes takes the form of mocking the language and cultures of Americans of color. On a mid-1990s radio show, U.S. Senator Alfonse D'Amato (R-New York) spoke in a mock foreign-Asian accent as he criticized the Japanese American judge, Lance Ito, presiding over the O. J. Simpson trial in California. Yet, Judge Ito has no such foreign accent and he, like D'Amato himself, is a third generation American![26]

Controversy over the use of ethnic and racial group symbols and caricatures as mascots for sports teams has increased in recent years. We discussed this issue in the chapter on Native Americans and noted that a number of sports teams have discontinued the use of stereotyped symbols of various American racial and ethnic groups. Shoreline Community College in Seattle abandoned its Japanese Samurai Warrior mascot, a Japanese caricature, because of its racist overtones.

Michael Crichton's best-selling novel, *Rising Sun*, and the movie of the same name, develop a negative caricature of the Japanese. Japanese businesspeople and other Japanese characters in this Los Angeles–based murder mystery are portrayed, to quote one reviewer, as "inscrutable, technologically proficient, predatory aliens who … subsist through unpalatable foods, manipulate *everything* and *everyone*, and enjoy kinky, violent sex with white women."[27] The novel's characters embody several age-old anti-Asian stereotypes. The Media Action Network (MANAA), an Asian American organization formed to combat anti-Asian stereotyping, initiated talks about the film's volatile racial content with Twentieth Century-Fox, the studio that made the film version of the novel. When the talks broke down, MANAA organized demonstrations in several cities against the use of racially stereotyped images of the Japanese in the film.[28]

New debates about negative Asian images in the mass media emerged in 2001 with the release of the major Disney movie *Pearl Harbor*. The film's use of the derogatory epithet, "Japs," as well as its one-sided portrayal of Japanese military aggression in the World War II period, resulted in some increase in anti-Japanese sentiment across the United States. Numerous Japanese Americans reported derogatory comments from non-Asians because of the movie, responses that indicate that certain old prejudices are still alive. One recent California news report quoted a number of Japanese American students who stated that other students blamed them for starting World War II. The Japanese American students faced derogatory epithets such as "'Nips" or "Chino." One student noted that, "People are still against Japan. They treat us like we did something wrong." Other students noted that non-Asians often believe that somehow the Japanese are the same as Japanese Americans. Such non-Asian reactions support Asian Americans' fear that this film has increased or reinforced anti-Asian sentiment across the United States.[29]

In the mid-1990s a white disc jockey for a San Francisco radio station was suspended for anti-Asian on-the-air comments and for allowing callers to make racist anti-Asian remarks. He reportedly spoke of the "stinking Japanese" and told a Japanese American caller that he would hate the Japanese until he died. He even predicted yet another war with Japan. The station received vigorous complaints from Asian American groups, including the Japanese American Citizens League (JACL).[30]

Repression and Violent Attacks

Japanese Americans have suffered not only from hostile prejudices but also from economic discrimination and physical attacks. The first major acts of violence against Japanese immigrants came within a decade of their arrival in large numbers. After the 1906 San Francisco earthquake, mob violence directed at Japanese Americans increased. Scientists sent by Japan to help with earthquake relief were attacked by white men and boys, and local newspapers condoned the vicious actions. Japanese American businesses were boycotted, and shopkeepers were attacked.[31]

The anti-Japanese exclusion movement sometimes turned to violence, such as in California in 1921, when large numbers of Japanese farm workers were driven out of some farm areas. In the 1930s, white farmers in Arizona petitioned the governor to throw out Japanese American farmers. When this failed, attempts were made to drive them out by force. Violent attacks escalated at the beginning of World War II. In 1942 alone, there were dozens of violent attacks by whites on Japanese Americans and their property, from Seattle to San Diego.[32]

The Ugly Specter of U.S. Concentration Camps

Japanese military victories in Asia and the Pacific in the 1930s and 1940s, including the attack on Pearl Harbor, increased fear of a Japanese invasion of the U.S. mainland. Members of Congress and the media parroted old anti-Japanese stereotypes and escalated fear of Japanese Americans across the country. By early 1942, the evacuation and imprisonment of Americans of Japanese ancestry was suggested. Some whites were motivated by economic self-interest; the Western Growers Protective Association and other groups seemed committed to destroying Japanese American business competition.[33]

In the first major phase of federal action against Americans whose ancestry was linked to countries at war with the United States, a small number of Japanese, German, and Italian aliens were moved from sensitive areas and their travel was restricted. The second stage began with Executive Order 9066, issued on February 19, 1942, by President Franklin

Japanese Americans forced out of their homes in San Francisco await transportation to U.S. concentration camps.

Roosevelt and validated by Congress, which instructed the secretary of war to establish areas from which any person could be excluded. The West Coast military commander established the western parts of California, Washington, and Oregon, as well as the southern part of Arizona, as areas where no Japanese, Italian, or German aliens could reside. However, it was only those of Japanese ancestry—U.S. citizens and non-citizens alike—who as a result were detained in large numbers in assembly centers and later transported under guard to barbed-wire concentration camps in the West.[34]

Japanese American businesses usually had to be sold at a loss. By fall 1942, inland areas in the West housed about 120,000 Japanese Americans, more than two-thirds of them native-born U.S. citizens whose only crime was to be perceived by whites as racially different.[35] Racist oppression behind the barbed wire took many forms. The white administration at California's Tule Lake Camp arranged for inmates to be hired out to whites as domestics at the very low wage of $30 per month. The camp administration took part of these earnings to spend on recreational facilities for white personnel. Barracks were typically bare-board buildings with few furnishings. Whole families were forced to live in small rooms or partitioned-off areas. Men, women, and children faced severe racism and the consequent psychological and physical stress. Valerie Matsumoto has written about the difficulties faced by Japanese American women, who "faced severe racism and traumatic family strain."[36]

Japanese Americans protested their racist treatment in numerous demonstrations; six thousand renounced their citizenship. Gradually, several thousand college students and workers on agricultural assignments were released, and others were allowed to join the U.S. Army, where, ironically, many served in Europe with extraordinary valor in segregated units under white officers.[37]

In late 1944, the order to evacuate was rescinded. Most of those imprisoned returned to the West Coast and found their farms and businesses in white hands or in ruin, household goods destroyed, and local whites hostile if not violent. The U.S. government spent about $250 million on the evacuation; Japanese American economic losses are estimated to have been at least $400 million. The psychological costs and other human losses were of course huge.[38]

Why the Camps Were Created

The U.S. Supreme Court upheld the military decision without investigation—even though two-thirds of those evacuated were U.S. citizens. This evacuation was a clear violation of the civil rights guaranteed all citizens by the U.S. Constitution.[39] The record shows that President Franklin Roosevelt and other high political officials held racist attitudes toward Japanese and other Asian Americans. Roosevelt believed that people of Japanese descent were racially inferior, and he and other leaders saw the emerging struggle in the Pacific as a racial war. Racist attitudes made it easier for top officials to order internment of large numbers of U.S. citizens of Asian descent (but not large numbers of citizens of German descent) in barbed-wire camps.[40]

Japanese Americans fought unsuccessfully in the courts and in demonstrations. When Japanese American evacuees confronted authorities at California's Santa Anita Assembly Center, angry members of the group destroyed camp property and attacked a police officer. The rioting was suppressed by armed military police. In fall 1942, internees called a strike at the Poston camp to protest the imprisonment of two Japanese Americans.[41] In December 1942, at the Manzanar camp in California, an assault on a Japanese American who had collaborated with whites and the imprisonment of the attacker led to a meeting attended by 4,000 and demands for an investigation of camp conditions. The director, escorted by military police armed with machine guns, met the crowd. A crowd again formed at night and was fired upon; two Japanese Americans were killed.[42] Ironically, this authoritarian oppression of Americans occurred at a time when the U.S. government was proclaiming the values of "freedom" and "democracy" to a war-torn world.

Recent Violence

After World War II, most Japanese Americans moved back to California where they continued to face oppression in the form of economic discrimination as well as violent attacks. The epithet "Jap" became part of commonplace anti-Japanese graffiti. As we will see later, hate crimes—including murders, assaults, threats, and harassment—targeting Japanese and other Asian Americans in their homes, businesses, and places of employment have persisted into the twenty-first century.[43]

THE POLITICAL ARENA

Because of racist U.S. naturalization laws, the Issei and other first-generation Asian Americans were not allowed to become citizens until the 1950s. They could not be active politically. Some political and civic organizations were created in the 1930s, when older Nisei formed Democratic political clubs in a few West Coast cities. The Japanese American Citizens League (JACL), under Nisei leadership, advocated accommodation strategies of self-help and individual enterprise and pressed moderately for civil rights and for citizenship for the Issei. Voter-registration campaigns were also inaugurated, but attempts to persuade candidates to run usually stopped at the planning stage.[44]

Compensation Pressures and Political Progress

Since World War II, the JACL, together with other Japanese American organizations, has won some important political and legal victories. By 1946, the JACL and some newer organizations were pressing for compensation for evacuation losses, for citizenship for the first generation, and for changes in discriminatory laws. Meager compensation for business and property losses finally came in the form of the 1948 Japanese American Evacuation Act. Japanese Americans were paid less than 10 percent of their losses.[45]

The JACL and other Japanese American organizations pressed the U.S. government for more adequate repayment for losses suffered. As advocates for the nation's "liberty and justice for all" tradition, these civil rights organizations helped secure public admission of discrimination against Japanese Americans. Belatedly, in September 1987, after years of foot-dragging by congressional leaders and initial opposition from the Reagan White House, Congress passed a bill, which President Reagan signed into law, that provided $1.2 billion in *reparations* to Japanese Americans. The law contained an admission that the "basic civil liberties" of Japanese Americans were violated as a result of "racial prejudice" and included a formal apology for internment.[46] Federal funding of compensation took two more years. Finally, by 1994, all checks were mailed. Each internee, or his or her heirs, received $20,000. President George H. Bush wrote each internee a letter of apology.

Some internees, such as U.S. Representative Robert Matsui of California, refused the check but accepted the apology, saying, "All of us feel like we are home again." Matsui and California's other Japanese American congressman at the time, Norman Mineta, had led the House effort to pass the bill.[47]

Not all Americans were willing to see these Japanese Americans receive justice. In one Japanese American community in Oxnard, California, for example, non-Asians who were unable to distinguish between Japanese Americans, who are U.S. citizens, and the Japanese government, circulated anti-Japanese leaflets that claimed that no apology to Japanese Americans for their unconstitutional imprisonment was necessary because the Japanese government had detained U.S. soldiers in World War II.[48]

In June 2001, a well-designed memorial to the Japanese Americans who were incarcerated and the Japanese American soldiers who served in the U.S. military during World War II was dedicated in downtown Washington, D. C. near the Capitol dome.[49]

We should note also that pressure from the JACL and other Japanese American organizations helped win two very important political victories during the 1970s: the repeal of the infamous Title II of the 1950 Internal Security Act, which permitted government imprisonment of citizens deemed potential collaborators with an enemy in time of crisis, and the rescinding of Executive Order 9066, which ordered the wartime imprisonment of Japanese Americans.[50] These were political victories of significance for the civil rights of all U.S. citizens.

Government Officials

Political organization aimed at electoral victories has increased decade by decade. Some second-generation Japanese Americans (Nisei) were registered to vote in Hawaii as early as 1917, and in 1930, the first two Japanese Americans were elected to the territorial legislature there. Returning World War II veterans, intent on expanding their political participation, became active in Democratic attempts to overthrow the traditional Republican domination of the islands, and several were elected to the legislature. Their efforts facilitated Congress's conferral of statehood on Hawaii in the late 1950s, after years of anti-Asian opposition. Statehood was opposed by U.S. politicians who held openly racist views. For example, the segregationist Senator Strom Thurmond (R-S.C.) opposed statehood stating that "East is East and West is West and never the twain shall meet" and that there was an "impassable difference" between Asian and European Americans.[51]

War hero Daniel Inouye was elected the first U.S. representative from the new state and the first Japanese American to serve in Congress. In 1962, Spark Matsunaga became the second to serve in the House when Inouye was elected to the U.S. Senate. In 1964, a second House seat was won by Patsy Takemoto Mink, the first Japanese American woman to serve in Congress.[52] In 2001, Inouye and Daniel Akaka, a native Hawaiian American, were Hawaii's U.S. senators, and Mink remained in the U.S. House.

Political victories on the mainland have been difficult because of the dilution of Japanese American votes in the predominantly non-Asian populations of most western areas. Few have been elected to office until recent decades. In the 1960s, a few were elected to city council offices in Los Angeles County, Oakland, and San Jose. In 1972, Carl Ooka was elected county commissioner in the state of Washington, the first Japanese American elected to office in that state.[53]

Since the early 1970s, only a handful of mainland Japanese Americans have held elected positions at higher government levels. In 1976, Samuel I. Hayakawa, a prominent semanticist, was elected U.S. senator from California, the first Japanese American senator from the mainland. In the mid-1970s, Norman Mineta of California became the first mainland representative of Japanese descent to the U.S. House. Robert Matsui was elected to the California delegation in 1978 and remained in the U.S. House in 2001 when he was joined by fellow Californian, Michael Honda, also a Japanese American. In 2001, one of every eight Californians was Asian American, although only two of the state's fifty-two-member congressional delegation were Asian American. In addition, only four Asian Americans served in the state's eighty-member Assembly, and none were in the state's forty-member senate.

Only one Japanese American has ever held a presidential cabinet post. Norman Mineta was appointed Secretary of Commerce by President Bill Clinton in 2000. In 2001 he became Secretary of Transportation in the George W. Bush administration.

Norman Mineta, a leading Japanese American official, has served in the cabinets of Democratic and Republican presidents.

Political empowerment has come slowly in western states. Historically, many Asian Americans, including Japanese Americans, have been reluctant to participate actively in politics out of fear of intensifying discrimination against their group. Even in the past decade or so, Japanese Americans are less likely than whites to be registered to vote. Some analysts have speculated that Japanese and other Asian Americans tend to view politics and politicians as corrupt or disreputable or that Asian Americans tend to vote for white politicians rather than run their own candidates because they feel that whites have "more political clout."[54]

Japanese and other Asian Americans who venture into the political arena sometimes encounter overtly racist reactions. For example, in 1992, a Democratic party leader at a Spokane, Washington party meeting reportedly referred to owners of a local hotel as "chinks," provoking strong protests from Asian Americans. Later, at a meeting to examine the incident, the party's white vice-chair bowed and clasped her hands in front of her in response to a Japanese American participant who would not shake her hand. This mocking, offensive gesture combined with the other leader's racial slur led the JACL to sue the state Democratic party for discrimination.[55]

Politics, Stereotyping, and Competition with Japan

Acts of violence and vandalism by whites against Japanese Americans have often been motivated by fear of economic competition from Japan, which might be seen as a variation of the classic racist view of "Oriental hordes" threatening white America. For example, an exhibit at a 1980s Flint, Michigan auto show portrayed a car with a Japanese face falling like a bomb on Detroit.[56] In recent decades, Japan's economic development has surpassed that of the United States in a number of manufacturing areas. In response, "buy-American" cartoons featuring caricatures of "wily Japs" and "crafty Orientals" have appeared in U.S. print media. Old stereotypes have reappeared in conversations among whites and in newspaper articles. Increasing unemployment in local and national recessions of the 1980s, 1990s, and early 2000s have fueled a tendency among some non-Asians to blame the Japanese and other Asians for U.S. economic troubles. This scapegoating is sometimes reflected in political action. Anti-Japanese protectionist bills have periodically been introduced in Congress. Yet, congressional leaders have frequently ignored Japanese investments in the United States that have created thousands of new jobs. U.S. recessions are not the result of Japan's investments or its competitive economy; the real causes lie elsewhere—often in poor U.S. corporate management and capital flight.[57]

Japanese executives and investors who have come to the United States in recent years have sometimes faced racist reactions. In 1992, a Japanese businessperson was killed in the Los Angeles area. Police investigations discovered that not long before his death, the victim had been threatened by a man who blamed him for a 1990s economic recession.[58] In Baton Rouge, Louisiana, a white butcher shot and killed a 16-year-old Japanese exchange student, mistaking the youth for a robber. A Louisiana jury found the white man not guilty of murder, and in court some white spectators applauded the decision. Just across the border in the Beaumont, Texas area, a Japanese American resident who tried to get a road sign reading "Jap Road" changed received hate mail and death threats with references to Pearl Harbor. Today, some anti-Japanese hostility among non-Asians still turns to threats or violence.[59]

Protest Organizations and Group Pride

Japanese Americans have long protested racial discrimination. Voluntary associations, such as the Japanese Association, were formed in the early 1900s to combat exclusion and other anti-Japanese discrimination. In the five decades after 1870, Japanese workers in Hawaii participated in at least sixty work stoppages to protest poor working conditions. Substantial labor organizing also took place on the mainland. There were strikes for better wages and working conditions from the 1890s onward. In 1903, more than 1,000 Japanese American and Mexican American agricultural workers jointly struck white farmers in California. Japanese American workers were involved in agricultural and mining strikes in California, Utah, Colorado, and Washington. Yet, white labor leaders often blocked the admission of Japanese Americans into older unions with the common racist argument that the latter were racially unassimilable.[60]

As we have seen, during the 1940s, Japanese Americans protested their incarceration in World War II concentration camps; thousands renounced their citizenship and returned to Japan after the war. During the 1960s, new pan-Asian organizations and publications appeared, often established by the younger generations. *Amerasia Journal* and similar journals urged collective action and attention to problems of Asian Americans. Distorted and sugar-coated images of Asian American success were increasingly challenged.[61]

In order to develop new scholarship on Asian Americans that will question traditional white views and provide a more honest appraisal of U.S. history and society, a number of colleges and universities have developed important Asian American studies programs. These include several campuses of the University of California and of California State University as well as the University of Washington and the University of Hawaii. Most of these programs have become institutionalized with a significant core of faculty.[62]

In recent years, hate crimes directed against Japanese and other Asian Americans have increased on college campuses. Recently, 700 Asian American students at Indiana University received hate (e-mail) messages in three separate incidents. In 1998, a naturalized U.S. citizen from El Salvador, writing under the alias, "Asian hater," and upset by the large number of successful Asian American students at the University of California (Irvine), was sentenced to a year in prison for e-mailing death threats to Asian American students.[63] He was the first American to serve time for violating civil rights laws in cyberspace.[64] Because of such hostility, which often increases as the number of Asian American students grows at a campus, many Japanese American and other Asian American students have become even more interested than before in the development of strong Asian American organizations and academic programs on their campuses.

THE ECONOMY

Most Japanese immigrants started out at the bottom levels of the U.S. economic pyramid, filling the hard farming, mining, and construction jobs. One California study in 1909 found 65 percent of Japanese American workers in agriculture, 15 percent in domestic service work, 15 percent in small businesses, and 5 percent in other lines of work.[65] In many areas Japanese workers did much of the "dirty work" and generally were paid less than whites.[66]

Finding an Economic Niche

Gradually, many first-generation immigrants (Issei) found land to farm on their own. Although the amount of land Japanese Americans owned was not large, their economic role was concentrated and important. In some areas they grew almost 100 percent of certain food crops. Some created small businesses in urban areas in which institutionalized discrimination barred them from manufacturing and white-collar employment. The Issei came to play what has been called a "middleman minority" role in western states (see Chapter 2). Operated on a small scale, some enterprises catered primarily to a Japanese American clientele, but many eventually served non-Asians as well. Issei group solidarity helped create a niche economy, and this small-business economy in turn reinforced group solidarity.

Edna Bonacich and John Modell conclude that "the Japanese minority filled a particular and specialized niche in the western economy and was important to it, providing key products and services."[67]

Most early immigrants came from just eleven Japanese prefectures, and each was represented by an association in the United States. These prefectural clubs became mutual-aid associations for immigrants caught in an often hostile environment. They aided immigrants' movement into the economy by providing training for workers and directing clients to small businesses. Businesses succeeded because they could usually draw on prefectural networks for workers and loans. Informal money-pooling organizations called *tanomoshi* often provided capital for small entrepreneurs who could not secure funds from banks.[68]

White opposition to these immigrant workers and entrepreneurs came swiftly. In urban areas, the white-controlled labor movement often led the opposition, using boycotts and anti-Japanese advertising. One such action by the Anti-Jap Laundry League attempted to drive Japanese Americans out of the laundry business.[69] A 1913 California Alien Land Law, passed under pressure from white farmers, stipulated that "aliens" could not buy land or lease it for more than three years. (All Issei were *forced* to remain "aliens" because of discriminatory naturalization laws.) This California land law interfered with agricultural activity, but some found ways to circumvent it, such as by registering land ownership under children's names. Discriminatory land laws reduced the number of Japanese American farms from more than five thousand in 1920 to four thousand in 1930.[70]

Those forced out of farming or otherwise attracted to the booming cities often became gardeners or nursery operators. The 1930 California census showed that half of male Japanese workers were in agriculture or gardening, one-fourth were in trade or business, 2 percent were in the professions, and most of the rest were in other urban occupations.[71] By the beginning of World War II, some Japanese American urbanites were moving into white-collar positions. One study estimated that half the Japanese American men in Los Angeles County in 1940 held white-collar positions and about 40 percent had semiskilled and unskilled blue-collar jobs.[72] Then the economy collapsed. Median economic losses per family in Los Angeles from the forced wartime evacuation were estimated at about $10,000 (in 1940 dollars) in goods, property, income, and expenses. The figures were similar elsewhere.

In research on the labor of women before World War II, Evelyn Nakano Glenn found that "from the moment they arrived, Japanese American women labored alongside the men to secure their own and their families' livelihood."[73] Much of the hard work done by the women was unpaid family labor on farms and in small businesses, but some Issei women and their daughters worked as domestic servants to whites. Before World War II, discrimination kept Japanese American women out of white-collar work that had been available to European immigrant women and their daughters. Domestic workers often resisted oppression in covert ways, such as by evading work pressed on them by exploitative employers. This resistance gave them a sense of self-reliance that was critical for their personal and political development and for that of their children. They sometimes struggled against husbands as well; their subordination to white women in domestic employment was often reinforced by subordination to husbands at home. Yet, they struggled to maintain dignity, and "despite the menial nature of employment, the Issei achieved a sense of their own strength, and in some cases, superiority to employer and husband within their own area of competence."[74]

The Postwar Economy

As the need for labor grew in the booming postwar economy, many white employers hired Japanese Americans. However, racial discrimination continued, keeping members of the second generation out of certain occupations. For example, University of California education departments discouraged Japanese American students from considering the teaching profession because of the difficulty of placement in the state's schools.[75] Self-employment continued to be important. By 1960 there were 7,000 Japanese-owned businesses, mostly small businesses, in the Los Angeles area. The "middleman minority" model seems to fit the Issei generation well, but the second and later generations have gradually moved away from the small business niche economy to professional and other white-collar jobs. In 1960 about half the Nisei were involved in niche businesses, but many others used the education provided by parents to move into white-collar jobs.[76]

Occupational Mobility, Income, and Persisting Employment Barriers

In recent decades, numerous books and articles have accurately related the postwar Japanese American experience as a story of major achievement. The usual socioeconomic indicators in census data do show that Japanese American progress since the 1950s has been dramatic. For example, in 1990 both Japanese American women and men were more likely to hold managerial or professional jobs than were their white counterparts (33 percent, compared with 30 percent, for women; and 40 percent, compared with 27 percent, for men). Some 29 percent of Japanese Americans held blue-collar jobs, compared with 38 percent of whites. Japanese Americans' unemployment rate was half that of whites and less than half that of all Asian Americans as a group.[77]

Income data also reveal economic success. Nationally, according to the most recent data available (1990), the median income for Japanese American families was more than one and one-third times as much as that for white families. In addition, only a small percentage of Japanese American families (3.4 percent) fell below the federal poverty line, a figure lower than those for whites (7.0 percent) and for all Asian Americans as a group (11.4 percent). Note, however, that Japanese American workers are concentrated in two states, Hawaii and California, which have high wages and a high cost of living. The difference in median incomes between Japanese American families and white families in California ($53,151 compared with $46,291) was not as great in 1990 as that between Japanese American families and white families nationally ($51,550 versus $37,628). *Per capita income* for Japanese Americans in California is actually a little lower than that for whites. Significantly, Japanese American families are somewhat more likely than white families to have two or more paid workers per family.[78]

Although Japanese Americans as a group have achieved significant economic success, they still face exclusion from prominent or top positions in many business, entertainment, political, and certain civil service areas, regardless of their abilities. Examinations of television and Hollywood filmmaking in recent decades have found few Japanese or other Asian American actors, except in stereotypical positions such as gardener, cook, geisha, and Japanese tourist.[79] Indirect discrimination in the form of white-normed height and weight requirements has played a restrictive role for some occupations such as firefighters and police officers. Moreover, positions at the highest administrative, managerial, and professional levels are often off limits to Japanese and other Asian Americans, and whites with lesser credentials or ability are sometimes promoted at a faster rate.[80]

Few of the thousands of directors and top executives of the one thousand largest U.S. firms are Asian Americans, even though Asian Americans now make up about 4 percent of the U.S. population.[81] One *Wall Street Journal* story noted that Asian Americans have a very hard time climbing corporate ladders because "ironically, the same companies that pursue them for technical jobs often shun them when filling managerial and executive positions."[82] Top corporate executives have been quoted as saying that Asian Americans, including Japanese Americans, are best as technical workers and not as corporate executives. Because of this stereotype, Asian Americans may be hired as engineers, computer experts, and technicians but are not usually considered for major or top management positions. Knowing that discrimination awaits them if they depart from the stereotype, many younger Asian Americans have pursued scientific and technical educations and rejected the humanities and social sciences. The promotional ceiling also exists in higher education.[83]

Blatant discrimination occurs in some employment settings. For example, in 1989, a third-generation Japanese American, Bruce Yamashita, entered the Marine Corps' Officer Candidate School at Quantico, Virginia. A talented young man with a law degree, Yamashita faced racist discrimination from the first day, when a sergeant told him to "go back to your own country." Other sergeants called him by the names of Japanese-made motor vehicles. A fellow officer candidate enquired as to why he had not joined the Japanese army. None of the Marine Corps officers intervened to stop the racial harassment, and Yamashita was terminated for "leadership failure." In 1994, after a long legal battle during which Yamashita, with the assistance of the JACL, uncovered a pattern of discrimination against non-European American officer candidates, the U.S. Navy Secretary finally commissioned Yamashita a captain in the Marine Corps reserves.[84]

Overall trends in the U.S. economy have affected employment opportunities. Many student career choices are influenced by the past discrimination that channeled Japanese Americans into certain occupations such as public school teaching. Business opportunities are still sometimes limited by the anti-Japanese sentiment. Japanese and other Asian Americans periodically report a glass ceiling in corporations or exclusion from white business networks. Response to discrimination has often come in the form of organization. For example, in 1992 several businesspeople created the Japanese American Chamber of Commerce to foster business development. That Japanese Americans have achieved remarkable economic success against enormous odds is indicated in statistics from the past several decades. What they could have achieved without persisting racial discrimination can only be imagined.

EDUCATION

Racism and Early Segregation

Like other immigrant groups, the Issei had a strong commitment to education. Most viewed education as a way to escape arduous farm and nursery jobs and secure better-paying positions. Issei parents enrolled their children in school more often than most other immigrant group parents, and many pursued formal education for themselves.[85]

In 1906, the mayor of San Francisco, in a move supported by local newspapers, secured a resolution from the board of education to establish a segregated public school for Asian children. Reflecting classic white fears of "racial mixing," one white member of the California legislature spoke of the danger to the "pure maids of California" posed by older Japanese students in primary grades. The Japanese government protested the segregation, and the U.S. government took court action to force the San Francisco Board of Education to give Japanese American children the equal rights promised by a U.S.–Japan treaty. Some whites were so angered by this rare federal show of support for Japanese Americans that they talked of state secession. President Theodore Roosevelt and San Francisco officials worked out a compromise that allowed most Japanese American children to return to integrated schools. In exchange, Roosevelt executed the infamous Gentlemen's Agreement, which effectively terminated most Japanese immigration.[86]

Japanese Americans developed their own schools to educate children in the Japanese language and in traditional values. By 1928 there were more than 4,000 pupils in 118 schools. White supremacists vigorously attacked the language schools as centers of emperor worship and Buddhism that allegedly sought to make children disloyal to the United States. The California legislature even passed a bill, vetoed by the governor, abolishing the schools.[87]

Educational Progress

By the 1930s, Japanese Americans were making great strides in education, from the primary grades to the college level, despite widespread discrimination. At several University of California branches, the ratio of Japanese American students to the Japanese American population was a little larger than the comparable figure for the total California population. A 1930 survey showed that Japanese Americans' educational attainments were already at least equal to those of whites in California.[88]

The wartime imprisonment interrupted these educational pursuits. Second- and third-generation Japanese Americans received part of their schooling behind barbed-wire. After the war, educational discrimination was relaxed, and major gains resumed. In recent decades the median educational level for adult Japanese Americans has been substantially greater than that for all adult Americans. The most recent data available show that among Japanese Americans over twenty-four years old, 88 percent are high-school graduates and 35 percent are college graduates, compared with 79 percent and 22 percent of whites, respectively, in this age group. Only about 3 percent of Japanese Americans aged 16 to 19 are high-school dropouts, compared with 9 percent of their white counterparts. Among those between the ages of 18 and 24, some 64 percent of Japanese Americans are enrolled in college, compared with 37 percent of whites.[89]

Nonetheless, elements of racial discrimination persist in the educational sphere. There is the commonplace underrepresentation of Japanese Americans in higher administrative positions in public education. Japanese and other Asian Americans continue to be underrepresented, relative to their abilities and personal goals, or differentially treated in certain graduate programs and departments at U.S. universities, often because of stereotypes about their scientific and technical abilities. Moreover, although the education levels of Japanese Americans are significantly higher than those of the white population, some research studies indicate that their income levels are lower than one would predict on the basis of their very high levels of education. The financial benefits of a college education still vary according to racial group or ethnicity.[90]

RELIGION

Japanese immigrants brought Buddhism and Shintoism with them. These religious traditions are now significant and growing in the United States. Once the Japanese arrived, Protestant missionaries converted many to Christian beliefs. Missions were often crucibles of acculturation in which young Japanese Americans began to absorb the language and values of the dominant culture. Many missions grew into full-scale Japanese Protestant churches segregated from other churches.[91]

By the 1920s, there were many Buddhist temples in the West. Buddhist groups often adapted to the new environment with Christian-style Sunday schools and church organizations. Some white racists and exclusionists, ignorant of the fact that Buddhism does *not* involve emperor worship, claimed that the temples were hotbeds of emperor worship and anti-patriotic teaching.[92] Before and during World War II, jingoistic agitation branded Buddhism (and Shintoism) as un-American, and many temples were vandalized. After the war, the number of temples increased as Buddhism regained its important position in local communities.[93]

Today there are many Protestant churches in the Japanese Southern California Ministerial Fellowship, with numerous others up and down the West Coast and across the country. By the 1990s the Jodo Shinshu Buddhist Churches of America had sixty-five temples across the country, and there were a number of smaller Buddhist groups. One study of Japanese Americans in San Francisco found that churches were second in importance only to family in cementing the community; two-thirds of the respondents were at least occasional participants in church activities. Still, the percentage of Buddhists among

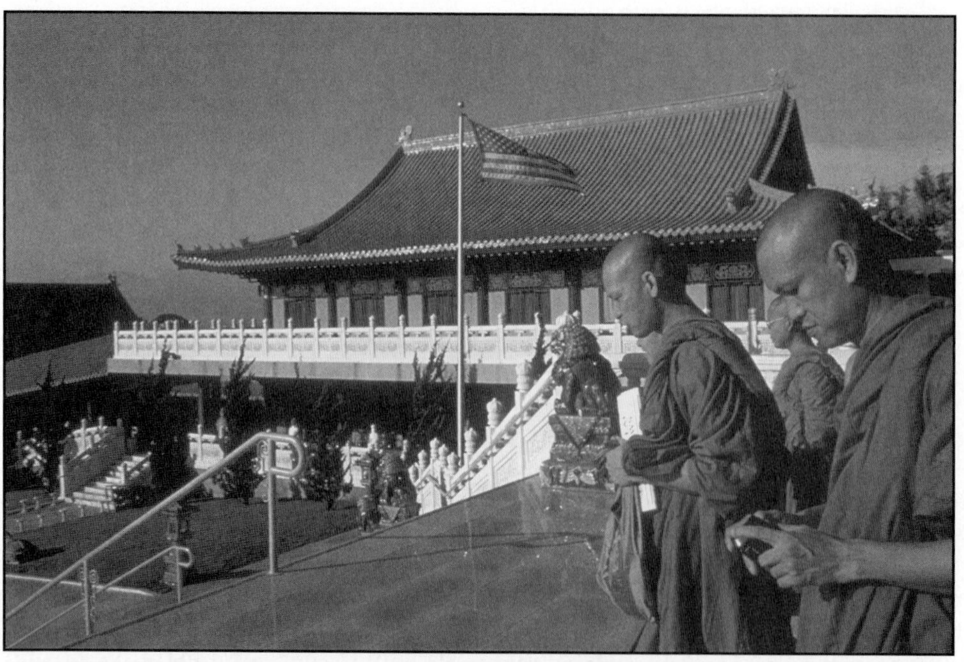

A Buddhist temple in Los Angeles, California.

Japanese Americans is declining. Buddhist groups tend to attract older members; younger Japanese Americans have preferred Protestant churches.[94]

There has been a resurgence of interest in Buddhism in the past decade or two among Asian and non-Asian Americans. Buddhist festivals have been celebrated in Japanese and other Asian American communities. Lt. Colonel Ellison Onizuka, the first Asian American in space and one of those who died in the 1986 space shuttle explosion, was a member of the Buddhist Churches of America. Onizuka's Buddhist funeral made many Americans aware of the growing presence of Buddhists in the United States.[95]

ASSIMILATION PERSPECTIVES

Japanese Americans are the Asian American group that historically has received the most attention in social science and popular theorizing about group adaptation in the United States. Many analysts have used an assimilation perspective to assess the socioeconomic situation of Japanese Americans. We have seen that early on many whites considered Japanese Americans to be "unassimilable." However, in recent decades, white social scientists and other analysts have often heralded Japanese Americans as the most assimilated of all Asian American groups, or of all Americans of color. These assimilation analysts sometimes emphasize that the younger generations of Japanese Americans have intermarried at relatively high rates and often have little facility in the Japanese language.

Today, most Japanese Americans are not immigrants. Because relatively few Japanese immigrants have come to the United States in recent decades, Japanese Americans' ties to the home country are not generally as strong as for other Asian American groups. Most were born in the United States and have grown up under the pressures and influence of the dominant Euro-American culture and institutions.

An assimilation theorist might argue that assimilation came at an early point for most Issei, although some acculturated to the language and other aspects of the dominant culture more rapidly than others. Some Issei sought to survive discrimination by socially isolating themselves and immersing themselves in things Japanese; many others sought to acculturate rapidly, at least in those areas where acculturation was permitted, while maintaining strong ties to relatives and friends. Cultural assimilation, especially in regard to language, religion, and orientation to white-collar employment, has come rapidly for later generations. Historically, Issei influence in the Japanese community was wide-ranging, but their ability to cope with the dominant culture was restricted by the massive discrimination they faced.

The second-generation Nisei, in contrast, became bicultural; they have operated successfully in Japanese American communities and in mainstream institutions. Studies of the Sansei have underscored the apparent closing of the gap with some aspects of the dominant culture. In one study, Nisei and Sansei respondents showed substantial acculturation in that they spoke mostly English at home and did not often read Japanese literature. Kitano and Daniels reported in 1988 that 49 percent of all Japanese Americans in Los Angeles County spoke only English, the highest proportion for any Asian American group there.[96]

A 1990s study of Japanese and Chinese Americans in California found that those who were third or fourth generation were highly oriented to the cultural styles of the white middle-class mainstream and retained few Japanese and Chinese traditions. They chose the parts of their ancestral cultures that fit their current way of life. "What they have retained of cultural traditions is largely symbolic and a novelty."[97] Yet, a deeper assessment of their values and world view would likely show strong continuity with some of the basic values of their parents and grandparents, particularly in regard to family, community, and educational values.

By the 1990s and early 2000s, some key community institutions were apparently in decline. Several important Japanese American newspapers have ceased publication in recent years. In the early 2000s, *Rafu Shimpo*, a Los Angeles newspaper in publication since 1903, struggled to remain in operation with a few thousand subscriptions. This is the largest remaining Japanese American paper and has moved to cover issues of interest to all Asian Americans. Readers of these newspapers are primarily Nisei who are being replaced by younger generations that appear to be less interested in these traditional publications.[98]

Structural assimilation at secondary-group levels has been significant for Japanese Americans, particularly in the economic sphere. Many analysts have argued that Japanese Americans represent a remarkable success story in their economic progress. Typically, second- and later-generation families have achieved relatively high levels of education, income, and occupational attainment. Explanations for this success tend to focus on work or family values and community or economic organization. Ivan Light, for example, has opted for a traditional-culture explanation for the development of Japanese Americans' small-business economy, a niche economy that in his view sets them apart from African and Mexican Americans. Light emphasizes the role of a "culturally preferred style of economic organization," by which he means rotating-credit associations and similar organizations established by Japanese immigrants. In addition, most Japanese American families own their homes and have adhered to homeownership values even more so than white Americans.[99]

What Milton Gordon refers to as behavior-receptional assimilation and attitude-receptional assimilation showed little change for Japanese Americans until after World War II. Blatant discrimination and prejudice marred the lives of Issei and Nisei for the first sixty years. Since World War II, discrimination and prejudice have decreased. In the early 1900s, Japanese Americans were seen by whites as the "lowest of the low" and were often grouped with black Americans, but, according to Paul Spickard, in recent years whites do "not see them as very different from themselves, and that fact is remarkable."[100] He judges white attitudes indirectly from intermarriage rates; approximately 30 percent of third-generation Japanese Americans have married non-Japanese. The third-generation figures are in the same range as those of some white ethnic groups and contrast sharply with the low intermarriage rate for black Americans. Spickard argues in effect that whites generally do not feel hostile about Japanese–white marriages.

However, Spickard may be too optimistic in equating intermarriage rates with positive white views. In recent years we have seen periodic white hostility and discrimination directed toward Japanese and other Asian Americans, especially during economic downturns. In one 1980s survey, one-fifth of those surveyed (31 percent of the Nisei and 13 percent of the Sansei) reported experiencing considerable discrimination as adults, and another 65 percent reported a little discrimination. Only 13 percent reported *never* having experienced discrimination. Three-fourths of the sample felt that Japanese Americans as a group did experience discrimination. Given the reluctance of many Japanese Americans to speak about personal matters or to speak ill of their country, these responses likely underestimated the actual amount of discrimination they faced.[101]

Assimilation analysts tend to focus on assimilation at the level of primary social ties and voluntary associations. Integration in these areas did not occur to any significant degree until after World War II. A number of researchers have found that primary-group integration with outsiders has been limited for the Nisei but is more extensive for the Sansei. One study of 148 Japanese American men found that two-thirds had mostly Japanese Americans as close friends; the Sansei were somewhat more integrated with whites than the Nisei. Yet, majorities in both groups lived in neighborhoods where 50 percent or more of their neighbors were white.[102] Other data suggest a trend toward primary-group assimilation since the 1960s, especially for those in the third and fourth generations who have moved away from areas with a critical mass of Japanese Americans.[103]

Until the late 1940s, antimiscegenation laws in western states made Asian–European marriages officially illegal. Los Angeles data show an outmarriage rate of 2 percent in the years between 1924 and 1933 and a rate of 11 to 20 percent for the 1950s. However, a 1967 national survey of young Sansei discovered that one-third had outmarried or were planning to outmarry.[104]

The most recent data (1990) on intermarriage indicate that, for Japanese Americans in California, outmarriage rates to *whites* are relatively high but not yet at a majority level—13 percent for men as a group and 28 percent for women as a group. These are the highest figures for any large Asian American group. In addition, the younger generation has even higher rates, some 27 percent for men and 30 percent for women. Perhaps most significant is the fact that many Japanese and other Asian Americans marry outside their own group yet interethnically, that is, to other Asian Americans. One recent analysis of census data found that *interethnic* marriages now exceed interracial marriages in California. Some 21 percent of Japanese American men in California had married someone in another Asian American group; 4 percent married someone who was black or Latino, and only 13 percent married a white person. Most had married within their own group. About 20 percent of women had married someone from another Asian American group; 4 percent married someone who was black or Latino, and 28 percent married a white person. While just over half the women had married outside the Japanese American group, the overwhelming majority had married a Japanese American or other Asian American. Most Japanese American marriages, at least in the key state of California, are currently within the Asian American umbrella group.[105]

Using Milton Gordon's concept of identificational assimilation, it seems clear that few Japanese Americans have rejected their cultural heritage for a purely "American" identity. They hold this identity for positive reasons, and it is also imposed on them by the many non-Asians who still see them as "foreigners." The sense of Japanese identity is strong in all generations. Most Japanese Americans are now bicultural, with a foot in both worlds. Substantial differences in value orientations between Japanese and white Americans have been found in recent decades. The authors of one study asked Japanese Americans whether they saw differences in Japanese American and white orientations toward social affairs, church life, and family relations. Large percentages saw significant differences, from 42 percent for social life to 65 percent for family life and 75 percent for church life. Interestingly, the Sansei were more likely to see differences than the Nisei. Most of these Japanese Americans did *not* consider that they were assimilating rapidly to the dominant culture in regard to such areas as family and the church.[106]

There are signs that younger Japanese Americans are retaining at least some of their distinctive organizations and traditions. Japanese American athletic leagues established by the Nisei have survived through subsequent generations, and where possible many younger Japanese and other Asian American college students have joined Asian American fraternities and sororities rather than white-dominated organizations.[107] The Sansei and Yonsei have also maintained numerous Japanese American parades and festivals in places like Los Angeles and Honolulu.

Recent surveys of Japanese American college students also reveal that, while the students show signs of significant acculturation to the core culture and support interracial dating and marriage, they hold many views and values that reveal close ties to those of their parents. For example, most held part-time jobs and placed great value on family, community, hard work, and education. They reported being most comfortable with other people of Asian descent, and they often were members of Asian or Asian American organizations.[108]

Developing a broad view of assimilation, Harry Kitano and Roger Daniels have suggested that Japanese and other Asian Americans can be grouped into three major categories based on (1) degree of overall assimilation to the dominant culture and institutions and (2) the strength of "ethnic identity." They argue that, among Japanese and other Asian Americans, many in the third and later generations, and those isolated from large communities, are in a "high assimilation, low ethnic identity" category; that is, they have made many adaptations to the dominant culture in terms of language and lifestyle and retain only weak ties to the old language and culture. Japanese Americans in this category have strong social ties to whites or have married whites. In addition, a large group of Japanese Americans belongs to a "high assimilation, high ethnic identity" category. These people move easily in both the Japanese American culture and community and in the dominant culture. In contrast with the first group, they are more knowledgeable about Japanese American history and culture and have a stronger racial-ethnic identity. A third and much smaller group includes those who have immigrated in recent decades and those who have spent most of their lives within Japanese American communities; they belong to a "low assimilation, high ethnic identity" category. Marriages are within the Japanese American group, and their Japanese identity is strong. Kitano and Daniels are careful to note that the degree of assimilation is relative even for the first two subgroups because many whites in the larger society still regard Japanese Americans as racially and ethnically distinct, and this visibility forces "the retention of ethnic identity, no matter how slight."[109]

An assimilation theorist might conceivably view Japanese Americans as a clear example of Andrew Greeley's concept of ethnogenesis—partly in but partly outside the dominant white culture and society. To our knowledge, no analyst has developed this perspective for Japanese Americans, although some time ago Petersen argued that this group had become a "subnation" in the United States, achieving integration in the economic sphere and making some cultural adaptation, but often maintaining cohesive, family-centered communities.[110]

The younger generations of Japanese Americans seem to be among the most integrated of all non-European groups into European American culture and communities. Still, how this assimilation and integration will develop in the future is unclear. We have already seen the high level of intermarriage to other Asian Americans, which has increased in recent years as the Asian American population has grown. Integration with whites may not be as important, at least in the primary-social sphere, as integration with other Asian Americans. In addition, some Japanese Americans view the children of mixed marriages as Japanese American and are working to integrate them into traditional Japanese American culture or communities. Sometimes called *Hapa*, those of mixed ancestry are seen by some as the leading edge of change among Japanese Americans. Japanese American leader Greg Mayeda has explained that eventually the typical Japanese American will be a Hapa:

> Community leaders must recognize this and encourage Hapas and their multicultural families to participate in Japanese-American organizations and customs. If given the opportunity, Hapas can unify and reinvigorate the Japanese-American community.[111]

A Power-Conflict View

Few analysts have interpreted the Japanese American experience systematically from a power-conflict perspective. One such analyst, Robert Blauner, has suggested that Japanese Americans might be viewed as a partially colonized racial group. This was certainly true in the first half-century of Japanese American life in the United States. Many early immigrants worked in a position of debt servitude or migrated to the United States under pressure.

Over the centuries there has usually been an important economic relationship between the labor needs of U.S. capitalism and the streams of immigrant workers. For some time Asian labor filled the needs of frontier capitalism on the West Coast. Chinese and Japanese laborers were seen by whites as "colored" labor with far fewer rights than whites. Because the United States was an imperial power in the Pacific, U.S. agents had easy entry into Asian countries and could often more or less dictate agreements benefiting employers. U.S. capitalists recruited Asian laborers because they could be made to work for very low wages. U.S. employers had the backing of their government in securing low-wage labor from Japan and China. Neither country then possessed the power that European nations had to protect their immigrant workers. Because Japanese immigrants could not become citizens under U.S. law, they could easily be excluded if employers later found them unsuitable.[112]

In the beginning, Japanese Americans, much like Mexican Americans, were forced by discrimination to become low-wage field laborers. Alien-labor laws that barred land ownership, the race-based exclusion of Japanese immigrants in 1924, and the massive imprisonment in World War II constitute semicolonial treatment. Japanese Americans' experiences were clearly quite different from the experiences of European immigrants on which assimilation models are typically based.

Acculturation might be viewed differently from a systematic power-conflict perspective. Pressures to acculturate were largely coercive for the first two generations. Early commitment to cultural assimilation in Japanese communities can be seen as a reaction to severe discrimination. In public schools, acculturation pressures took the form of attacks on the Japanese cultural heritage. By about 1910, numerous Japanese American leaders were exhorting their constituents to be exemplary in their hard work and deference to whites in order to gain some acceptance. In the early decades, Japanese Americans' experiences with the racist system were similar to those of African, Mexican, and Native Americans.

Some Asian American scholars have raised a question about the *bias* in the assimilation model itself. The assimilation theory of Robert Park and other early social scientists emerged in a period of intense white agitation against Japanese immigration and reflected those scholars' often racist views of the Japanese. Applying the assimilationist perspective to Japanese and other Asian Americans prior to the 1950s is very inappropriate in one fundamental respect. Asians were generally *prevented* from even trying to assimilate politically and in other important ways. Unlike European immigrants, Japanese and other Asian immigrants were denied the right to become naturalized citizens.

U.S. government agencies and officials have long played a central role in defining racial groups. In the 1922 *Ozawa* case, the Supreme Court ruled that Asian immigrants were *not white* and thus could not become citizens. In a similar case the following year, *U.S. v. Bhagat Singh Thind*, the same racist reasoning was applied to an Asian Indian who sought to become naturalized. The Court declared that, in contrast to the children of Asian parentage, "the children of English, French, German, Italian, Scandinavian, and other European parentage quickly merge in to the mass of our population and lose the distinctive hallmarks of their European origin."[113] This explicitly racist reasoning by an arm of the federal government misses the point that at the time—and indeed into the 1950s—Asian immigrants were legally barred from political and civic assimilation in the United States.

Returning to the present situation of Japanese Americans, the intermarriage data cited earlier might also be viewed from a power-conflict perspective. There is an increasing tendency for Japanese and other Asian Americans to marry within the Asian American umbrella group rather than to intermarry with whites, especially on the West Coast. Even among second and later generations of Asian Americans, for all major Asian American groups including Japanese Americans, the proportions of marriages to other Asian Americans is greater than the proportion of marriages to whites. The interethnic marriage rate has been growing. The reasons for this include the growing size of the Asian American population, the consequent expansion of social and personal networks, the similarity in economic achievements for many Asian American groups, and a shared Asian American identity. Moreover, as Larry Shinagawa and Gin Yong Pang have expressed it, the "most important factor is a growing racial consciousness in American society, which is perceived by many Asian Americans as increasingly racially polarized and stratified.... Race, more so than ethnicity, shapes the experiences and the development of identity among Asian Americans."[114]

Criticizing the "Model Minority" Stereotype

Paramount among the weaknesses in many assimilation perspectives is what is called the "model minority" stereotype. In recent decades most major newsmagazines and television networks have periodically carried glowing reports on the achievements of Japanese and other Asian Americans in various occupational categories and in education.[115] The success of Japanese Americans, frequently viewed as rooted in values and family styles, is cited not only in the media but also by prominent whites as a reflection of the great opportunities in the United States and as a model for what other people of color, particularly African Americans and Latinos, could achieve if they would only follow the Japanese American example.[116] However, stereotypes of Japanese Americans as paragons of hard work and docility often carry a negative undercurrent. Suzuki has suggested that the "model minority" image of groups such as Japanese Americans was created not by these groups but rather by white outsiders, including non-Asian scholars and media analysts, for their own ideological reasons.[117] During the period when African Americans protested during the 1960s, these whites *created* the model minority image to suggest that African Americans could achieve the American dream by working harder rather than by protesting discrimination. This view assumes that Asian Americans are more like whites in their attitudes toward work and family.

As we have noted, recent scholarship has questioned much of this imagery. Pre–World War II educational opportunities greater than those available to legally segregated African Americans in states like California helped prepare many Japanese Americans for white-collar jobs opening up after that war. It was not Asian values alone that brought success but better access to education and white-collar jobs. Critics of the model minority notion have also noted other factors in the economic success of Japanese Americans: the Japanese government's early support of immigrants and the availability of an important small-business niche in West Coast areas. At an early point, Japanese Americans created many successful businesses through which they served one another and the basic needs of a frontier economy of the West. Out of economic necessity, Japanese American employers and employees, many with kinship or regional ties, worked together against hostile white competitors.

Success often came at the price of being ghettoized in the small-business economy and, later, in certain professions. As with Jewish Americans, Japanese Americans have, to a substantial degree, succeeded economically in U.S. society by carving a distinctive niche or two for themselves—a process of adaptation not completely in line with the idealistic assimilation models. The long-term effects of racial discrimination are still reflected in the disproportionate concentration of Japanese Americans in the small-business economy and in certain professional and technical occupations. The movement of Japanese Americans into white-collar jobs does not necessarily indicate full emancipation from racial discrimination. A study of Japanese American workers in the San Francisco metropolitan area found that those in white-collar jobs were clustered in such occupations as computer programming, clerical work, architecture, engineering, dentistry, and pharmacy. The highest level white-collar personnel, such as managers, financial officers, and management analysts, still tended to be white men.[118]

A study of businesses owned by Americans of color found that most of those owned by Asian Americans were in retail trade (such as grocery stores and restaurants) and selected services (such as laundries). Gross annual receipts were modest for the majority of Japanese American firms. In addition, as we have noted, some research has revealed that Japanese Americans receive smaller economic benefits from their high levels of education than do comparably educated whites. Japanese American families have higher incomes but they also have more workers per family compared with white families.[119]

Paul Takagi has pointed to another bias in the traditional cultural-background explanation of Japanese American success—the idea that the racial and ethnic groups whose values are closest to those of the dominant white group are the ones who will be, and should be, successful. Success is evaluated in terms of values prized by the dominant white group. Although Japanese Americans have acculturated in numerous ways, the price they have often paid in terms of conformity, lost creativity, and lost contributions to this society has been great.[120]

In her recent documentary work, Japanese American media analyst Janice Tanaka has examined the negative impact of the great pressures for assimilation on the third-generation Sansei. Tanaka's innovative interviews with the Sansei found that most of their parents were interned as youth in the wartime camps by racist white officials. These Nisei were greatly affected by that incarceration, and during and after World War II they placed great pressure on themselves and their children to *conform* to white perspectives, norms, and customs. Fearful of a reoccurrence of extreme oppression, they responded to this brutal racism with the orientation that would later get them labeled, in an ironic twist of stereotyping, as "model minorities." Many Nisei and Sansei conformed to white ways in an effort to prevent such a racist outrage as the concentration camps from targeting Japanese Americans again. However, the Nisei and their children have paid a heavy price for having to respond to racism in this fashion. The effects of this aggressive conformity often have been negative: Many have encountered, and continue to endure, great personal distress, painful self-blame, mental and physical illnesses, or alcoholism and drug abuse. Some have committed suicide because the conformity pressures have been too great. Not surprisingly, the negative reactions of the Sansei have in turn affected their own children, the Yonsei. The costs of racism persist over several generations. The racist internment continues to exert a terrible price from many Japanese Americans. The tepid U.S. government response in terms of modest reparations has not been enough to lift this burden from Japanese Americans.[121]

Over the past decade or two, many Japanese Americans have also reported that no amount of cultural assimilation protects them from whites who insist on continuing to stereotype Japanese and other Asian Americans as outsiders. Ronald Takaki, a professor at the University of California, visited an East Coast city where a taxicab driver congratulated him on his good English and inquired how long he had been in the country. Takaki told the driver his family had been here for *three* generations—since 1886.[122] Despite the fact that many Japanese Americans have grown up in mostly white neighborhoods and gone to mostly white schools and colleges, they too often report blatant or subtle discrimination and do not feel they are fully accepted by large numbers of white Americans.[123]

From the beginning, Japanese immigration and Japanese American integration into the dominant culture and society have been shaped by U.S. intervention in the capitalist world economy. The action of the U.S. government in forcing Japan into the world economy in the nineteenth century was eventually followed by the recruitment of many low-wage laborers for U.S. business enterprises. Today, as the Japanese economy vies successfully with the U.S. economy for Pacific and world dominance, the world economy still forms the backdrop. New economic alliances on the Pacific Rim, such as the Association of Southeast Asian Nations, are bypassing the United States. Japan is today the most powerful economy in these alliances, and that economic success is one major reason there has been relatively little recent migration from Japan to the United States.

There is a negative side to the prosperity of Japan and other Asian nations in the world economy: Some non-Asian Americans, angry over domestic economic troubles, confuse Japanese Americans and other Asian Americans with the Japanese and blame them unfairly for economic troubles caused by U.S. employers investing overseas or by the federal government. These stereotypes are yet another constant indication to Japanese Americans that somehow they have not been accepted as "true Americans" by many non-Asian Americans. As with African Americans and Latinos, Japanese and other Asian Americans pay a heavy cost for this stereotyping and related discrimination.

SUMMARY

Japanese Americans are a very important group in U.S. racial and ethnic history. In the beginning they were severely exploited and treated as a greatly "inferior race." Many entered as laborers, facing violence and intense discrimination. They later endured complete exclusion as a result of racist immigration legislation. During World War II, they suffered the only large-scale imprisonment of U.S. citizens in concentration camps. Against these terrible odds they prospered. Yet, for all their cultural and other assimilation, Japanese Americans are still not fully integrated into the dominant European American institutions.

Students of racial and ethnic relations should realize that the success story of Japanese and other Asian Americans is partially a myth. Japanese Americans have suffered in the past and still suffer from discrimination. Fewer Japanese Americans than whites fully realize earnings levels that parallel their high educational levels. Few rise to top management in Fortune 1000 corporations, major law firms, or major government agencies. Although Asian Americans have lived in the United States for much more than a century, not one has ever been nominated for the U.S. Supreme Court or for president or vice-president of the United States.

In general, Japanese Americans have been stereotyped by whites, including state and federal government officials. Across the United States white employers and government officials have spoken of Japanese Americans and other Asian Americans as though they were "foreigners," not "true Americans." Japanese Americans are considered by most whites and many other Americans to be a "model minority" with no need of special government protection against discrimination. Yet, as we have seen, there is still anti-Japanese sentiment among white Americans that results in discrimination and violence. White Americans must change their attitudes and practices if Japanese Americans are to enjoy full equality. David Mura, author of *Turning Japanese: Memoirs of a Sansei*, has argued that whites must see that the "problem of race is one of giving up power." In his view, whites must begin to take part in "dismantling racism and redistributing power."[124]

Working harmoniously together, the seven-person crew of the ill-fated space shuttle Challenger included an African American born to sharecroppers (Ronald McNair), a Jewish American of the Orthodox faith (Judith Resnik), and a Japanese American of the Buddhist faith (Ellison Onizuka). Onizuka, the grandson of Japanese laborers who immigrated to Hawaii to work on a coffee plantation in the 1890s, was born on a coffee farm. He became an aerospace engineer and participated in two space missions. As the first Asian American astronaut, Onizuka has come to symbolize for many the heroic character of the Asian American struggle for success.

Hawaii was the first U.S. state in which no racial or ethnic group constituted a majority of the population. Today Japanese Americans are the single largest group in Hawaii, but they are not a majority. Compared with other areas of the United States, racial and ethnic relations in Hawaii have long been more cooperative and less conflict ridden. While Hawaii has seen some interracial tensions, and native Hawaiians have suffered much poverty and discrimination, some observers have suggested that multiracial, multiethnic Hawaii can provide a few lessons on how diverse racial and ethnic groups can work with each another to build a viable multiracial society and real democracy.[125]

11 Chinese, Filipino, Korean, Vietnamese, and Asian-Indian Americans

ELAINE H. KIM, A KOREAN AMERICAN PROFESSOR AT THE UNIVERSITY OF CALIFORNIA, Berkeley has written insightfully about the major Los Angeles riot that took place in the early 1990s. She has noted how the media played up visual images of conflict between black and Latino rioters and Korean American merchants, while ignoring the important histories and social contexts of these groups. Korean Americans, African Americans, and Latinos have been the victims of a long tradition of violence and discrimination at the hands of whites. Recalling her own experiences, Kim noted the following:

> My schooling offered nothing about Chicanos or Latinos, and most of what I was taught about African-Americans was distorted to justify their oppression and vindicate the forces of that oppression.[1]

Then she added:

> Likewise, Korean-Americans have been and continue to be used for someone else's agenda and benefit, whether we are hated as foreigners who refuse to become "good

> Americans," stereotyped as diligent work machines or simply treated as if we do not exist. Throughout my childhood, the people who continually asked, "What are you?" knew nothing of Korea or Koreans.[2]

Korean Americans are one of five major Asian American groups—each with a strong identity and a rich history and culture—that are analyzed in this chapter. The others are Chinese, Filipino, Vietnamese, and Asian-Indian Americans. Although these groups have contributed much to the dynamic development of the United States, they still suffer greatly from stereotyping and discrimination at the hands of white and other non-Asian Americans.

MIGRATION: AN OVERVIEW

Since the 1980s, Filipinos, Chinese, Koreans, Vietnamese, and Asian-Indians have been among the fastest-growing immigrant groups in the United States. Table 11.1 documents the changing scale of this immigration since the early nineteenth century.[3]

Relatively few Filipinos, Koreans, Vietnamese, or Asian Indians immigrated to the U.S. mainland before the 1960s. Thereafter, immigration increased dramatically. The number of Filipino, Korean, and Vietnamese immigrants rose from so few that records of their arrival were not kept to a total of nearly 2 million since 1981. Most Asian Indians have also come in this recent period. Chinese immigration has followed a different pattern, with two major periods. The first began about 1850 and lasted until the passage of the 1882 Chinese Exclusion Act, which prohibited direct immigration from China. Although some Chinese immigration occurred in the years following the 1882 act, large-scale immigration did not resume until the immigration reforms in 1965. As can be seen in Table 11.1, a substantial majority of all Chinese immigrants to the United States have come recently.

The 1924 Immigration Act excluded people in Asian countries from immigrating to the United States. The 1952 Immigration and Nationality Act began to eliminate some of the anti-Asian racism inherent in the 1924 act. That 1952 act established three principles for immigration policy: (1) reunification of families; (2) protection of the domestic labor force; and (3) immigration of persons with needed skills. It permitted small-scale Asian immigration and for the first time made immigrants from Asia eligible for citizenship. In 1965, Congress took a major step toward providing Asians the opportunity to immigrate on a scale similar to that of earlier European groups. The 1965 Immigration Act abolished the national-origins quota system and established an annual quota of 20,000 for individual Asian countries. The proportion of Chinese, Filipinos, Koreans, Vietnamese, and Asian Indians among the total number of immigrants rose from 0.2 percent for 1901–1920 to 27 percent in the decade of the 1970s and remained well above one-fifth at the end of the 1990s.

Because the 1965 act and its amendments give preference to family members of people already in the United States, many Asian immigrants are family sponsored. The majority of immigrants have gone to areas where earlier Asian immigrants settled, particularly on the West Coast. Today, the largest Asian-Pacific American populations are in the nation's largest cities; Los Angeles, New York, Honolulu, and San Francisco lead the list. Because of past immigration barriers, the majority of Asian Americans today are foreign-born. Only the Chinese

TABLE 11.1 ASIAN IMMIGRATION, 1820–1998

	1820–1900	1901–1920	1921–1940	1941–1960	1961–1980	1981–1998
Chinese*	305,455	41,833	43,835	41,910	347,564	888,683
Filipino	**	**	**	19,307	453,363	982,534
Korean	**	**	**	6,231	302,164	470,397
Vietnamese	**	**	**	335	177,160	522,423
Asian Indian	694	6,795	2,830	4,843	207,930	546,419

*Figures include Hong Kong after 1951.

**Data not reported before 1951.

American and Japanese American populations have sizeable third- and later-generation components. Today, most Asian-Pacific Americans are either immigrants or the children of immigrants.

Chinese Americans

Over time the Chinese have been the largest single group of Asian immigrants to the United States. Chinese migration began in substantial numbers in the decade before the Civil War, with a quarter million coming during the three decades after 1860. Most men entered as low-wage workers, brought in to do the "dirty work" for white employers on the West Coast. Many were recruited to remedy labor shortages in railroad work or to fill menial positions in such personal service areas as laundry and restaurant work that whites did not want to do.

Few women were among the immigrants, and those who did immigrate usually came alone, often brought by force to work as prostitutes. Some escaped to missions run by religious denominations. In 1875, Congress passed a law prohibiting the importation of Chinese women for prostitution—the first direct regulation of immigration in U.S. history. Significant numbers of women were not permitted to enter again until the 1940s. Between 1946 and 1952, almost 90 percent of Chinese immigrants were women, typically wives of men who had immigrated earlier.[4]

As the 1870s began, the U.S. economy entered a depression; at the same time, Chinese Americans were becoming numerous and more successful. White labor leaders, newspapers, politicians, and the general public accused Chinese Americans of driving wages to a substandard level and of taking jobs away from whites. They often blamed the Chinese for the country's economic difficulties.[5] The 1882 Chinese Exclusion Act officially prohibited direct immigration from China. Over the next few decades, the Exclusion Act reduced the flow of Chinese immigrants, which had reached a high of 123,201 in the years between 1871 and 1880. Because most early immigrants were male, the exclusion of new immigrants resulted in a 40 percent decline in the Chinese American population between 1880 and 1920.[6] In 1905 the "progressive" President Theodore Roosevelt strongly affirmed his support for the racist act, stating that Chinese laborers must be kept out of this country "absolutely."[7] Significantly, this highly racist Exclusion Act was not repealed *until 1943* when China became a wartime ally against Japan. At that time, a tiny quota of 105 was set for Chinese immigrants.[8]

The second major period of immigration took place after the 1960s immigration reform legislation. Between 1961 and 1980, nearly 348,000 Chinese, mainly from Hong Kong and Taiwan, came to the United States. Larger numbers have entered since 1981. During this most recent period the proportion from Hong Kong and Taiwan has fallen as the proportion from the mainland has grown. Between 1980 and 2000, the Chinese American population tripled, from 806,000 to more than 2.4 million. In the 2000 census, Chinese Americans constituted about one-fourth of all Asian Americans, and more than 45 percent lived in western states.[9]

Filipino Americans

When the islands that make up the Philippines were taken by the U.S. government after the Spanish-American War, an imperialistic relationship was established. The U.S. government ignored Filipino desires for independence, and U.S. military forces killed many Filipinos who fought for the country's independence. After seizing the islands, the U.S. government sent a commission to determine how to Americanize them. Between 1901 and 1913, a U.S. form of government was established, and a new system of education was introduced in which U.S. teachers taught Filipino children U.S. cultural values.

By the 1920s and 1930s, the overwhelming majority of Filipino immigrants were peasant farmers who sought employment as laborers. Since the Philippines was a U.S. territory, Filipinos were exempt from the anti-Asian exclusionary provisions of the 1917 and 1924 Immigration Acts. This allowed them to immigrate freely, and employers actively recruited them to work on sugar plantations in Hawaii and in fields on the West Coast. However, few came to the mainland; by 1924 only 6,000 lived in the continental United States.[10]

After passage of the 1924 Immigration Act, employers increased recruitment of Filipinos as laborers to replace the Asian and other workers excluded by the act. Between 1924 and 1929, approximately 24,000 Filipinos came to California to do low-wage work. As their numbers increased, so did anti-Filipino sentiment among white workers. In 1934, Congress responded to this sentiment by passing an act that granted deferred independence to the Philippines and imposed an immigration quota of only fifty persons per year.[11]

Although Filipinos could enter the United States without restriction until 1934, the advantages ended there. Filipino Americans held an ambiguous legal position that was not resolved until 1946 when they were finally declared eligible for U.S. citizenship. Most states did not allow Filipinos to practice law, medicine, or other professions. Congress began moving toward citizenship for Filipinos during World War II, since it was hard to defend the idea of freedom for the Philippines from Japanese rule while denying citizenship to Filipino Americans.

During World War II, some 30,000 Filipinos were recruited to fight with U.S. forces battling the Japanese in the Philippines. President Franklin Roosevelt promised these fighters that they could come to the United States and become U.S. citizens. The government soon backed out of the promise and left thousands of veterans stranded. These veterans were not granted the right to U.S. citizenship until passage of the Immigration Act of 1990.[12] Most of those who now live in the United States have not been eligible for veteran's benefits. A recent study of Filipino American veterans in California found that most have lived on low incomes and many have had serious medical problems. In recent years the Filipino American Veterans Campaign and the Filipino-American Service Group have fought hard to secure belated justice for these veterans.[13]

Between the 1950s and the 1970s, the number of Filipinos residing in the United States almost doubled. Since 1970, Filipino immigration has continued. The 2000 census counted more than 1.85 million Filipino Americans, making this group the second largest group in the Asian–Pacific category. Today, a large majority of Filipino Americans are foreign-born; more than half live in western states. In 2000, Filipino Americans were the second largest Asian American group in California, and more than a quarter million lived in the Los Angeles area alone. Filipino Americans are also numerous in several midwestern cities.[14]

Korean Americans

The immigration of Koreans began in the early 1900s. Approximately 7,000 emigrated to Hawaii between 1903 and 1905, and by 1905 some 1,000 Korean Americans lived in California. Most came seeking better living and working conditions, but they too confronted discrimination and low wages. They were segregated, refused housing in all but the poorest areas, and denied service in public facilities. After learning of these conditions, Japan, which occupied Korea beginning in 1910, pressured the Korean government to ban emigration. This ban restricted the entry of Koreans into the United States for many years.[15]

Even after these restrictions were imposed, a few—primarily "picture brides" and students—managed to emigrate to the United States. Because most who arrived before the 1910 restrictions were single men, and since interracial marriage was not an option because of anti-intermarriage laws, Korean men sent pictures to prospective brides in their homeland. From 1910 to 1924, more than one thousand Korean brides came to the United States.[16]

During the heavy U.S. involvement in the Korean War in the 1950s, the people of South Korea saw prosperous Americans up close and came to admire the United States. U.S. support for the South Korean government, which then allowed little political freedom, built strong ties between the two countries. Most Koreans who immigrated from 1950 to 1965 were the brides of U.S. soldiers and as such escaped the regular immigration system. The children and grandchildren stemming from these marriages are today part of a growing and substantial multiracial population that is making its voice heard for greater respect for intermarriage and multiracial ancestry across the United States.

Changes in immigration laws in 1965 opened up new possibilities. The lack of economic or educational opportunities in Korea compared with those in the United States has prompted many young people to emigrate. Some immigrants have been political dissidents who opposed the dictatorial regimes that dominated South Korea for decades. Others have been students who completed their education and stayed. Once established, early immigrants also used the immigration law's family reunification clause to bring in more family members. Between 1960 and 1965, only a few thousand entered each year, but after 1965 the numbers increased; within a decade the annual number exceeded 30,000. Immigration peaked at 35,849 in

1987 and dropped to less than 14,000 annually in the late 1990s.[17] Improvements in South Korea's economy over the past two decades has contributed to this decline, as has Korean disenchantment with the United States as a land of opportunity. Nonetheless, since the 1980s a growing number of Korean business people and students have come to the United States on temporary visas.

The 2000 census counted almost 1.1 million Korean Americans, almost 11 percent of the Asian American population. About 40 percent lived in the western states. By the early 2000s, many Korean Americans were moving from the West Coast, often settling in midwestern or eastern cities.[18]

Vietnamese Americans

Most Vietnamese immigrants to the United States have come since 1975, when U.S. involvement in the Vietnam War ended abruptly. When French military forces withdrew from their war in Vietnam in 1954, and Vietnam was divided in two, the United States became a military ally of the South Vietnamese government, a non-Communist political dictatorship. U.S. troops and dollars flowed to an increasingly unpopular war. In the face of advancing enemy forces at the end of the war, U.S. plans to evacuate South Vietnamese included those (and their families) who had been employed by the U.S. government or U.S. businesses. In just one week, thousands fled their country.[19]

The large numbers of Vietnamese refugees who began to enter the United States in 1975 were admitted outside the usual immigration process because they were political refugees.[20] As Table 11.1 (on page 290) shows, few immigrated before 1961, in part because of the anti-Asian immigration laws. Following changes in U.S. immigration laws and the end of U.S. involvement in Vietnam, more than 166,000 Vietnamese entered the United States between 1975 and 1980.

In the 1980–1990 period, the number of Vietnamese Americans grew 142 percent—the largest percentage increase for the larger Asian American groups. Between 1990 and 2000, this population increased another 189 percent. A very large percentage of Vietnamese Americans are foreign-born, and approximately half live in western states. The nation's largest Vietnamese community is in Orange County, California.[21]

Asian-Indian Americans

Of all the major Asian–Pacific groups in the United States, perhaps the least well known is the group the census bureau calls "Asian Indians"—those who have immigrated from India. The first immigrants were Sikhs who worked on the railroads or in agriculture on the West Coast in the 1800s, but the number remained very small until the 1960s. Asian Indians have immigrated in significant numbers only since the 1965 Immigration Act. The 1990 census reported almost 787,000 Asian-Indian Americans. More than three-fourths were foreign-born, and more than four in ten had come since 1980. By 2000, this population had more than doubled.[22]

Three periods are evident in the recent Asian-Indian migration. In the 1960s, many immigrants were male professionals and managers, and most easily found jobs. Their wives were generally not well educated. Today, their children are a new adult generation. A second group came in the 1970s; it included a mixture of immigrants, with more well-educated professional women than in the previous group. A third group has come since the 1980s and includes many relatives sponsored by the earlier immigrants. Compared with earlier immigrants, this latter group tends to be less well educated and more likely to move into service work such as taxi driving or into family-owned small businesses.[23]

Unlike other Asian Americans, the majority of Asian-Indian Americans do not live on the West Coast, although the number there is growing rapidly. The 2000 census counted more than 314,000 Asian Indians in California. Still, almost 40 percent live in the Northeast, and a large proportion live in the Midwest and the South. Almost 200,000 live in the greater New York City area, and more than 71,000 live in the Chicago area.[24]

In several metropolitan areas, many Asian-Indian Americans have had the economic resources to move directly into suburbs rather than settling first in central-city areas like other recent immigrants. As a result, they are more scattered geographically than other recent Asian immigrants. There are no large central city concentrations as there are for other Asian American groups. Even so, wherever there is a substantial Asian-Indian population in a large metropolitan area, there are usually numerous community organizations, such as Indian houses of worship.

Asian Women as Immigrants

Many discussions of Asian immigrants, and Asian Americans in general, stereotype the women in these groups as being rather subordinate and docile. Yet Asian immigrant families do include many women who are strong figures in their own right. Min Zhou and James Gatewood write, "As immigrants, Asian American women are agents in their own destiny, often making painful decisions to come to America but, more often than not, having some control over their choices. They play an active role."[25] The immigration experience often reshapes traditional gender relationships so that these women immigrants take a much more active role in providing economic and other support for their families than they typically did in the home country. This in turn can reshape their relationships with the men in their families. As with earlier immigrant groups, such as the Irish and the Jews, Asian women are often important decisionmakers in the immigration process.[26]

STEREOTYPES

Anti-Asian stereotyping and hostility have a long history in the United States. One common stereotype about Asian Americans is that they are basically the same, both physically and culturally. Japanese Americans are commonly mistaken by non-Asians for Chinese Americans, who in turn may be mistaken for Vietnamese or Korean Americans. Asian Americans are often viewed by non-Asians as "foreigners" rather than as "Americans" because of their non-European appearance. Historically, U.S. films and television programs have often portrayed Asians as criminal, faceless, fanatic, or willing to die because they do not value life. Stereotyped images, such as the "evil Jap" of World War II and the "Communist gook" in China and Vietnam, were created primarily by white Americans and have been recycled as U.S. foreign policy has changed from decade to decade. This uninformed and stereotypical way of thinking, sometimes called *Orientalism*, is common among non-Asian Americans and shapes much anti-Asian discrimination.[27]

One Chinese American leader has commented: "To the larger society, Asian Americans are either invisible, or forever foreigners, or honorary whites, or problems."[28] Chinese and other Asian Americans are still often viewed as foreigners, aliens, or problems. These stereotypes have serious implications. Recently a white member of the State Board of Education in South Carolina made this comment at a board meeting: "Screw the Buddhists and kill the Muslims." Even with this type of stereotyped outburst, he was able to keep his educational position.[29]

As we have noted previously, several Asian American groups have been stereotyped as "model minorities." According to this stereotyped view, which many who use it think is only a positive view, Asian Americans have moved ahead rapidly in U.S. society, generally unhindered by prejudice or discrimination, mainly by dint of hard work and thrift. There are indeed many exemplary individuals in Asian American communities, but the model minority stereotype overstates their economic situation and progress, and has certain negative implications.

Specific Images of Asian Americans

Coming to the West Coast, the first Chinese workers soon became subjects of white workers' anger and suspicion. They were called "coolies" and maligned as "heathen," "mice-eaters," or "Chinks." For decades most white leaders, as well as the white public, viewed Chinese Americans not as Americans in any sense, but as an alien "race." Sociologist Claire Jean Kim has noted how Asian immigrants have been negatively evaluated by whites along the axes of superior/inferior and insider/foreigner.[30] The Chinese were inferior foreigners. In 1896, even as he defended some rights for black Americans as the lone dissenter in the famous *Plessy v. Ferguson* segregation decision (see Chapter 7), Supreme Court Justice John Marshall Harlan added this racist comment: "There is a race so different from our own that we do not permit those belonging to it to become citizens of the United States. Persons belonging to it are, with few exceptions, absolutely excluded from our country. I allude to the Chinese race."[31] Such "alien race" images of Asian Americans have persisted to the present.

Some modest change in white attitudes came in the 1940s. After the United States declared war on Japan in 1941, China and the United States became allies against Japan. The Chinese were suddenly friends. Soon after the United States entered World War II, the influential *Time* magazine printed the following racialized explanation of the differences between the Chinese and the Japanese:

> HOW TO TELL YOUR FRIENDS FROM THE JAPS: Virtually all Japanese are short. Japanese are likely to be stockier and broader-hipped than short Chinese. Japanese are seldom fat; they often dry up and grow lean as they age. Although both have the typical epicanthic fold on the upper eyelid, Japanese eyes are usually set closer together. The Chinese expression is likely to be more placid, kindly, open; the Japanese more positive, dogmatic, arrogant. Japanese are hesitant, nervous in conversation, laugh loudly at the wrong time. Japanese walk stiffly erect, hard heeled. Chinese, more relaxed, have an easy gait, sometimes shuffle.[32]

Ironically, those white editors who published this wildly stereotyped statement likely thought they were saying something positive about their "friends" the Chinese. Yet, this is an example of the crude and negative stereotyping that has long been part of white thinking in the United States.

Historically, the stereotypes of Filipino immigrants have fluctuated according to this group's usefulness to employers recruiting them as low-wage labor, such as for the plantations of Hawaii. When white employers were recruiting male Filipinos, they frequently characterized them as "not too intelligent" and "docile." But when these workers were no longer needed, they were stereotyped as "lazy, shiftless, and unmanageable."[33]

The Vietnamese arrived in the United States when unemployment was relatively high, and many non-Asian Americans feared that these new refugees would take jobs or drain sources of public assistance. During the mid-1970s, this anti-Vietnamese sentiment was reflected in a Gallup poll in which 54 percent of the respondents felt that Vietnamese refugees should not be permitted to stay.[34] Many white leaders and the public apparently wanted to forget Vietnam and its people. Some non-Asian Americans still see the Vietnamese as "the enemy" because of the U.S. experience in Vietnam and use the racist epithet *gooks*. Indeed, Senator John McCain, a man who ran in the Republican presidential primaries in 2000, recently used the term "gook" for the Vietnamese who took him captive. Vietnamese Americans represent a culture different from that of a large segment of U.S. society, and many non-Asians still regard them as strange, clannish, and hard to approach.[35] One survey of the Vietnamese residents of Orange County, California found that six in ten thought anti-Vietnamese prejudice was still a problem there.[36]

Stereotyping in the Media and Popular Entertainment

In the 1990s and early 2000s, negative stereotyping has targeted various Asian American groups. Television series such as "The Simpsons" have derided Indian and other South Asian store clerks, while the David Letterman show has made fun of Bangladeshi newsstand operators.[37] In 1990 the musical *Miss Saigon*, produced in London and New York, was sharply criticized by Vietnamese Americans who charged that the central character, a Vietnamese "bar girl" abandoned by a white GI, is a crude racial stereotype. Vietnamese and other Asian American leaders called on Asian American theatergoers and actors to boycott the popular play.[38] Moreover, a recent study of images of people of color in news coverage found numerous portrayals of Asian Americans as manipulative, mysterious, and inscrutable. The study found widespread trivialization of Asian customs, ridicule of Asian American pronunciation, and use of derogatory clichés and inflammatory phrases such as "Asian invasion," terminology that reinforces views of Asian Americans as undesirable foreigners.[39]

In the late 1990s, Chinese Americans and other Asian Americans became targets of widespread stereotyping in the investigation of alleged illegal contributions to political campaigns. Under heavy pressure to raise money for the Democratic party in the mid-1990s, John Huang, a Chinese American, and a few other Asian American fundraisers raised several million dollars in contributions, some of which were alleged to have been illegally contributed by overseas donors, including the major political party in Taiwan. Media discussions included considerable stereotyping of Chinese and other Asian Americans as mysterious, underhanded, or corrupt. Old racist images of "Orientals" were often resurrected. While investigation of illegal campaign contributions is legitimate, stereotyping is another matter. Indeed, the media did *not* so vigorously target for investigation other foreign contributions, such as those from overseas corporations and organizations, to Democratic party and Republican party activities. And the ethnicity of other contributors was not singled out.[40]

Investigations of illegal contributions by the Democratic Party focused disproportionately on Asian Americans. This small minority among fundraisers was unfairly targeted. Commenting on Huang's testimony before a U.S. Senate investigating committee regarding fundraising, a white U.S. senator from Kansas made fun of what he thought to be Chinese American speech patterns: "No raise money, no get bonus."[41] Amazingly enough, the senator contended that his mocking language was not intended as a slight. A Georgia representative also made what he thought was a witty comment about illegal donations being the "tip of the egg roll." As Mia Tuan has suggested, "That both men felt free enough from recrimination to engage in such racist witticisms speaks volumes about the atmosphere during the hearings."[42] Such commentary suggests that elite white Americans, not just the general white public, still harbor strong negative stereotypes of Asian Americans.

A graphic commentary on the fundraising investigations that appeared on the cover of a spring 1997 issue of the magazine *National Review* showed caricatures of President Bill Clinton and his wife Hilary as slant-eyed, buck-toothed Chinese in Mao suits and Chinese hats and drew strong protests. Daphne Kwok, of the Organization of Chinese Americans, described these images as racist and offensive because they resurrected stereotypes about Asian Americans' physical characteristics and dress. Since the nineteenth century, white cartoonists have portrayed Chinese and other Asian Americans in such stereotyped terms to express fear of the so-called Yellow Peril. Appearing on NBC's "Today" show with Daphne Kwok, the editor of *National Review* admitted the caricatures were an attempt to portray Asian characteristics but refused to apologize. In April 1997, representatives of several civil rights groups protested outside the magazine's New York offices and called for a boycott of the magazine.[43]

Clearly, media and elite stereotypes of Asians and Asian Americans still include notions of the latter as unassimilated and racialized foreigners. Robert Lee has argued that such racist humor only works "because the first family is always presumably white—an enduring, if anachronistic, symbol of America as a white nation in the popular imagination."[44]

Negative stereotypes of Asian Americans have deep roots in the current language of everyday discourse among whites, including many children. One Asian American journalist has recently noted some of the harsh and hostile words she heard from whites as she was growing up: "Ching chong Chinaman sitting on a rail, along came a white man and snipped off his tail"; "Ah so. No tickee, No washee. So sorry, so sollee"; and "Chinkee, Chink, Jap, Nip, zero, Dothead ... Flip, Hindoo."[45]

DISCRIMINATION AND CONFLICT

Hate Crimes and Other Ethnoviolence

Violence, harassment, and vandalism directed against Americans of Asian descent have occurred since the earliest days of Asian immigration. Until recently, few local or state governments have collected data on the scale of this ethnoviolence. Where data have been collected, Asian Americans are often disproportionately represented among victims.[46] In 1996 alone, for example, 534 anti-Asian hate crimes were reported to law enforcement, according to data collected by the National Asian Pacific American Legal Consortium. Since 1998, at least nine Asian Americans have died in hate crime attacks.[47] Hate crimes range from killings to verbal slurs and hate messages painted on homes and businesses.

Periodically, some anti-Asian discrimination is thoroughly reported in the mass media. In 1997 several Asian American students were denied service at a Syracuse restaurant. When they left, they were beaten by white patrons, and the restaurant's security personnel reportedly did not try to intervene. Some Asian American leaders have attributed the increase in these hate crimes and other discrimination to anti-immigrant sentiment and anti-Asian images in the media.[48]

The U.S. Commission on Civil Rights has noted that ethnoviolence is underreported, especially in the case of Asian Americans. Many of the latter are immigrants who distrust the police, have a limited understanding of their civil rights, and may have a limited knowledge of English. Some have been mistreated or killed by police officers.[49] Orange County, California reported 169 hate crimes in 1998, up from the previous year. While black residents were the most frequent targets, Asian Americans were singled out for a variety of hate crimes, which ranged from racist graffiti—painted on homes or businesses or circulated on the Internet—to violent threats and attacks.[50]

The U.S. Civil Rights Commission has found that adequate police protection is not provided to many communities. In cities from Boston to Los Angeles, Asian American community organizations are urging officials to investigate and prosecute hate crimes vigorously.[51] Many white-dominated police departments seem insensitive or hostile to Asian American communities and cultures. When Asian Americans do have contact with white officers, their rights are sometimes jeopardized by language barriers, and few police departments have adequate interpretive services for non-English-speaking Americans. The California attorney general's office has estimated that fewer than half the crimes against Asian Americans are reported. When Asian Americans report a crime, they frequently do not receive justice. The Asian and Pacific Islander Advisory Committee of the California attorney general's office has reported that "one of the most commonly repeated experiences is one in which the perpetrator is allowed to go free and the victim [an Asian American] is arrested."[52]

One controversial police strategy is photographing youths because they fit a "gang profile." Asian Americans—like African Americans, Latinos, and Arab Americans—are sometimes the targets of racial profiling by white authorities. Some communities have organized to challenge the police harassment. A spokesperson for one such community organization explained, "Culturally, the Asian community does not speak out against such things as police harassment. By nature, our people do not complain or report abuse, so by having some speak out, we hope to encourage others to do the same."[53] This is beginning to change, for a growing number of Asian Americans are attending community-sponsored forums on citizens' rights.

Chinese Americans

During the nineteenth century, openly anti-Chinese sentiments and discrimination were common in union policies and political platforms, as well as in the press. Chinese immigrants were violently attacked by whites in western states. In recent decades, Chinese Americans have continued to be the targets of racially motivated attacks, if on a smaller scale. For example, a Chinese American woman in New York was pushed in front of a subway train by a man with a "phobia about Asians."[54] And an eighteen-year-old white supremacist in California was charged with numerous felony crimes, including the attempted murder of a Chinese American city council member and the firebombing of NAACP and Japanese American Citizens League (JACL) offices.[55]

In Detroit in 1982, the murder of Vincent Chin, a Chinese American, brought racially motivated actions against Asian Americans to public attention. Two white auto workers, apparently believing Chin was Japanese and blaming him for auto industry problems, started an argument with him, then beat him to death with a baseball bat. A Michigan judge sentenced each to only three years' probation and a fine of $3,780. Many Americans expressed outrage at the extraordinarily lenient punishment. The U.S. Commission on Civil Rights concluded that the leniency was "suggestive of very little value being placed on an Asian American life."[56] The U.S. Department of Justice later brought federal charges against the assailants for civil rights violations. A U.S. district court jury found one of the defendants guilty of violating Chin's civil rights, thereby acknowledging the racial motivation of the attack. The other, apparently not directly involved in the beating, was acquitted. The guilty defendant was sentenced to twenty-five years in prison, but his conviction was overturned by an appellate court for technical reasons. In a retrial he was acquitted.[57]

A similar incident took place in Raleigh, North Carolina in 1989. This time the Chinese American victim, Ming Hai Loo, was killed by two white brothers who thought he was Vietnamese and were angry about U.S. battle deaths in Vietnam. In 1990, the brother who struck the fatal blow was sentenced to thirty-seven years in prison for second-degree murder and simple assault, but with the possibility of parole after serving four-and-a-half years. The maximum penalty for such crimes under North Carolina's law is life in prison. The other assailant, who made hostile racist remarks, received a six-month misdemeanor sentence. The following year he was found guilty in federal court of violating the victim's civil rights and received a four-year sentence, which was shorter than the minimum sentence specified by federal guidelines. Significantly, this case was the *first* successful federal prosecution of a civil rights case in which the target was Asian American. Yet, it received little media attention, a neglect that perpetuates non-Asian Americans' lack of awareness of anti-Asian violence.[58]

Anti-Asian attacks often illustrate not only racist violence but also the confusion of non-Asians about Asian Americans. Many non-Asians are not aware that Asian–Pacific Americans include many nationality groups, and many non-Asians mistake a person from one Asian American group for someone from another. This confusion may have been reflected in several incidents since the late 1990s in which Secret Service guards have treated with suspicion, as though they were foreigners, Asian Americans (including in one case White House interns) entering the White House.[59]

In the late 1990s, the federal government's Los Alamos National Laboratory was investigated for security compromises, and Dr. Wen Ho Lee, a naturalized U.S. citizen from Taiwan, was fired for allegedly being a major spy for the Chinese government. He was indicted on 59 counts of "mishandling classified information." In fall 2000, after months of media and political speculation about Chinese intrigues and Lee's involvement, and after Lee had served nine months in solitary confinement, he was freed on a plea bargain in which all but one relatively minor charge (downloading secret files to an unsecured computer) were dropped. Some news stories on the events seemed to view Chinese Americans as mysterious or disloyal. President Bill Clinton was openly critical of the investigation and long incarceration, yet said that no anti-Asian animosity lay behind what happened. However, many Asian Americans protested the stereotyping of Chinese Americans as somehow disloyal and criminal, as well as the scapegoating and mistreatment of Dr. Lee himself. Moreover, in fall 1997 the U.S. Commission on Civil Rights held a briefing on an ACLU petition from northern California that charged the U.S. Congress, the Democratic National Committee, and the Republican National Committee with creating a hostile environment for Asian Americans in the United States.[60]

Filipino Americans

Among the earliest of Asian-Pacific immigrants, Filipino Americans have suffered many violent attacks from white Americans. In the 1910s–1930s period, there were many clashes in California between Filipino and white farm laborers. Revealing racial discrimination, Filipino wages were considerably lower than the wages of whites, yet white workers still wanted to get rid of the Filipino workers. On October 24, 1929, whites rioted against Filipino workers in a farming community in the San Joaquin Valley. White workers were openly bitter about white farmers' use of Filipino workers for harvesting. The attacks began at a carnival where whites were shooting young Filipinos with rubber bands as the latter walked with white women. After days of harassment, a young Filipino farm laborer used a knife to defend himself when a white group attempted to corner him. He escaped, but a white mob formed. Whites went to a nearby labor camp, ordered all Filipinos out, then burned the camp to the ground. The local police chief refused to take action against the mob despite their criminal acts.[61]

The most prolonged riot by whites in California occurred near Watsonville in 1930. This riot reflected a decade of increasing tension between white and Filipino American workers. Local tension was exacerbated by a newspaper interview with a local white official who blamed the Filipino Americans for tensions. A series of anti-Filipino demonstrations erupted, and a vigilante mob of 500 whites marched on a Filipino dance hall. The white-dominated press misreported the incident as Filipino Americans marching and rioting in the streets. On January 22, 1930, the anti-Filipino attacks reached a peak when 400 white vigilantes attacked the Northern Monterey Filipino Club. One person was killed, and a large number of Filipino Americans were severely beaten.[62]

In more recent decades, whites have also directed their hostility toward Filipino Americans. In the early 1990s, white guests at a party at Chicago mayor Richard Daley's Michigan estate called two Filipino American youths racist names and threw them out. The youths came back with some white friends, and there was a violent brawl. In this case, whites both attacked and defended Filipino Americans.[63] In 1999, Joseph Ileto, a Filipino American mail carrier, was killed in Los Angeles by a white supremacist who admitted he killed him because of the color of his skin. (White supremacist groups often attack all Americans of color as inferior "mud" people.) In response to the killing, Ileto's family has become active in rallies and protests against hate crimes, including pressing the U.S. Congress to pass hate crimes legislation. Filipino American organizations rallied against this hate crime in several cities, including Chicago and San Francisco.[64]

Korean Americans

Koreans are relatively recent immigrants, yet they too have been hit by anti-Asian violence. Like white ethnic merchants, Korean American merchants in some black communities have faced hostility and their businesses have been targets of economic boycotts. Local black residents have charged that the merchants treat black customers rudely and refuse to hire black employees. Korean American merchants, in turn, cite the high level of crime they often face at the hands of poor black criminals.

During the past decade, black residents in New York and California have boycotted and demonstrated against Korean American businesses. Each group has accused members of the other of racially motivated violence. In 1991 a Korean American storekeeper in Los Angeles killed a fifteen-year-old black girl (Latasha Harlins) whom the storekeeper mistakenly thought was shoplifting. Black rage over this incident, which intensified after a judge imposed a lenient sentence on the merchant, played a role in the major 1992 Los Angeles riot (see Chapter 7).[65] Historian Mike Davis has described the looting and burning of 2,000 Korean-owned businesses during that 1992 riot as the product of "the black community's unassuaged grief over Harlins's murder."[66]

During the 1992 riot, Los Angeles's Korean Americans felt betrayed by the U.S. justice system as they saw white police officers protect large shopping centers owned by wealthy whites while smaller, Korean-owned stores were destroyed by the black and Latino rioters. Social scientist Elaine Kim has commented that "the so-called black–Korean problem masks a deeper racism in this country.... When the Los Angeles Police Department and the state government failed to respond to the initial outbreak of violence in South Central, I suspected that Korean Americans were being used as human shields to protect the real source of rage."[67]

One factor that contributes to continuing tensions between African Americans and Korean Americans is that many Korean and other Asian immigrants already have strong negative stereotypes of black Americans when they come to the United States. Asian immigrants, like other recent immigrants, pick up negative stereotypes from U.S.-made movies and television programs that are seen by hundreds of millions in countries across the globe. In one recent study, Asian respondents in rural Taiwan were interviewed about their views of African Americans. Although they had never been to the United States, and although some respondents realized that the U.S. mass media (television, movies, newspapers) were engaged in stereotyping, most still accepted the negative stereotypes of African Americans that they had learned from the now-global U.S. media.[68]

The negative stereotypes that some Korean and other Asian immigrants bring with them can thus become a basis for negative interactions with African Americans. In their turn, African Americans sometimes develop negative views of the Asian immigrants who stereotype them. Negative stereotyping of Asian Americans that African Americans pick up from the same white-controlled media can affect how they see the Asian American merchants in their communities. The negative attitudes of immigrants toward African Americans—and the negative attitudes of African Americans toward Asian immigrants—are thus part of a much larger, indeed global, system of white-generated and white-circulated racist imagery.[69]

Moreover, sociologist Claire Jean Kim has shown that the conflict between Korean Americans and African Americans must be set in the larger context of systemic racism. Black–Asian conflict is not just about stereotyping and scapegoating by African Americans or Korean Americans, but reflects the larger white-racist framework and its racial hierarchy. In this racial hierarchy whites are at the top, and blacks are at the bottom, while other racially oppressed groups, such as Korean Americans, are in between. This white-created hierarchy stimulates conflict among the racial groups positioned differently in it. It also generates *legitimate* protests against a group's hierarchical placement and the racist barriers associated with that placement. "The differential positioning of Blacks and Asian Americans (including Korean immigrants) in the American racial order and their physical juxtaposition in the urban economy creates an immanent tendency for conflict between the two groups."[70] Collective black actions against Korean American merchants in black communities are not simply about black stereotyping of these merchants but are part of centuries of black resistance to outside control of their communities.

This resistance arises no matter who (Irish, Jewish, or Korean) the outside merchants are.

Another source of bitterness on the part of some African Americans is the largely unfounded belief that the federal government helps Korean Americans start their small businesses. In fact, Korean Americans usually pool family resources to purchase businesses in low-income black and Latino neighborhoods.[71] Many Korean immigrants have started businesses in black and Latino communities because such businesses only require modest capital and can be very profitable. The gamble the Korean American entrepreneurs take in poor communities is "necessitated by the constraints they face—the near impossibility of a professional career or white-collar work, and the daunting difficulties in opening a store in an affluent neighborhood."[72] Contrary to the "American dream," these Korean immigrants are usually not able to start businesses in heavily white areas because they face anti-Asian discrimination or do not have enough capital to start businesses there. Many have graduated from Korean colleges, yet are unable to find employment in line with their educations, in part because of discrimination and in part because they do not yet have the language skills. Like white ethnic merchants before them, Korean Americans have sometimes become the latest "middleman minorities."[73]

In recent years, conflict has erupted between Korean Americans and Latinos in California. Some researchers and reporters have found strong antagonism between the two groups. For example, many of the rioters looting Korean American businesses during the 1992 L.A. riot were Latinos. In addition, Korean American garment industry subcontractors are often seen by their low-wage Latino employees as profit-seeking exploiters who are indifferent to workers' well-being. In their turn, these Korean American contractors report frequent verbal disputes in the workplace and acts of vandalism by Latino workers. The Korean American subcontractors are themselves exploited by white manufacturers who make use of a subcontracting system designed for flexible and profitable production of garments.[74]

Vietnamese Americans

Many recent Vietnamese immigrants fished as a livelihood in their homeland, and it is natural for them to do so in their new country. To pursue this dream, some have moved to fishing communities on the Gulf Coast. In the late 1970s, they had been encouraged to move to that area because of its labor shortage. They generally took low-paying jobs, such as cleaning fish or working in restaurant kitchens, and in these positions they were tolerated by the white community. But as they began to buy fishing boats and offer competition to white fishers, white attitudes toward them changed. Many whites in the area have resented the Vietnamese Americans' success and have even blamed them for economic recessions that have come to the Gulf Coast.

Vietnamese Americans have faced open hostility and violence at the hands of whites. A 1979 conflict between Vietnamese Americans and whites in Seadrift, Texas culminated in the shooting death of a white fisher. Two Vietnamese refugees were arrested for the shooting, which followed an argument over the placement of crab traps. Within hours of the death, three Vietnamese boats were burned, one house was fire-bombed, and an attempt was made to bomb a packing plant where Vietnamese Americans worked. The attacks caused most of the Vietnamese Americans there to flee to another town. The Vietnamese Americans were eventually acquitted of the shooting. In response to this verdict, some whites turned to the white supremacists in the Ku Klux Klan for "protection of their industrial interest."[75]

Vietnamese Americans have faced racial violence in a number of other areas as well. For example, between 1983 and 1987, the Boston police department reported that nearly one-fourth of the racial violence in the city was directed at Vietnamese and other Asian Americans. And in 1989 one Vietnamese and four Cambodian children were gunned down in Stockton, California by a white man in army fatigues with a semi-automatic weapon. He attacked the children at his old school, which now had mostly Asian American children. He had often expressed hostility toward Asians. Significantly, some of the major media reports on the killings ignored the issue of anti-Asian racism raised by the incident.[76]

Asian-Indian Americans

Asian-Indian Americans have also faced racial hostility and discrimination. For example, anti-Indian leaflets have been circulated in New Jersey cities. In New Jersey schools, Asian-Indian children have been called derogatory names (e.g., "dot heads") and physically abused because of their Indian ancestry.[77] Some Asian-Indian Americans have also faced racial violence. In a middle-class area of Queens, New York in 1998, Rishi Maharaj, an Indian whose family came to the United States from the Caribbean, received multiple head injuries when he was beaten with baseball bats by three white men as they shouted racist epithets and threats. Two days later, a Pakistani American gas attendant was killed with a baseball bat on Long Island.[78]

Exaggerated stereotypes of the successfulness of Asian Indians have also contributed to interracial political struggles in several states, including California. For example, some non-Asians in the San Francisco area have vigorously opposed attempts to include Indians as Asians in several affirmative action programs designed to help small Asian American businesses.[79]

ORGANIZING AND ACTIVISM IN THE POLITICAL ARENA

A number of Asian Americans have distinguished themselves politically, despite anti-Asian prejudices. Yet, except in the state of Hawaii, Asian Americans still have limited political representation. Even in the early 2000s, federal appointed offices, including congressional staff positions, have largely been inaccessible. As we mentioned in Chapter 10, Norman Mineta, a Japanese American, has held two presidential cabinet posts. In 2001, President George W. Bush appointed Elaine Chao as Secretary of Labor, making her the *first* Chinese American and the *first* Asian American woman to hold such a Cabinet post. As of 2001, however, no member of any other Asian American group has been represented at this political level. As of 2001, there were only six Asian American voting members in the U.S. Congress, only three of whom were from outside of Hawaii. In 1999, David Wu (D-Oreg.) became the first Chinese American to serve in the U.S. House and he remained in that office in 2001. Jay Kim, who served three terms in the U.S. House during the 1990s, was the first and only Korean American to hold federal elected office.

Advances at the state level have also come slowly. In 2001, California, whose more than 4 million Asian Americans made up more than 12 percent of its population, had only two Asian American members of Congress and four Asian American members in its state Assembly. The state of Washington had one Asian American state senator, three Asian American state representatives, and a Chinese American

Taiwanese-born U.S. Congressman David Wu from Oregon (left) is greeted by Taiwanese President Chen Shui-bian at the Presidential Palace in Taipei.

ASIAN AMERICANS AND NEW YORK CITY POLITICS

A survey of 2,800 voters leaving New York City polling places on Election Day 2000 found that at least one-fifth were foreign-born; 13 percent of the foreign-born identified themselves as Asian American. The large number of first-time voters who cast ballots in New York City in the 2000 national election helped increase the city turnout from 58 percent in 1996 to 67 percent in 2000. Two-thirds of the new voters were foreign-born. This turnout likely signals coming changes in political representation in New York City, two-thirds of whose population is now made up of immigrants and their children. While Asian Americans have had little representation in New York City politics in the past, Asian American leaders forecast imminent changes. Reflecting on the poll, Christopher Kui, director of Asian Americans for Equality, stated, "It's encouraging to see so many Asian Americans voting and running for City Council in this year's elections, but that's only part of what needs to happen." He noted that recognition of Asian Americans' role in city politics is long overdue and added that following the 2000 census, "the drawing of new political lines in the redistricting process must respect our communities."

Source: "The Immigrant Vote in New York City Is Topic of Panel Discussion," *Barnard Campus News*, Wednesday, May 2, 2001, p. 1.

governor, Gary Locke, the first Asian American elected governor outside of Hawaii. A serious lack of representation in government also exists in most local areas with substantial Asian American populations, although the number of such officials, and candidates for office, has grown since the 1990s. For example, until 2002, when Chinese American John C. Liu became a councilmember from the district of Queens, no Asian American had ever served on New York City's council. New York's Asian American population is now almost 900,000. Nationally, a large proportion of Asian Americans have immigrated too recently to be eligible to vote, and the registration rate of eligible (native born and naturalized) Asian Americans has until recently been relatively low (53 percent versus 69 percent for whites), although this trend appears to be changing. Many Asian Americans have not registered or voted because they come from (or fled) countries with undemocratic political systems, and they still do not trust politicians or political systems.[80]

Anti-Asian prejudice and discrimination on the part of white officials and the white public also play a role in the modest level of Asian American political involvement. Participants in Civil Rights Commission conferences have pointed to several barriers to political participation: (1) apportionment policies that dilute the voting strength of Asian American voting blocs; (2) the unavailability of Asian-language election materials; and (3) anti-Asian sentiments among non-Asian voters and in the mass media.[81]

Pan-Asian Organizations and Coalitions

Nineteenth-century and early twentieth-century Asian immigrants, divided by language and cultural differences and historical tensions between their countries of origin, held fast to distinctive cultural identities, resisting the tendency of non-Asian Americans to lump all Asians together. This has remained true for most first generation immigrants in recent decades. However, among the large number of second- and later-generation Asian Americans, language and cultural barriers are not as significant, and a pan-Asian identity and solidarity have developed in many cities. Beginning on college campuses in the late 1960s—especially in the 1968 San Francisco State student strike over multicultural education—and spreading to community activists and professional organizations by the mid-1970s, pan-Asian organizations and news media have helped to forge a group consciousness among many students, artists, professionals, and other Asian Americans. This movement to *panethnicity* is fostered by shared cultural backgrounds, common experiences of racial and/or ethnic oppression in the United States, and a common interest in fighting that oppression. All Asian American groups have experienced being considered "foreigners" by other Americans, especially white Americans.[82]

The term *Asian American* has developed since the 1960s, in part because the term *Oriental*, with its roots in European colonialism and imperialism, is strongly rejected. Asia is East (Oriental) only if the point of reference is Europe. The term *Oriental* has long been associated with stereotypes of deviousness, passivity, and acquiescence. For many, *Asian American* means respect and empowerment.[83]

Yet, not all Asian Americans were empowered by the early pan-Asian movement of the 1960s and 1970s. Asian American women reported that they were too often restricted to subordinate roles in organizations, and those who challenged sexism in the movement were often ridiculed as "traitors" to Asian American unity.[84] Feeling alienated from the mainstream women's movement, as have other racially oppressed women, Asian American women have formed their own groups within the context of their Asian American identity, often emphasizing their triple oppression based on their gender, their racial group, and their class.[85] Indeed, these organizations of racially oppressed women have helped bring the issue of multiple forms of stratification—of race, gender, and class—into sharper focus in much new scholarship in recent decades.

Asian American groups' reactions to the early pan-Asian movement ranged from support to apprehension and hostility.[86] Not until the 1980s did a national pan-Asian political organization specifically address broad Asian American concerns. The first major political effort began in 1986 with the founding of the Asian-American Voters Coalition, which included organizations representing Japanese, Chinese, Asian-Indian, Filipino, Korean, Vietnamese, and Thai Americans.[87] The organization sought to consolidate Asian Americans into an effective bloc of voters that could influence elections in states from California to New York; protect Asian Americans' civil rights; and fight anti-Asian legislation, distorted media images, hate crimes, and employment discrimination.[88] Since the 1990s, the Asian Pacific American Legal Center of Southern California has taken action to protect Asian immigrants' rights to speak their own languages in workplaces and has addressed other important community issues.

In the late 1990s, twenty organizations, including the Japanese American Citizens League and the Organization of Chinese Americans, joined to form the National Council of Asian Pacific Americans (NCAPA). The Council is concerned with such problems as hate crimes, discrimination, immigration restrictions, and the unfair singling out of Asian Americans during various official investigations.[89]

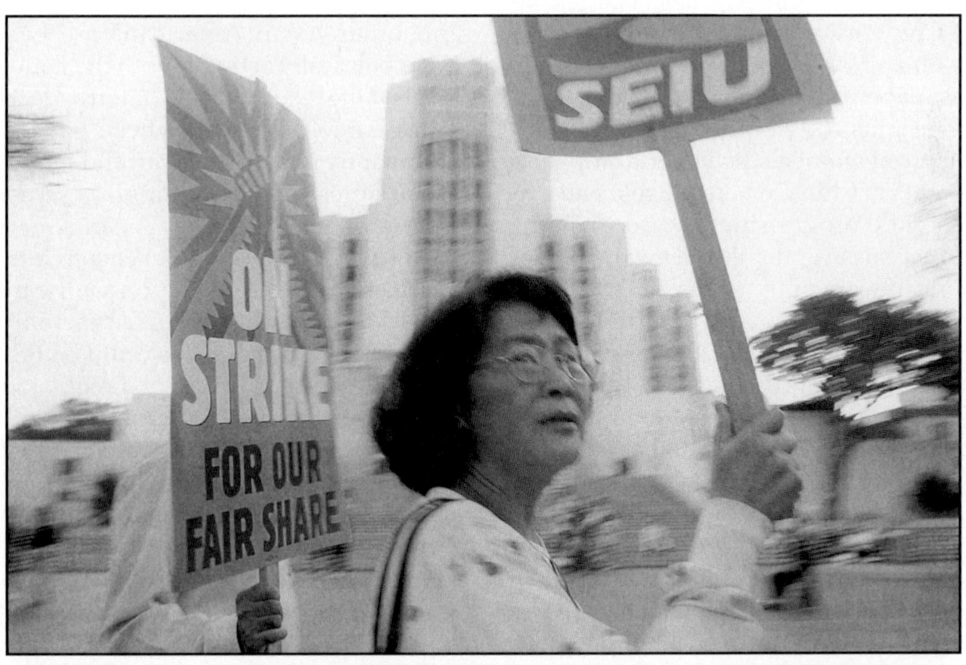

Unionized Asian American health-care workers picket for better wages and working conditions in Los Angeles.

Coalitions with non-Asian groups have also been created. Latino, African, Vietnamese, Korean, Chinese, and other Asian American leaders in Los Angeles created the Multicultural Association for Voter Registration to encourage all people of color to register to vote and become more active politically. Such coalitions reflect a growing awareness that cooperation generates greater political power. Recently, Korean American community organizations' support for Latino hotel workers' unions involved in a dispute with a Los Angeles hotel owner was hailed by Latino union leaders as a major example of coalition building among people of color.[90]

Chinese Americans

Perhaps because Chinese Americans have had a long history of immigration, they have been the most politically active of the groups discussed in this chapter. Political activity was modest until about 1920. Increasingly, Chinese Americans became involved in a variety of political organizations and spent much time discussing new political developments in China and in the United States. A number of labor-oriented organizations were created; some tried to organize laborers in New York's Chinese American communities, where a large concentration of Chinese Americans then lived.[91] Between 1900 and 1930, the important Chinese language newspaper *Chung Sai Yat Po* was an advocate of civil rights for Chinese Americans, including the rights of women. The paper's emphasis on political events in China, where the role and status of women were progressing toward equality, contributed to the social and political awakening of Chinese American women.[92]

With the new immigration after the reforms of 1965 came renewed political activity. Explaining barriers to expanded political activity, Michael Woo, one of the few Chinese Americans yet to hold a major city government position, has argued that one challenge in getting out the vote is that Chinese and other Asian Americans "traditionally view all political activity as suspect." Woo added, however, that more Asian Americans are becoming active in election campaigns.[93] Earlier, Irving Chin, chair of the Chinatown Advisory Committee to the Borough President of Manhattan, had told a U.S. Senate committee that Chinese American political activity was limited because of problems with English, fear of and lack of familiarity with government, and a traditional reluctance to engage in political action. In addition, Professor Ling-chi Wang, a San Francisco community activist and chair of Asian American studies at the University of California (Berkeley), spoke to this committee in support of social welfare programs. Wang, sometimes called the "Chinese Martin Luther King, Jr.," has been active in many civil rights causes. He testified to the Senate Committee that unemployment in San Francisco's Chinatown was double the citywide average, that available housing was often substandard, and that the incidence of tuberculosis was far above the national average.[94]

Wang has also played a key role in persuading immigrant parents to press a lawsuit for bilingual education in public schools, an effort that resulted in a 1974 U.S. Supreme Court decision ordering such bilingual education. More recently, Wang has been active in efforts to get rid of discriminatory height requirements for San Francisco police officers and fire fighters, to eliminate disproportionately tough admissions standards for Asian American students at elite universities, and to have SAT-type tests given in Asian languages.[95]

Concerned about a range of local and national issues, including attacks on immigrants, Chinese and other Asian Americans are becoming ever more politically active at both the national and local levels. One example is Monterey Park, California, a Los Angeles suburb whose population is predominantly Asian American and Latino. This is one of the largest Chinese immigrant settlements in the United States, and other Asian American groups are also well represented. When white city council members passed a resolution saying that Monterey Park did not consider itself a sanctuary for "illegal aliens" and that English should be the official U.S. language, many of the city's Asian American residents were outraged. Some 4,000 people signed petitions demanding that the city council rescind the resolution, which it did. The controversy indicated a serious rift within the community between fearful whites, who contended that the Asians are not trying "to assimilate" and are "taking over," and Asian Americans who only seek the middle-class American dream.[96]

By the early 2000s, Chinese Americans were growing in influence in California cities. They sat on city councils in Los Angeles–area communities and in San Francisco. In 1996, Gary Locke, the son of immigrants, became governor in the state of Washington, the first Chinese American to serve as governor of a mainland state. Locke also campaigned in Oregon for David Wu, who in 1998 became the first Taiwan-born American to serve in Congress. As we have noted, Chinese Americans have become increasingly active in national politics. They have pressed both major political parties to select Chinese American candidates. Yet few Chinese Americans have so far served in the U.S. Congress. Daniel K. Akaka, currently senator from Hawaii, is the *only* person of Hawaiian or Chinese American ancestry to ever serve in the U.S. Senate. Moreover, as a group, Chinese Americans have financially supported the Democratic party, and a majority of Chinese Americans still vote for state and national Democratic party candidates.

Like many other U.S. groups with a substantial number of immigrants, Chinese Americans are often concerned about U.S. foreign policy. Since the 1980s many Chinese Americans have pressed for changes in U.S. government policy toward China. The killing of protesting students in Beijing's Tiananmen Square in 1989 prompted the creation of a new organization called the Committee of 100. Headed by influential Chinese Americans, including architect I. M. Pei, the organization has sought to change U.S. government policy on China. Many Chinese Americans have pressured the U.S. government to take stronger action to persuade China to improve its labor and human rights policies.[97] Even though there is continuing concern about the Chinese government's authoritarian human rights record, in 2001, Chinese Americans throughout the United States were pleased when Beijing, China was chosen to host the 2008 Olympic Games. Many Chinese Americans reportedly felt that bringing the world's mass media to Beijing, and focusing the world's attention on China, would have a beneficial, liberalizing effect on that nation.[98]

Filipino Americans

The nation's most successful farm workers' union, the United Farm Workers (see Chapter 8), was created by a merger between a Mexican American organizing drive and a Filipino labor organization, the Agricultural Workers' Organizing Committee (AWOC). These groups conducted a major strike against poor working conditions on the grape farms of California. Larry Itliong, head of AWOC and an energetic Filipino American activist, worked to organize farm laborers from Alaska to California to South America.[99] A number of other Filipino American labor and political organizations have been created, including the Filipino Organizing Committee, which was created in the San Francisco area in the 1970s to facilitate greater political participation for Filipino Americans.[100]

New resistance tactics have emerged since the 1980s. The National Filipino American Council, a group of 3,000 Filipino social, community, and civil rights groups across the nation, has fought for fairer immigration laws. Since the 1990s, Filipino Americans have held national conferences to generate political strategies to win elected and appointed offices in cities where they make up a significant percentage of the population. For example, at a 1997 conference, organized by the Council and other Filipino organizations, one issue was getting the Filipino Veterans Equity Act passed, legislation that would finally give Filipino veterans of World War II the veterans benefits long promised by the U.S. government.[101]

According to one study of 1969–1978 naturalization data by Elliot Barkan, Filipinos have one of the highest naturalization rates of any U.S. immigrant group; in that study their rate was a high 60 percent, and much higher than the 45 percent naturalization rate for non-Asians. We should note that, despite the stereotyped images of "foreigners," Filipinos and other groups of Asian American immigrants have long been eager to become naturalized citizens of the United States.[102]

In spite of this commitment to becoming good citizens, Filipino Americans have rarely been elected or appointed to major political offices, even in areas such as California where their numbers are large. As of 2001, the California legislature still had no Filipino American members. In 1992, the first Filipino American was elected to the city council in Carson, a community near Los Angeles. In 1994, Benjamin Cayetano became the *first* Filipino American ever elected to a top political office in the United States, as governor of Hawaii. In addition, in recent years a few Filipino Americans have been elected as state senators and representatives, mayors, city council members, and school board members in some western states.

A number of Filipino American organizations have responded to the Philippine government's call for investment in the islands to help overcome recurring economic crises. Once again, we see the global influences on U.S. racial and ethnic groups. In addition, the overthrow of the Ferdinand Marcos dictatorship in the Philippines in the late 1980s boosted Filipino American pride. Filipino identity was strengthened by the advent of political democracy in the Philippines. This trend reinforced the commitment of Filipino Americans to greater political participation in the United States. Significantly, in 1997, Filipino American leaders in San Francisco protested the installation of a huge granite column celebrating Commodore George Dewey's victory over the Spanish in Manila Bay in 1898.[103] Dewey is seen as having brought U.S. imperialism to Pacific countries like the Philippines.

Korean Americans

Korean American political activity has also been inspired by events in the homeland. For example, during the years between 1905 and 1919, Korean Americans were active in the fight for Korean independence from Japan.[104] Yet, it is only in recent years that Korean Americans have gained significant political visibility. Although Korean Americans have been active in the Asian-American Voters Coalition discussed earlier, until the early 1990s, not one had held major political office in western states. In 1992 in California, Jay C. Kim became the first Korean American—and the first Asian immigrant—ever elected to the U.S. House of Representatives.

After the 1992 Los Angeles riot, the local Korean-American Coalition there became more active. Jerry Yu, a member of the coalition, has noted that during the riot "Korean Americans really saw with their own eyes the lack of political strength that we as a community have."[105] In the 1996 and 2000 presidential elections, Korean and other Asian Americans became very active in registering voters and in supporting Democratic party candidates. During the Democratic party's 1997 inaugural celebrations, 1,000 Korean and other Asian Americans attended the first ever Asian American inaugural ball, an indication of growing political influence.[106]

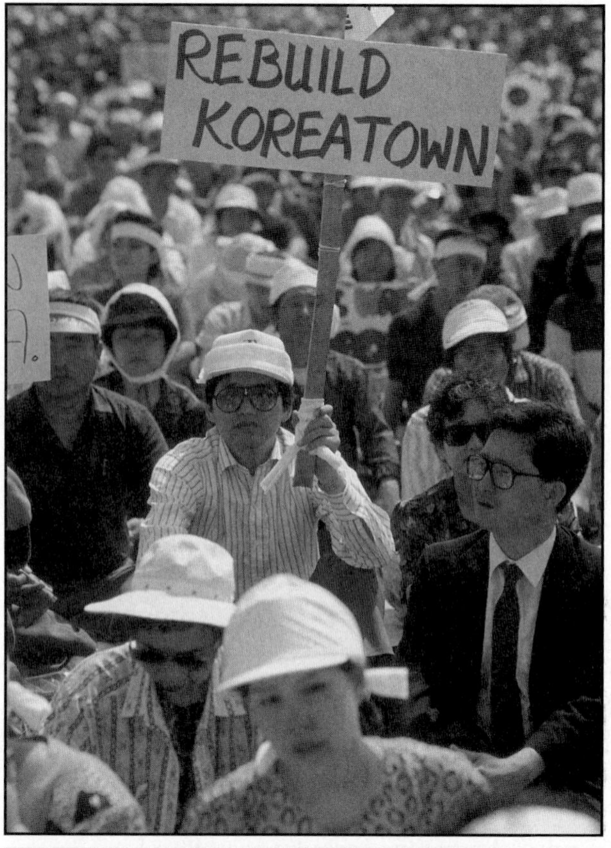

Calling for rebuilding, Korean Americans protest the destruction of Korean businesses in a major Los Angeles riot.

Korean Americans have sometimes vigorously demonstrated against discrimination and other mistreatment. Not long after the 1992 Los Angeles riot in which numerous Korean American businesses were destroyed, more than thirty thousand Korean Americans marched through their community protesting police brutality, the lack of justice in the criminal justice system, and media bias. This was the largest protest demonstration ever carried out by Asian Americans against injustice, yet it received little media attention.[107]

Many Korean Americans maintain close ties to Korea. After the 1992 Los Angeles riot, several officials from the Republic of Korea promptly visited the riot areas of Los Angeles, arriving even before U.S. presidential candidates in that election year. When North Korea faced serious food shortages in the late 1990s, Korean Americans sent more than a million dollars for food and other assistance.[108] In 2001 many Korean Americans signed a petition to the U.S. Secretary of State supporting U.S. government negotiations with the North Korean government to unite Korean families that were divided long ago by the Korean War. An estimated half million Korean Americans have relatives in North Korea.[109]

Vietnamese Americans

The home country also remains important for Vietnamese Americans. In recent years the icy political and economic relationship between Vietnam and the United States has begun to thaw. A 1989 survey of Vietnamese Americans in Orange County, California found that about half favored establishing diplomatic ties with Vietnam and felt that they might return for a visit under such conditions.[110] The issue of reestablishing ties to a Communist homeland has been a topic of debate within Vietnamese American communities since the 1980s, just as it has been in Cuban American communities.

Like other Asian Americans, Vietnamese Americans are still stereotyped as "foreigners." In Orange County a group of Vietnamese Americans seeking a parade permit for a parade to honor the Vietnamese war dead were turned down by the city council because local whites did not consider the parade to be truly "American." Vietnamese stores and signs were also defaced by white vandals. A white city council member remarked, "If they want to be South Vietnamese, go back to South Vietnam." After protests from the Asian American community, however, the council member apologized. Today, Orange County has an active Vietnamese-American Political Action Committee working for expanded political participation and influence for Vietnamese Americans.[111] Indeed, as concern over domestic political and economic issues in recent years has replaced the intense anti-Communist views that brought many Vietnamese immigrants to the United States, many Vietnamese Americans have moved their political allegiance from the Republican Party to the Democratic Party.

Vietnamese Americans have gradually begun to move up the social, political, and legal ladders like other immigrants before them. In recent decades they have created numerous important community organizations and institutions, including Buddhist temples and Vietnamese radio stations. In the 1990s, the Vietnamese Community of Southern California was created to unify some 300 local Vietnamese American organizations and to develop employment, immigrant, and youth programs. Very slowly, Vietnamese Americans are moving into important government positions. For example, in 1997, Thang Nguyen Barrett became a Santa Clara County Municipal Court Judge, the first Vietnamese American to serve as a judge in California. In 1992, Tony Lam, a restaurant owner, was elected to the Westminster city council in Orange County and became the *first* Vietnamese American elected to political office in the United States. In 2001 he was serving a third term.[112] Lam came to the United States as a political refugee in the 1970s and soon became camp manager at the Orange County Marine base where Vietnamese immigrants were housed before resettlement.[113] Still, as of the early 2000s, very few Vietnamese American have served as elected officials in the United States.[114]

Vietnamese Americans have developed important national advocacy organizations working for southeast Asian American concerns. One such group, the Southeast Asia Resource Action Center (SEARAC) in Washington, D.C. engages in political action and educational efforts on behalf of the southeast Asian American community and has worked on domestic social program, foreign policy, and civil rights issues. SEARAC provides training and technical assistance for numerous southeast Asian American community organizations. One of their programs helps local organizations fight the stereotyping faced by Asian Americans in the mass media.[115]

Asian-Indian Americans

Because of their relatively recent arrival in large numbers in the United States, Asian Indians also have relatively little political visibility. In the history of the U.S. Congress, only one Asian-Indian American has served, Californian Dalip Singh Saund, a representative elected in the mid-1950s. Saund was also the *first* Asian American member of Congress. However, by the early 1990s, Asian-Indian Americans were starting to form a number of organizations designed to increase political influence. Resulting in part from this activity, Pitambar Somani was appointed Ohio's director of health in the mid-1990s and became the first Asian-Indian American to serve in a state governor's cabinet. Since the 1990s, the number of Asian-Indian Americans running for political office has slowly grown in New Jersey and other states with rapidly increasing Asian-Indian American populations. In the past decade Asian-Indian Americans have also organized to fight racial discrimination in a number of U.S. cities.[116] One Hartford, Connecticut group has pressed for changes in discriminatory licensing requirements for foreign-born physicians and lobbied for expanded U.S. government aid for India. This is another example of the influence of the international context on the political orientations of recent immigrant groups.[117]

In the 1990s the New York Taxi Workers Alliance organized a large group of south Asian American taxi drivers to protest poor working conditions and poor treatment at the hands of city government officials. South Asians are a majority of New York taxi drivers. The group included Asian-Indians as well as taxi drivers from Pakistan and Bangladesh. Faced with twelve-hour shifts, constant traffic jams and exhaust fumes, low incomes, and no fringe benefits, the drivers staged a successful one-day strike in May 1998 against New York officials' attempts to impose unfair regulations on taxis. The strike helped organize taxi drivers from a diverse array of south Asian nationality groups to work together for better working conditions.[118] Broad Asian American coalitions like the Alliance are increasing in number across the United States.

THE ECONOMY

The U.S. Civil Rights Commission, among others, has documented the exploitation of Asian and other immigrants who are unaware of their rights by white employers who violate laws regarding safe working conditions, wages, and hours. The commission has noted that U.S. Supreme Court decisions since the 1980s have so far failed to protect Asian American workers from harassment and other discrimination. The 1991 Civil Rights Act was designed to undo the effects of some of these conservative Court decisions but has not yet had a major impact.[119]

Even well-educated Asian immigrants with professional experience in their homelands have faced employment barriers in the United States. Employers often discount immigrants' experience and credentials. Eventually, many are hired for research, engineering, and other technical positions, yet they remain underrepresented at the management levels in most large U.S. companies. A Civil Rights Commission study found that U.S.-born Asian American men with good English proficiency were less likely to hold managerial positions than white men with comparable qualifications. Asian Americans are even *less* likely to hold top executive positions in corporations. Asian American managers and professionals report a "glass ceiling." In the early 1990s, they made up just 0.3 percent of top executives in Fortune 500 companies—about one-tenth of their population percentage. This low percentage had changed little by the early 2000s. Moreover, a large majority of Chinese and Filipino American professionals and managers responding to a survey in San Francisco also reported that racism was a problem in their jobs.[120]

A mid-1990s study found that in the field of health care and research, where Asian Americans make up more than one-fourth of the work force, fewer than 1 percent of senior executives are Asian American. Another study of Asian American managers in California found that they were often seen as docile workers who could be hired and fired at will because they would not complain. White stereotypes of Asian American professionals and managers still result in economic exploitation and other discrimination.[121]

The previously noted Civil Rights Commission study found racially based employment discrimination to be even more severe for Asian American women. These workers are vulnerable not only to racial discrimination but also to sexual harassment and other gender discrimination on the job, and many have little knowledge of their legal rights. They are frequently excluded from the critical informal networks of white co-workers and enjoy fewer sources of support than white women when confronted with harassment. In one instance, an Asian American woman working at a San Francisco military base encountered severe retaliation after reporting sexual harassment. The Civil Rights Commission report noted that "because of the stereotypic expectation of compliance and docility, a formal complaint from an Asian American woman might have been considered as a personal affront or challenge."[122]

Discrimination based on language proficiency or accent is common. In a major decision, the Ninth Circuit Court of Appeals upheld an employer's right to consider an applicant's verbal skills when these were relevant to job performance, although the court cautioned employers not to misuse language proficiency to discriminate on the basis of national origin. Recent Asian and Latin American immigrants are adversely affected by English-only rules in the workplace, many of which are inappropriate because no business necessity for them can be demonstrated.[123]

Chinese Americans

In the nineteenth century, Chinese immigrants were recruited to fill the lower rungs of the occupational ladder in the United States. The first large-scale use of Chinese labor—more than 12,000 workers—was in the construction of the transcontinental railroad, which was completed in 1869. Early Chinese immigrant workers converted swampland in California to farmland; their planting, cultivating, and harvesting skills were used extensively at white-owned vineyards, orchards, and ranches. Chinese factory workers were also an important part of the California economy. Most labored long hours in poor working conditions for very low wages.[124]

Later on, the demand for large numbers of factory workers in World War II defense plants opened opportunities for thousands of Chinese Americans. Between 1940 and 1950, more than one-third of Chinese American men remained in service occupations, but the percentages in craft, technical, and professional occupations more than doubled. War industries also provided Chinese American women with clerical and technical jobs in defense plants.[125]

In recent decades, many Chinese immigrants' prospects have not been very good because many lack money, skills, and the ability to speak English well. Most have settled in preexisting urban Chinese American communities, where the men typically find restaurant or other service jobs and the women work in nonunion garment factories in or near Chinese American residential areas. Working conditions are often substandard or dangerous, and pay is often very low.[126]

The well-educated among postwar immigrants—such as engineers, doctors, mathematicians, and scientists trained in China, Taiwan, or the United States—have usually found better jobs in U.S. industries and universities and generally have had an easier time adjusting to their new country than the large number of poorer working class immigrants.[127]

The globalization of the U.S. economy since the 1970s can be seen in the major growth in high-tech industries, including those on the West Coast. The shortage of highly skilled workers in the United States and employers' desire for cheaper labor have led many high-tech employers to recruit skilled labor from overseas, especially from China, India, and the Philippines. Attracted by high-tech employment in the United States, many new U.S. engineers and medical personnel since 1980 have been immigrants from abroad, often from Asia. Many of these Asians have been educated in overseas colleges and universities oriented to a Western curriculum or have been international students at Western universities.[128] Some have become entrepreneurs. Thus, one 1999 study of Silicon Valley high-tech firms found that about one-fourth were headed by Chinese and Asian-Indian Americans.[129]

Table 11.2 (at the top of page 310) presents the most recent data available (1990) on the occupational distribution of the groups considered in this chapter as well as that of white Americans.[130] Today, Chinese Americans are heavily concentrated in white-collar jobs; 35.8 percent hold professional and managerial positions. The proportion rises to 43 percent for those born in the United States. The proportion of Chinese Americans exceeds that of whites in this category. However, Chinese Americans are also overrepresented in service-sector jobs compared with whites. They are about half as likely to hold skilled blue-collar jobs as are whites and somewhat less likely to hold less-skilled blue-collar jobs in the operators, fabricators, and laborers category. In 1990, Chinese Americans' unemployment rate was lower than that of the population as a whole.[131]

The Chinese American community is represented at both extremes of the economic spectrum. An Wang, former head of Wang Laboratories computer firm who died in 1990, became a billionaire. At one point he was fifth on Forbes's list of the wealthiest Americans. I. M. Pei, one of the nation's leading architects, is perhaps the most famous Chinese American, at least among non-Chinese. Several Chinese American women, including Amy Tan and Jade Snow Wong, are prominent novelists.[132] At the other

TABLE 11.2 OCCUPATIONAL DISTRIBUTION BY ASIAN AMERICAN GROUP

	CHINESE AMERICAN	FILIPINO AMERICAN	KOREAN AMERICAN	VIETNAMESE AMERICAN	ASIAN-INDIAN AMERICAN	WHITE AMERICAN
Managerial and professional specialty	35.8%	26.6%	25.5%	17.6%	43.6%	28.5%
Technical, sales, and administrative support	31.2	36.7	37.1	29.5	33.2	32.6
Precision production, craft, and repair	5.6	7.4	8.9	15.7	5.2	11.6
Operators, fabricators, and laborers	10.6	11.0	12.8	20.9	9.4	13.4
Service occupations	16.5	16.8	15.1	15.0	8.1	11.5
Farming, forestry, and fishing	0.4	1.5	0.7	1.4	0.6	2.4
Totals	100.1%	100.0%	100.1%	100.1%	100.1%	100.0%

end of the economic continuum, some 11 percent of Chinese American families lived below the poverty line in 1990.

Table 11.3 presents the most recent data available (1990) on income and poverty for the Asian American groups considered in this chapter and for white Americans.[133]

The median family income for Chinese Americans ($41,316 for all Chinese American families and $56,762 for the U.S.-born group) was higher than that of white families in 1990, and a larger percentage of Chinese American families reported incomes of $100,000 or more. Yet the proportion of Chinese American families living in poverty in 1990 was also greater than that of white families. The economic range is related to length of residence. U.S.-born Chinese Americans tend to be better educated, to hold managerial or professional jobs, and to live outside the so-called Chinatowns of the larger cities. In 1990 their poverty rate was only 3 percent. However, more recent immigrants tend to have less education, be unemployed or hold low-wage jobs, and live in inner cities. The 1990 poverty rate of this group was high—more than 20 percent.[134]

One study of Manhattan's Chinese American community revealed that the area did not fit the common image, sometimes seen on television crime shows such as "NYPD Blue," of an exotic urban zone with dangerous and mysterious "Orientals" and red light districts. Instead, it is peopled by hard-working Chinese Americans, many of them immigrants, who have created a booming local economy and enclave "that is the center of economic and social life for the Chinese population throughout the New York City metropolitan area."[135] Yet, this vital community periodically faces major redevelopment

TABLE 11.3 INCOME LEVEL BY ASIAN AMERICAN GROUP

	CHINESE AMERICAN	FILIPINO AMERICAN	KOREAN AMERICAN	VIETNAMESE AMERICAN	ASIAN-INDIAN AMERICAN	WHITE AMERICAN
Median family income	$41,316	$46,698	$33,909	$30,550	$49,309	$37,628
Percentage of families: with incomes of $100,000 or more	10	8	7	4	14	6
below poverty level	11	5	15	24	7	7

pressures from outside, such as when white officials who view the area in "exotic" terms propose redevelopment projects to "clean up" the area. The community is also shaped by the U.S. government's changing immigration policies and by cycles of investment by overseas Chinese investors.

The economic discrimination faced by Asian Americans takes many forms and affects consumers and businesses as well as workers. A recent study by Leland Saito examined the redevelopment of a shopping center in Monterey Park, which is now a majority Asian American community. The white minority forced an important redevelopment project to be done their way. "Rather than reflecting the city's current and future position as a major node for Asian-themed businesses, the shopping center was remodeled [with a Mediterranean design] to provide a place where whites could shop and 'feel at home.'"[136]

Filipino Americans

Filipinos were first recruited as farm workers for Hawaiian sugar plantations and West Coast farms. Most were single men who endured a grueling schedule and meager wages. In the early 1930s, thousands of Filipino American workers, constituting 40 percent of California's Salinas Valley agricultural work force, formed the Filipino Labor Union (FLU). An FLU-led strike of lettuce workers was met with violence from white growers supported by white police officers. Strikers eventually won wages of $.40 an hour and recognition of the union. "The FLU represented ... the entrance of Filipinos into the labor movement in America.... The involvement of the Filipinos in the labor movement reflected a changing consciousness—a sober recognition of shattered dreams and a new sense of ethnic unity."[137]

Military-related Filipino communities were created on the West Coast in the 1950s and 1960s, when the U.S. armed forces, especially the Navy, began recruiting Filipinos into its civilian workforce. For several decades U.S. hospitals have recruited Filipino nurses. Many Filipino scientists, engineers, and other professionals have emigrated because of political and economic crises at home.[138]

Table 11.2 shows a concentration of Filipino Americans in white-collar jobs, although they are less heavily represented in managerial and professional positions and more heavily represented in technical, sales, and administrative support jobs than Chinese Americans. Filipino Americans are more likely to hold service sector jobs and less likely to hold skilled blue-collar jobs than are whites. Significantly, the 1990 unemployment rate for Filipino Americans was lower than that of the general population.[139]

Filipino Americans have a relatively high median family income, one-third greater than the national average. The median family income for foreign-born Filipinos who arrived in the United States prior to 1980 is even higher. However, these figures are somewhat misleading because on average more family members work among Filipino Americans than among the general population, and most Filipino Americans work and live on the West Coast where wages and living costs are higher. This is generally the case for most Asian American groups.

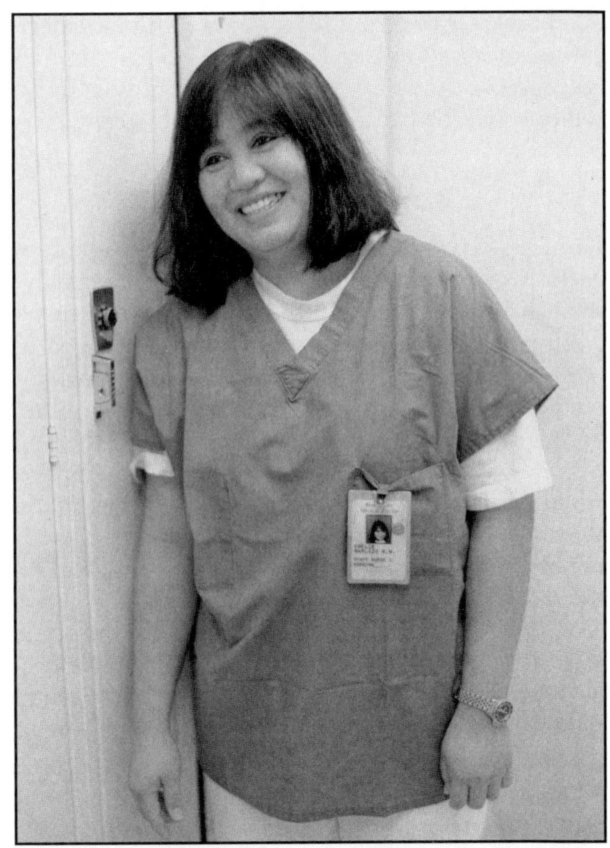

An example of the job discrimination faced by Filipino Americans is the Los Angeles hospital that prohibits its Filipino nurses from speaking their native language, even when they are on break.

Note too that Filipino Americans have the lowest family poverty rate of any Asian American group.

Filipino Americans have faced serious job discrimination, including language discrimination. A 1988 class action lawsuit filed with the Equal Employment Opportunity Commission charged that the San Francisco city government systematically discriminated against Filipino Americans. Statistical data cited in the suit indicated that Filipino Americans held only 1 percent of the city's administrative and supervisory positions although they made up 12 percent of the city's professional workers. The Filipino American organizations behind the lawsuit charged that whites in the city government stereotyped Filipino American professionals as incapable of leadership and penalized them because of their accents.[140] In 1991, a federal judge upheld a Los Angeles hospital's ban on speaking Tagalog, the native language of many Filipinos. The hospital prohibited its Filipino nurses from speaking Tagalog, even on their breaks. In Hawaii, a Filipino American unsuccessfully sued officials who discriminated against him by turning him down for a white-collar job because of his Filipino accent.[141]

Korean Americans

Language barriers and racial discrimination kept early Korean immigrants from obtaining employment in accordance with their abilities. The early-twentieth-century Korean immigrants engaged in hard physical labor for extremely low wages. Many, including professionals, worked as agricultural laborers or as dishwashers, houseboys, or janitors in urban areas. During World War I, a few opened small, family-operated shops, mainly in Hawaii. By World War II, Korean Americans owned approximately fifty small and medium-sized businesses on the mainland.[142]

Koreans arriving after 1965 have included some scientists and other professionals. A significant percentage have become entrepreneurs, starting small retail stores, often in low-income areas. Korean Americans have filled an important small-business niche in New York, Philadelphia, Los Angeles, and other large cities. In the early 1990s, about 17 percent of Korean American workers nationwide were self-employed, compared with 7 percent of the general population.[143] Surveys of Korean American small-business owners have found that few had been small-business owners in Korea; most had held white-collar jobs in their homeland.[144]

As we noted earlier, many immigrants have been forced into self-employment because of *exclusion* from professions for which they were trained. Limited English proficiency is one factor, but overt anti-Asian discrimination is also significant. Korean Americans who hold white-collar jobs are often passed over for promotions, especially to higher management ranks, regardless of language skills. Several news reports have recently indicated that some managers and professionals have moved back to Korea where their skills allow them to move up the corporate ladders.[145]

Given these barriers, many Korean Americans prefer the freedom and dignity afforded by self-employment. Recent Korean immigrants have arrived at a time when earlier immigrant groups are moving out of the inner-city small-business niche into white-collar jobs. Many female immigrants have little knowledge of spoken English, and thus their main employment option is a family business. Indeed, one of the dramatic changes brought by international immigration is the greatly increased participation of Korean women in the workforce, often as unpaid workers in family businesses. This increased participation has had some impact on the strong patriarchal values, associated with Confucian thought, that Korean immigrants brought with them from Korea. These new roles for Korean American women have often "reduced their husbands' patriarchal authority, creating new sources of marital conflict and sometimes leading to separation and divorce."[146]

Many Korean immigrants arrived with some capital, and they often have the support of the larger Asian American community, including Asian American banks. One Los Angeles survey found that those merchants whose customers are primarily black or Latino earn more than those whose customers are primarily white. Many of these merchants take the money they earn in low-income communities and move out to middle-class areas. As we have seen, black resentment over Korean merchants taking money out of the black community has contributed to the hostility many black urbanites feel toward Korean American entrepreneurs in their areas.[147] Researchers have found a high degree of geographic mobility among Korean Americans in Los Angeles. Many live for only a short time in a heavily Korean inner-city area before moving to a suburb.[148]

Table 11.2 (on page 310) shows that Korean Americans are somewhat less likely to hold professional and managerial jobs and more likely to hold technical, sales, and administrative support jobs than whites. Korean Americans are more likely to be in service occupations and less likely to hold skilled blue-collar jobs than whites. In 1990 the unemployment rate for Korean Americans was well below that of the general population. The 1990 median family income for Korean Americans ($33,909) was also below the white median ($37,628). Korean Americans have the second-highest poverty rate of the groups considered here.[149]

Vietnamese Americans

Vietnamese Americans have a relatively short economic history in the United States. Those who came immediately after the fall of Saigon were often more affluent and better educated than those who came later. Some immigrants had been in business in their home country. However, after immigration, many immigrants suffered downward occupational mobility. One survey found that more than six in ten immigrants with white-collar jobs in Vietnam held blue-collar jobs in the United States. The remainder held white-collar jobs, primarily clerical or sales work. Professionals also experienced downward mobility.[150]

Vietnamese Americans still face overt discrimination. In the 1990s, one large convenience store chain settled a class action lawsuit charging that one of its managers had ordered discrimination against Vietnamese American employees. Two supervisors reported that in the mid-1980s they had been told to fire Vietnamese workers and hire whites. In the settlement, the company agreed to hire more Vietnamese American managers. Soon, however, the employees of the chain were back in court protesting continuing discrimination in some company stores in the 1990s.[151]

Many later Vietnamese immigrants have faced low-wage jobs and poverty in the United States. They have not been as economically successful as earlier arrivals.[152] As we see in Table 11.2, in the early 1990s, Vietnamese Americans held professional or managerial positions at half the rate of Chinese Americans; they held about the same proportion of technical, sales, and administrative support positions as well as service-sector jobs as did Chinese Americans. Vietnamese Americans held the highest proportion of blue-collar jobs of any of the Asian groups in this chapter. More than half held blue-collar or service jobs. This occupational situation was reflected in the median family income ($30,550), which was substantially below that of European Americans ($37,628) and other Asian groups (see Table 11.3 on page 310). Nearly one-fourth of Vietnamese American families fell below the poverty line. In 1990 the unemployment rate was one-third higher than the national average and the highest of any Asian group considered in this chapter.[153] The socioeconomic status of many Vietnamese Americans has been lower than it was before immigration. As with other Asian Americans, discrimination in business and the job market still remains a problem to the present day.

Asian-Indian Americans

Most of the nation's more than 1.6 million Asian-Indian Americans have roots in recent immigration. Most have not settled in pre-existing communities on the West Coast like other Asian immigrants, but rather have created new neighborhoods, mostly in East Coast cities. Many have brought substantial monetary capital and cultural capital in the form of college educations and professional training. Today, the majority are white-collar workers or business people. The rate of creation of Asian-Indian American businesses has been twice that for the nation as a whole. In the 1990s, Asian-Indian Americans owned 93,000 businesses, compared with 153,000 businesses owned by Chinese Americans and 68,000 by Japanese Americans. Most have been in retail trade or the services.[154]

Since the late 1980s, many skilled Asian-Indian immigrants have gone to California, especially to the high-tech Silicon Valley. Many have prospered in the economic boom there, but some have been hurt by the high-tech downturn since the early 2000s. Those with limited work visas have had to return to India, which many have considered a disgrace. Others have scrounged for low-wage jobs in order to remain in the United States.[155]

Asian-Indian Americans have by far the largest proportion of college graduates and professional and managerial employees of all Asian–Pacific American groups (see Table 11.2 on page 310). The proportions are much higher than for whites. In the early 1990s, they also had the second-highest median family income among Asian Americans (after Japanese Americans). Still, all in this group have not achieved economic success; in the same year, 7 percent of families were below the poverty level.[156] Certainly, the large numbers of less well-educated Asian-Indian immigrants in Silicon Valley, who tend to hold service jobs such as taxi drivers and restaurant workers, have had a much harder economic struggle in recent years than most of the Asian-Indian American professionals who work in this same region.[157]

EDUCATION

In earlier decades, Chinese, Japanese, and other Asian American children were often segregated in separate schools. A 1927 decision by the U.S. Supreme Court, for example, upheld the state of Mississippi's segregation of children of the "Mongolian race." This racial segregation began to break down after World War II, but de facto school segregation persisted in many cities because discriminatory housing covenants kept Asian Americans out of white housing areas.[158] Still, this overt racial discrimination did not keep Asian Americans from pressing hard for better educational opportunities for their children.

High Achievement amid Persisting Problems

Most Asian American groups place heavy stress on educational success. Over the past decade Asian American students have often been overrepresented among students doing well in various science competitions, such as the Westinghouse scholars program. However welcome these prizes are to the student winners, they are a mixed blessing for Asian Americans as a group. Winning science competitions has served to reinforce popular stereotypes of Asian Americans as "naturally" gifted in science and technical fields. Asian Americans have often criticized such "model minority" stereotypes, pointing out that many Asian Americans excel in areas other than the natural sciences. Being stereotyped as especially high achievers also puts a great burden on Asian American students who are not at the top of their class. In addition, many Asian American children, especially poorer children, do not have well-funded educational environments. Yet the "model" stereotype reduces the likelihood of government action to meet their needs.

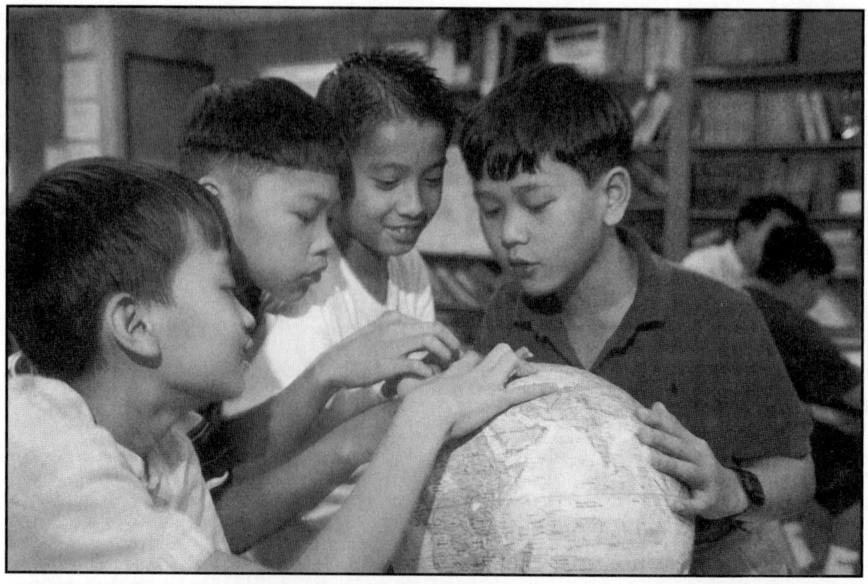

In Austin, Texas, Vietnamese American children work on their geography lesson.

Some Asian Americans, particularly youth growing up in predominantly white suburbs, come to accept these stereotypes themselves. Some Asian American youth may come to view themselves or their group in terms of the white-crafted model minority imagery because it appears to be only positive. These young people do not yet understand the ideological purpose for which this stereotyped imagery was created by whites, and their acceptance of it may limit their own opportunities and life choices, as well as their ability to work with Americans of color in coalitions against discrimination.[159]

Many immigrant children, along with some American-born children of recent immigrants, face problems of limited English proficiency and the shock of an unfamiliar culture when they enter public schools. Non-Asian teachers and administrators are often ignorant of Asian cultures and insensitive to the needs of these students. Some non-Asian teachers have also been unwilling to protect Asian American students from mistreatment by non-Asian students. In addition, many from Southeast Asia still have vivid memories of the horrors of war in their homeland; for many, a war-generated post-traumatic stress syndrome may also interfere with success in school.

In the 1990s, the U.S. Civil Rights Commission reported that only a small proportion of limited-English-proficiency Asian American students had teachers who spoke their native languages, despite the legal obligation of public schools to help students develop English proficiency. Contrary to media stories, recent immigrants not proficient in English frequently have low grades and high dropout rates. A study of San Diego high-school students found that Vietnamese, Cambodian, and Pacific Islander students had higher dropout rates than white students.[160]

A late 1990s report of the organization Asian-American/Pacific Islanders in Philanthropy showed that only 1.2 percent of teachers in U.S. schools were Asian American. Yet 3.2 percent of the children in these schools were Asian American. School authorities often have shown little concern for these children's language problems or for the hostility they receive from non-Asian children.[161] Indeed, public schools have been settings for substantial hostility and violence against Asian Americans.

One 1990s report examined Asian American and Pacific Islander students in urban and suburban New England schools. More than half of the respondents in a survey of 266 students reported that they had been called names or racially harassed, and nine in ten had seen others being harassed. One-fourth had been attacked; more than half had seen other Asian and Pacific American students being attacked. Not surprisingly, many of those harassed had considered dropping out.[162] Hate crimes are also common on college campuses. Recently, at the University of California (Davis), a group of whites, including students, beat up five Korean American students while spouting racist epithets.[163]

Educational Attainment

Many observers have noted the fact that as a group Asian Americans have a higher educational level than the population as a whole. They are almost twice as likely to have a college degree as the average American.[164] This figure is misleading, however, because of wide variations *among* the Asian American groups as well as *within* each group. Using the latest available data (1990) for persons over twenty-four years of age, Table 11.4 compares the educational attainment of the five groups in

TABLE 11.4 EDUCATIONAL ATTAINMENT BY ASIAN AMERICAN GROUP

	CHINESE AMERICAN	FILIPINO AMERICAN	KOREAN AMERICAN	VIETNAMESE AMERICAN	ASIAN-INDIAN AMERICAN	WHITE AMERICAN	TOTAL POPULATION
Less than 5 years of school completed	9.4%	4.2%	4.6%	11.4%	3.8%	1.3%	2.7%
High-school graduate or more	73.6	82.6	80.2	61.2	84.7	79.1	75.2
Bachelor's degree or more	40.7	39.3	34.5	17.4	58.1	22.0	20.3

this chapter with that of whites and with the total population.[165]

Vietnamese Americans ranked the lowest in educational attainment. They were the only Asian American group to fall below the national percentage for college completion. While Chinese Americans fell slightly below the national percentage for high-school graduation, the rate at which this group completed college was double the national rate. Asian-Indian and Filipino Americans are much more likely to have graduated from college than the general population. Note the wide variation *within* Asian American groups. The proportion with less than a fifth-grade education is higher for all Asian American groups than for the total population.

Various explanations have been offered to explain Asian American success in education. Some observers argue that it is rooted in Asian cultures' traditional reverence for learning or in strong family support. In one national Educational Testing Service poll of Asian-Indian high-school seniors, every student said parents had pressed them to secure a college degree.[166] However, other groups also have high expectations for their youth. Yet, other analysts have noted the significant educational benefits that bilingualism brings to those Asian Americans who learned English at a young age. In addition, many Asian Americans aggressively pursue education as a weapon against anti-Asian prejudice and discrimination; educational effort has become part of an oppositional culture in which education is viewed as a family rather than individual achievement.

Asian American achievement is often compared, especially by whites, with that of African American and Latino achievements. However, this comparison is problematical. As a group Asian American students have greater access to educational institutions, such as those in California cities, that facilitate economic and educational mobility better than the schools attended by many black and Latino students in southern or southwestern states. Even though most Asian American students reside in large metropolitan areas, they are not as likely as other students of color to be segregated from white middle class students, whose schools typically have first-rate facilities.

Nonetheless, continuing discrimination in the job market has kept many Asian Americans from achieving the economic success that they might have expected based on their abilities and relatively high educational achievements.[167]

Controversy in Higher Education

In recent decades some elite colleges and universities have reportedly discriminated against Asian American applicants. For example, Ivy League universities began admitting a large percentage of Asian American applicants in the 1970s, but acceptance rates often dropped as the number of Asian American applications increased. Critics accused some universities of using such nonacademic pretexts as lack of alumni parents and the necessity for a regional distribution to exclude Asian American students.[168]

For example, the proportion of Asian Americans among the students admitted at Brown University rose from 2.6 percent for the class of 1979 to 14.8 percent for the class of 1993, although the proportion of Asian American applicants admitted fluctuated between 14 percent and 41 percent during this period. Studying the sharp drop in the proportion of Asian applicants admitted between 1982 and 1983, investigators found that the admissions staff had assigned comparatively low nonacademic ratings to Asian American applicants and had sought to hold steady the number of Asian American students admitted, even though their applicant pool had tripled. The Brown administration then took action to ensure that the percentage of qualified Asian American applicants admitted would not fall below the percentage of qualified non-Asian applicants.[169] Both Harvard and Yale have faced similar charges of discrimination against Asian American applicants.

FULL ASSIMILATION FOR ASIAN AMERICANS?

Assimilation Views

The influential assimilation theorist Milton Gordon argued that his assimilation theory applied to a wide range of ethnic and racial groups. While Gordon did not apply his assimilation scheme to Asian Americans, other assimilation-oriented analysts have argued that most Asian American groups are on their way to full integration into the core society—at least at the dominant-culture level and at the secondary-structural level in terms of job placement. Assimilation-oriented analysts tend to be optimistic about the eventual, and thorough-going, assimilation of Asian American groups, including full incorporation into the American middle class.

Numerous assimilation-oriented analysts have underscored Asian American progress in economic integration. Sociologist Talcott Parsons argued that racial and ethnic inclusion is a basic, powerful, and ongoing process in U.S. society, and this includes Americans of color (see Chapter 2). Numerous scholarly analysts of Asian Americans argue that anti-Asian discrimination is collapsing and assimilation into the dominant institutions is well underway. Some media analysts of Filipino Americans have argued similarly: "With a command of English, light brown skin, and Spanish-sounding names, Filipinos have few problems assimilating into American society," asserted James T. Madore, a reporter for the *Christian Science Monitor*.[170] Not surprisingly, many assimilation-oriented analysts view Filipino and other Asian Americans as "model minorities." In their view, a non-European group has succeeded when its economic attainments, measured by the quantitative socioeconomic indicators of occupation, education, and income, are comparable to those of the dominant white group.[171]

Interestingly, the National Asian Pacific American Bar Association (NAPABA) opposed Supreme Court nominee Clarence Thomas at his 1991 Senate confirmation hearings, challenging Thomas's publicly asserted image of Asian Americans as "model minorities." Thomas argued that Asian Americans "transcended the ravages caused even by harsh legal and social discrimination" and should not be the beneficiaries of affirmative action because they are "overrepresented in key institutions." The NAPABA pointed out the racial hostility and discrimination still faced by many Asian Americans. In their experienced view, affirmative action programs have been critical to Asian American workers' employment in historically white job categories.[172]

Recall Kitano and Daniels' assimilation model, discussed in Chapter 10, that distinguishes three major types of group adaptation: (1) high assimilation, low ethnic identity; (2) high assimilation, high ethnic identity; and (3) low assimilation, high ethnic identity. In this view Asian Americans who fall into the high assimilation/low ethnic identity category are more "core American" than they are Asian. Their language, lifestyle, and expectations are more like those of whites, and their traditional culture is mostly forgotten. High rates of marriage to non-Asians occur in this group. While a significant (although still modest) proportion of Japanese Americans seem to fall into this category of assimilation, the proportions for the groups in this chapter appear to be smaller.

Those Asian Americans in the high assimilation/high ethnic identity category differ from those in the first because they retain a strong group identity. They move easily in and out of both cultures, and their friendship patterns and interests reflect a bicultural perspective. They are usually comfortable with their identity, and they resist persisting discrimination. A significant proportion of Filipino and Asian-Indian Americans appear to fall into this category. Yet even they remain substantially bicultural. One scholar has suggested that Asian-Indian children are constantly operating in two cultures. According to Marcia Mogelonsky, most speak English well and are influenced by American pop music and movies, yet they also watch Indian movies and often "follow the ways of their elders when it comes to such traditions as marriage and child-rearing." Most Asian-Indian American young people have a strong sense of their group identity.[173]

A study of Chinese and Japanese Americans, mentioned in Chapter 10, found that those in the third or fourth generation were often highly oriented to mainstream, white middle-class cultural styles. They were very assimilated culturally and retained little traditional culture. However, most of these culturally assimilated Asian Americans still had a strong sense of group identity. One reason is that many whites expect them to accept and accent their Asian identity. Unlike white ethnics such as Italian or Polish Americans, Asian Americans do not have a choice, for their racial-ethnic position is constantly imposed on them by whites and other outsiders who ask repeatedly, "What are you?" or "Where are you from?" Answers such as "American" or "New York City" often anger these questioners.[174]

Asian Americans in Kitano and Daniels's third major category, low assimilation/high group identity, are usually recent immigrants or those who have spent most of their lives in traditional urban enclaves. Most have made some adaptations to the dominant culture but prefer their own communities. They typically form friendship and marriage bonds within their own group.[175] Many if not most recent Korean and Vietnamese immigrants fall into this category. A significant proportion of recent Filipino and Chinese immigrants also seem modestly assimilated at the cultural level but firmly rooted culturally and socially in their communities.[176] Moreover, tensions between recent immigrants and the native-born are often seen in many Asian American communities. Immigrants in some Chinese American communities mockingly call the native-born "ABCs" (American-born Chinese). New immigrants criticize ABCs' lack of touch with traditional Chinese culture. In return, native-born Chinese and other Asian Americans sometimes call the new immigrants "FOBs" (fresh off boats) and mock their traditional ways.[177]

A 1989 survey of Vietnamese American adults in Orange County found that the Vietnamese language was dominant in 83 percent of households. Two-thirds said that their families remained strongly Vietnamese in customs and traditions, and most of the rest said they were somewhat involved in traditional culture. Three-fourths reported regular contact with relatives and friends in Vietnam.[178] Yet, many were also concerned about accelerating group acculturation. One-third said the greatest community need was more English classes—the largest percentage for any community need noted. They expressed a strong desire to master English in order to acculturate and advance economically.[179]

As in other Asian American communities, generational conflicts are increasingly conspicuous. A recent southern California poll found that, after crime, assimilation was considered the most serious problem facing the Vietnamese American community. In recent years, Vietnamese American parents have complained that their children have given up the Vietnamese language, are not interested in entering the family business, and often move from old neighborhoods. For their part, young Vietnamese Americans today refer to the conflict in the hyphenated term "Vietnamese-American" as "riding the hyphen."[180] Recently a group of Vietnamese American leaders in Garden Grove, California met to establish an institute of Vietnamese studies that will offer courses in the Vietnamese language and history. One of this institute's unstated purposes is to combat what is viewed as the too-rapid assimilation of the younger generation. Southern California's Vietnamese-language radio and television programs also help to keep Vietnamese culture and language alive.[181]

Most first-generation Korean immigrants are also committed to their language and culture and to maintaining close ties to relatives, and they have built strong institutions within their communities. In "Koreatown," in Los Angeles, Korean Americans have created many important institutions, including newspapers, schools, an orchestra, and churches.[182] Religion has often facilitated the adjustment of many Koreans. South Korea has one of the largest Protestant populations of any Asian nation, and many Korean immigrants come to this country as Christians. These immigrants have established many new churches, which typically combine Western practices with Korean ceremonies and Korean-language services.[183]

A recent study by Karen Pyke examined the views that seventy-three children of Korean and Vietnamese immigrants had of their family life. Most accepted the dominant U.S. conception of the "normal" American family as their framework. They often criticized their parents as too strict or emotionally distant and thought the latter should more closely resemble the "normal" family. These children had assimilated the dominant view of the favored family style. However, when they discussed plans for taking care of their parents in later life, they expressed strong traditional Korean and Vietnamese values and described their parents' family practices in positive terms. They retained important filial values drawn from their parents' culture of origin. The adaptation pattern for these children of Asian immigrants blends aspects of the culture of origin with aspects of the dominant U.S. culture, as is suggested by Greeley's ethnogenesis perspective.[184]

Many Asian-Indian Americans are well integrated into the dominant culture. They know English well, and many families reside in predominantly white neighborhoods, where the children spend much time with white teachers and students. The majority of Asian-Indian adults work in predominantly white settings. Most have adopted key aspects of the European American core culture. One recent study of 629 first-generation Asian-Indian Americans found that most came from urban areas in India and were already exposed to many aspects of U.S. culture through the mass media. The majority spoke English well. The group as a whole scored in the middle range on a cultural assimilation scale that included language use and music, food, and media preferences.[185] Yet, most families also maintain essential aspects of traditional culture. The majority still marry within the group. Asian-Indian Americans have also built numerous Hindu temples in U.S. cities. For example, the Hindu temple in Silicon Valley opened in a warehouse in 1994 with 380 families, but with immigration had grown to 4800 families by 2001.[186] Asian-Indian Americans are highly acculturated on some dimensions of adaptation and highly Indian on other dimensions. They are indeed straddling two cultures.

One sign of the generally slower overall assimilation of most Asian–Pacific groups in this chapter, compared with the assimilation rate for Japanese Americans, may be their lower outmarriage rates to non-Asians. The most recent data (1990) show relatively high outmarriage rates to whites for California's younger-generation Japanese Americans—27 percent for men and 30 percent for women. The rates of outmarriage to whites are generally lower for the younger adults in four other Asian American groups discussed in this chapter: Chinese Americans, 16 percent (men) and 17 percent (women); Filipino Americans, 16 and 29 percent; Korean Americans, 6 and 16 percent; and Vietnamese Americans, 9 and 11 percent. Assimilation with whites at this key primary-structural level is still moderate for these Asian American groups.[187]

Significantly, a recent analysis of these census data found that, in California, *interethnic* marriages (within the Asian American umbrella group) are increasing to the point that they now exceed interracial marriages (outside the umbrella group) for almost all generations in the major Asian American groups. In California, 71 percent of all Asian American and Pacific Islander (the data include small numbers of Pacific Islanders) men had married inside their own Asian American group; 18 percent married someone in another Asian American group, 3 percent married a black or Latino, and only 8 percent married a white person. For all Asian American women, 64 percent had married someone from their own group and another 16 percent married someone from another Asian American group. Three percent married a black or Latino man, and 16 percent married a white man. Women are thus somewhat more likely to intermarry than men. Perhaps surprisingly, 89 percent of men and 80 percent of women married *within* the Asian American group.[188]

Public discussion of intermarriage may exaggerate the rate, for most Asian American marriages in the key state of California are within the Asian American umbrella group, and, most importantly, the rate of marriage within the Asian American group has grown in recent years. As we noted in Chapter 10, this is in part because of the larger population of Asian Americans, especially on the West Coast, and, perhaps more importantly, because of the growing racial consciousness among Asian Americans, especially in regard to their continuing discriminatory treatment at the hands of whites and others just because they are Asian.[189]

Nazli Kibria has used the ethnogenesis model to assess the adaptations of Asian groups to each other. Her research on second-generation middle-class Chinese and Korean Americans revealed what she terms a Pan-Asian ethnogenesis. Members of each second-generation group are developing a sense of a shared Asian American identity in addition to their own group identities. The construction of this Asian American identity is a "process that involves recognition of the shared personal experiences and orientations of Asian-origin persons, including that of being racially labeled as Asian by the dominant society, of growing up in an Asian home, and of adhering to the Asian values of an emphasis on family, education, hard work, and respect for elders."[190] Being defined as racially different plays a significant role in the shaping of this Asian American identity. Racial consciousness is particularly strong on the West Coast, with its recent history of anti-immigrant political campaigns, hate crimes, and white flight.[191]

Some Questions from a Power-Conflict Perspective

Power-conflict analysts of Asian Americans reject optimistic assimilationist perspectives, including the model minorities imagery. Among other things, the model minority view ignores the origins of many Asian immigrants who came as middle-class immigrants with good educations and some capital. It also exaggerates Asian American progress and downplays continuing problems with racial discrimination.[192]

The image of Asian immigrants is often one of poor immigrants working their way up by dint of hard work. However, while they were certainly hardworking, the majority of the Asian immigrants that came between the mid-1960s and the mid-1970s were middle-class with white-collar backgrounds. Their monetary capital or educational backgrounds often enabled them to establish themselves as middle-class Americans and to provide advantages for their children. In contrast, the Asian immigrants who came after the mid-1970s included more working-class people, many of whom secured low-wage jobs in the needlework and electronic assembly industries. Asian Americans, "particularly immigrant Asian workers, have a highly visible position in both ends" of the economy. "Despite the fact that a large number of Asian Americans are successful, a disproportionate number of Asian Americans are poor."[193]

Recall from Chapter 10 that, in response to black and Latino American protesting in the 1960s, some whites developed the model minority stereotype to suggest that all Americans of color could achieve the American dream not by protesting discrimination but simply by working as hard as Asian Americans. This negative assessment of African Americans is illustrated in a 1966 *U.S. News & World Report* article entitled "Success Story of One Minority Group in U.S." that compared Chinese Americans and African Americans. By praising the hard work, thrift, and morality of Chinese Americans, the article implied that if black Americans possessed these virtues, it would not be necessary to spend "hundreds of billions to uplift" them. The article omitted any mention of the widespread racial discrimination suffered by African Americans.[194]

Power-conflict analysts have shown how, over centuries, white Americans have positioned non-European groups in the hierarchical framework of racial oppression. As we saw in Chapter 2, the earliest and most fundamental of the racial oppressions generated within the early colonies themselves, and later within the new United States, targeted the enslaved African Americans brought in to do hard labor to build up white wealth. Later on, white employers brought other non-European groups, such as Mexican, Chinese, Japanese, and Filipino immigrants, into the United States as low-wage labor. Whites have usually judged and evaluated these later non-European immigrants and their descendants from within the earlier, well-established framework of white-on-black oppression, a framework with a strong ideology of white cultural and social superiority. New immigrant groups of color are placed, principally by dominant whites, somewhere in the long-established white-to-black hierarchy of exploitation and social status. In white practice and in white minds, the white rung of this hierarchy is the superior, privileged, and preferred rung, while the black rung is the most inferior, impoverished, and denigrated rung.[195]

At certain times in U.S. history, whites have elevated some Asian Americans, as individuals or as groups, to an intermediate rung in this white-to-black hierarchy of status. At least in their images of contemporary society, white leaders and the white public place certain non-Europeans groups in an intermediate, or even near-white, status. This helps to maintain an intact but flexible racist system. For example, when white commentators, analysts, and politicians write or say positive things about the success of selected Asian American groups, they usually single out those who are most white-oriented and acculturated. They point to achievements of groups like middle-class Japanese Americans and Asian-Indian Americans to suggest that Asian Americans are working harder and thereby succeeding better than black or Latino Americans.[196]

Some power-conflict analysts note that at earlier points in U.S. history, most Asian Americans were placed on or near the bottom rung of the racial hierarchy for intensive exploitation and were thus typed negatively as black or near-black in status. Chinese American scholar Frank Wu has noted how various racially oppressed people, such as Asian Americans, have often been seen as "constructive blacks," at or near the black end of the racist hierarchy.[197]

Today, in contrast, certain Asian American groups are publicly constructed as "nearer-to-white," but once again generally to serve white purposes. Given this construction, whites can then move to criticize African or Latino Americans for not being like the Asian American model minorities in efforts and achievements. However, as Gary Okihiro has noted, historically whites have "upheld Asians as 'near-whites' or 'whiter than whites' in the model minority stereotype, and yet Asians experienced and continue to face white racism 'like blacks' in educational and occupational barriers and ceilings and in anti-Asian abuse and physical violence.... This ... 'disciplines' both Africans and Asians and constitutes the essential site of Asian American oppression."[198] In addition, the model minority perspective obscures the problems and needs of those many Asian Americans who face continuing discrimination, stereotyping, and poverty. Recent studies have shown that many Southeast Asian immigrants, especially those from rural backgrounds with little education, have experienced severe economic strain from the 1980s to the present. Instead of dealing with these difficult socioeconomic realities, the mass media often celebrate particular Asian American individuals who have been highly successful, even portraying them in Horatio Alger "rags to riches" terms. For example. Chang-Lin Tien, the distinguished former chancellor of the University of California (Berkeley) is portrayed as a poor immigrant who came to the United States at age twenty-one without knowing English. What is less often noted is that he was from a wealthy Chinese family with close ties to the pre-Communist ruler of China, Chiang Kai Shek. Numerous other leading Asian Americans have also come from families with substantial economic or educational resources.[199]

Indeed, given the variation in assimilation among Asian groups and subgroups, the segmented assimilation view of analysts such as Min Zhou seems appropriate. Those Asian immigrants with greater family and group resources, such as the affluent or elite Chinese immigrants, generally have had a different experience adapting to U.S. culture and society than those with fewer resources, such as the many working class Vietnamese and Hmong immigrants.[200]

The secondary-structural integration of many Asian Americans into the U.S. economy is not as untroubled as optimistic assimilation analysts suggest. Many still suffer discrimination in employment and educational institutions. We have noted the informal quotas sometimes used to reduce Asian American participation, such as those at some universities in the past decade or two. Once in an historically white institution, moreover, many Asian Americans report an array of blatant and subtle barriers that are thrown in their paths. In employment settings, for example, many find that the jobs available are not as good as what their credentials should have secured. Asian Americans tend to excel in their college studies, but many receive a lower rate of return on their educational investment than whites do. In addition, although many are hired by major companies, many also find that promotions to higher management levels are unlikely.[201]

Optimistic assimilation analysts rarely discuss the continuing problems of anti-Asian violence in U.S. society. Few pay sufficient attention to the continuing racial violence and profiling that handicap Asian Americans and affect long-term assimilation probabilities. Many non-Asian Americans still view Asian Americans in racial terms and as "mud people" or non-American foreigners. We have seen recent violence on both coasts, such as the killing of Joseph Ileto in California, and the attacks on Asian-Indian Americans in New Jersey cities. Asian-bashing has increased since the 1990s.

Recall too the study of third- and later-generation Chinese and Japanese Americans noted earlier. Even though most are culturally assimilated, most also have a strong sense of their group identity. This is in part because many whites constantly impose the identity of "oriental" or "foreigner" on them. Many whites, even recent immigrants, often view them in racialized terms—as somehow not "real Americans." A power-conflict analyst might suggest that for this reason it is unlikely that most Asian Americans will soon be absorbed into the white middle-class mainstream. As Mia Tuan has noted, "Generations of highly acculturated Asian ethnics who speak without an accent have lived in this country, and yet most white Americans have not heard of or ever really seen them. They are America's invisible citizenry."[202]

Asian Americans have long struggled to protect their civil rights and growing political power. In 1992, for example, the Asian American Legal Defense Fund fought hard for an extension of the 1965 Voting Rights Act in order to protect the right of non-English speakers to bilingual election materials. White senators argued that Asian American voters needed no protection, even though the Senate itself included no Asian Americans from the forty-eight mainland states. In addition, in 1997 the confirmation of Bill Lann Lee, a brilliant Chinese American lawyer, as assistant attorney general was blocked by conservative white senators who disagreed with his moderate views on affirmative action. From the perspective of most Asian Americans, the struggle over power and resources continues, and full inclusion in U.S. society is still far from being realized.[203]

SUMMARY

Many Korean, Filipino, Asian-Indian, and Vietnamese Americans—and the newest Chinese Americans—are among the most recent of the immigrant additions to the bubbling cauldron that is the United States. Yet, as with immigrants before them, they have been targets of much racial and ethnic prejudice, hostility, and violence. In general, their socioeconomic success has been so significant that they have been stereotyped as model minorities. Some who portray Asian Americans in this way have had the ulterior motive of criticizing certain non-Asian groups, such as African and Latino Americans, for their alleged deficiencies. Numerous assimilation-oriented social scientists are inclined to focus on Asian American progress but to downplay persisting problems of discrimination and poverty.

In contrast, from a power-conflict perspective, an Asian American group has not achieved complete success until it can participate fully in the mainstream of the economy, politics, and society without paying higher social, material, and psychological costs than the dominant white group for that participation. No Asian American group has attained comfortable equality with the oldest white immigrant groups, such as English and German Americans. As physically distinguishable groups, Asian Americans have remained disadvantaged and have experienced economic problems, recurrent hostility and racial discrimination, and only modest recent gains in political power.[204]

Since the 1980s, immigration has taken "a central position on the American social agenda" and much talk has focused on regaining "control of U.S. borders."[205] Much white opposition to immigration seems to go beyond the question of immigrants taking jobs to the issue of their racial characteristics, since most recent immigrants have been Asian and Latin American. Recent Asian immigrants continue to be the victims of anti-Asian stereotyping, some of which suggests that they are a new "yellow peril."

Yet, Asian and Latino immigrants are at the heart of what makes U.S. society great. They are the ones who have supplied much of the energetic imagination and new labor necessary as the older immigrant groups and their descendants age. The hard work and abilities of these new immigrants have helped to make the United States a vigorous nation, yet one that is still very much in the making. The new-immigrant dimension of this process has helped the United States, time and again, to surge out of economic and social stagnation into new societal developments and enhanced creativity.

12 Arab Americans

MOST AMERICANS ARE NOT AWARE OF THE FACT THAT EUROPEAN CIVILIZATION WAS heavily influenced and shaped by the advanced Arab cultures of the tenth to the twelfth centuries. In that early period, Arab scholars made critical breakthroughs in mathematics, such as the development of the place-value decimal system, well before European scholars. They also made major contributions to the development of the sciences, such as optics and medicine, and to seafaring. They were the first to develop the compass. Much knowledge developed by these Arab scholars was later imported into European civilizations.[1]

The widespread use of the Arabic language indicates just how far the Arab empire once spread. Today, Arabic is a language spoken by more than 300 million people, the seventh most commonly spoken language across the world. It is spoken in the Middle East and north Africa, Malta, and Sicily, and was spoken in Spain for several centuries prior to 1500. In addition, modern Persian (in Iran) and Urdu (in Pakistan and India) are written in Arabic script, which is also used in some areas of China, Russia, and the Philippines.[2] From the eight century to the fifteenth century, during the years of the Moorish domination, Arab Islamic culture was especially influential in Spain, and thus in the important Spanish diaspora across the globe.

From this Moorish period and other avenues of Arabic influence, an estimated 2,400 Arabic-origin words and place-names have found their way into the contemporary English language. These include words such as algebra, almanac, camel, chemistry, cipher, coffee, cotton, jar, mattress, nadir, orange, sofa, syrup, and zero. These words often reveal what was borrowed from Arabic sources, such as from the sciences and commerce, but only hint at the large-scale impact of Arabic civilization on European and American societies.[3]

Today the Arab World ranges from Mauritania and Morocco in western North Africa to Iraq and Saudi Arabia in what is now termed the *Middle East*. It includes those countries that are part of the League of Arab States, those with the Arabic language and cultures. (We should note that some countries in the Middle East, such as Turkey and Iran, are *not* Arab states, although they do have large Muslim populations.) While many Americans with origins in the Arab World consider themselves to be Arab Americans, others from these areas—such as some Lebanese Maronites, Coptic Americans, Armenians, and Chaldean Americans—often do not. They prefer instead to accent their ethno-religious origins.[4]

Since 1980 most people with their origins in the Arab World have coalesced under the rubric Arab Americans, an umbrella term that has gained wider use and acceptance relatively recently. There was cooperation and interaction between the various Middle Eastern communities prior to 1980, such as in facilitating the development of Middle Eastern businesses in U.S. cities. Yet, prior to the Arab–Israeli conflicts of the 1960s, most immigrants from Arab countries usually identified themselves by religion, village, nation state, or family. After these important conflicts, a stronger pan-Arab identity developed across the numerous groups. This umbrella Arab American identity is also a political reaction to the stereotyping of Arab peoples in the United States and to a perceived anti-Arab tilt by the U.S. government in Middle Eastern conflicts. Numerous pan-Arab organizations, including the National Association of Arab Americans, the Arab American Institute, and the Arab American University Graduates, have been created since the 1960s conflicts.[5]

We should note that this pan-Arab sentiment and orientation are not unique to the United States, nor have they only arisen in recent decades. The concept of pan-Arabism initially developed in the early twentieth century and grew during the 1950s, especially under Gamal Abdel Nasser of Egypt. Even with the political, religious, and cultural differences in the Middle East and in the United States, a strong Arab identity continues to exist in both areas.

According to the 1990 census, about half of Arab Americans are Lebanese, while the next largest percentage is Syrian. This chapter focuses on Arab Americans. However, we should be clear that not all Americans who are from Muslim countries are Arab Americans, and not all Arab Americans are Muslim. There are an estimated 6 million Muslim Americans in the United States, at least half of whom are not Arab American. There are an estimated 2–3 million Arab Americans, including those of both Christian and Muslim backgrounds. The actual numbers are not known, in part because the U.S. census has no Arab American category. Indeed, the Arab American Institute and other groups have criticized the Census Bureau for not including a census category for Arab Americans.

MIGRATION

The Early Period

Many Arab Americans are immigrants or children of immigrants. There have been two major periods of immigration from Arab areas and countries to the United States—one from 1880 to 1945, and a second migration from 1946 to the present.

Between 1880 and World War II, the first immigrants entered in modest numbers. They were primarily Christians from rural villages who, like most recent immigrants, viewed the United States as a land of economic opportunity. Many planned to make some money and return home, a type of "sojourner immigration." They were generally from what was then Greater Syria, an area that included what would later be known as Lebanon, Syria, Jordan, and historical Palestine/Israel. By the mid-1920s, Arab Americans numbered an estimated 200,000. The descendants of these early immigrants now make up about half the Arab American population.[6] Significantly, the discriminatory 1924 Immigration Act sharply reduced immigration from the Middle East, as well as southern Europe.

Later Immigration

Far more Arab immigrants have entered the United States since World War II than before. The greatest number have come since 1970, more than a half million. Many of these have fled various conflicts and wars in the Middle East and Africa. These immigrants have come from some twenty different countries, ranging from Morocco in western Africa to the United Arab Emirates in the Middle East. The 1970s' Lebanese civil war and the 1980s' Israeli invasion of Lebanon generated numerous immigrants, including many who were Muslims. Other immigrants were fleeing the wars been Iraq and Iran and between Iraq and Kuwait, as well as the civil war in Yemen. Whether Muslim or Christian, they often entered with a strong sense of Arab nationalism and a greater inclination to criticize U.S. governmental policy in the Middle East than earlier immigrants.[7] The largest numbers have been people from Lebanon, Syria, and Egypt, as well as Palestinians. Most have been Muslim. The majority have settled in the metropolitan areas of New York, Chicago, Detroit, and Los Angeles. Indeed, the Arab American population is today more urban than the general U.S. population.[8]

These various groups of immigrants have important cultural differences and similarities. Although there are some cultural variations, as we will see later, common linkages in areas such as language help them coalesce and work together. As we noted earlier, in recent decades most of these later groups have more or less coalesced into an Arab American umbrella group for social and political reasons. Most of the third-generation descendants of the earlier "Greater Syrian" immigrants have also come to see themselves as Arab Americans. Interestingly, one recent study in Detroit surveyed the leaders of Middle Eastern organizations to discern if there were cultural traits shared across the diverse groups. The research found that most leaders accented the importance of the extended family. One respondent commented: "The most important [thing] in our tradition is respect for the family. And closeness of family."[9] Not surprisingly, many of these leaders were concerned that modern American culture tends to break up families through divorce and lenient supervision of children.

Many of these Detroit respondents also accented the importance of religion. Religion has long been central to the Arab and other Middle Eastern cultures. One scholar argues that most Arab Americans come from backgrounds with a "common language, tradition, cultural traits, and values," even though they have diverse national and religious identities.[10] While there are some differences (e.g., in marriage practices) within the Arab American community between Christians, Muslims, and Jews, the dominant society's anti-Arab stereotypes and hostility have provided some social forces that, ironically enough, unite the Arab American community. In addition to family and religion, other cultural traits accented by this study's respondents included an emphasis on tracing ancestry to Arab or Middle Eastern history and lands, an orientation to Arabic and other Middle Eastern languages, and a strong commitment to independent entrepreneurship as a way of building community economies.[11] Americans whose origins lie in Arab and Middle Eastern areas may have different physical features and religious backgrounds, but they generally share some cultural traits and political concerns. Only in this loose way can one speak of an umbrella group called "Arab Americans" or "Middle Eastern Americans."

Stereotyping and Prejudice

Classified as an "Inferior Race"

In the first period of Arab immigration to the United States, government officials sometimes classified these immigrants as "Turks" and sometimes as "Syrians." In 1914 a South Carolina court ruled that while a Syrian immigrant "may be Caucasian," he or she was *not* what the 1790 Naturalization Act called a "free white person"—and thus could not become a U.S. citizen. In 1915 this decision was reversed on the grounds that the relevant laws were those of 1873 and 1875, which allowed Syrians to be considered as close enough to Europeans to be officially classified as "white."[12]

Still, the right of Arab immigrants to citizenship and to a claim of whiteness continued to be strongly challenged in many institutional arenas, at least until the 1940s. Racist writers of the early 20th century saw these immigrants as "parasites" and "Mongolian plasma" that would "contaminate the pure American stock."[13] Syrian immigrants were often catalogued with southern and eastern Europeans as "inferior races" by leading European American intellectuals such as Madison Grant. European American nativists sometimes called the Syrians the "most foreign" of all immigrants.[14]

Recent Stereotyping and U.S. Politics

In more recent decades, Arab Americans have continued to face widespread prejudice and stereotypes, although of a somewhat more complex variation. A 1975 undergraduate course guide at Columbia University described one Arabic course by suggesting that every other word in Arabic was about violence and that this signalled the character of the Arab mind.[15] One survey of portraits of Arab peoples in U.S. textbooks reported that they showed Arabs as ignorant about other peoples and asserted that anti-Jewish sentiment was the ultimate link holding Middle Eastern peoples together.[16] One public opinion survey in 1981 found that 44 percent of the respondents considered Arabs to be "barbaric" or "cruel," while about half thought they were "treacherous" or "cunning." More than half thought they were "warlike" and that they "mistreat women." Forty percent thought Arabs were anti-Christian and anti-Semitic. Such strong images have been circulating among non-Middle Eastern Americans for at least three decades now.[17]

Since the late 1960s, U.S. political and military policies regarding the Middle East have often generated or accelerated the spread of negative stereotypes of Arabs and Arab Americans. For example, Terrel Bell, Ronald Reagan's Secretary of Education, reported that in the 1980s, mid-level aides in the White House and other government agencies made blatantly racist comments about Arab peoples as "sand niggers," as well as derogatory comments about African Americans. These racist perspectives on the part of national political leaders were often accompanied by a weakening of civil rights laws.[18] The common labeling of Arab and other Middle Eastern peoples with terms such as "camel jockies" and "sand niggers" during the early 1990s' Gulf War and more recent Middle Eastern conflicts has also helped to rationalize the conflicts in the minds of many non-Middle Eastern Americans.

Today, as in the recent past, political figures in the Middle East are sometimes characterized in biologically racist terms. Cartoons have long shown Arab leaders as evildoers with "sharply hooked noses" and a "mustachioed leer on their faces."[19] Palestinian leader Yasser Arafat has recently been portrayed by a leading New York newspaper as having "pendulous lips," and other Arab leaders are sometimes portrayed in the media and elsewhere as having "beak-like noses." Significantly, these are similar to old anti-Jewish stereotypes.[20] The mass media have often stereotyped Arab men as militaristic extremists and Arab women as distinctively servile. The errors in Arab and Arab American stereotypes can be seen in Evelyn Shakir's comments on her family: "Terrorist, oil sheik, master of the seraglio—it was impossible for me to connect these terms with my uncle who baked blueberry muffins for his wife's breakfast and washed out her underthings by hand, or with my other uncle who belonged to the Rotary Club, voted Republican, and was a deacon in the Baptist church."[21] Both television and the movies have often circulated harshly stereotyped images and have largely ignored the important differences among Middle Eastern peoples. The influential Arab scholar, Edward Said, has described these generally negative and stereotyped views of Middle Eastern peoples as an ideology of *Orientalism*. This Orientalism goes back some centuries in Western thought, pervading much scholarly work as well as popular thinking.[22]

Challenging Stereotyping

Until recently, few U.S. leaders outside Arab American communities have been willing to challenge these racialized images. In a speech to the 1984 Democratic Party national convention, Jesse Jackson, an African American leader, was perhaps the first major U.S. politician to speak publicly of Arab Americans in strongly positive terms and as a people facing the "pain and hurt of racial and religious rejection."[23] Yet, Jackson paid a price for speaking out against this stereotyping. For a time, whenever he spoke positively about Arab Americans or questioned what he saw as the one-sided U.S. emphasis on the Israeli side of Arab–Israeli conflicts, Jackson was attacked in the mass media or by other non-Middle Eastern politicians.

In a recent survey, Arab and other Middle Eastern American leaders expressed concern about the commonplace stereotyping and discrimination directed at their communities. They cited the frequency of negative images of Muslims as well as the infrequency of positive commentaries in the mass media. They were disturbed that Arab Americans have been targeted as a "bad image" community. These leaders noted that among Arab Americans, those of the Muslim faith are the most likely to be targets of hostility and discrimination. They also noted that Arab Americans who possess the physical or cultural traits associated with Arab or Middle Eastern Americans in the minds of other Americans are more likely to be targeted for hostility than those who do not fit these images or stereotypes.[24]

Stereotypes and Arab American Women

Arab and Arab American women, as well as women from other Middle Eastern countries such as Iran and Turkey, have faced a range of negative stereotypes. In the United States they have frequently been portrayed as members of harems, exotic belly dancers, or as totally dominated by their husbands, with the latter also being stereotyped as hot-tempered bullies. In the United States, the religion of Islam and Arab culture are often viewed as extremely oppressive of women.[25] Even European American feminists have sometimes accepted uncritically the stereotyped accounts of so-called "savagery" among Arab men and "passivity" among women. For some decades, numerous Western writers have circulated the notion that marital arrangements such as the "harem" are typical of Arab societies, when in fact such arrangements of several wives have never involved more than a small elite in certain countries. Most Arab women are poor or working class. The "harem" has been much more important in European fantasy life than in the real world of Arab societies.[26]

The reality of life for Arab women in both Arab countries and in the United States is more complex and varied and should be put in a broader comparative context. Historically, most women in Arab societies have lived under strong patriarchal conditions, yet this condition of strong patriarchal dominance was also true of most non-Arab families in Western societies until the past few decades—a reality that Western missionaries and travellers in previous decades rarely criticized. And patriarchal dominance is still significant in many U.S. families that are not Arab American. Today, as in the past, many Middle Eastern wives and mothers in both Muslim and Christian Arab families have substantial decisionmaking power, a fact left out of many discussions of patriarchy. The image of Arab patriarchy has some truth at its core, but as with many such popular images it often involves a stereotyped exaggeration well beyond the reality. Generally speaking, traditional values in Arab countries have emphasized family honor and stipulated that women be modest and protected when around men who are strangers. For Arab women in the United States, this value system sometimes comes into conflict with prevailing American values relating to such behaviors as dating. Some Arab American women "have engaged in outright rebellion against their parents' or husbands' authority. Others have been able to invoke traditional values to justify unconventional behavior; in the name of service to family and community, much has been permitted."[27] Over time many Arab American women have gained greater autonomy, sometimes creating tensions in their families. Moreover, women are particularly important to the persistence of Arab culture in the United States; some studies have found them to be the "anchor of the group's sense of identity."[28]

Another problem facing many Arab American women is the commonplace image of ideal female beauty. The centrality of European American body imagery in the mass media can be seen in the typically thin, light-skinned, and often blonde models in advertising and other media contexts. As a result, "dark pigmentation and, especially, dark body hair, have been sources of shame to [Arab American] girls growing up in the United States." Some feminist groups have emerged among Arab American women, in part because of their concern with the common American images of ideal female beauty.[29]

Oppression, Discrimination, and Conflict

Early Discrimination

The first few generations of Arab immigrants and their children sometimes faced a clearly racialized discrimination, especially in southern areas where whites often classified them with black Americans. Considered as "not white," Arab Americans were sometimes turned away from voting places, restaurants, and rest rooms by racist whites in southern states such as Alabama.[30] While across the nation they faced less discrimination than did African Americans, they were nonetheless often seen as not being white Americans.

Current Patterns of Discrimination

Before World War II, most Arab immigrants were Christian, but since then most have been Muslim. This has affected how they are seen by many other Americans. While the U.S. Census Bureau now defines Arab immigrants as "white," many non-Arab Americans still view them as "not white." Classification as "white, non-European" by the U.S. Census Bureau has not kept them from suffering intense racial-ethnic prejudice and discrimination.

For several decades, and up to the present day, racial-ethnic discrimination remains a problem for Arab Americans. For example, since the late 1990s several Arab American women have been dismissed from jobs because they refused to remove their head coverings (the hijab), part of the traditional dress adopted by some Muslim women. Protests against this discrimination by the Council on American Islamic Relations did lead to the rehiring of several of these women.[31] Discrimination also affects Arab Americans in the U.S. legal system. Some lawyers have reportedly feared going to jury trials for Arab American clients because of negative depictions of Arab peoples in the U.S. media.[32] Unlike older white ethnic groups, most of these Americans do not yet have the choice of escaping their racial-ethnic identities, even if they wished to do so.

International Politics and Discrimination

Edward Said has pointed out that the commonplace "Orientalist" distortions of Arab and other Middle Eastern peoples have serious implications for U.S. government policies regarding overseas matters. This is especially true for U.S. policies in the Middle East, a region where the U.S. government has long been heavily invested, in part because of its continuing concern for oil supplies for U.S. industry and consumers. For some decades many U.S. policymakers in Washington, D.C. and numerous U.S. diplomats in the Middle East have not been well informed about the region's history or cultures. "The Middle East experts who advise policymakers are imbued with Orientalism almost to a person.... If in the meantime the Arabs, the Muslims, or the Third and Fourth Worlds go unexpected ways after all, we will not be surprised to have an Orientalist tell us that this testifies to the incorrigibility of Orientals and therefore proves that they are not to be trusted."[33]

Much recent discrimination, including violent attacks on Arab Americans, is linked to international issues and conflicts and to the misconceptions and stereotypes held by many non-Arab Americans. Since the 1960s, the United States has had a "negative atmosphere for Americans of Arab descent, due to the stereotyping, harassment, defamation, and exclusion of Arab Americans brought on by the widespread perception of Arabs as immigrants from hostile, enemy lands."[34] For example, influenced by this negative perception of Arabs, President Richard Nixon responded to the 1972 killing of Israeli Olympic athletes in Germany by some Palestinians by establishing Operation Boulder, a secret U.S. government operation targeting people of "Arab ancestry." Even though the attacks in Europe on the Israelis had nothing directly to do with the United States, the CIA and the FBI collected information on Arab American individuals and groups and harassed and intimated thousands of people.[35]

The anti-Arab stereotyping has persisted since the 1970s, at the highest levels of the U.S. government. Thus, the 1996 Anti-Terrorism and Effective Death Penalty Act and the Illegal Immigration Reform and Immigrant Responsibility Act have given federal authorities new powers to detain and interrogate immigrants suspected of being linked to terrorist organizations, without the usual civil rights protection such as the right to a speedy and fair hearing at which the evidence for detention is presented. These laws have primarily been used against U.S. immigrants and citizens with Arab or Muslim backgrounds.[36] As we have seen in earlier chapters, such as those on Japanese and Italian Americans, some American citizens have been viewed by their government as guilty until proven innocent, and only because of their racial or ethnic backgrounds.

Since the 1970s, Arab American community and political activists, especially those who articulate critical views of U.S. government policies in the Middle East, have periodically been targets of harassment and violence. Some have received threatening phone calls, had their property vandalized, or found dead animals on their front steps. In 1985 a regional director for one Arab American organization was killed by a bomb that exploded at his office. Some police authorities attributed the bombing to the extremist Jewish Defense League, which expressed satisfaction at the bombing. In addition, the U.S. government has periodically conducted secret surveillance operations targeting some activist Arab Americans solely because of their political views.[37]

U.S. government involvement in the Middle East, especially in recent conflicts such as the Gulf War or the intervention in Afghanistan, has periodically generated outbreaks of overt hostility and violence against Arab Americans. Hate crimes often seem linked to media reports of particular events. Since 1989 several Islamic mosques in the United States have been bombed or set on fire, and others have been vandalized, often in response to media reports of conflicts or terrorism involving Middle Eastern groups. Many physical attacks on Americans of Middle Eastern descent took place following the 1991 Gulf War between Iraq and the United States and its allies. In the early 1990s more than 150 anti-Arab hate crimes were reported to the police.[38] Since that war, Arab Americans have been blamed for events such as the April 1995 Oklahoma City bombing plot targeting a federal building by the white-racist terrorist Timothy McVeigh and his white associates. In the three days after that bombing, there were more than 200 attacks on Arab and Muslim Americans. In addition, in the 1990s the FBI and the Immigration and Naturalization Service developed a plan to imprison Arab Americans in the event that war broke out between the United States and Arab countries.[39] It appears from this planning that these federal government agencies have not yet learned the lessons that were clear during and after the 1940s imprisonment of Japanese American citizens solely because of their racial characteristics. Government actions based on racial stereotyping and profiling are not only unconstitutional and a violation of international human rights treaties, but they also rarely enhance national security (see Chapter 10).

The Impact of the Attacks on the World Trade Center and the Pentagon: 2001 and After

The September 11, 2001 attacks by Middle Eastern terrorists—who were apparently angry about U.S. policies and involvement in the Middle East—on the World Trade Center and the Pentagon generated many hate crimes against Arab Americans or those who were thought to look like people of Arab or other Middle Eastern ancestry. These hate crimes were principally about racial-ethnic stereotyping and ignorance, for they were committed in spite of the fact that no Arab American citizen had been implicated in the attacks and that seventeen of the nineteen men thought to have been the terrorists (connected to the international al Qa'eda terrorist network) were from Saudi Arabia and the United Arab Emirates, the countries of origin for few Arab Americans. According to one anti-discrimination group's tally, in the first nine weeks after the September 11 attacks, there were at least 520 *violent* attacks on people thought to be of Arab or Middle Eastern ancestry. These attacks included assaults, arson, and six murders. Some of those assaulted or killed were not Arab, but were assumed to be Arab by their ignorant attackers. In addition to these crimes, hundreds of cases of employment discrimination were reported in this brief period, as well as increased discrimination in the form of racial profiling and other discrimination by law enforcement officers and airline personnel. Since the 2001 report, many more cases of violent discrimination, employment discrimination, and racial profiling targeting Arab Americans have also been reported.[40]

In addition, the 2001 USA Patriot Act, passed quickly after the September 11 attacks, gave the federal government broad new authority to detain noncitizens with little or no due process and to proceed with searches and surveillance with less judicial review than before. Many Americans concerned for civil liberties feared that this and related laws said to be designed to reduce the future possibility of terrorism would be used, like the 1996 anti-terrorism law, to target immigrants of color, particularly those who looked like Middle Eastern Americans. As the American-Arab Anti-Discrimination Committee (ADC) recently put it, "These serious civil liberties concerns should be alarming to all Americans, but there can be little doubt that it is the Arab American and Muslim communities who are facing the gravest threats to their rights and that these communities will bear the brunt of any major diminution of civil liberties in the United States."[41]

Taking Action against Discrimination

Arab Americans have taken action against some of this stereotyping and discrimination. For example, recent protests have targeted the Chicago *Sun-Times* newspaper for stereotyping Arabs and for neglecting reporting on the Arab American community. Some Arab American groups organized a boycott of the paper; protests called attention to editorials that claimed Palestinian Authority leader Yasser Arafat was primarily responsible for recent Middle Eastern violence. Anti-discrimination groups have also strongly protested movies such as *The Siege* (1998), which shows Arabs as terrorists and a threat to the United States, further feeding hostile images in the general population. The film directly links the religion of Islam to terrorism, showing Muslim rituals being conducted before acts of violence. Hala Maksoud, head of one anti-discrimination organization, described this film as "insidious, dangerous, and incendiary" and as inciting "hate which leads to harassment, intimidation, discrimination, and even hate crimes."[42]

A number of Arab American and Islamic organizations are taking action against religious discrimination. Recently, Eric Shakir, civil rights coordinator for the Council on American-Islamic Relations (CAIR), noted the growing reports of employment discrimination faced by millions of Muslims in the United States. Many cases involve workplace prohibitions against religious practices, such as not allowing Muslim men to wear beards in the workplace, not permitting Muslim women to wear the hijab (a religious headscarf), or not permitting daily prayers. Reportedly, CAIR first attempts mediation with employers to make them more sensitive to the religious needs of their Muslim employees. If that fails, they may go to court.[43]

Local Conflict and Cooperation with Other Groups

In areas such as Detroit, where Arab Americans have established many small businesses, periodic conflicts with several other racial and ethnic groups

People celebrate at the Arab American International Festival in Michigan.

have occurred. Black groups have reported that the relatively new Arab American merchants sometimes treat black customers with disrespect or discrimination. Arab American merchants have complained that black youngsters sometimes steal from their stores. This conflict is reminiscent of similar conflicts between Korean and African Americans. Some local efforts—for example at Detroit's Wayne State University and on Youth Day at Belle Isle in Detroit—have been directed at increasing communication between the African American and Arab American communities in the Detroit metropolitan area.[44]

In recent years some local Jewish American and Arab American groups have also made substantial efforts to increase contacts and dialogue. For example, in Chicago, members of the Arab-American Bar Association and the Decalogue Society of Jewish lawyers have committed themselves to more positive intergroup contacts, especially among their young people.[45] In fall 2000, groups of New York Muslims, Jews, and Arab Christians, including religious leaders, met to work for increasing understanding between these groups and to reduce local interpersonal and intergroup violence.[46]

Politics and Political Emergence

Gradual Increase in Political Activity

By the 1930s a few Syrian Americans held elected public office, but it was not until 1958 that the first Arab American was elected to the U.S. Congress. Greater political representation has come slowly at the national level. The first U.S. senator of Arab descent, South Dakota's James Abourezk, was not elected until 1980. In the late 1980s a few Arab Americans were named to major appointed positions in government, including the White House Chief of Staff. Over the past few decades, Arab Americans have gradually moved into some positions of influence in the U.S. political system.

Recent Political Involvement

In fall 2000, a majority of New York City's council members passed a strong resolution on the Palestinian–Israeli conflict that condemned Palestinian violence against Israel and called Palestinian leader Yasser Arafat a terrorist, but did not criticize Israel's role in the continuing conflict. Several council members left that meeting in protest over its one-sided character.[47] Such protest actions show once again how international tensions spill over into local and national politics in the United States.

In the years since 1990, we have seen increasing political activity and representation for Muslim and Arab Americans. Numerous Arab and Muslim Americans have been elected at state and local levels across the country. The fall 2000 political campaigns saw more Muslim and Arab American candidates (approximately 700) than ever. Major voter registration drives by Arab American organizations led to a substantial increase in Arab voter participation. In addition, some Arab Americans have been appointed as ambassadors and placed on national and local political commissions. As of the early 2000s, at least a dozen Muslim or Arab Americans were serving on the Capitol Hill staffs of U.S. representatives and senators.[48] The presence of these officials has had an impact, in both large and small ways. For example, there is now a Friday (Muslim) prayer service on Capitol Hill, and more attention is being given to the Arab American view of ongoing Middle Eastern conflicts.

For the first time in U.S. history, the year 2000 Republican and Democratic national conventions had Muslim clergy giving prayers. In fall 2000 there were an estimated one million Arab American voters in the United States, mostly located in New Jersey, Ohio, Pennsylvania, and Michigan.[49] In this presidential election, states with significant numbers of Arab American voters, such as Michigan, received substantial attention from both major presidential candidates. In the fall campaign, candidate George W. Bush surprised the voters by condemning racial profiling of Arab immigrants as "terrorists" by U.S. government agencies. This stance gained him substantial support from Arab American voters in Michigan as well as other states. While the majority of Arab Americans had voted for the Democratic Party candidate in 1996, the majority voted Republican in 2000.[50] When he became president in 2001, Bush appointed Spencer Abraham, an Arab (Lebanese) American, as Energy Secretary.

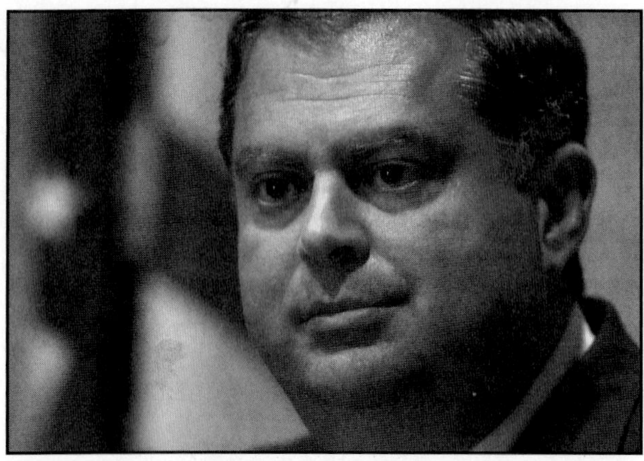

Spencer Abraham, a Lebanese American, has served as U.S. Secretary of Energy.

Politics and Discrimination

After a long campaign, political pressures exerted by Arab American leaders and community activists forced changes in the discriminatory use of secret evidence in immigrant deportation hearings, evidence allowed under U.S. immigration law but mostly used against Muslim and Arab entrants and immigrants. Eventually, the secretive and discriminatory process was condemned or questioned by some 250 articles and editorials in U.S. newspapers.[51]

Negative images of Arab Americans have sometimes frustrated their ability to participate fully in U.S. politics. In recent decades some political candidates have returned the contributions of Arab Americans, often with a public display, because the candidates were afraid to be seen as accepting contributions from Arab or Muslim Americans. For example, during the fall 2000 New York state senate campaign, the Democratic campaign returned a contribution by Muslim donors because of public reaction. Conventional stereotyping of Arab Americans seems to be just below the surface of such discriminatory reactions to political contributions, which are usually eagerly sought by non-Arab politicians.[52]

International Politics and Linkages

We have seen throughout this textbook that social and political ties to countries or lands of origin often remain important to immigrants and their descendants, even generations after they have become fully established in the United States. Today, for many Arab Americans, such as Lebanese Americans or Palestinian Americans, ties to their homelands or other Middle Eastern countries are still of importance. They closely watch political events in the Middle East and the U.S. government's involvement in those events. To a substantial degree, their political concerns are international and are linked to developments in the Middle East.

In recent years many Arab and Muslim Americans have been critical of U.S. foreign policy in the Middle East, faulting it for tilting too far in support of Israel (Israel is currently the largest recipient of U.S. foreign aid) and too much against the interests of the nearly two dozen Arab countries in the region. For example, they are often critical of Israel's historical and contemporary treatment of the Palestinians and their lands. Ibrahim Hooper, communications director of the Council on American-Islamic Relations, has put it this way: "You're not going to find a Muslim who is not going to support the Palestinians' efforts to free themselves from occupation." Nonetheless, like most other Americans, most Arab and Muslim Americans do *not* support terroristic violence as a strategy to change things. They do not support terrorism in any country. As Dr. Agha Saeed, chair of the American Muslim Alliance, an organization working for civic education and leadership training, has noted: "We are critical of Israel but not supporters of terrorism."[53] Not surprisingly, then, Arab Americans in cities from Atlanta, Georgia to Riverside, California have openly and peacefully protested Israeli treatment of the Palestinians and called for increased efforts to bring peace to the area.

The influence of Arab American organizations' efforts to bring their perspective into U.S. discussions of the Middle East can be seen in recent opinion polls. The majority of U.S. respondents in one general poll expressed a desire for an evenhanded approach to the Israeli–Palestinian conflict. Moreover, while Israel is still favored over the Palestinians by the general public, the gap may be narrowing.[54]

Arab American political activists have made it clear that the Arab–Israeli conflict is not their only political and social concern. They have actively focused on critical domestic issues such as immigration reform and health care.[55] Arab Americans and other Middle Eastern Americans have created a large array of important voluntary associations and organizations to provide aid and support for their communities. Cities with large Arab and Middle Eastern communities have many voluntary associations, including both Islamic and Christian religious groups, mass media groups, family and village societies, professional groups, educational associations, human service groups, and political organizations such as the Arab American Political Action Committee.[56]

Many Middle Eastern American community leaders are working to build greater community and political cooperation and coordination across the various Arab American and other Middle Eastern organizations. One leader in Detroit has noted that, "The one thing I wish is for a united community with one organization and leaders ... who are most qualified and can accomplish things whether they're Palestinian, Lebanese, Yemeni, Shi'a, Sunni, Muslims, non-Muslims."[57] To promote such cooperation, organizations such as the American Muslim Political Coordinating Committee have recently been formed to link Arab and other Middle Eastern Americans politically across the country. Moreover, today the American Muslim Alliance, another relatively new political organization, has 7,000 members in 31 states.[58]

THE ECONOMY

Like other immigrants, some early Arab immigrants were attracted by the relatively high wages paid by Henry Ford in his new automobile plant in Michigan. However, unlike large numbers of European immigrants, most of the early-twentieth-century Arab immigrants, those from Greater Syria, did not enter the new manufacturing and other industrial occupations that were expanding dramatically in the decades just after 1890, but rather became peddlers or small merchants. As a result, they often had somewhat higher incomes than the new industrial workers. Most settled in a few major cities, where they often established small grocery stores, fruit stands, and dry goods stores.[59] There they built distinctive enclaves much like those of certain other immigrant groups, such as Italian and Cuban Americans.

While those in the earliest period of immigration were generally poor, many who have immigrated since the 1960s have been educated professionals such as teachers, doctors, and engineers. Today, Arab Americans as a group are disproportionately self-employed. This group has above average percentages of workers in professional, managerial, and sales occupations compared with the general population. Arab Americans are also less likely than the general population to hold government jobs.[60] Numerous Arab Americans have achieved prominence in professional and managerial occupations. They include Dr. Michael DeBakey (inventor of the heart pump), Gibran Khalil Gibran (poet), Christa McAuliffe (teacher and astronaut), Ralph Nader (consumer advocate and presidential candidate), and Donna Shalala (HEW Secretary in the 1990s).

Arab Americans, as we have noted, are concentrated in a few major cities, with the largest number living in the Detroit area. Although Detroit is often seen as a distinctively African American city, its population now includes more than 300,000 Middle Eastern Americans. Metropolitan Detroit now has the largest Arab American population of any city and the largest Arab-origin population of any place outside the Middle East. The central areas of the city have significant Iraqi, Egyptian, Lebanese, Palestinian, and Syrian communities. Metropolitan Detroit is home to the national headquarters of the Chaldean church in the United States and an Islamic Institute. Many Middle Eastern restaurants can be found in the area, as well as Arabic language signs advertising an array of shops and professional offices. Early 1900s' Arab American immigrants went into the automobile industry in the Detroit area, and during the 1960s and 1970s, Lebanese Muslims and Chaldeans (Catholics from northern Iraq) migrated to the Detroit area. Many of the latter group became merchants with small retail stores. By 2001 some 13,000 Arab American businesses were located in metropolitan Detroit, including service stations and liquor stores.[61] Dearborn, located within metropolitan Detroit, has been called the center of Arab America because of its large Arab American population. Once principally known for being the home of the automobile industry and Henry Ford, this area has become a city of mosques and Middle Eastern restaurants and shops.[62]

Arab Americans are more prosperous economically than numerous other recent immigrant groups. The 1990 census reported that Arab Americans had a higher average household income than the U.S. population average.[63] Yet the proportion of Arab

American families below the poverty level is also higher than for the general population. This is partially because many recent immigrants earn relatively low wages. In some low-income urban neighborhoods a large proportion of Arab Americans receive some type of public assistance.[64]

EDUCATION

The average Arab American is better educated than the average American. Both the 1980 and 1990 censuses reported that Arab Americans had higher average educational levels than the U.S. population averages.[65] Not surprisingly, thus, the commitment to education is high in Arab American and other Middle Eastern American communities. For example, a survey of leaders of Middle Eastern organizations in Detroit found a strong emphasis on the importance of education, an emphasis that has served to unite the various subcommunities there. These leaders stressed education in part because education and knowledge have long been important within Islamic and other Middle Eastern cultures and in part because of its importance in facilitating economic advancement in U.S. society.[66]

Some Arab American parents send their children to private Muslim schools, but most send their children to the public schools attended by most of the nation's children. As with earlier immigrants and their children, significant tensions have sometimes arisen between public school teachers and administrators, on the one hand, and students or their parents, on the other. One Arab American educator recently noted that non-Arab teachers often fail to realize that not all Arab Americans share the same cultural background. They or their ancestors have come from many different countries. Tensions or conflicts may arise when teachers are unaware that their Arab students come from numerous countries and cultures or when teachers make incorrect assumptions about the cultural backgrounds of their students. For example, one teacher made the assumption that Lebanese women were not allowed to walk freely in the street. Others are unaware of the strong tradition of education and the extensive system of schools in many Arab countries. Misunderstandings about appropriate roles and behaviors are another source of conflict. Non-Arab teachers often see Arab American parents as too strict with their children, while the Arab parents may view the teachers as too lax with disruptive students.[67]

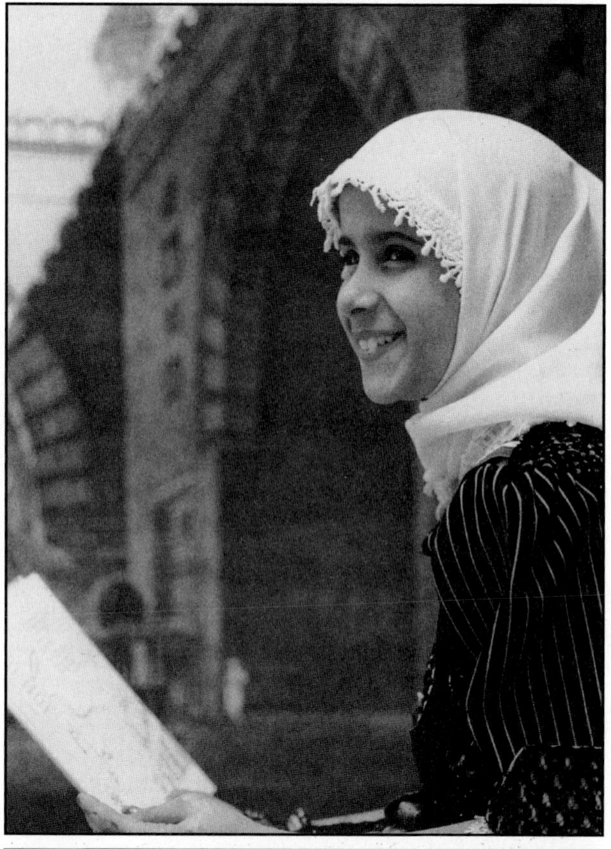
An Arab American girl attends school in Dearborn, Michigan.

Columbia University educator Wendy Schwartz notes that public schools have a responsibility to deal with the racial and ethnic stereotyping faced by Arab American children: "Because prejudice against Arab Americans increases when political events involve Arabs, or are even speculated to involve them, educators need to be prepared to respond to possible harassment of Arab American students resulting from negative news reporting, and to invoke school policies against hate crimes and discrimination as appropriate."[68] Most are not prepared. Schwartz also calls on educators to become more sensitive to the major cultural practices of Arab Americans, such as by respecting major Islamic holidays, and to become better informed about Middle Eastern history and contemporary political issues.

RELIGION

As we have noted, religion has long been central to most Middle Eastern countries and cultures. Not surprisingly, many Arab Americans take their religion seriously. However, today there is great diversity among Arab Americans; some are Christian, a few are Jewish, and many are Muslim in their religious commitments. Among the Christians and the Muslims there are also distinctive subgroups.

Most early Arab immigrants were Christian. Generally, they immigrated from the Maronite, Melkite, and Syrian Orthodox areas in Greater Syria. As late as the 1960s, most Arab Americans were Christian in religion. However, since the 1960s most Arab immigrants have been Muslim. They and their descendants account for a significant proportion of the current U.S. Muslim population.

Islam has been practiced in North America since the first century of settlement (some enslaved Africans were Muslims), but it did not become very visible in the United States until the 1950s. By the early 1950s, when the Federation of Islamic Associations of the United States and Canada was created, there were at least 52 mosques in the United States, not including the African American mosques. By 2000 there were more than 1,250 mosques and Islamic centers in the United States, double the number that had existed in the mid-1980s.[69] Soon, Muslims will become the second largest religious group in the United States.

The arrival of many new Muslim immigrants since the 1970s has brought some conflicts to some Islamic mosques and other organizations. The new arrivals have sometimes expressed surprise at the deviations in U.S. mosques from what they regard as traditional Islamic teachings. Like Christian churches and Jewish synagogues, mosques have been significantly shaped by the U.S. sociocultural environment. For example, Sunday schools have been set up, and Sunday prayer services have become more popular than traditional Friday prayer services. Some conservative Islamic revivalists have sometimes worked to bring U.S. mosques back to more traditional practices. They have sought to eliminate such things as raffles and teenage dances and to reduce the participation of women in mosque affairs.[70]

People gather outside a new mosque in Orange County, California.

Recent surveys of U.S. Muslims indicate that only 3–4 percent attend Friday prayers weekly. This is much lower than the 40 percent of Christians who attend church at least once a week. However, 47 percent of U.S. Muslims report that they fast for the month of Ramadan.[71]

Nationwide there are at least one hundred Islamic day schools and more than one thousand Sunday and weekend schools. As of 2001, only an estimated 3 percent of children with Muslim backgrounds were receiving direct schooling in Islam outside the home.[72] In the late 1990s a religious training program for religious leaders was established in Herndon, Virginia by the International Institute of Islamic Thought. This Institute offers degrees in Imamate Studies and seeks to provide Islamic communities in the United States with religious leaders (Imams) educated in the United States. Until this program was established, most religious leaders came from overseas, and the inability of some of these leaders to understand U.S. society sometimes created tensions with those whom they served, especially with Muslim young people influenced by the dominant culture in the United States.[73]

Islamic scholar Yvonne Haddad has recently noted that while practicing Islam in the United States is becoming easier, some problems remain: "The practice of religion is to pray five times a day, to perform ablutions before the prayers, to fast the month of Ramadan, to give alms, to go on the hajj once in a lifetime. Fasting is not as easy as fasting in a Muslim country, where the workday is shortened."[74] Finding places to do ablutions and to pray in the workplace can be difficult, but the rapidly growing numbers of practicing Muslims are pressuring numerous employers to become aware of the need to provide facilities. The growing number of mosques and Islamic centers is also making the practice of Islam much easier than in previous decades.

However, unlike the various denominations of Christianity (Catholicism, several Orthodox groups, and numerous Protestant groups), Islam is not yet a fully accepted religion in the United States. Its practitioners still suffer widespread prejudice and stereotyping. In this regard the practitioners of Islam suffer much as Jewish Americans once did for practicing Judaism in the United States. (Indeed, Jewish synagogues are still sometimes the targets for anti-Jewish hate crimes.) The U.S. media sometimes connect mainstream Islam to extremist terrorism. The U.S. media refer to some incidents as involving "Islamic terrorists"—as though the religion of Islam routinely generated this terrorism. Yet the same U.S. reporters and editors would never refer to the terrorists in northern Ireland as "Christian terrorists," even though Christian sectarianism (Catholics versus Protestants) is centrally linked to bloody terrorism on that island. Clearly, in neither case is the broader religion, Islam or Christianity, responsible for extremist terrorism. Today, as Suad Joseph has noted, the portrayal of Islam in the United States is often "achieved by misrepresenting and then essentializing and homogenizing a highly complex and diverse religion that has many different sects, legal systems, beliefs, and practices."[75]

The recurring linkage of the general religion of Islam to extremist terrorism creates serious dilemmas for many Muslim Americans. Religious intolerance still confronts them in their everyday lives. Continuing anti-Arab and anti–Middle Eastern stereotyping and discrimination also can create serious problems of identity and self-esteem for Arab and other Middle Eastern Americans. Indeed, some have decided to deny or "de-emphasize their Arab or Islamic background."[76]

ADAPTATION AND ASSIMILATION ISSUES

Patterns of Assimilation

Partial cultural assimilation has come relatively quickly for most Arab immigrants and their children. Most of the earlier immigrants, the Greater Syrian immigrants, soon adapted to their new cultural and social environments, picking up English and certain American folkways. Yet, most also maintained a commitment to their own distinctive religious traditions. Intentional discrimination by European Americans often played a role in frustrating the rise of first-generation Arab Americans and their children. In response to discrimination, they often anglicized their names, gave up the Arabic language, and tried to appear as Anglo-American as they could in public.[77]

In the sphere of structural assimilation at the secondary level of the economy and politics, these Arab

Americans soon advanced and achieved substantial economic success. They often came with the intention of starting a small business and returning home with some wealth. In the early period most white Americans saw them as "Syrians," not as Arabs. And they did not see themselves as "Arabs" at that point, although most did draw heavily on their Arab cultural roots. While they had come to make money, which most did, in the entrepreneurial process they came to be proud of their efforts in America. Their constant contacts with other Americans drew them into the individualistic culture and language habits of the dominant culture. As they became more attached to their new homeland, their attachment to the areas of Syria and Lebanon declined.[78]

In contrast, Arab immigrants who entered after the 1960s have assimilated more slowly at most levels, perhaps because their numbers have been much larger and because of the more intense anti-Arab sentiment in the United States in this recent period. We can now look in more detail at some of the adaptation issues in current Arab American communities, particularly for these more recent immigrants and their children.

Contemporary Assimilation Issues and Patterns

The recent survey of Middle Eastern American leaders in Detroit found that the issues receiving the greatest emphasis there were immigration and residency, cultural and language preservation, citizenship, and assimilation and acculturation. The preservation of Arab and other Middle Eastern cultures, especially language and religion, is of great concern in Middle Eastern American communities.[79]

Generally speaking, significant language and related cultural assimilation is taking place in the Arab American communities today. While almost half of Arab Americans over the age of seventeen speak some language besides English in their homes, and only one-third of Arab Americans speak only English at home, in most homes two languages are the norm. Moreover, probably because of the growing Arab American population and the continuing Middle East crisis, interest in the Arabic language and culture among many second- and third-generation, native-born Arab Americans has risen, resulting in an increase in Arabic language classes across the nation.[80]

While some Arab Americans oppose intermarriage because it threatens the solidarity of the Arab American community, intermarriage is increasing with each new generation. Many second- and third-generation Arab Americans, as well as other Middle Eastern Americans, are moving out of enclave residential communities and are intermarrying outside their traditional religious and nationality groups. Along with vertical progress in the economy has come a degree of horizontal mobility in the form of suburbanization. First-generation Arab immigrants, like other immigrant groups, are primarily concentrated in central-city or other older urban areas, while subsequent generations have been the most likely to move to suburban areas. Indeed, many Arab Americans of all generations have moved from the city to the suburbs.[81] Some observers suggest that, among other things, this suburbanization has reduced attendance at mosques and weakened commitment to other Islamic traditions.

Assimilation and Generational Conflicts

Today, Arab American and other Middle Eastern American groups are relatively young populations; nearly half are under the age of twenty-five. This pattern is characteristic of populations containing large numbers of recent immigrants.[82] As with earlier Arab immigrants, assimilation pressures have led postwar immigrants and their children to adopt the English language and some of the mainstream values that are constantly articulated and reinforced in the mass media and public school system. As they become better educated, Arab and other Middle Eastern Americans, especially the young, are being drawn away from their cultures of origin to the mainstream U.S. culture. Education is essential for advancement, but it also results in greater acculturation to the Eurocentric core culture.

Like the children of many other immigrants, Arab American children are usually caught between their parents' home culture and the dominant U.S. culture, and family conflicts are often the result. Indeed, many Arab American parents and community leaders worry that their young people are being enticed away from important traditional values and practices by the negative aspects of U.S. culture and society—drinking, drugs, sexual promiscuity, and violence. As in other racial and ethnic groups, many

Arab American teenagers often prefer the more permissive core culture. Many U.S.-born teenagers seek to fit in by adopting such practices as coloring their hair unusual colors, wearing blue jeans, or listening to rap music. Some Arab American young people arrange their dates at shops or in malls away from their parents.[83] While parents are often disturbed at their children's lack of respect for the old ways, the children frequently feel they are unfairly criticized and restricted. As one young Yemeni American recently put it, "I think it is not fair; I was born in a different society. I am in America." Some of the children have even revolted against parental discipline by running away from home. On the opposite extreme, one young Jordanian American was sent for counseling because he had beaten his younger sister who was dating a boy at school without permission.[84]

Some Middle Eastern community leaders fear that anti-Arab prejudice and discrimination will also cause the youth to desire to more rapidly abandon their heritage or ancestry.[85] Indeed, there is evidence that some young Arab Americans do try to hide their identities. In one interview, an Arab American girl told of a friend who passed herself off as half-black and half-Puerto Rican in order to avoid anti-Arab racism. However, she herself said, "I could constantly find an excuse to deny my culture, but I'm not."[86]

Creating a Hybrid Culture

Recall Andrew Greeley's *ethnogenesis* perspective that was discussed in Chapter 2. This perspective recognizes the reality of cultural differences within contemporary ethnic groups and seems to fit the Arab American experience in certain ways. Arab Americans constitute more than a single Middle Eastern group. Their origins lie in two dozen differing countries and cultures. Today they are becoming a composite group of diverse origins. Within the U.S. context, immigrants from a variety of Arab countries and their descendants have increasingly forged a distinctive Arab American umbrella group shaped both by their Arab heritages and by their adaptation to the European American core culture. Despite substantial adaptive changes, significant Arab American cultural distinctiveness remains.

One study of Arab Americans in Detroit found that Arab American organizations help young people to become assimilated to the good features of U.S. society while at the same time cautioning them about the bad features and emphasizing the traditional family and religious values of their Arab heritage. As one Middle Eastern American leader has put it, "We even actually encourage our kids to assimilate in American society."[87]

David and Ayouby have defined *mediated assimilation* as the process whereby Arab American organizations act as cultural filters to screen out some undesirable features of U.S. culture and society. The pattern of using community organizations for both assimilation and resistance to the dominant culture has been typical of immigrants to the United States. This view of the impact and role of community organizations differs from the view that these organizations are only interested in promoting ancestral traditions and maintaining old cultural ways. In the mediated assimilation model, these organizations do attempt to maintain some adherence to tradition, but they also help to create a new "Arab American" mixture. A hybrid Arab American culture appears to be developing in U.S. cities, one that includes elements of the ancestral practices but that also adapts these elements to the pre-existing patterns within a specific city or community. The new Arab culture is "specific to the community's experiences both in the new and old lands."[88] This new hybrid culture particularly helps to blend together groups of young people whose ancestral roots are in different countries into an Arabic culture at the local or national level.

Some Power-Conflict Issues: Racial and Ethnic Identities in the Face of Hostility

A power-conflict perspective might accent or underscore certain other aspects of the Arab American experience. It is the dominant European American majority that has the major say in how Arab Americans are portrayed in the mass media and how they are viewed and treated in many other institutions of the society. In public discussions and settings, it is the dominant European American view of Arab Americans that customarily decides whether they as a group are placed toward the darker, more socially undesirable end of the prevailing racial-ethnic continuum or toward the lighter, more socially desirable end. Indeed, one important dimension of daily interaction with European Americans for Arab Americans is that as a group the latter are treated as, at worst, "sand niggers" or, with less overt hostility, as "not quite white," even as they are officially listed as "white" by the U.S. Census Bureau.

As we noted earlier, continuing anti-Arab and anti-Middle Eastern stereotyping and discrimination have pressed some Arab Americans to deny or deemphasize their Islamic or Arab ties. While the majority continue to claim their nationality and religious backgrounds, they often restrain their reactions to anti-Arab prejudices and discrimination even as they may also work quietly to eliminate them. Moreover, some Arab Americans, such as those represented by the Arab American Institute, have sought to have Arab Americans officially classified as a distinctive non-European group like the "Hispanic" category earlier devised by the Census Bureau. Also, some Arab Americans publicly identify themselves as "people of color," and thus link themselves to the long struggle of movements against white-generated racism in the United States.[89]

Clearly, the racial-ethnic identity of Arab Americans today is much more than a "symbolic identity" without lasting significance—the view some analysts hold of group identity in certain white ethnic groups such as Irish Americans. In a color-conscious U.S. society, Arab Americans' array of physical characteristics presents a continuing problem for the group and for European Americans who think in racist terms about that group. Arab Americans vary from very dark-skinned to blue-eyed and blond, although most have brown eyes, dark hair, and olive or light brown skin.[90] Although some can and do pass as phenotypically white, many others reject this option and emphasize certain differences from European Americans. They are usually proud of their national origins, which are not in Europe. Some openly and intentionally assert their identities as not white.[91] Most European Americans, for their part, seem to view Arab Americans and other Middle Eastern Americans, taken as groups, as "not white," at least not yet. Today, the persistence of anti-Arab stereotyping and hostility can both encourage and discourage movement away from a strong Arab American identity.

SUMMARY

Middle Eastern immigrants have come to the United States for more than a century. The largest group among these are Arab immigrants from more than twenty countries. By the mid-1920s there were an estimated 200,000 Arab Americans, most being Christian in religion. They and their descendants make up about half of today's Arab American population. The other half of this group encompasses the many recent immigrants from Arab countries, most of whose religious background is Muslim. These immigrants and their descendants will soon make Islam the second largest religion in the United States. As has been the case for other immigrant groups before them, economic and political conditions in their countries of origin are major reasons for the recent Arab migration. Many Arab immigrants have fled wars in the Middle East, including the 1970s' civil war in Lebanon. Most have a strong sense of their Arab origins and an inclination to be critical of many traditional U.S. government policies in the Middle East.

Today, Arab Americans have established strong communities in a number of large U.S. cities. The largest number live in metropolitan Detroit. Many have become successful professionals or businesspeople, and some are beginning to move into important political offices. In the United States today, Arab Americans still face widespread stereotyping and significant and sometimes violent discrimination. Frequent hate crimes have targeted Islamic mosques and centers, as well as individuals and their families or homes. Negative images of Arabs and Arab Americans are common in some mass media; the men are often portrayed as distinctively extremist or domineering and the women as distinctively servile or repressed. Few U.S. leaders outside Arab American communities have yet been willing to challenge these stereotyped images in a sustained way.

Arab Americans are today in the forefront of those Americans fighting against racial-ethnic stereotyping and racial or religious discrimination. Like other groups of Americans currently facing serious discrimination, they have created important community and civil rights organizations that have pressed for expanded civil rights not only for Middle Eastern Americans but also for all Americans.

13 The Future of Racial and Ethnic Relations in the United States

In the early 1990s, David Spritzler, a twelve-year-old student at the distinguished Boston Latin School, refused to stand up and do the Pledge of Allegiance with other students. He explained that, because "liberty and justice for all" does not exist in the United States, he did not want to do something that violated his principles. Facing disciplinary action, the boy went to the Massachusetts Civil Liberties Union, which sent the headmaster a letter noting that Supreme Court and other court decisions supported the boy's understanding of free speech. Inside and outside the school, the reaction to the boy's courageous assertion of his free speech rights was both positive and negative. One hostile letter that he received was accompanied by a copy of his newspaper photograph marked with a bullet-riddled Star of David and a swastika.[1]

The United States began as a land of great hope and promise for the European immigrants who came to North America. Early poets such as Philip Freneau, in his 1788 poem "The Pictures of Columbus," spoke of the new land as "paradise anew" and "another Canaan" excelling the old. Thomas Jefferson and other founders used strong language about liberty, freedom, and democracy for the new nation that was created in the late 1700s.[2] Yet, as Latino scholar Ilan Stavans has noted, this celebrated image is not the reality of the past four centuries. Instead, America has always been "the crossroads of hope and violence, democracy and intolerance. America the beautiful and America the ugly."[3] Today, the United States is still a country of hope with the ideals of equality and democracy, yet it is also "America the ugly," where certain "others" are often second-class citizens who face racial or ethnic oppression that is substantially under the control of the still-dominant European Americans.

Currently, U.S. society is undergoing important changes in its racial and ethnic composition. The challenges and conflicts brought by these demographic changes will likely continue for at least the next century. Among these are challenges to the white domination of U.S. society, both in terms of the white population majority and of white power and privilege. The proportion of whites in the population is now decreasing. Significant challenges to white social, political, and educational domination are already arising from large-scale population changes and the new organizational developments that those changes usually bring. People of European descent are today a modest, decreasing fifth of the world's population. They are also a decreasing proportion of the U.S. population. White Americans are today a statistical minority in the metropolises of New York City, Los Angeles, Chicago, and Houston. They are a minority in nearly half of the nation's 100 largest cities. Whites are also a minority of the population in California, New Mexico, and Hawaii, and they soon will be in Texas. If future birth and immigration rates are at least roughly similar to those of the present day, more than half the U.S. population will be Americans of color no later than the 2050s.[4]

This ongoing demographic shift is significant, for whites have not been a statistical minority of the North American population since the 1700s. Today, much private and public discussion of these demographic changes, especially among Americans of European descent, has a fearful and alarmist tone. Many of the latter have a deep concern about non-European challenges to the dominant culture. For example, Patrick Buchanan, a former contender for the Republican presidential nomination and recent presidential candidate under the banner of the Reform Party, has often expressed the concerns of many whites about a nation no longer predominantly white. Buchanan has asserted that "Our Judeo-Christian values are going to be preserved and our Western heritage is going to be handed down to future generations and not dumped on some landfill called multiculturalism."[5] Writing in the policy journal *Foreign Affairs*, influential Harvard professor Samuel Huntington asserted the same point, with a similar metaphor: "If multiculturalism prevails and if the consensus on liberal democracy disintegrates, the United States could join the Soviet Union on the ash heap of history."[6] He, too, fears that the domestic forces pushing toward heterogeneity, diversity, and multiculturalism are disintegrating the nation.[7] Other conservatives use even wilder language and compare modest government programs of multiculturalism to "Stalinism" or "Nazism."[8]

Some liberal analysts have also expressed variations on this view of multiculturalism. Distinguished historian Arthur Schlesinger, Jr., has written about the multiculturalism that he sees as dominating all levels of U.S. education. In his view this involves "an astonishing repudiation" of the idea of "a unifying American identity." He fears the great "assault on the Western tradition" by multiculturalism, which he also terms "tribalism."[9] Many white analysts, thus, see efforts to create a multiracial democracy whose core culture is no longer predominantly European as a disturbing challenge to white values and interests, if not to white European "civilization."

A Nation of Immigrants

The United States has long been a *nation of immigrants*. Recurring immigration is its uniqueness and one of its strengths. In numbers and diversity the many millions who have come to these shores from all corners of the globe are unparalleled in the rest of the world. These millions have brought dozens of languages and cultures, a great diversity of resources, and an array of physical characteristics. This diversity can be seen in something as simple as the array of Asian, African, European, Middle Eastern, Asian-Indian, and South American restaurants in many cities, or in something as complex as recent voting patterns in California or New York and ongoing debates over multicultural education in the schools across the country.

IMMIGRANTS TO THE UNITED STATES, 1820–1998

Official government records show that between 1820 and 1998, some 64,599,082 immigrants entered the United States. Interestingly, only a small number of countries have sent more than 700,000 people. Listed below are the countries from which at least 700,000 immigrants have arrived during this long period. The asterisked countries are those from which at least two million immigrants have come during this period.[10]

- Europe (Total = 38,233,062)
  - Austria and Hungary*
  - France
  - Germany*
  - Greece
  - Ireland*
  - Italy*
  - Norway and Sweden*
  - Poland
  - Soviet Union*
  - United Kingdom*
- North America (Total = 10,273,115)
  - Canada*
  - Mexico*
- Asia and Middle East (Total = 8,365,931)
  - China
  - India
  - Korea
  - Philippines
- The Caribbean (Total = 3,525,703)
  - Cuba
  - Dominican Republic
- Central America, South America, Africa, Oceania (Total = 3,800,416; immigration from no individual country has exceeded 700,000)

European countries have supplied nearly 60 percent of the 64.6 million immigrants who have legally entered the United States over this 179-year period. Numerous European countries have supplied at least 700,000 immigrants to the growth of the United States; Austria/Hungary, Germany, Ireland, Italy, Norway/Sweden, the Soviet Union, and the United Kingdom have each contributed more than two million immigrants each. Canada, populated mostly by European immigrants and their descendants until relatively recently, has also supplied more than two million immigrants. Significantly, only four countries from the populous areas of Asia and the Middle East have contributed 700,000 immigrants or more to the U.S. mix, and not one of these has contributed as many as two million immigrants. Only two countries from the Caribbean have reached the level of 700,000 immigrants, and *no* country in Central America, South America, Africa, or Oceania has sent as many as 700,000 immigrants in this period. Indeed, Mexico is the *only* country outside of Europe and Canada that has contributed more than two million immigrants to the U.S. mix. These patterns reflect the highly discriminatory effects of U.S. immigration laws before the 1965 Immigration Act went into effect. Some groups of immigrants do not appear in these official statistics for various reasons. One group is Puerto Ricans, who are not counted because they are officially U.S. citizens whether on the island of Puerto Rico or on the mainland. We should also note that from the early 1600s to the 1860s many Africans were forced to immigrate from the continent of Africa. For most African immigrants to the colonies, and later the United States, the particular point of origin on that continent is unknown because of the brutal conditions of the forced migration. These involuntary immigrants numbered an estimated half million people, but are not counted in official immigration records.

Why do people migrate to the United States? What affects their migration? We have traced out some of these issues in Chapter 2 and elsewhere in this book. Distinctive economic and political conditions in the United States and in sending countries for particular historical periods have shaped which countries supply immigrants and how many immigrants come. As we have seen in numerous chapters, for many decades between the late nineteenth century and the mid-1960s, the United States imposed major barriers to immigrants from many areas. For those who were able to come voluntarily to the United States, economic and political conditions in their homelands that were distressing or inhospitable to personal and family development pressed people to leave. During boom times, when many low-wage jobs are available, the U.S. economy has attracted poor immigrants such as many of the Irish, Jews, Koreans, Italians, Mexicans, and Asian-Indians—all groups studied in this book. Most have come more or less voluntarily.

In thinking about ancestry and migration patterns, one must keep in mind that numerous Native American nations were already present in what would later be named "North America" when strangers from many distant shores arrived. The ancestors of contemporary Native Americans had migrated to these shores, probably from Asia, thousands of years before the first Europeans and Africans stepped off their boats. Immigration from Europe brought genocide, forced migration to reservations, and many material and other losses to Native Americans.

Immigration should also be analyzed within the relevant economic and political contexts. Political actions by the colonial and U.S. governments have helped determine immigration patterns. Historically, the U.S. empire has expanded as the U.S. government and corporations have expanded activities around the globe. U.S. ties overseas, which are more extensive than those for any previous economic or political empire, include many corporate linkages as well as military linkages, often from military interventions overseas; extensive government aid; and far-reaching mass media linkages, including television and advertising. As we have seen in this book, the history of large-scale immigration often parallels the development of U.S. linkages internationally. We saw this in the first great migrations of workers to North America, the migration of English and Irish laborers in the eighteenth and nineteenth centuries. We have also seen it in later migrations, such as the Chinese laborers who built transportation and other infrastructure projects in western states, the Mexican laborers who have done much of the hard labor in agriculture and services since the early 1900s, and the Korean immigrants who have established thousands of small businesses in U.S. cities.

In the United States, leading politicians and other government officials have used restrictive laws to control migration according to their racial and ethnic prejudices and preferences. As an article in a 1914 literary magazine noted: "Immigrants who came earlier and their descendants have always tried to keep this country for those who were already here and for their kinfolk."[11] The Chinese Exclusion Act (1882) and restrictive national-origin quotas in the 1924 Immigration Act guaranteed that by the early

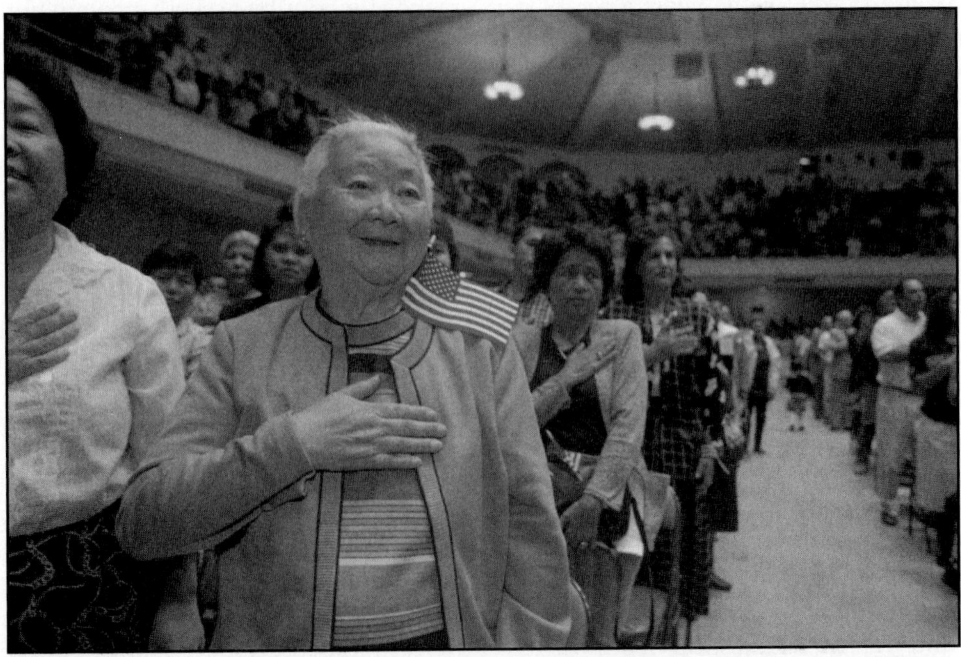

An elderly Chinese American woman recites the pledge of allegiance with a diverse group of 1,700 other new U.S. citizens in San Jose, California.

2000s the U.S. population mix would include fewer Americans from Asia or southern and eastern Europe than would otherwise have been the case. The 1924 law sharply reduced the number of Catholic immigrants from countries such as Italy and Poland and the number of Jews from eastern Europe. As a result, the United States is today majority Protestant; a minority of the population is Catholic, Jewish, or Islamic in religious faith. And Asian Americans today constitute only about 4 percent of the total U.S. population.[12]

Beginning in 1965, exclusionary racial or national-origin quotas in U.S. immigration laws were replaced with limits on the number of immigrants allowed to enter from any one country. Still, both the 1986 Immigration Reform and Control Act and 1990 Immigration Act reflected dominant-group concerns about immigration. The 1986 act was intended to limit the number of immigrants from south of the U.S. border, particularly from Mexico. Latinos and other Americans have been troubled by several provisions of that act, including intrusive governmental documentation of legal work status and sanctions for businesses that employ undocumented aliens.

The 1990 Immigration Act set the annual limit of all immigrants at 675,000 for the years after 1994. This limit most affects immigrants from those countries, such as certain Asian countries, in which many people seek to enter the United States and contrasts with the generally unlimited immigration allowed before about 1910, when most potential immigrants were European in origin. The 1990 act established several visa categories, the largest of which is for family members of legal U.S. residents in order to facilitate family reunification. The 140,000 employment-based visas are primarily reserved for highly skilled workers; visas for unskilled workers are virtually unavailable. The act also designated a special category of visas to provide legalization for certain illegal immigrants from some (mostly European) countries and to set aside some visas for wealthy immigrants willing to invest at least $1 million to create jobs in the United States.[13]

In recent years, immigration has been debated by Congress and by the public. Many native-born business leaders and politicians question the character and values of the Latin Americans and Asians who constitute the majority of recent newcomers. Some native-born Americans doubt that the country can absorb, economically or politically, even the legally permitted number of new immigrants. Some worry that current immigrants are a threat to jobs of those already here, especially during recessions, or that immigrants are likely to depend on public welfare programs. Interestingly, these arguments are similar to those made by opponents of immigration in the late nineteenth century against immigrants from southern and eastern Europe.

Most respondents in a 2000 opinion survey felt that the diverse cultural composition of the United States was one of its assets. However, a substantial minority (44 percent) of the sample thought that immigrants were a drain on the economy. Just over half felt that there were too many people now immigrating to the United States. While 43 percent felt that Americans should encourage acceptance of minority groups and their customs, just over half (52 percent) thought that minority groups should be encouraged to change to be like other Americans.[14]

Although many respondents in this and other polls *believe* that immigrants are taking away many jobs, most research studies have shown that immigrants do not generally take away more jobs than they create. Immigrants' presence creates new demands for housing and other commodities. Drawing on several studies showing that immigrants actually create more jobs than they take, one report of the Council of Economic Advisors concluded that the low-wage jobs "taken by immigrants in years past have ... increased employment and income for the population as a whole."[15]

However, the impact of job competition from immigrants is not evenly felt. Native-born, lower-wage workers are hurt more than better-off Americans because immigrants are often hired for lower-wage jobs. (Numerous defenders of continuing immigration suggest that the federal government should deal actively with these negative job consequences of immigration.) Surprisingly, perhaps, it is often those Americans who are unlikely to suffer serious job competition from immigrants who are among the strongest supporters of, if not the leaders of, anti-immigrant campaigns.[16]

In 1994, the U.S. Commission on Immigration Reform issued a report asking Congress to police the borders and work sites vigorously and to establish a computerized citizen identification system for the purpose of decreasing the number of undocumented immigrants. The Commission also asked that these immigrants be barred from public services except in emergencies.[17]

Over the past decade or two, the growing misinformation about and hostility toward immigrants, both those who are legal and those who are not, have too seldom been countered by educators and public officials willing to speak out effectively on the truth about immigration. For example, contrary to public belief, recent government data indicate that the immigration from Asia and Latin America since the late 1960s is not fueling a uniquely large population expansion in the United States. The 1980s saw a population increase of only 10 percent, the second-lowest rate of increase for any decade in U.S. immigration history. The 1990s saw a somewhat faster increase (13 percent), but this, too, was smaller than the increases for most other decades over the past century and a half. For example, in the decades from the 1850s to the 1920s, the percentage increases in population ranged from a low of 15 percent over the 1910s to a high of 36 percent over the 1850s.[18]

Between 1901 and 1910, the decade that has so far seen the heaviest immigration to the United States, some 8.8 million immigrants entered the United States, mostly from Europe. Immigration and Naturalization Service (INS) data for the 1990s are incomplete at this point in time. For 1991–1998, total immigration was about 7.6 million. If the rate of immigration for these years continues for 1999 and 2000, the total number of immigrants in the decade may reach or modestly exceed that of the 1901–1910 decade. Yet, during that early-twentieth-century decade, the U.S. population was much smaller than it is today—92 million in 1910 compared with 281 million in 2000.[19] The ratio of immigrants to the native-born population is thus much lower today than it was in the late nineteenth and early twentieth centuries. Today, the United States has not only a smaller percentage of foreign-born than it had in the 1920s but also a smaller percentage of foreign-born than several European nations. Given its long history of successful absorption of immigrants and the size of its native-born population and geographical area, the United States is unlikely to be overwhelmed by the current rate of immigration.

Some social analysts argue that immigrants make mostly positive contributions to this country: As a group, immigrants are "upwardly mobile, ambitious, saving; they have traditional values, care about their children, all that sort of stuff. They've done something very dramatic to upgrade themselves."[20] Immigrants are generally hardworking and seek to make a good life for themselves and their families. If it were not for the many immigrants who have come to the United States in recent decades, numerous cities would now have significantly declining populations. The 2000 census showed that several major cities, including Chicago, Boston, and New York City, whose populations have declined over the past half century, are growing again. Other major cities, including Pittsburgh and Philadelphia, without as great an immigrant influx, have continued to decline. Some city officials have sought to support their urban economies by encouraging greater immigration. Immigrants, especially from Latin America and Asia, have repopulated declining residential areas and filled many of the low-wage jobs that often facilitate central city economic growth. In the late 1990s, the city of Boston even established an Office of New Bostonians to assist immigrant settlement there. Other cities, such as Philadelphia, are now looking to this model as one possibility for stemming their own urban decline.[21]

Interestingly, over the next half century, the United States will likely face a shortage of young workers as baby boomers retire. Over the next few decades, the aged population will gradually grow to more than one-fifth of the total population, and additional numbers will be near retirement age. The current U.S. workforce is not sufficient to meet the heavy demand for health care and social services that this aging population will require or to provide the private services such as restaurants that the more affluent among them will seek. Latin America and Asia have workers who will likely attempt to fill this gap. Increasing numbers of social analysts today are asking whether the United States can survive without the constant infusion of younger immigrants.[22]

It is significant that those immigrants who now help fill, and will increasingly fill, the low-wage worker gap are mostly workers of color, especially workers from Latin America and Asia. Many public discussions of immigration restrictions today express concern that new immigrants from Latin America and Asia are not compatible with, or assimilable to, a substantially European American culture. For more than a century, many opponents of immigration have worried about new immigrants and their physical (and thus racial) characteristics.

Most anti-immigration groups have sought to protect the dominant (north) European American culture and ensure the structural domination of new immigrants by prior immigrant groups. Today, as in the past, anti-immigrant groups would like to stop or at least substantially curtail the U.S. experiment as a "nation of immigrants."

Americans whose sentiments tap the pluralistic values that are part of U.S. history offer strong opposition to this anti-immigrant view. As they see it, the United States is still a "golden land" of opportunity and freedom for the poor or oppressed peoples of the world. Recent immigrants, like their predecessors from Europe, generally bring skills, intelligence, hard work, and/or cultural invigoration to the United States. A deeper understanding of these contributions, and a full recognition that most Americans are immigrants or the descendants of immigrants, might encourage native-born Americans to be more accepting of the present and future immigrants coming across U.S. borders.

THE MELTING POT: EARLY IMAGES OF IMMIGRANT INCORPORATION

There has never been a consensus on how new immigrants are to be incorporated into this society. Pressures for assimilation are often matched by immigrants' desire to maintain their own cultures and values. For nearly a century one prominent idealized image for the incorporation of immigrants has been that of the "melting pot." In the early 1900s, the immigrant playwright Israel Zangwill made an influential statement of this optimistic idea in his play, *The Melting Pot*, in which a struggling Russian immigrant argued the following:

> America is God's Crucible, the great Melting-Pot where all races of Europe are melting and re-forming! Here you stand, good folks, think I, when I see them at Ellis Island, here you stand in your fifty groups, with your fifty languages and histories, and your fifty blood hatreds and rivalries. But you won't be long like that, brothers, for these are the fires of God.... A fig for your feuds and vendettas! Germans and Frenchmen, Irishmen and Englishmen, Jews and Russians—into the Crucible with you all! God is making the American.[23]

Zangwill's idealistic image of a crucible that melts many different groups to form a new "American blend" symbolizes a mutual adaptation process in which old and new groups blend together on a more or less equal basis. Yet actual intergroup adaptation has usually involved much more one-way assimilation and group conflict than Zangwill envisioned. Also, Americans of color—including African, Asian, Latino, and Native Americans—are conspicuously absent from this melting pot image.

Assimilation theorists such as Milton Gordon argue that in practice the melting pot has diverged greatly from Zangwill's ideal. Immigrant adaptation has typically been in the direction of Anglo-conformity as those in each new group of immigrants have given up much of their cultural heritage for the dominant Euro-American culture. Recall Gordon's argument: "If there is anything in American life which can be described as an overall American culture which serves as a reference point for immigrants and their children, it can best be described, it seems to us, as the middle-class cultural patterns of, largely, white Protestant, Anglo-Saxon origins."[24]

MULTICULTURAL AND MULTIRACIAL DEMOCRACY ISSUES

In recent years the melting pot and pluralistic imagery have again become fairly common. Some modern-day assimilationists have expressed concern over the integration of groups from Asia and Latin America into the U.S. mix. Popular and scholarly debates over the meaning of the melting pot image today occur in colleges, corporate boardrooms, the Congress, and the White House. Indeed, in 1997–1998, President Bill Clinton set up a White House advisory panel to hold hearings across the nation on how to deal with the growing diversity and to preserve "One America." Contemporary discussions are often filled with terms, such as *multiculturalism* and *cultural diversity*, that stress the importance of respecting the many racial and ethnic groups and subcultures that have contributed to U.S. development, especially the contributions of non-European groups. A variation of the cultural pluralism perspective (see Chapter 2), multiculturalism, emerged out of the racial and ethnic protest movements of the 1960s and has spread across the United States. Yet multiculturalism itself includes substantial variations. Some multiculturalists seek only modest changes in existing institutions, while others, often called "strong" multiculturalists, seek more fundamental structural and cultural changes, especially in patterns of institutionalized racial and ethnic discrimination.

Numerous U.S. colleges and universities, as well as many elementary and secondary schools, have developed a few multicultural courses or programs to give voice to the racially oppressed people (and sometimes white women) who have done much of the hard work that has built this society. Since the 1980s, universities from Stanford University and the University of California at Irvine to the University of Florida and Tufts University have added a few courses that focus on some aspects of cultural diversity to their B.A. requirements. Multicultural programs, usually modest in scope, have been implemented at many public schools. For instance, teachers at one high school in Brooklyn's predominantly white Bensonhurst section, where a black man shopping for a used car was brazenly killed by a mob of whites, pioneered a successful multicultural class that was soon added to the curriculum in other high schools. Their goal was to shatter racial and ethnic stereotypes and provide students with an opportunity to discuss causes of intergroup stereotyping and strife.[25]

Some publishers and voluntary organizations have made multicultural teaching materials more readily available to colleges and public schools. The Southern Poverty Law Center in Montgomery, Alabama has developed a program for public schools that includes the high-quality magazine, *Teaching Tolerance*, and other curriculum materials for multicultural programs.

A "strong" version of multiculturalism has been enthusiastically embraced by numerous scholars and other Americans with roots in Africa, Asia, Latin America, and the Middle East who seek a sharp reduction in ideological racism and racial-ethnic discrimination, as well as a greater respect for their home countries and cultures. Some white analysts view this stronger variant of multicultural thought as an attack on the dominant Euro-American culture and institutions. As we noted before, Arthur

Many U.S. colleges and universities, like the University of California (Berkeley), have become more racially and ethnically diverse over the past few decades.

Schlesinger, Jr. has called the multiculturalism perspective a repudiation of the idea of the melting pot: "The contemporary ideal is not assimilation but ethnicity. We used to say *e pluribus unum*. Now we glorify *pluribus* and belittle *unum*. The melting pot yields to the Tower of Babel."[26]

Social scientists and popular writers who make such arguments usually reflect the "order theory" framework we have discussed throughout this textbook. Critics of an assertive multiculturalism, fearful of losing the centripetal forces of the Euro-American culture, argue that Anglo-conformity is the best assimilation model for non-European groups. Their "melting pot" is not so much a mutual blending of diverse groups as a melting of newcomers (and some older groups) into the dominant Euro-American culture. While they may recognize some contributions of non-Europeans to the core culture, many strong critics of multiculturalism emphasize a version of the Anglo-conformity assimilation theory when they assert, for example, that the United States is founded on the European philosophy of individualism, not on a philosophy of ethnic and racial pluralism. A Eurocentric bias is evident in Schlesinger's argument: "It is not that the Western cultures are superior to other cultures as much as it is, for better or worse—our culture."[27] From this perspective, the Eurocentric bias generally found in the U.S. educational system, as well as in other sectors of the society, is not problematic, but rather essential to the integration of diverse racial and ethnic groups into one societal whole. Eurocentric observers are concerned that non-Europeans, including recent immigrants, assimilate rapidly to the dominant culture in order to prevent, as they often say, a "Balkanization" of the United States.

The strong version of multicultural thought sometimes suggests that the United States should be viewed, not as a melting pot, but as a grand mosaic, a nation that celebrates its racial and ethnic diversity with "rainbow" language.[28] The traditional images of the melting pot and assimilation assume that European culture and institutions do and should form the foundation of U.S. society. None of the early melting pot analysts paid serious attention to Americans of color. And many later pluralists have "presupposed a set of criteria for successful participation in American plural society: middle-class values, English-language dominance, and acceptance of Western political and cultural ideas."[29] In contrast, mosaic theorists do not see the European culture as necessarily central to the American identity, but rather see the United States evolving as an increasingly rainbow nation. "Ironically, it is in minority communities that the idea of the 'gorgeous mosaic' has been embraced most enthusiastically: the least powerful are advancing the most encompassing and egalitarian notion of social relations."[30] As Amitai Etzioni has noted, "The mosaic is enriched by continuous elements of different colors and shapes, but it is held together by a frame and glue. The mosaic depicts a society in which various communities maintain their religious, culinary, and cultural particularities, proud and knowledgeable about their specific traditions—while recognizing that they are integral parts of a more encompassing whole."[31]

Strong multicultural analysts and activists believe that vigorous multiculturalism and cultural diversity programs provide a necessary corrective to the dominance of Euro-American culture. Such programs should be greatly expanded in number and scope. One reason for this is that relatively few Americans, of any age, know much about the country's variegated history. One survey, using multiple-choice questions, found that most respondents could *not* choose 1775 as the year the Revolutionary War started, nor could they pick Virginia as the area where that war ended. In addition, a government survey of high school seniors found that most lacked knowledge of simple historical facts.[32] Even those who think they know U.S. history often accept many misconceptions and myths they were taught in school. Research by James Loewen, for example, shows that high school textbooks communicate much inaccurate, distorted, or elliptical information about U.S. history, particularly in regard to racial and ethnic matters. Typical high school and college textbooks try to put a pleasant face on an often brutal and bloody racial and ethnic history. For example, most textbooks leave out inconvenient historical information—such as the fact that New York's Wall Street was one of the large colonial markets where whites sold enslaved Africans, a savage business that lasted in New York until 1862, after the Civil War started.[33]

Many multicultural studies, sociologist Margaret Andersen suggests, "have encouraged us to look at traditionally excluded cultures and study them on their own terms rather than seeing them through the eyes of the dominant class." From this point of view, multiculturalism is not separatist but rather encourages "people to see in plural ways, so that they are not seeing through the lens of any single culture, but understanding the relationships of cultures to each other."[34] Analyses such as that of Schlesinger miss the fact that multicultural education is in tune with the changing demographic reality of the United States. For many, a strong multiculturalism provides a needed challenge to white (or white male) dominance in most major U.S. institutions.

Debates over multiculturalism and cultural diversity programs often become heated when they encompass issues of racial and ethnic inequality and white privilege and power. As we have noted, some analysts view the function of multicultural courses as simply to expose students to diverse racial and ethnic groups and their cultures, but other analysts want such courses to analyze the oppressive stratification that underlies much of U.S. racial and ethnic relations. Some have called this strongest version a "revolutionary multiculturalism." Its focus is power and resource inequality, and its goal is to effect major societal change through large-scale restructuring of U.S. society.

Some power-conflict analysts argue that multiculturalism in college curricula should acquaint students with the perspectives of non-dominant racial and ethnic groups and also scrutinize and change the curricula in all college disciplines so that they "fairly represent the variegated nature of American culture."[35] From this perspective, multiculturalism should also change college and university hierarchies so that people of color (and white women) are fairly represented at all levels of the faculty and administration and are an empowered presence in policy making on such matters as the admission and funding of students, hiring of administrators and faculty, drafting of curricula, and the makeup of college investments.[36] These analysts also believe that a strong commitment to multiculturalism should lead to a major alteration of the hierarchies of all private and public organizations, including corporations and government agencies, so that people of color (and white women) are substantially and meaningfully represented at all levels of decision making.

EQUALITY AND A PLURALISTIC DEMOCRACY

An Egalitarian Society?

The equality and social justice sought by all subordinated racial and ethnic groups has an ancient heritage. Indeed, the view that "all men are created equal" was articulated for this society by Thomas Jefferson and the other white male "founders" in the Declaration of Independence. Many groups since that time have taken this ideal very seriously. However, these words were initially meant to apply only to white, European, Protestant male immigrants and their male descendants—and generally only those with property. This very limited equality of access to political institutions was certainly a dramatic and democratic step forward in an autocratic and feudalistic era, but it still excluded the American majority, which at the time included women, African Americans, and Native Americans. Even the few Jewish and Catholic Americans in the country at the time usually had limited citizenship.

Over the following centuries, the conception of who could claim this equality and justice has become more inclusive. Numerous commentators see the ideal of equality as a major driving force in U.S. history as the social, economic, and political systems have gradually become more inclusive and egalitarian. The concept of equality has evolved to include equality of worth among individuals, equality of opportunity for all, equality before the law (civil rights), and, for many, equality of results in the socioeconomic system. Many scholars and popular analysts, as well as politicians and business leaders, have praised what they see as an egalitarian trend. Over time, most poor and subordinated ethnic and racial groups have achieved greater equality in some or all of these categories.

Between the early 1800s and the early 1900s, dramatic economic development in the new United States brought opportunity and prosperity to the many millions of immigrants from Europe. Although they often suffered some initial discrimination, substantial majorities of these white ethnic groups eventually achieved socioeconomic and political success. Many assimilation analysts argue that non-European groups are also moving, if more slowly, toward substantial social, economic, and political equality.

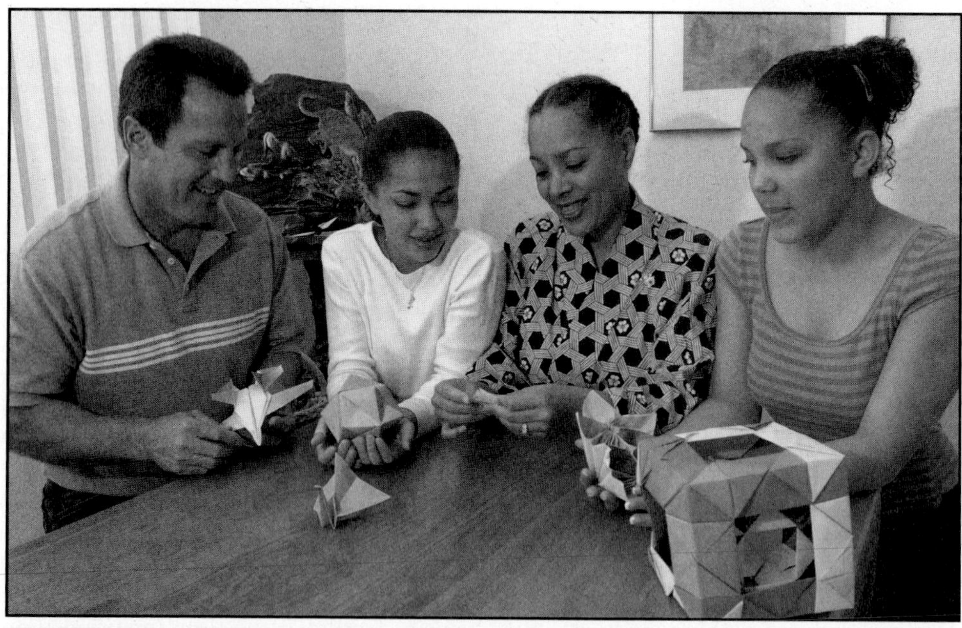

Family members, who are proud of their mixed racial and ethnic ancestries, explore the art of origami at their home in Arizona.

However, the rosy view of U.S. society as committed to "liberty and justice for all" remains today, as always, problematical. Substantial movement up the economic and political ladders did indeed come for white ethnic immigrants from Europe. But an overly optimistic view ignores the great misery and discrimination that many white ethnics endured, for a generation at least, as poorly paid laborers, servants, or peddlers in an exploitative economic system. In this book we have documented the capitalistic exploitation of workers such as Italian, Irish, and Jewish Americans. In addition, immigration for the allegedly "inferior races" from southern and eastern Europe was severely restricted by the racist immigration law that was in effect in the United States until 1965; this law also presented serious obstacles for immigrant families trying to reunite. White ethnic Americans usually faced stereotyping for several decades; for some, such as Jewish and Italian Americans, this stereotyping persists, sometimes resulting in discrimination. In assessing the present scene, one should not overlook the discrimination that some white ethnic Americans still face.

The optimistic picture of equality and freedom glosses over the continuing subordination and widespread discrimination faced by Americans with roots outside of Europe. Historically, Native, Asian, African, Latino, and Middle Eastern Americans have pressed hard for expanded equality and an end to racial and ethnic discrimination and other oppression. Periodically, over the course of U.S. history, significant improvements have occurred in legal rights and socioeconomic opportunities, such as those that followed the civil rights movement of the 1960s. Nonetheless, today's major problems of continuing racial and ethnic discrimination remain imbedded in the informal operation of U.S. economic, educational, political, and other social institutions, in which prejudiced whites still frequently discriminate against people of color, often without fear of punishment under the law. Today, most U.S. civil rights laws are weakly enforced.

Racial Discrimination: The Present Day

The year 1992 marked the 500th anniversary of the landing of Christopher Columbus and his soldiers in the Americas. Many celebrations were planned for this anniversary. As we have noted previously, the Quincentenary celebrations generated protests from many Americans, especially Native Americans, who have worked hard to counter the mythical images of brave and beneficent European explorers "discovering" America. They have shown how arrogant and imperialistic it was for these Europeans to claim to discover a land that had already been occupied by millions of people for thousands of years. The European invasion certainly benefited Europe, but it created major new problems for Native Americans, who were forced into a long and continuing struggle to maintain their lands, cultures, and institutions in the face of land theft, genocide and attempted genocide, and omnipresent racial oppression.

"Liberty and justice for all" has largely bypassed the original Americans, who generally remain the forgotten Americans. As Native American leader LaDonna Harris has stated, "How do our children feel when they read the textbooks and they're not included? What does it do to their psyche?" Harris has emphasized the vital pluralism of the Native American tribes that survived white attempts to destroy them. Indeed, respect for this early pluralism could help all Americans prepare for a future of diversity that seems to frighten many. "The browning of America is coming whether or not we like it. It's coming, and we're not prepared for it, because we haven't incorporated it into our thinking."[37]

Asian Americans, too, have provided lessons in cultural pluralism. The broad category of Asian Americans is composed of many diverse groups, including Chinese, Korean, Filipino, Vietnamese, Asian-Indian, and Japanese Americans. Today they must struggle with anti-Asian sentiment among non-Asian Americans who are concerned about job losses and economic restructuring in the United States. Asian countries have sometimes replaced the former Soviet Union as "enemies" of the United States that are somehow responsible for U.S. economic troubles. "Asia loathing" targets not only Asian countries but often the character and color of Asian peoples, once again revealing the persistence of U.S. racism.[38]

Anti-Asian sentiment has recently generated violence by whites against Asian-Pacific Americans in cities across the nation. We have noted the killing in Los Angeles in 1999 of Joseph Ileto, a Filipino American mail carrier, by a white supremacist who admitted he hated the color of the victim's skin. We also noted the killing of one Vietnamese and four Cambodian children in Stockton, California by a white man known for his hostility toward Asians.[39] "Liberty and justice" for Asian Americans is also frustrated today by the continuing bias in the justice system. For example, a group of Asian Californians testified before a distinguished panel of state judges and lawyers about problems in the state court system regarding punishment for racial violence. Dennis Hayashi, director of the Japanese American Citizens League, told the panel that the courts must become tougher on the growing number of hate-motivated criminals: "Hate violence is at an all-time high in America. But acts of racial violence are assigned a low priority [by the courts]."[40] Recent events have confirmed this perspective.

Latinos, including Puerto Ricans, Mexican Americans, and Cuban Americans, also continue to face many problems in securing justice and equality. Newspapers across the country provide evidence that anti-Latino discrimination continues to be a serious problem. One newspaper story reported that the chief executive of a health insurance firm in the Southwest had publicly defended insurance companies' discrimination against Latinos, noting that people "who cannot speak, understand or read English are considered ineligible for coverage."[41] Recent media stories have reported protests against the absence of Latino actors in major roles on television and stereotyped mass-media portrayals of Latinos as drug dealers, maids, and "Latin lovers." Research studies reported in the media have documented discrimination by white employers against Latinos in New York as well as high levels of discrimination against Latinos seeking rental housing in Fresno, California and San Antonio, Texas. Today, numerous research reports show that Latinos continue to find their progress toward equality and justice limited by stereotyping and discrimination.[42]

African Americans, too, face major obstacles in securing the equality and justice promised by the American creed. Only a little more than a century ago, Reconstruction, a period of progress in opportunities for African Americans (from about 1865 to 1885), was followed by a dramatic resurgence of white-generated oppression and legal segregation. And in the late twentieth and early twenty-first centuries, only a few decades after public policy shifted significantly in favor of expanded opportunities for African Americans and other Americans of color (in the 1960s and 1970s), U.S. society and its federal, state, and local governments again moved in a backward direction. From 1981 to 1992, and again since 2001, powerful Republican political leaders, including Republican presidents since Ronald Reagan, have cut back or kept ineffective various equal opportunity, affirmative action, and other civil rights programs designed to redress racial discrimination against Americans of color. In the 1990s the Democratic (Clinton) presidential administration placed somewhat greater emphasis on enforcing civil rights laws and expanding equal opportunity, but the election of more conservative Congresses in 1995 and 1997 brought renewed efforts to curtail affirmative action and other anti-discrimination programs. Since the 2000 election of George W. Bush, the United States has moved even farther away from an aggressive commitment to end racial discrimination in the United States. Indeed, in its first year this conservative administration turned a blind eye to matters of U.S. and international racism. For example, President Bush withdrew early a delegation to the major international conference on racism held in South Africa in August–September, 2001, an action that even European political leaders criticized.

In his book, *Turning Back: The Retreat from Racial Justice in American Thought and Policy*, Stephen Steinberg has documented a movement backward on civil rights over the past two or three decades. He suggests that both conservatives and liberals have evaded "any reckoning with America's greatest crime—slavery—and its legacy in the present."[43] Decades after civil rights laws were passed, racial and ethnic discrimination is widespread in the United States, and many of the nation's federal, state, and local government agencies and private institutions have backed away from effective programs to counter discrimination. No large-scale and lasting changes in racial composition and influence have yet occurred at or near the top levels in most major U.S. institutions. White men still, overwhelmingly, dominate upper-level (and often middle-level) positions in most major organizations, from the executive branch of the U.S. government to Fortune 1000 corporations, major universities, state legislatures, major banks, and large supermarket chains.

Discrimination against African Americans remains common. In one Los Angeles study, about 60 percent of black employees reported experiencing job discrimination; those with the most education faced especially high rates of discrimination. A majority of highly educated Asian and Latino American workers also reported discrimination.[44] Just under half (45 percent) of the black respondents in one late 1990s nationwide Gallup survey—and 70 percent of black men aged 18–34—reported experiencing discrimination in one of the following areas just during the previous month: at work, dining out, shopping, with police, or in public transportation.[45]

Since the 1980s, most white Americans have shifted their attention away from eradicating racial and ethnic discrimination. Indeed, in recent years a majority of whites seem to be in denial about the severity of continuing racial discrimination. Yet the reality and pain of discrimination can be seen by any person who wishes to see it. For example, when asked what it is like being black in America, a retired professor who has lived in several regions of the country replied as follows:

> I feel angry. I feel betrayed. Sometimes I feel very cynical. Most of the time I feel that I live in a country where I'm still not respected as a person. I lived at a time when I was told that if I got a good education, did all the right things, that I could be anything I wanted to be. I got a good education. I did all the right things, but even today I run into situations where my opportunity structure is limited because I am black. So I found that all along, no matter what I did, no matter how hard I tried, limitations were placed on me strictly because of the color of my skin. So I feel betrayed by the Constitution that guaranteed me certain rights. I feel betrayed by the Pledge of Allegiance to the flag, which says "liberty and justice for all."[46]

In the aftermath of protests by African Americans in recent years, many whites have asked why they still rebel. As they did in earlier decades, some white officials have asserted that urban protests are not about racism or civil rights; instead they speak of wild youngsters, "deviants," and the need for more police. However, across the country African Americans (and other Americans of color) in all income groups have spoken out and protested because of continuing frustration, disillusionment, anger, and rage over persisting racial and ethnic discrimination. The age-old equality-and-justice agenda remains substantially unfinished for the United States. Contrary to the views of many whites, protests by African Americans and other Americans of color are usually realistic and are indeed about racism, economic equality, and civil rights. These protests are often about inequality in a criminal justice system that too often winks at police officers who engage in racial profiling or excessive force directed against people of color. They are often about the persistence of racial discrimination that keeps many men and women of color from having jobs at decent wages or from moving into better housing. And they are often about the discrimination that many Americans of color routinely encounter on the streets and in restaurants, department stores, workplaces, and historically white neighborhoods.

CONCLUSION: AN INCREASINGLY BALKANIZED NATION?

We began this chapter with a brief discussion of some major demographic changes now taking place in the United States. In some ways the country is becoming more geographically segregated along racial and ethnic lines. Most new immigrants, who are primarily Asian and Latin American, have settled in Los Angeles, New York City, San Francisco, Chicago, Miami, Baltimore, Houston, San Diego, and Boston, even as large numbers of whites have left these cities in favor of towns and cities (Atlanta, Las Vegas, Phoenix, Portland, Denver, and Seattle) in the south Atlantic, Pacific, and Mountain regions.

Even though the U.S. population has grown substantially over the past few decades, without immigration many major cities from which whites have fled would have experienced serious population declines in recent years. The ten highest-immigration metropolitan areas are becoming heavily populated by Americans of color, while much of the rest of the United States remains disproportionately white.[47] The outmigration of whites, including older whites and less-skilled whites, from states with the highest levels of new immigration from outside the United States—California, New York, Texas, Illinois, Massachusetts, Florida, and New Jersey—has been characterized by some as "white flight" from the large numbers of immigrants of color.[48]

As of the late 1990s, about half the white population lived in the Northeast or Midwest, but only one-third of Americans of color lived in those areas. This pattern continues today. Americans of color are already a majority of the populations in California, New Mexico, and Hawaii, and they will be a majority in Texas during this decade. The populations of eight additional states, including New York, New Jersey, and Florida, are projected to be more than 40 percent Americans of color by the 2020s. In contrast, twelve states, including several in New England and in the Mountain and North Central areas, are projected to be overwhelmingly white.[49]

Such population trends will likely increase the separation and informal segregation of the nation's major racial and ethnic groups and will pose a further serious challenge not only for the lives of ordinary Americans of all backgrounds but also for the nation's ability to live up to its proclaimed ideals of peaceful pluralism, tolerance, equality, and justice. Increasing separation is generally in conflict with these traditional ideals.

The ongoing population shift from a predominantly white nation to one in which no racial or ethnic group has a population majority has significant economic, social, and political implications. In our view, much more thought needs to be given by all Americans, including social researchers and policy makers, to the likely impact of these changes.

For example, consider the educational system. No later than about 2040, the U.S. educational system as a whole will be predominantly composed of students of color. Well before 2040, most city school systems will have a non-white majority. Such a population change will increasingly pose major challenges to the traditional white control of the structure, administration, and curriculum of public schools. Increasingly, parents, students, and teachers of color will likely press for more input into how public schools are structured and run. The current discrimination, subtle and blatant, against Americans of color is not likely to be tolerated when these groups have significant organizational and political power. Schools will likely become much more concerned with issues of multiculturalism, diversity, group conflict, and institutional racism.

In addition, by the 2050s, if not before, demographic forecasts suggest that a majority of working Americans will no longer be white, while a majority of the older retired population will be white. One can wonder how, to take just one issue, workers of color will view paying taxes to support elderly whites on social security and other support programs when many of those whites were the ones who created and maintained the patterns of racial discrimination that have oppressed these workers of color or their parents over many decades.

Intergroup debates about and conflict over discrimination, assimilation, diversity, and related public policy issues—such as the dismantling of affirmative action programs or movements to restrict immigrants—are likely to increase. Areas in which a majority of voters are people of color are not likely to elect white politicians who have a history of strong opposition to legal immigration, affirmative action, and other anti-discrimination programs. We already see this in California and New York. Recall that the 2000 survey of voters leaving New York City polling places found that at least one-fifth of the voters were foreign-born (mostly voters of color). Some 13 percent of the foreign-born were Asian American voters, who are doubtless seeking expanded political representation in a city where they have had little representation. Not surprisingly, Asian American leaders forecast major political changes for that city, including more attention to the needs of the city's Asian American communities. As voting constituencies change to reflect ongoing demographic changes, the composition of political bodies, juries and justice systems, educational systems, and other government institutions at all levels is likely to change significantly—unless, as some analysts fear, reactionary political and business leaders take action to stop these likely changes in the direction of expanded democracy.[50]

Is it possible to move in the direction of much greater racial and ethnic equality and justice? These ideals have long been part of an authentic American dream. The roots of that dream lie in many Americans' aspirations for liberty, human rights, and social justice over nearly four centuries. These ideals were articulated in the Declaration of Independence, a pathbreaking document that more than two centuries ago reflected this nation's movement in the direction of expanded liberty and democracy. However, as we have seen, the Declaration and the U.S. Constitution were seriously marred by a capitulation to white supporters of the slavery system. After the abolitionist movement and the Civil War, the Constitution was amended to abolish slavery and to expand the liberties of African Americans, although Supreme Court and other government decisions soon severely limited the benefits stemming from the constitutional changes. Later, in the mid- and late-twentieth century, under pressure from the civil rights and women's movements, Supreme Court decisions and new civil rights laws brought formal equality and greater opportunities for Americans of color (and women). Still, anti-discrimination laws and court decisions have often gone unenforced or have been weakly enforced. It is also important to note that civil rights laws do not protect against, and thus cannot eradicate, many informal types of racial and ethnic discrimination that persist in the twenty-first century.

Whether equality and social justice for subordinated racial and ethnic groups can become the reality in the United States remains to be seen. In the recent and distant past, the expansion of human rights, equality, and justice has often resulted from the effective organization of racially and ethnically oppressed people and their allies against racial and ethnic oppression. The likelihood of a further expansion seems to be conditional on renewed and successful political action and organization by Americans of all backgrounds and creeds who are committed to the eradication of racial and ethnic oppression and to the full implementation of these ideals of human rights, equality, and justice.

PART III

Global Realities

TODAY, there is much racial and ethnic oppression and conflict in countries across the globe. In this third section we go beyond the United States to look at some major racial and ethnic issues as they have arisen on other continents—Latin America, Europe, and Africa.

Until European imperialism began in the 1400s, most local intergroup oppressions and conflicts overseas were shaped only by local histories and contexts. In the long period of European imperialism, numerous European countries sent explorers and colonists to seize the labor, lands, and other material resources that would expand the wealth of the home countries. Eventually, most of the globe was under European domination. This colonialism involved the organized theft (exploitation) of the labor and land of many indigenous societies.

In *The World and Africa* (1946), sociologist W. E. B. Du Bois summarized the bloody impact of much European colonialism:

> There was no Nazi atrocity—concentration camps, wholesale maiming and murder, defilement of women and ghastly blasphemy of childhood—that the Christian civilization of Europe had not long been practicing against colored folk in all parts of the world in the name of and for the defense of a Superior Race born to rule the world.

Indigenous societies were usually destroyed or greatly reshaped by the impact of the European invaders and their military, political, and economic organizations. This colonization was usually defended by an ideology of white European superiority.

In addition, if there was already intergroup conflict in the colonized country, it was usually shaped or redirected by the European intervention. European imperialism also had a rebound impact on racial-ethnic oppression and conflicts in the colonizing societies. We see this in the example of France in the next chapter, as we have already seen evidence of this impact in the United States.

After centuries of direct European colonialism, colonizers and colonized have often remained linked. In *The World and Africa* Du Bois examined how the poverty and disease of Europe's African colonies were a major generating cause of the wealth and prosperity that developed in numerous European countries. A full understanding of that prosperity must incorporate how European colonialism took by force labor and other resources from many colonized countries.

Today, economic neo-colonialism often continues the process of resource exploitation. We see the impact of this colonialism and neo-colonialism in the cases of South Africa and Brazil, which are examined in the next chapter. In major ways the stolen resources of land and labor created the basis for much wealth in contemporary European countries, while leaving the former colonies with a range of major, and lasting, social and economic problems.

The histories and current racial-ethnic realities of the three countries examined in the next chapter are closely connected to the colonization of Africa. These important case studies show the major and continuing effects of Europe's overseas colonization on both the colonized and the colonizers.

14 Colonialism and Post-Colonialism

The Global Expansion of Racism

IN THE SPRING OF 1994, AFTER THE FIRST ELECTIONS IN WHICH BLACKS AND WHITES voted together, South Africa's new black president, Nelson Mandela, commented: "Today is a day like no other before it. Today marks the dawn of our freedom.... We are starting a new era of hope, reconciliation and nation-building."[1] After casting his ballot in this historic election, Anglican Archbishop Desmond Tutu remarked, "I am about two inches taller than when I arrived."[2] A black worker stated that voting day was the best day of his life: "I don't have to carry a pass. I can work anywhere in the country I want. I am free."[3] That day, thirty million South Africans felt free of apartheid, the legally institutionalized system of extensive racial segregation and social, economic, and political inequality that had long invaded every aspect of daily life in South Africa.

The newly elected South African government outlawed apartheid and promised to move toward equality in rights and in black access to everything whites had in

Most of this chapter was written by Pinar Batur of Vassar College.

South Africa. With this assurance, Nkosingthi Msesizwe, a black miner, believed he could now ride the same elevator with white miners in post-apartheid South Africa. But Msesizwe was beaten by white miners who shouted that "this hoist is for whites. It is not for you."[4] Even though South Africa's new government assured South Africans that equality would be achieved through constitutional changes, the transition has been difficult. Institutionalized racism, including overt discrimination, is still the everyday reality in contemporary South African society.

In this chapter, we move away from racial and ethnic relations and stratification in the United States to look at patterns of racial and ethnic discrimination and institutional racism in other parts of the world. We will examine the cases of South Africa, Brazil, and France in order to illustrate how colonialism and the global culture of racism and institutionalized discrimination have been implemented by and maintained by whites, including white Europeans, European Americans, and whites of European ancestry in non-European countries. The case of South Africa demonstrates the major life-determining and life-threatening consequences of colonialism and the thorough-going institutionalization of anti-black racism, whereas Brazil exhibits how a racist culture links to and maintains racist institutions. Turning to France, we explore the legacy and impact of colonialism in one major colonizing society. In our view, students of contemporary racial and ethnic relations must know about more than intergroup relations and stratification in their own country. In order to understand the global realities of this twenty-first century, students must know about the history and development of colonialism, imperialism, and racialized societies across the globe.

COLONIALISM AND RACISM

In F. Scott Fitzgerald's classic 1920s novel, *The Great Gatsby*, one discussion among wealthy white characters focuses on a racist book that argued that, if not prevented, "the white race will be ... utterly submerged. It's all scientific stuff; it's been proved.... It is up to us, who are the dominant race, to watch out or these other races will have control of things." One of the white characters then whispers, "We've got to beat them down."[5] As revealed in novels as well as in policy decisions, ideological racism has long validated for the white public imperialist expansion and colonialism around the world. Economic and political racism has long exploited people who are not of the dominant racial group, while the ideology of racism has rationalized this oppression. White racism has been the framework for rationalizing the subordination of people of color in many societies colonized by Europeans, including not only the United States but also South Africa and Brazil.

The expansion of Western capitalism around the globe since the 1500s has fostered the division of people according to racial group, including the assignment of superior and inferior characteristics to certain designated "races." As we noted in Chapter 2, the dynamics of this Western capitalistic expansion, which created numerous colonies of subordinated peoples, made racial inequality a permanent part of global existence through the discriminatory practices and ideologies of institutionalized racism. The international development of Western capitalism also fostered the advancement of ideological and "scientific" racism, integrating them into a global culture of systemic racism. The examination of racism as a global culture is important to the study of racial and ethnic relations because racism's global culture superimposes itself on most institutions in the societies it invades, and those institutions shape the construction of the personal identities and everyday experiences of both colonizers and colonized.[6]

White racism has long been a global reality. By the 19th century it had become a process of defining and building communities and societies based on racialized privileges and a continuing hierarchy of power with whites of European background at the top and racially oppressed people at or near the bottom. The global expansion of Western capitalism through colonialism gave white racism a new and global scope; indeed, by the early 1900s a majority of the earth's peoples were more or less under the control of European colonizers.

THE HISTORY AND LEGACY OF COLONIALISM

Western colonialism began with the major overseas expansion of Spain and Portugal, whose rulers sought to enhance their treasuries with gold, silver, and other goods taken by force from the world's peoples. The legal and ideological rationale for this colonialism was provided by Roman Catholic popes in several papal bulls, declarations echoing papal justifications for the Christian crusades against Muslims in earlier centuries.[7] On May 3, 1493, Pope Alexander VI issued a bull of demarcation, a document resolving Spanish and Portuguese disputes over colonization. As revised by the Treaty of Tordesillas in 1494, this bull put all the world's non-Christian ("pagan") peoples at the economic disposal of these growing colonial powers.[8] The Christian justification for expansion was for a time in tension with the profit-making desire of European entrepreneurs for land and slave labor. For a short period, some Catholic theologians and priests, most notably the Spanish priest Las Casas, opposed the ruthless enslavement of the indigenous populations. However, in a 1550 debate with Las Casas in Spain, theologian Gaines de Sepulveda carried the day with his argument that it was lawful to make war on and enslave the native populations because of their heathen, sinful, and barbarous "natures," which obligated them to serve those (the Spanish) with the "superior" culture and virtues.[9]

By the 1500s, freewheeling capitalism was developing in several nations of northern and western Europe. Over the next few centuries, a number of nations, especially the Netherlands, England, and France, spurred the global expansion of capitalism, in the process fostering great economic and racial inequality between colonizers and colonized.[10] These nations generated scholars, theologians, and politicians who developed theories of the superiority of Europeans and the animal-like inferiority of peoples caught in the web of colonialism. Europeans distinguished themselves from the so-called "savages" in many ways. Often, the colonized peoples were demonized and considered to have the vices that the English and other Europeans feared in themselves: wildness, brutishness, cruelty, laziness, sexual promiscuity, and heathenism. "Far from English civilization, they had to remind themselves constantly what it meant to be civilized—Christian, rational, sexually controlled, and white. And they tried to impute to peoples they called 'savages' the instinctual forces they had within themselves."[11] By the 1700s and 1800s, well-developed theories of the cultural and racial inferiority of the "savages" were developed by the English and other Europeans, as we noted in Chapter 1. As the major racist advocate of the nineteenth century, Joseph de Gobineau, put it:

> [White people] are gifted with reflective energy, or rather with an energetic intelligence.... They have a remarkable, even extreme love of liberty, and are openly hostile to the formalism under which the Chinese are glad to vegetate, as well as the strict despotism which is the only way of governing the Negro.[12]

At an early point in time, colonialism became a system of control based on a colonial political administration, an exploitative commercial trade, and a missionary zeal to convert indigenous populations to Christianity and Western "civilization." In Asian, African, and American societies, this threefold domination fostered colonial administrations' oppressive rule, unequal trade practices, and the imposition of Christianity and Western culture.

Desire for raw materials motivated European colonial expansion, such as the desire to obtain black pepper and lumber from Brazil or tea and spices from India. Securing these resources required use of military violence—which violence, after the military conquest, was carried out by a colonial administration. Colonial oppression was supported directly and indirectly by Christian religious groups. In India, British colonialism served as a vehicle for the spread of Christian missionary schools and activities, which were aimed at assimilating Hindus and Muslims to Western culture and ideas and fostering their acceptance of autocratic British rule. The colonized were to be violently repressed if they resisted. The North American colonists experienced British oppression in the 1700s. The people of India experienced British oppression in the 1800s and 1900s. On April 13, 1919, fearing insurrection, a British-led army unit fired on an unarmed assembly of Indians celebrating the Hindu New Year, killing 379 people and wounding 1,200—an event still well remembered in India as the Amritsar Massacre.[13]

Everyday life in the colonies was reshaped by the European oppressors, who controlled colonized societies politically, economically, and culturally. Exploitation of colonized peoples and their natural resources was accompanied by systematic violence. Violence and exploitation were justified through an ideology of cultural and racial superiority that penetrated religious and political views and even language. This institutional racism was not only an integral aspect of the dominant group's racial identity, it also seeped into the subordinate group's racialized construction of its self-conception. Pervasive material and ideological racism fostered the view of the colonized as subordinate and powerless.[14] Albert Memmi, a north African author educated in French colonial schools, wrote about the impact of colonial rule:

> I am ill at ease in my own land and I know of no other. My culture is borrowed and I speak my mother tongue haltingly. I have neither religious beliefs nor tradition and am ashamed of whatever particle of them has survived deep within me.... I am Tunisian, but of French culture.[15]

For centuries, European colonialism has had a major impact on colonizers and their home countries. The flow of raw materials from the colonies demanded a docile working class in both the colonized and the colonizing societies. The British Empire not only subjugated India, but the system of economic subjugation and racism reached back into British society, thereby shaping conditions for the white working class in Great Britain. The white working class accepted colonialism and white racism, with its sense of racial superiority. British racism has long fostered a false sense of superiority and contributed to many British workers' uncritical acceptance of their own political and economic system. Today, the impact of ideological racism is seen in white British workers' hostility to immigrants from countries in the former Empire and elsewhere. As Britain has moved into the European Union, the British government has begun to cater to xenophobia. For example, the government has used union laws to prevent the migration of "unwanted" people into the United Kingdom, such as Gypsies immigrating from the Czech Republic.[16]

Similarly, French colonialism long oppressed Algerians in Africa, and in today's post-colonial France racist views and arguments still influence the political and economic positions of first- and second-generation Algerians residing in France.[17] In the United States, as we have documented, colonial oppression included African slavery, the extermination of Native Americans, and the conquest of Puerto Rico and the Philippines. The scars of colonial oppression likewise continue to influence contemporary social and political events in the United States.

Drawing on old racist ideologies and verbally or physically attacking racially oppressed people in their midst, neo-Nazi groups and racist political parties have reemerged in most of the former colonizer societies of Europe and North America. The ongoing relationships between colonizing and colonized societies have firmly established ideological racism as a mode of global thinking—an ideology that shapes images of the colonized as well as institutionalized practices and everyday life. The ideology of racism and the practices of institutional racism are continuing global realities.

We now turn to an exploration of the impact and the legacy of colonialism in the colonized societies of South Africa and Brazil and in the colonizing society of France.

To Whom Does Southern Africa Belong?

In many countries those who occupy the land often ask, "To whom does this land really belong?" According to racist constructions of colonial history, the land is usually "discovered" by "civilized" white people who are the first to "use the land in a productive way." For white colonizers, the real history of a place begins with colonization.

An examination of land ownership in southern Africa reveals the following: The Khoisan, who were hunters and gatherers, were living in what is now South Africa when the ancestors of the current Bantu-speaking black majority began to settle there around A.D. 300.[18] The first European expedition to the area came much later in the form of Portuguese explorers in 1487. The first European settlement in southern Africa dates only to 1652, when Jan van Riebeeck established a station for the Dutch East India Company. As Dutch colonial settlements spread, confrontations with the Bantu peoples led to a series of what Europeans call "Kaffir Wars."

In Arabic, kaffir originally meant "infidel"; today it is a degrading term (like "nigger" in the United States) that whites have long applied to black South Africans. Early European occupiers saw their colonization as a religious and civilizing mission that justified the killing, subjugation, and enslavement of indigenous Khoisan and Bantu peoples. These Europeans rated themselves as religiously and racially superior to Africans, whom they considered to be animal-like, and stereotyped them as heathens, "idolatrous and licentious, thieving and lying, lazy and dirty."[19] Europeans often rationalized what they saw as the inferiority of Africans through "scientific" racism, arguing that the tropical environment was responsible for producing immature, childish, and "beastlike" creatures who would be civilized only by the European work ethic and Christian discipline. Europeans legitimated brutal enslavement of Africans as a vehicle to lift the latter from their "barbarism."[20] This view of native inferiority, a critical aspect of a colonizing ideology, was well established among the first white occupiers of southern Africa.

The Dutch colonial interest in southern Africa collided with British determination to control the sailing route to India around the tip of Africa. Britain's conquest of southern Africa's Cape Colony in 1806 and British colonial settlement beginning in 1820 fueled the out-migration of 15,000 Dutch farmers (called "Boers") into the interior, a movement these whites called the Great Trek. The Great Trek became an important symbol for their descendants. The British imperialists abolished slavery and changed the regulations on black labor. The Boers interpreted British actions as putting the Khoisan and Bantus "on an equal footing with Christians, contrary to the laws of God and the natural distinction of race."[21] These views were asserted by Christian ministers and reflected the goals of the Dutch East India Company, which had tried to create a racially divided society to buttress the slave trade and the theft of raw materials.[22]

During this period, a white mythology about land ownership developed. Some Dutch settlers began calling themselves "Afrikaners," or the "white tribe of Africa."[23] Defending slavery, the white colonizers argued that "we make the people work for us in consideration of allowing them to live in our country."[24] According to the white ideology, there were "no native blacks" prior to the arrival of Europeans. This erroneous view persists today: "Basically we came here more or less at the same time. We both belong to South Africa. There is no one black man who can say that this is his country more so than a white. We belong here as much as they do."[25] From the beginning, European colonizers in Africa often justified the subjugation of and violence against Africans in openly racist terms, and their descendants have often claimed the land as more or less for whites only.

The colonial subjugation of indigenous peoples was violent. In 1838, Boer farmers defeated the once-powerful Zulu army. In 1848, British and local forces defeated the Xhosa, and in 1879, they conquered the remaining Zulu domains. In addition to these wars, forced labor was also imposed on indigenous peoples as well as a coercive tax system. Under growing colonial control, the oppressive conditions in European-controlled mines and on agricultural plantations contributed to the brutality of everyday life for indigenous Africans.

Formation of the State and Apartheid

European interest in southern Africa was further stimulated by the discovery of diamonds and gold in the late nineteenth century. In 1910, the Union of South Africa was created, which united British areas with Boer areas. The new white-controlled state imposed racial segregation on the politically defined population of "blacks" and "coloreds," the latter being those of mixed white–black ancestry. The 1913 Native Lands Act limited land ownership and settlement for blacks and coloreds, but not for whites, to restricted areas. Voting rights and political representation were reserved for whites. At the beginning of the twentieth century, these British and Dutch colonists were not homogeneous, but did feel that they shared a common heritage of Christianity and a mission of "civilizing" Africa.

As gold and other mining expanded, the racial structure of the preindustrial colonial society became part of the new capitalist industry. The labor force was divided between white workers, who held skilled and supervisory positions with better wages and working conditions, and black workers, who were unskilled and worked under severe conditions with little pay.[26]

Black South Africans drew on their home cultures to resist the apartheid system. Organized opposition to increasingly racist policies came from the African National Congress (ANC), founded in 1912 to demand voting rights, freedom of residence, and land ownership for black Africans. The ANC was resisting a growing and openly racist state. White voters elected the National Party in 1948 on a platform of apartheid that mandated separate development and complete racial segregation. The supporters of apartheid drew on fascist ideas that had recently been dominant in Europe. Afrikaner whites, like Germans in the Nazi ideology, were constructed as a "special nation with a special mission: The Afrikaner believes that it is the will of God that there should be a diversity of races and nations and that obedience to the will of God therefore requires the acknowledgment and maintenance of that diversity."[27] Afrikaner nationalist defenders argued that "the preservation of the pure race tradition of the Boerevolk must be preserved at all costs.... Any movement, school, or individual who sins against this must by dealt with as a racial criminal by the effective authorities." Church-sanctioned racism was a great buttress for apartheid; the Dutch Reform Church of South Africa became a citadel for the National Party.[28]

Apartheid had several connected aspects. One was the hierarchical structure in which whites, about 18 percent of the population, ruled over the 82 percent who were called "colored" or "black." This racial hierarchy was fostered by a white-controlled nation state that denied citizenship to black Africans. Another aspect of racial apartheid was widespread institutional discrimination, which included extensive racial segregation in everyday life.[29]

Apartheid was reinforced by many racist laws. For example, the 1950 Population Registration Act established legal registration by racial group; the Group Areas Act prohibited black South Africans from residing outside of racially zoned areas. In 1950, the government sought to control opposition to apartheid by passing security legislation against so-called Communist activities. Since the white Minister of Justice was empowered to decide just who were "Communists," this law permitted the state to silence any blacks or whites opposed to government racial policies through the use of intimidation, imprisonment, and police violence. To control the transfer of knowledge, in 1953 the white government also took control of education from the missionary schools, creating a separate and inferior educational system for black South Africans. The government desired education that would produce unskilled laborers to meet the needs of South African industries.[30]

In addition, the Bantu Self-Government Act forced much of the black population into territorially fragmented areas, the so-called homelands, with limited resources. Recognized by white South Africans, and only by them, as "independent countries," these homelands were yet another form of racial apartheid. Another example of the brutality of apartheid was the 1956 decision to order 100,000 non-Europeans to leave their homes in the city of Johannesburg within one year in order to make space available for whites. In 1964, new laws expanded apartheid by regulating black employment, giving the police power to hold suspects for months without trial, and prohibiting mixed-race political organizations.

Scholars have debated the role of South African capitalists in maintaining apartheid. Clearly, these white capitalists have benefited from apartheid, yet some have been opposed to its more extreme manifestations. A good example is Harry Oppenheimer, who in 1957 inherited the Anglo-American Corporation and DeBeers Consolidated Mines, which control 40 percent of South African gold, 80 percent of the world's diamonds, one-sixth of the world's copper, and almost all coal production in South Africa. After 1959, Oppenheimer supported the Progressive Party, which advocated incorporation of black Africans into the political system. In 1976, he established the Urban Foundation for social support projects in black areas. Yet Oppenheimer also took advantage of the racist labor structure by holding down the wages of his black workers. Even though some capitalists objected to apartheid because it was bad for the country's image, they played a key role in prolonging apartheid because it kept labor costs down.[31]

Opposition to Apartheid

As apartheid intensified, so did efforts of the African National Congress (ANC) and another resistance group called the Pan-African Congress (PAC), both banned by the government in 1960.[32] In 1964, after the infamous Sharpeville massacre, in which the police killed sixty-nine black demonstrators in an urban area, Nelson Mandela and other ANC and PAC leaders were sentenced to life in prison. These imprisonments were followed by the torture and deaths of some leaders held in police custody. As the support of apartheid became more violent, the anti-apartheid movement in South Africa became stronger and more violent in response. A growing number of demonstrations,

Black South Africans line up to use their new voter rights in democratic municipal elections in Cape Town.

including numerous student demonstrations, resulted in hundreds of deaths of black protesters at the hands of brutal police forces.[33]

By the late 1970s, open opposition to apartheid in black townships near the larger cities forced the government to search for new ways to legitimize control. White leaders first tried co-optation. Beginning in 1978, the restrictions on labor unions among black workers and on multiracial political parties were lifted. Meanwhile, the ANC enlarged its political base and changed its emphasis from armed struggle to mass political mobilization.[34]

In the most recent period, critical issues for South Africa have included (1) "black on black violence," which reflects group differences among black South Africans; (2) the political and economic problems plaguing the segregated homelands, which began to receive attention from both the South African government and the ANC; and (3) the question of who is indeed a South African, an issue debated by black and white intellectuals.

For a time, the white government attempted to continue its control by exacerbating divisions in the black and colored populations. Differences among black South Africans have been used by white leaders to channel black anger away from white oppression. Thus, the South African government funded the black Inkatha Zulu separatist movement and secretly provided it with military training in order to fuel Zulu (one black group) hostility toward the ANC and its primary supporters, especially the Xhosa people (a different black group).[35]

By providing for some limited political participation by Asian and colored (mixed-race) people in the 1984 constitution, the white-controlled government tried to further divide the South African population, provoking widespread opposition among black Africans. Demonstrations in townships were again met with brutal suppression. Declaring a state of emergency, the government tried to prevent the press from reporting clashes and detained thousands; 250,000 black mineworkers responded to these actions with a three-week strike.[36] For a few years, such divide-and-conquer strategies allowed the white government to continue to impose its rule on black South Africans. However, by accentuating racial and ethnic divisions, these actions produced lasting problems for the development of a democratic South Africa in the current era.

White resistance to the anti-apartheid movement had its limits. Black protests, together with an international economic boycott, made life difficult for many whites in the country. The white elite, particularly the economic elite, was disturbed by the social chaos and loss of profits. In 1989, after becoming the head of the government, F. W. deKlerk began to dismantle the policies of racial apartheid under the pressure of black and white opponents of the old racist regime. After 12,000 deaths in political clashes over four years, the South African government finally moved to hold the first free elections. In April 1994, two and one-half years after being freed from prison, Nelson Mandela, the head of the ANC, was elected to the presidency of South Africa. This marked a dramatic shift in political power, from oppressors to oppressed, something rarely seen in human history without large-scale revolutions.

The Future of South Africa

In a major speech the white South African leader, F. W. deKlerk, looked back into the nation's history. On the anniversary of the Sharpeville massacre, he said: "Let the memory of those who died at Sharpeville, and all others who died as a result of the conflicts of the past, be an inspiration for the new beginning—not as a reason for dwelling in the past."[37] Yet, today the racist past is still integral to South African society. Racism is well institutionalized in everyday life, from the city of Pretoria—which white Afrikaner separatists see as their spiritual capital—to the rural Zulu homelands, where many Zulus still consider the ANC and its leaders to be the continuation of white oppression.[38]

In June 1999 a new South African president was elected to replace Mandela: the ANC leader Thabo Mbeki. So far, the black-led ANC has had a mixed record in political office. The ANC party has facilitated a peaceful transition from white to black political rule, and it has provided some economic help for poor black South Africans. To this point, however, it has mostly failed in its policies in reducing unemployment and stimulating regional development that will benefit the entire black population. It has also dismayed outside observers in its failure to acknowledge the seriousness of the AIDS epidemic in South Africa. Mbeki was elected because the new political opposition, called the Democratic Alliance, represents white power to many of the nation's black citizens. In the presidential election, the ANC distributed pamphlets showing that the opposition included among its members white supremacists who use old Nazi salutes. Yet, many black South African voters now seem to be losing hope for real economic development and prosperity. Many blacks and whites are growing disinterested in politics. For example, the turnout for regional elections dropped from 89 percent in 1999 to 50 percent in 2000.[39]

Frantz Fanon, a strong critic of European colonialism, once asked: "What is South Africa?" He answered his own question: "A boiler into which thirteen million blacks are clubbed and penned in by two and a half million whites."[40] Today, South Africa is changing, but whites still have economic control, and most black South Africans feel the nation is not changing fast enough.

The case of South Africa shows how European colonialism has historically operated through a trilogy of domination—administration, trade, and religion—to establish a system of white control and anti-black violence. Through long-term white domination, institutional racism has become an integral part of most social institutions and of white culture. Racial discrimination has shaped the construction of racial and ethnic identities and everyday experiences. The segregated patterns of housing, education, and employment reveal persisting patterns of overt racist practices by white South Africans that still target black South Africans. After three centuries of colonial exploitation, the lives of the black people of southern Africa have been changed fundamentally and irrevocably. These changes have made the struggle against systemic white racism integral to the present and future of South Africa.

Brazil: The Legacy of Slavery and the Illusion of Equality

The country of Brazil in South America is second in population only to the United States in the Western Hemisphere. It has the *largest* African-origin population outside of Africa—more than 60 million, almost half of its population. Slavery was abolished in Brazil more than one hundred years ago, but a culture of institutional racism still has a major impact on black Brazilians today. For example, in many restaurants, black customers are excluded by being told that all empty tables are reserved. A major television soap opera that showed a white man and black woman kissing received numerous protests. Black women complain that in apartment buildings they are presumed to be maids and are shown the service elevator. Almost all of the many thousands of teenagers on whom the police reportedly have detailed files are not white. Many employers routinely choose white over black applicants for better-paying jobs.[41]

Today, 40 percent of the black population works in minimum-wage jobs.[42] Though nearly half the population, black Brazilians constitute just 1 percent of the students enrolled in the universities. At the University of São Paulo, for instance, only five of the five thousand faculty members are black. Overall, blacks in Brazil have the highest rates of illiteracy, unemployment, underemployment, and marginal housing.[43] This social, economic, and political situation is the legacy of European colonization and slavery.

Brazil was colonized during the early period of the expansion of Spain and Portugal, when European knowledge of the world beyond Europe was sketchy. The Portuguese sought to establish a commercial empire, and explorer Pedro Alvarez Cabral claimed this land for the Portuguese crown. The Portuguese named the land after a dye extracted from native trees. The emerging European textile industry consumed so much of the dye that, by the end of the 1500s, one hundred ships traveled regularly between Brazil and Portugal. The Portuguese established sugar cane plantations in numerous colonial settlements. Some indigenous inhabitants were enslaved, although most were slaughtered during wars between indigenous groups and the European colonizers or in wars between the Portuguese and other European powers coming into Brazil. Or, like Native Americans in the United States, the indigenous peoples died from European diseases because they had no immunity to them.[44]

By the nineteenth century, Brazil resembled the U.S. South. Large numbers of enslaved Afro-Brazilians worked on large plantations to produce sugar, coffee, and rubber for the ever-expanding capitalist world market.[45] Brazil's slave population numbered about five million—more than half its total population—just before the late abolition of slavery in 1888. Brazil became independent of Portugal in 1822, and in 1889 the local military overthrew the monarch and declared a republic. Since that time, Brazilian history has been marked by recurring military intervention in national politics and by continuous debates about the establishment of real democracy.

A Racial Democracy?

Since Brazil's slave system ended, great racial inequality has been maintained, often in slavelike conditions, for most Afro-Brazilians. Nonetheless, a

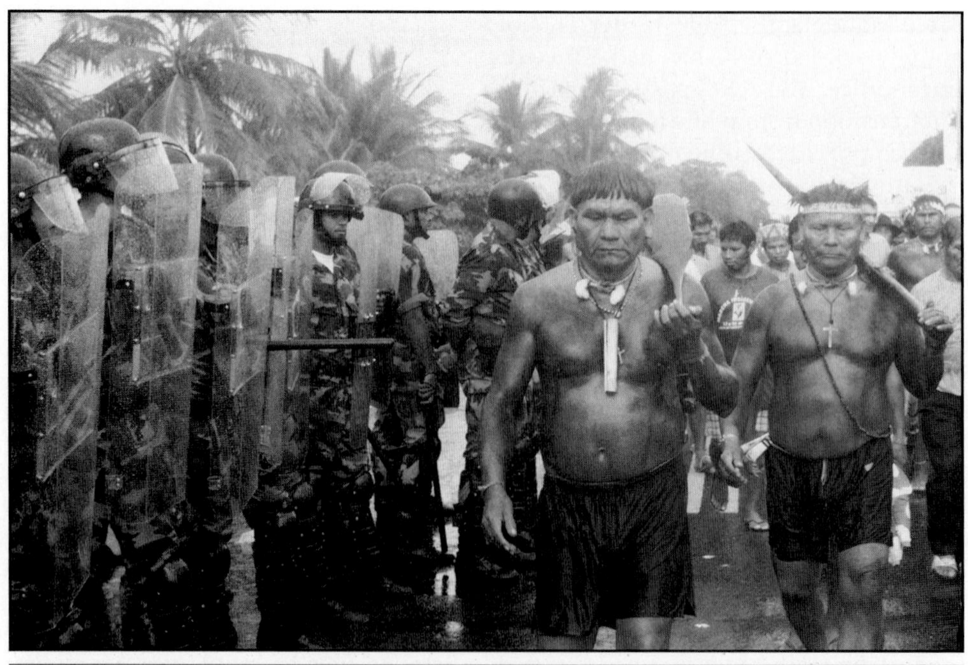

Brazilian Indians protest Brazil's 500th birthday celebration.

grand myth emerged that Brazil had "benign patterns" of racial relations and that Brazil was, and currently is, a unique "racial democracy." Many Brazilians, especially those who are white, have loudly proclaimed their society to be a true racial democracy.

Those who hold this view typically make the assumption that Portuguese colonialism was a benign form of colonial rule and that the Roman Catholicism it brought as the nation's new religion was actually oriented to black inclusion and assimilation. The Catholic church, these whites argue, encouraged the freeing of slaves and more humane treatment of enslaved Africans than existed in North America. Furthermore, the influence of the Muslim, darker-skinned North African Moors, who conquered and controlled Spain and Portugal from 711 to 1492, is seen as making the Spanish and Portuguese colonizers more accommodating than northern European colonizers on racial matters.[46] However, this interpretation of the Portuguese and Spanish past overlooks the Catholic church's long support of slavery and its brutal inquisition and torture of Jews and Muslims in the fifteenth and sixteenth centuries, as well as the unyielding hostility of the Spanish and Portuguese to the Moors' rule.

This notion of Brazil's unique "racial democracy" usually does recognize the existence of some prejudice and discrimination, but, in an extension of the assumption of the benign nature of slavery, it claims that such occurrences are isolated and that Afro-Brazilians are roughly equal in this multicultural society. The mainstream white ideology in Brazil argues that because of "Brazilian exceptionalism," meaning the allegedly equal treatment of the former slave population and the equal opportunities available to all, multicultural Brazil is not so starkly divided along racial lines as the United States and South Africa.[47] However, this view ignores Brazil's continuing patterns of institutional racism and its associated racist ideologies.

In the late nineteenth century, one aspect of Brazil's racist ideology was a focus on racial mixing. Many white Brazilians, including scholars and intellectuals, argued that people of mixed descent exhibit the worst characteristics of their parents' racial groups, and Brazilian society would degenerate with the increased "mixing" of the "races." This societal-degeneration view was imported from the United States and Europe. Based on nineteenth-century assumptions about the origins and hierarchy of "races" (see Chapter 1), this racist notion fit in well with white fears of losing control to a growing Afro-Brazilian population. Opponents of racial mixing supported their argument with a "whitening thesis," which claimed that the "stronger and better white genes" are essential to the progressive evolution of the Brazilian population.

Even though these racist notions assume the superiority of the white race, they are contradictory. On the one hand, the fear of racial mixing seems to encourage racial segregation, while on the other, the whitening notion seems to favor interracial marriages that would supposedly improve society's "gene pool."[48] Emerging together in the nineteenth century, these racist views still remain part of Brazil's culture of racism and still influence many white Brazilians' thinking about the future of the country. Today, this perspective can be seen in immigration policies favoring white Europeans, in white attitudes to interracial marriages, and even in many blacks' adherence to a color hierarchy that also shows preference for lighter skin tones.

Many light-skinned Brazilians believe that differences between their racial groups are less important than such differences in South Africa or the United States. However, Brazilians use at least 125 words for racial identification; the word for "black" does not have the same meaning in Brazil as in the United States or South Africa. In Brazil, *preto* (black) describes a person with mostly or all African ancestry. Yet, a racially mixed person who would likely be called "black" in the United States is identified in Brazil as *moreno*. *Morenos* are further divided into light (*morenos claros*) and dark (*morenos escuros*). The term *mulatto* is used to refer specifically to a person of mixed African and European backgrounds. In addition, since the term *Negro* includes *pretos* and *morenos*, it has provided a political term for black-power movements, as in Brazil's Movimento Negro.[49] Despite this diverse terminology, however, the country's racial hierarchy is supported by strong white stereotypes that view blacks as "bad-smelling, dirty, unhygienic, ugly" and view mulattoes as "pushy and envious of whites." According to one revealing Brazilian ditty, "The white man goes to heaven, the *mulatto* stays on earth, the *caboclo* (*mestizo*) goes to purgatory, the black goes to hell."[50]

Today, as in the past, whiteness is a symbol of superiority and the key to social and political power. Indeed, in national censuses the number of people who identify as *mulatto* has grown faster than is statistically possible. Many people who are not white seem to be choosing this term because they believe that "brownness" (*pardo*) is an escape hatch allowing them to achieve greater upward mobility by acquiring an intermediate, and whiter, racial status. Moreover, by downplaying real racial differences in much public discussion and debate, Brazil's white elites and political leaders avoid addressing problems of racially based economic inequality as well as racial inequalities in education and mortality rates. Brazil had an economic boom between 1950 and 1980, but the benefits flowed heavily to the upper class, which was and remains almost exclusively white. The racial disparity in income increased during this period to a level similar to that in the United States. It remains at a high level.[51]

A Century of Lies?

The colonial histories of Brazil and the United States are different, but racial inequality is similar in both countries. The inequality between Brazil's racial groups sharpened between the 1960s and the early 2000s during the nation's movement to "modernization." Transnational corporations, many headquartered in the United States, have sought low wages and new markets and thus invested heavily in Brazil. Afro-Brazilians have confronted elites and demanded equal-opportunity legislation to secure greater access to education and employment. They have developed a political movement resembling U.S. civil rights and black power movements. Since the 1980s, several conservative U.S. presidential administrations have sought to reduce federal commitments to civil rights and affirmative action and to curtail government efforts to reduce inequality (see Chapter 7). Brazil's government has acted in a similar fashion. As in the United States, powerful whites have rejected affirmative action for Afro-Brazilians as "reverse racism."[52]

May 13, 1988, marked the centennial of slavery's abolition in Brazil. The government organized a celebration, but Afro-Brazilian groups put together counter demonstrations. Demonstrators protested the persisting racial inequality and institutionalized discrimination. Labeling the celebration a "farce" and "100 years of lies," they called for a "march for the real liberation of the race." Afro-Brazilians demanded the elimination of inequality in jobs and political power; they addressed issues of racial categorization and the African influence in Brazilian culture. They advocated a strengthening of cultural and other ties between blacks in Brazil and in other parts of the African diaspora in order to challenge white racism everywhere.[53]

Helio Santos, a black university professor, has underscored the contradictions in his country today: "Brazilian society discriminates against blacks at every point, but it is hidden, disguised.... There is an illusion of social democracy in Brazil.... Blacks internalize discrimination so often they can't see it."[54] As in the United States, the illusion of equality serves elites' political purposes while discrimination remains integral to the society. As another black professor argues, "It is an illusion to think [their] situation will automatically get better as the [economic] situation of the country improves. Inequality will continue."[55] The promise of economic success frames the European colonizers' persisting myth that equality will come, along with prosperity, in the near future. In this sense, Brazil differs little from the United States and South Africa. Institutional racism and its racist culture continue to shape debates on equality and democracy. Recently, Carlos Hasenbalg has asked this question, "Is it possible that the Brazilian racial dilemma could be redefined in these terms: how to legitimate cultural diversity and at the same time insure the equal social integration of ethnic and racial groups?"[56]

In urban and rural areas, a person's racial group often coincides with class position. Because 5 percent of the Brazilian population, which is overwhelmingly white, controls 95 percent of the land, more than 50,000 rural poor marched in the late 1990s to protest the slow pace of land reform. President Fernando Henrique Cardoso was criticized for not undertaking reforms that would confront white elites. These reforms include investing in national infrastructure and education and carrying out much-needed land reform.[57] Under Cardoso's administration, visible gains have mainly been in the bureaucracy. His advisory council on racial issues is chaired by the *first* black government minister in Brazil. Under this administration, Brazil also gained its second black general and first black police commander.[58] Not surprisingly, many Brazilians want faster change. Interestingly, some rap groups, such as Racionais MC'S and Thaide & DJ Hum, are strengthening the black rights movement by using popular music to criticize racial prejudice and discrimination in the society.[59]

Another growing social movement is that of indigenous people. Even though the recent census indicates a rapid growth of the indigenous population, from 294,000 in 1991 to 386,000 in 2001, twelve of the 216 indigenous groups in Brazil are facing extinction. These indigenous groups make up 3.5 percent of the population, yet their voices have been largely undermined or ignored for centuries.[60]

The Brazilian case shows the impact of European colonialism not only on economic and political institutions but also on ideological racism's development and its penetration of popular culture. Afro-Brazilian subordination, although considered by whites to be a thing of the past, remains a central part of Brazil's present and promises to continue to influence the nation's future through the dominance of ideological racism in elite thinking, institutionalized practices, and popular culture. The Brazilian case illustrates that colonialism not only enslaved colonized people and forced them into physical labor, but it also tried to colonize their thoughts and imaginations, their relationships with each other, and the way in which they construct their identities.

COLONIALISM AND COLONIZER IN FRANCE: THE VIOLENCE OF EXCLUSION

The African theorist of race, Frantz Fanon, argued that European colonialism brought violence on subordinated peoples in part through a construction of the new colonial world in terms of "good" and "evil." Through totalitarian "colonial exploitation the settler paints the native as a sort of quintessence of evil."[61] This symbolism of good Europeans and evil colonials has religious roots and has long been part of the European culture of racism. It helped to legitimate violence against many colonized peoples. The ideology was an integral aspect of racial subordination and conflict during the colonial period and during the subsequent post-colonial period. While there are many examples of this, contemporary France is one very important case.

The Character of French Colonialism

French colonialism differed from British and Portuguese colonialism in that it claimed the newly colonized peoples as "citizens of France." To realize this fiction, colonial administrators propagated French culture and language in a vigorous attempt to assimilate colonized peoples into the French culture and empire. However, at no point in its history has France itself been unified or monocultural. Subordinated racial and ethnic groups in France, such as the Jews, have long been targets of racial hostility and exclusion. In a famous case, Alfred Dreyfus, a Jewish captain in the French army, was falsely accused by his superiors and convicted in 1898 of selling military secrets to the Germans. The trial became a major political issue in the elections of that year, and many candidates adopted anti-Semitic platforms. Yet French Jews made up a tiny 0.2 percent of the population at the time. In the first two months of 1898, French Jews were the targets of no fewer than sixty-nine anti-Semitic riots in which 4,000 people participated; the rioters destroyed Jewish businesses and synagogues and attacked individuals.[62]

France's anti-Semitic orientation emerged again during World War II in the southern pro-Nazi Vichy area of France. While the Vichy government opposed the exportation of French Jews to German extermination camps, it did not resist deportation of foreign Jews in the region.[63] When former French President Francois Mitterand's association with the pro-Nazi Vichy government was later revealed in the press, he only responded that at the time "I did not think about the anti-Semitism of Vichy."[64] Official and popular obliviousness to racism, even among some "left" politicians, is integral to a culture of racism and its allied racist practices.

Since the period of overseas colonialism, debates surrounding immigration to France have reflected the overt racism in government policies. Today, it is estimated that one in every four French citizens has a non-French parent or grandparent.[65] So immigration is of continuing importance in France. Significantly, both popular and official analyses of the problems of immigration focus on immigrants from Africa, most of whom settled in France after the Algerian War of 1954–1962.

Algeria, a country in north Africa, became a French colony in the 1830s, although the Algerians vigorously resisted the French invasion. French colonists confiscated land and stripped Algerians of political and economic rights. In response some Algerians advocated complete assimilation into French society; others demanded total independence from France through organized resistance. Interestingly, when France itself was controlled by the Germans during World War II, Algiers (in Algeria) became the capital of Free France. Algerians even fought in the French army against Germans in expectation of Algerian independence from France after the war. Yet, this political liberation did not happen. Following the war, a growing Algerian nationalist movement led by the National Liberation Front met with violent suppression from the French government. The war of independence did not end until 1962, when Algeria finally gained political independence from France.

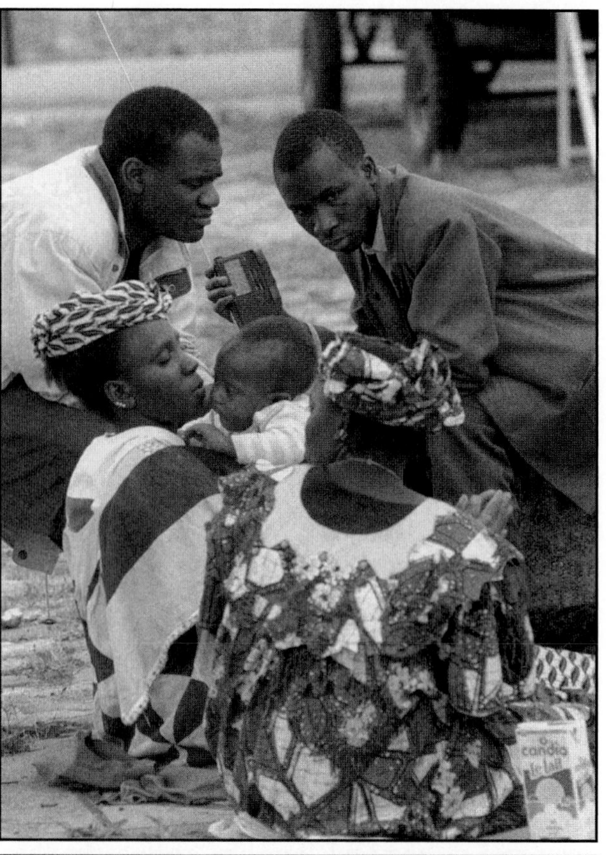

Sitting in a courtyard, these undocumented African immigrants await a court decision on whether they can stay in France.

Immigrants and Racism

Since the early 1960s, the migration of Algerians to France has made Islam the nation's second major religion, after Roman Catholicism. The large number of Muslims in France has kept alive memories of the brutal colonial war and brought a hostile reaction from many whites who fear the loss of the essence of French culture.[66] Many native-born French people have argued that cultural differences between the native-born and the African immigrants are more important than the racial division. Intellectual and popular debates focus on individual assimilation into, or conflict with, existing French culture rather than a recognition of the racialized perceptions of whites and "others," a view that is also common in the United States.[67] When French whites view racial segregation in housing as a result of immigrants' individual "choices," they miss the dynamics of the institutional racism that is routinely directed against African immigrant groups in urban housing markets in France.

Indeed, the term "immigrant" in French (as increasingly, in English) is popularly used to define only those of non-European origin, and especially Africans. According to one social worker, "immigrant" is a pejorative word: "I am a foreigner. You and I are foreigners. We are not victims of racism. An immigrant is someone who is forced to leave his country, the poor bloke—Arabs and so on."[68] Officially, people in France are classified in terms of nationality as "foreigners" or "nationals." There is no popular recognition that those Africans who are naturalized are also actual citizens of France. Unlike naturalized citizens from other parts of Europe, even naturalized Africans somehow remain "undesirable immigrants."

In recent years, the French far-right has engaged in much agitation against African immigrants. Yet, the proportion of immigrants in the French population has not increased: Immigrants account for about the same proportion of the population today (7 percent) as in 1931. In addition, 80 percent of those popularly classified as immigrants have lived in France more than ten years, and one-fourth were born in France. Most under fifteen have never lived in another country.[69]

Especially since 1980, the issue of African immigration has come to the forefront of political debate, pressed there in particular by the reactionary

Jean-Marie Le Pen and the French far right, which has received as much as 15 percent of the vote in recent elections. Le Pen's support is greatest from non-African French voters in urban areas with sizable numbers of Africans. Far-right groups advocate ending African immigration, providing job priority only for native-born French whites, forcing Africans to return to Africa, and reimposing the death penalty for criminals.[70] The far-right particularly objects to the acquisition of French nationality by second-generation Africans, whose parents are often criticized for their attachment to their cultural values and for teaching these values to their French-born children.[71] Some rightist politicians have even argued that the increasing numbers of Muslims in Europe are a threat to the supposedly Christian core of Western civilization. Indeed, such religious-right arguments have roots going back to the Crusades.

In an effort to attract voters who support the racist right, the French government has pursued some repressive policies against African immigrants and their supporters. For example, in summer 1996, when three hundred African immigrants, as well as non-African intellectuals, staged a mass protest in a church, the government sent 1,000 police officers to break down the gates of the church "so that law and order be respected."[72]

Today, racism is dividing France. An anti-racist association called SOS Racism, which includes native-born French and immigrants, is actively challenging the xenophobia, anti-Semitism, and racism fostered by the French Right. SOS Racism advocates equality of rights and favors giving immigrants the right to vote. SOS Racism had 350 local committees and fifty thousand followers at its inception and attracted media attention in the mid-1980s when it organized an anti-racism demonstration that was attended by hundreds of thousands.[73]

Still, the attacks on African (especially Arab) immigrants continue. The most extreme form of discrimination is "Arabicide," a term some use for the more than two hundred unsolved murders of the Arab residents of France over the past two decades. French law includes no category for hate crimes, and the French police do not classify the killings in a way that shows the pattern of violence against the French Arab community. These murders are often dismissed by whites as the settling of accounts between rival Arab factions. This official government attitude is similar to the French government's response to the 1961 Papon Massacre during the Algerian War. In that case, a demonstration in Paris organized to protest the nightly curfew for Algerians in France was met with massive police violence. Protesters were clubbed, machine gunned, or driven into the Seine River by the police. At least 140 Algerians were killed, and 400 people were declared missing. According to the official government report, these were all "gangland killings" between the National Liberation Front and the Algerian National Movement. The police were thereby excused for their killings.[74]

In addition to the anti-African violence, racial discrimination in housing, workplaces, and education is commonplace. Muslim communities also face attacks on their culture and traditions. One issue is the right of Muslim girls to wear traditional head scarves in French schools. Depending on the circumstances, the wearing of these head scarves has different meanings. Some Muslim feminists have argued that the traditional head scarves for women represent the oppression of patriarchy if forced on women by men. However, other feminists have argued the head scarves can represent an assertion of women's rights if they are worn by women of their own free will. They can thus represent a political statement.

The controversy began in 1989, when three Arab students wearing head scarves were excluded from school classes. In 1994, the French government banned the wearing of head scarves in public schools, arguing that the practice violated the tradition of secular education. The Education Minister claimed, "We must respect the culture and faith of Muslims, but the history and will of our people was to build a united secular society specifically where schools were concerned." In this view, scarves divided Muslims from non-Muslims, therefore violating the separation of church and state.[75] The French government has interpreted the increasing number of students wearing head scarves in schools as an indication of the increasing appeal of Muslim fundamentalism, including French Muslim support for Algeria's Islamic Salvation Front, which is fighting to establish an Islamic government in Algeria. In fact, the Education Ministry's ban on head scarves coincided with police raids in which the residents of Arab neighborhoods in French cities were arrested on suspicion of being Muslim militants.[76]

Since the 1990s, the French government has been deeply involved in the civil war between militant

Islamic groups and the government in Algeria. The French government has supported the Algerian government. In addition, France's President Jacques Chirac has aroused the racist sentiments of whites in France by accusing Algerian immigrants of being "welfare cheats" who produce many children in order to drain the welfare system.[77]

France's movement into the European Union (EU) has brought the complexities of the "New Europe" into its own society. The European Union stresses workers' rights, the standardization of policies in regard to communities of color, and a stable immigration policy. But European Union politics have also fostered a resurgence of rightist, protectionist, racist, anti-immigration, and anti–community rights political platforms in the regional areas of several countries. Le Pen supporters in France would like to expel foreigners from the country. These pressures are fostering anti–European Union movements, sometimes known as "EuroNat."[78] Hate crimes against people of color have risen significantly. One survey of young people in the EU countries found them to be dangerously nationalistic.[79] Indeed, racist music, such as the song "Beating Up Blacks," has had some popularity. A French television executive was fined for allowing this song to be performed on air, with lines like, "can't stand the foreigners, the darkies ... flick on the lighters, we're going to set them on fire."[80]

Colonialism brings oppression and violence not only to the land of the colonized but also to the land of the colonizer, especially if the colonized migrate to the colonizing country. In the post-colonial era institutional discrimination and the culture of racism persist in countries like France. Immigrants to France experience the violent legacy of African colonialism in the land of the colonizer. Their expressions of identity and culture are suppressed again with racial hatred. Their social and political participation is restricted even though the French system claims to be democratic. Their economic participation is channeled mostly into the low-wage jobs usually spurned by whites. Frantz Fanon, who participated in the original Algerian struggle for independence against the French, noted that violence "has ruled over the colonial world ... has ceaselessly drummed the rhythm for the destruction of native social forms and broken up without reserve the systems of reference of the economy, the customs of dress and external life."[81]

THE FUTURE OF COLONIALISM AND POST-COLONIALISM

During the era of European colonialism and during the post-colonial era, Europeans and European Americans have believed that the seeds of "westernization" and "modernization" will eventually bring "civilization" to the colonial or formerly colonial areas. Expecting a slow evolution, modernization theorists have argued that Euro-colonialism spread Western culture and ideology to the lands of the uncivilized and inferior. Following westernization, conflict between the colonizers and the colonized was expected to eventually disappear as the colonized peoples gradually assimilated into the superior European culture.

Clearly, this westernization view is not only racist but also unrealistic. First, the westernization process often requires colonized peoples to accept racist stereotypes of themselves as "inferior." Secondly, the westernization process demands that colonized peoples acquiesce to the continuation of global patterns of racial and ethnic inequality by accepting external European and U.S. economic and political domination. These two aspects of westernization reinforce one another and re-create another version of colonialism (some call it "coloniality") in the post-colonial era. One example can be seen in the maintenance of non-European countries as extractive economies that continue to provide important natural resources for Europeans; this arrangement perpetuates the colonial exploitation of human and natural resources and the destruction of cultures, bodies, and spirits.[82]

Some Western analysts argue that colonial control of "underdeveloped" countries brought new economic development and strong state administrations and thus helped most colonized societies advance into the "modern world." One goal of Western colonization, however, was to create local elites that were assimilated to Western cultures. The well-educated indigenous elites created by the colonial administrations are then offered as evidence of the success of this modernization process, even though many of the elites are considered by their own peoples to be as foreign as the European colonizers.[83]

Challenging this colonialism and racism, power-conflict analysts reject the assimilationist westernizing perspective. They argue that today as in the past white-generated racism is a global reality, although it has not yet been globally confronted. From the power-conflict perspective, the awareness of global diversity should emphasize the creation of new terms of human coexistence and equality in order to establish real peace. Current world conditions do not allow for the careful exploration of alternatives to external colonialism or its post-independence variants (for example, economic colonialism), in part because warring factions in many post-colonial countries continue to practice oppression and violence. And in the United States, South Africa, Brazil, and France institutional racism and discrimination continue to destroy the lives and communities of racially oppressed people.

The enslavement of human beings, whether of indigenous or imported populations, that was a common aspect of colonialism had effects that have lasted to the present. As slavery destroyed human beings and their cultures, it and its ideology became integrated into social institutions that still dominate post-colonial societies. For example, South Africa is today confronting the lingering effects of slavery and its ideology under its slowly disintegrating apartheid system; African Americans and Afro-Brazilians are demanding an abolition of the contemporary effects of slavery in their lives and communities.

From a power-conflict perspective, colonialism is an exploitative system that has brought great racial and ethnic inequalities and misery to many nations. Racial subordination integrated segregation and racial inequality into the everyday lives of North Americans, South Africans, and Brazilians, as well as people in many other countries. In the post-colonial era the painful realities of Euro-colonialism are evident in the continuing racial inequality in education, housing, business, employment, public accommodations, and health care. Around the globe this inequality influences the life chances of all people who were (and are) racially, ethnically, and religiously oppressed. Although the modes of inequality and segregation may be different, oppression and violence have been perpetuated in the post-colonialist era in both colonizing and colonized societies.

From a strong power-conflict perspective, a realistic assessment of the present and future of post-colonial societies requires a confrontation with entrenched racial inequality and segregation and a major struggle against the practices and effects of institutionalized racism and its global culture. After World War II, the conditions of the cold-war era defined the possibilities for the colonial societies as they revolted against their colonial masters. The cold war between the Soviet Union and the United States and its European allies shaped the economic dependency and cultural experiences of many post-colonial societies. Neocolonialism—the continuation of the economic and cultural dominance of the former colonial states—was often an extension of the cold war. When the Soviet Union and its empire broke up in the late 1980s and early 1990s and the cold war ended, many people in the former Soviet Union and in its satellites pressed toward full independence, with the expectation that colonialism and neocolonialism, including that of the former Soviet Union, would end. However, this has not been the case. In most of these countries, Communism has been replaced by a form of capitalism that constitutes a new type of economic and political colonialism with its close ties to Western banks and corporations. And many former European colonies in Africa and Asia face a similar neocolonialism. As the capitalist system recreates itself in new colonial forms, it creates new modes of inequality and segregation that usually remain imbedded in a culture of racial and ethnic hostility and racism.[84]

SUMMARY

European racism became a global reality through colonialism, which operated through bureaucratic administrations, exploitative trade, and a missionary type of Christian culture. European, and later U.S., colonizers rationalized colonial expansion and violence by defining themselves as superior peoples whose duty it was to modernize the "uncivilized." The construction of colonized peoples as racially inferior was a fundamental aspect of the legitimizing of this colonial exploitation. Colonialism was deadly. It destroyed local economies and political arrangements, and it even shaped many colonized peoples' conceptions of themselves and of their future possibilities. Racist culture and institutions were integral to European colonialism, and Euro-racism has persisted into the post-colonial era. Across the globe, institutional racism can be seen in racial prejudices, emotions, practices, and institutions.

The colonization of black South Africans by European states began in the seventeenth century. Over a 300-year period, a powerful racist ideology and culture evolved that has shaped most aspects of the existence of black South Africans from housing to education to employment. The racist system of apartheid created separate racial communities. Since the free election of 1994, white and black South Africans have attempted to reconcile differences within a post-apartheid system. Yet, they still face major obstacles because of persisting racism and discrimination, as well as continuing neocolonialism in the form of white control of the economy.

In contrast to racism in South Africa, Brazilian racism is often more subtle and is wrapped in the myth of "racial democracy." Brazil was colonized in the sixteenth century. Yet, today, Brazilian politics, economy, and society reveal the impact of European colonization and the slave system imposed by whites. Even though slavery was abolished more than 100 years ago, the culture of racism is evident in institutionalized racial discrimination, media and intellectual discussions, popular culture, and other aspects of everyday life. White racism penetrates the images Brazilians have of who they are and works to divide Brazilians, including those with African ancestry, according to shades of skin color. More than a century after slavery's abolition, white racism persists in the way that whites treat people of African ancestry and in the way that most Brazilians view themselves and their communities.

Colonialism left major scars on the colonized lands and also on colonizer countries. The post-colonial lives of colonized and colonizers have been plagued by social disruption and group violence. For example, France, a colonizer, has experienced continuing racial violence in the post-colonial era. Racialized thinking and practice still target French Muslims from Africa, who experience the destruction of property and attacks on their Muslim cultures.

Nonetheless, the European community, the United States, and even the United Nations have been hesitant to condemn the many acts, both violent and otherwise, that underpin global racism. They have often been reluctant to name and confront institutional racism around the globe. Today, the world appears to be in the increasingly tight grip of a culture of racial and ethnic hostility and a structure of racism long propagated by European colonialism and neocolonialism—a world in which racial and ethnic discrimination and violence are generally accepted as everyday occurrences.

Glossary

affirmative action programs Private and governmental programs that seek to improve the economic and educational opportunities for formerly excluded racial, ethnic, and gender groups.

Anglo-Protestant A more accurate term for those often referred to as Anglo-Saxon Protestant Americans.

Anglo-Saxon A term that originally referred to Germanic tribes, the Angles and the Saxons, that came to the area now called England in the fifth and sixth centuries A.D.; it was later applied to the inhabitants of England and to those English who came to North America.

anti-Semitism Stereotyping of, prejudice toward, or discrimination against Jews.

assimilation An incoming group's adoption of the cultural traits (e.g., language) and identity of the host group or integration into the primary networks and secondary organizations of the host group.

attitude-receptional assimilation Milton Gordon's term for the absence of prejudice and stereotyping.

authoritarian personalities Personalities characterized by a high degree of submission to authority, a tendency to stereotype, great concern for status, a view of the world as threatening, and an intolerance of out-groups that occupy socially subordinate positions.

behavior-receptional assimilation Milton Gordon's term for the absence of intentional discrimination.

bilingualism The ability to speak two or more languages; school (and similar) programs for children speaking two languages.

braceros Farm workers on seasonal contracts (for example, Mexican farm workers).

caste school of racial relations Power-conflict theory that emphasizes institutionalized discrimination as the foundation of a caste-like system of U.S. apartheid.

Chicano political movement A militant political movement that began during the 1960s and that has sought increased power and respect for Mexican Americans.

civic assimilation Milton Gordon's term for the absence of value and power conflict between two racial or ethnic groups.

civil rights movement A collective movement to establish or improve the legal and political rights of a subordinate racial or ethnic group.

color coding Social discrimination or stratification based on skin color.

competition theory A view of ethnicity that emphasizes the stability of ethnic boundaries over time and the intergroup competition over resources that results from shifts in these boundaries because of migration.

competitive capitalism An economic system dominated by competition between small and medium-sized for-profit businesses.

conformity function of prejudice Prejudiced attitudes held in order to conform to the expectations of an important social reference group.

covert discrimination Harmful treatment of members of subordinate racial and ethnic groups that is hidden and difficult to document.

cultural assimilation The change of one group's cultural patterns to those of the host or dominant group.

cultural pluralism The view that each racial or ethnic group has the democratic right to preserve and practice its own cultural heritage without being forced to assimilate to a dominant culture.

direct institutionalized discrimination Organizationally prescribed or community-prescribed action that by intention has a differential and negative impact on members of subordinate racial and ethnic groups.

discrimination Actions carried out by members of dominant groups, or their representatives, that have a differential and harmful impact on members of subordinate racial or ethnic groups.

dominant group A racial or ethnic group with the greatest power and resources in a society; also called a majority group.

ethnic enclave The economic (often market) and social niche that certain racial and ethnic groups have developed as a way of surviving or prospering in U.S. cities.

ethnic group A group socially distinguished or set apart, by others or by itself, primarily on the basis of cultural or national-origin characteristics.

ethnogenesis The sociological theory that over time immigrant groups not only share cultural traits with the host group but also retain major nationality characteristics.

ethnoviolence Violence directed at an individual or group because of their ethnic or racial identity.

external colonialism The economic or political exploitation of societies by powerful groups, such as (imperialistic) aristocrats or capitalists, in another geographically separate society.

externalization function of prejudice The transfer of an individual's internal psychological problem to an external racial or ethnic group as a way of repressing or denying that problem.

gendered racism The interaction of racial discrimination and gender discrimination that affects women of color.

genocide The deliberate and systematic extermination of a nationality or racial group.

hate crimes Crimes motivated by hatred or fear of a racial or ethnic group, usually an outgroup.

identification assimilation Milton Gordon's term for an incoming group's development of a sense of identity linked to that of the host group.

ideological racism An ideology that considers a group's unchangeable physical characteristics to be linked in a direct, causal way to psychological or intellectual characteristics, and that on this basis distinguishes between superior and inferior racial groups.

illegals Undocumented immigrants.

indigenous superordination A societal condition in which immigrant groups are placed in a subordinate position to a host-dominant group.

indirect institutionalized discrimination Dominant-group practices that have a harmful impact on members of subordinate racial and ethnic groups even though the organizationally- or community-prescribed norms (informal or legal rules) guiding the actions were established with no intent to harm.

individual racism Racially hostile acts of an individual directed at one or more members of another racial group.

institutional racism Institutionalized practices that differentially and negatively affect members of a subordinate racial group.

intermarriage Marriage between members of different racial or cultural groups.

internal colonialism The colony-like control and exploitation of subordinate groups by a dominant group *within* a given society.

"IQ" tests Paper-and-pencil or object/symbol manipulation tests that advocates claim can measure a global human intelligence.

isolate discrimination Harmful action taken intentionally by a member of a dominant racial or ethnic group against members of a subordinate group without direct and significant support from the immediate social or community context.

lynching The illegal killing of a person by a mob, such as by hanging.

"Mafia" myth A stereotype of Italian Americans as substantially involved in organized crime.

marital assimilation Significant intermarriage between one racial or ethnic group and another racial or ethnic group.

Marranos Jews who were forced to publicly convert to Christianity during the Spanish Inquisition under threat of death but who privately maintained allegiance to Judaism.

melting pot The view that immigrants to the United States lose their racial and ethnic identities as they mix together in one new American blend.

middleman minority A racial or ethnic group that occupies an in-between position in terms of societal power and resources.

migrant superordination A societal condition in which immigrants assume a dominant position over an indigenous population.

millenarian movements Movements among indigenous groups, such as Native Americans, that have included the belief in a golden age in which supernatural events would change present oppressive conditions.

minority group A group that is singled out because of physical or cultural characteristics for differential and unequal treatment and whose members become objects of discrimination; it typically has less power and resources than the dominant group; also called a subordinate group.

model minority stereotype The stereotype that views certain Asian American groups as exemplary in socioeconomic and moral characteristics, often as compared to other people of color.

modern racism Symbolic racism.

movements of forced labor Involuntary immigration, such as the forcible removal of Africans to North America.

multiculturalism Cultural pluralism; the political or educational movement to respect the human rights of all Americans and to recognize the diverse cultural ways of the many racial and ethnic groups in the United States, particularly those that have suffered widespread racial or ethnic discrimination.

multinational capitalism An economic system dominated by large-scale, for-profit corporations that operate in many different countries, thereby creating an international market system.

nativism An anti-immigrant ideology that advocates the protection of the native-born inhabitants of a country from immigrants who are seen as threatening or dangerous.

oppositional culture The culture of resistance often found among subordinate groups; somewhat or greatly distinct from the dominant culture, it reflects in part the struggle with that dominant culture.

order theories Racial and ethnic theories that accent group adaptation patterns involving the orderly and progressive assimilation of particular racial and ethnic groups to a dominant culture and its related institutions.

patriarchal system A social system in which men generally predominate in power and status over women and in which men work to maintain or reinforce the subordinate social roles for women.

power-conflict theories Racial and ethnic theories that accent the persisting and great inequality in the power and resource distributions associated with racial or ethnic subordination in a society.

prejudice An antipathy (negative feeling), felt or expressed, that is usually based upon a faulty generalization and directed toward a group as a whole or toward individual members of a group.

race A term developed in the 1700s by European analysts to refer to what is also called a racial group (see *racial group*).

race relations cycle Robert E. Park's view of a progressive sequence of intergroup events that usually results from one group's migration into a host society: contact, competition, accommodation, and eventual assimilation.

racial and ethnic hierarchy Stratification of, and substantial inequality among, a society's racial and ethnic groups.

racial formation theory The view that racial and ethnic relations and identities in a society are socially defined, especially by the historical actions of governments.

racial group A social group that persons inside or outside the group have decided is important to single out as inferior or superior, typically on the basis of real or alleged physical characteristics that are subjectively selected.

Reconstruction The period in U.S. history following the Civil War during which an attempt was made by the federal government to disenfranchise the slaveholding oligarchy and to improve the economic, educational, political, and human rights conditions for poor whites and blacks in the South.

Scotch-Irish immigrants Immigrants from northern Ireland some of whose ancestors are said to have immigrated to Ireland from Scotland.

slavery The legal ownership and exploitation of one human being by another; the system that makes the trade in and ownership of human beings possible.

small-group discrimination Harmful action taken intentionally by a small number of dominant-group individuals acting in concert against members of subordinate racial and ethnic groups without the support of the immediate social context.

split labor market view A power-conflict perspective that argues that the white employer class and the white part of the working class both discriminate, to a substantial degree independently, against the racially subordinated part of the working class.

stereotype An overgeneralized image, usually negative, of a racial or ethnic outgroup that is false or that greatly distorts the real characteristics of the outgroup.

structural assimilation Milton Gordon's term for an incoming group's penetration of the primary social networks of the host group.

subordinate group A group that is singled out because of physical and/or cultural characteristics for differential and unequal treatment and whose members become objects of discrimination; it typically has less power and fewer resources than the dominant group.

subtle discrimination Unequal and harmful treatment of members of subordinate racial and ethnic groups that is obvious to the victim but not as overt as traditional "door-slamming" varieties of discrimination.

symbolic racism Beliefs held by many whites that serious anti-black discrimination does not exist today and that African Americans or other people of color are making illegitimate demands for social and racial change.

systemic discrimination Institutionalized patterns of discrimination that cut across most political, economic, and social organizations in a society.

systemic racism The white prejudices, stereotypes, emotions, discriminatory practices, and institutions that are integral to the long-term domination of Americans of color.

undocumented immigrants Immigrants without legal immigration papers.

voluntary migration Migration primarily by choice.

white Anglo-Saxon Protestant Americans A label often applied to white Protestant Americans whose ancestry is English or British.

Zionism A worldwide movement for the establishment in Palestine of a national homeland for the world's Jewish communities.

Notes

Part I

1. Leonard Dinnerstein and Frederic C. Jaher, "Introduction," in *The Aliens*, ed. Leonard Dinnerstein and Frederic C. Jaher (New York: Appleton-Century-Crofts, 1970), p. 4.
2. Leonard Dinnerstein and Frederic C. Jaher, "The Colonial Era," in *The Aliens*, ed. Dinnerstein and Jahr, p. 17.
3. Quoted in Peter M. Bergman, *The Chronological History of the Negro in America* (New York: Harper & Row, 1969), p. 52.
4. John Hope Franklin, *From Slavery to Freedom*, 2nd ed. (New York: Knopf, 1963), pp. 141–143.
5. Ibid., p. 143.
6. Samuel E. Morison, *The Oxford History of the American People* (New York: Oxford University Press, 1965), p. 353.

Chapter 1

1. Frances F. Marcus, "Louisiana Repeals Black Blood Law," *New York Times*, July 6, 1983, p. A10.
2. Wilton M. Krogman, "The Concept of Race," in *The Science of Man in the World Crisis*, ed. Ralph Linton (New York: Columbia University Press, 1945) p. 38.
3. Winthrop D. Jordan, *White over Black* (Baltimore, MD: Penguin, 1969), p. 217.
4. Stephen J. Gould, "The Geometer of Race," *Discover*, November 1994, pp. 65–66.
5. Audrey Smedley, *Race in North America* (Boulder, CO: Westview, 1993), pp. 303–305.
6. Ibid, p. 26.
7. Peter I. Rose, *The Subject Is Race* (New York: Oxford University Press, 1968), pp. 32–33; Thomas F. Gossett, *Race* (New York: Schocken Books, 1965), p. 3.
8. M. Annette Jaimes, "Liberating Race," in *The State of Asian America: Activism and Resistance in the 1990s*, ed. Karin Aguilar-San Juan (Boston: South End Press, 1994), p. 369.
9. Ibid., p. 370.
10. See Pierre L. van den Berghe, *Race and Racism* (New York: Wiley, 1967), p. 11.
11. Robert Bennett Bean, *The Races of Man* (New York: University Society, 1935), pp. 94–96, quoted in *In Their Place: White America Defines Her Minorities, 1850–1950*, ed. Lewis H. Carlson and George A. Colburn (New York: Wiley, 1972), p. 106.
12. Eugenia Shanklin, *Anthropology and Race* (Belmont, CA: Wadsworth, 1994).
13. James Shreeve, "Terms of Estrangement," *Discover*, November 1994, p. 60; see also Paul Hoffman, "The Science of Race," *Discover*, November 1994, p. 4.
14. Jared Diamond, "Race without Color," *Discover*, November 1994, p. 84.
15. Michael Banton and Jonathan Harwood, *The Race Concept* (New York: Praeger, 1975), pp. 13–50.
16. See Nathan Rutstein, *Healing Racism in America* (Springfield, MA: Whitcomb, 1993), pp. 1–51, 121–129.
17. Ashley Montagu, *Race, Science and Humanity* (Princeton, NJ: D. Van Nostrand, 1963).
18. Oliver C. Cox, *Caste, Class, and Race* (Garden City, NY: Doubleday, 1948), p. 402.
19. Van den Berghe, *Race and Racism*, p. 9.
20. Michael Banton, *Race Relations* (New York: Basic Books, 1967), p. 57; see also p. 58.
21. Charles Wagley and Marvin Harris, *Minorities in the New World* (New York: Columbia University Press, 1958), p. 7.
22. Thomas F. Pettigrew, *A Profile of the Negro American* (Princeton, NJ: D. Van Nostrand, 1964), p. 69.
23. Bill Zimmerman and Bob Herzog, "Golf: From Sheep to Tiger," *Newsday*, August 13, 1997, p. A34.

24. Denene Millner, "In Creating a Word to Describe His Racial Makup, Golfer Tiger Woods Has Also Stirred Up a Round of Controversy among Blacks," *New York Daily News*, June 8, 1997, p. 2.
25. Wire reports, *Newsday*, May 20, 1997, p. A57.
26. Joe Drape, "Woods Meets Zoeller for Lunch," *New York Times*, May 21, 1997, p. B13.
27. Barbara Vobejda, "Hill Reassured on Racial Checkoff Plan for Census," *Washington Post*, July 26, 1997, p. A4; Art Shriberg and Carol Lloyd, "Interracial Marriages Still Taboo," *Tampa Tribune*, June 5, 1997, p. 1.
28. Milton M. Gordon, *Assimilation in American Life* (New York: Oxford University Press, 1964), p. 27.
29. Werner Sollors, *The Invention of Ethnicity* (New York: Oxford University Press, 1989).
30. William M. Newman, *American Pluralism* (New York: Harper & Row, 1973), p. 19.
31. W. Lloyd Warner and Leo Srole, *The Social Systems of American Ethnic Groups* (New Haven, CT: Yale University Press, 1945), pp. 284–286.
32. Van den Berghe, *Race and Racism*, p. 10.
33. See Nathan Glazer, "Blacks and Ethnic Groups: The Difference, and the Political Difference It Makes," *Social Problems* 18 (spring 1971): 447.
34. D. John Grove, *The Race vs. Ethnic Debate: A Cross-National Analysis of Two Theoretical Approaches* (Denver, CO: Center on International Race Relations, University of Denver, 1974); Robert Blauner, *Racial Oppression in America* (New York: Harper & Row, 1972).
35. Philomena Essed, *Understanding Everyday Racism* (Newbury Park, CA: Sage Publications, Inc., 1991), p. 28.
36. Letter to authors from Edna Bonacich, October 1994.
37. St. Clair Drake, *Black Folk Here and There* (Los Angeles: UCLA Center for Afro-American Studies, 1987), 1: xxiii. See also vol. 2 of this work.
38. Frank Snowden, *Color Prejudice* (Cambridge, MA: Harvard University Press, 1983), pp. 3–4, 107–108.
39. Max Weber, "Ethnic Groups," in *Theories of Society*, ed. Talcott Parsons, et al. (Glencoe, IL: Free Press, 1961), vol. 1, p. 306.
40. Joane Nagel, "Constructing Ethnicity: Creating and Recreating Ethnic Identity and Culture," *Social Problems* 43 (February 1994): 152.
41. Mary Waters, *Ethnic Options: Choosing Identities in America* (Berkeley, CA: University of California Press, 1990).
42. Mary Waters, "The Intersection of Race and Ethnicity." Paper presented at annual meeting of the American Sociological Association, Cincinnati, Ohio, 1991.
43. This term was suggested by Donald M. Young in *American Minority Peoples* (New York: Harper, 1932), p. xviii.
44. Louis Wirth, "The Problem of Minority Groups," in *The Science of Man in the World Crisis*, ed. Linton, p. 347.
45. Clifford Goertz, *The Interpretation of Cultures* (New York: Basic Books, 1973), p. 89.
46. Wendy Griswold, *Cultures and Societies in a Changing World* (Thousand Oaks, CA: PinForge Press, 1994), p. xiv.
47. Milton M. Gordon, *Assimilation in American Life* (New York: Oxford University Press, 1964), pp. 72–73.
48. See Bonnie Mitchell and Joe Feagin, "America's Racial-Ethnic Cultures: Opposition within a Mythical Melting Pot," In *Toward the Multicultural University*, ed. Benjamin Bowser, Gale Auletta, and Terry Jones (Westport, CT: Praeger, 1995), pp. 65–86; Patricia Hill Collins, *Black Feminist Thought: Knowledge, Consciousness, and the Politics of Empowerment* (Boston: Unwin Hyman, 1990).
49. William G. Sumner, *Folkways* (New York: Mentor Books, 1960), pp. 27–28.
50. Robin M. Williams, Jr., *Strangers Next Door* (Englewood Cliffs, NJ: Prentice Hall, 1964), pp. 22–25.
51. Gordon Allport, *The Nature of Prejudice*, abridged ed. (New York: Doubleday Anchor Books, 1958), p. 7 (italics omitted); see also pp. 6–7.
52. Ibid., p. 10 (italics added).
53. Jane H. Hill, "Mock Spanish: A Site for the Indexical Reproduction of Racism in American English," unpublished research paper, University of Arizona, 1995; I draw here on Joe R. Feagin, *Racist America: Roots, Current Realities, and Future Reparations* (New York: Routledge, 2000), p. 119.
54. Rosina Lippi-Green, *English with an Accent* (New York: Routledge, 1997), p. 201.
55. Hill, "Mock Spanish"; Jane H. Hill, "Junk Spanish, Anglo Identity, and the Forces of Desire," paper presented at Symposium on "Hispanic Language and Social Identity," Albuquerque, New Mexico, February 10–12, 1994.
56. See Thomas F. Pettigrew, *Racially Separate or Together?* (New York: McGraw-Hill, 1971), pp. 134–135.
57. T. W. Adorno et al., *The Authoritarian Personality* (New York: Harper, 1950), pp. 248–279.
58. Williams, *Strangers Next Door*, pp. 110–113; Pettigrew, *Racially Separate or Together?*, p. 131.
59. R. A. Schermerhorn, *Comparative Ethnic Relations* (New York: Random House, 1970), p. 6.
60. Herbert Blumer, "Race Prejudice as a Sense of Group Position," *The Pacific Sociological Review* 1 (spring 1959): 3–7.
61. Cox, *Caste, Class, and Race*, p. 400.
62. See Charles R. Lawrence, "The Id, the Ego, and Equal Protection," *Stanford Law Review* 39 (January 1987): 317–323; Gerald D. Jaynes and Robin Williams, Jr., eds. *A Common Destiny: Blacks and American Society* (Washington, D.C.: National Academy Press, 1989).

63. David M. Wellman, *Portraits of White Racism* (Cambridge: Cambridge University Press, 1977).
64. David O. Sears, "Symbolic Racism," in *Eliminating Racism*, ed. Phyllis A. Katz and Dalmas A. Taylor (New York: Plenum, 1988), pp. 55–58; John B. McConahay, "Modern Racism," in *Prejudice, Discrimination and Racism*, ed. John F. Dovidio and Samuel L. Gaertner (Orlando, FL: Academic Press, 1986).
65. Lawrence Bobo, "Group Conflict, Prejudice, and the Paradox of Contemporary Racial Attitudes," in *Eliminating Racism*, ed. Katz and Taylor, pp. 99–101.
66. Marylee Taylor and Thomas Pettigrew, "Prejudice," in *Encyclopedia of Sociology*, ed. Edgar F. Borgatta and Marie L. Borgatta (New York: Macmillan, 1992), p. 1,538.
67. Figure 1.1 and portions of this discussion are adapted from Joe R. Feagin, "Affirmative Action in an Era of Reaction," in *Consultations on the Affirmative Action Statement of the U.S. Commission on Civil Rights* (Washington, D.C.: U.S. Government Printing Office, 1982), pp. 46–48.
68. Allport, *The Nature of Prejudice*, p. 14.
69. Gunnar Myrdal, *An American Dilemma* (New York: McGraw-Hill, 1964; originally published 1944), vol. 1, p. 52.
70. Robert K. Merton, "Discrimination and the American Creed," in *Discrimination and National Welfare*, ed. Robert MacIver (New York: Harper, 1949), p. 103. See also Graham C. Kinloch, *The Dynamics of Race Relations* (New York: McGraw-Hill, 1974), p. 54.
71. Faye Crosby, Stephanie Bromley, and Leonard Saxe, "Recent Unobtrusive Studies of Black and White Discrimination and Prejudice," *Psychological Bulletin* 87 (1980): 546–563. See also Lester Hill, "Prejudice and Discrimination" (Ph.D. dissertation, University of Texas, 1978), and Joe R. Feagin and Douglas L. Eckberg, "Discrimination: Motivation, Action, Effects, and Context," in *Annual Review of Sociology*, ed. Alex Inkeles, Neil J. Smelser, and Ralph H. Turner (Palo Alto, CA: Annual Reviews, 1980), pp. 3–4.
72. Ninety percent of the smaller group gave an "approve" answer to the short question. Eduardo Bonilla-Silva and Tyrone A. Forman, "'I Am Not a Racist But ...': Mapping White College Students' Racial Ideology in the U.S.A.," *Discourse and Society* 11(2000): 51–86.
73. Charles Hamilton and Stokely Carmichael, *Black Power* (New York: Random House/Vintage Books, 1967), p. 4. See also *Institutional Racism in America*, ed. Louis L. Knowles and Kenneth Prewitt (Englewood Cliffs, NJ: Prentice Hall, 1969), p. 5.
74. Anthony Downs, *Racism in America and How to Combat It* (Washington, D.C.: U.S. Commission on Civil Rights, 1970), pp. 5, 7.
75. Thomas F. Pettigrew, "Racism and the Mental Health of White Americans: A Social Psychological View," in *Racism and Mental Health*, ed. Charles V. Willie, Bernard M. Kramer, and Bertram S. Brown (Pittsburgh, PA University of Pittsburgh Press, 1973), p. 271.
76. Essed, *Understanding Everyday Racism*, p. 39.
77. Joe R. Feagin, "Indirect Institutionalized Discrimination," *American Politics Quarterly* 5 (April 1977): 177–200.
78. Diana M. Pearce, "Black, White, and Many Shades of Gray: Real Estate Brokers and Their Racial Practices" (Ph.D. dissertation, University of Michigan, 1976); Diana Kendall, "Square Pegs in Round Holes: Nontraditional Students in Medical Schools" (Ph.D. dissertation, University of Texas, 1980).
79. Joe R. Feagin, "The Continuing Significance of Race: Antiblack Discrimination in Public Places, " *American Sociological Review* 56 (February 1991): 101–116.
80. Allport, *The Nature of Prejudice*, pp. 14–15.
81. Nijole V. Benokraitis and Joe R. Feagin, *Modern Sexism*, 2nd ed. (Englewood Cliffs, NJ: Prentice Hall, 1995), pp. 39–43.
82. Ed Jones, "What It's Like to Be a Black Manager," *Harvard Business Review* 64 (May/June 1986): 84–93; Thomas Pettigrew and Joanne Martin, "Shaping the Organizational Context for Black American Inclusion," *Journal of Social Issues* 43 (spring 1987): 41–78; Joe R. Feagin and Melvin Sikes, *Living with Racism: The Black Middle Class Experience* (Boston: Beacon Press, 1994).
83. Benokraitis and Feagin, *Modern Sexism*, p. 135.
84. Quoted in Itabari Njeri, "Words to Live or Die By," *Los Angeles Times Magazine*, May 31, 1992, p. 23.
85. Quoted in Joe R. Feagin and Melvin P. Sikes, *Living with Racism*, pp. 145–147.
86. See Joe R. Feagin and Herna Vera, *White Racism: The Basics* (New York: Routledge, 1995), Chap. 8; Feagin and Sikes, *Living with Racism.*
87. See Joe R. Feagin and Aaron Porter, "Affirmative Action and African Americans: Rhetoric and Practice," *Humboldt Journal of Social Relations* 21 (1995): 81–104. Nijole Benokraitis and Joe R. Feagin, *Affirmative Action and Equal Opportunity: Action, Inaction, Reaction* (Boulder, CO: Westview, 1978).
88. The last two paragraphs draw on Feagin and Porter, "Affirmative Action and African Americans: Rhetoric and Practice."

CHAPTER 2

1. See Tamotsu Shibutani and Kian M. Kwan, *Ethnic Stratification* (New York: Macmillan, 1965), pp. 28–33; and Donald L. Noel, "A Theory of the Origin

of Ethnic Stratification," in *Majority and Minority*, ed. Norman R. Yetman and C. Hoy Steele (Boston: Allyn & Bacon, 1971), p. 32.

2. William M. Newman, *American Pluralism* (New York: Harper & Row, 1973), pp. 30–38.
3. Ernest A. T. Barth and Donald L. Noel, "Conceptual Frameworks for the Analysis of Race Relations: An Evaluation," *Social Forces* 50 (March 1972): 336.
4. Charles Tilly, *Migration to an American City* (Wilmington, DE: University of Delaware Agricultural Experiment Station, 1965).
5. Barth and Noel, "Conceptual Frameworks," pp. 337–339.
6. R. A. Schermerhorn, *Comparative Ethnic Relations* (New York: Random House, 1970), p. 98.
7. Ibid., p. 99.
8. Stanley Lieberson, "A Societal Theory of Racial and Ethnic Relations," *American Sociological Review* 29 (December 1961): 902–910.
9. Charles Hirschman, "America's Melting Pot Reconsidered," *Annual Review of Sociology* 9 (1983): 397–423.
10. Robert E. Park, *Race and Culture* (Glencoe, IL: Free Press, 1950), p. 150 (italics added).
11. Robert E. Park and Ernest W. Burgess, *Introduction to the Science of Society* (Chicago: University of Chicago Press, 1924), p. 735.
12. Janice R. Hullum, "Robert E. Park's Theory of Race Relations." (Master's thesis, University of Texas, 1973), pp. 81–88; Park and Burgess, *Introduction to the Science of Society*, p. 760.
13. Milton M. Gordon, *Assimilation in American Life* (New York: Oxford University Press, 1964), pp. 72–73.
14. On the levels, see ibid., p. 71. On residential assimilation, see Doug Massey and Nancy Denton, "Suburbanization and Segregation in U.S. Metropolitan Areas," *American Journal of Sociology* 94 (1988): 592–626.
15. Silvia Pedraza, *Political and Economic Migrants in America: Cubans and Mexicans* (Austin: University of Texas Press, 1985), pp. 5–7; Richard Alba, *Ethnic Identity: The Transformation of White America* (New Haven, CT: Yale University Press, 1990), p. 311; Richard Alba and Victor Nee, "Rethinking Assimilation Theory for a New Era of Immigration," *International Migration Review* (1997): 829–837; J. Allen Williams and Suzanne T. Ortega, "Dimensions of Assimilation," *Social Science Quarterly* 71 (1990): 697–709.
16. Milton M. Gordon, *Human Nature, Class, and Ethnicity* (New York: Oxford University Press, 1978), pp. 67–89.
17. Gordon, *Assimilation in American Life*, pp. 78–108.
18. See Will Herberg, *Protestant–Catholic–Jew*, rev. ed. (Garden City, NY: Doubleday/Anchor Books, 1960).
19. Milton M. Gordon, "Models of Pluralism: The New American Dilemma," *Annals of the American Academy of Political and Social Science* 454 (1981): 178–188.
20. Alba, *Ethnic Identity*, p. 3; Herbert J. Gans, "Symbolic Ethnicity," *Ethnic and Racial Studies* 2 (1979): 1–20
21. Stanley Lieberson and Mary Waters, "Ethnic Mixtures in the United States," *Sociology and Social Research* 70 (1985): 43–53; Cookie White Stephan and Walter Stephan, "After Intermarriage," *Journal of Marriage and the Family* 51 (May 1989): 507–519; Alba and Lee, "Rethinking Assimilation Theory for a New Era of Immigration," p. 846; Mia Tuan, *Forever Foreigners or Honorary Whites?: The Asian American Experience Today* (New Brunswick, NJ: Rutgers University Press, 1998).
22. Milton R. Konvitz, "Horace Meyer Kallen (1882–1974)," in *American Jewish Yearbook, 1974–1975* (New York: American Jewish Committee, 1974), pp. 65–67; Milton Gordon, *Assimilation in American Life*, pp. 142–159.
23. Nathan Glazer and Daniel P. Moynihan, *Beyond the Melting Pot* (Cambridge, MA: M.I.T. Press and Harvard University Press, 1963).
24. Andrew M. Greeley, *Ethnicity in the United States* (New York: Wiley, 1974), p. 293.
25. Ibid., pp. 295–309.
26. William L. Yancey, D. P. Ericksen, and R. N. Juliani, "Emergent Ethnicity: A Review and Reformulation," *American Sociological Review* 41 (June 1976): 391–393. See also Greeley, *Ethnicity in the United States*, pp. 290–317.
27. Gunnar Myrdal, *An American Dilemma* (New York: McGraw-Hill, 1964), vol. 2, p. 929.
28. Talcott Parsons, "Full Citizenship for the Negro American? A Sociological Problem," in *The Negro American*, ed. Talcott Parsons and Kenneth B. Clark (Boston: Houghton Mifflin, 1965–1966), p. 740.
29. Ruben G. Rumbaut, "Paradoxes (and Orthodoxies) of Assimilation," *Sociological Perspectives* 40 (1997): 483.
30. Steven J. Gold, "Transnationalism and Vocabularies of Motive in International Migration: The Case of Israelis in the United States," *Sociological Perspectives* 40 (1997): 410–411.
31. Gordon, *Human Nature, Class, and Ethnicity*, pp. 73–78; See also Clifford Geertz, "The Integrative Revolution," in *Old Societies and New States*, ed. Clifford Geertz (New York: Free Press, 1963), p. 109.
32. Edna Bonacich, "Class Approaches to Ethnicity and Race," *Insurgent Sociologist* 10 (fall 1980): 11.
33. Frederik Barth, "Introduction," in *Ethnic Groups and Boundaries: The Social Organization of Culture Difference* (Oslo: Universitets Forlaget, 1969), pp. 10–17.
34. Susan Olzak, "A Competition Model of Collective Action in American Cities," in *Competitive Ethnic Relations*, ed. Susan Olzak and Joane Nagel (Orlando, FL: Academic Press, 1986), pp. 17–46.

35. Susan Olzak, "Have the Causes of Ethnic Collective Action Changed over a Hundred Years?" (technical report, Department of Sociology, Cornell University, 1987), p. 18.
36. Susan Olzak, *The Dynamics of Ethnic Competition and Conflict* (Stanford, CA: Stanford University Press, 1992).
37. Joane Nagel, "Resource Competition Theories," *American Behavioral Scientist* 38 (January 1995): 442.
38. W. Lloyd Warner, "Introduction," in Allison Davis et al., *Deep South* (Chicago: University of Chicago Press, 1941), pp. 4–6; W. Lloyd Warner and Leo Srole, *The Social Systems of American Ethnic Groups* (New Haven, CT: Yale University Press, 1945), pp. 295–296.
39. Compare Robert Blauner, *Racial Oppression in America* (New York: Harper & Row, 1972), p. 7.
40. William E. B. Du Bois, "Is Man Free?" *Scientific Monthly* 66 (May 1948): 432–434. See also Manning Marable, *How Capitalism Underdeveloped Black America* (Boston: South End Press, 1983), pp. 3–15.
41. Oliver C. Cox, *Caste, Class, and Race* (Garden City, NY: Doubleday, 1948), p. 332.
42. Ronald Bailey and Guillermo Flores, "Internal Colonialism and Racial Minorities in the U.S.: An Overview," in *Structures of Dependency*, ed. Frank Bonilla and Robert Girling (Stanford, CA: privately published by a Stanford faculty–student seminar, 1973), pp. 151–153.
43. G. Balandier, "The Colonial Situation: A Theoretical Approach," in *Social Change*, ed. Immanuel Wallerstein (New York: Wiley, 1966), p. 35.
44. Pablo Gonzalez-Casanova, "Internal Colonialism and National Development," in *Latin American Radicalism*, ed. Irving L. Horowitz, et al. (New York: Random House, 1969), p. 130; Bailey and Flores, "Internal Colonialism," p. 156.
45. Bailey and Flores, "Internal Colonialism," p. 156.
46. Blauner, *Racial Oppression in America*, p. 55. Our analysis draws throughout on Blauner's discussion.
47. Ramón Grosfoguel and Chloe S. Georas, "'Coloniality of Power and Racial Dynamics: Notes Toward a Reinterpretation of Latino Caribbeans in New York City," *Identities: Global Studies in Culture and Power* 7 (2000): 85–125.
48. Mario Barrera, *Race and Class in the Southwest* (Notre Dame, IN: University of Notre Dame Press, 1979), pp. 214–217.
49. Guillermo B. Flores, "Race and Culture in the Internal Colony: Keeping the Chicano in His Place," in *Structures of Dependency*, ed. Bonilla and Girling, p. 192.
50. Bonnie Mitchell and Joe Feagin, "America's Racial-Ethnic Cultures: Opposition within a Mythical Melting Pot," in *Toward the Multicultural University*, ed. Benjamin Bowser, Gale Auletta, snd Terry Jones (Westport, CT: Praeger, 1995), pp. 65–86. See also Michael Hechter, Debra Friedman, and Malka Appelbaum, "A Theory of Ethnic Collective Action," *International Migration Review* 16 (1982): 412–434.
51. See Carol B. Stack, "Sex Roles and Survival Strategies in an Urban Black Community," in *Woman, Culture and Society*, ed. Michelle Zimbalist Rosaldo and Louise Lamphere (Stanford, CA: Stanford University Press, 1974), p. 128; Ronald Angel and Marta Tienda, "Determinants of Extended Household Structure: Cultural Pattern or Economic Need?" *American Journal of Sociology* 87 (1981–1982): 1360–1383.
52. James C. Scott, *Domination and the Arts of Resistance* (New Haven, CT: Yale University Press, 1990); John Gaventa, *Power and Powerlessness* (Urbana, IL: University of Illinois Press, 1980).
53. Scott, *Domination and the Arts of Resistance*, p. 116.
54. Sterling Stuckey, *Slave Culture* (New York: Oxford University Press, 1987), pp. 27, 42–46.
55. W. E. B. Du Bois, "The Future of Africa," *Advocate of Peace* 81 (January 1919): 12, as quoted in Manning Marable, *W. E. B. Du Bois: Black Radical Democrat* (Boston: Twayne, 1986), p. 100.
56. Marable, *W. E. B. Du Bois*, p. 101.
57. Michael Omi and Howard Winant, *Racial Formation in the United States*, 2nd ed. (New York: Routledge, 1994), p. 40.
58. Omi and Winant, *Racial Formation in the United States*, p. 41.
59. Molefi Kete Asante, *The Afrocentric Idea* (Philadelphia: Temple, 1987); Molefi Kete Asante, *Afrocentricity* (Trenton, NJ: Africa World Press, 1988).
60. Marimba Ani, *Yurugu: An African-Centered Critique of European Cultural Thought and Behavior* (Trenton, NJ: Africa World Press, 1994), p. 567.
61. Ani, *Yurugu*, p. 570.
62. Joan W. Moore, "American Minorities and 'New Nation' Perspectives," *Pacific Sociological Review* 19 (October 1976): 448–455.
63. Bonacich, "Class Approaches to Ethnicity and Race," p. 14.
64. Cox, *Caste, Class, and Race*; Al Szymanski, *Class Structure* (New York: Praeger, 1983), pp. 420–440; Al Szymanski, "Racial Discrimination and White Gain," *American Sociological Review* 41 (1976): 403–414.
65. Stanley B. Greenberg, *Race and State in Capitalist Development* (New Haven, CT: Yale University Press, 1980), p. 349.
66. Barrera, *Race and Class in the Southwest*, pp. 201–203; Bonacich, "Class Approaches to Ethnicity and Race," p. 14.
67. W. E. B. Du Bois, *Black Reconstruction in America 1860–1880* (New York: Atheneum, 1992 [1935]), p. 700; Joe R. Feagin, *Racist America: Roots, Current Realities and Future Reparations* (New York: Routledge, 2000), pp. 30–31, 178.

68. Bonacich, "Class Approaches to Ethnicity and Race," pp. 14–15.
69. Edna Bonacich and John Modell, *The Economic Basis of Ethnic Solidarity* (Berkeley, CA: University of California Press, 1980), pp. 1–37.
70. Alejandro Portes and Robert D. Manning, "The Immigrant Enclave: Theory and Empirical Examples," in *Competitive Ethnic Relations*, ed. Olzak and Nagel, pp. 47–68.
71. Rumbaut, "Paradoxes (and Orthodoxies) of Assimilation," p. 483; Alejandro Portes, "Segmented Assimilation among New Immigrant Youth: A Conceptual Framework," in *California's Immigrant Children*, ed. Ruben Rumbaut and Wayne Cornelius (La Jolla, CA: Center for Mexican American Studies, University of California, 1995), pp. 71–76; and Min Zhou, "Growing Up American: The Challenge Confronting Immigrant Children and Children of Immigrants," *Annual Review of Sociology*, 23 (1997): 63–95.
72. Quoted in Michael Albert et al., *Liberating Theory* (Boston: South End Press, 1986), p. 35.
73. Philomena Essed, *Understanding Everyday Racism* (Newbury Park, CA: Sage, 1991), pp. 30–32.
74. Patricia Hill Collins, *Black Feminist Thought: Knowledge, Consciousness, and the Politics of Empowerment* (Boston: Unwin Hyman, 1990), pp. 40–48.
75. Denise A. Segura, "Chicanas and Triple Oppression in the Labor Force," in *Chicana Voices: Intersections of Class, Race and Gender*, ed. Teresa Cordova, et al. (Austin, TX: Center for Mexican American Studies, 1986), p. 48.
76. Omi and Winant, *Racial Formation in the United States*, pp. 75–76.
77. William E. B. Du Bois, *The World and Africa* (New York: International Publishers, 1965 [1946]), p. 37; for a more detailed development of these ideas, see Feagin, *Racist America*.
78. Cox, *Caste, Class, and Race: A Study in Social Dynamics*, p. 578.
79. Ibid., p. 332.
80. Andrew Hacker, *Two Nations: Black and White, Separate, Hostile, Unequal* (New York: Scribner's, 1992).
81. Trina, Williams. "The Homestead Act—Our Earliest National Asset Policy," paper presented at the Center for Social Development's symposium, Inclusion in Asset Building, St. Louis, Missouri, September 21–23, 2000. See also, Feagin, *Racist America*, chapter 6.
82. Ian Craib, *Modern Social Theory: From Parsons to Habermas* (New York: St. Martin's Press, 1984), p. 53.
83. Iris Young, *Justice and the Politics of Difference* (Princeton, NJ: Princeton University Press, 1990), p. 52.
84. See Tomas Almaguer, *Racial Fault Lines* (Berkeley, CA: University of California Press, 1994), p. 7.
85. Aldon Morris, *The Origins of the Civil Rights Movement* (New York: Free Press, 1984).
86. Juan F. Perea, "The Black/White Binary Paradigm of Race: The 'Normal Science' of American Racial Thought," *California Law Review* 85 (October 1997): 1219–1221.
87. See Lewis R. Gordon, *Her Majesty's Other Children: Sketches of Racism from a Neocolonial Age* (Lanham: Rowman and Littlefield, 1997), pp. 5, 53; Feagin, *Racist America*, chapter 7. This section draws in part on chapter 7.
88. Gary Y. Okihiro, "Is Yellow Black or White?" in *Asian Americans: Experiences and Perspectives*, ed. Timothy P. Fong and Larry H. Shinagawa (Upper Saddle River, NJ: Prentice Hall, 2000), p. 75.

Part II

1. Edna Bonacich, "United States Capitalist Development: A Background to Asian Immigration," in *Labor Immigration under Capitalism*, ed. Lucie Cheng and Edna Bonacich (Berkeley, CA: University of California Press, 1984), p. 82.
2. Herbert Aptheker, lectures on American history, University of Minnesota, 1984.
3. Lucie Cheng and Edna Bonacich, "Imperialism, Distorted Development, and Asian Emigration to the United States," in *Labor Immigration under Capitalism*, ed. Cheng and Bonacich, pp. 214–217.
4. Bonacich, "United States Capitalist Development," pp. 99–110.
5. Coretta Scott King, "It's a Bit Late to Protest Preferential Treatment," *Detroit Free Press*, December 13, 1985, p. 9A.
6. Stephen Steinberg, *The Ethnic Myth* (New York: Atheneum, 1981), p. 36.
7. Bonacich, "United States Capitalist Development," pp. 112–115.
8. Irving Kristol, "The Negro Today Is Like the Immigrant of Yesterday," *New York Times Magazine*, September 11, 1966, pp. 50–51, 124–142.
9. Theodore Hershberg et al., "A Tale of Three Cities: Blacks, Immigrants, and Opportunity in Philadelphia: 1850–1880, 1930, 1970," in *Philadelphia*, ed. Theodore Hershberg (New York: Oxford University Press, 1981), pp. 462–464.
10. William Yancey, E. P. Ericksen, and R. N. Juliani, "Emergent Ethnicity," *American Sociological Review* 41 (June 1976): 393.
11. Stanley Lieberson, *A Piece of the Pie* (Berkeley, CA: University of California Press, 1980), pp. 377–383.
12. Robert Blauner, *Racial Oppression in America* (New York: Harper & Row, 1972), p. 62.

13. H. Sitkoff, *A New Deal for Blacks* (New York: Oxford University Press, 1978), pp. 37–38; C. G. Wye, "The New Deal and the Negro Community," *Journal of American History* 59 (December 1972): 634.
14. Charles B. Keeley, "Population and Immigration Policy: State and Federal Roles," in *Mexican American and Central American Population Issues and U.S. Policy*, ed. Frank D. Bean, Jurgen Schmandt, and Sidney Weintraub (Austin, TX: Center for Mexican American Studies, 1988).

Chapter 3

1. Cleveland Amory, *The Proper Bostonians* (New York: Dutton, 1947), p. 11.
2. U.S. Census Bureau, *Census 2000 Supplementary Survey*. Table PCT 024. Ancestry-First Reported, <http://factfinder.census.gov/home>; U.S. Census Bureau, *Census 2000 Supplementary Survey*. Table PCT 025. Ancestry-Second Reported, <http://factfinder.census.gov/home> (retrieved January 28, 2002); U.S. Bureau of the Census, *1990 Census of Population: Social and Economic Characteristics: United States*, CP-2-1 (Washington, D.C.: 1993), p. 166.
3. Carl Wittke, "Preface to the Revised Edition," in *We Who Built America*, rev. ed. (Cleveland, OH: Case Western Reserve University Press, 1967).
4. Milton M. Gordon, *Assimilation in American Life* (New York: Oxford University Press, 1964), p. 72.
5. Rowland T. Berthoff, *British Immigrants in Industrial America* (Chicago: University of Chicago Press, 1953), p. 1.
6. John Jay, Alexander Hamilton, and James Madison, *The Federalist* (London: Penguin Classics, 1987 [1788]), p. 91.
7. Wilbur S. Shepperson, *British Emigration to North America* (Oxford: Basil Blackwell, 1957), p. 3.
8. Conrad Taeuber and Irene B. Taeuber, "Immigration to the United States," in *Population and Society*, ed. Charles B. Nam (Boston: Houghton Mifflin, 1968), p. 316.
9. Immigration and Naturalization Service, *1975 Annual Report* (Washington, D.C.: 1975), pp. 62–64.
10. Alice Marriott and Carol K. Rachlin, *American Epic* (New York: Mentor Books, 1969), p. 105.
11. Samuel Eliot Morison, *The Oxford History of the American People* (New York: Oxford University Press, 1965), pp. 48–49.
12. Klaus E. Knorr, *British Colonial Theories*, 1570–1850 (Toronto: University of Toronto Press, 1944), p. 126.
13. Marriott and Rachlin, *American Epic*, pp. 104–106; Winthrop D. Jordan, *White over Black* (Baltimore, MD: Penguin, 1969), p. 89.
14. The remainder of this paragraph and the following paragraph draw on Morison, *Oxford History of the American People*, pp. 50–154; and Maldwyn A. Jones, *American Immigration* (Chicago: University of Chicago Press, 1960), pp. 10–38.
15. Morison, *Oxford History of the American People*, p. 74.
16. David Hackett Fischer, *Albion's Seed: Four British Folkways in America* (New York: Oxford University Press, 1989), pp. 6, 13–205, 785–786.
17. Ibid., pp. 207–418.
18. Ibid., pp. 419–603.
19. Ibid., pp. 605–782.
20. *Proceedings of the American Historical Association*, vol. 1 of *Annual Report of the American Historical Association* (Washington, D.C.: American Historical Association, 1932), p. 124.
21. Jones, *American Immigration*, pp. 34–35.
22. Berthoff, *British Immigrants in Industrial America*, pp. vii, 28–29; Charlotte Erickson, "English," in *Harvard Encyclopedia of American Ethnic Groups*, ed. Stephan Thernstrom (Cambridge, MA: Harvard University Press, 1980), pp. 324–332.
23. Shepperson, *British Emigration to North America*, pp. 27–32, 84; Berthoff, *British Immigrants in Industrial America*, pp. 46–87, 122; Charlotte Erickson, "Agrarian Myths of English Immigrants," in *In the Trek of the Immigrants*, ed. O. Fritiof Ander (Rock Island, IL: Augustana Library Publications, 1964), pp. 59–64.
24. Berthoff, *British Immigrants in Industrial America*, p. 125.
25. Stanley Lieberson and Mary C. Waters, *From Many Strands* (New York: Russell Sage, 1988), pp. 40–41.
26. Charles H. Anderson, *White Protestant Americans* (Englewood Cliffs, NJ: Prentice Hall, 1970), pp. 28–71, 79–87. See also Ian C. Graham, *Colonists from Scotland* (Ithaca, NY: Cornell University Press, 1956); and Albert B. Faust, *The German Element in the United States* (New York: Steuben Society, 1927).
27. Ronald Takaki, *Iron Cages* (New York: Oxford University Press, 1990), pp. 12–14.
28. William E. B. Du Bois, *Black Reconstruction in America: An Essay Toward a History of the Part Which Black Folk Played in the Attempt to Reconstruct Democracy in America, 1860–1880* (New York: Atheneum, [1935] 1992). This and the following paragraph draw on Joe R. Feagin and Aaron Porter, "White Racism: Bibliographic Essay," *Choice* 33 (February 1996): 903–914.
29. Theodore W. Allen, *The Invention of the White Race* (New York: Verso, 1994), pp. 21, 184; David Roediger, *Towards the Abolition of Whiteness: Essays on Race, Politics, and Working Class History* (New York: Verso, 1994).
30. John Higham, *Strangers in the Land* (New York: Atheneum, 1963), p. 4.

31. Henry P. Fairchild, *Immigration* (New York: Macmillan, 1920), p. 47; Jones, *American Immigration*, p. 44.
32. Jordan, *White over Black*, p. 86.
33. Ibid., p. 87.
34. Jones, *American Immigration*, pp. 41–46.
35. Fairchild, *Immigration*, pp. 57–58.
36. Michael Kammen, *People of Paradox* (New York: Knopf, 1972), p. 66.
37. Quoted in Nancy F. Conklin and Margaret A. Lourie, *A Host of Tongues* (New York: Free Press, 1983), p. 69.
38. Higham, *Strangers in the Land*, p. 6; Marcus L. Hansen, *The Immigrant in American History* (New York: Harper Torchbooks, 1964), pp. 111–136; Wittke, *We Who Built America*, p. 505.
39. Quoted in Richard Hofstadter, *Social Darwinism in American Thought*, rev. ed. (Boston: Beacon Press, 1955), pp. 171–172.
40. Higham, *Strangers in the Land*, p. 33.
41. Hofstadter, *Social Darwinism in American Thought*, pp. 178–179; Lewis H. Carlson and George A. Colburn, *In Their Place* (New York: Wiley, 1972), pp. 305–308. Carlson and Colburn provide excerpts from the writings of Strong.
42. Higham, *Strangers in the Land*, pp. 96–152.
43. E. Digby Baltzell, *The Protestant Establishment* (New York: Random House/Vintage Books, 1966), pp. 96–98; Higham, *Strangers in the Land*, pp. 148–157.
44. Richard Alba, *Ethnic Identity: The Transformation of White America* (New Haven, CT: Yale University Press, 1990), p. 365.
45. Jones, *American Immigration*, pp. 36–38.
46. W. Lloyd Warner and Leo Srole, *The Social Systems of American Ethnic Groups* (New Haven, CT: Yale University Press, 1945), p. 287.
47. Quoted in Juan F. Perea, "Demography and Distrust: An Essay on American Languages, Cultural Pluralism and Official English," *Minnesota Law Review* 77 (1992): 269.
48. Susanna McBee, "A War over Words," *U.S. News & World Report*, October 6, 1986, p. 64.
49. "National English Campaign Supports English as the Official Language of the United States," *Business Wire*, February 11, 1997.
50. "English for the Children—California English Campaign Endorses Initiative," *Business Wire*, August 28, 1997.
51. Clarence Petersen, "Tribune Books," *Chicago Tribune*, October 31, 1993, p. C8.
52. Bill Piatt, *Only English? Law and Language Policy in the United States* (Albuquerque: University of New Mexico Press, 1990), p. 159.
53. Amado Padilla et al., "The English-Only Movement," *American Psychologist* 46 (February 1991): 120–130; National Education Association, *Official English/English Only* (Washington, D.C.: National Education Association, 1988), pp. 5–7.
54. Perea, "Demography and Distrust."
55. National Education Association, *Official English/English Only*, p. 7; Carl J. Veltman, *Language Shift in the United States* (Berlin: Mouton, 1983).
56. Fischer, *Albion's Seed*, pp. 795–797.
57. Edwin S. Gaustad, *Historical Atlas of Religion in America* (New York: Harper & Row, 1962), pp. 1–20.
58. Will Herberg, *Protestant–Catholic–Jew*, rev. ed. (Garden City, NY: Doubleday/Anchor Books, 1960), p. 82.
59. Marshall Sklare, *Conservative Judaism* (Glencoe, IL: Free Press, 1955), pp. 31–117.
60. Takaki, *Iron Cages*, p. 7.
61. Max Weber, *The Protestant Ethic and the Spirit of Capitalism*, trans. Talcott Parsons (New York: Scribner's, 1958), p. 17; see also p. 50.
62. David Ewen, *History of Popular Music* (New York: Barnes & Noble, 1961), pp. 1–10.
63. See Samuel Bowles and Herbert Gintis, *Schooling in Capitalist America* (New York: Basic Books, 1976).
64. Morison, *Oxford History of the American People*, p. 55.
65. Samuel P. Huntington, "Political Modernization: America versus Europe," *World Politics* 18 (April 1966): 147–148.
66. Jack P. Greene, *The Quest for Power* (Chapel Hill: University of North Carolina Press, 1963), pp. 1ff.
67. Roscoe Pound, *The Formative Era of American Law* (Boston: Little, Brown, 1938), pp. 7–8.
68. Ibid., p. 12.
69. Elizabeth G. Brown and William W. Blume, *British Statutes in American Law, 1776–1836* (Ann Arbor: University of Michigan Law School, 1964), p. 44. See also Lawrence M. Friedman, *A History of American Law* (New York: Simon & Schuster, 1973), pp. 96–100.
70. Pound, *The Formative Era of American Law*, p. 81.
71. Maurice R. Davie, *World Immigration* (New York: Macmillan, 1939), p. 36.
72. Henry J. Ford, *The Scotch-Irish in America* (Princeton, NJ: Princeton University Press, 1915), p. 491.
73. Charles A. Beard, *An Economic Interpretation of the Constitution of the United States* (New York: Macmillan, 1947), p. 17.
74. Joseph N. Kane, *Facts about the Presidents*, 3rd ed. (New York: Wilson, 1974).
75. John R. Schmidhauser, "The Justices of the Supreme Court: A Collective Portrait," *Midwest Journal of Political Science* 3 (February 1959): 1–57.
76. William Miller, "American Historians and the Business Elite," *Journal of Economic History* 9 (November 1949): 202–203.
77. On Protestant presidents before Kennedy, see ibid., p. 21.

78. Robert A. Dahl, *Who Governs?* (New Haven, CT: Yale University Press, 1961), pp. 15–16.
79. Matthew Holden, Jr., "Ethnic Accommodation in a Historical Case," *Comparative Studies in Society and History* 8 (January 1966): 172.
80. Rowland Berthoff, *An Unsettled People* (New York: Harper & Row, 1971), p. 13; Oliver C. Cox, *Caste, Class, and Race* (Garden City, NY: Doubleday, 1948), pp. 338–339; Barrington Moore, Jr., *Social Origins of Dictatorship and Democracy* (Boston: Beacon Press, 1966), pp. 112–113.
81. Frank Thistlewaite, *The Anglo-American Connection in the Early Nineteenth Century* (Philadelphia: University of Pennsylvania Press, 1959), pp. 5–11.
82. Jesse Lemisch, "The American Revolution Seen from the Bottom Up," in *Toward a New Past*, ed. Barton J. Bernstein (New York: Random House, 1968), p. 8; J. O. Lindsay, ed., *The Old Regime*, vol. 7 of *The New Cambridge Modern History* (Cambridge: Cambridge University Press, 1957), pp. 509–511.
83. Morison, *Oxford History of the American People*, p. 89.
84. Abbot E. Smith, *Colonists in Bondage* (Chapel Hill: University of North Carolina Press, 1947), pp. 25, 336; Jordan, *White over Black*, p. 47; Howard Zinn, *The Politics of History* (Boston: Beacon Press, 1970), p. 68.
85. Lee Soltow, *Men and Wealth in the United States, 1850–1870* (New Haven, CT: Yale University Press, 1975), p. 149.
86. Matthew Josephson, *The Robber Barons* (New York: Harcourt, Brace & World, 1934), pp. 32–35, 315–452.
87. John N. Ingham, *The Iron Barons* (Westport, CT: Greenwood Press, 1978), pp. 14–16.
88. Miller, "American Historians and the Business Elite," p. 202.
89. Elin L. Anderson, *We Americans* (Cambridge, MA: Harvard University Press, 1937), p. 137; see also pp. 21–247.
90. E. Digby Baltzell, *An American Business Aristocracy* (New York: Collier Books, 1962), p. 267.
91. Baltzell, *The Protestant Establishment*, p. 321.
92. Thomas R. Dye, *Who's Running America?* (Englewood Cliffs, NJ: Prentice Hall, 1976), pp. 3–8, 150–153. See also Thomas R. Dye, *Who's Running America? The Carter Years* (Englewood Cliffs, NJ: Prentice Hall, 1979), pp. 171–177.
93. Thomas R. Dye, letter to author, April 11, 1977.
94. Julia Reed, "The New American Establishment," *U.S. News & World Report*, February 8, 1988, p. 38.
95. Richard D. Alba and Gwen Moore, "Ethnicity in the American Elite," *American Sociological Review* 47 (June 1982); see also Thomas R. Dye, *Who's Running America? The Clinton Years* (Upper Saddle River, NJ: Prentice Hall, 1995), pp. 170–173.
96. U.S. Bureau of the Census, *1990 Census of Population: Ancestry of the Population of the United States*, CP-3-2 (Washington, D.C.: 1993), p. 33; U.S. Bureau of the Census, *1990 Census of Population: Social and Economic Characteristics: United States*, p. 166; also, see note 2.
97. Calculated from data in U.S. Bureau of the Census, *1990 Census of Population: Ancestry of the Population of the United States*, pp. 33, 237. U.S. Bureau of the Census, *1990 Census of Population: Social and Economic Characteristics: United States*, pp. 40, 42.
98. U.S. Bureau of the Census, *1990 Census of Population: Ancestry of the Population of the United States*, p. 441; U.S. Bureau of the Census, *1990 Census of Population: Social and Economic Characteristics: United States*, pp. 48, 49.
99. Calculated from data in U.S. Bureau of the Census, *1990 Census of Population: Ancestry of the Population of the United States*, p. 339; U.S. Bureau of the Census, *1990 Census of Population: Social and Economic Characteristics: United States*, p. 45.
100. U.S. Bureau of the Census, *1990 Census of Population: Ancestry of the Population of the United States*, p. 339; U.S. Bureau of the Census, *1990 Census of Population: Social and Economic Characteristics: United States*, pp. 44, 47.
101. The tabulation was done in 1997 by Joe R. Feagin using Mead Data Central's Nexis database.
102. Lieberson and Waters, *From Many Strands*, p. 173.
103. Alba, *Ethnic Identity*, pp. 49–82.
104. Fischer, *Albion's Seed*, pp. 199–205, 412, 597, 777–782, 897–898.
105. Ibid., pp. 887–897, quotation on p. 896.
106. Lieberson and Waters, *From Many Strands*, pp. 53–56.
107. Lewis M. Killian, *White Southerners* (New York: Random House, 1970), p. 16.
108. Peter Schrag, *The Decline of the WASP* (New York: Simon & Schuster, 1971), p. 164.

Chapter 4

1. U.S. Department of Justice, Immigration and Naturalization Service, *Annual Report* (Washington, D.C., 1973), pp. 53–55. The figures for the period between 1820 and 1867 represent "alien passengers arrived"; for later periods they represent immigrants arrived or admitted.
2. Cited in William Peterson, *Population*, 2nd ed. (New York: Macmillan, 1969), p. 260.
3. U.S. Bureau of the Census, *Statistical Abstract of the United States 1991* (Washington, D.C., 1991), p. 10; U.S. Bureau of the Census, *Statistical Abstract of the United States 1994* (Washington, D.C., 1994), p. 11.

4. U.S. Bureau of the Census, *1990 Census of Population: Ancestry of the Population in the United States*, CP-3-2 (Washington, D.C., 1993), pp. 50, 65.
5. U.S. Bureau of the Census, *1990 Census of Population: Social and Economic Characteristics: United States*, CP-2-1 (Washington, D.C., 1993), p. 166; U.S. Census Bureau, *Census 2000 Supplementary Survey*. Table PCT 024. Ancestry-First Reported, <http://factfinder.census.gov/home>; U.S. Census Bureau, *Census 2000 Supplementary Survey*. Table PCT 025. Ancestry-Second Reported, <http://factfinder.census.gov/home> (retrieved January 28, 2002).
6. Philip H. Bagenal, *The American Irish* (London: Kegan Paul, Trench, 1882), pp. 4–5.
7. Henry Jones Ford, *The Scotch-Irish in America* (Princeton, NJ: Princeton University Press, 1915), pp. 125–128.
8. Ibid., pp. 183–186; James G. Leyburn, *The Scotch-Irish* (Chapel Hill: University of North Carolina Press, 1962), pp. 160ff.
9. Michael J. O'Brien, *A Hidden Phase of American History* (New York: Devin-Adair, 1919), p. 249; see also pp. 287–288.
10. Ibid., p. 267.
11. Thomas D'Arcy McGee, *A History of Irish Settlers in North America* (Boston: Office of American Celt, 1851), pp. 25–34.
12. Leyburn, *The Scotch-Irish*, pp. 331–332.
13. Quoted in Ford, *The Scotch-Irish in America*, pp. 520–521.
14. Winthrop D. Jordan, *White over Black* (Baltimore, MD: Penguin, 1969), pp. 86–88.
15. McGee, *A History of Irish Settlers in North America*, p. 79.
16. Arnold Shrier, *Ireland and the American Emigration, 1850–1900* (Minneapolis: University of Minnesota Press, 1958), pp. 13–16; T. A. Jackson, *Ireland Her Own* (New York: International Publishers, 1970), pp. 243–245; Kerby A. Miller, *Emigrants and Exiles* (New York: Oxford University Press, 1985), p. 556.
17. Carl Wittke, *The Irish in America* (Baton Rouge: Louisiana State University Press, 1956), pp. 24–27; Theodore Hershberg et al., "A Tale of Three Cities," in *Majority and Minority*, 3rd ed., ed. Norman Y. Yetman and C. Hoy Steele (Boston: Allyn & Bacon, 1982), pp. 184–185.
18. Bagenal, *The American Irish*, p. 72 (the statistics on crime and poverty are found on pp. 70–71); Wittke, *The Irish in America*, p. 46.
19. Ronald Takaki, *A Different Mirror* (Boston: Little, Brown, 1993), pp. 154–160; Hasia R. Diner, *Erin's Daughters in America* (Baltimore, MD: Johns Hopkins, 1983), pp. xiii–xv.
20. Dale T. Knobel, *Paddy and the Republic* (Middletown, CT: Wesleyan University Press, 1986), pp. 24–27; Bill Bryson, *The Mother Tongue: English and How It Got That Way* (New York: Morrow, 1990).
21. Lewis P. Curtis, Jr., *Apes and Angels: The Irish in Victorian Caricature* (Washington, D.C.: Smithsonian Institution Press, 1971), p. 103. See also p. 59.
22. Andrew M. Greeley, *That Most Distressful Nation* (Chicago: Quadrangle, 1972), pp. 119–120.
23. Leonard Gordon, "Racial and Ethnic Stereotypes of American College Students over a Half Century" (paper presented at meetings of the Society for the Study of Social Problems, Washington, D.C., August 1985), pp. 14–15.
24. American Institute of Public Opinion, *Roper Center*, 1982.
25. Richard D. Alba, *Ethnic Identity: The Transformation of White America* (New Haven, CT: Yale University Press, 1990), p. 156; Nick Carter, "In a Tip of the Hat to Tradition, Pubs Are Hubs of Festivities," *Milwaukee Journal Sentinel*, March 8, 1996, p. 17.
26. Leonard Dinnerstein and Frederic C. Jaher, "Introduction," in *The Aliens*, ed. Leonard Dinnerstein and Frederic C. Jaher (New York: Appleton-Century-Crofts, 1970), p. 4.
27. Leyburn, *The Scotch-Irish*, pp. 234, 301–316.
28. Ford, *The Scotch-Irish in America*, pp. 291–324; Leyburn, *The Scotch-Irish*, pp. 225–230.
29. Dennis Clark, *The Irish in Philadelphia* (Philadelphia, PA: Temple University Press, 1973), p. 21.
30. Wittke, *The Irish in America*, p. 120.
31. Wayne G. Broehl, Jr., *The Molly Maguires* (Cambridge, MA: Harvard University Press, 1964), pp. 198–199.
32. Anthony Bimba, *The Molly Maguires* (New York: International Publishers, 1932), pp. 70–73.
33. Takaki, *A Different Mirror*, pp. 150–152; Oscar Handlin, *Boston's Immigrants, 1790–1865* (Cambridge, MA: Harvard University Press, 1941), p. 137.
34. James McCague, *The Second Rebellion* (New York: Dial Press, 1968).
35. Theodore W. Allen, *The Invention of the White Race* (London: Verso, 1994), p. 21; David Roediger, *Towards the Abolition of Whiteness* (London: Verso, 1994), p. 12.
36. Allen, *The Invention of the White Race*, pp. 21–50. This paragraph draws on Joe R. Feagin and Hernan Vera, *White Racism: The Basics* (New York : Routledge, 1995), pp. 1–18.
37. Roediger, *Towards the Abolition of Whiteness*, p. 140.
38. Ford, *The Scotch-Irish in America*, pp. 246, 462, 491; McGee, *A History of Irish Settlers in North America*, p. 71; Shane Leslie, *The Irish Issue in Its American Aspect* (New York: Scribner's, 1919), p. 8.
39. Wittke, *The Irish in America*, p. 104; Edward M. Levine, *The Irish and Irish Politicians* (Notre Dame, IN: University of Notre Dame Press, 1966), pp. 6–9.
40. Leo Hershkowitz, *Tweed's New York* (New York: Doubleday/Anchor Books, 1987), pp. xiii–xx.

41. Nathan Glazer and Daniel P. Moynihan, *Beyond the Melting Pot* (Cambridge, MA: M.I.T. Press and Harvard University Press, 1963), pp. 218–262; Robert A. Dahl, *Who Governs?* (New Haven, CT: Yale University Press, 1963), p. 41.
42. Mike Royko, *Boss: Richard J. Daley of Chicago* (New York: Dutton, 1971); Sam Roberts, "In Search of Irish, or the Greening of the Suburbs," *New York Times*, March 17, 1988, p. B1; Alba, *Ethnic Identity*, p. 156.
43. Greeley, *That Most Distressful Nation*, pp. 206–209.
44. Dennis J. Clark, "The Philadelphia Irish," in *The Peoples of Philadelphia*, ed. Allen F. Davis and Mark H. Haller (Philadelphia, PA: Temple University Press, 1973), p. 145.
45. Terry N. Clark, "The Irish Ethnic and the Spirit of Patronage," *Ethnicity* 2 (1975): 305–359; Mark R. Levy and Michael S. Kramer, *The Ethnic Factor* (New York: Simon & Schuster, 1972), pp. 130–135; Andrew M. Greeley, *The Irish Americans* (New York: Harper & Row, 1981), pp. 168–169.
46. William Miller, "American Historians and the Business Elite," *Journal of Economic History* 9 (November 1949): 202–203.
47. John Aloysius Farrell, "Clinton Staff Alters Blair Brown's Status," *Boston Globe*, March 19, 1994, p. 3.
48. Linda Greenhouse, "Supreme Court Ruling Clears Way for Deportation of an I.R.A. Man," *New York Times*, January 16, 1992, p. A1; "O'Connor Seeks Aid for I.R.A. Fugitive," *New York Times*, February 1, 1992, sec. 1, p. 25; Cal McCrystal, "Notebook: A Tug-of-War for America's Irish Soul," *Independent*, February 2, 1992, p. 23.
49. Steve Fainaru, "Adams, in New York Limelight, Asks for U.S. Help on Peace," *Boston Globe*, February 2, 1994, p. 1; Gerald Renner, "Sinn Fein Leader Urges Peace Plan Support," *Hartford Courant*, September 26, 1994, p. A1; Kevin Cullen, "Loyalist Extremists Call Ulster Cease-Fire," *Boston Globe*, October 14, 1994, p. 1; "Northern Ireland Peace Talks," National Public Radio, "Weekend Edition," September 21, 1997.
50. William V. Shannon, *The American Irish* (New York: Macmillan, 1963), pp. 151–181.
51. Glazer and Moynihan, *Beyond the Melting Pot*, p. 287; Shannon, *The American Irish*, pp. 395–411; Levy and Kramer, *The Ethnic Factor*, pp. 126–127.
52. *Reporting for the Russell Sage Foundation*, no. 6, May 1985, p. 6.
53. Stephen Steinberg, *The Ethnic Myth* (New York: Atheneum, 1981), pp. 160–164.
54. Handlin, *Boston's Immigrants*, p. 67.
55. Greeley, *That Most Distressful Nation*, p. 120; Clark, "The Philadelphia Irish," p. 143; Wittke, *The Irish in America*, pp. 217–227.
56. Lloyd Warner and Leo Srole, *The Social Systems of American Ethnic Groups* (New Haven, CT: Yale University Press, 1945), pp. 93–95.
57. Ronald P. Formisano, *Boston against Busing: Race, Class, and Ethnicity in the 1960s and 1970s* (Chapel Hill: University of North Carolina Press, 1991), p. 15; Harold J. Abramson, *Ethnic Diversity in Catholic America* (New York: Wiley, 1973), pp. 41–44; Levy and Kramer, *The Ethnic Factor*, p. 125. See also Greeley, *The Irish Americans*, p. 111.
58. U.S. Bureau of the Census, *1990 Census of Population: Ancestry of the Population in the United States*, pp. 353, 371, 455, 473; U.S. Bureau of the Census, *1990 Census of Population: Social and Economic Characteristics: United States*, pp. 45, 48, 49; Andrew Hacker, *Money: Who Has How Much and Why* (New York: Scribner International, 1997).
59. Roberts, "In Search of Irish," p. B1; Tim Unsworthy, "The Irish: Faith Persuasive as Metamucil in an Old Priest's Diet," *National Catholic Reporter*, March 15, 1996, p. 16.
60. John T. Ellis, *American Catholicism* (Garden City, NY: Doubleday/Image Books, 1965), p. 62; Clark, *The Irish in Philadelphia*, p. 123.
61. David O. Moberg, *The Church as a Social Institution* (Englewood Cliffs, NJ: Prentice Hall, 1962), p. 193.
62. Andrew M. Greeley, *Ethnicity, Denomination and Inequality* (Beverly Hills, CA: Sage, 1976), pp. 45–53.
63. U.S. Bureau of the Census, *1990 Census of Population: Ancestry of the Population in the United States*, pp. 251, 269; U.S. Bureau of the Census, *1990 Census of Population: Social and Economic Characteristics: United States*, p. 42; Andrew M. Greeley, review letter on chapter, September 1997.
64. "Bill to Require Teaching of Irish Famine," United Press International, March 17, 1997.
65. Wittke, *The Irish in America*, pp. 52–61, 205.
66. Owen B. Corrigan, "Chronology of the Catholic Hierarchy of the United States," *Catholic Historical Review* 1 (January 1916): 267–389; Edwin S. Gaustad, *Historical Atlas of Religion in America* (New York: Harper & Row, 1962), p. 103; Ellis, *American Catholicism*, p. 56; Wittke, *The Irish in America*, p. 91; Greeley, *That Most Distressful Nation*, p. 93; correspondence between Andrew Greeley and the authors.
67. National Opinion Research Center, 1990 General Social Survey. Tabulations by authors.
68. Greeley, *The Irish Americans*, pp. 130–132.
69. *Saturday Evening Post*, December 12, 1901; *Saturday Evening Post*, August 28, 1902. Quoted in Rita J. Simon and Susan H. Alexander, *The Ambivalent Welcome: Print Media, Public Opinion, and Immigration* (Westport, CT: Praeger, 1993), pp. 66–67.
70. Clark, *The Philadelphia Irish*, p. 178.
71. Stephan Thernstrom, *Poverty and Progress* (Cambridge, MA: Harvard University Press, 1964), p. 179.

72. Abramson, *Ethnic Diversity in Catholic America*, p. 111; Greeley, *The Irish Americans*, pp. 149–151.
73. Andrew M. Greeley, "The Success and Assimilation of Irish Protestants and Irish Catholics in the United States," *Sociology and Social Research* 72, no. 4 (July 1988): 236; Raymond E. Wolfinger, "The Development and Persistence of Ethnic Voting," *American Political Science Review* 60 (1965): 907
74. Joseph P. O'Grady, *How the Irish Became American* (New York: Twayne, 1973), p. 141; Marjorie R. Fallows, *Irish Americans: Identity and Assimilation* (Englewood Cliffs, NJ: Prentice Hall, 1979), p. 147.
75. Abramson, *Ethnic Diversity in Catholic America*, p. 53; Alba, *Ethnic Identity*, p. 47; Nona Claren, "The Trouble with the Melting Pot," *Baltimore Sun*, June 24, 1997, p. 9a.
76. Fallows, *Irish Americans*, pp. 148–149. See also Richard D. Alba, "Social Assimilation among American Catholic National-Origin Groups," *American Sociological Review* 41 (December 1976): 1,032.
77. Alba, *Ethnic Identity*, pp. 55, 61.
78. Greeley, *The Irish Americans*, p. 206. See also Andrew M. Greeley, *Ethnicity in the United States* (New York: Wiley, 1974), p. 311.
79. S. L. Berry, "In Step with the Irish Heritage; Irish-Americans Struggle to Learn Ancestral Language," *Indianapolis Star*, March 17, 1997, p. E1.
80. Giovanni Schiavo, *The Italians in America before the Civil War* (New York: Vigo Press, 1934), pp. 55–180.
81. U.S. Department of Justice, Immigration and Naturalization Service, *Annual Report* (Washington, D.C., 1973), pp. 52–54 (figures for 1820 to 1867 represent alien passengers arrived; for 1868–1891 and 1895–1897, immigrant aliens arrived; for 1892–1894 and 1898–1973, immigrant aliens admitted); Schiavo, *The Italians in America*, p. 204; Carl Wittke, *We Who Built America*, rev. ed. (Cleveland, OH: Case Western Reserve University Press, 1964), p. 441; Humbert S. Nelli, *The Italians in Chicago, 1880–1930* (New York: Oxford University Press, 1970), p. 5; Grazia Dore, "Some Social and Historical Aspects of Italian Emigration to America," in *The Italians*, ed. Francesco Cordasco and Eugene Bucchioni (Clifton, NJ: Augustus M. Kelley, 1974), p. 7.
82. Joseph Lopreato, *Italian Americans* (New York: Random House, 1970), pp. 23–27; John S. MacDonald, "Agricultural Organization, Migration, and Labor Militancy in Rural Italy," *Economic History Review*, 2d ser., 16 (1963–1964): 61–75. We are indebted to Phyllis Cancilla Martinelli for her useful suggestions concerning the sections that follow.
83. Luciano J. Iorizzo and Salvatore Mondello, *The Italian-Americans* (New York: Twayne, 1971), pp. 57–59; Michael La Sorte, *La Merica* (Philadelphia, PA: Temple University Press, 1985), pp. 1–13, 189–202.
84. Antonia Stella, *Some Aspects of Italian Immigration to the United States*, reprint ed. (San Francisco: R & E Associates, 1970), p. 33; Rudolph J. Vecoli, "Contadini in Chicago," in *Divided Society*, ed. Colin Greer (New York: Basic Books, 1974), p. 220.
85. William Petersen, *Population*, 2nd ed. (New York: Macmillan, 1969), p. 260; La Sorte, *La Merica*, pp. 189–202.
86. John Higham, *Strangers in the Land*, rev. ed. (New York: Atheneum, 1975), pp. 312–324.
87. U.S. Bureau of the Census, *Statistical Abstract of the United States 1994* (Washington, D.C., 1994), p. 11.
88. U.S. Bureau of the Census, *1990 Census of Population: Ancestry of the Population in the United States*, CP-3-2 (Washington, D.C., 1993), p. 50.
89. U.S. Census Bureau, *Census 2000 Supplementary Survey*. Table PCT 024. Ancestry-First Reported, <http://factfinder.census.gov/home>; U.S. Census Bureau, *Census 2000 Supplementary Survey*. Table PCT 025. Ancestry-Second Reported, <http://factfinder.census.gov/home> (retrieved January 28, 2002).
90. Stanley Lieberson, *Ethnic Patterns in American Cities* (Glencoe, IL: Free Press, 1963), pp. 209–218; La Sorte, *La Merica*, pp. 61–158.
91. William F. Whyte, *Street Corner Society*, 2nd ed. (Chicago: University of Chicago Press, 1955), pp. 272–273; Walter Firey, *Land Use in Central Boston* (Cambridge, MA: Harvard University Press, 1947), pp. 187–188; Wittke, *We Who Built America*, p. 446.
92. Eliot Lord, John J. D. Trenor, and Samuel J. Barrows, *The Italian in America*, reprint ed. (San Francisco: R & E Associates, 1970), pp. 17–18.
93. Simon and Alexander, *The Ambivalent Welcome*, pp. 84, 131.
94. Kenneth L. Roberts, *Why Europe Leaves Home*, excerpted in "Kenneth L. Roberts and the Threat of Mongrelization in America, 1922," in *In Their Place*, ed. Lewis H. Carlson and George A. Colburn (New York: Wiley, 1972), p. 312.
95. Cited in Leon J. Kamin, *The Science and Politics of I.Q.* (New York: Wiley, 1974), pp. 15–16.
96. Ibid., pp. 16–19.
97. Carl C. Brigham, *A Study of American Intelligence* (Princeton, NJ: Princeton University Press, 1923), especially pp. 124–125 and 177–210. Later Brigham recanted.
98. See Roberts, *Why Europe Leaves Home*; for earlier views, see Woodrow Wilson, *A History of the American People* (New York: Harper, 1902), 5: 212–214.
99. See Kamin, *The Science and Politics of I.Q.*, p. 30.
100. Quoted in E. Digby Baltzell, *The Protestant Establishment* (New York: Random House/Vintage Books, 1966), p. 30.
101. See ibid.

102. Irving L. Allen, *Unkind Words* (New York: Bergin and Garvey, 1990), pp. 32, 60.
103. Iorizzo and Mondello, *The Italian-Americans*, pp. 35–36; quotation cited in Nelli, *The Italians in Chicago*, p. 126.
104. Stella, *Some Aspects of Italian Immigration*, pp. 60–61, 73.
105. Philip di Franco, *The Italian American Experience* (New York: Tom Doherty Associates, 1988), pp. 84–86; Richard Gambino, *Blood of My Blood* (Garden City, NY: Doubleday / Anchor Books, 1975), pp. 293–298; Lopreato, *Italian Americans*, p. 126; Nelli, *The Italians in Chicago*, pp. 154–155.
106. Mary C. Waters, *Ethnic Options: Choosing Identities in America* (Berkeley, CA: University of California Press, 1990), pp. 142–143.
107. "Italian American Group Rips CBS for 'Mafia' Stereotypes," *Daily News* (New York), November 18, 1997, p. 96; William F. Miller, "Lawyer Fights Italian American Stereotypes," *Plain Dealer*, June 15, 1996, p. 7B.
108. Gambino, *Blood of My Blood*, pp. 300–301; Selwyn Raab, "The Mob in Decline," *New York Times*, October 22, 1990, p. A1.
109. Robert Lichter and Linda Lichter, "Italian-American Characters in Television Entertainment" (report prepared for the Commission for Social Justice, Order of Sons of Italy, May 1982).
110. Quotation cited in Micaela di Leonardo, *The Varieties of Ethnic Experience* (Ithaca, NY: Cornell University Press, 1984), pp. 160–161; Susanna Tardi, *Family and Society: The Case of the Italians in New Jersey* (Ann Arbor, MI: UMI Dissertation Service, 1991), p. 189.
111. Donna Haupt, Jan Mason, and Penny W. Moser, "The Embattled Queen of Queens," *Time*, October 1, 1984, p. 34; Vivienne Walt, "Cuomo: Hurt by Prejudice toward Italians," *Newsday*, July 23, 1991, p. 19.
112. Alba, *Ethnic Identity*, pp. 141–142; Waters, *Ethnic Options*, pp. 142–43; see also Ross Harano and Jeryl Levin, "Capone Image Hurts Italian-Americans," *Chicago Tribune*, August 3, 1993, p. N16.
113. William F. Whyte, "Race Conflicts in the North End of Boston," *New England Quarterly* 12 (December 1939): 626; Iorizzo and Mondello, *The Italian-Americans*, pp. 35, 66.
114. Luciano J. Iorizzo, "The Padrone and Immigrant Distribution," in *The Italian Experience in the United States*, ed. Silvano Tomasi and M. H. Engel (New York: Center for Migration Studies, 1970), pp. 49–51; Gambino, *Blood of My Blood*, p. 119; Higham, *Strangers in the Land*, p. 169.
115. di Franco, *The Italian American Experience*, p. 85; Gambino, *Blood of My Blood*, pp. 118, 280–281; quotation cited in Gambino, *Blood of My Blood*, p. 118.
116. See, for example, William Young and David E. Kaiser, *Postmortem* (Amherst: University of Massachusetts Press, 1985). See also a work from the 1970s, Gambino, *Blood of My Blood*, pp. 120–21.
117. Iorizzo and Mondello, *The Italian-Americans*, p. 207; Gerald D. Suttles, *The Social Order of the Slum* (Chicago: University of Chicago Press, 1968), pp. 102–103; Richard Krickus, *Pursuing the American Dream* (Garden City, NY: Doubleday / Anchor Books, 1976), p. 280.
118. Curtis Rist, "Prosecutor: Race Riot in Bensonhurst," *Newsday*, April 17, 1990, p. 4.
119. Cited in Levy and Kramer, *The Ethnic Factor*, p. 174.
120. National Opinion Research Center, General Social Surveys, 1989 and 1990. Tabulations by authors.
121. Schiavo, *The Italians in America before the Civil War*, pp. 163–166.
122. Nelli, *The Italians in Chicago*, pp. 75–76; Wittke, *We Who Built America*, p. 447; Lopreato, *Italian Americans*, pp. 113–117; Giovanni Schiavo, *Italian American History* (New York: Vigo Press, 1947), 1: 499–504.
123. di Franco, *The Italian American Experience*, pp. 146–147. Salvatore J. LaGumina, "Case Studies of Ethnicity and Italo-American Politicians," in *The Italian Experience in the United States*, ed. Tomasi and Engel, p. 147; Krickus, *Pursuing the American Dream*, pp. 174–181.
124. "World War II Italian American Internment," Bill Ritter, Charles Gibson, ABC "Good Morning America," October 30, 1997.
125. Wittke, *We Who Built America*, p. 450; Iorizzo and Mondello, *The Italian-Americans*, pp. 200–205, 208; Gambino, *Blood of My Blood*, p. 316.
126. Richard Alba, *Italian Americans* (Englewood Cliffs, NJ: Prentice Hall, 1985), pp. 78–81.
127. Alba, *Italian Americans*, p. 143; General Social Surveys, 1989 and 1990. See also Andrew M. Greeley, *Ethnicity in the United States* (New York: Wiley, 1974), pp. 94–101.
128. "Italian Americans: Big Swing?" *Campaigns & Elections*, August 1996, p. 63.
129. John M. Goshko, "Italian Americans Lobbying UN for Their Motherland," *International Herald Tribune*, September 18, 1997, p. 10.
130. Iorizzo, "The Padrone and Immigrant Distribution," p. 43.
131. Stella, *Some Aspects of Italian Immigration*, p. 94.
132. Gambino, *Blood of My Blood*, p. 85; Leonard Covello, "The Influence of Southern Italian Family Mores upon the School Situation in America," in *The Italians*, ed. Cordasco and Bucchioni, p. 513; Lord, Trenor, and Barrows, *The Italian in America*, pp. 16–19; E. P. Hutchinson, *Immigrants and Their Children, 1850–1950* (New York: Wiley, 1956), pp. 137–138.
133. Higham, *Strangers in the Land*, p. 48.
134. Gambino, *Blood of My Blood*, p. 77.
135. Stephan Thernstrom, *The Other Bostonians* (Cambridge, MA: Harvard University Press, 1973), p. 161.

136. John J. d'Alesandre, "Occupational Trends of Italians in New York City," *Italy-America Monthly* 2 (February 1935): 11–21.
137. W. Lloyd Warner and Leo Srole, *The Social Systems of American Ethnic Groups* (New Haven, CT: Yale University Press, 1945), pp. 96–97; Gambino, *Blood of My Blood*, p. 101; Wittke, *We Who Built America*, p. 443.
138. Nelli, *The Italians in Chicago*, pp. 211–214; Smith, *The Mafia Mystique*, p. 322.
139. Ianni, *A Family Business*, p. 193.
140. Smith, *The Mafia Mystique*, p. 323.
141. Andrew F. Rolle, *The American Italian* (Belmont, CA: Wadsworth, 1972), pp. 89–93.
142. Thernstrom, *The Other Bostonians*, p. 171.
143. U.S. Bureau of the Census, *1990 Census of Population: Ancestry of the Population in the United States*, p. 356; U.S. Bureau of the Census, *1990 Census of Population: Social and Economic Characteristics: United States*, p. 45.
144. Personal correspondence with Dr. Alfred Rotondaro, executive director of the National Italian American Foundation, June 12, 1991.
145. U.S. Bureau of the Census, *1990 Census of Population: Ancestry of the Population in the United States*, pp. 307, 356, 458; U.S. Bureau of the Census, *1990 Census of Population: Social and Economic Characteristics: United States*, pp. 48.
146. National Center for Urban Ethnic Affairs Newsletter 1, no. 5 (1976): 8.
147. Robert Viscusi, "Giving the Boot to Italians," *Newsday*, May 30, 1991, p. 74
148. "CUNY Settles Suit by Italian Institute," *New York Times*, January 9, 1994, section 1, p. 22.
149. Lawrence A. Cremin, *The Transformation of the School* (New York: Knopf, 1961), pp. 67–68; Colin Greer, *The Great School Legend* (New York: Basic Books, 1972), pp. 3–6.
150. U.S. Bureau of the Census, *U.S. Census of Population, 1950: Special Reports—Nativity and Parentage*, p. 155; U.S. Bureau of the Census, *U.S. Census of Population, 1950: Vol. II, Characteristics of the Population*, Part 1 (Washington, D.C., 1953), p. 96; U.S. Bureau of the Census, *U.S. Census of Population, 1970: Subject Reports—National Origin and Language*, PC(2)-1A (Washington, D.C., 1973), p. 165; U.S. Bureau of the Census, *U.S. Census of Population, 1970: General Social and Economic Characteristics*, PC(1)-C1 (Washington, D.C., 1972), p. 368.
151. U.S. Bureau of the Census, *1990 Census of Population: Ancestry of the Population in the United States*, p. 254; U.S. Bureau of the Census, *1990 Census of Population: Social and Economic Characteristics: United States*, p. 42.
152. Rudolph J. Vecoli, "Contadini in Chicago: A Critique of The Uprooted," in *The Aliens*, ed. Leonard Dinnerstein and Frederic C. Jaher (New York: Appleton-Century-Crofts, 1970), p. 226; Harold J. Abramson, *Ethnic Diversity in Catholic America* (New York: Wiley, 1973), pp. 136–139.
153. Silvano M. Tomasi, "The Ethnic Church and the Integration of Italian Immigrants in the United States," in *The Italian Experience in the United States*, ed. Tomasi and Engel, p. 167.
154. Ibid., pp. 187–188; Nelli, *The Italians in Chicago*, p. 195; di Franco, *The Italian American Experience*, pp. 269–270.
155. National Opinion Research Center, *A Profile of Italian Americans: 1972–1991*, March 1992; Stuart Vincent, "Devotion to Saints a Part of Life; Festivals Have an Italian Flavor," *Newsday*, May 1, 1996, p. A6.
156. Covello, "The Influence of Southern Italian Family Mores," p. 515.
157. Paul J. Campisi, "Ethnic Family Patterns: The Italian Family in the United States," *American Journal of Sociology* 53 (May 1948): 443–449; Covello, "The Influence of Southern Italian Family Mores," pp. 525–530.
158. Irvin L. Child, *Italian or American?* (New Haven, CT: Yale University Press, 1943) (an important excerpt from this book can be found in *The Italians*, ed. Cordasco and Bucchioni, pp. 321–336); Alba, *Italian Americans*, p. 114.
159. Alba, *Italian Americans*, p. 166.
160. See ibid.
161. Colleen L. Johnson, *Growing Up and Growing Old in Italian American Families* (New Brunswick, NJ: Rutgers University Press, 1985), pp. 221–228; Richard D. Alba, *Ethnic Identity*, pp. 47–48, 59–61, 70–71, 224–226; Tardi, *Family and Society*, pp. 179–192.
162. Anthony L. LaRuffa, *Monte Carmelo: An Italian-American Community in the Bronx* (New York: Gordon & Breach, 1988), pp. 135–139.
163. Commentary from Richard Alba given to authors, May 1994 and June 1997.
164. Francis X. Femminella and Jill S. Quadagno, "The Italian American Family," in *Ethnic Families in America*, ed. Charles H. Mindel and Robert W. Habenstein (New York: Elsevier, 1976), pp. 74–75; Ruby Jo Reeves Kennedy, "Single or Triple Melting Pot? Intermarriage in New Haven, 1870–1950," *American Journal of Sociology* 58 (July 1952): 56–59; Nelli, *The Italians in Chicago*, p. 196; James A. Crispino, *The Assimilation of Ethnic Groups: The Italian Case* (New York: Center for Migration Studies, 1980), p. 105; Alba, *Italian Americans*, pp. 146–147; Waters, *Ethnic Options*, p. 104; Nona Claren, "The Trouble with the Melting Pot," *Baltimore Sun*, June 24, 1997, p. 9a.
165. Alba, *Italian Americans*, pp. 159–162; Alba, *Ethnic Identity*, p. 47.
166. LaRuffa, *Monte Carmelo*, pp. 17–28.
167. Phyllis Cancilla Martinelli, *Ethnicity in the Sunbelt* (New York: AMS Press, 1989), pp. 234–258; Alba, *Ethnic Identity*, pp. 59–60, 70.

168. Marcus Lee Hansen, "The Third Generation," in *Children of the Uprooted*, ed. Oscar Handlin (New York: Harper & Row, 1966), pp. 255–271; P. J. Gallo, *Ethnic Alienation* (Rutherford, NJ: Fairleigh Dickinson University Press, 1974), p. 194; John M. Goering, "The Emergence of Ethnic Interests," *Social Forces* 49 (March 1971): 381–382; Tardi, *Family and Society*, pp. 179–192.
169. di Leonardo, *The Varieties of Ethnic Experience*, p. 156.
170. Richard D. Alba, "Identity and Ethnicity among Italians and Other Americans of European Ancestry," in *The Columbus People: Perspectives in Italian Immigration to the Americas and Australia*, ed. Lydio Tomasi, Piero Gautaldo, and Thomas Row (Staten Island, NY: Center for Migration Studies, 1994), pp. 21–41.
171. U.S. Census Bureau, *Census 2000 Supplementary Survey*. Table PCT 024. Ancestry-First Reported; Table PCT 025. Ancestry-Second Reported.

Chapter 5

1. Alan Dershowitz, *Chutzpah* (Boston: Little, Brown, 1991), p. 202.
2. Ibid., pp. 198–199, 206, 343–354; Arthur Hertzberg, *The Jews in America* (New York: Simon & Schuster, 1989), pp. 377–388; Bernard J. Wolfson, "African American Jews: Dispelling Myths, Bridging the Divide," in *Black Zion: African American Religious Encounters with Judaism* ed. Yvonne Chireau and Nathaniel Deutsch (New York: Oxford University Press, pp. 34–38.
3. Hertzberg, *The Jews in America*, pp. 13–28.
4. Charles E. Silberman, *A Certain People* (New York: Summit Books, 1985), pp. 42–45; Chaim I. Waxman, *America's Jews in Transition* (Philadelphia, PA: Temple University Press, 1983), pp. 6–8.
5. Silberman, *A Certain People*, pp. 42–49; Hertzberg, *The Jews in America*, pp. 102–104.
6. Hertzberg, *The Jews in America*, pp. 152–154, 185; Silberman, *A Certain People*, p. 49; Waxman, *America's Jews in Transition*, p. 43.
7. Hertzberg, *The Jews in America*, pp. 160–176, 224; Silberman, *A Certain People*, pp. 49–51.
8. Milton Meltzer, *Never to Forget: The Jews of the Holocaust* (New York: Harper and Row, 1976), p. 45.
9. Douglass Stanglin, Kenneth Walsh, Edward Pound, Charles Fenyvesi, Josh Chetwynd, "Quale's Newest Place in the Sun," *U.S. News & World Report*, August 26, 1996, pp. 16, 19.
10. Maurice J. Karpf, *Jewish Community Organization in the United States* (New York: Arno, 1971), p. 33; Sidney Goldstein, "American Jewry: A Demographic Analysis," in *The Future of the Jewish Community in America*, ed. David Sidorsky (New York: Basic Books, 1973), p. 71; Alvin Chenkin, "Jewish Population in the United States," in *American Jewish Yearbook, 1973* (New York: American Jewish Committee, 1973), pp. 307–309; Arthur A. Goren, "Jews," in *Harvard Encyclopedia of American Ethnic Groups* (Cambridge, MA: Harvard University Press, 1980), pp. 591–592; Rita J. Simon and Julian L. Simon, "Social and Economic Adjustment," in *New Lives*, ed. Rita J. Simon (Lexington, MA: Heath/Lexington Books, 1985), pp. 26–41; Stanglin et al., "Quale's Newest Place in the Sun," pp. 16, 19.
11. Annelise Orleck, *The Soviet Jewish Americans* (Westport, CT: Greenwood Press, 1999), p. 7.
12. Calvin Goldscheider and Sidney Goldstein, *The Jewish Community of Rhode Island* (Providence: Jewish Federation of Rhode Island, 1988), pp. 3–35.
13. "Religion in Brief," *Atlanta Journal and Constitution*, September 6, 1997, p. 6E; Jerome A. Chanes, "A Primer on the American Jewish Community," <http://www.ajc.org/pre/primer.asp> (retrieved March 13, 2001).
14. See David Sidorsky, "Introduction," in *The Future of the Jewish Community in America*, ed. Sidorsky, pp. xix–xxv; and Stephen D. Isaacs, *Jews and American Politics* (Garden City, NY: Doubleday, 1974), pp. ix–x.
15. Charles Y. Glock and Rodney Stark, *Christian Beliefs and Anti-Semitism* (New York: Harper & Row, 1966), p. 64 et passim.
16. Carey McWilliams, *A Mask for Privilege* (Boston: Little, Brown, 1948), pp. 164–165, 170–173; John Higham, "Social Discrimination against Jews in America, 1830–1930," *Publication of the American Jewish Historical Society* 47 (September 1957): 5.
17. Silberman, *A Certain People*, p. 48; Hertzberg, *The Jews in America*, pp. 86–87, 188–189; Higham, "Social Discrimination against Jews in America," p. 47.
18. Leonard Dinnerstein, *Antisemitism in America* (New York: Oxford University Press, 1994), pp. 80–82.
19. Gustavus Meyers, *History of Bigotry in the United States*, rev. ed. (New York: Capricorn Books, 1960), pp. 277–313; McWilliams, *A Mask for Privilege*, pp. 110–111; T. W. Adorno et al., *The Authoritarian Personality* (New York: Harper, 1950), pp. 69–79; Isaacs, *Jews and American Politics*, pp. 51, 98.
20. Gary A. Tobin, *Jewish Perceptions of Anti-Semitism* (New York: Plenum, 1988), pp. 106–112.
21. Silberman, *A Certain People*, pp. 22–27, 335–337, 360–366; Dershowitz, *Chutzpah*, pp. 116–129.
22. Barry A. Kosmin, et al., *Highlights of the CJF 1990 National Jewish Population Survey* (New York: Council of Jewish Federations, 1991), p. 29; American Jewish Committee, "2000 Annual Survey of American Jewish Opinion," <http://www.ajc.org/pre/Survey2000.asp> (retrieved March 13, 2001).

23. "Anti-Semitism Concerns Surveyed," *San Diego Union-Tribune*, June 6, 1997, p. E5.
24. American Jewish Committee, "Introduction," *Television's Changing Image of American Jews*, <http://www.ajc.org/pre/journal12-index.asp> (retrieved March 13, 2001).
25. Joyce Antler, "Introduction," in *Talking Back: Images of Jewish Women in American Popular Culture*, ed. Joyce Antler (Hanover, NH: Brandeis University press, 1998), p. 1.
26. Ibid, p. 10.
27. Henry L. Feingold, *Zion in America* (New York: Twayne, 1974), pp. 143–144; C. Vann Woodward, *Tom Watson* (New York: Oxford University Press, 1963), pp. 435–445.
28. Rufus Learski, *The Jews in America* (New York: KTAV Publishing House, 1972), pp. 290–291; John Higham, *Strangers in the Land* (New York: Atheneum, 1975), pp. 298–299; Woodward, *Tom Watson*.
29. Milton R. Konvitz, "Inter-group Relations," in *The American Jew*, ed. O. I. Janowsky (Philadelphia, PA: Jewish Publication Society of America, 1964), pp. 78–79; Donald S. Strong, *Organized Anti-Semitism in America* (Washington, D.C.: American Council on Public Affairs, 1941), pp. 14–20.
30. Strong, *Organized Anti-Semitism in America*, p. 67.
31. Lucy S. Dawidowicz, *The War against the Jews: 1933–1945* (New York: Holt, Rinehart & Winston), p. 148; see also pp. 164, 403.
32. Lewis H. Carlson and George A. Colburn, "The Jewish Refugee Problem," in *In Their Place*, ed. Lewis H. Carlson and George A. Colburn (New York: Wiley, 1972), pp. 290–291; Stephanie Chavez, "Anti-Semitic Incidents Reported Rising," *Los Angeles Times*, February 7, 1992, p. A3.
33. "ADL Demands Full Investigation into Pike County Alabama School Practices," PR Newswire, August 6, 1997.
34. Lenni Brenner, *Jews in America Today* (Secaucus, NJ: Lyle Stuart, 1986), pp. 205–206, 209; Chavez, "Anti-Semitic Incidents Reported Rising," p. A3.
35. Kevin Johnson, "Hate-motivated Murders Reach 5-year High," *USA Today*, February 14, 2001, p. 3A.
36. Greg Wilson, "Hate Crimes Law to Make Debut in Attack on Bronx Synagogue," *Daily News* (New York), October 20, 2000, p. 30.
37. Konvitz, "Inter-group Relations," pp. 85–95.
38. Dershowitz, *Chutzpah*, p. 326; Linda Greenhouse, "Justices Affirm Ban on Prayers in Public School," *New York Times*, June 25, 1992, p. A1.
39. Robert F. Drinan, "The Supreme Court, Religious Freedom and the Yarmulke," *America*, June 12, 1986, pp. 9–11.
40. Gerald S. Strober, *American Jews* (Garden City, NY: Doubleday, 1974), pp. 149–176.
41. Anti-Defamation League, *Extremism in the Name of Religion: The Violent Legacy of Meir Kahane* (Washington, D.C.: ADL, 1995).
42. Ronald Takaki, *A Different Mirror: A History of Multicultural America* (Boston: Little, Brown, 1993), p. 406.
43. "Two Deaths Ignite Racial Clash in Tense Brooklyn Neighborhood," *New York Times*, August 21, 1991, p. A1; Scott Minerbrook and Miriam Horn, "Side by Side, Apart," *U.S. News & World Report*, November 4, 1991, p. 44.
44. Silberman, *A Certain People*, p. 340.
45. Ibid., p. 41.
46. Ibid., pp. 333, 339–343; Dershowitz, *Chutzpah*, pp. 241, 301–302.
47. Letty Cottin Pogrebin, *Deborah, Golda, and Me: Being Female and Jewish in America* (New York: Crown, 1991).
48. Joe R. Feagin and Leslie Inniss, "Racial Attitudes in Four Socio-religious Groups" (research paper, University of Florida, spring 1992).
49. *Highlights from an Anti-Defamation League Survey on Racial Attitudes in America* (New York: Anti-Defamation League, 1993), pp. 51, 55, 61, 80–86.
50. Tom Tugend, "L.A. Jews Step Up Aid to Riot-Hit Areas," *Jerusalem Post*, May 12, 1992, n.p.
51. Buddy Nevins, "Idea of Saving Bucks Doesn't Compute with School Officials," *Ft. Lauderdale Sun-Sentinel*, December 18, 1994, p. B4.
52. Gene Warner, "Black, Jewish Teens Team Up to Honor King Legacy," *Buffalo News*, January 21, 1997, p. 1B; and Judith Reitman, "Black, Jewish Teens Look to Past to Find New Understanding," *Times-Picayune*, March 9, 1997, p. A3.
53. Waxman, *America's Jews in Transition*, pp. 5–10, quotation from p. 10; Hertzberg, *The Jews in America*, pp. 62–69; Lawrence H. Fuchs, *The Political Behavior of American Jews* (Glencoe, IL: Free Press, 1956), pp. 23–25; Silberman, *A Certain People*, p. 44.
54. Hertzberg, *The Jews in America*, pp. 108–109; Mark R. Levy and Michael S. Kramer, *The Ethnic Factor* (New York: Simon & Schuster, 1972), p. 101; William R. Heitzmann, *American Jewish Voting Behavior* (San Francisco: R & E Research Associates, 1975), pp. 27–28.
55. Irving Howe, *World of Our Fathers* (New York: Simon & Schuster, 1976), pp. 362–364; Emanuel Hertz, "Politics: New York," in *The Russian Jew in the United States*, ed. Charles S. Bernheimer (Philadelphia, PA: John Winston, 1905), pp. 256–265.
56. Edward M. Levine, *The Irish and Irish Politicians* (Notre Dame, IN: University of Notre Dame Press, 1966); Isaacs, *Jews and American Politics*, pp. 23–24; Feingold, *Zion in America*, p. 321.
57. Hertz, "Politics," pp. 265–267; Heitzmann, *American Jewish Voting Behavior*, p. 37; Fuchs, *The Political Behavior of American Jews*, pp. 57–58.
58. Hertzberg, *The Jews in America*, pp. 282–283.

59. Heitzmann, *American Jewish Voting Behavior*, p. 49; Fuchs, *The Political Behavior of American Jews*, pp. 99–100.
60. American Jewish Committee, "2000 Annual Survey of American Jewish Opinion," <http://www.ajc.org/pre/Survey2000.asp> (retrieved March 13, 2001).
61. Isaacs, *Jews and American Politics*, pp. 23, 201; Levy and Kramer, *The Ethnic Factor*, pp. 102–103; Howe, *World of Our Fathers*, p. 118; Milton Plesur, *Jewish Life in Twentieth Century America* (Chicago: Nelson Hall, 1982), pp. 143–145; Andrew Herrmann, "Buddhists See Cup as Half Full," *Chicago Sun-Times*, January 21, 1995, p. 13.
62. Chanes, "A Primer on the American Jewish Community."
63. Isaacs, *Jews and American Politics*, pp. 12, 118–119.
64. Nathan Reich, "Economic Status," in *The American Jew*, ed. Janowsky, pp. 70–71; Karpf, *Jewish Community Organization in the United States*, pp. 11–12; Howe, *World of Our Fathers*, pp. 391–393; Feingold, *Zion in America*, pp. 235–236.
65. Karpf, *Jewish Community Organization in the United States*, pp. 62–65; Naomi Cohen, *Not Free to Desist* (Philadelphia, PA: Jewish Publication Society of America, 1972), pp. 3–18, 37–80, 433–452.
66. Jonathan S. Woocher, *Sacred Survival* (Bloomington: Indiana University Press, 1986), pp. vii–viii.
67. Arnold Foster and Benjamin R. Epstein, *The New Anti-Semitism* (New York: McGraw-Hill, 1974), pp. 155–284; Strober, *American Jews*, pp. 7–42.
68. Leonard, Mary, "Many Jews Hit Faith Plan Funding," *Boston Globe*, February 28, 2001, p. A2.
69. Brenner, *Jews in America Today*, p. 10.
70. Hertzberg, *The Jews in America*, pp. 17–28, 63.
71. Feingold, *Zion in America*, p. 12; McWilliams, *Brothers under the Skin*, pp. 305–306.
72. Wittke, *We Who Built America*, p. 325; George Cohen, *The Jews in the Making of America* (Boston: Stratford, 1924), pp. 120–122; Silberman, *A Certain People*, pp. 44–45; Waxman, *America's Jews in Transition*, pp. 22–24.
73. Nathan Goldberg, *Occupational Patterns of American Jewry* (New York: Jewish Teachers Seminary Press, 1947), pp. 15–17; Marshall Sklare, *America's Jews* (New York: Random House, 1971), p. 61; Isaac M. Rubinow, "Economic and Industrial Conditions: New York," in *The Russian Jew in the United States*, ed. Bernheimer, pp. 110–111.
74. Jacob Lestschinsky, "Economic and Social Development of American Jewry," in *The Jewish People* (New York: Jewish Encyclopedic Handbooks, 1955), 4:74–77; Rubinow, "Economic and Industrial Conditions," pp. 103–107; Waxman, *America's Jews in Transition*, p. 58; Hertzberg, *The Jews in America*, p. 198.
75. Charlotte Baum, Paula Hyman, and Sonya Michel, *The Jewish Woman in America* (New York: Dial Press, 1976), p. 98; Hertzberg, *The Jews in America*, pp. 198–201.
76. Karpf, *Jewish Community Organization in the United States*, pp. 9–14; Lestschinsky, "Economic and Social Development of American Jewry," pp. 91–92; W. Lloyd Warner and Leo Srole, *The Social Systems of American Ethnic Groups* (New Haven, CT: Yale University Press, 1945), p. 112; Silberman, *A Certain People*, pp. 127–130.
77. McWilliams, *A Mask for Privilege*, pp. 38, 40–41; Karpf, *Jewish Community Organization in the United States*, pp. 20–21; Higham, "Social Discrimination against Jews in America," pp. 18–19.
78. For the February 1936 *Fortune* survey, see Karpf, *Jewish Community Organization in the United States*, pp. 9–11.
79. See McWilliams, *A Mask for Privilege*, pp. 143–150.
80. Lestschinsky, "Economic and Social Development of American Jewry," pp. 71, 87; McWilliams, *A Mask for Privilege*, p. 159; Reich, "Economic Status," pp. 63–65; Dershowitz, *Chutzpah*, p. 74.
81. Cited in Barry R. Chiswick, "The Labor Market Status of American Jews," in *American Jewish Handbook*, ed. M. Himmelfarb and D. Singer (New York: American Jewish Committee, 1984), p. 137.
82. Mabel Newcomer, *The Big Business Executive* (New York: Columbia University Press, 1955), pp. 46–48.
83. Kosmin et al., *Highlights of the CJF 1990 National Jewish Population Survey*, p. 19; U.S. Bureau of the Census, *Statistical Abstract of the United States 1991* (Washington, D.C., 1991), pp. 449, 450. Median household income is usually lower than median family income in census data.
84. American Jewish Committee, "Responding to Intermarriage Survey, Analysis, Policy," January 2001, <http://www.ajc.org/jl/intermarriageindex.asp> (retrieved March 13, 2001).
85. Goren, "Jews," p. 593; Sklare, *America's Jews*, pp. 61–62; Goldscheider and Goldstein, *The Jewish Community of Rhode Island*, pp. 11–12; Kosmin et al., *Highlights of the CJF 1990 National Jewish Population Survey*, p. 12.
86. Abraham K. Korman, *The Outsiders: Jews and Corporate America* (Lexington, MA: Heath/Lexington Books, 1988), pp. 79–82.
87. Richard L. Zweigenhaft and G. William Domhoff, *Jews in the Protestant Establishment* (New York: Praeger, 1982), p. 46.
88. Korman, *The Outsiders*, pp. 66–88.
89. Ibid., pp. 35–41.
90. Dov B. Levy, "Top Jobs," *Jerusalem Post*, March 30, 1997, p. 6.
91. "Florida Legislature Passes Bill," PR Newswire,

March 13, 1992; Sklare, *America's Jews*, p. 65; McWilliams, *Brothers under the Skin*, pp. 310–311.

92. American Jewish Committee, "2000 Annual Survey of American Jewish Opinion."
93. Allen Myerson, "At Rental Counters, Are All Drives Created Equal? Avis Finds Itself at the Center of Discrimination Complaints," *New York Times*, March 18, 1997, p. D1; Ellen Neuborne, "Car Renters Outline Charges at State Hearing," *USA Today*, April 1, 1997, p. 1B.
94. Hertzberg, *The Jews in America*, pp. 50, 273; Silberman, *A Certain People*, p. 51; Waxman, *America's Jews in Transition*, p. 53.
95. J. K. Paulding, "Educational Influences: New York," in *The Russian Jew in the United States*, ed. Bernheimer, pp. 186–197; Cohen, *The Jews in the Making of America*, pp. 140–141; Karpf, *Jewish Community Organization in the United States*, p. 57; Hertzberg, *The Jews in America*, p. 200; Waxman, *America's Jews in Transition*, p. 137.
96. Silberman, *A Certain People*, pp. 52–55; Hertzberg, *The Jews in America*, pp. 246–247; Higham, "Social Discrimination against Jews in America," p. 22; Karpf, *Jewish Community Organization in the United States*, p. 19; McWilliams, *A Mask for Privilege*, pp. 128–129.
97. Silberman, *A Certain People*, pp. 98–100; Hertzberg, *The Jews in America*, p. 309; Dershowitz, *Chutzpah*, pp. 73–74.
98. Strober, *American Jews*, pp. 120–130; Maurice R. Berube and Marilyn Gittell, "The Struggle for Community Control," in *Confrontation at Ocean Hill–Brownsville*, ed. Maurice R. Berube and Marilyn Gittell (New York: Praeger, 1969), pp. 3–12 et passim; Joe R. Feagin and Harlan Hahn, *Ghetto Revolts* (New York: Macmillan, 1973), pp. 327–328; Nathan Glazer, *Affirmative Discrimination* (New York: Basic Books, 1975), pp. 33–76, 196–221.
99. Dershowitz, *Chutzpah*, pp. 75–79, quotation from pp. 78–79.
100. Hertzberg, *The Jews in America*, p. 309; Kosmin et al., *Highlights of the CJF 1990 National Jewish Population Survey*, pp. 10–11; Holly J. Lebowitz, "High Holy Days Can Be Lonely for Students," *Plain Dealer*, September 7, 1996, p. 6E.
101. American Jewish Committee, "Responding to Intermarriage Survey, Analysis, Policy."
102. Silberman, *A Certain People*, pp. 171–172; Goldscheider and Goldstein, *The Jewish Community of Rhode Island*, pp. 11, 25–28; Kosmin et al., *Highlights of the CJF 1990 National Jewish Population Survey*, pp. 10–11; Robert Alter, "What Jewish Studies Can Do," *Commentary* 58 (October 1974): 71–74.
103. Waxman, *America's Jews in Transition*, p. 10; Hertzberg, *The Jews in America*, pp. 117–123, 146–147, 254–262, quotation from p. 120. See also Silberman, *A Certain People*, p. 46.
104. Hertzberg, *The Jews in America*, pp. 159–161, 167–168, 195, 214–236.
105. Ibid., pp. 277–279; Waxman, *America's Jews in Transition*, p. 17.
106. Wolfe Kelman, "The Synagogue in America," in *The Future of the Jewish Community in America*, ed. Sidorsky, pp. 157–158; Louis Lipsky, "Religious Activity: New York," in *The Russian Jew in the United States*, ed. Bernheimer, pp. 152–154; Silberman, *A Certain People*, pp. 170–177; Hertzberg, *The Jews in America*, pp. 277–279.
107. Silberman, *A Certain People*, pp. 176–181.
108. American Jewish Committee, "2000 Annual Survey of American Jewish Opinion."
109. J. L. Blau, *Judaism in America* (Chicago: University of Chicago Press, 1976), as summarized in Samuel C. Heilman, "The Sociology of American Jewry," in *Annual Review of Sociology*, ed. Ralph Turner, vol. 8 (Palo Alto, CA: Annual Reviews, 1982), p. 147.
110. Michael Greenstein, *The American Jew: A Contradiction in Terms* (New York: Gefen, 1990), pp. 1–5.
111. Dershowitz, *Chutzpah*, p. 209.
112. American Jewish Committee, "2000 Annual Survey of American Jewish Opinion."
113. Monty Noam Penkower, *At the Crossroads: American Jewry and the State of Israel* (Haifa, Israel: University of Haifa, 1990), p. 27.
114. Stanley Reed, "Will Palestine's Peace Dividend Buy Peace?" *Business Week*, May 16, 1994, p. 53.
115. "U.S. Jews Favor Palestinian State: Poll," Agence France Presse, September 29, 1997.
116. American Jewish Committee, "2000 Annual Survey of American Jewish Opinion."
117. Howe, *World of Our Fathers*, p. 645; Karpf, *Jewish Community Organization in the United States*, pp. 37–39, 49–50; Tobin, *Jewish Perceptions of Anti-Semitism*, p. 84.
118. Milton R. Konvitz, "Horace Meyer Kallen (1882–1974)," in *American Jewish Yearbook, 1974–1975* (New York: American Jewish Committee, 1974), pp. 65–67; Milton Gordon, *Assimilation in American Life* (New York: Oxford University Press, 1964), pp. 142–159.
119. Hertzberg, *The Jews in America*, pp. 102–130, 167–176, 195.
120. Sidney Goldstein and Calvin Goldscheider, *Jewish Americans* (Englewood Cliffs, NJ: Prentice Hall, 1968), p. 226; Silberman, *A Certain People*, pp. 173–181.
121. Riv-Ellen Prell, *Fighting to Become Americans: Jews, Gender, and the Anxiety of Assimilation* (Boston: Beacon, 1999), p. 8. See also pp. 6–10.
122. Nathan Glazer, "The American Jew and the Attainment of Middle-class Rank: Some Trends and

Explanations," in *The Jews*, ed. M. Sklare (Glencoe, IL: Free Press, 1958), p. 143, as quoted in Stephen Steinberg, *The Ethnic Myth* (New York: Atheneum, 1981), p. 93.

123. Steinberg, *The Ethnic Myth*, pp. 94–102.
124. Hertzberg, *The Jews in America*, pp. 167–171, 195, 254–255, quotation from p. 171; Waxman, *America's Jews in Transition*, pp. 55–58.
125. Calvin Goldscheider, *Jewish Continuity and Change* (Atlanta, GA: Scholars Press, 1986), pp. 17–18, quotation from p. 17.
126. Quoted in Sidney Goldstein, "Jews in the United States: Perspectives from Demography," in *American Jewish Yearbook, 1981* (New York: American Jewish Committee, 1980–1981), p. 28.
127. Kosmin, et al., *Highlights of the CJF 1990 National Jewish Population Survey*, p. 35.
128. Gordon, *Assimilation in American Life*, pp. 76–77.
129. American Jewish Committee, "2000 Annual Survey of American Jewish Opinion."
130. Paul R. Spickard, *Mixed Blood* (Madison: University of Wisconsin Press, 1989), pp. 180–228; Kosmin, et al., *Highlights of the CJF 1990 National Jewish Population Survey*, p. 14; Judith Dunford, "An Inside View of Interfaith Marriage," *Newsday*, September 28, 1997, p. B12.
131. American Jewish Committee, "Responding to Intermarriage Survey, Analysis, Policy."
132. Goldscheider, *Jewish Continuity and Change*, pp. 15–19, quotation from p. 16.
133. Alan Dershowitz, *The Vanishing American Jew: In Search of Jewish Identity for the Next Century* (New York: Little Brown, 1997).
134. Marilyn Henry, "Israeli Immigrants to the United States Moving Up the Ladder," *Jerusalem Post*, August 13, 1996, p. 12; Henry summarizes a report in the 1996 *American Jewish Yearbook* by Steven Gold and Bruce Phillips.
135. Simon and Simon, "Social and Economic Adjustment," pp. 27–38.
136. Orleck, *The Soviet Jewish Americans*, p. 3.
137. Steven J. Gold, *Refugee Communities* (Newbury Park, CA: Sage, 1992), pp. 39–44, 67–89.
138. Orleck, *The Soviet Jewish Americans*, pp. 190–193.
139. American Jewish Committee, "2000 Annual Survey of American Jewish Opinion."
140. David Biale, "The Melting Pot and Beyond," in *Insider/Outsider: American Jews and Multiculturalism*, ed. David Biale, Michael Galchinsky, and Susan Heschel (Berkeley: University of California Press, 1998), p. 31.
141. Kosmin, et al., *Highlights of the CJF 1990 National Jewish Population Survey*, p. 28.
142. Ibid., pp. 3–6, 14–17.
143. Sylvia Barack Fishman, *Jewish Life and American Culture* (Albany, NY: SUNY Press, 2000), pp. 1–16.
144. Herbert J. Gans, "Symbolic Ethnicity," *Ethnic and Racial Studies* 2 (1979): 1–20; Richard Alba, *Ethnic Identity: The Transformation of White America* (New Haven, CT: Yale University Press, 1990), p. 306.
145. Hertzberg, *The Jews in America*, p. 386.
146. The report is cited in Ira Rifkin, "Jewish Social Agency Finds Support Eroding," *Sacramento Bee*, December 2, 1995, p. G5.
147. Ariela Keysar, Barry A. Kosmin, and Jeffrey Scheckner, *The Next Generation: Jewish Children and Adolescents* (Albany, NY: SUNY press, 2000), pp. 103–104.
148. American Jewish Committee, "A Statement on Jewish Education," <http: / /www.ajc.org/pre/jewisheducation.asp> (retrieved March 13, 2001).
149. Alba, *Ethnic Identity*, p. 310.
150. Silberman, *A Certain People*, pp. 25, 159–324.
151. American Jewish Committee, "Responding to Intermarriage Survey, Analysis, Policy."
152. Karen Brodkin, *How The Jews Became White Folks: And What That Says about Race in America* (New Brunswick: Rutgers, 1998), pp. 139–178.
153. Ibid., p. 187.

CHAPTER 6

1. Peggy Lowe, "Columbus Day Case Dropped; Charges to Be Dismissed Against 139 Protesters Arrested at October March," *Rocky Mountain News*, March 7, 2001, p. 5A.
2. "Counter-Quincentenary Protesters Encounter Celebrators at Kickoff of Quincentenary Year," *Indigenous Thought* 1, nos. 4 and 5 (October 1991): 1–3.
3. "We Have No Reason to Celebrate an Invasion," *Rethinking Columbus* (Milwaukee, WI: Rethinking Schools, 1991), p. 4.
4. For a discussion of the development of the designations *white* and *red*, see David R. Roediger, *The Wages of Whiteness* (New York: Verso, 1991), pp. 21–23.
5. Henry F. Dobyns, "Estimating Aboriginal American Population," *Current Anthropology* 7 (October 1960): 395–416; Kirkpatrick Sale, *The Conquest of Paradise* (New York: Knopf, 1990); Lenore A. Stiffarm and Phil Lane, Jr., "The Demography of Native North America," in *The State of Native America*, ed. M. Annette Jaimes (Boston: South End Press, 1992), pp. 23–28; see also Russell Thornton, *American Indian Holocaust and Survival* (Norman: University of Oklahoma Press, 1987); C. Matthew Snipp, *American Indians: The First of This Land* (New York: Russell Sage Foundation, 1989).
6. U.S. Census Bureau, "Overview of Race and Hispanic Origin, Census 2000 Brief, March 2001, pp. 2–5.
7. U.S. Bureau of the Census, *1990 Census of Population:*

Social and Economic Characteristics: United States, CP-2-1 (Washington, D.C., 1993), p. 105; U.S. Bureau of the Census, *We the First Americans* (Washington, D.C., 1993), pp. 2–3, 7–8; Public Information Office, U.S. Census Bureau, "Census Bureau Facts for Features," November 2000, CB00-FF.13, <http://www.census.gov> (retrieved June 7, 2001).

8. Carol Morello, "Native American Roots, Once Hidden, Now Embraced," *Washington Post*, April 7, 2001, p. A01.
9. Joane Nagel, *American Indian Ethnic Renewal: Red Power and the Resurgence of Indian Identity and Culture* (New York: Oxford University Press, 1996).
10. Morello, "Native American Roots, Once Hidden, Now Embraced."
11. Edward H. Spicer, *Cycles of Conquest* (Tucson: University of Arizona Press, 1962), pp. 20–23; Clyde Kluckhohn and Dorothy Leighton, *The Navaho*, rev. ed. (Garden City, NY: Doubleday/Anchor Books, 1962), pp. 23–27 et passim.
12. Devon A. Mihesuah, *American Indians: Stereotypes and Realities* (Atlanta, GA: Clarity Press, 1996), p. 20.
13. Ibid., p. 43.
14. Jack Weatherford, *Indian Givers: How the Indians of the Americas Transformed the World* (New York: Ballantine, 1988), pp. 39–133.
15. Peter Linebaugh and Marcus Rediker, *The Many-Headed Hydra: Sailors, Slaves, Commoners, and the Hidden History of the Revolutionary Atlantic* (Boston: Beacon Press, 2000), pp. 32–34.
16. Howard M. Bahr, "An End to Invisibility," in *Native Americans Today*, ed. Howard M. Bahr, Bruce A. Chadwick, and Robert C. Day (New York: Harper & Row, 1972), pp. 407–409; James E. Officer, "The American Indian and Federal Policy," in *The American Indian in Urban Society*, ed. Jack O. Waddell and O. Michael Watson (Boston: Little, Brown, 1971), pp. 45–60.
17. U.S. Bureau of the Census, *1990 Census of Population: General Population Characteristics: Urbanized Areas*, CP-1-1C (Washington, D.C., 1992), p. 48.
18. Spicer, *Cycles of Conquest*, pp. 5, 306–307; Murray L. Wax, *Indian Americans* (Englewood Cliffs, NJ: Prentice Hall, 1971), pp. 6–7; Lynn R. Bailey, *Indian Slave Trade in the Southwest* (Los Angeles: Westernlore Press, 1966), pp. 73–140.
19. D'Arcy McNickle, *The Indian Tribes of the United States* (London: Oxford University Press, 1962), pp. 13–17; Alice Marriott and Carol K. Rachlin, *American Epic* (New York: Mentor Books, 1969), pp. 104–108; John Collier, *Indians of the Americas* (New York: Mentor Books, 1947), p. 115.
20. William T. Hagan, *American Indians* (Chicago: University of Chicago Press, 1961), p. 14. The discussion of these wars is taken from ibid., pp. 12–15.
21. McNickle, *The Indian Tribes of the United States*, pp. 23–28; Ruth M. Underhill, *Red Man's America* (Chicago: University of Chicago Press, 1953), pp. 321–322; Wax, *Indian Americans*, p. 13.
22. Alexis de Tocqueville, *Democracy in America* (New York: Random House/Vintage Books, 1945), 1:364.
23. Virgil J. Vogel, "The Indian in American History, 1968," in *This Country Was Ours*, ed. Virgil J. Vogel (New York: Harper & Row, 1972), pp. 284–287; McNickle, *The Indian Tribes of the United States*, pp. 40–41.
24. Ralph K. Andrist, *The Long Death* (London: Collier-Macmillan, 1964), p. 3.
25. John D. Unruh, *The Plains Across* (Urbana: University of Illinois Press, 1979), p. 185 et passim.
26. Vogel, "The Indian in American History, 1968," p. 285; Wendell H. Oswalt, *This Land Was Theirs* (New York: Wiley, 1966), pp. 501–502.
27. Andrist, *The Long Death*, pp. 31–68, 78–91.
28. William Meyer, *Native Americans* (New York: International, 1971), p. 32. See also Thornton, *American Indian Holocaust and Survival*.
29. Andrist, *The Long Death*, pp. 240–250, 350–353; Alvin M. Josephy, *The Indian Heritage of America* (New York: Bantam, 1968), pp. 284–342; Theodora Kroeber and Robert F. Heizer, *Almost Ancestors* (San Francisco: Sierra Club, 1968), pp. 14–20.
30. Spicer, *Cycles of Conquest*, pp. 216–221, 247–270.
31. Robert F. Spencer, Jesse D. Jennings, et al., *The Native Americans* (New York: Harper & Row, 1965), pp. 495–496; David Miller, "The Fur Men and Explorers View the Indians," in *Red Men and Hat Wearers*, ed. Daniel Tyler (Fort Collins, CO: Pruett, 1976), pp. 26–28; Roediger, *The Wages of Whiteness*, pp. 21–23.
32. Peter Farb, *Man's Rise to Civilization as Shown by the Indians of North America from Primeval Times to the Coming of the Industrial State* (New York: Dutton, 1968), pp. 246–249; Tyler, ed., *Red Men and Hat Wearers*, passim.
33. Lewis H. Carlson and George A. Colburn, "Introduction," in *In Their Place*, ed. Lewis H. Carlson and George A. Colburn (New York: Wiley, 1972), p. 44.
34. Vogel, "The Indian in American History, 1968," pp. 288–289; Tocqueville, *Democracy in America*, 1:355–357.
35. Rayna Green, "The Pocahontas Perplex: The Image of Indian Women in American Culture," in *Unequal Sisters*, ed. Ellen Carol DuBois and Vicki L. Ruiz (New York: Routledge, 1990), pp. 15–21, quotation from p. 17.
36. "Children's Secret Lessons," *Indigenous Thought* 1, nos. 4 and 5 (October 1991): 24.
37. James W. Loewen, *Lies My Teacher Told Me: Everything Your American History Textbook Got Wrong* (New York: The New Press, 1995), p. 91.
38. See Jacquelyn Kilpatrick, *Celluloid Indians: Native*

Americans and Film (Lincoln, NE: University of Nebraska Press, 1999).

39. Snipp, *American Indians*, pp. 23–25; Jimmie Durham, "Cowboys and … ," in *The State of Native America*, ed. Jaimes, pp. 423–425.
40. Ward Churchill, *Fantasies of the Master Race* (Monroe, ME: Common Courage Press, 1992), pp. 243–247, quotation from p. 246.
41. Jacquelyn Kilpatrick, *Celluloid Indians: Native Americans and Film*, p. 152.
42. Ibid., pp. 151–153.
43. Howard M. Bahr, Bruce A. Chadwick, and Robert C. Day, "Introduction: Patterns of Prejudice and Discrimination," in *Native Americans Today*, ed. Bahr, Chadwick, and Day, pp. 44–45; Emory S. Bogardus, *Immigration and Race Attitudes* (Boston: Heath, 1928); Beverly Brandon Sweeney, "Native American: Stereotypes and Ideologies of an Adult Anglo Population in Texas" (M.A. thesis, University of Texas at Austin, 1976), pp. 125–133.
44. Alexandra Witkin-New Holy, "American Indian Religious Rights: Inside Montana Prisons," Center for Native American Studies, Montana State University (Bozeman), <http://tlc.wtp.net/american_indian_religious_rights.htm> (retrieved June 7, 2001).
45. Gayle Pollard Terry, "Los Angeles Times Interview with Suzane Shown Harjo: Fighting to Preserve the Legacy and Future of Native Americans," *Los Angeles Times*, November 27, 1994, p. M3.
46. Jeff Cohen and Norman Solomon, "Using History, CNN Delivers Improved Coverage of Indians," *Star Tribune*, November 30, 1994, p. A17.
47. "Nationwide poll shows support for Native issues; Saginaw-Chippewa commissions Zogby research firm to reach average Americans," *Oklahoma Indian Times Online*, <http://www.okit.com/gaming/2001/feb/poll.htm> (retrieved June 6, 2001).
48. Mihesuah, *American Indians: Stereotypes and Realities*, pp. 61–63.
49. Loewen, *Lies My Teacher Told Me*, p. 104.
50. Mihesuah, *American Indians: Stereotypes and Realities*, pp. 63–65.
51. U.S. Bureau of Indian Affairs, *Federal Indian Policies* (Washington, D.C., 1975), p. 6.
52. Ibid., p. 7; Spicer, *Cycles of Conquest*, p. 348.
53. *Elk v. Wilkins*, 112 U.S. 94 (1884); see also Vine Deloria, Jr., *Of Utmost Good Faith* (New York: Bantam, 1972), pp. 130–132.
54. Spicer, *Cycles of Conquest*, pp. 351–353; McNickle, *The Indian Tribes of the United States*, p. 59; Alison R. Bernstein, *American Indians and World War II* (Norman: University of Oklahoma Press, 1991), pp. 4–10.
55. Virgil J. Vogel, "Introduction," in *This Country Was Ours*, ed. Vogel, pp. 196–197.
56. M. Annette Jaimes, "Federal Indian Identification Policy: A Usurpation of Indigenous Sovereignty in North America," in *The State of Native America*, ed. Jaimes, p. 124.
57. Ibid., pp. 95–98; U.S. Bureau of Indian Affairs, *Federal Indian Policy*, p. 9.
58. W. A. Brophy and S. D. Aberle, *The Indian* (Norman: University of Oklahoma Press, 1966), pp. 179–193; Rebecca L. Robbins, "Self-Determination and Subordination: The Past, Present, and Future of American Indian Governance," in *The State of Native America*, ed. Jaimes, pp. 98–100.
59. U.S. Bureau of Indian Affairs, *Federal Indian Policy*, p. 12.
60. Jaimes, "Federal Indian Identification Policy," pp. 123–137; Susan Campbell, "A Mohegan Family," *Hartford Courant*, March 1, 1992, p. 10; Anne Fullam, "Tribe Seeks U.S. Recognition," *Newsday*, February 11, 1992, p. 20.
61. Jack Forbes, *Native Americans of California and Nevada* (Berkeley, CA: Far West Laboratory for Educational Research and Development, 1968), pp. 80–82; Alan L. Sorkin, *American Indians and Federal Aid* (Washington, D.C.: Brookings Institution, 1971), pp. 48–65; Vogel, "Introduction," p. 205; James S. Olson and Raymond Wilson, *Native Americans in the Twentieth Century* (Provo, UT: Brigham Young University Press, 1984), p. 209; E. S. Cahn, *Our Brother's Keeper* (New York: World, 1969), pp. 157–158.
62. Robbins, "Self-Determination and Subordination," pp. 98–112, quotation from p. 109.
63. Elouise Cobell, "After five years of delay, will the Bush Administration treat the Trust Accounts lawsuit any differently?" *Oklahoma Indian Times Online*, <http://www.okit.com/opinion/2001/janfeb/trust.htm>.
64. Brophy and Aberle, *The Indian*, pp. 33–44; Olson and Wilson, *Native Americans in the Twentieth Century*, pp. 189, 191.
65. Virgil J. Vogel, "Famous Americans of Indian Descent," in *This Country Was Ours*, ed. Vogel, pp. 310–351.
66. Public Information Office, U.S. Census Bureau, "Census Bureau Facts for Features."
67. Olson and Wilson, *Native Americans in the Twentieth Century*, p. 186.
68. "Indians Flashing Casino Profits in D.C.: The Mashantucket Pequot Tribe, for Example, Employs a Full-time Lobbyist in Washington," *Providence Journal-Bulletin*, July 13, 1997, p. 5A.
69. Hazel W. Hertzberg, *The Search for an American Indian Identity* (Syracuse, NY: Syracuse University Press, 1971), pp. 20–21, 42–76, 180–200.
70. Ibid., pp. 200–208, 291–293; Isabel Wilkerson, "Indignant Indians Seeking Changes," *New York Times*, January 26, 1992, p. 14.

71. Robert C. Day, "The Emergence of Activism as a Social Movement," in *Native Americans Today*, ed. Bahr, Chadwick, and Day, pp. 516–517.
72. Robbins, "Self-Determination and Subordination," p. 103.
73. Meyer, *Native Americans*, p. 88; "Pine Ridge after Wounded Knee: The Terror Goes on," *Akwesasne Notes* 7 (summer 1975): 8–10.
74. Greg Toppo, "Group Wants a Peltier Pardon," *Santa Fe New Mexican*, December 8, 1996, p. B1.
75. Richard Meryhew, "Be It Redskins, Chiefs, or Lions, Indians to Protest," *St. Paul Star Tribune*, January 3, 1992, p. 1B; Wilkerson, "Indignant Indians Seeking Changes," p. 14.
76. "Doby's Best Pitch Comes at Playground," *Austin American-Statesman*, July 9, 1997, p. C4.
77. C. Richard King and Charles Fruehling Springwood, "Introduction," in *Team Spirits: The Native American Mascots Controversy*, ed. C. Richard King and Charles Fruehling Springwood (Lincoln, NE: University of Nebraska Press, 2001), p. 7.
78. Susan Dodge, "Illiniwek Not Going Anywhere," *Chicago Sun-Times*, March 08, 2001, p. 1.
79. David Prochaska, "At Home in Illinois: Presence of Chief Illiniwek, Absence of Native Americans," in *Team Spirits*, ed. King and Springwood, pp. 165–169.
80. Laurel R. Davis, "Protest Against the Use of Native American Mascots: A Challenge to Traditional American Identity," *Journal of Sport and Social Issues* 17 (April 1993): 9–22; quotation on p. 13.
81. Ibid., p. 19.
82. Quoted in "Newspaper Defends Dropping Native American Names from Teams," *Reuters News Service*, February 19, 1992.
83. Terry, "Los Angeles Times Interview with Suzane Shown Harjo"; "Indian Mascots Are Out, Says Vote in L.A.," *Los Angeles Times*, September 10, 1997, p. A6; C. Richard King and Charles Fruehling Springwood, "Introduction," in *Team Spirits*, ed. King and Springwood, p. 5.
84. Zach Maxwell, "Rally for Repatriation," Oklahoma Indian Times Online, <http://www.okit.com/news/2001/feb/rally.htm> (retrieved June 7, 2001).
85. U.S. Commission on Civil Rights, *Indian Tribes: A Continuing Quest for Survival* (Washington, D.C., 1981), pp. 61–99; Institute for Natural Progress, "In Usual and Accustomed Places," in *The State of Native America*, ed. Jaimes, pp. 223–226.
86. Institute for Natural Progress, "In Usual and Accustomed Places," pp. 224–226.
87. U.S. Commission on Civil Rights, *Indian Tribes*, p. 103.
88. Olson and Wilson, *Native Americans in the Twentieth Century*, p. 195.
89. Ward Churchill, "The Earth Is Our Mother," in *The State of Native America*, ed. Jaimes, pp. 151–169.
90. Peter Carlson, "The Un-Fashionable: In the Year of *'Dances with Wolves,'* Everybody Wanted to Be on the Senate Indian Affairs Committee. Nearly a Decade Later, It Can Hardly Get a Quorum," *Washington Post Magazine*, February 23, 1997, p. W6.
91. U.S. Commission on Civil Rights, *Indian Tribes*, pp. 1–2 (Hatfield quotation from p. 1; quotation from tribal leader from p. 2); Institute for Natural Progress, "In Usual and Accustomed Places," pp. 223, 231, 233–234.
92. "Shattering the Myth of the Vanishing American," *Ford Foundation Letter* 22, no. 3 (winter 1991): 1–5.
93. "The Hidden Victims: Hate Crimes Against American Indians Under-Reported, *Southern Poverty Law Center Intelligence Report*, October 1994, pp. 1–4; quotation on p. 4.
94. Jeff Shaw, "Bitter Harvest; Indian Farmers Allege Years of Discrimination at the USDA," *In These Times*, October 2, 2000, p. 20.
95. Ibid.
96. Alvin M. Josephy, Jr., Joane Nagel, and Troy Johnson "Introduction: 'You Are on Indian Land!'" in *Red Power: The American Indians' Fight for Freedom*, ed. Alvin M. Josephy, Jr., Joane Nagel, and Troy Johnson (Second edition; Lincoln, NE: University of Nebraska Press, 1999), p. 5. We draw here on pp. 3–6.
97. Alvin M. Josephy, Jr., Joane Nagel, and Troy Johnson, "The National Museum of the American Indian Act," in *Red Power*, ed. Josephy, Nagel, and Johnson, p. 228; Alvin M. Josephy, Jr., Joane Nagel, and Troy Johnson, "The Native Americans Graves Protection and Repatriation Act," in *Red Power*, ed. Josephy, Nagel, and Johnson, p. 233.
98. Churchill, *Fantasies of the Master Race*, pp. 5–7 (quotation from p. 5); Ward Churchill and Winona LaDuke, "Native North America: The Political Economy of Radioactive Colonialism," in *The State of Native America*, ed. Jaimes, pp. 241–262; Campbell, "A Mohegan Family," p. 10. See also Sar A. Levitan, Garth L. Mangum, and Ray Marshall, *Human Resources and Labor Markets*, 2nd ed. (New York: Harper & Row, 1976), p. 441.
99. Joseph G. Jorgensen, "Indians and the Metropolis," in *The American Indian in Urban Society*, ed. Waddell and Watson, p. 85. This paragraph draws on Jorgensen's theory.
100. Quoted in Deloria, *Of Utmost Good Faith*, pp. 380–381.
101. Hagan, *American Indians*, pp. 126–127; Spicer, *Cycles of Conquest*, pp. 349–356.
102. Cahn, *Our Brother's Keeper*, pp. 69–110; Rupert Costo, "Speaking Freely," *Wassaja* 4 (November–December 1976): 2; Sorkin, *American Indians and Federal Aid*, pp. 70–71; Jorgensen, "Indians and the Metropolis," pp. 96–99.

103. Olson and Wilson, *Native Americans in the Twentieth Century*, p. 181; Robert Bryce, "Indians Seek Control of Tribal-Land Resources," *Christian Science Monitor*, September 14, 1994, p. 4.
104. Churchill and LaDuke, "Native North America," pp. 247–248.
105. Michael Parfit, "Keeping the Big Sky Pure," *Perspectives* 13 (spring 1981): 44.
106. Bryce, "Indians Seek Control of Tribal-Land Resources."
107. U.S. Bureau of the Census, *Population, 1940: Characteristics of the Nonwhite Population by Race* (Washington, D.C., 1943), pp. 83–84; U.S. Bureau of the Census, *Population, 1960: Nonwhite Population by Race* (Washington, D.C., 1963), p. 104; U.S. Bureau of the Census, *1990 Census of Population: Social and Economic Characteristics: United States*, p. 45. Data for 1960 do not include states with less than 25,000 Native Americans.
108. U.S. Bureau of the Census, *1990 Census of Population: Social and Economic Characteristics: United States*, p. 45.
109. Daniel Gonzalez, "TV Reporter Keeps Ties to Heritage," *Arizona Republic*, February 25, 2001, p. B3.
110. U.S. Bureau of the Census, *Sixteenth Census of the United States: The Labor Force, Part I: U.S. Summary* (Washington, D.C., 1943), p. 39; U.S. Department of Health, Education and Welfare, *A Study of Selected Socio-economic Characteristics of Ethnic Minorities Based on the 1970 Census*, vol. 3, *American Indians* (Washington, D.C., 1974), p. 49.
111. U.S. Bureau of the Census, *1990 Census of Population: Social and Economic Characteristics: United States*, p. 44.
112. U.S. Bureau of the Census, *1990 Census of Population: Social and Economic Characteristics: American Indian and Alaska Native Areas*, CP-2-1A (Washington, D.C., 1993), p. 56.
113. Public Information Office, U.S. Census Bureau, "Census Bureau Facts for Features."
114. Nagel, *American Indian Ethnic Renewal.*
115. U.S. Department of Health and Human Services, *Regional Differences in Indian Health* (Washington, D.C., 1994), pp. 33, 45, 56–61, 90.
116. National Indian Gaming Association, "Tribes lead in the stringent regulation of Indian gaming," *Oklahoma Indian Times Online*, <http://www.okit.com/gaming/2001/feb/tribes.htm>.
117. National Indian Gaming Commission, "Helping Indian Nations recover from centuries of economic and social neglect," *Oklahoma Indian Times Online*, <http://www.okit.com/gaming/2001/feb/helping.htm> (retrieved June 7, 2001).
118. Bob Doucette, "Tribes compete and contribute," *The Oklahoman*, June 6, 2001, <http://www.oklahoman.com/cgi-bin/show_article?ID=696797&TP> (retrieved June 7, 2001); and National Indian Gaming Commission, "Helping Indian Nations recover from centuries of economic and social neglect."
119. Bob Doucette and Mark A. Hutchison, "Tribes build businesses from gaming," *The Oklahoman*, June 4, 2001, <http://www.oklahoman.com/cgi-bin/show_article?ID=696799&pic=none&TP=getarticle> (retrieved June 7, 2001).
120. "Nationwide poll shows support for Native issues; Saginaw-Chippewa commissions Zogby research firm to reach average Americans," *Oklahoma Indian Times Online.*
121. Bill Lueders, "Casino Cowboys Take Indians for a Ride," *Progressive*, August 1994, pp. 30–33.
122. Quoted in Bob von Sternberg, "Tribe Fights Storage of Reactor's Spent Fuel," *St. Paul Star Tribune*, November 27, 1991, p. 2B. See also Dan Fagin, "Badlands in Demand," *Newsday*, October 21, 1991, p. 5; David Seals, "Sacred Ground Must Not Be Abused," *Newsday*, October 31, 1991, p. 129.
123. U.S. Bureau of Indian Affairs, *Federal Indian Policies*, p. 5; Jorge Noriega, "American Indian Education in the United States," in *The State of Native America*, ed. Jaimes, pp. 371–383.
124. U.S. Bureau of Indian Affairs, *Federal Indian Policies*, pp. 5–6; Spicer, *Cycles of Conquest*, p. 349; Noriega, "American Indian Education in the United States," pp. 381–383; U.S. Bureau of Indian Affairs, *Federal Indian Policies*, p. 9.
125. Noriega, "American Indian Education in the United States," pp. 384–385.
126. Interview with Phyllis Young, quoted in ibid., p. 387.
127. *Indian Nations at Risk: An Educational Strategy for Change*, report of U.S. Department of Education Task Force (Washington, D.C., 1991), cited in Kenneth Cooper, "Multicultural Focus Recommended for Education of Native Americans," *Washington Post*, December 27, 1991, p. A19; U.S. Bureau of the Census, *1990 Census of Population: Social and Economic Characteristics: United States*, p. 42.
128. Public Information Office, U.S. Census Bureau, "Census Bureau Facts for Features."
129. Noriega, "American Indian Education in the United States," pp. 391–392; Office of Indian Education Programs, *Fingertip Facts: 1994* (Washington, D.C.: U.S. Bureau of Indian Affairs, 1994), p. 16.
130. U.S. Bureau of the Census, *1990 Census of Population: Social and Economic Characteristics: United States*, p. 42.
131. *Indian Nations at Risk*, in Cooper, "Multicultural Focus Recommended for Education of Native Americans."
132. Paul Hammel, "Tribes Offered Help In Preserving Relics, Treasured Artifact," *Omaha World-Herald*, February 26, 2001, p.1

133. Vine Deloria, Jr., *Custer Died for Your Sins* (London: Collier-Macmillan, 1969), pp. 108–116.
134. Vittorio Lanternari, *The Religions of the Oppressed* (New York: Mentor Books, 1963), pp. 110–132; Spencer, Jennings, et al., *The Native Americans*, pp. 498–499; Wax, *Indian Americans*, p. 141.
135. Lanternari, *The Religions of the Oppressed*, pp. 99–100; Hertzberg, *The Search for an American Indian Identity*, pp. 239–240, 251, 280.
136. Hertzberg, *The Search for an American Indian Identity*, pp. 246, 257, 271–274, 280–284; Elaine G. Eastman, "Does Uncle Sam Foster Paganism?" in *In Their Place*, ed. Carlson and Colburn, pp. 29ff.
137. Deloria, *Of Utmost Good Faith*, pp. 177–180; idem, *Custer Died for Your Sins*, pp. 110–115.
138. Quoted in Olson and Wilson, *Native Americans in the Twentieth Century*, p. 219. See also Vine Deloria, Jr., *Custer Died for Your Sins* (London: Collier-Macmillan, 1969), pp. 122–124; and Cahn, *Our Brother's Keeper*, pp. 175–190.
139. For example, Lurie, as quoted in John A. Price, "Migration and Adaptation of American Indians to Los Angeles," *Human Organization* 27 (summer 1968): 168–175.
140. Snipp, *American Indians*, pp. 23–25
141. Olson and Wilson, *Native Americans in the Twentieth Century*, p. 212; see also pp. 210–211.
142. Alvin M. Josephy, Jr., Joane Nagel, and Troy Johnson, "Native American Languages Act," in *Red Power*, ed. Josephy, Nagel, and Johnson, p. 199.
143. Prodipto Roy, "The Measurement of Assimilation: The Spokane Indians," *American Journal of Sociology* 67 (March 1962): 541–551; Price, "Migration and Adaptation of American Indians to Los Angeles," pp. 169–174; U.S. Department of Health, Education and Welfare, *A Study of Selected Socio-economic Characteristics*, p. 35; Oswalt, *This Land Was Theirs*, pp. 513–514.
144. Lynn C. White and Bruce A. Chadwick, "Urban Residence, Assimilation, and Identity of the Spokane Indian," in *Native Americans Today*, ed. Bahr, Chadwick, and Day, p. 243; Brophy and Aberle, *The Indian*, p. 10; Spicer, *Cycles of Conquest*, p. 577.
145. Joan Weibel-Orlando, *Indian Country, L.A.* (Urbana: University of Illinois Press, 1991), pp. 22–43.
146. Josephy, Nagel, and Johnson "Introduction," in *Red Power*, ed. Josephy, Nagel, and Johnson, pp. 7–8.
147. Robert Blauner, *Racial Oppression in America* (New York: Harper & Row, 1972), p. 54; Spicer, *Cycles of Conquest*, pp. 573–574.
148. Quoted in Francis McKinley, Stephen Bayne, and Glen Nimnicht, *Who Should Control Indian Education?* (Berkeley, CA: Far West Laboratory for Educational Research and Development, 1969), p. 13 (italics added).
149. Quoted in Shirley Hill Witt, "Pressure Points in Growing Up Indian," *Perspectives* 12 (spring 1980): 31.
150. Wilbur J. Scott, "Attachment to Indian Culture," *Youth and Society* 17 (June 1986): 392–394.
151. Witt, "Pressure Points in Growing Up Indian," pp. 28–31; Robert W. Blum, et al., "American Indian–Alaska Native Youth Health," *Journal of the American Medical Association* 267 (March 25, 1992): 1,637–1,644; see also U.S. Department of Health and Human Services, *Trends in Indian Health* (Washington, D.C., 1993), pp. 60–61; U.S. Department of Health and Human Services, *Regional Differences in Indian Health* (Washington, D.C., 1994), p. 56.
152. Albert L. Wahrhaftig and Robert K. Thomas, "Renaissance and Repression: The Oklahoma Cherokee," in *Native Americans Today*, ed. Bahr, Chadwick, and Day, p. 81.
153. Richard B. Williams, "The Indian Renaissance in America," *Denver Post*, June 6, 2001, p.B7.
154. Institute for Natural Progress, "In Usual and Accustomed Places," pp. 228–236.

Chapter 7

1. Bebe Moore Campbell, "To Be Black, Gifted, and Alone," *Savvy* 5 (December 1984): 69.
2. James H. Dorman and Robert R. Jones, *The Afro-American Experience* (New York: Wiley, 1974), pp. 72–74; Thomas R. Frazier, preface to Chapter 1, in *Afro-American History: Primary Sources*, ed. Thomas R. Frazier (New York: Harcourt, Brace, & World, 1970), pp. 3–5.
3. Olaudah Equiano, "The Interesting Narrative of the Life of Olaudah Equiano," in *Afro-American History*, ed. Frazier, pp. 18, 20.
4. Dorman and Jones, *The Afro-American Experience*, pp. 80–82.
5. Philip D. Curtin, *The Atlantic Slave Trade* (Madison: University of Wisconsin Press, 1969), pp. 87–93; U.S. Bureau of the Census, *Historical Statistics of the United States* (Washington, D.C., 1960), p. 770.
6. Carl N. Degler, *Out of Our Past* (New York: Harper, 1959), pp. 161–163; John Hope Franklin, *From Slavery to Freedom*, 4th ed. (New York: Knopf, 1984), p. 88.
7. Franklin, *From Slavery to Freedom*, pp. 132–133.
8. U.S. Bureau of the Census, *Historical Statistics of the United States*, p. 11; Degler, *Out of Our Past*, pp. 163–164; Ulrich B. Phillips, *Life and Labor in the Old South* (Boston: Little, Brown, 1929), pp. 339ff; Kenneth M. Stampp, *The Peculiar Institution* (New York: Random House/Vintage Books, 1956), pp. 383–418.
9. Ben Simpson, "Ben Simpson: Georgia and Texas," in

Lay My Burden Down, ed. B. A. Botkin (Chicago: University of Chicago Press, 1945), p. 75.

10. John W. Blassingame, *The Slave Community* (New York: Oxford University Press, 1972), pp. 155–160.
11. Quoted in Jacqueline Jones, *Labor of Love, Labor of Sorrow: Black Women, Work, and the Family, from Slavery to the Present* (New York: Random House/Vintage Books, 1985), p.16. We have emended the quotation slightly for clarity.
12. Quoted in ibid., p.19.
13. Herbert Gutman, *The Black Family in Slavery and Freedom, 1750–1925* (New York: Pantheon, 1976); Stanley Elkins, "The Slavery Debate," *Commentary* 46 (December 1975): 46–47.
14. Patricia Williams, "Alchemical Notes: Reconstructing Ideals from Deconstructed Rights," *Harvard Civil Rights and Civil Liberties Review* 22 (1987): 415.
15. Bonnie Mitchell and Joe Feagin, "America's Racial-Ethnic Cultures: Opposition within a Mythical Melting Pot," in *Toward the Multicultural University*, ed. Benjamin Bowser, Gale Auletta, and Terry Jones (Westport, CT: Praeger, 1995), pp. 65–86; see also Patricia Hill Collins, *Black Feminist Thought: Knowledge, Consciousness, and the Politics of Empowerment* (Boston: Unwin Hyman, 1990), pp. 40–48.
16. Eugene G. Genovese, *Roll, Jordan, Roll* (New York: Random House, 1974), p. 650.
17. Herbert Aptheker, *American Negro Slave Revolts* (New York: International, 1943), pp. 12–18, 162.
18. Ibid., pp. 165, 220–225, 249–250, 267–273.
19. Herbert Aptheker, *Essays in the History of the American Negro* (New York: International, 1945), pp. 39, 49–51.
20. Sterling Stuckey, *Slave Culture* (New York: Oxford University Press, 1987), pp. 42–46.
21. Cited in *Bartlett's Familiar Quotations*, 15th ed., ed. Emily M. Beck (Boston: Little, Brown, 1980), p. 556.
22. Benjamin B. Ringer, *"We the People" and Others* (New York: Tavistock, 1983), p. 533.
23. A. L. Higginbotham, *In the Matter of Color* (New York: Oxford University Press, 1978), pp. 144–149.
24. Jerry Fresia, *Toward an American Revolution: Exposing the Constitution and Other Illusions* (Boston: South End, 1988), pp. 1–2; Dinitia Smith and Nicholas Wade, "DNA Evidence Links Thomas Jefferson to Slave's Offspring," *Gainesville Sun*, November 1, 1998, p. 4A.
25. Thomas F. Gossett, *Race* (New York: Schocken Books, 1965), pp. 42–43.
26. See, for example, Samuel Cartwright's infamous 1850s article "The Prognathous Species of Mankind," in *Slavery Defended*, ed. Eric L. McKitrick (Englewood Cliffs, NJ: Prentice Hall, 1963).
27. Williams, "Alchemical Notes," pp. 401–434. See also Duncan J. MacLeod, *Slavery, Race, and the American Revolution* (London: Cambridge University Press, 1974), p. 158.
28. Richard J. Herrnstein, *IQ in the Meritocracy* (Boston: Little, Brown, 1973); Arthur R. Jensen, "How Much Can We Boost IQ and Scholastic Achievement?" *Harvard Education Review* 39 (1969): 1–123; Tom Wilkie, "The American Association for the Advancement of Science: Research Revives Dispute over IQ," *Independent*, February 19, 1991, p. 7.
29. Richard J. Herrnstein and Charles Murray, *The Bell Curve: Intelligence and Class Structure in American Life* (New York: Free Press, 1994), p. 311; see also pp. 295–316.
30. Cited in Richard Brookhiser, "Fear and Loathing at City College," *National Review*, June 11, 1990, p. 20.
31. An unsigned editorial, "Buchanan Campaign Rhetoric," *Boston Globe*, January 12, 1992, p. 68. Samuel Francis, "Out of the Mouths of Japanese," *Washington Times*, February 11, 1992, p. F1.
32. See data gathered by Otto Klinberg as cited in I. A. Newby, *Challenge to the Court* (Baton Rouge: Louisiana State University Press, 1967), p. 74. See also Thomas F. Pettigrew, *A Profile of the Negro American* (Princeton, NJ: D. Van Nostrand, 1964), pp. 123–126.
33. Leon J. Kamin, *The Science and Politics of IQ* (New York: Wiley, 1974), pp. 175–178.
34. N. J. Block and Gerald Dworkin, "IQ, Heritability, and Inequality," in *The IQ Controversy*, ed. N. J. Block and Gerald Dworkin (New York: Random House, 1976), pp. 410–540.
35. *Highlights from an Anti-Defamation League Survey on Racial Attitudes in America* (New York: Anti-Defamation League, 1993), pp. 3–33; Lawrence Bobo, "Inequalities that Endure?: Racial Ideology, American Politics, and the Peculiar Role of the Social Sciences," paper presented at conference on "The Changing Terrain of Race and Ethnicity," University of Illinois, Chicago, Illinois, October 26, 2001.
36. Doris Wilkinson, "Minority Women: Social-Cultural Issues," in *Women and Psychotherapy*, ed. Annette M. Brodsky and Rachel T. Hare-Mustin (New York: Guilford, 1980), pp. 295–297. See also A. Thomas and S. Sillen, *Racism and Psychiatry* (New York: Bruner-Mazel, 1972), pp. 57–58.
37. Kevin A. Schulman, et al., "The Effect of Race and Sex on Physicians' Recommendations for Cardiac Catherization," *New England Journal of Medicine* (February 25, 1999): 618–626; Peter B. Bach, et al., "Racial Differences in the Treatment of Early-Stage Lung Cancer," *New England Journal of Medicine* (October 14, 1999): 1,198–1,205.
38. National Opinion Research Center (NORC), General Social Survey, 1994. Tabulation by author.
39. John B. McConahay and Joseph C. Hough, "Symbolic Racism," *Journal of Social Issues* 32 (1976): 38.

40. National Opinion Research Center (NORC), General Social Survey, 1994. Tabulations by authors. "Survey Finds Minorities Resent Whites And Each Other," *Jet*, March 28, 1994, p. 14.
41. Matthew P. Smith, "Bridging the Gulf Between Blacks and Whites," *Pittsburgh Post-Gazette*, April 7, 1996, p. A1.
42. Richard L. Berke, "The 1994 Campaign; Survey Finds Voters in U.S. Rootless and Self-Absorbed," *New York Times*, September 21, 1994, p. A21.
43. Joe R. Feagin and Melvin P. Sikes, *Living with Racism: The Black Middle Class Experience* (Boston: Beacon Press, 1994).
44. John F. Dovidio, John C. Brigham, Blair T. Johnson, and Samuel L. Gaertner, "Stereotyping, Prejudice, and Discrimination: Another Look," in *Stereotypes and Stereotyping*, ed. C. Neil Macrae, Miles Hewstone, and Charles Stangor (New York: Guilford, 1995), pp. 276–319.
45. Eduardo Bonilla-Silva and Tyrone A. Forman, "'I Am Not A Racist But ...': Mapping White College Students' Racial Ideology in the U.S.A.," *Discourse and Society* 11 (2000): 51–86; I draw in this section on Joe R. Feagin, *Racist America: Roots, Current Realities, and Future Reparations* (New York: Routledge, 2000), chapter 5.
46. Nancy Krieger and Stephen Sidney, "Racial Discrimination and Blood Pressure," *American Journal of Public Health* 86 (1996): 1,370–1,378.
47. Gallup, *Black/White Relations in the United States* (Princeton, NJ: The Gallup Organization, 1997), pp. 29–30, 108–110.
48. U.S. Bureau of the Census, *Historical Statistics of the United States*, p. 218.
49. W. J. Cash, *The Mind of the South* (New York: Random House/Vintage Books, 1960), p. 125.
50. Note a 1940 pamphlet written by a white southerner for U.S. senators and congressmen, quoted in Gunnar Myrdal, *An America Dilemma* (New York: McGraw-Hill, 1964), 2:1,198.
51. Gilbert Osofsky, *Harlem: The Making of a Ghetto* (New York: Harper & Row, 1963), pp. 45–51; Arthur I. Waskow, *From Race Riot to Sit-In, 1919 and the 1960s* (Garden City, NY: Doubleday, 1966), pp. 209–210 et passim; Elliot M. Rudwick, *Race Riot at East St. Louis* (Carbondale: Southern Illinois University Press, 1964), pp. 3–30.
52. "Active White Supremacist Groups in 1993," *Intelligence Report*, March 1994, pp. 15–17; "White Supremacist Movement Reels from Severe Setbacks in 1993," *Intelligence Report*, March 1994, p. 12; "Active Hate Groups in the United States in 2000," *Intelligence Report*, spring 2001, pp. 32–33. See also pp. 34–45.
53. Linda Diebel, "Darkest Iowa," *Toronto Star*, February 23, 1992, p. F1; John Turner, *The Ku Klux Klan: A History of Racism and Violence* (Montgomery, AL: Southern Poverty Law Center, 1982), pp. 48–56; "Going after the Klan," *Newsweek*, February 23, 1987, p. 29.
54. "Violent Hate Crime Remains at Record Levels Nationwide," *Intelligence Report*, March 1994, pp. 1, 4–5.
55. "Hate Crime Violence," *Race Relations Reporter*, August 15, 1994, p. 2; "Residential Terrorism," *Race Relations Reporter*, August 15, 1994, p. 4.
56. Thomas Fields-Meyer, Bob Stewart, Michelle McCalope and Michael Haederle, "One Deadly Night: Deep in the Woods of East Texas, James Byrd Died a Terrible Death, Leaving a Town and a Nation in Shock," *People*, June 29, 1998, p. 46; Howard Chua-Eoan and Hilary Hylton-Austin "Beneath the Surface; A 'New South' Town is Haunted by 'Deep South' Ghosts—And a Fresh, Ugly Murder," *Time*, June 22, 1998, p. 34.
57. "U.S. Supreme Court Upholds Stiffer Sentences for Hate Crimes," *Intelligence Report*, September 1993, pp. 4–5.
58. Joe R. Feagin and Harlan Hahn, *Ghetto Revolts* (New York: Macmillan, 1973), p. 134.
59. "The Mood of Ghetto America," *Newsweek*, June 2, 1980, pp. 32–34.
60. Lara Parker, "Violence after Police Shooting Exposes Miami Racial Tensions," *Washington Post*, June 29, 1991, p. A2.
61. Associated Press, "Cincinnati City Manager Resigns," *New York Times*, May 2, 2001, <http://www.nytimes.com> (retrieved May 3, 2001).
62. Gallup, *Black/White Relations in the United States*, pp. 29–30, 108–110.
63. Kim Lersch, "Current Trends in Police Brutality: An Analysis of Recent Newspaper Accounts." (Master's thesis, University of Florida, 1993.)
64. "Accidents or Police Brutality?" *Time*, October 26, 1981, p. 70; Charles Leerhsen, "L.A.'s Violent New Video," *Newsweek*, March 18, 1991, pp. 33, 53.
65. William M. Wiecek, "The Origins of the Law of Slavery in British North America," *Cardozo Law Review* 17 (1996): 1,711–1,792; Robert S. Browne, "Achieving Parity through Reparations," in *The Wealth of Races: The Present Value of Benefits from Past Injustices*, ed. R. F. America (New York: Greenwood Press, 1990), pp. 199–206.
66. Cited in David H. Swinton, "Racial Inequality and Reparations," in *The Wealth of Races*, pp. 153–162.
67. Ibid.
68. Trina Williams, "The Homestead Act—Our Earliest National Asset Policy," paper presented at the Center for Social Development's symposium, Inclusion in Asset Building, St. Louis, Missouri, September 21–23, 2000.

69. Stephen J. DeCanio, "Accumulation and Discrimination in the Postbellum South," in *Market Institutions and Economic Progress in the New South 1865–1900*, ed. G. Walton and J. Shepherd (New York: Academic Press, 1981), pp. 103–125.
70. Doris Y. Wilkinson, "The Segmented Labor Market and African American Women from 1890 to 1960," in *Research in Race and Ethnic Relations*, vol. 6, ed. Rutledge M. Dennis (Greenwich, CT: JAI Press, 1991), p. 89. See also Ray Marshall, *The Negro Worker* (New York: Random House, 1967), pp. 7–12; MacLeod, *Slavery, Race, and the American Revolution*, pp. 151–153; Pete Daniel, *The Shadow of Slavery: Peonage in the South* (London: Oxford University Press, 1972); and Myrdal, *An American Dilemma*, 1:228.
71. Quoted in Jones, *Labor of Love, Labor of Sorrow*, p. 123.
72. Karl E. Taeuber and Alma F. Taeuber, *Negroes in Cities* (Chicago: Aldine, 1965), pp. 12–13.
73. Charles Tilly, "Race and Migration to the American City," in *The Urban Scene*, ed. Joe R. Feagin (New York: Random House, 1973), p. 35; Taeuber and Taeuber, *Negroes in Cities*, pp. 144–147.
74. Edna Bonacich, "Class Approaches to Ethnicity and Race," *Insurgent Sociologist* 10 (fall 1980): 11. See also Bennett Harrison, *Education, Training, and the Urban Ghetto* (Baltimore, MD: Johns Hopkins, 1972).
75. W. E. B. Du Bois, *Black Reconstruction in America: An Essay Toward a History of the Part Which Black Folk Played in the Attempt to Reconstruct Democracy in America, 1860–1880* (New York: Atheneum, [1935] 1992).
76. Wilkinson, "The Segmented Labor Market and African American Women from 1890 to 1960," pp. 90–94.
77. U.S. Bureau of the Census, *Negroes in the United States, 1920–1932* (Washington, D.C., 1935), p. 289.
78. Jones, *Labor of Love, Labor of Sorrow*, p. 179; Myrdal, *An American Dilemma*, 1:304–306.
79. Marshall, *The Negro Worker*, pp. 23–24, 56–57.
80. U.S. Bureau of the Census, *Population*, vol. 3, *The Labor Force* (Washington, D.C., 1943); see also Sidney M. Wilhelm, *Who Needs the Negro?* (Cambridge, MA: Schenkman, 1970), p. 57.
81. U.S. Bureau of Labor Statistics, "Annual Average Tables from the January 2001 Issue of Employment and Earnings, Table 10: "Employed persons by occupation, race, and sex," published June 14, 2001, <ftp://ftp.bls.gov/pub/special.requests>.
82. Ibid., "Table 11: Employed persons by detailed occupation, sex, race, and Hispanic origin."
83. "*Washington Post*/Kaiser/Harvard Racial Attitudes Survey," *Washington Post*, July 11, 2001, p. A01; Richard Morin, "Misperceptions, Cloud Whites' View of Blacks," *Washington Post*, July 11, 2001, p. A01.
84. Feagin and Sikes, *Living with Racism*, pp. 191–192.
85. Ibid.
86. Margery Austin Turner, Michael Fix, and Raymond J. Struyk, *Opportunities Denied: Discrimination in Hiring* (Washington, D.C.: Urban Institute, 1991).
87. Sharon M. Collins, "The Making of the Black Middle Class," *Social Problems* 30 (April 1983): 369–381; Sharon Collins, "Blacks on the Bubble: The Vulnerability of Black Executives in White Corporations," *Sociological Quarterly* 34 (August 1993): 429–447.
88. Kenneth B. Clark, "The Role of Race," *New York Times Magazine*, October 5, 1980, p. 30.
89. David Hatchett, "Corporate America and Affirmative Action: The Struggle Continues," *Crisis*, October 1994, pp. 8–9.
90. Kurt Eichenwald, "Texaco Executives, On Tape, Discussed Impeding a Bias Suit," *New York Times*, November 4, 1996, p. A1.
91. Kurt Eichenwald, "The Two Faces Of Texaco," *New York Times*, November 10, 1996, sec. 3, p. 1.
92. Ibid.
93. "The Multi-City Study of Urban Inequality," Russell Sage Foundation Newsletter, fall, 1999, pp. 1–3, and on an attached supplement to that newsletter; and Philip Moss and Chris Tilly, *Stories Employers Tell: Race, Skill, and Hiring in America* (New York: Russell Sage, 2001).
94. Glass Ceiling Commission, *Good for Business: Making Full Use of the Nation's Human Capital* (Washington, D.C., 1995), pp. 12–60.
95. Jacquelyn Scarville et al., *Armed Forces Equal Opportunity Survey* (Arlington, VA: Defense Manpower Data Center, 1999), pp. 46–85; Office of the Under Secretary of Defense Personnel and Readiness, *Career Progression of Minority and Women Officers* (Washington, D.C.: Department of Defense, 1999), pp. 83–85.
96. Ian Ayres, "Fair Driving: Gender and Race Discrimination in Retail Car Negotiations," *Harvard Law Review*, February 1991, 104 Harv. L. Rev. 817.
97. *Wards Cove Packing Co. v. Atonio* 109 S. Ct. 2115 (1989).
98. U.S. Bureau of the Census, *The Social and Economic Status of the Black Population in the United States, 1971* (Washington, D.C., 1972), p. 52; Bureau of Labor Statistics, "Labor Force Statistics from the Current Population Survey," <http://stats.bls.gov/cpsatabs.htm> (retrieved July 16, 2001).
99. U.S. Bureau of Labor Statistics, *Employment and Earnings*, March 1994, p. 35.
100. U.S. Census Bureau "Historical Income Tables–Families, Table F-5: Race and Hispanic Origin of Householder—Families by Median and Mean Income: 1947 to 1999," published October 30, 2000, <http://www.census.gov/hhes/income/histinc/incfamdet.html>. The census category "nonwhite" consists mostly of blacks.

101. U.S. Census Bureau, *Money Income in the United States, 1999*, Current Population Reports, P60-209 (Washington, D.C., 2000), p. viii.
102. U.S. Census Bureau, "Historical Income Tables—Families, Table F-7B: Type of Family—Black Families by Median and Mean Income: 1967 to 1999," published October 30, 2000, <http://www.census.gov/hhes/income/histinc/incfamdet.html>.
103. Joseph Dalaker and Bernadette D. Proctor, U.S. Census Bureau, Current Population Reports, Series P60-210, *Poverty in the United States, 1999* (U.S. Government Printing Office, Washington, D.C., 2000), pp. B-15, B-17.
104. Robert B. Hill, "The Economic Status of Black Americans," in *The State of Black America, 1981*, ed. J. D. Williams (New York: Urban League, 1981), pp. 5–6, 33.
105. Dalaker and Proctor, *Poverty in the United States, 1999*, pp. vi, B-9, B-15, B-16.
106. U.S. Census Bureau, "Asset Ownership of Households: 1995, Table 1: Median Value of Assets for Households, by Type of Asset Owned and Selected Characteristics: 1995," published April 9, 2001, <http://www.census.gov/hhes/www/wealth/1995/wealth95.html>; U.S. Census Bureau, "Asset Ownership of Households: 1995, Table 2: Asset Ownership Rates for Households, by Selected Characteristics: 1995," published April 9, 2001, <http://www.census.gov/hhes/www/wealth/1995/wealth95.html>; The middle class data are from Rhonda V. Magee, "The Master's Tools, from the Bottom Up: Responses to African-American Reparations Theory in Mainstream and Outsider Remedies Discourse," *Virginia Law Review* 79 (May 1993): 863.
107. See William J. Wilson, *The Declining Significance of Race* (Chicago: University of Chicago Press, 1978); Ken Auletta, *The Underclass* (New York: Random House, 1982); William J. Wilson, *The Truly Disadvantaged* (Chicago: University of Chicago Press, 1987).
108. See Joe R. Feagin, *Subordinating the Poor* (Englewood Cliffs, NJ: Prentice Hall, 1975), p. 22.
109. See Joe R. Feagin and Clairece B. Feagin, *Discrimination American Style*, 2nd ed. (Malabar, FL: Robert Krieger, 1986), pp. 207–234.
110. See, for example, Fair Housing Council of Fresno County, "Audit Uncovers Blatant Discrimination against Hispanics, African Americans and Families with Children in Fresno County," press release, Fresno, California, October 6, 1997.
111. Shanna L. Smith and Cathy Clous, "Documenting Discrimination by Homeowners Insurance Companies through Testing," in *Insurance Redlining: Disinvestment, Reinvestment, and the Evolving Role of Financial Institutions*, ed. Gregory D. Squires (Washington, D.C.: Urban Institute, 1997), pp. 106–117.
112. Isabel Wilkerson, "The Tallest Fence: Feelings on Race in a White Neighborhood," *New York Times*, June 21, 1992, sec. 1, p. 18.
113. The discussion in this subsection draws on a course given by Thomas F. Pettigrew at Harvard University.
114. Franklin, *From Slavery to Freedom*, pp. 252–253; Chuck Stone, *Black Political Power in America*, rev. ed. (New York: Dell, 1970), pp. 30–31.
115. Stetson Kennedy, *After Appomattox: How the South Won the War* (Gainesville: University Press of Florida, 1995), p. 3; see also Cedric J. Robinson, *Black Movements in America* (New York: Routledge, 1997), pp. 86–88.
116. I draw here on Feagin, *Racist America*, pp. 57–58.
117. *Plessy v. Ferguson*, 163 U.S. 551–552.
118. Hanes Walton, Jr., *Black Politics* (Philadelphia, PA: Lippincott, 1972), pp. 100, 119.
119. Chandler Davidson and Bernard Grofman, "The Voting Rights Act and the Second Reconstruction," in *The Quiet Revolution in the South* (Princeton, NJ: Princeton University Press, 1994), p. 386; the data here are from the Joint Center for Political and Economic Studies, retrieved from <http://nuance.dhs.org/ibotalk/0012/0083.html> (retrieved May 3, 2001).
120. Chandler Davidson, *Minority Vote Dilution: An Overview*, Reprint 85-1 (Houston, TX: Institute for Policy Analysis, Rice University, 1985), pp. 17–18; Frank R. Parker, *Black Votes Count* (Chapel Hill: University of North Carolina Press, 1990).
121. Davidson, *Minority Vote Dilution*, pp. 17–18.
122. Ibid.
123. Earl Ofari Hutchinson, "Bamboozled at the Voting Booth," *Mother Jones*, November 16, 2000, <http://www.motherjones.com/reality_check/bamboozled.html> (retrieved May 3, 2001).
124. William E. Forbath, "Civil Rights, Economic Justice, and the Meaning of the Guinier Affair," *Legal Times*, June 28, 1993, p. 21; Michael Isikoff, "Readings in Controversy: Guinier's Pivotal Articles," *Washington Post*, June 4, 1993, p. A10; Lani Guinier, *The Tyranny of the Majority: Fundamental Fairness and Representation Democracy* (New York: Free Press, 1994).
125. Quotes are from James W. Button, *Blacks and Social Change* (Princeton, NJ: Princeton University Press, 1989), pp. 226–227.
126. Data are from the Joint Center for Political and Economic Studies, personal communication, 1995.
127. Myrdal, *An American Dilemma*, 1:503; Raymond Wolters, *Negroes and the Great Depression* (Westport, CT: Greenwood Press, 1970), p. xi and elsewhere.
128. Congressional Black Caucus, *Directory of the 104th Congress* (Washington, D.C., 1995).
129. Stone, *Black Political Power in America*, pp. 68–72.

130. Ibid., p. 47. Stone draws here on Henry L. Moon, *Balance of Power* (Garden City, NY: Doubleday, 1948).
131. Kevin Phillips, *The Emerging Republican Majority* (New Rochelle, NY: Arlington House, 1969).
132. Joe R. Feagin, "White Elephant: Race and Electoral Politics in Texas," *Texas Observer*, August 23, 1991, pp. 15–16.
133. The discussions of oppositional culture in this chapter draw on Mitchell and Feagin, "America's Racial–Ethnic Cultures," pp. 65–86.
134. Feagin and Hahn, *Ghetto Revolts*, pp. 81–85; Loren Miller, *The Petitioners* (New York: Random House, 1966), pp. 250–256.
135. Miller, *The Petitioners*, pp. 260–347.
136. Lerone Bennett, Jr., *Confrontation: Black and White* (Baltimore, MD: Penguin, 1966), pp. 164–169.
137. Ibid., pp. 223–234; Bryan T. Downes and Stephen W. Burks, "The Historical Development of the Black Protest Movement," in *Blacks in the United States*, ed. Norval D. Glenn and Charles Bonjean (San Francisco: Chandler, 1969), pp. 322–344.
138. Feagin and Hahn, *Ghetto Revolts*, pp. 92–94; Bennett, *Confrontation*, pp. 234–237; Inge P. Bell, *CORE and the Strategy of Nonviolence* (New York: Random House, 1968), pp. 13–16.
139. Aldon Morris, *The Origins of the Civil Rights Movement* (New York: Free Press, 1984).
140. U.S. Commission on Civil Rights, *The Federal Civil Rights Enforcement Effort: Fiscal Year 1983* (Washington, D.C., 1982), pp. 5–7; Andrew Rosenthal, "Reagan Hints Rights Leaders Exaggerate Racism to Preserve Cause," *New York Times*, January 14, 1989, p. 8.
141. Joe R. Feagin and Hernan Vera, *White Racism: Basic Principles* (New York: Routledge, 1995), pp. 52–57.
142. Sheila D. Collins, *The Rainbow Challenge* (New York: Monthly Review Press, 1986), pp. 128–143.
143. Collins, *Black Feminist Thought*.
144. Franklin, *From Slavery to Freedom*, pp. 280–281; Myrdal, *An American Dilemma*, 1:337–344; Henry A. Bullock, *A History of Negro Education in the South* (New York: Praeger, 1967), pp. 1–99.
145. Bullock, *A History of Negro Education in the South*, pp. 170–186; Franklin, *From Slavery to Freedom*, pp. 284–286.
146. U.S. Bureau of the Census, *Statistical Abstract of the United States 1993*, p. 152; U.S. Census Bureau, "Educational Attainment, Table A-2: Percent of People 25 Years Old and Over Who Have Completed High School or College, by Race, Hispanic Origin and Sex: Selected Years 1940 to 2000," published December 19, 2000, <http://www.census.gov/population/www/socdemo/educ-attn.html>.
147. Bullock, *A History of Negro Education in the South*, pp. 211–212, 225–230; Miller, *The Petitioners*, pp. 347–358.
148. U.S. Commission on Civil Rights, *Twenty Years after Brown* (Washington, D.C., 1975), pp. 11–41; *Milliken v. Bradley*, 418 U.S. 717.
149. Russell W. Irvine and Jacqueline Jordan Irvine, "The Impact of the Desegregation Process on the Education of Black Students: Key Variables," *Journal of Negro Education* 53 (1983): 410–421.
150. Quoted in William H. Freivogel, "Black, White, and Brown: Desegregation Ruling Established a Legal Landmark, Unkept Promises," *St. Louis Post-Dispatch*, May 15, 1994, p. 1B.
151. Harvard Graduate School of Education, "Press Release: School Segregation on the Rise Despite Growing Diversity Among School-Aged Children," July 17, 2001, <http://www.gse.harvard.edu/nv/features/orfield07172001.html>.
152. Quoted in Peter Applebome, "Schools See Re-emergence Of 'Separate but Equal,'" *New York Times* (April 8, 1997): A10.
153. Gail Russell Chaddock, "U.S. Schools Slip Back Toward Segregation," *Christian Science Monitor*, July 18, 2001, <http://www.csmonitor.com>.
154. Diana Pearce, "Breaking Down Barriers: New Evidence on the Impact of Metropolitan School Desegregation on Housing Patterns." Research report, School of Law, Catholic University, 1980, pp. 48–53.
155. New York ACORN Schools Office, *Secret Apartheid: A Report on Racial Discrimination against Black and Latino Parents and Children in the New York City Public Schools* (New York: ACORN, 1996).
156. Ibid., p. 2.
157. Amy Stuart Wells, Robert L. Crain, and Susan Uchitelle, *Stepping Over the Color Line: African American Students in White Suburban Schools* (New Haven, CT: Yale University Press, 1997).
158. Ibid.
159. Feagin and Feagin, *Discrimination American Style*, pp. 201–204.
160. Juan Williams, "The Seduction of Segregation, and Why King's Dream Still Matters," *Washington Post*, January 16, 1994, p. C1.
161. Gary Orfield, as quoted in George J. Church, "The Boom Towns," *Time*, June 15, 1987, p. 17.
162. "Black Students and Educational Aspirations," *Race Relations Reporter*, August 15, 1994, p. 1
163. U.S. Census Bureau, "School Enrollment, October 2000, Social and Economic Characteristics of Students, Table 13: Enrollment and Employment Status of Recent High School Graduates 16 to 24 Years Old, by Type of School, Attainment Level for People Not Enrolled, Sex, Race, and Hispanic Origin," published June 1, 2001, <http://www.census.gov/population/www/socdemo/school.html>.
164. U.S. Census Bureau, "Educational Attainment in the United States, March 2000, Table 1: Educational

Attainment of the Population 15 Years and Over, by Age, Sex, Race, and Hispanic Origin," published December 19, 2000, <http://www.census.gov/population/www/socdemo/education.html>.

165. Mary Jordan, "Black College Enrollment Up," *Washington Post*, January 20, 1992, p. A14; "Is the Dream Over?" *Newsweek on Campus*, February 1987, pp. 10–14.
166. Komanduri S. Murty and Julian B. Roebuck, "The Case for Historically Black Colleges and Universities," *Journal of Social and Behavioral Sciences* 36 (1992): 177–178.
167. Walter R. Allen, "Correlates of Black Student Adjustment, Achievement, and Aspirations at a Predominantly White Southern University," in *Black Students in Higher Education*, ed. Gail E. Thomas, (Westport, CT: Greenwood Press, 1981), pp. 128–137; Walter R. Allen, "Black and Blue: Black Students at the University of Michigan." Research report, University of Michigan, n.d., pp. 8–12.
168. See Joe R. Feagin, Hernan Vera, Nikitah Imani, *The Agony of Education* (New York: Routledge, 1996), p. 55.
169. Stampp, *The Peculiar Institution*, pp. 156–162; Aptheker, *American Negro Slave Revolts*, pp. 56–60.
170. Stuckey, *Slave Culture*, p. 27.
171. James Scott, *Domination and the Arts of Resistance* (New Haven, CT: Yale University Press, 1990).
172. Richard C. Wade, *Slavery in the Cities* (New York: Oxford University Press, 1964), pp. 161–163; Winthrop Jordan, *White over Black* (Baltimore, MD: Penguin, 1969), pp. 422–425.
173. E. Franklin Frazier, *The Negro Church in America* (New York: Schocken Books, 1964), pp. 35–39; Myrdal, *An American Dilemma*, 2:938–939; E. U. Essien-Udom, *Black Nationalism* (New York: Dell, 1964).
174. Quoted in Michael Hirsley, "Churches Are Sources of Power," *Chicago Tribune*, February 5, 1992, p. C6.
175. Frazier, *The Negro Church in America*, p. 44; Joseph R. Washington, Jr., *Black Religion* (Boston: Beacon Press, 1964), pp. 2–29.
176. David L. Lewis, *King* (Baltimore, MD: Penguin, 1970), p. 390.
177. This paragraph draws heavily on contributions by Bonnie Mitchell to Feagin and Mitchell, "America's Non-European Cultures."
178. Joe Klein, "Can Colin Powell Save America?" *Newsweek*, October 10, 1994, p. 26.
179. Jeffrey S. Passel and Barry Edmonston, "Immigrating and Race: Recent Trends in Immigration to the United States," in *Immigration and Ethnicity: The Integration of America's Newest Arrivals*, ed. Barry Edmonston and Jeffrey S. Passel (Washington, D.C.: Urban Institute Press, 1994), pp. 52–53.
180. U.S. Bureau of the Census, *1990 Census of Population: Ancestry of the Population in the United States*, CP-3-2 (Washington, D.C., 1993), p. 73; U.S. Bureau of the Census, *1990 Census of Population: Social and Economic Characteristics: United States*, CP-2-1 (Washington, D.C., 1993), pp. 167–172.
181. Ibid., pp. 42, 44, 45, 48, 49; U.S. Bureau of the Census, *1990 Census of Population: Ancestry of the Population in the United States*, pp. 277, 379, 481.
182. U.S. Bureau of the Census, *1990 Census of Population: Ancestry of the Population in the United States*, pp. 87–88; U.S. Bureau of the Census, *1990 Census of Population: Social and Economic Characteristics: United States*, pp. 168, 170.
183. U.S. Bureau of the Census, *1990 Census of Population: Ancestry of the Population in the United States*, pp. 94–95.
184. Personal communication between authors and Haitian American professor Dr. Yanick St. Jean, September 1994.
185. Felix Robert Masud-Piloto, *With Open Arms: Cuban Migration to the U.S.* (Totowa, NJ: Rowman and Littlefield, 1988), pp. 111–125; see also Paul Farmer, *The Uses of Haiti* (Monroe, ME: Common Courage Press, 1994); Amy Wilentz, *The Rainy Season: Haiti Since Duvalier* (New York: Simon & Schuster/Touchstone, 1989).
186. Gwen Ifill, "President Names Black Democrat Advisor on Haiti," *New York Times*, May 9, 1994, p. A1; Eric Schmitt, "Tents for Haitians Rise Again at Guantanamo," *New York Times*, July 2, 1994, p. 1.
187. Eric Schmitt, "U.S. Ready to Declare Haiti 'Secure,'" *New York Times*, January 15, 1995, p. 8.
188. U.S. Bureau of the Census, *1990 Census of Population: Social and Economic Characteristics: United States*, p. 45; U.S. Bureau of the Census, *1990 Census of Population: Ancestry of the Population in the United States*, p. 393.
189. U.S. Bureau of the Census, *1990 Census of Population: Ancestry of the Population in the United States*, p. 394.
190. Mary C. Waters, "Ethnic and Racial Identities of Second Generation Black Immigrants in New York City," *International Migration Review* 28 (winter 1994): 795–820; Ramón Grosfoguel and Chloe S. Georas, "'Coloniality of Power and Racial Dynamics: Notes Toward a Reinterpretation of Latino Caribbeans in New York City," *Identities: Global Studies in Culture and Power* 7 (2000): 85–125.
191. U.S. Bureau of the Census, *1990 Census of Population: Social and Economic Characteristics: United States*, pp. 47, 48, 49; U.S. Bureau of the Census, *1990 Census of Population: Ancestry of the Population in the United States*, pp. 393, 495.
192. U.S. Bureau of the Census, *1990 Census of Population: Ancestry of the Population in the United States*, p. 496.
193. U.S. Bureau of the Census, *1990 Census of Population:*

Social and Economic Characteristics: United States, p. 42; U.S. Bureau of the Census, *1990 Census of Population: Ancestry of the Population in the United States*, pp. 291–292.

194. U.S. Bureau of the Census, *1990 Census of Population: Ancestry of the Population in the United States*, p. 292.
195. Barbara J. Fields, "Ideology and Race in American History," in *Region, Race, and Reconstruction: Essays in Honor of C. Vann Woodward*, ed. J. Morgan Kousser and James M. McPherson (New York: Oxford University Press, 1982), p. 146.
196. Waters, "Ethnic and Racial Identities of Second Generation Black Immigrants in New York City."
197. Personal communication between authors and Yanick St. Jean, September 1994.
198. Waters, "Ethnic and Racial Identities of Second Generation Black Immigrants in New York City."
199. Personal communication between authors and Yanick St. Jean, September 1994.
200. Paul Farmer, *AIDS and Accusation* (Berkeley, CA: University of California Press, 1992), pp. 215–226.
201. Milton Gordon, *Assimilation in American Life* (New York: Oxford University Press, 1964), p. 78.
202. Talcott Parsons, "Full Citizenship for the Negro American? A Sociological Problem," in *The Negro American*, ed. Talcott Parsons and Kenneth B. Clark (Boston: Houghton Mifflin, 1965), p. 740; see also pp. 714–715.
203. Nathan Glazer, *Affirmative Discrimination* (New York: Basic Books, 1975), pp. 40–76; Daniel P. Moynihan, *The Negro Family* (Washington, D.C., 1965); Frazier, *The Negro Church in America*; Myrdal, *An American Dilemma.*
204. Robert Blauner, *Racial Oppression in America* (New York: Harper & Row, 1972), pp. 51–110.
205. Wade, *Slavery in the Cities*, pp. 273–275; Herman D. Bloch, *The Circle of Discrimination* (New York: New York University Press, 1969), pp. ix–xiii.
206. Wilhelm, *Who Needs the Negro?*; Robert L. Allen, *Black Awakening in Capitalist America* (Garden City, NY: Doubleday/Anchor Books, 1970), pp. 4–6; *Report of the National Advisory Commission on Civil Disorders* (New York: Bantam, 1968), pp. 278–279.
207. Marimba Ani, *Yurugu: An African-Centered Critique of European Cultural Thought and Behavior* (Trenton, NJ: Africa World Press, 1994), pp. 567–569.
208. Feagin and Sikes, *Living with Racism*, p. vii.

Chapter 8

1. Juan Gonzalez, *Harvest of Empire: A History of Latinos in America* (New York: Penguin Books, 2000), p. xii.
2. U.S. Census Bureau, "The Hispanic Population," Census 2000 Brief, May 2001, pp. 1–2, <www.census.gov/prod/cen2000>.
3. Edward Múrguía, "On Latino/Hispanic Ethnic Identity," *Latino Studies Journal* 2, no. 3 (September 1991): 8–18.
4. U.S. Census Bureau, "Census 2000 Summary File 1," published May 2001, <www.census.gov/prod/cen2000>.
5. Teresa L. Amott and Julie A. Matthaei, *Race, Gender, and Work* (Boston: South End Press, 1991), pp. 64–67.
6. Ilan Stavans, *The Hispanic Condition: Reflections on Culture and Identity in America* (New York: HarperCollins, 1995), p. 22.
7. Américo Paredes, *With His Pistol in His Hand* (Austin: University of Texas Press, 1958), pp. 3–14; Rodolfo Acuña, *Occupied America* (San Francisco: Canfield Press, 1972), pp. 10–12.
8. Acuña, *Occupied America*, p. 15; S. Dale McLemore, "The Origin of Mexican American Subordination in Texas," *Social Science Quarterly* 53 (March 1973): 665–667; Rodolfo Alvarez, "The Psycho-historical and Socioeconomic Development of the Chicano Community in the United States," *Social Science Quarterly* 53 (March 1973): 925; David Montejano, *Anglos and Mexicans in The Making of Texas, 1836–1986* (Austin: University of Texas Press, 1987).
9. William Lord, "Myths and Realities of the Alamo," *American West* 5 (May 1968): 20–25.
10. Carl N. Degler, *Out of Our Past* (New York: Harper, 1959), pp. 109–110; Acuña, *Occupied America*, pp. 23–29.
11. Joan Moore and Harry Pachon, *Hispanics in the United States* (Englewood Cliffs, NJ: Prentice Hall, 1985), pp. 18, 22–23; Leo Grebler, Joan W. Moore, and Ralph G. Guzmán, *The Mexican-American People* (New York: Free Press, 1970), pp. 43–44; Acuña, *Occupied America*, p. 105; Joan W. Moore, "Colonialism: The Case of the Mexican Americans," *Social Problems* 17 (spring 1970): 468–469.
12. Moore and Pachon, *Hispanics in the United States*, p. 21; Ellwyn R. Stoddard, *Mexican Americans* (New York: Random House, 1973), pp. 9–13; Carey McWilliams, *North from Mexico* (New York: Greenwood Press, 1968), pp. 70–76; Acuña, *Occupied America*, pp. 60–62; Grebler, Moore, and Guzmán, *The Mexican American People*, pp. 43–44; Nancie L. Gonzales, *The Spanish-Americans of New Mexico* (Albuquerque: University of New Mexico Press, 1967), pp. 204–210.
13. Alvarez, "Psycho-Historical and Socioeconomic Development," p. 925.
14. Oscar J. Martinez, "On the Size of the Chicano Population: New Estimates: 1850–1900," *Aztlán* 6 (spring 1975): 55–56; U.S. Department of Justice, Immigration and Naturalization Service, *Annual Report*

(Washington, D.C., 1975), pp. 62–64; Julian Samora, *Los Mojados: The Wetback Story* (Notre Dame, IN: University of Notre Dame Press, 1971), pp. 7–8.

15. Leo Grebler, *Mexican Immigration to the United States: The Record and Its Implications* (Los Angeles: UCLA Mexican-American Study Project, 1965), pp. 20–21.
16. Mark Reisler, *By the Sweat of Their Brow: Mexican Immigrant Labor in the United States, 1900–1940* (Westport, CT: Greenwood, 1976); Grebler, *Mexican Immigration to the United States*, pp. 23–24; Manuel Gamio, *Mexican Immigration to the United States* (New York: Dover, 1971), pp. 171–174; Ronald Takaki, *A Different Mirror* (Boston: Little, Brown, 1993), pp. 326–334.
17. Samora, *Los Mojados*, pp. 48–52.
18. Gilberto Cardenas, "United States Immigration Policy toward Mexico," *Chicano Law Review* 2 (summer 1975): 73–75; Grebler, *Mexican Immigration to the United States*, p. 26.
19. Samora, *Los Mojados*, pp. 18–19, 24–25, 44–46, 57; Joan Moore, *Mexican Americans*, 2nd ed. (Englewood Cliffs, NJ: Prentice Hall, 1976), pp. 49–51; Strategy Research Corporation, *1991 U.S. Hispanic Market* (Miami, FL, 1991), pp. 39, 51.
20. Cardenas, "United States Immigration Policy toward Mexico," pp. 84–85; Cheryl Anderson, "Immigration Bill under Attack on Several Fronts," *Austin American-Statesman*, December 12, 1982, p. C1.
21. Luis Alberto Urrea, *By the Lake of Sleeping Children: The Secret Life of the Mexican Border* (New York: Anchor Books), 1996, p. 18.
22. Stavans, *The Hispanic Condition*, p. 22.
23. See Gonzalez, *Harvest of Empire*, pp. 234–236.
24. Michael Fix and Jeffrey S. Passel, *Immigration and Immigrants: Setting the Record Straight* (Washington, D.C.: Urban Institute, 1994), p. 24.
25. Leo R. Chávez, *Shadowed Lives: Undocumented Immigrants in American Society* (Orlando, FL: Harcourt Brace Jovanovich, 1992), pp. 19–20, 29–30, 39, 70, 79–80, 126–129, 148–151.
26. Fix and Passel, *Immigration and Immigrants*, pp. 24–25, 51, 60, 62, 71, 81; Chávez, *Shadowed Lives*, pp. 143, 151.
27. Stephen Koepp, "Rotten Shame: Who Will Pick the Crops?" *Time*, June 22, 1987, p. 49.
28. Jacqueline Maria Hagan and Susan González Baker, "Implementing the U.S. Legalization Program," *International Migration Review*, 27 (fall 1993): 514; Susan González Baker and Frank Bean, "The Legalization Programs of the 1986 Immigration Reform and Control Act," in *In Defense of the Alien*, ed. Lydio F. Tomasi (New York: Center for Migration Studies, 1990), pp. 3–11; Susan González Baker, *The Cautious Welcome: The Legalization Programs of the Immigration Reform and Control Act* (Washington, D.C.: Urban Institute, 1990); data provided by Demographics Statistics Branch, Immigration and Naturalization Service, January 1995.
29. Jose A. Pagan and Alberto Davila, "On-the-Job Training, Immigration Reform, and the True Wages of Native Male Workers," *Industrial Relations* 35 (January 1996): 45–58.
30. Lisa Lollock, *The Foreign Born Population in the United States: March 2000*, Current Population Reports, P20-534, Census Bureau, Washington, D.C., 2001; Karen A. Woodrow and Jeffrey S. Passel, "Post-IRCA Undocumented Immigration to the United States" in *Undocumented Migration to the United States*, ed. Frank Bean, Barry Edmonston, and Jeffrey Passel (Santa Monica, CA: Rand Corporation, 1990), p. 42.
31. Quoted from *Los Angeles Times* in Donaldo Macedo, "Foreword," in Enrique T. Trueba, *Latinos Unidos: From Cultural Diversity to the Politics of Solidarity*, pp. xviii–xix.
32. Lynda Gorov, "Poor Immigrants Face New Hurdles," *Boston Globe*, November 30, 1997, p. A1.
33. This research by David Hayes-Bautista is summarized in "Immigrants and Cohesion," *Orange County Register*, June 17, 1997, p. B8.
34. Gonzalez, *Harvest of Empire*, p. 197.
35. Quotations are from Arnoldo De León, "Initial Contacts: Niggers, Redskins, and Greasers," in *The Latino/a Condition: A Critical Reader*, ed. Richard Delgado and Jean Stefancic (New York: New York University Press, 1998), p. 161.
36. Quoted in Philip D. Ortego, "The Chicano Renaissance," in *Introduction to Chicano Studies*, ed. Livie I. Duran and H. Russell Bernard (New York: Macmillan, 1973), p. 337.
37. Ricardo Romo, *East Lost Angeles: History of a Barrio* (Austin: University of Texas Press, 1983), pp. 89–111.
38. Cardenas, "United States Immigration Policy toward Mexico," pp. 70–71.
39. Quoted in Ralph Guzmán, "The Function of Anglo-American Racism in the Political Development of Chicanos," in *La Causa Politica*, ed. F. Chris Garcia (South Bend, IN: University of Notre Dame Press, 1974), p. 22.
40. McWilliams, *North from Mexico*, p. 213.
41. William Sheldon, "Educational Research and Statistics: The Intelligence of Mexican-American Children," in *In Their Place*, ed. Lewis H. Carlson and George A. Colburn (New York: Wiley, 1972), pp. 149–151.
42. Quoted in Guillermo V. Flores, "Race and Culture in the Internal Colony: Keeping the Chicano in His Place," in "Structures of Dependency," ed. Frank Bonilla and Robert Girling. Manuscript, research seminar, Stanford, CA, 1973, p. 194.
43. Quoted in George A. Martinez, "Mexican Americans and Whiteness," in *The Latino/a Condition*, p. 178.

44. Quoted in Otto Santa Ana, "'Like an Animal I was Treated': Anti-Immigrant Metaphor in U.S. Public Discourse," *Discourse & Society* 10 (1994): 220.
45. Octavio Ignacio Romano, "The Anthropology and Sociology of the Mexican-Americans," *El Grito* 2 (fall 1968): 13–19; Oscar Lewis, *Five Families* (New York: Wiley, 1962); William Madsen, *Mexican Americans of South Texas* (New York: Holt, Rinehart & Winston, 1964).
46. G. Marin, "Stereotyping Hispanics," *International Journal of Intercultural Relations* 8 (1984): 17–27.
47. Americo Paredes, *With His Pistol in His Hand*; Romano, "The Anthropology and Sociology of the Mexican Americans"; Stoddard, *Mexican Americans*, pp. 42–44; Lea Ybarra, "Empirical and Theoretical Developments in the Study of the Chicano Family," in *The State of Chicano Research on Family, Labor, and Migration*, ed. Armando Valdez, Albert Camarillo, and Tomás Almaguer (Stanford, CA: Stanford Center for Chicano Research, 1983), p. 96.
48. Linda A. Jackson, "Stereotypes, Emotions, Behavior, and Overall Attitudes Toward Hispanics by Anglos," Research Report 10, Julian Samora Research Institute, Michigan State University, January 1995, <http://www.jsri.msu/RandS/research/irr/rr10.htm> (retrieved June 9, 2001).
49. National Conference of Christians and Jews, *Taking America's Pulse: The National Conference Survey on Inter-Group Relations* (New York: National Conference, 1994).
50. Charles N. Weaver, "Work Attitudes of Mexican Americans," *Hispanic Journal of Behavioral Sciences* 22 (August 2000): 275–295.
51. John Dillin, "Immigration Proposals Get Mixed Reviews," *Christian Science Monitor*, March 20, 2001, <http://www.csmonitor.com/durable/2001> (retrieved June 19, 2001).
52. James H. Johnson, Jr., Karen D. Johnson-Webb, and Walter C. Farrell, Jr., "A Profile of Hispanic Newcomers to North Carolina," *Popular Government* 65 (fall 1999): 2–12.
53. "Blood on the Border," *Intelligence Report* (Southern Poverty Law Center), spring 2001, pp. 8–11.
54. National Council of La Raza, "Distorted Reality: Hispanic Characters in TV Entertainment," September 1994. See also Gregory Freeman, *Crisis*, October 1994, p. 5.
55. Ansel Martinez, "Study Shows Television Shows Stereotype Hispanics." Washington, D.C.: National Public Radio, *All Things Considered*, September 10, 1994.
56. Marco Portales, *Crowding Out Latinos: Mexican Americans in the Public Consciousness* (Philadelphia, PA: Temple Press, 2000), p. 101.
57. Ibid., p. 31.
58. Santa Ana, "'Like an Animal I was Treated'", pp. 194–220; see also Otto Santa Ana, *Brown Tide Rising: Metaphors of Latinos in Contemporary American Public Discourse* (Austin, TX: University of Texas Press, forthcoming, 2001). We draw on a foreword for this volume written by Joe Feagin.
59. Jane H. Hill, "Mock Spanish: A Site for the Indexical Reproduction of Racism in American English," unpublished research paper, University of Arizona, 1995.
60. Ibid.
61. David Lopez and Ricardo Stanton-Salazar, "The Mexican American Second Generation: Yesterday, Today, and Tomorrow," in *Ethnicities: Coming of Age in Immigrant America*, ed. Ruben Rumbaut and Alejandro Portes (Berkeley, CA: University of California Press, forthcoming).
62. Clara E. Rodríguez, *Changing Race: Latinos, The Census, and the History of Ethnicity in the United States* (New York: New York University Press, 2000), p. 19.
63. Tatcho Mindiola, Néstor Rodríguez, and Yolanda Flores Niemann, "Intergroup Relations between African Americans and Hispanics in Harris County," unpublished research report, Center for Mexican American Studies, University of Houston, 1996.
64. U.S. Census Bureau, "Overview of Race and Hispanic Origin," Census 2000 Brief, March 2001, pp. 2–5, <www.census.gov/prod/cen2000>.
65. E. J. Hobsbawm, *Primitive Rebels* (New York: W. W. Norton, 1959), pp. 15–16.
66. Paredes, *With His Pistol in His Hand*, pp. 27–32; McWilliams, *North from Mexico*, p. 127; Moore, "Colonialism," p. 466; Stoddard, *Mexican Americans*, p. 181.
67. Ralph H. Turner and Lewis M. Killian, *Collective Behavior* (Englewood Cliffs, NJ: Prentice Hall, 1957), pp. 125–128; McWilliams, *North from Mexico*, pp. 229–238.
68. Armondo Morales, *Ando Sangrando* (Fair Lawn, NJ: R. E. Burdick, 1972), pp. 100–108.
69. U.S. Commission on Civil Rights, *Mexican Americans and the Administration of Justice in the Southwest* (Washington, D.C., 1970), pp. 6–10; Robert Lee Maril, *Poorest of Americans* (South Bend, IN: University of Notre Dame Press, 1989), p. 52; Andrea Ford and Sheryl Stolberg, "Latinos Tell Panel of Anger at Police Conduct," *Los Angeles Times*, May 21, 1991, p. A1; Louis Sahagun, "Shooting Spurs Latinos to Reassess Law Enforcement," *Los Angeles Times*, August 8, 1991, p. A1; George Ramos, "Latinos Push Demand for Sheriff's Dept. Probe," *Los Angeles Times*, September 19, 1991, p. B3.
70. Patrick J. McDonnell, "Latinos Recover Optimism Lost in '90s," *Los Angeles Times*, March 11, 2001.
71. Raymond Smith, "The Chase and Beating Incident," *Press-Enterprise* (Riverside), March 30, 1997, p. B1.

72. Antonio H. Rodríguez and Carlos A. Chávez, "Latinos Unite in Self-Defense on Proposition 187," *Los Angeles Times*, October 21, 1994, p. B7; Beth Shuster and Chip Johnson, "Hundreds of Students Stage Walkouts to Protest Proposition 187," *Los Angeles Times*, October 21, 1994, p. B3.
73. Frank Trejo, "Thousands of Hispanics March in Washington; Texas Residents Join Call for End to Discrimination, Rights Abuses," *Dallas Morning News*, Oct 13, 1996, p. 1.
74. Abel G. Rubio, *Stolen Heritage* (Austin, TX: Eakin Press, 1986).
75. Clark Knowlton, "Recommendations for the Solution of Land Tenure Problems among the Spanish Americans," in *Chicano: The Evolution of a People*, ed. Renato Rosaldo, Robert A. Calvert, and Gustav L. Seligmann (San Francisco: Rinehart Press, 1973), pp. 334–335; George I. Sánchez, *Forgotten People* (Albuquerque: University of New Mexico Press, 1940), p. 61; Arnoldo Deleón, *The Tejano Community, 1836–1900* (Albuquerque: University of New Mexico Press, 1982), pp. 63–91.
76. Tomas Almaguer, "Historical Notes on Chicano Oppression: The Dialectics of Racial and Class Domination in North America," *Atzlán* 5 (spring–fall 1974): 38–39; Richard del Castillo, "Myth and Reality: Chicano Economic Mobility in Los Angeles, 1850–1880," *Atzlán* 6 (summer 1975): 153–154; McWilliams, *North from Mexico*, pp. 127–128; Gamio, *Mexican Immigration to the United States*, pp. 39–40; Charles Wollenberg, "Huelga, 1928 Style: The Imperial Valley Canteloupe Workers' Strike," in *Chicano*, ed. Rosaldo, Calvert, and Seligmann, pp. 185–188; Amott and Matthaei, *Race, Gender, and Work*, pp. 76–77.
77. Samora, *Los Mojados*, p. 130; Grebler, Moore, and Guzmán, *The Mexican-American People*, p. 91.
78. Ruth H. Tuck, *Not with the Fist* (New York: Harcourt, Brace, & World, 1946), pp. 173–183.
79. McWilliams, *North from Mexico*, pp. 217–218; U.S. Commission on Civil Rights, *Mexican American Education Study*, vol. 1, *Ethnic Isolation of Mexican Americans in the Public Schools of the Southwest* (Washington, D.C., 1971), p. 11.
80. Anne Brunton, "The Chicano Migrants," in *Introduction to Chicano Studies*, ed. Duran and Bernard, pp. 489–492.
81. Roberto Suro, "Border Boom's Dirty Residue Imperils U.S.–Mexico Trade," *New York Times*, March 31, 1991, p. 1; Patrick McDonnell, "Foreign-Owned Companies Add to Mexico's Pollution," *Los Angeles Times*, November 18, 1991, p. A1; Richard W. Stevenson, "Economic Scene: The Hidden Costs of Mexico Plants," *New York Times*, July 19, 1991, p. D2; Judy Pasternak, "Firms Find a Haven from U.S. Environmental Rules," *Los Angeles Times*, November 19, 1991, p. A1; Patrick McDonnell, "Mexico: Progress and Promise," *Los Angeles Times*, October 22, 1991, p. 11.
82. Chávez, *Shadowed Lives*, pp. 19, 139–155.
83. Teresa Puente, "When Hope Turns into Slavery," *Chicago Tribune*, August 10, 1997, p. 1C; Pierrette Hondagneu-Sotelo, *Domestica: Immigrant Workers Cleaning and Caring in the Shadows of Affluence* (Berkeley: University of California Press, 2001), p. 210.
84. "A Time for Courage," *Newsday*, April 6, 2001, p. A48.
85. H. Cross, G. Keeney, J. Mell, and W. Zimmerman, *Employer Hiring Practices: Differential Treatment of Hispanic and Anglo Job Seekers* (Washington, D.C.: Urban Institute, 1990).
86. Philip Moss and Chris Tilly, *Stories Employers Tell: Race, Skill, and Hiring in America* (New York: Russell Sage, 2001), pp. 130–150.
87. Lopez and Stanton-Salazar, "The Mexican American Second Generation," in *Ethnicities*, n.p.
88. Lawrence D. Bobo and Susah A. Suh, "Surveying Racial Discrimination: Analyses from a Multiethnic Labor Market," in *Prismatic Metropolis: Inequality in Los Angeles*, ed. Lawrence D. Bobo, Melvin L. Oliver, James H. Johnson, Jr., and Abel Valenzuela, Jr. (New York: Russell Sage, 2000) p. 528.
89. Edward Iwata, "Race Issues Shake Tech World: What looks like meritocracy can brim with bias, experts say as more lawsuits are filed," *USA Today*, July 24, 2000, p. 1B.
90. Jim Doyle, "Court Curbs 'English-Only' Company Rules," *San Francisco Chronicle*, October 5, 1991, p. A12; Juan Perea, "English-Only Rules and the Right to Speak One's Primary Language in the Workplace," *University of Michigan Journal of Law Reform* 23, no. 2 (winter 1990): 265–318.
91. *Garcia v. Gloor* 618 F.2d 264 (5th Cir. 1980), *cert. denied*, 449 U.S. 1113 (1981).
92. *Gutierrez v. Municipal Court*, 838 F.2d at 1039, quotations from Perea, "English-Only Rules," pp. 271–272; *Gutierrez v. Municipal Court, vacated as moot*, 109 S. Ct. 1736 (1989).
93. *Garcia v. Spun Steak Co.*, DC NCalif, No. C91-1949 RHS, October 14, 1991; Doyle, "Court Curbs 'English-Only' Company Rules."
94. Associated Press, "School Settles Bias Suit; Texas University to Pay $2 Million," April 21, 2001.
95. Gilda Laura Ochoa, " Mexican Americans' Attitudes toward and Interactions with Mexican Immigrants: A Qualitative Analysis of Conflict and Cooperation," *Social Science Quarterly* 81 (March 2000): 84–105.
96. Bureau of Labor Statistics, "Annual Average Tables from the January 2001 Issue of Employment and Earnings, Table 6: Employment status of the Mexican, Puerto Rican, and Cuban-origin population by sex and age," published June 14, 2001; Bureau of Labor Statistics, "Annual Average Tables from the

January 2001 Issue of Employment and Earnings, Table 12: Employed white, black, and Hispanic-origin workers, by sex, occupation, class of worker, and full- or part-time status," published June 14, 2001; U.S. Census Bureau, "Hispanic Population of the United States, Table 10.2: Occupation of the Employed Civilian Population 16 Years and Over by Sex, Hispanic Origin, and Race: March 2000," published March 6, 2001, <http://www.census.gov/population/www/socdemo/hispanic.html>; U.S. Census Bureau, "Hispanic Population, Table 10.3: Occupation of the Employed Civilian Population 16 Years and Over by Sex, Hispanic Origin, and Race: March 2000," published March 6, 2001, <http://www.census.gov/population/www/socdemo/hispanic.html>.

97. Edward E. Telles and Edward Múrguía, "Phenotypic Discrimination and Income Differences among Mexican Americans," *Social Science Quarterly* 71, no. 4 (December 1990): 682–696.
98. U.S. Census Bureau, "Hispanic Population, Table 1: Selected Summary Measures of Age and Income by Hispanic Origin and Race: March 2000," published March 6, 2001, <http://www.census.gov/population/www/socdemo/hispanic.html>; U.S. Census Bureau, "Hispanic Population, Table 13.1: Total Money Income in 1999 of Families by Type, and by Hispanic Origin and Race of Householder; published March 6, 2001, <http://www.census.gov/population/www/socdemo/hispanic.html>; U.S. Census Bureau, "Hispanic Population, Table 14.1: Poverty Status of the Population in 1999 by Sex, Age, Hispanic Origin, and Race," published March 6, 2001, <http://www.census.gov/population/www/socdemo/hispanic.html>; U.S. Census Bureau, "Hispanic Population, Table 15.1: Poverty Status of Families in 1999 by Family Type, and by Hispanic Origin and Race of Householder," published March 6, 2001, <http://www.census.gov/population/www/socdemo/hispanic.html>.
99. U.S. Census Bureau, "Hispanic Population, Table 11.2: Earnings of Full-Time, Year-Round Workers 15 Years and Over in 1999 by Sex, Hispanic Origin, and Race (Male)," published March 6, 2001, <http://www.census.gov/population/www/socdemo/hispanic.html>; U.S. Census Bureau, "Hispanic Population, Table 11.3: Earnings of Full-Time, Year-Round Workers 15 Years and Over in 1999 by Sex, Hispanic Origin, and Race (Female)," published March 6, 2001, <http://www.census.gov/population/www/socdemo/hispanic.html>.
100. Lopez and Stanton-Salazar, "The Mexican American Second Generation." We draw on this article in this section.
101. Joan Moore and Raquel Pinderhughes, *In the Barrios: Latinos and the Underclass Debate* (New York: Russell Sage, 1993).
102. Avelardo Valdez, "Persistent Poverty, Crime, and Drugs: U.S.–Mexican Border Region," in *In the Barrios: Latinos and the Underclass Debate*, ed. Joan Moore and Raquel Pinderhughes (New York: Sage, 1993), pp. 184–194.
103. Nestor Rodríguez, "Economic Restructuring and Latino Growth in Houston," in *In the Barrios: Latinos and the Underclass Debate*, ed. Moore and Pinderhughes, pp. 101–126.
104. Joan Moore and James Diego Vigil, "Barrios in Transition," in *In the Barrios: Latinos and the Underclass Debate*, ed. Moore and Pinderhughes, pp. 27–47.
105. National Fair Housing Advocate, "Farmworkers Represented by CRLA and the County of Riverside Settle Major Fair Housing Case," <http://www.fairhousing.com/news_archive/releases/crla5-23-00.html> (retrieved March 1, 2001).
106. Dan Rozek, "Elgin Denies Housing Bias against Hispanics," *Chicago Sun-Times*, October 3, 2000, p. 32.
107. Fair Housing Council of Fresno County, "Audit Uncovers Blatant Discrimination against Hispanics, African Americans and Families with Children in Fresno County," press release, Fresno, California, October 6, 1997; San Antonio Fair Housing Council, "San Antonio Metropolitan Area Rental Audit 1997," San Antonio, Texas, 1997.
108. Daryl Strickland, "O. C. Business Plus; Yoder-Shrader Settles Housing Bias Suit," *Los Angeles Times*, August 1, 2000, p. C3.
109. Moore, *Mexican Americans*, p. 33.
110. *Garza v. County of Los Angeles*, 918 F.2d 763; 1990 U.S. App.; *Williams v. City of Dallas*, 734 F. Supp. 1317; 1990 U.S. Dist.
111. Gonzalez, *Harvest of Empire*, p. 168.
112. The data on Mexican American officials in this and the following paragraph come from Juan Gómez-Quiñones, *Chicano Politics: Reality and Promise, 1940–1990* (Albuquerque: University of New Mexico Press, 1990), pp. 167–169, 173; *National Association of Latino Elected and Appointed Officials, National Report* 11, no. 1 (Fourth Quarter 1991): 1, 3; and personal communications with Rodolfo de la Garza and Robert Brischetto.
113. Hector Tobar and Richard Simon, "Molina's First Goal Expand County Board," *Los Angeles Times*, February 21, 1991, p. A1; Carla Rivera, "Heated Meeting Marks Burke's Debut as Leader," *Los Angeles Times*, December 8, 1993, p. B3.
114. The National Association of Latino Elected and Appointed Officials Educational Fund, press release, May 9, 2001.
115. Juan Gonzalez, *Harvest of Empire*, p. 169.
116. Gregory Rodriguez, "Mayoral Election; A Novel

Latino Strategy," *Los Angeles Times*, June 3, 2001, p. M1.

117. National Association of Latino Elected and Appointed Officials Educational Fund, press release, November 9, 2000.
118. Rodolfo O. de la Garza, Nestor Rodríguez, and Harry Pachon, "The Domestic and Foreign Policy Consequences of Mexican and Central American Immigration: Mexican-American Perspectives," in *Immigration and International Relations*, ed. Georges Vernes (Santa Monica, CA: Rand Corporation, 1990), pp. 135–147.
119. Ray Suarez, "Latinos Politics," National Public Radio, Talk of the Nation, August 5, 1997.
120. Southwest Voter Registration Project, *The Hispanic Electorates* (San Antonio, TX Hispanic Policy Development Project, 1984), pp. 145–149; Robert R. Brischetto, "Chicano Voting and Views in the 1986 Elections" (typescript, Southwest Voter Research Institute, San Antonio, 1987); U.S. Commission on Civil Rights, *Ethnic Isolation of Mexican Americans in the Public Schools of the Southwest*, p. 55; Gómez-Quiñones, *Chicano Politics*, p. 163; Marjorie Connelly, "The 1994 Elections," *New York Times*, November 13, 1994, p. 24; Bob Wing, "White Power in Election," *ColorLines*, spring 2001, <http://www.arc.org/C_Lines/CLArchive retrieved> (June 19, 2001).
121. *Hernandez v. Texas*, 347 U.S. 482 (1954). Cited in Ricardo Romo, "Mexican Americans in the New West," in *The Twentieth-Century West*, ed. Gerald D. Nash and Richard W. Etulian (Albuquerque: University of New Mexico Press, 1989), p. 135.
122. U.S. Commission on Civil Rights, *Mexican Americans and the Administration of Justice in the Southwest*, pp. 79–86.
123. Ibid., pp. 66–69.
124. *Hernandez v. New York*, 1991, 111 S. Ct. 1859; Juan Perea, "*Hernandez v. New York*: Courts, Prosecutors, and the Fear of Spanish," *Hofstra Law Review*, 21 (fall 1992): 1–61.
125. See Romo, "Mexican Americans in the New West," pp. 136–139.
126. Michael V. Miller and James D. Preston, "Vertical Ties and the Redistribution of Power in Crystal City," *Social Science Quarterly* 53 (March 1973): 772–782; John S. Shockley, *Chicano Revolt in a Texas Town* (Notre Dame, IN: University of Notre Dame Press, 1974), pp. 28–148, 162–177.
127. Maril, *Poorest of Americans*, p. 52.
128. Armando Gutiérrez and Herbert Hirsch, "The Militant Challenge to the American Ethos: 'Chicanos' and the 'Mexican Americans,'" *Social Science Quarterly* 53 (March 1973): 844–845; Carlos Muñoz, Jr., *Youth, Identity, Power: The Chicano Movement* (New York: Verso, 1989); Ignacio M. Garcia, *United We Win* (Tuscon: University of Arizona Press, 1989), pp. 228–231.
129. Marta Cotera, "Feminism, the Chicana and Anglo Versions," in *Twice a Minority*, ed. Margarita B. Melville (St. Louis: C. V. Mosby, 1980), p. 231.
130. Amott and Matthaei, *Race, Gender, and Work*, pp. 83–84; Cotera, *Feminism*, pp. 213–233.
131. McWilliams, *North from Mexico*, pp. 191–193; Grebler, Moore, and Guzlán, *The Mexican-American People*, pp. 91–92; Stoddard, *Mexican Americans*, p. 180; Gamio, *Mexican Immigration to the United States*, pp. 135–138.
132. Grebler, Moore, and Guzmán, *The Mexican-American People*, pp. 543–545; Stoddard, *Mexican Americans*, p. 188; Moore, *Mexican Americans*, p. 152.
133. U.S. Commission on Civil Rights, *Mexican Americans and the Administration of Justice in the Southwest*, pp. 15–17; Rees Lloyd and Peter Montague, "Ford and La Raza: 'They Stole Our Land and Gave Us Powdered Milk,'" in *Introduction to Chicano Studies*, ed. Duran and Bernard, pp. 376–378; Frances L. Swadesh, "The Alianza Movement: Catalyst for Social Change in New Mexico," in *Chicano*, ed. Rosaldo, Calvert, and Seligmann, pp. 270–274.
134. Robert Pear, "U.S. Sues Houston to Block Election," *New York Times*, October 22, 1991, p. A16; William Grady and Thomas Hardy, "Court Orders New Remap," *Chicago Tribune*, December 14, 1991, p. 1; Kenneth Weiss, "Latinos to Challenge Court Plan," *Los Angeles Times*, December 17, 1991, p. B1.
135. Mark Bixler, "Latino advocacy groups plan offices here for anti-bias efforts," *Atlanta Journal and Constitution*, May 30, 2001, p. 3B.
136. Mary Pardo, "Mexican American Women Grassroots Community Activists: 'Mothers of East Los Angeles,'" *Frontiers* XI, no. 1 (1990): 4.
137. Jacques E. Levy, *César Chávez* (New York: W. W. Norton, 1975), pp. 182–201; Peter Matthiessen, *Sal Si Puedes* (New York: Delta Books, 1969), pp. 59–216; John G. Dunne, *Delano* (New York: Farrar, Straus & Giroux, 1967), pp. 110–167.
138. Levy, *César Chávez*, pp. 495, 522–535.
139. J. Craig Jenkins, *The Politics of Insurgency* (New York: Columbia University Press, 1985), pp. x–xi; Robert Reinhold, "Environmental Agency Moves to End Most Uses of Deadly Agricultural Pesticide," *New York Times*, September 6, 1991, p. A17.
140. Ann Bancroft, "10,000 at Rally for Farm Workers," *San Francisco Chronicle*, April 25, 1994, p. A1.
141. Mark Arax, "UFW Pledges New Activism as March Ends," *Los Angeles Times*, April 25, 1994, p. A3.
142. Letisia Marquez, "Farm workers union has work cut out for it," *Ventura County Star*, March 29, 2001, <http://web.insidevc.com/news/372065.shtml> (retrieved July 2, 2001).

143. Hector L. Delgado, *New Immigrants, Old Unions: Undocumented Workers in Los Angeles* (Philadelphia, PA: Temple University Press, 1993).
144. Margaret M. Zamudio, "Organizing Labor among Difference: the Impact of Race/Ethnicity, Citizenship, and Gender on Working-Class Solidarity," in *Places and Politics in the Age of Global Capitalism*, ed. Arif Dirlik (Lanham, MD: Rowman and Littlefield, 2001), p. 116.
145. Antonio Olivo, "Hotel Workers, Riot Police Clash During Protest," *Los Angeles Times*, August 4, 2000, p. B1.
146. Frank D. Bean and Stephanie Bell-Rose, "Immigration and Its Relation to Race and Ethnicity in the United States," in *Immigration and Opportunity: Race, Ethnicity, and Employment in the United States*, ed. Frank D. Bean and Stephanie Bell-Rose (New York: Russell Sage, 1999), pp. 13–14.
147. Martin Kasindorf and Maria Puente, "Hispanics, blacks find futures entangled," *USA Today*, September 10, 1999, p. 4.
148. Ibid.
149. Chandler Davidson and Charles M. Gaitz, "Ethnic Attitudes as a Basis for Minority Cooperation in a Southwestern Metropolis," *Social Science Quarterly* 53 (March 1973): 747–748.
150. Néstor Rodríguez, "U.S. Immigration and Intergroup Relations in the Late 20th Century: African Americans and Latinos," *Social Justice* 23 (1996): 111–124; Ricardo Romo, Néstor Rodríguez, Luis Plascencia, and Ximena Urrutia-Rojas, "Houston Evaluation of Community Priorities," unpublished report, University of Houston, Tomas Rivera Center, 1994.
151. Thomas P. Carter, *Mexican Americans in School* (New York: College Entrance Examination Board, 1970), pp. 204–205.
152. George I. Sánchez, "History, Culture, and Education," in *La Raza*, ed. Julian Samora (Notre Dame, IN: University of Notre Dame Press, 1966), pp. 1–26; Paul Taylor, *An American-Mexican Frontier* (Chapel Hill: University of North Carolina Press, 1934), pp. 196–204; Guadalupe San Miguel, Jr., *Let All of Them Take Heed: Mexican Americans and the Campaign for Educational Equality in Texas, 1910–1981* (Austin: University of Texas Press, 1987), pp. 1–58.
153. Charles Wollenberg, *All Deliberate Speed: Segregation and Exclusion in California Schools, 1855–1975* (Berkeley: University of California Press, 1976), pp. 125–135.
154. Carter, *Mexican Americans in School*, pp. 97–102; Thomas P. Carter, "The Negative Self-concept of Mexican-American Students," *School and Society* 96 (March 30, 1968): 217–220.
155. George I. Sánchez, "Bilingualism and Mental Measures, a Word of Caution," *Journal of Applied Psychology*, December 1934, pp. 767–769. See also Wollenberg, *All Deliberate Speed*, pp. 118–119.
156. Jane Mercer, *Labelling the Mentally Retarded* (Berkeley, CA: University of California Press, 1973), pp. 96–189; U.S. Commission on Civil Rights, *Mexican American Education Study*, vol. 6, *Toward Quality Education for Mexican Americans* (Washington, D.C., 1974), pp. 21–22.
157. Harvard Graduate School of Education, "Press Release: School Segregation on the Rise Despite Growing Diversity Among School-Aged Children," July 17, 2001, <http://www.gse.harvard.edu/nv/features/orfield07172001.html>.
158. Quoted in Gail Russell Chaddock, "U.S. Schools Slip Back Toward Segregation," *Christian Science Monitor*, July 18, 2001, <http://www.csmonitor.com>.
159. San Miguel, Jr., *Let All of Them Take Heed*, p. 217.
160. Juan F. Perea, "Demography and Distrust: An Essay on American Languages, Cultural Pluralism, and Official English," *Minnesota Law Review* 77 (1992): 269.
161. See Kenji Hakuta and Eugene E. Garcia, "Bilingualism and Education," *American Psychologist* 44 (February 1989): 374–379; Dick Kirschten, "Speaking English," *National Review*, June 17, 1989, pp. 1,556–1,561; Manuel Ramirez and Alfredo Castaneda, *Cultural Democracy, Bicognitive Development, and Education* (New York: Academic Press, 1974); San Miguel, Jr., *Let All of Them Take Heed* (Austin: University of Texas Press, 1987).
162. Susan Baker and Kenji Hakuta, "Bilingual Education and Latino Civil Rights," <http://www.law.harvard.edu/groups/civilrights/papers/bilingual/bilingual.html> (retrieved July 2, 2001).
163. Ibid.
164. U.S. Bureau of the Census, *1950 Census of Population*, P-E no. 3C, Table 3.
165. U.S. Census Bureau, "Hispanic Population, Table 7.1: Educational Attainment of the Population 25 Years and Over by Sex, Hispanic Origin, and Race: March 2000," published March 6, 2001, <http://www.census.gov/population/www/socdemo/hispanic.html>.
166. U.S. Census Bureau, "The Foreign-Born Population, Table 4.1: Latin American Foreign-Born Population by Sex, Age, and Region of Birth: March 2000," published January 03, 2001, <http://www.census.gov/population/www/socdemo/foreign.html>.
167. Quoted in Beth Barrett, "College Disparity Costly: Mexican-Americans' Wage Gap Up, Study Says," *Daily News of Los Angeles*, May 27, 1997, p. N1.
168. U.S. Census Bureau, Current Population Survey, October 1999, p. 4; Barbara Kantrowitz with Lourdes Rosado, "Falling Further Behind," *Newsweek*, August

19, 1991, p. 60; Maril, *Poorest of Americans*, pp. 117–118.

169. The research discussed in this and the following paragraph is reported in Harriett Romo and Toni Falbo, *Defying the Odds: Keeping Latino Youth in School* (Austin: University of Texas Press, 1995).
170. Ibid.
171. Lopez and Stanton-Salazar, "The Mexican American Second Generation," in *Ethnicities*.
172. Concha Delgado-Gaitan and Henry Trueba, *Crossing Cultural Borders: Education for Immigrant Families in America* (Philadelphia, PA: The Falmer Press, 1991).
173. Catherine Walsh, *Pedagogy and the Struggle for Voice* (New York: Bergin and Garvey, 1991), pp. 95–113, quotation on p. 112.
174. Moore, *Mexican Americans*, pp. 67–69; Carter, *Mexican Americans in School*, pp. 30–31; National Commission for Employment Policy, *Hispanics and Jobs: Barriers to Progress* (Washington, D.C., 1982), p. 11.
175. Edward H. Spicer, *Cycle of Conquest* (Tucson: University of Arizona Press, 1962), pp. 285–365; Patrick H. McNamara, "Bishops, Priests, and Prophecy: A Study in the Sociology of Religious Protest." (Ph.D. dissertation, UCLA, 1968.)
176. Moore, *Mexican Americans*, pp. 88–89.
177. Ibid., p. 91; Stoddard, *Mexican Americans*, p. 93; Grebler, Moore, and Guzmán, *The Mexican-American People*, pp. 459–460; Gómez-Quiñones, *Chicano Politics*, p. 179; "Latinos Shift Loyalties," *Christian Century*, April 6, 1994, p. 344.
178. Grebler, Moore, and Guzmán, *The Mexican-American People*, pp. 436–439, 473–477. See also Jane M. Christian and Chester C. Christian, "Spanish Language and Loyalty in the Southwest," in *Language Loyalty in the United States*, ed. Joshua A. Fishman (London: Mouton, 1966), pp. 296–297.
179. Report by Allan F. Beck, as described in "Latinos Shift Loyalties," *Christian Century*, April 6, 1994, p. 344.
180. Jill Leovy, "More Hispanics Hear Call of Witnesses," *Seattle Times*, March 25, 1991, p. E1.
181. "The Mixture as Never Before," *The Economist*, March 11, 2000.
182. Edward Múrguía, *Assimilation, Colonialism, and the Mexican American People* (Austin: University of Texas Press, 1975), pp. 4–5.
183. Rodolfo Alvarez, "The Unique Psycho-historical Experience of the Mexican-American People," *Social Science Quarterly* 52 (June 1971): 15–29; Stoddard, *Mexican Americans*, p. 103; Benjamin S. Bradshaw and Frank Bean, "Trends in the Fertility of Mexican Americans, 1950–1970," *Social Science Quarterly* 53 (March 1973): 696–697.
184. Strategy Research Corporation, *1991 U.S. Hispanic Market*, pp. 107–108.
185. U.S. Bureau of the Census, *1990 Census of Population: Social and Economic Characteristics: Urbanized Areas*, CP-2-1C (Washington, D.C., 1993), p. 2,844.
186. Charles Oliver, "Is American Culture Changing?" *Investor's Business Daily*, October 4, 1994, p. A1; Gonzalez, *Harvest of Empire*, pp. 224–225.
187. Edward E. Telles and Edward Múrguía, "Phenotypic Discrimination and Income Differences among Mexican Americans" (Typescript, University of Texas, 1987); Edward Múrguía and Edward E. Telles, "Phenotype and Schooling Among Mexican Americans," *Sociology of Education* 69 (October 1996): 276–289.
188. Lopez and Stanton-Salazar, "The Mexican American Second Generation," in *Ethnicities*.
189. Strategy Research Corporation, *1991 U.S. Hispanic Market*, pp. 111–115.
190. Edward Múrguía, *Chicano Intermarriage: A Theoretical and Empirical Study* (San Antonio, TX: Trinity University Press, 1982), pp. 45–51; Amitai Etzioni, "The Monochrome Society," *Heritage Foundation Policy Review*, February 2001, p. 53.
191. Linda Chávez, *Out of the Barrio: Toward a New Politics of Hispanic Assimilation* (New York: Basic Books, 1991).
192. Nathan Glazer, "The Political Distinctiveness of the Mexican Americans," in *Mexican-Americans in Comparative Perspective*, ed. Walter Connor (Washington, D.C.: Urban Institute, 1985), pp. 212–216.
193. Walter Connor, "Who Are the Mexican Americans? A Note on Comparability," in *Mexican-Americans in Comparative Perspective*, ed. Connor, pp. 4–28.
194. Lopez and Stanton-Salazar, "The Mexican American Second Generation," in *Ethnicities*.
195. "The Mixture as Never Before," *The Economist*.
196. Peter Skerry, "Not Much Cooking," *Brookings Review*, June 22, 1993, p. 42.
197. Montejano, *Anglos and Mexicans in the Making of Texas, 1836–1986*.
198. Múrguía, *Assimilation, Colonialism, and the Mexican American People*, p. 112.
199. Strategy Research Corporation, *1991 U.S. Hispanic Market*, pp. 109–120.
200. Ibid., pp. 78–120; Jim Loretta, "Latin Population Pressure Mounts," *Inside Strategy* 3, no. 2 (September 1990): 2.
201. Strategy Research Corporation, *1991 U.S. Hispanic Market*, pp. 80–94.
202. Mireya Navarro, "Complaint to Spanish TV: Not Enough Americans; Few U.S. Plots for Growing U.S. Audience," *New York Times*, August 21, 2000, p. B1.
203. See Achy Obejas, "A Changing Nation: Shades of Future Seen in Census Report on Hispanics," *Chicago Tribune*, March 31, 1996, p. 1.
204. Acuña, *Occupied America*, p. 3.

205. Alvarez, "Psycho-historical and Socioeconomic Development," pp. 928–930.
206. Múrguía, *Assimilation, Colonialism, and the Mexican American People*, pp. 8–9.
207. John U. Ogbu, *Minority Education and Caste* (New York: Academic Press, 1987), pp. 236–237; see also John Obgu, "Variability in Minority Responses to Schooling: Nonimmigrants vs. Immigrants," in *Interpretive Ethnography of Education*, ed. George Spindler and Louise Spinder (Hillsdale, NJ: Lawrence Erlbaum, 1987), pp. 255–275.
208. Barrera, *Race and Class in the Southwest*, p. 213.
209. Geoffrey Fox, *Hispanic Nation: Culture, Politics, and the Constructing of Identity* (Tucson, AZ: University of Arizona Press, 1996), pp. 240–241.
210. Rodolfo Acuña, *Anything But Mexican: Chicanos in Contemporary Los Angeles* (London: Verso, 1996), p. 8.
211. Nestor Rodriguez, personal communication with authors, March 1996.
212. Nancy Abelmann and John Lie, *Blue Dreams: Korean Americans and the Los Angeles Riots* (Cambridge: Harvard, 1995); and Yolanda Flores-Niemann, Tatcho Mindiola, and Nestor Rodriguez, "U.S.-Born and Foreign-Born Latinas' Perceptions of Black/Brown Relations: Implications for Future Inter-Group Relations," unpublished research paper, University of Houston, 1997, pp. 12–13.
213. Fox, *Hispanic Nation*, p. 241.
214. Felix M. Padilla, *Latino Ethnic Consciousness: The Case of Mexican Americans and Puerto Ricans in Chicago* (Notre Dame, IN: University of Notre Dame Press, 1985), pp. 138–139.
215. Ibid, p. 7.
216. Múrguía, "On Latino/Hispanic Ethnic Identity."

CHAPTER 9

1. Daniel Adams, "Puerto Ricans Vote on Independence from U.S.," *The Independent*, December 9, 1991, p. 14.
2. U.S. Census Bureau, *The Hispanic Population*, Census 2000 Brief, May 2001, pp. 1–2.
3. U.S. Census Bureau, Census 2000 Data on American FactFinder, "Population and Housing: Puerto Rico," acccessed July 23, 2001, <http://factfinder.census.gov.html>.
4. Enrique Fernandez, "Puerto Rican Independence: Is It a Dream?" *Newsday*, February 27, 1992, p. 94.
5. Manuel Maldonado-Denis, *Puerto Rico, A Socio-historic Interpretation*, trans. Elena Vialo (New York: Random House/Vintage Books, 1972), pp. 13–19; Luis Antonio Cardona, *A History of the Puerto Ricans in the U.S.A.* (Rockville, MD: Carreta Press, 1990), pp. 8–9; Eric Williams, *From Columbus to Castro: The History of the Caribbean 1492–1969* (London: André Deutsch: 1970), pp. 109, 291.
6. U.S. Commission on Civil Rights, *Puerto Ricans in the Continental United States: An Uncertain Future* (Washington, D.C., 1976), pp. 11–12; Jorge Heine, "A People Apart," *Wilson Quarterly* 4, no. 2 (spring 1980): 119–123.
7. Maldonado-Denis, *Puerto Rico*, p. 77.
8. U.S. Commission on Civil Rights, *Puerto Ricans in the Continental United States*, p. 12.
9. Maldonado-Denis, *Puerto Rico*, pp. 305–306; Heine, "A People Apart," p. 123.
10. U.S. Bureau of the Census, *Statistical Abstract of the United States 1994*, Table 1,342 (Washington, D.C., 1994), p. 835.
11. Kristin S. Krause, "Post-incentive Puerto Rico; Island's Future as Manufacturing Center in Doubt as Congress Phases Out Income Tax Break," *Traffic World*, October 27, 1997, p. 20.
12. Adalberto Lopez, "The Puerto Rican Diaspora: A Survey," in *Puerto Rico and Puerto Ricans: Studies in History and Society*, ed. Adalberto Lopez and James Petras (New York: Wiley, 1974), p. 318; Clara E. Rodríguez, *Puerto Ricans: Born in the U.S.A.* (Boston: Unwin Hyman, 1989), pp. 1–10.
13. Jack Agueros, "Halfway to Dick and Jane," in *The Immigrant Experience: The Anguish of Becoming American*, ed. Thomas C. Wheeler (New York: Dial Press, 1971), p. 93.
14. Cardona, *A History of the Puerto Ricans in the U.S.A.*, pp. 95–96.
15. U.S. Commission on Civil Rights, *Puerto Ricans in the Continental United States*, p. 25; Rodríguez, *Puerto Ricans*, pp. 4–13; Cardona, *A History of the Puerto Ricans in the U.S.A.*, pp. 95–112; Felix M. Padilla, *Puerto Rican Chicago* (Notre Dame, IN: University of Notre Dame Press, 1987), pp. 66–72.
16. U.S. Commission on Civil Rights, *Puerto Ricans in the Continental United States*, pp. 19–25; Pedro A. Rivera, "Angel and Aurea," *Wilson Quarterly* 4, no. 2 (spring 1980): 146–152; "The Spending Power of Puerto Ricans," *American Demographics*, April 1991, pp. 46–49; Rodríguez, *Puerto Ricans*, pp. 4–8, 28; correspondence with U.S. representative Jose Serrano's staff.
17. U.S. Census Bureau, *The Hispanic Populatoin*, Census 2000 Brief, May 2001, pp. 2, 4.
18. Candice Choi, "Fewer Puerto Ricans in NYC, But More Mexicans, Asian Indians," DiversityInc.com, <http://www.diversityinc.com> (retrieved July 8, 2001).
19. Bart Jones, "Census 2000: Island's Little El Salvador," *Newsday*, May 23, 2001, p. A2.
20. Ibid.

21. Quoted in Frank Bonilla, "Beyond Survival: Porque Sequiremos Siendo Puertoriquenos," in *Puerto Rico and Puerto Ricans*, ed. Lopez and Petras, p. 439.
22. Alfredo Lopez, *The Puerto Rican Papers* (Indianapolis, IN: Bobbs-Merrill, 1973), p. 120.
23. Quoted in ibid., p. 211.
24. Rose Marie Arce, "Crime, Drugs, and Stereotypes," *Newsday*, December 2, 1991, p. 5.
25. Kristal Brent Zook, "Esai Morales, Good Cop; 'NYPD Blue' Casts New Recruit Against Type," *Washington Post*, May 21, 2001, p. C1.
26. Quoted in Juan Gonzalez, *Harvest of Empire: A History of Latinos in America* (New York: Penguin Books, 2000), p. 253.
27. Nathan Glazer and Daniel P. Moynihan, *Beyond the Melting Pot* (Cambridge: M.I.T. Press and Harvard University Press, 1963), pp. 88–90.
28. Oscar Lewis, *La Vida* (New York: Random House, 1965).
29. Mirta Ojito, "A Movement Is Born; New Britain Puerto Ricans React to Report Revealing Bias," *New York Times*, June 28, 1997, p. 23.
30. Associated Press, "Congressman criticized for Vieques 'Welfare' Slam," June 20, 2001, <http://salon.com/politics/wire/2001/06/20/welfare/index.html>; Dexter Filkins, "Racial Slurs and Intrigue on City Island," *New York Times*, February 16, 2001, p. B3.
31. Rodríguez, *Puerto Ricans*, pp. 51–56.
32. Ramón Grosfoguel and Chloe S. Georas, "'Coloniality of Power" and Racial Dynamics: Notes Toward a Reinterpretation of Latino Caribbeans in New York City," *Identities: Global Studies in Culture and Power* 7 (2000): 85–125.
33. Piri Thomas, *Down These Mean Streets* (New York: Knopf, 1967), pp. 85–86.
34. Rodríguez, *Puerto Ricans*, pp. 56–59, 79.
35. Angel R. Martínez, "The Effects of Acculturation and Racial Identity on Self-Esteem and Psychological Well-Being among Young Puerto Ricans" (Ph.D. dissertation, City University of New York, 1988); cited in ibid., pp. 60–61.
36. Rodríguez, *Puerto Ricans*, pp. 61–68.
37. Jesús Colon, "The Early Days," in *The Puerto Ricans: A Documentary History*, ed. Kal Wagenheim (Garden City, NY: Doubleday/Anchor Books, 1973), p. 286.
38. Thomas, *Down These Mean Streets*, pp. 102–104.
39. Rodríguez, *Puerto Ricans*, p. 2; U.S. Commission on Civil Rights, *Puerto Ricans in the Continental United States*, p. 54; Frank Bonilla and Ricardo Campos, "A Wealth of Poor: Puerto Ricans in the New Economic Order," *Daedalus* 110 (spring 1981): 158.
40. U.S. Census Bureau, "Hispanic Population of the United States, Table 10.2: Occupation of the Employed Civilian Population 16 Years and Over by Sex, Hispanic Origin, and Race: March 2000," published March 6, 2001, <http://www.census.gov/population/www/socdemo/hispanic.html>; U.S. Census Bureau, "Hispanic Population, Table 10.3: Occupation of the Employed Civilian Population 16 Years and Over by Sex, Hispanic Origin, and Race: March 2000," published March 6, 2001, <http://www.census.gov/population/www/socdemo/hispanic.html>.
41. Juan Gonzalez, "Puerto Ricans on the Mainland," *Perspectives* 13 (winter 1982): 16; U.S. Commission on Civil Rights, *Puerto Ricans in the Continental United States*, p. 52; Bonilla and Campos, "A Wealth of Poor," p. 160.
42. Bureau of Labor Statistics, "Annual Average Tables from the January 2001 Issue of Employment and Earnings, Table 6: Employment status of the Mexican, Puerto Rican, and Cuban-origin population by sex and age," published June 14, 2001, <http://www.bls.gov/cpsaatab.html>; Bureau of Labor Statistics, "Annual Average Tables from the January 2001 Issue of Employment and Earnings, Table 12: Employed white, black, and Hispanic-origin workers, by sex, occupation, class of worker, and full- or part-time status," published June 14, 2001, <http://www.bls.gov/cpsaatab.html>.
43. Gonzalez, *Harvest of Empire*, p. 95.
44. U.S. Commission on Civil Rights, *Puerto Ricans in the Continental United States*, pp. 59–62.
45. Western Regional Office, U.S. Commission on Civil Rights, *Puerto Ricans in California* (Washington, D.C., 1980), p. 17.
46. Rodríguez, *Puerto Ricans*, pp. 92–93, quotation on p. 93. See also Herbert Hill, "Guardians of the Sweatshops: The Trade Unions, Racism, and the Garment Industry," in *Puerto Rico and Puerto Ricans*, ed. Lopez and Petras, pp. 386–388.
47. U.S. Commission on Civil Rights, *Puerto Ricans in the Continental United States*, p. 60; Vilma Ortiz, "Latinos and Industrial Change in New York and Los Angeles" (paper, 1990); Clara E. Rodríguez, "Economic Factors Affecting Puerto Ricans in New York," in *Labor Migration under Capitalism: The Puerto Rican Experience*, ed. History Task Force (New York: Center for Puerto Rican Studies, 1979), pp. 208–210; Rodríguez, *Puerto Ricans*, pp. 85–91.
48. Marta Tienda and William A. Diaz, "Puerto Ricans' Special Problems," *New York Times*, August 28, 1987, p. A30; Marta Tienda and William Diaz, letter to *New York Times*, October 10, 1987, p. A30.
49. Mercer L. Sullivan, "Puerto Ricans in Sunset Park, Brooklyn: Poverty Amidst Ethnic and Economic Diversity," in *In the Barrios*, ed. Joan Moore and Raquel Pinderhughes (New York: Russell Sage, 1993), pp. 1–25.

50. U.S. Census Bureau, "Hispanic Population in the United States, Table 1. Selected Summary Measures of Age and Income by Hispanic Origin and Race: March 2000," published March 6, 2001, <http://www.census.gov/population/www/socdemo/hispanic.html>.
51. U.S. Census Bureau, "Hispanic Population in the United States, Table 11.1: Earnings of Full-Time, Year-Round Workers 15 Years and Over in 1999 by Sex, Hispanic Origin, and Race," published March 6, 2001, <http://www.census.gov/population/www/socdemo/hispanic.html>.
52. U.S. Census Bureau, "Hispanic Population in the United States, Table 14.1: Poverty Status of the Population in 1999 by Sex, Age, Hispanic Origin, and Race: March 2000," published March 6, 2001, <http://www.census.gov/population/www/socdemo/hispanic.html>.
53. Agueros, "Halfway to Dick and Jane," pp. 96–102; Rivera, "Angel and Aurea," p. 148.
54. See Padilla, *Puerto Rican Chicago*, pp. 117–123.
55. U.S. Bureau of the Census, *The Hispanic Population in the United States: March 1993*, Current Population Reports P20–475 (Washington, D.C., 1994), pp. 16–17.
56. Rodríguez, *Puerto Ricans*, pp. 106–116.
57. Jordan Green, "City Life; Gentrification Puts Whites on the Hook, "*Newsday*, June 21, 2001, p. A45.
58. Joseph Mallia, "Matter of Rights in Freeport," *Newsday*, February 11, 2001, p. G17; Joseph Mallia, "Complaints against Inspectors," *Newsday*, January 25, 2001, p. A8.
59. Randal Archibold, "Mount Kisco Agrees to Extend Ban on Bias against Hispanics," *New York Times*, February 8, 2001, p. B7.
60. Lance Freeman, "A Note on the Influence of African Heritage on Segregation: The Case of Dominicans," *Urban Affairs Review* 35 (September 1999): 137–146; Grosfoguel and Georas, "'Coloniality of Power and Racial Dynamics," p. 110.
61. Clay F. Richards, "Jobs Top Latinos' List of Concerns," *Newsday*, October 13, 1991, p. 27.
62. U.S. Census Bureau, "Hispanic Population in the United States, Table 7.1: Educational Attainment of the Population 25 Years and Over by Sex, Hispanic Origin, and Race: March 2000," published March 6, 2001, <http://www.census.gov/population/www/socdemo/hispanic.html>.
63. Rodríguez, *Puerto Ricans*, pp. 122–123, 127; George Borjas and Marta Tienda, eds. *Hispanics in the U.S. Economy* (New York: Academic Press, 1985), cited in Rodríguez, *Puerto Ricans*, p. 91.
64. Milga Morales-Nadal, "Puerto Rican/Latino(a) Vistas on Culture and Education" (paper, 1991), n.p.
65. Rodríguez, *Puerto Ricans*, pp. 139–140.
66. Ibid., pp. 122–123, 149–150.
67. Quoted in U.S. Commission on Civil Rights, *Puerto Ricans in the Continental United States*, p. 99.
68. Rodríguez, *Puerto Ricans*, pp. 126.
69. Quoted in U.S. Commission on Civil Rights, *Puerto Ricans in the Continental United States*, p. 103.
70. Rodríguez, *Puerto Ricans*, pp. 139–140.
71. Ibid., pp. 147–148.
72. Catherine Walsh, *Pedagogy and the Struggle for Voice* (New York: Bergin and Garvey, 1991), pp. 101, 127.
73. Ibid., p. ix.
74. Ibid., pp. vii–xi, 1–27, 65–68, quotations from p. vii.
75. Migration Division, Department of Labor and Human Resources, Commonwealth of Puerto Rico, *Puerto Rican Voter Registration in New York City* (New York: Commonwealth of Puerto Rico, 1988), pp. 5–6.
76. Information provided by the Midwest–Northeast Voter Registration Education Project.
77. In this and the following section we draw on comments provided by Maria Merrill-Ramirez.
78. Information provided by the Midwest–Northeast Voter Registration Education Project.
79. David Medina, "Racial Land Mines Line Road to Perez Victory," *Hartford Courant*, June 14, 2001, p. A17.
80. Information provided by the Midwest–Northeast Voter Registration Education Project.
81. Lopez, "The Puerto Rican Diaspora," p. 329; Western Regional Office, U.S. Commission on Civil Rights, *Puerto Ricans in California*, p. 16.
82. Information provided by the Midwest–Northeast Voter Registration Education Project.
83. *Building a Road Towards Tomorrow*, Midwest–Northeast Voter Registration Education Project Newsbulletin (Chicago, 1991); David E. Pitt, "Puerto Rico Expands New York Voter Drive," *New York Times*, October 14, 1987, p. A18; conversation with Carmen Ambert at the Department of Puerto Rican Community Affairs for the United States, New York City, December 23, 1991.
84. Shannah Kurland, "Brown Power vs. Black Power," *ColorLines*, spring 2001, <http://www.ard.org/C_Lines/CLArchive.htm>.
85. Lopez, *The Puerto Rican Papers*, pp., 55–58.
86. Bonilla and Campos, "A Wealth of Poor," pp. 166–167; Larry Rohter, "Puerto Rico Votes to Retain Status as Commonwealth," *New York Times*, November 15, 1993, p. A1.
87. Gonzalez, *Harvest of Empire*, pp. 263–266.
88. Ruben Berrios Martinez, "Puerto Rico's Decolonization," *Foreign Affairs*, November/December, 1997; "Puerto Rico Crosscurrents Likely to Wash over Florida," *Broward Daily Business Review*, March 21, 1997, p. A5.

89. Georgie Anne Geyer, "Puerto Rico Should Teach the Language That Binds," *Tulsa World*, September 5, 1997, p. A21.
90. Associated Press, "Congressman Criticized for Vieques 'Welfare' Slam," June 20, 2001, <http://salon.com/politics/wire> (retrieved July 3, 2001).
91. Joseph Fitzpatrick, "Puerto Ricans," in *Harvard Encyclopedia of Ethnic Groups*, ed. Stephen Thernstrom (Cambridge, MA: Harvard University Press, 1981), p. 866; Padilla, *Puerto Rican Chicago*, pp. 54, 99–143.
92. John Adam Moreau, "My Parents, They Cry for Joy," in *The Puerto Ricans*, ed. Wagenheim, pp. 327–330.
93. Lopez, "The Puerto Rican Diaspora," p. 331.
94. Ibid., pp. 331–332.
95. Gonzalez, "Puerto Ricans on the Mainland," p. 17; Padilla, *Puerto Rican Chicago*, pp. 117–125; Steven A. Holmes, "Puerto Ricans' Alienation Is Cited in Miami Rampage," *New York Times*, December 5, 1990, p. A24.
96. Jennifer Weil, Joe Williams, and Alice McQuillan, "Violence Follows Parade: 42 arrested as cops and angry crowd clash in Bronx," *Daily News*, June 12, 2001, p. 7.
97. Lopez, "The Puerto Rican Diaspora," p. 332.
98. Quoted in Gigi Anders, "Talking the Talk," *American Journalism Review*, November 2000, p. 30.
99. Joseph Torres, "Racism Mars Puerto Rican Parade," New America News Service, September 10, 1997.
100. Fitzpatrick, "Puerto Ricans," p. 865.
101. Joseph P. Fitzpatrick, *Puerto Rican Americans: The Meaning of Migration to the Mainland* (Englewood Cliffs, NJ: Prentice Hall, 1971), pp. 22–43.
102. Milton Gordon, *Assimilation in American Life* (New York: Oxford University Press, 1964), pp. 75–77; Elena Padilla, *Up from Puerto Rico* (New York: Columbia University Press, 1958); Walsh, *Pedagogy and the Struggle for Voice*, pp. 101–102.
103. Maldonado-Denis, *Puerto Rico*, p. 319.
104. Lloyd H. Rogler and Rosemary Santana Cooney, *Puerto Rican Families in New York City: Intergenerational Processes* (Maplewood, NJ: Waterfront Press, 1984), pp. 76–79.
105. Strategy Research Corporation, *1991 U.S. Hispanic Market* (Miami, FL, 1991), p. 78.
106. Fitzpatrick, *Puerto Rican Americans*, p. 43.
107. "Interview with Leonard Covello," *Urban Review* 3 (January 1969): 53–61.
108. U.S. Commission on Civil Rights, *Puerto Ricans in the Continental United States*, p. 29; Rogler and Cooney, *Puerto Rican Families in New York City*, p. 204.
109. Rogler and Cooney, *Puerto Rican Families in New York City*, pp. 76–79.
110. Nancy Rivera Brooks, "Barbie's Online Critics See Guise in Dolls; Toys: Puerto Rican Incarnation Is at Center of Latest Mattel Brouhaha. First, the Hair ... ," *Los Angeles Times*, November 21, 1997, p. D1.
111. Gonzalez, *Harvest of Empire*, p. 95.
112. See Lopez, "The Puerto Rican Diaspora," p. 343.
113. Bonilla and Campos, "A Wealth of Poor," p. 172.
114. Felix Robert Masud-Piloto, *With Open Arms: Cuban Migration to the U.S.* (Totowa, NJ: Rowman and Littlefield, 1988), pp. 7–11.
115. Ibid., pp. 11–16.
116. Ibid., pp. 13, 20.
117. Ibid., p. 11.
118. Ibid., pp. 20–35.
119. Ibid., pp. 1, 32–35, 39–41; "U.S. Hispanics: Who They Are, Whence They Came, and Why," in *The Hispanic Almanac* (Washington, D.C.: Hispanic Policy Development Project, 1984), pp. 17–18; Antonio Jorge and Raul Moncarz, *The Political Economy of Cubans in South Florida* (Miami, FL: Institute of Interamerican Studies, 1987), pp. 4, 18; Hugh Thomas, *Cuba: The Pursuit of Freedom* (New York: Harper & Row, 1971), p. 117; Silvia Pedraza-Bailey, "Cuba's Exiles: Portrait of a Refugee Migration," *International Migration Review* 19, no. 1 (spring 1985): 9–11, 23; Silvia Pedraza, "Cubans in Exile (1959–1989): The State of the Research," *Scholarship on the Cuban Experience: A Dialogue Among Cubanists*, ed., Damian Fernandez (Gainesville: University of Florida, 1992).
120. Masud-Piloto, *With Open Arms*, pp. 1–5, 83–87.
121. Pedraza-Bailey, "Cuba's Exiles," pp. 15–17; Michael G. Wenk, "Adjustment and Assimilation: The Cuban Refugee Experience," *International Migration Review* 3, no. 1 (fall 1968): 44, 48.
122. Pedraza-Bailey, "Cuba's Exiles," pp. 22–26; Masud-Piloto, *With Open Arms*, pp. 92–108.
123. Masud-Piloto, *With Open Arms*, pp. 83–87.
124. Zulema E. Suarez, "Cuban Americans in Exile: Myths and Reality," in *Family Ethnicity: Strength in Diversity*, ed. Harriette P. McAdoo (Thousand Oaks, CA: Sage, 1999), pp. 135–152.
125. Tim Golden, "U.S.-Cuban Accord Sets Off a Surge of New Refugees," *New York Times*, September 11, 1994, p. 1; "Prepared Statement of the Honorable Phylis E. Oakley, Assistant Secretary of State, Bureau of Population, Refugees and Migration, Before the Senate Committee on the Judiciary, Subcommittee on Immigration," Federal News Service, July 31, 1997.
126. Andrew I. Schoenholtz and Thomas F. Muther, Jr., "Immigration and Nationality," *The International Lawyer* 33 (summer 1999): 517.
127. U.S. Census Bureau, *The Hispanic Population*, Census 2000 Brief, May 2001, pp. 1, 7, 8.
128. Lisandro Perez, "Immigrant Economic Adjustment and Family Organization: The Cuban Success Story Reexamined," *International Migration Review* 20, no. 1 (spring 1986): 13.

129. "Trouble in Paradise," *Time*, November 23, 1981, pp. 24–32; Max J. Castro and Guillermo J. Grenier, "Black–Latino Relations under Conditions of Latino Empowerment: The Miami Case" (research proposal, Miami, 1991), pp. 3–4; Jeffrey Schmalz, "Miami Tensions Simmering 3 Months after Violence," *New York Times*, April 10, 1989, p. A8; Holmes, "Puerto Ricans' Alienation Is Cited in Miami Rampage," p. A24.
130. Mike Clary, "Black, Cuban Racial Chasm Splits Miami," *Los Angeles Times*, March 23, 1997, p. A1.
131. "757 Haitians Cleared to Seek Refuge in U.S.," *New York Times*, December 10, 1991, p. A8.
132. Mirta Ojito "Best of Friends, Worlds Apart," *New York Times*, June 5, 2000, p. 1A.
133. Ibid.
134. Myriam Marquez, "'Ugly Cuban-American' a Malicious Stereotype," *Houston Chronicle*, April 20, 2000, p. A29.
135. U.S. Census Bureau, "Hispanic Population in the United States, Table 11.1: Earnings of Full-Time, Year-Round Workers 15 Years and Over in 1999 by Sex, Hispanic Origin, and Race, March 2000," published March 6, 2001, <http://www.census.gov/population/www/socdemo/hispanic.html>; U.S. Census Bureau, "Hispanic Population in the United States, Table 14.1: Poverty Status of the Population in 1999 by Sex, Age, Hispanic Origin, and Race: March 2000," published March 6, 2001, <http://www.census.gov/population/www/socdemo/hispanic.html>.
136. Matt Spetalnick, "Florida Declares English Official Language," *Reuter Library Report*, November 9, 1988, n.p.
137. Neil A. Lewis, "Committee Rejects Bush Nominee to Key Appellate Court in South," *New York Times*, April 12, 1991, pp. A1, A11.
138. Philip Shenon, "FBI Suspends Veteran Agent," *New York Times*, March 5, 1990, p. A1.
139. David Kidwell, "Miami Agent Lashes Out at DEA," *Miami Herald*, February 22, 2001, p. 1B.
140. Jorge and Moncarz, *The Political Economy of Cubans in South Florida*, pp. 16–19.
141. Ibid., p. 9.
142. Wenk, "Adjustment and Assimilation," pp. 39–42.
143. Perez, "Immigrant Economic Adjustment and Family Organization," pp. 4–7; Silvia Pedraza-Bailey, "Cubans and Mexicans in the United States: The Functions of Political and Economic Migration," *Cuban Studies* 11, no. 2/12, no. 1 (July 1981–January 1982); Alejandro Portes and Robert L. Bach, *Latin American Journey* (Berkeley, CA: University of California Press, 1985), pp. 200–220.
144. Grosfoguel and Georas, "'Coloniality of Power and Racial Dynamics," p. 113; other data here are from David E. Hayes-Bautista and Robert M. Stein, "Los Angeles; A Choice of Two Destinies: Will It Be Miami or San Antonio?" *Los Angeles Times*, March 11, 2001 p. 1M.
145. Perez, "Immigrant Economic Adjustment and Family Organization," pp. 4–20.
146. Ibid., quotation on p. 18.
147. Ibid.
148. U.S. Census Bureau, "Hispanic Population, Table 1: Selected Summary Measures of Age and Income by Hispanic Origin and Race: March 2000," published March 6, 2001, <http://www.census.gov/population/www/socdemo/hispanic.html>; U.S. Census Bureau, "Hispanic Population, Table 13.1: Total Money Income in 1999 of Families by Type, and by Hispanic Origin and Race of Householder; published March 6, 2001, <http://www.census.gov/population/www/socdemo/hispanic.html>; U.S. Census Bureau, "Hispanic Population, Table 14.1: Poverty Status of the Population in 1999 by Sex, Age, Hispanic Origin, and Race," published March 6, 2001, <http://www.census.gov/population/www/socdemo/hispanic.html>; U.S. Census Bureau, "Hispanic Population, Table 15.1: Poverty Status of Families in 1999 by Family Type, and by Hispanic Origin and Race of Householder," published March 6, 2001, <http://www.census.gov/population/www/socdemo/hispanic.html>; U.S. Census Bureau, "Hispanic Population, Table 7.1: Educational Attainment of the Population 25 Years and Over by Sex, Hispanic Origin, and Race: March 2000," published March 6, 2001, <http://www.census.gov/population/www/socdemo/hispanic.html>.
149. U.S. Census Bureau, "Hispanic Population, Table 14.1: Poverty Status of the Population in 1999 by Sex, Age, Hispanic Origin, and Race"; U.S. Census Bureau, "Hispanic Population, Table 15.1: Poverty Status of Families in 1999 by Family Type, and by Hispanic Origin and Race of Householder."
150. Quoted in "Widespread Political Efforts Open New Era for Hispanics," *Congressional Quarterly*, October 23, 1982, p. 2,709.
151. Jorge and Moncarz, *The Political Economy of Cubans in South Florida*, p. 30; Masud-Piloto, *With Open Arms*, p. 16.
152. Information provided by the Midwest–Northeast Voter Registration Education Project; Clary, "Black, Cuban Racial Chasm Splits Miami."
153. Andrew Gumbel, "U.S. Presidential Election: Mayor Denies 'Betrayal' of Democrats," *The Independent* (London), December 4, 2000, p. 12.
154. See Samuel P. Huntington, "The Erosion of American National Interests," *Foreign Affairs*, September/October, 1997, p. 28.
155. Jorge Mas Santos, "Make a difference. Have a purpose. Shine a light," February 7, 2001, <http://www.canfnet.org> (retrieved July 12, 2001).

156. Richard Boudreaus, "Cuba Strikes Democracy Movement," *Los Angeles Times*, January 19, 1992, p. A1; Deborah Sharp, "Execution in Cuba," *USA Today*, January 22, 1992, p. 3A.
157. Peter Kornbluh and Jon Elliston, "Will Congress Kill TV Marti?" *Nation*, August 22/29, 1994, pp. 194–196.
158. Kirk Nielsen, "Sail Away and Stay and Stay," *Miami New Times Online*, May 10, 2001, <http://www.miaminewtimes.com> (retrieved July 12, 2001).
159. "Protesters Disrupt 'Peace for Cuba' Rally," *Los Angeles Times*, January 26, 1992, p. A5; Arun Gupta, "5,000 Oppose Crunching Cuba at N.Y. Rally," *Guardian*, February 5, 1992, p. 13.
160. Jon Nordheimer, "Where Old Havana Plays," *New York Times*, April 3, 1991, p. C1.
161. Deborah Sontag, "The Lasting Exile of Cuban Spirits," *New York Times*, September 11, 1994, section 4, p. 1.
162. Kelly M. Barlow, Donald M. Taylor, and Wallace E. Lambert, "Ethnicity in America and Feeling 'American'," *Journal of Psychology* 134 (November 2000): 581–600.
163. Portes and Bach, *Latin American Journey*, pp. 91–93, 193–199.
164. Hayes-Bautista and Stein, "Los Angeles: A Choice of Two Destinies."
165. Amie Parnes, "First Communions Turn Lavish in South Florida; Cuban-Americans among Big Spenders," *Boston Globe*, June 27, 2001, p. A2.
166. Portes and Bach, *Latin American Journey*, pp. 246–247.
167. "Trouble in Paradise," pp. 30–31.
168. Data in this and the following paragraph are from Strategy Research Corporation, *1991 U.S. Hispanic Market*, pp. 78–130.
169. Matea Gold, "Cultural Celebration Sways to a Cuban Beat; Heritage: About 20,000 Attend L.A.'s Third Annual Cuban American Festival of Art, Music, and Food in Echo Park," *Los Angeles Times*, May 19, 1997, p. B1.
170. Andrew Meadows, "Catering to Latin Tastes; Tapping the Hispanic Market," *Tampa Tribune*, April 20, 2001, p. 1, Business & Finance.
171. Private communication with Maria Merril-Ramirez, July 1982.
172. Stephanie Armour, "Welcome Mat Rolls Out for Hispanic Workers: Corporate America Cultivates Talent as Ethnic Population Booms," *USA Today*, April 12, 2001, p. 1B.

CHAPTER 10

1. U.S. Bureau of the Census, *U.S. Census of Population, 1980: Asian and Pacific Islander Population in the United States*, PC80-2-1E (Washington, D.C., 1988), p. 1; U.S. Bureau of the Census, *1990 Census of Population: Social and Economic Characteristics: United States*, CP-2-1 (Washington, D.C., 1993), pp. 105–106; U.S. Census Bureau, *Census 2000*, Table DP-1: Profile of General Demographic Characteristics of the United States: 2000, <http://www.census.gov/pressrelease/2001/tables/dpus/2000> (published July 27, 2001).
2. U.S. Commission on Civil Rights, *Civil Rights Issues Facing Asian Americans in the 1990s* (Washington, D.C.: U.S. Government Printing Office, 1992), p. 15; Robert Daniels, *Coming to America* (New York: HarperCollins, 1990), p. 350.
3. Kathryn Tolbert, "Pacific Grim," *Boston Globe Sunday Magazine*, March 29, 1992, p. 14.
4. Ronald Takaki, *Strangers from a Different Shore: A History of Asian Americans* (New York: Penguin, 1989), p. 7.
5. Alan T. Moriyama, *Imingaisha: Japanese Immigration Companies and Hawaii, 1894–1908* (Honolulu: University of Hawaii Press, 1985); Wayne Patterson, *The Korean Frontier in America: Immigration to Hawaii, 1896–1910* (Honolulu: University of Hawaii Press, 1988).
6. Roger Daniels, *The Politics of Prejudice* (New York: Atheneum, 1969), pp. 3–6; Hilary Conroy, *The Japanese Frontier in Hawaii, 1868–1898* (Berkeley, CA: University of California Press, 1953), passim; Moriyama, *Imingaisha*, pp. xvi–xix.
7. Takaki, *Strangers from a Different Shore*, p. 179.
8. U.S. Immigration and Naturalization Service, *1975 Annual Report* (Washington, D.C., 1975), pp. 62–66.
9. Arinori Mori, *The Japanese in America* (Japan Advertiser Press, 1926), pp. 19–21; Kaizo Naka, *Social and Economic Conditions among Japanese Farmers in California* (San Francisco: R & E Research Associates, 1974), p. 6; John Modell, "On Being an Issei: Orientations toward America" (paper presented to the American Anthropological Association, San Diego, November 1970), p. 4.
10. Sucheng Chan, *Asian Americans: An Interpretive History* (Boston: Twayne, 1991), pp. 103–117; Roger Daniels, *Asian America: Chinese and Japanese in the United States Since 1850* (Seattle: University of Washington Press, 1988), pp. 100–154.
11. Jacobus tenBroek, Edward N. Barnhart, and Floyd W. Matson, *Prejudice, War, and the Constitution* (Berkeley, CA: University of California Press, 1968), pp. 42–43; *Takao Ozawa v. United States*, 260 U.S. 178 (1922); Takaki, *Strangers from a Distant Shore*, pp. 14–15.
12. Hillary Conroy and T. Scott Miyakawa, "Foreword," in *East across the Pacific*, ed. Hillary Conroy and T. Scott Miyakawa (Santa Barbara, CA: ABC-CLIO, 1972), pp. xiv–xv.

13. The statistics are from U.S. Census Bureau publications.
14. Takaki, *Strangers from a Different Shore*, pp. 479–481.
15. Robert G. Lee, *Orientals: Asian Americans in Popular Culture* (Philadelphia, PA: Temple University Press, 1999), p. 8.
16. E. Manchester-Boddy, *Japanese in America* (San Francisco: R & E Research Associates, 1970), pp. 25–30.
17. V. S. McClatchy, *Japanese Immigration and Colonization*, reprint ed. (San Francisco: R & E Research Associates, 1970), p. 42.
18. Quoted in Edward K. Strong, Jr., *The Second-Generation Japanese Problem* (Stanford, CA: Stanford University Press, 1934), p. 133.
19. tenBroek, Barnhart, and Matson, *Prejudice, War, and the Constitution*, p. 31.
20. Dennis M. Ogawa, *From Japs to Japanese* (Berkeley: McCutchan, 1971), p. 12; Carey McWilliams, *Brothers Under the Skin*, rev. ed. (Boston: Little, Brown, 1964), pp. 148–149; Stanley Sue and Harry H. L. Kitano, "Stereotypes as a Measure of Success," *Journal of Social Issues* 29 (1973): 83–98.
21. tenBroek, Barnhart, and Matson, *Prejudice, War, and the Constitution*, pp. 66–70.
22. Quoted in Ogawa, *From Japs to Japanese*, p. 11.
23. U.S. Department of the Interior, War Relocation Authority, *Myths and Facts about the Japanese American* (Washington, D.C., 1945), pp. 7–8; Ogawa, *From Japs to Japanese*, pp. 35–54. Survey data document attitude changes in the period 1942–1961. See also Roger Daniels, "Why It Happened Here," in *The Social Reality of Ethnic America*, ed. R. Gomez et al. (Lexington, MA: D. C. Heath, 1971), p. 236.
24. Council on Interracial Books for Children, *Stereotypes, Distortions and Omissions in U.S. History Textbooks* (New York: Racism and Sexism Resource Center for Educators, 1977), pp. 42–46.
25. Letta Tayler, "Dateline: Washington," States News Service, May 8, 1987, n.p.; Takaki, *Strangers from a Different Shore*, p. 6.
26. Mia Tuan, *Forever Foreigners or Honorary Whites?: The Asian American Experience Today* (New Brunswick, NJ: Rutgers University Press, 1998), p. 1.
27. Karl Taro Greenfield, "Return of the Yellow Peril," *Nation*, May 11, 1992, p. 636; Michael Crichton, *Rising Sun* (New York: Knopf, 1991).
28. Helen Zia, *Asian American Dreams: The Emergence of an American People* (New York: Farrar, Straus, and Giroux, 2000), p. 134.
29. Erika Hayasaki, "'Pearl Harbor' Making Its Marks," *Los Angeles Times*, May 29, 2001, p. 6-1
30. Steven A. Chin, "KFRC Deejay Draws Suspension for On-Air Derogatory Remarks," *San Francisco Examiner*, December 6, 1994, p. A2.
31. Herbert B. Johnson, *Discrimination against the Japanese in California* (Berkeley, CA: Courier, 1907), pp. 73–74; Daniels, *The Politics of Prejudice*, pp. 33–34; Howard H. Sugimoto, "The Vancouver Riots of 1907: A Canadian Episode," in *East across the Pacific*, ed. Conroy and Miyakawa, pp. 92–110.
32. Jean Pajus, *The Real Japanese California* (San Francisco: R & E Research Associates, 1971), pp. 164–166; Daniels, *The Politics of Prejudice*, p. 87; tenBroek, Barnhart, and Matson, *Prejudice, War, and the Constitution*, p. 73.
33. Lemuel F. Ignacio, *Asian Americans and Pacific Islanders* (San Jose, CA: Pilipino Development Associates, 1976), pp. 95–96; tenBroek, Barnhart, and Matson, *Prejudice, War, and the Constitution*, passim.
34. Dorothy Swaine Thomas and Richard S. Nishimoto, *The Spoilage* (Berkeley, CA: University of California Press, 1946), pp. 8–16; tenBroek, Barnhart, and Matson, *Prejudice, War, and the Constitution*, pp. 118–120.
35. tenBroek, Barnhart, and Matson, *Prejudice, War, and the Constitution*, pp. 120, 126–129, 130; Thomas and Nishimoto, *The Spoilage*, pp. 10–20; Edward H. Spicer et al., *Impounded People* (Tucson: University of Arizona Press, 1969), pp. 141–241.
36. Richard Drinnon, *Keeper of Concentration Camps* (Berkeley, CA: University of California Press, 1987), pp. 47, 153; quotation from Valerie Matsumoto, "Japanese American Women during World War II," in *Unequal Sisters*, ed. Ellen C. DuBois and Vicki L. Ruiz (New York: Routledge, 1990), p. 373.
37. Thomas and Nishimoto, *The Spoilage*, pp. 54–71; tenBroek, Barnhart, and Matson, *Prejudice, War, and the Constitution*, pp. 126–132, 149–155; Spicer et al., *Impounded People*, pp. 252–280.
38. Leonard Bloom and Ruth Riemer, *Removal and Return* (Berkeley; University of California Press, 1949), pp. 124–157, 198–204; tenBroek, Barnhart, and Matson, *Prejudice, War, and the Constitution*, pp. 155–177, 180–181.
39. Bradford Smith, *Americans from Japan* (New York; Lippincott, 1948), pp. 10–12, 202–276; Carey McWilliams, *Prejudice* (Boston: Little, Brown, 1944), p. 4; tenBroek, Barnhart, and Matson, *Prejudice, War, and the Constitution*, pp. 211–223; Harry H. L. Kitano, *Japanese Americans*, 2nd ed. (Englewood Cliffs, NJ: Prentice Hall, 1976), pp. 82–88; S. Frank Miyamoto, "The Forced Evacuation of the Japanese Minority during World War II," *Journal of Social Issues* 29 (1973): 11–29.
40. Drinnon, *Keeper of Concentration Camps*, pp. 255–256. See also Christopher Thorne, *Allies of a Kind* (New York: Oxford University Press, 1978).
41. Kitano, *Japanese Americans*, p. 73.
42. Gary Y. Okihiro, "Japanese Resistance in America's Concentration Camps: A Re-evaluation," *Amerasia Journal* 2 (fall 1973): 20–34; Arthur A. Hansen and

David A. Hacker, "The Manzanar Riot: An Ethnic Perspective," *Amerasia Journal* 3 (fall 1974): 112–142. See also Roger Daniels, *Concentration Camps, U.S.A.* (New York: Holt, Rinehart & Winston, 1971).

43. See the Southern Poverty Law Center's *Intelligence Report*, March 1994, pp. 17–29; and the *Intelligence Report*, October 1994, pp. 9–14.
44. Ivan H. Light, *Ethnic Enterprise in America* (Berkeley, CA: University of California Press, 1972), pp. 174–179; Bill Hosokawa, *The Nisei* (New York: Morrow, 1969), pp. 199–200; Kitano, *Japanese Americans*, pp. 55–58.
45. Hosokawa, *The Nisei*, pp. 439–446; Kitano, *Japanese Americans*, pp. 89–90.
46. Nathaniel C. Nash, "House Votes Payments to Japanese Americans," *New York Times*, September 18, 1987, p. A15.
47. Ken Miller, "U.S. Pays Japanese Internees $20,000—and Apologies," Gannett News Service, October 9, 1990, n.p.
48. Santiago O'Donnell and Psyche Pascual, "Kato Slaying Raises Fears of Hate Crime," *Los Angeles Times*, March 1, 1992, p. B1.
49. Benjamin Forgey, "Imagery Says It All at New Monument; Artistry, Apology Merge at Japanese American Memorial," *Washington Post*, June 30, 2001, p. C1.
50. Rodolfo Acuña, *Occupied America* (San Francisco: Canfield Press, 1972), pp. 212–213.
51. Quoted in Harry H. L. Kitano and Roger Daniels, *Asian Americans: Emerging Minorities*, 3rd ed. (Englewood Cliffs, NJ: Prentice Hall, 2001), p. 47.
52. Kitano, *Japanese Americans*, pp. 174–186; Daniel Inouye and Lawrence Elliot, *Journey to Washington* (Englewood Cliffs, NJ: Prentice Hall, 1967), pp. 248–250; Hosokawa, *The Nisei*, pp. 460–469.
53. Hosokawa, *The Nisei*, pp. 486–487.
54. Stanley Karnow, "Apathetic Asian Americans?" *Washington Post*, November 29, 1992, p. C1.
55. "Slur Stirs Party In-fighting," *Commercial Appeal*, May 4, 1994, p. 5A.
56. U.S. Commission on Civil Rights, *Recent Activities against Citizens and Residents of Asian Descent* (Washington, D.C., 1986), pp. 3–6.
57. Kenneth Walsh, Gloria Borger, Susan Dentzer, and Carla A. Robbins, "The 'America First' Fallacies," *U.S. News & World Report*, February 3, 1992, p. 22.
58. O'Donnell and Pascual, "Kato Slaying Raises Fears of Hate Crime," p. B1.
59. Kitano and Daniels, *Asian Americans*, 3rd ed., p. 83.
60. Yuji Ichioka, "A Buried Past," *Amerasia Journal* 1 (July 1971): 1–25; Karl Yoneda, "100 Years of Japanese Labor History in the U.S.A.," in *Roots*, ed. Amy Tachiki et al. (Los Angeles, CA: UCLA Asian American Studies Center, 1971), pp. 150–157; Takaki, *Strangers from a Different Shore*, p. 200.
61. See the various articles in *Roots*, ed. Tachiki et al.
62. Russell Endo and William Wei, "On the Development of Asian American Studies Programs," in *Reflections on Shattered Windows*, ed. Gary Y. Okihiro et al. (Pullman: Washington State University Press, 1988), pp. 6–12.
63. "Prepared Testimony of Karen Narasaki, Executive Director, National Asian Pacific American Legal Consortium, Before the House Judiciary Committee," Subcommittee on the Constitution, Subcommittee Hearing on H.R. 1909: The Civil Rights Act of 1997, Federal News Service, June 26, 1997; Randal C. Archibold, "UC Irvine Expected to Offer Asian Studies Major; Education: On a Campus Where More Than Half the Students Are of Asian Background, Absence of Such a Program Has Been a Concern and a Topic of Protests," *Los Angeles Times*, May 13, 1997, p. A3.
64. Wired News Report, "E-mail Hate Scribe Sentenced," Wired News, <http://www.wired.com/news/print/0,1294,12090,00.html> (retrieved August 12, 2001).
65. Cited in Sidney L. Gulick, *The American Japanese Problem* (New York: Scribner's, 1914), p. 11.
66. Japanese Association of the Pacific Northwest, *Japanese Immigration* (San Francisco: R & E Research Associates, 1972), pp. 22–25; Daniels, *The Politics of Prejudice*, pp. 7, 10–12.
67. Edna Bonacich and John Modell, *The Economic Basis of Ethnic Solidarity* (Berkeley, CA: University of California Press, 1980), pp. 38–47.
68. Kitano, *Japanese Americans*, pp. 19–21; Light, *Ethnic Enterprise in America*, pp. 27–29; S. Frank Miyamoto, "An Immigrant Community in America," in *East across the Pacific*, ed. Conroy and Miyakawa, pp. 223–225.
69. Gulick, *The American Japanese Problem*, pp. 11, 32–33; Light, *Ethnic Enterprise in America*, p. 71; Roger Daniels, "Japanese Immigrants on the Western Frontier: The Issei in California, 1890–1940," in *East across the Pacific*, ed. Conroy and Miyakawa, p. 85.
70. Pajus, *The Real Japanese California*, pp. 147–151; Light, *Ethnic Enterprise in America*, p. 76.
71. Bloom and Riemer, *Removal and Return*, pp. 115–117; Strong, *The Second-Generation Japanese Problem*, pp. 209–211.
72. Bloom and Riemer, *Removal and Return*, pp. 17–20.
73. Evelyn Nakano Glenn, "The Dialectics of Wage Work: Japanese American Women and Domestic Service, 1905–1940," in *Unequal Sisters*, ed. DuBois and Ruiz, p. 345.
74. Ibid., p. 369.
75. Bloom and Riemer, *Removal and Return*, pp. 44, 144.
76. Bonacich and Modell, *The Economic Basis of Ethnic Solidarity*, pp. 256–259.

77. U.S. Bureau of the Census, *1990 Census of Population: Social and Economic Characteristics: United States*, CP-2-1 (Washington, D.C., 1993), pp. 44, 45, 111, 115.
78. Ibid., pp. 48, 49, 105–106, 117, 119; U.S. Bureau of the Census, *1990 Census of Population: Social and Economic Characteristics: California*, CP-2-6 (Washington, D.C., 1993), pp. 186, 252, 256, 286.
79. Kitano and Daniels, *Asian Americans*, 3rd ed., p. 81.
80. U.S. Commission on Civil Rights, *Success of Asian Americans: Fact or Fiction?* (Washington, D.C., 1980), pp. 14–15.
81. Harry H. L. Kitano and Roger Daniels, *Asian Americans: Emerging Minorities* (Englewood Cliffs, NJ: Prentice Hall, 1988), p. 171.
82. Winfred Yu, "Asian Americans Charge Prejudice Slows Climb to Management Ranks," *Wall Street Journal*, September 11, 1985, n.p., quoted in Takaki, *Strangers from a Different Shore*, p. 476.
83. Takaki, *Strangers from a Different Shore*, pp. 475–477.
84. Art Pine, "Marines Pin Bars on Man They Dismissed," *Los Angeles Times*, March 19, 1994, p. A4; Judy Tachibana, "Triumph over Racism in the Marines," *Sacramento Bee*, April 20, 1994, p. B3.
85. K. K. Kawakami, *The Japanese Question* (New York: Macmillan, 1921), pp. 143–145; John Modell, "Tradition and Opportunity: The Japanese Immigrant in America," *Pacific Historical Review* 40 (May 1971): 163–182.
86. Johnson, *Discrimination against the Japanese in California*, pp. 3–20, 40–47; Franklin Hichborn, *The Story of the Session of the California Legislature of 1909* (San Francisco: James H. Barry Press, 1909), p. 207; Pajus, *The Real Japanese California*, pp. 170–178; Kawakami, *The Japanese Question*, pp. 168–169.
87. William Petersen, *Japanese Americans* (New York: Random House, 1971), p. 183; Strong, *The Second-Generation Japanese Problem*, pp. 201–204; Kawakami, *The Japanese Question*, pp. 146–151; Pajus, *The Real Japanese California*, p. 181.
88. Pajus, *The Real Japanese California*, p. 183; Strong, *The Second-Generation Japanese Problem*, pp. 185–188.
89. U.S. Bureau of the Census, *1990 Census of Population: Social and Economic Characteristics: United States*, pp. 42, 107.
90. Kitano, *Japanese Americans*, pp. 93, 174–175; U.S. Commission on Civil Rights, *Social Indicators of Equality for Minorities and Women* (Washington, D.C., 1978), pp. 24–26; U.S. Bureau of the Census, *1990 Census of Population: Social and Economic Characteristics: California*, pp. 181, 246.
91. Manchester-Boddy, *Japanese in America*, p. 118.
92. Petersen, *Japanese Americans*, p. 177; Manchester-Boddy, *Japanese in America*, pp. 114–118.
93. Andrew W. Lind, *Hawaii's Japanese* (Princeton, NJ: Princeton University Press, 1946), pp. 212–257; Petersen, *Japanese Americans*, pp. 177–178, 185.
94. Hosokawa, *The Nisei*, p. 131; Kitano, *Japanese Americans*, p. 115; Christie Kiefer, *Changing Cultures, Changing Lives* (San Francisco: Jossey-Bass, 1974), pp. 34–38; Petersen, *Japanese Americans*, p. 187.
95. John Dart, "Military Opens Chaplain Ranks to Buddhists," *Los Angeles Times*, October 27, 1987, p. 1.
96. John Modell, "The Japanese American Family: A Perspective for Future Investigations," *Pacific Historical Review* 37 (February 1968): 79; Joe R. Feagin and Nancy Fujitaki, "On the Assimilation of Japanese Americans," *Amerasia Journal* 1 (February 1972): 15–17.
97. Tuan, *Forever Foreigners*, p. 155.
98. Peter Y. Hong, "Japanese American Newspaper's Layoffs Anger Community," *Los Angeles Times*, November 15, 1997, p. B1. See newspaper at <http://www.rafu.com>.
99. Petersen, *Japanese Americans*, pp. 6–7; Light, *Ethnic Enterprise in America*, passim; William Caudill, "Japanese American Personality and Acculturation," *Genetic Psychology Monographs* 45 (1952): 3–102; Kitano and Daniels, *Asian Americans*, p. 179.
100. Paul Spickard, *Mixed Blood* (Madison: University of Wisconsin Press, 1988), p. 347.
101. David J. O'Brien and Stephen S. Fugita, "Generational Differences in Japanese Americans' Perceptions and Feelings about Social Relationships between Themselves and Caucasian Americans," in *Culture, Ethnicity, and Identity*, ed. William McCready (New York: Academic Press, 1983), pp. 235–236.
102. Darrel Montero, *Japanese Americans: Changing Patterns of Ethnic Affiliation over Three Generations* (Boulder, CO: Westview Press, 1980), p. 80; Petersen, *Japanese Americans*, pp. 220–224; Modell, "The Japanese American Family," pp. 76–79; Kitano, *Japanese Americans*, pp. 189, 196; George Kagiwada, "Assimilation of Nisei in Los Angeles," in *East Across the Pacific*, ed. Conroy and Miyakawa, p. 273.
103. Feagin and Fujitaki, "On the Assimilation of Japanese Americans," p. 23.
104. Akemi Kikumura and Harry H. L. Kitano, "Interracial Marriage: A Picture of Japanese Americans," *Journal of Social Issues* 29 (1973): 67–81; John N. Tinker, "Intermarriage and Ethnic Boundaries: The Japanese American Case," *Journal of Social Issues* 29 (1973): 55; John W. Connor, *Tradition and Change in Three Generations of Japanese Americans* (Chicago: Nelson-Hall, 1977), p. 308; Gene N. Levine and Colbert Rhodes, *The Japanese American Community* (New York: Praeger, 1981), p. 145.
105. Larry H. Shinagawa and Gin Yong Pang, " Asian American Panethnicity and Intermarriage," in *Asian Americans: Experiences and Perspectives*, ed. Timothy P. Fong and Larry H. Shinagawa (Upper Saddle River, NJ: Prentice Hall, 2000), pp. 334–343.

106. O'Brien and Fugita, "Generational Differences," pp. 231–235.
107. Kitano and Daniels, *Asian Americans: Emerging Minorities*, 3rd ed., p. 80.
108. Ibid., p. 81.
109. Ibid., pp. 191–192.
110. Petersen, *Japanese Americans*, pp. 214–221.
111. Greg Mayeda, "Japanese Americans Don't Lose Identity," *New York Times*, December 28, 1995, p. A20.
112. Edna Bonacich, "United States Capitalist Development: A Background to Asian Immigration," in *Labor Immigration under Capitalism*, ed. Lucie Cheng and Edna Bonacich (Berkeley, CA: University of California Press, 1984), p. 82.
113. *U.S. v. Bhagat Singh Thind*, 261 U.S. 215 (1923).
114. Shinagawa and Pang, "Asian American Panethnicity and Intermarriage," in Fong and Shinagawa, *Asian Americans*, pp. 343–344.
115. See Takaki, *Strangers from a Different Shore*, p. 474.
116. This section draws on Robert Blauner, *Racial Oppression in America* (New York: Harper & Row, 1972), pp. 54–55; Paul Takagi, "The Myth of 'Assimilation in American Life,'" *Amerasia Journal* 2 (fall 1973): 149–158; Peter Uhlenberg, "Demographic Correlates of Group Achievement: Contrasting Patterns of Mexican-Americans and Japanese-Americans," *Demography* 9 (February 1972): 119–128.
117. B. Suzuki, "Education and the Socialization of Asian Americans," in *Asian Americans: Social and Psychological Perspectives*, ed. R. Endo, S. Sue, and N. Wagner (Palo Alto, CA: Science & Behavior Books, 1980), 2:155–178; William Petersen, "Success Story, Japanese-American Style," *New York Times*, January 9, 1966, p. 21; "Success Story of One Minority Group in the U.S.," *U.S. News & World Report*, December 26, 1966, pp. 73–76; Thomas Sowell, *Ethnic America* (New York: Basic Books, 1981).
118. Amado Cabezas and Gary Kawaguchi, "Empirical Evidence for Continuing Asian American Inequality: The Human Capital Model and Labor Market Segmentation," in *Reflections on Shattered Windows*, pp. 144–164.
119. Studies cited in Amado Cabezas, "Testimony to U.S. Commission on Civil Rights," in *Civil Rights Issues of Asian and Pacific Americans* (Washington, D.C.: U.S. Government Printing Office, 1980), pp. 389–393. See also Takaki, *Strangers from a Different Shore*, p. 475.
120. Takagi, "The Myth of 'Assimilation in American Life,'" pp. 149–158; Ogawa, *From Jap to Japanese*, pp. 43ff.
121. "When You're Smiling: The Deadly Legacy of Internment," a documentary produced and directed by Janice D. Tanaka, Visual Communications, 1999.
122. Brad Knickerbocker, "U.S. Japanese Retain Cultural Ties," *Christian Science Monitor*, July 27, 1993, p. 11.
123. See, for example, the comments of a woman in Miranda Ewell, "Japanese American Still Trying to Find a Way to Belong in U.S.; Asians Have Achieved Measurable Success but Continue to Face a Complex Racial and Ethnic Landscape," *Orange County Register*, August 19, 1996, p. A10.
124. David Mura, "Whites: How to Face the Angry Racial Tribes," *Utne Reader*, July/August 1992, p. 80. See also David Mura, *Turning Japanese: Memoirs of a Sansei* (New York: Atlantic Monthly Press, 1991).
125. Charles Burress, "Looking to Hawaii for Harmony: Japanese American Panel Wants a Model for the New California," *San Francisco Chronicle*, October 21, 1997, p. A17.

CHAPTER 11

1. Elaine H. Kim, "They Armed in Self-Defense," *Newsweek*, May 18, 1992, p. 10.
2. Ibid.
3. Data provided by Statistics Division, U.S. Immigration and Naturalization Service, 2001.
4. Ronald Takaki, *A Different Mirror* (Boston: Little, Brown, 1993), pp. 211–214; Roger Daniels, *Asian America: Chinese and Japanese in the United States Since 1850* (Seattle: University of Washington Press, 1988), pp. 16–17, 44; Bill Ong Hing, *Making and Remaking Asian America Through Immigration Policy: 1850–1990* (Stanford, CA: Stanford University Press, 1993), p. 23, 48–49, 80.
5. U.S. Commission on Civil Rights, *Recent Activities against Citizens and Residents of Asian Descent* (Washington, D.C., 1986), p. 7.
6. Immigration and Naturalization Service, *1985 Statistical Yearbook*, pp. 2–5; Ronald Takaki, *Strangers from a Different Shore: A History of Asian Americans* (Boston: Little, Brown, 1989), pp. 111–112.
7. U.S. Commission on Civil Rights, *Recent Activities against Citizens and Residents of Asian Descent*, p. 8.
8. U.S. Commission on Civil Rights, *The Tarnished Golden Door: Civil Rights Issues in Immigration* (Washington, D.C., 1980), p. 10.
9. Immigration and Naturalization Service, *1985 Statistical Yearbook*, pp. 2–5; U.S. Census Bureau, Table DP-1: Profile of General Demographic Characteristics for the United States: 2000, <www.census.gov> (retrieved August 29, 2001; U.S. Census Bureau, <http://factfinder.census.gov/basicfacts.html> (retrieved August 29, 2001).
10. Stephan Thernstrom, ed., *Harvard Encyclopedia of American Ethnic Groups* (Cambridge, MA: Harvard University Press, 1981), pp. 357–359.

11. U.S. Commission on Civil Rights, *Recent Activities against Citizens and Residents of Asian Descent*, p. 9.
12. Vanessa Ho, "Filipinos' American Dream Comes True," *Seattle Times*, April 29, 1992, p. B1.
13. David Pierson, "Plight of Filipino Vets Studied," *Los Angeles Times*, August 1, 2001, Part 2, p. 8
14. U.S. Census Bureau, Table DP-1: Profile of General Demographic Characteristics for the United States: 2000; U.S. Census Bureau, <http://factfinder.census.gov/basicfacts.html>.
15. Wayne Patterson, *The Korean Frontier in America: Immigration to Hawaii, 1896–1910* (Honolulu: University of Hawaii Press, 1988), p. 177; Takaki, *Strangers from a Different Shore*, pp. 270–271; U.S. Commission on Civil Rights, *Recent Activities against Citizens and Residents of Asian Descent*, p. 9.
16. Warren Y. Kim, *Koreans in America* (Seoul: Po Chin Chai Printing Co., 1971), pp. 22–25.
17. David M. Reimers, *Still the Golden Door: The Third World Comes to America* (New York: Columbia University Press, 1985), pp. 110–111; data from the Statistics Division, U.S. Immigration and Naturalization Service, 2001.
18. U.S. Census Bureau, Table DP-1: Profile of General Demographic Characteristics for the United States: 2000; U.S. Census Bureau, <http://factfinder.census.gov/basicfacts.html>.
19. Darrel Montero, *Vietnamese Americans: Patterns of Resettlement and Socioeconomic Adaptation in the United States* (Boulder, CO: Westview Press, 1979), pp. 1–3.
20. Morrison G. Wong and Charles Hirschman, "The New Asian Immigrants," in *Culture, Ethnicity, and Identity*, ed. William C. McCready (New York: Academic Press, 1983), p. 381.
21. U.S. Bureau of the Census, *1990 Census of Population: United States Summary*, CP-2-1 (Washington, D.C., 1993), p. 4; U.S. Census Bureau, Table DP-1: Profile of General Demographic Characteristics for the United States: 2000; U.S. Census Bureau, <http://factfinder.census.gov/basicfacts.html>.
22. Ibid.
23. This paragraph draws on research of Arun Jain, as cited in Marcia Mogelonsky, "Asian-Indian Americans," *American Demographics*, August 1995, p. 36.
24. U.S. Census Bureau, <http://factfinder.census.gov/basicfacts.html>.
25. Min Zhou and James V. Gatewood, "Introduction: Revisiting Contemporary Asian America," in *Contemporary Asian America: A Multidisciplinary Reader*, ed. Min Zhou and James V. Gatewood (New York: New York University Press, 2000), p. 35.
26. Ibid., p. 10.
27. Harry H. L. Kitano and Roger Daniels, *Asian Americans: Emerging Minorities* (Englewood Cliffs, NJ: Prentice Hall, 1988), p. 176.
28. Quoted in K. Connie Kang, "Building Bridges to Equality," *Los Angeles Times*, January 7, 1995, p. A1.
29. Quoted in "Prepared Testimony of Karen Narasaki, Executive Director, National Asian Pacific American Legal Consortium Before the House Judiciary Committee, Subcommittee on the Constitution," Subcommittee Hearing on H.R. 1909: The Civil Rights Act of 1997, Federal News Service, June 26, 1997.
30. Claire Jean Kim, "The Racial Triangulation of Asian Americans," *Politics and Society* 27 (March 1999): 105–138.
31. *Plessy v. Ferguson* 163 U.S. 537, 561 (1896).
32. Quoted in Takaki, *Strangers from a Different Shore*, p. 370.
33. Miriam Sharma, "Labor Migration and Class Formation among the Filipinos in Hawaii, 1940–1946," in *Labor Immigration under Capitalism*, ed. Lucie Cheng and Edna Bonacich (Berkeley, CA: University of California Press, 1984), pp. 583, 593.
34. Montero, *Vietnamese Americans*, pp. 3–4.
35. Paul Sweeney, "Tolerance in a Texas Town," *Texas Observer*, September 17, 1982, pp. 7–9; K. Connie Kang, "U.S. Asians Seen as 'Alien,' Study Finds," *Los Angeles Times*, March 2, 2000, p. A3.
36. Steve Emmons and David Reyes, "Gangs, Crime Top Fears of Vietnamese in Orange County," *Los Angeles Times*, February 5, 1989, p. 3.
37. Helen Zia, *Asian American Dreams: The Emergence of an American People* (New York: Farrar, Straus, and Co., 2000), p. 199.
38. Sonni Efron, "'Saigon' Is Under Fire Once More," *Los Angeles Times*, September 7, 1990, p. F1.
39. Center for Integration and Improvement of Journalism, *News Watch: A Critical Look at Coverage of People of Color* (San Francisco: San Francisco State University, 1994), pp. 40–43.
40. Ling-chi Wang, "Foreign Money is No Friend of Ours," in *Asian Americans: Experiences and Perspectives*, ed. Timothy P. Fong and Larry H. Shinagawa (Upper Saddle River, NJ: Prentice Hall, 2000), p. 402.
41. Steven Rosenfeld, Liane Hansen, "Asian Americans," NPR Weekend Sunday, November 23, 1997; Andrea Stone and Robert Silvers, "Asian Americans See Rising Racism," *USA Today*, July 15, 1997, p. 8A.
42. Mia Tuan, *Forever Foreigners or Honorary Whites?: The Asian American Experience Today* (New Brunswick, NJ: Rutgers University Press, 1998), p. 154.
43. "Daphne Kwok, Organization of Chinese Americans, and John O'Sullivan, *National Review*, Discuss Recent Cover Story for That Magazine That Asian Americans Are Saying Is Offensive and Racist," NBC News Transcripts, March 21, 1997; Mae M. Cheng, "Magazine Cover Ripped; Coalition Calls *National Review* Illustration Racist," *Newsday*, April 11, 1997, p. A4.

44. Robert G. Lee, *Orientals: Asian Americans in Popular Culture* (Philadelphia, PA: Temple University Press, 1999), p. 7.
45. Zia, *Asian American Dreams*, p. 109.
46. U.S. Commission on Civil Rights, *Civil Rights Issues Facing Asian Americans in the 1990s* (Washington, D.C.: U.S. Government Printing Office, 1992), pp. 5–6; U.S. Commission on Civil Rights, *Recent Activities against Citizens and Residents of Asian Descent*, pp. 3–6.
47. Jocelyn Y. Stewart, "Lest Hate Victim Be Forgotten," *Los Angeles Times*, January 25, 2001, p. A1.
48. U.S. Department of Justice, "Criminal Justice Information Services Uniform Crime Reports," press release for June 1994; Lena H. Sun, "Anti-Asian American Incidents Rising, Civil Rights Group Says; Organization Executives to Meet With Reno Today," *Washington Post*, September 9, 1997, p. A2; "Prepared Testimony of Karen Narasaki," Federal News Service, June 26, 1997.
49. U.S. Commission on Civil Rights, *Civil Rights Issues Facing Asian Americans in the 1990s*, pp. 22–48.
50. "Hate Crimes Rise in Orange County," *The Race Relations Reporter*, May 15, 1999, p. 1.
51. David Reyes, "Coalition Urges More Prosecutions of Hate Crimes," *Los Angeles Times*, September 9, 1994, p. B1; Mara Rose Williams, "Asian Americans Say Police Are Biased," *Atlanta Journal and Constitution*, September 9, 1994, p. C5; Sandy Coleman, "A Place to Turn for Victims of Hate," *Boston Globe*, June 26, 1994, p. 1.
52. U.S. Commission on Civil Rights, *Civil Rights Issues Facing Asian Americans in the 1990s*, pp. 49–69, quotation from p. 52.
53. Mimi Ko, "Forum to Examine Police Harassment," *Los Angeles Times*, June 11, 1994, p. B2.
54. U.S. Commission on Civil Rights, *Civil Rights Issues Facing Asian Americans in the 1990s*, pp. 5–6; U.S. Commission on Civil Rights, *Recent Activities against Citizens and Residents of Asian Descent*, pp. 3–6.
55. Ann Bancroft, "Jury Gets Racist Firebombings Case in Sacramento," *San Francisco Chronicle*, August 25, 1994, p. A20.
56. U.S. Commission on Civil Rights, *Recent Activities against Citizens and Residents of Asian Descent*, pp. 43–44; U.S. Commission on Civil Rights, *Civil Rights Issues Facing Asian Americans in the 1990s*, pp. 25–26; quotation from p. 28.
57. U.S. Commission on Civil Rights, *Civil Rights Issues Facing Asian Americans in the 1990s*, pp. 25–26.
58. Ibid., pp. 26–28.
59. Julie Chao, "Berkeley students claim bias in D.C.; Asian Americans Offended by Guards," *San Francisco Examiner*, September 30, 1997, p. A1.
60. Harry H. L. Kitano and Roger Daniels, *Asian Americans: Emerging Minorities*, 3rd ed. (Englewood Cliffs, NJ: Prentice Hall, 2001), pp. 54–55; ACLU press release, "Rights Commission Schedules Briefing On Scapegoating of Asian-Americans," October 23, 1997.
61. Howard A. DeWitt, *Anti-Filipino Movements in California: A History, Bibliography and Study Guide* (San Francisco: R & E Research Associates, 1976), pp. 27–66.
62. Ibid.
63. David Ibata, "Asians Seek Spot in America's Melting Pot," *Chicago Tribune*, April 26, 1992, p. 1.
64. Stewart, "Lest Hate Victim Be Forgotten," p. A1.
65. Andrea Ford, "Slain Girl Was Not Stealing Juice, Police Say," *Los Angeles Times*, March 19, 1991, p. B1; Itabari Njeri, "Perspectives on Race Relations," *Los Angeles Times*, November 29, 1991, p. B5; Mike Davis, "In L.A., Burning All Illusions," *Nation* 254, no. 21 (June 1, 1992): 743–746.
66. Davis, "In L.A., Burning All Illusions," 745.
67. Kim, "They Armed in Self-Defense," p. 10.
68. Hsia-Chuan Hsia, "Imported Racism and Indigenous Biases: the Impacts of the U.S. Media on Taiwanese Images of African Americans," paper presented at the Annual Meeting of the American Sociological Association, August 5–9, 1994, Los Angeles, California.
69. See Joe R. Feagin, *Racist America: Roots, Current Realities, and Future Reparations* (New York: Routledge, 2000), chapter 7.
70. Claire Jean Kim, *Bitter Fruit: The Politics of Black–Korean Conflict in New York City* (New Haven, CT: Yale University Press, 2000), p.11.
71. Moon H. Jo, "Korean Merchants in the Black Community: Prejudice Among the Victims of Prejudice," *Ethnic and Racial Studies* 15 (1992): 395–411; Robert L. Bach, *Changing Relations: Newcomers and Established Residents in U.S. Communities* (New York: Ford Foundation, 1993).
72. Nancy Abelmann and John Lie, *Blue Dreams: Korean Americans and the Los Angeles Riots* (Cambridge: Harvard, 1995), pp. 140–141.
73. Quoted in Njeri, "Perspectives on Race Relations," p. B5.
74. Ku-Sup Chin, "New Immigrants, Industrial Flexibility, and Ethnic Conflicts: Korean and Hispanic Immigrants in the Los Angeles Garment Industry," paper presented at the Annual Meeting of the American Sociological Association, August 5–9, 1994, Los Angeles, California.
75. U.S. Commission on Civil Rights, *Recent Activities against Citizens and Residents of Asian Descent*, pp. 50–52; Sweeney, "Tolerance in a Texas Town," pp. 7–10.
76. Michael McCabe, "U.S. Leaders Urged to Fight Hate Crimes," *San Francisco Chronicle*, February 29, 1992, p. A1; Zia, *Asian American Dreams*, p. 91.

77. Jonathan Schuppe and Aditi Kinkhabwala, "Education a Family Affair; Asian Indians Work Hard for Success in Classroom," *Asbury Park Press* (Neptune, NJ), August 17, 1997, p. 27A.
78. Zia, *Asian American Dreams*, pp. 219–221.
79. Arlene Newman, "Festival Reflects Indians' Growth," *New York Times*, August 18, 1991, sec. 12NJ, p. 1; Joel Kotkin, "Asian Indians in California Spotlight after Years in Shadows," *Washington Post*, May 6, 1990, p. H2.
80. K. Connie Kang, "Group Seeks to Boost Profile of Asian American Voters," *Los Angeles Times*, August 22, 2000, p. B1; Telephone interview with New York City Council office, January 18, 2002; Paul Ong and Don Nakanishi, "Becoming Citizens, Becoming Voters," in *Asian Americans*, ed. Fong and Shinagawa, pp. 380–383; "The Immigrant Vote in New York City Is Topic of Panel Discussion," *Barnard Campus News*, Wednesday, May 2, 2001.
81. U.S. Commission on Civil Rights, *Civil Rights Issues Facing Asian Americans in the 1990s*, pp.157–163.
82. Daniels, *Asian America*, p. 113; Zhou and Gatewood, "Introduction: Revisiting Contemporary Asian America," p. 27.
83. Yen Le Espiritu, *Asian American Panethnicity* (Philadelphia: Temple University Press, 1992), pp. 19–49.
84. Lisa Lowe, "Heterogeneity, Hybridity, Multiplicity: Marking Asian American Differences," *Diaspora* 1 (1991): 31.
85. Espiritu, *Asian American Panethnicity*, pp. 47–49.
86. Ibid., 50–51.
87. Paul Sweeney, "Asian Americans Gain Clout," *American Demographics* 8 (February 1986): 18–19.
88. Kang, "Building Bridges to Equality."
89. Frank Wu, "Asian Americans Finally Organize the NCAPA," New America News Service, November 27, 1997.
90. Carla Rivera, "Orange County Focus," *Los Angeles Times*, April 28, 1992, p. B3; K. Connie Kang, "Korean Groups Back Union Fight for Jobs," *Los Angeles Times*, November 17, 1994, p. B1.
91. Peter Kwong, *Chinatown, N.Y.: Labor and Politics, 1930–1950* (New York: Monthly Review Press, 1979), pp. 45–67.
92. Judy Yung, "The Social Awakening of Chinese American Women," in *Unequal Sisters*, ed. Ellen Carol DuBois and Vicki L. Ruiz (New York: Routledge, 1990), p. 196.
93. Martin F. Nolan, "California Confronts the Politics of Growth," *Boston Globe*, October 23, 1991, p. 1.
94. Kitano and Daniels, *Asian Americans*, p. 49.
95. K. Connie Kang, "Activist for a New Era of Civil Rights; Berkeley Professor has Fought Many Battles for the Asian American Community in the Past Three Decades," *Los Angeles Times*, July 6, 2001, part 2, p. 1.
96. Nicholas Lemann, "Growing Pains," *Atlantic Monthly*, January 1988, pp. 57–62.
97. Frank Wu, "What Do Chinese Americans Think of China?" New America News Service, October 30, 1997.
98. K. Connie Kang, "The 2008 Summer Games; Chinese Americans Feel Joy, Concern at Choice," *Los Angeles Times*, July 14, 2001, p. A10.
99. John Gregory Dunne, *Delano: The Story of the California Grape Strike* (New York: Farrar, Straus & Giroux, 1967), p. 77.
100. Lemuel F. Ignacio, *Asian Americans and Pacific Islanders* (San Jose, CA: Pilipino Development Associates, 1976), pp. 11–56; Kitano and Daniels, *Asian Americans*, p. 86.
101. Michelle Mizal, "Filipino Americans Hope to Build Unity; Group also Hopes to Build Political Clout at D.C. Event," *Virginian-Pilot* (Norfolk, VA), August 21, 1997, p. B1.
102. The study is cited in Kitano and Daniels, *Asian Americans*, 3rd ed., p. 117.
103. James T. Madore, "Long-quiet Asian Group Starts to Mobilize," *Christian Science Monitor*, May 20, 1988, p. 7; "Filipino Americans Protest S.F. Memorial," United Press International, March 31, 1997.
104. Bong-youn Choy, *Koreans in America* (Chicago: Nelson-Hall, 1979), pp. 141–189.
105. Quoted in Greg La Motte, "Asian Americans: A Diverse Voting Block," Cable News Network, June 1, 1992, transcript no. 76-5.
106. Julie Ha, "Korean American Political Power," New America News Service, March 18, 1997.
107. Zia, *Asian American Dreams*, p. 184.
108. "Korean Americans Send 100,000 Dollars in Aid to North Korea," Agence France Presse, April 3, 1997.
109. Barbara Slavin, "Korean-Americans Want Families on Agenda," *USA Today*, May 9, 2001, p. 13A.
110. Steve Emmons and David Reyes, "The Orange County Poll," *Los Angeles Times*, February 5, 1989, p. 1.
111. Ibid.
112. Quyen Do, "Little Saigon Readies for Community Balloting; Vietnamese Americans Will Elect Their Unofficial Leaders," *Orange County Register*, January 13, 1996, p. B1.
113. Bert Eljera, "Big Plans for Little Saigon," <http://www.asianweek.com/051796/LittleSaigon.html> (retrieved August 15, 2001).
114. Leland Saito, personal communication, April 18, 2001.
115. Carolyn Leung, "Redefining Advocacy for the Southeast Asian American Community," *Journal of Asian American Studies* 3 (2000): 237–241.
116. Kotkin, "Asian Indians in California Spotlight after Years in Shadows," p. H2.

117. Arlene Newman, "Festival Reflects Indians' Growth," sec. 12NJ, p. 1; Vindu P. Goel, "The Rise of Asian Indians," *Plain Dealer*, July 28, 1996, p. 8.
118. Zia, *Asian American Dreams*, pp. 198–202.
119. U.S. Commission on Civil Rights, *Civil Rights Issues Facing Asian Americans in the 1990s*, pp. 131–136, 145–148.
120. Ibid.
121. Paul Ong, ed., *Economic Diversity: Issues and Policies* (Los Angeles: Leadership Education for Asian Pacifics, 1994); E. J. Park, "Asian Americans in Silicon Valley: Race and Ethnicity in the Postindustrial Economy," unpublished doctoral dissertation, University of California, Berkeley, Department of Ethnic Studies, 1992; Cliff Cheng, "Are Asian American Employees a Model Minority or Just a Minority?" *Journal of Applied Behavioral Science* 33, no. 3 (September 1997): 277–290.
122. U.S. Commission on Civil Rights, *Civil Rights Issues Facing Asian Americans in the 1990s*, pp. 131–136, 153–156, quotation from pp. 155–156.
123. Ibid., pp. 136–148.
124. *Harvard Encyclopedia of American Ethnic Groups*, ed. Thernstrom, pp. 218–220.
125. Takaki, *Strangers from a Different Shore*, pp. 374–375.
126. Reimers, *Still the Golden Door*, p. 107.
127. Ibid.
128. Zhou and Gatewood, "Introduction: Revisiting Contemporary Asian America," in *Contemporary Asian America: A Multidisciplinary Reader*, ed. Zhou and Gatewood, p. 10.
129. The study is cited in Bettina Boxall, "Asian Indians Remake Silicon Valley; Immigrants: As Their Numbers Surge, High-Tech Skills Ease the Transition for Many," *Los Angeles Times*, July 6, 2001 p. A1.
130. U.S. Bureau of the Census, *1990 Census of Population: Social and Economic Characteristics: United States Summary*, p. 45; U.S. Bureau of the Census, *1990 Census of Population: Asians and Pacific Islanders in the United States*, p. 111.
131. U.S. Bureau of the Census, *1990 Census of Population: Social and Economic Characteristics: United States Summary*, pp. 44, 111–112.
132. Roger Daniels, *Coming to America* (New York: HarperCollins, 1990), p. 355.
133. U.S. Bureau of the Census, *1990 Census of Population: Social and Economic Characteristics: United States Summary*, CP-2-1 (Washington, D.C., 1993), pp. 48, 117; U.S. Bureau of the Census, *1990 Census of Population: Asians and Pacific Islanders in the United States*, p. 146.
134. U.S. Bureau of the Census, *1990 Census of Population: Asians and Pacific Islanders in the United States*, pp. 76, 111, 146.
135. Jan Lin, *Reconstructing Chinatown: Ethnic Enclave, Global Change* (Minneapolis, MN: University of Minnesota Press, 1998). p. ix.
136. Leland Saito, personal communication, fall 1998; Leland Saito, *Race and Politics: Asian Americans, Latinos, and Whites in a Los Angeles Suburb* (Urbana: University of Illinois Press, 1998), pp. 39–54.
137. Takaki, *Strangers from a Different Shore*, pp. 322–323, quotation from p. 323.
138. Steve Lohr, "Filipinos Flocking to the U.S. as Manila's Troubles Grow," *New York Times*, June 6, 1985, p. A14.
139. U.S. Bureau of the Census, *1990 Census of Population: Social and Economic Characteristics: United States Summary*, pp. 48, 111, 117; U.S. Bureau of the Census, *1990 Census of Population: Asians and Pacific Islanders in the United States*, p. 146.
140. United Press International, press release, March 30, 1988.
141. Irene Chang, "Ruling on Foreign Language Ban Criticized," *Los Angeles Times*, October 26, 1991, p. B3.
142. Choy, *Koreans in America*, pp. 123–133.
143. U.S. Bureau of the Census, *1990 Census of Population: Social and Economic Characteristics: United States Summary*, pp. 47, 113; U.S. Bureau of the Census, *1990 Census of the Population: Social and Economic Characteristics: Urbanized Areas*, CP-2-1C (Washington, D.C., 1993), p. 4,759.
144. Takaki, *Strangers from a Different Shore*, pp. 441–444; Reimers, *Still the Golden Door*, pp. 111–112; Ivan Light, "Immigrant Entrepreneurs in America: Koreans in Los Angeles," in *Clamor at the Gates*, ed. Nathan Glazer (San Francisco: ICS Press, 1985), p. 162.
145. "Korean Americans Adjust to Life in Korea," New America News Service, February 3, 1997.
146. Pyong Gap Min, *Changes and Conflicts: Korean Immigrant Families in New York* (Boston: Allyn and Bacon, 1998), p. 120.
147. Survey by Eui-Young Yu, cited in Emily MacFarquhar, "Fighting over the Dream," *U.S. News & World Report*, May 18, 1991, p. 34.
148. Ivan Light and Edna Bonacich, *Immigrant Entrepreneurs* (Berkeley, CA: University of California Press, 1988).
149. U.S. Bureau of the Census, *1990 Census of Population: Social and Economic Characteristics: United States Summary*, pp. 44, 48, 111, 117, 119.
150. Montero, *Vietnamese Americans*, p. 39.
151. "Prepared Testimony of Karen Narasaki," Federal News Service, June 26, 1997.
152. Dennis McLellan, "Writer Urges the U.S. to See 'A Hidden Treasure of Talents,'" *Los Angeles Times*, February 7, 1992, p. E3; Sonni Efron, "Few Viet Exiles Find U.S. Riches," *Los Angeles Times*, April 29, 1990, p. A1.
153. U.S. Bureau of the Census, *1990 Census of Population:*

Social and Economic Characteristics: United States Summary, pp. 44, 48, 112, 119.

154. "Asian, Indian Firms Growing," *Omaha World Herald*, August 5, 1996, p. 13.
155. The study is cited in Boxall, "Asian Indians Remake Silicon Valley."
156. U.S. Bureau of the Census, *1990 Census of Population: Social and Economic Characteristics: United States Summary*, pp. 107, 115, 117, 119.
157. Boxall, "Asian Indians Remake Silicon Valley."
158. "Prepared Testimony of Karen Narasaki," Federal News Service, June 26, 1997.
159. Leland Saito, personal communication, fall, 1998.
160. U.S. Commission on Civil Rights, *Civil Rights Issues Facing Asian Americans in the 1990s*, pp. 68–99.
161. Somini Sengupta, "Not All Asian Americans Prospering, Study Reports; Students' Academic Success Obscuring Needs," *Dallas Morning News*, November 14, 1997, p. 44A.
162. Michelle Ott, "The Incidence of Anti-Asian Violence in High Schools," Bates College, 1994, cited in Peter Nien-Chu Kiang, "We Could Shape It: Organizing for Asian Pacific American Student Empowerment," in *Asian Americans*, ed. Fong and Shinagawa, p. 126.
163. Donna Leinwand, "Racist Threats Set Penn State on Edge," *USA Today*, May 3, 2001, p. 3A.
164. U.S. Bureau of the Census, *Statistical Abstract of the United States 1994* (Washington, D.C., 1994), pp. 49, 157.
165. U.S. Bureau of the Census, *1990 Census of Population: Social and Economic Characteristics: United States Summary*, pp. 44, 107–108.
166. Schuppe and Kinkhabwala, "Education a Family Affair."
167. Quoted in Melita Marie Garza, "Asians Feel Bias Built on Perceptions," *Chicago Tribune*, August 7, 1994, p. C1.
168. Eloise Salholz et al., "Do Colleges Set Asian Quotas?" *Newsweek*, February 9, 1987, p. 60.
169. U.S. Commission on Civil Rights, *Civil Rights Issues Facing Asian Americans in the 1990s*, pp. 109–112.
170. Madore, "Long-Quiet Asian Group Starts to Mobilize," p. 7.
171. Ronald Takaki, "Is Race Surmountable? Thomas Sowell's Celebration of Japanese-American 'Success,'" in *Ethnicity and the Work Force*, ed. Winston A. Van Horne (Madison: University of Wisconsin Press, 1985), pp. 218–220.
172. Senate Judiciary Committee, "Capitol Hill Hearings," September 20, 1991; "Prepared Testimony of Karen Narasaki," Federal News Service, June 26, 1997.
173. Mogelonsky, "Asian-Indian Americans," pp. 32–38; Takaki, *Strangers from a Different Shore*, p. 473.
174. Tuan, *Forever Foreigners*, p. 155.
175. Kitano and Daniels, *Asian Americans*, pp. 190–192.
176. Takaki, *Strangers from a Different Shore*, p. 473.
177. Saito, *Race and Politics*, p. 61.
178. Emmons and Reyes, "Gangs, Crime Top Fears of Vietnamese in Orange County," p. 3.
179. Emmons and Reyes, "The Orange County Poll," p. 1.
180. Scott Gold, "A Generation Removed: Lessons and Legacies 25 Years After Vietnam," *Los Angeles Times*, April 28, 2000, p. M3.
181. Ibid.
182. Daniels, *Coming to America*, p. 367.
183. Reimers, *Still the Golden Door*, p. 111.
184. Karen Pyke, "'The Normal American Family' as an Interpretive Structure of Family Life among Adult Children of Korean and Vietnamese Immigrants," unpublished paper, Gainesville, University of Florida, 1997.
185. Durriya Z. Khairullah and Zahid Y. Khairullah, "Behavioural Acculturation and Demographic Characteristics of Asian Indian Immigrants in the United States of America," *International Journal of Sociology* 19 (1999): 57–80.
186. Boxall, "Asian Indians Remake Silicon Valley."
187. John Dillin, "More Blacks Enter Middle Class," *Christian Science Monitor*, August 9, 1991, p. 7; Shinagawa and Pang, "Asian American Panethnicity and Intermarriage," in *Asian Americans*, ed. Fong and Shinagawa, p. 341.
188. Shinagawa and Pang, "Asian American Panethnicity and Intermarriage," pp. 334–343.
189. Ibid.
190. Nazli Kibria, "The Construction of 'Asian American': Reflections on Intermarriage and Ethnic Identity among Second-Generation Chinese and Korean Americans," *Ethnic and Racial Studies*, 20 (July 1997): 523–544.
191. Shinagawa and Pang, "Asian American Panethnicity and Intermarriage," p. 343.
192. B. Suzuki, "Education and the Socialization of Asian Americans," in *Asian Americans: Social and Psychological Perspectives*, ed. R. Endo, S. Sue, and N. Wagner (Palo Alto, CA: Science & Behavior Books, 1980), 2:155–178.
193. Lee, *Orientals: Asian Americans in Popular Culture*, p. 188, 189.
194. Ishmael Reed, "America's Color Bind: The Modeling of Minorities," *San Francisco Examiner*, November 19, 1987, p. A20; "Success Story of One Minority Group in the U.S.," *U.S. News & World Report*, December 26, 1966, pp. 73–76.
195. We draw here on Feagin, *Racist America: Roots, Current Realities, and Future Reparations*, chapter 7.
196. See, for example, Dinesh D'Souza, *The End of Racism: Principles for a Multiracial Society* (New York: Free Press, 1995).

197. Frank Wu, "Neither Black nor White: Asian Americans and Affirmative Action," *Boston College Third World Law Journal* 15 (1995): 249–250.
198. Gary Y. Okihiro, "Is Yellow Black or White?" in *Asian Americans: Experiences and Perspectives*, ed. Fong and Shinagawa, p. 75.
199. Richard L. Zweigenhaft and William Domhoff, *Diversity in the Power Elite: Have Women and Minorities Reached the Top?* (New Haven: Yale, 1998).
200. Min Zhou, "Growing Up American: The Challenge Confronting Immigrant Children and Children of Immigrants," *Annual Review of Sociology* 23 (1997): 63–95.
201. Gloria Luz R. Martinez and Wayne J. Villemez, "Assimilation in the United States: Occupational Attainment of Asian Americans, 1980," paper presented at the American Sociological Association meetings, Chicago, 1987, pp. 31–32; U.S. Commission on Civil Rights, *Civil Rights Issues Facing Asian Americans in the 1990s*, pp. 103–136.
202. Tuan, *Forever Foreigners*, p. 159
203. Wendy Lin, "Asians, Latinos Rip Voting Plan," *Newsday*, May 29, 1992, p. 4.
204. See Kwang Chung Kim and Won Moo Hurh, "Korean Americans and the 'Success' Image: A Critique," *Amerasia* 10 (fall/winter 1983): 15.
205. Daniels, *Coming to America*, pp. 388–389.

Chapter 12

1. Joseph R. Haiek, *Arab American Almanac*, 3rd ed. (Glendale, CA: News Circle Publishing, 1984), pp. 20–32. We are indebted to Gary David, Amir Marvasti, and Pinar Batur for helpful comments on this chapter.
2. Ibid, p. 33.
3. Ibid., pp. 33–42.
4. Gary David, *The Mosaic of Middle Eastern Communities in Metropolitan Detroit* (Detroit, MI: United Way Community Services, 1999), pp. 7–9.
5. Nadine Naber, "Ambiguous Insiders: An Investigation of Arab-American Invisibility," *Ethnic and Racial Studies* 23 (January 2000), p. 41.
6. Naber, "Ambiguous Insiders," pp. 37–61; and John Zogby, "Arab America Today," 1990, <http://www.arab-aai.org> (retrieved January 26, 2001).
7. Alixa Naff, *Becoming American: The Early Arab Immigrant Experience* (Carbondale, IL: Southern Illinois University Press, 1985), pp. 3–4.
8. Zogby, "Arab America Today."
9. David, *The Mosaic of Middle Eastern Communities in Metropolitan Detroit*, p. 17.
10. Naff, *Becoming American*, p. 16.
11. David, *The Mosaic of Middle Eastern Communities in Metropolitan Detroit*, pp. 17–19.
12. Michael W. Suleiman, "Introduction: The Arab Immigrant Experience," in *Arabs in America: Building a New Future*, ed. Michael W. Suleiman (Philadelphia: Temple, 1999), p. 7.
13. Naber, "Ambiguous Insiders," p. 39.
14. Evelyn Shakir, *Bint Arab: Arab and Arab American Women in the United States* (Westport, CT: Praeger, 1997), p. 81.
15. Edward W. Said, *Orientalism* (New York: Vintage Books, 1979), p. 287.
16. Ibid.
17. Shelly Shade, "The Image of the Arab in America: Analysis of a Poll on American Attitudes," *Middle East Journal* 35 (spring 1981): 143–162.
18. Terrel Bell, *The Thirteenth Man: A Reagan Cabinet Memoir* (New York: Free Press, 1988), pp. 103–105.
19. Said, *Orientalism*, p. 286.
20. Therese Saliba, "Resisting Invisibility: Arab Americans in Academia and Activism," in *Arabs in America*, p. 310.
21. Shakir, *Bint Arab*, p. 1.
22. See Said, *Orientalism*.
23. Quoted in ibid., p. 79.
24. David, *The Mosaic of Middle Eastern Communities in Metropolitan Detroit*, p. 39.
25. Shakir, *Bint Arab*, p. 2.
26. Ibid., p. 5.
27. Ibid., p. 10. See also pp. 8–9.
28. Kristine Ajrouch, "Family and Ethnic Identity in an Arab-American Community," in *Arabs in America*, p. 129.
29. Shakir, *Bint Arab*, p. 112.
30. Ibid., p. 81.
31. Ibid., p. 116.
32. Fatima Agha Al-Hayani, "Arabs and the American Legal System: Cultural and Political Ramifications," in *Arabs in America*, p. 80.
33. Said, *Orientalism*, p. 321.
34. Zogby, "Arab America Today."
35. Mowahid Shah, "The FBI and the Civil Rights of Arab-Americans," ADC Issues, Number 5, Washington D.C., 1986.
36. Gary David, email communication, March 2001.
37. Shakir, *Bint Arab*, p. 86; Kathleen M. Moore, "A Closer Look at Anti-Terrorism Law," in *Arabs in America*, p. 80.
38. "Islam in the United States, A Tentative Ascent, A Conversation with Yvonne Haddad," <http://usinfo.state.gov/usa/islam/hadad.htm> (retrieved June 4, 2001).
39. Naber, "Ambiguous Insiders," p. 49; Leadership Conference on Civil Rights, "Faces of Hate Crimes," <http://www.civilrights.org/programs/hate_crimes/faces/index.htm1#3> (retrieved January 24, 2002).

40. American-Arab Anti-Discrimination Committee (ADC), "ADC Fact Sheet: The Condition of Arab Americans Post 9/11," <http://www.adc.org/terror_attack/9-11aftermath.pdf>, p. 1 (retrieved January 24, 2002); Peter Finn, "Hijackers Depicted as Elite Group," *Washington Post*, November 5, 2001, p. Al.
41. American-Arab Anti-Discrimination Committee (ADC), "ADC Fact Sheet: The Condition of Arab Americans Post 9/11," p. 2.
42. Mark Fitzgerald, "Arab Americans Boycott *'Chicago Sun-Times'*" *Jerusalem Post*, November 1, 2000, p. 1; quote is from Naber, "Ambiguous Insiders," p. 46.
43. " Muslim-American Activism: Discussion of Legal Issues Facing Muslim Communities in the United States," *Washington Report of Middle Eastern Affairs*, June 2000, pp. 88–89.
44. Nikki Tait, "Immigrants Earn Their Rewards: Arab-American Community," *Financial Times*, February 28, 2000, p. 6. See also Gary David, *Intercultural Relationships Across The Counter: An Interactional Analysis Of In-Situ Service Encounters*, unpublished dissertation, Detroit, Michigan, Wayne State University, 1999.
45. Abdon M. Pallasch, "Arab, Jewish Law Groups Convene; Attorneys Here Seeking Common Ground," *Chicago Sun-Times*, November 10, 2000, p. 12.
46. Albor Ruiz, "Group Fights Spread of Mideast Hate Here," *New York Daily News*, November 6, 2000, p. 6.
47. Leo Standora et alia, "Violence Shaking up Arabs, Jews in City," *New York Daily News*, October 13, 2000, p. 37.
48. Teresa Watanabe, "American Muslims Look for Ways to Harness Political Power," *Los Angeles Times*, October 1, 2000, p. B3.
49. Andrea Stone, "Arab Vote is Critical in Michigan," *USA Today*, November 1, 2000, p. 12A.
50. Zev Chafets, "Arab Enclave on Pols' Map," *New York Daily News*, November 3, 2000, p. 6.
51. Watanabe, "American Muslims Look for Ways to Harness Political Power," p. B3.
52. Shakir, *Bint Arab*, p. 88.
53. Quoted in E. R. Shipp, "Anti-Muslim Bigotry is Bad Political Strategy," *New York Daily News*, November 5, 2000, p. 45.
54. Bonnie Squires, "Americans Warming to Arab Cause?" *Philadelphia Daily News*, as reprinted on <http://www.arab-aai.org> (retrieved January 26, 2001).
55. Janine Zacharia, "Arab Americans Send Record Number of Delegates to Democratic Convention," *Jerusalem Post*, August 17, 2000, p. 2.
56. David, *The Mosaic of Middle Eastern Communities in Metropolitan Detroit*, p. 23.
57. Quoted in Ibid., p. 51.
58. Watanabe, "American Muslims Look for Ways to Harness Political Power," p. B3.
59. Naber, "Ambiguous Insiders," pp. 37–61; and Zogby, "Arab America Today."
60. Zogby, "Arab America Today."
61. Ibid.; David, *The Mosaic of Middle Eastern Communities in Metropolitan Detroit*, pp. 9–49; Tait, "Immigrants Earn Their Rewards: Arab-American Community," p. 6.
62. Chafets, "Arab Enclave on Pols' Map," p. 6.
63. Suleiman, "Introduction," p. 16.
64. Zogby, "Arab America Today."
65. Suleiman, "Introduction," p. 16.
66. David, *The Mosaic of Middle Eastern Communities in Metropolitan Detroit*, p. 40.
67. As reported in Jane Adas, "Museum of the City of New York Examines Local Arab Americans," *Washington Report of Middle Eastern Affairs*, April 2000, pp. 51–52, 83.
68. Wendy Schwartz, "Arab American Students in Public Schools," <http://eric-web.tc.columbia.edu/digests/dig142.htm> (retrieved June 4, 2001).
69. "Islam in the United States, A Tentative Ascent, A Conversation with Yvonne Haddad."
70. Shakir, *Bint Arab*, pp. 115–116.
71. Abdul Malik, "Muslims in America: Profile 2001," <http://www.soundvision.com/yearinreview/2001/profile.shtml> (retrieved June 4, 2001).
72. Abdul Malik, "Muslims in America: Profile 2001."
73. "Islam in the United States, A Tentative Ascent, A Conversation with Yvonne Haddad."
74. Ibid.
75. Suad Joseph, "Against the Grain of the Nation—The Arab," in *Arabs in America: Building a New Future*, ed. Suleiman, p. 261.
76. Suleiman, "Introduction," p. 15.
77. Naber, "Ambiguous Insiders," p. 40.
78. Naff, *Becoming American*, p. 15.
79. David, *The Mosaic of Middle Eastern Communities in Metropolitan Detroit*, pp. 32–34.
80. Zogby, "Arab America Today."
81. Shakir, *Bint Arab*, p. 116.
82. Zogby, "Arab America Today."
83. Gary David and Kenneth Kahtan Ayouby, "Being Arab and Becoming Americanized," unpublished research paper, Bentley College, Waltham, MA, 2001, p. 34.
84. Mariam Sami, "As Cap Replaces Kaffiyeh, Arab Parents Look for Help," *New York Times*, November 2, 1997, Section 14, p. 10.
85. David, *The Mosaic of Middle Eastern Communities in Metropolitan Detroit*, p. 39.
86. Richard A. Chapman, "Arab-American Teenagers Share Their Culture in Video," *Chicago Sun-Times*, November 28, 1996, p. 22.

87. Quoted in David, *The Mosaic of Middle Eastern Communities in Metropolitan Detroit*, p. 37.
88. David and Ayouby, p. 35. See also pp. 4, 37.
89. Ibid., p. 15.
90. Shakir, *Bint Arab*, p. 112.
91. Naber, "Ambiguous Insiders," pp. 50–51.

CHAPTER 13

1. Nat Hentoff, "Free Expression Comes to Boston Latin," *Washington Post*, February 8, 1992, p. A21.
2. Quoted in Ilan Stavans, *The Hispanic Condition: Reflections on Culture and Identity in America* (New York: HarperCollins, 1995), p. 166.
3. Stavans, *The Hispanic Condition: Reflections on Culture and Identity in America*, p. 167.
4. S. H. Murdock, *An America Challenged: Population Change and the Future of the United States* (Boulder, CO: Westview, 1995), pp. 33–47.
5. Quoted in Clarence Page, "U.S. Media Should Stop Abetting Intolerance," *Toronto Star*, December 27, 1991, p. A27.
6. Samuel P. Huntington, "The Erosion of American National Interests," *Foreign Affairs* (September 1997/October 1997): 28.
7. Ibid. p. 32.
8. Lawrence Auster, "The Forbidden Topic," *National Review*, April 27, 1992, p. 42.
9. Arthur Schlesinger, *The Disuniting of America: Reflections on a Multicultural Society* (New York: Norton, 1991), pp. 13, 124 125.
10. Immigration and Naturalization Service, *Fiscal Year 1998 Statistical Yearbook* (Washington, D.C.: Government Printing Office, 1999), Table 2, <http://www.ins.gov/graphics/aboutins/statistics/98immtbl.pdf> (retrieved August 31, 2001). Note that the data are incomplete for certain time periods and that the definition of some countries, such as the United Kingdom (and Northern Ireland), have sometimes changed at different points in time.
11. Andrew Piatt, "The Crux of the Immigration Question," *North American Review* 199 (June 1914): 866, quoted in Rita J. Simon and Susan H. Alexander, *The Ambivalent Welcome: Print Media, Public Opinion, and Immigration* (Westport, CT: Praeger, 1993), p. 59.
12. U.S. Census Bureau, Table DP-1: Profile of General Demographic Characteristics for the United States: 2000, <http://www.census.gov> (retrieved August 29, 2001).
13. Wendy Lin, "Stakes are High in Lottery for U.S. Green Cards," *Newsday*, October 13, 1991, p. 19.
14. "Canadians View Immigration as Having Positive Economic Effect, Reports Recent Canada–U.S. Public Opinion Poll," Canada NewsWire, <http://www.newswire.ca/releases/May2000/06/c2434.html> (retrieved August 27, 2001).
15. Cited in Shawn Foster, "Immigrants: Blessing or Curse for Utah?" *Salt Lake Tribune*, November 10, 1994, p. A1.
16. See David Cole, "Five Myths about Immigration," *Nation*, October 7, 1994, p. 410.
17. Josh Friedman, "Experts Tell of Boom among Immigrants," *Newsday*, November 3, 1994, p. A34.
18. Immigration and Naturalization Service, *Fiscal Year 1998 Statistical Yearbook* (Washington, D.C.: Government Printing Office, 1999), Tables 1–3, <http://www.ins.gov/graphics/aboutins/statistics/98immtbl.pdf> (retrieved August 31, 2001).
19. Ibid.
20. Quoted in Keith Henderson, "Immigration as an Economic Engine," *Christian Science Monitor*, March 27, 1992, p. 9. See also Ben Wattenberg, *The First Universal Nation* (New York: Free Press, 1990).
21. Hector Tobar and Robin Fields, "21st-Century Cities: What is Happening in Urban America?" *Milwaukee Journal Sentinel*, May 11, 2001, p. 19A.
22. Juan Gonzalez, *Harvest of Empire: A History of Latinos in America* (New York: Penguin Books, 2000), pp. xii–xix.
23. Israel Zangwill, *The Melting Pot* (New York: Macmillan, 1925), p. 33.
24. Milton M. Gordon, *Assimilation in American Life* (New York: Oxford University Press, 1964), pp. 72–73.
25. Terry Lefton, "Building Bridges in the Big Apple," *Teaching Tolerance* 1, no. 1 (spring 1992): 8–13; Ralph Blumenthal, "Black Youth Is Killed by Whites; Brooklyn Attack Is Called Racial," *New York Times*, August 25, 1989, p. A1.
26. Itabari Njeri, "Beyond the Melting Pot; In America, Blending In Was Once the Ideal," *Los Angeles Times*, January 13, 1991, p. E1.
27. Arthur Schlesinger, Jr., "Speaking Up: A Look at Noteworthy Addresses in the Southland," *Los Angeles Times*, February 7, 1992, p. B2.
28. Andres Torres, *Between Melting Pot and Mosaic: African Americans and Puerto Ricans in the New York Political Economy* (Philadelphia: Temple, 1995), pp. 2–6.
29. Ibid., p. 2.
30. Ibid., p. 4.
31. Amitai Etzioni, "Community of Communities," *Washington Quarterly*, 19 (summer 1996): 127–138.
32. Cited in Bobbie Harville, "History: Knowledge Is Lacking; Americans' Understanding of the Country's History Is Thin, a New Survey Reveals," *Dayton Daily News*, July 14, 1996, p. 15A.

33. James W. Loewen, *Lies My Teacher Told Me: Everything Your American History Textbook Got Wrong* (New York: The New Press, 1995), p. 163.
34. Quoted in Njeri, "Beyond the Melting Pot," p. E1.
35. Ted Gordon and Wahneema Lubiano, "The Statement of the Black Faculty Caucus," in *Debating P.C.*, ed. Paul Berman (New York: Dell, 1992), p. 251.
36. Ibid., pp. 251–253.
37. LaDonna Harris, "Rediscovering Native Americans," *Forum*, spring 1992, p. 8.
38. Robert J. Samuelson, "The Loathing of Japan," *Washington Post*, February 19, 1992, p. A19.
39. "Asian-Americans: Growing Racism; Major New Report Warns against the Vile Danger," *Los Angeles Times*, March 3, 1992, p. B6.
40. Quoted in Reynolds Holding, "Panel of Judges, Lawyers Chided for Courts' Toleration of Racism," *San Francisco Chronicle*, May 9, 1992, p. A15.
41. Scott Rothschild and Debra Beachy, "Insurance Bias Probe Requested," *Houston Chronicle*, February 14, 1992, p. 1.
42. Reuben Blades, "The Politics Behind the Latino's Legacy," *New York Times*, April 19, 1992, sec. 2, p. 31; Fair Housing Council of Fresno County, "Audit Uncovers Blatant Discrimination against Hispanics, African Americans, and Families with Children in Fresno County," press release, October 6, 1995.
43. Stephen Steinberg, *Turning Back: The Retreat from Racial Justice in American Thought and Policy* (Boston: Beacon, 1995), p. 136.
44. Larry Bobo and S. A. Suh, "Surveying Racial Discrimination: Analyses from a Multiethnic Labor Market," unpublished research report, Department of Sociology, University of California, Los Angeles, 1995.
45. Gallup, *Black/White Relations in the United States* (Princeton, NJ: The Gallup Organization, 1997), pp. 29–30, 108–110.
46. Joe R. Feagin and Melvin P. Sikes, *Living with Racism* (Boston: Beacon, 1994).
47. William H. Frey, "Immigration, Domestic Migration, and Demographic Balkanization in America: New Evidence from the 1990s," *Population and Development Review* 22 (December 1996): 741–763; see also William H. Frey, "Immigrant and Native Migrant Magnets," *American Demographics* (November 1996), pp. 1–4.
48. See William H. Frey, "The New White Flight," *American Demographics* (April 1994), pp. 1–6.
49. Frey, "Immigration, Domestic Migration, and Demographic Balkanization in America," p. 758.
50. See, for example, Joe R. Feagin, "The Future of U.S. Society in an Era of Racism, Group Segregation, and Demographic Revolution," paper presented to the International Sociology Association conference on The Heritage and Future of Sociology, Toronto, Canada, August 1997.

CHAPTER 14

1. Peter Turnley, et al., "Graceland," *Newsweek*, May 9, 1994, pp. 30–33.
2. Russell Watson, et al., "Black Power!" *Newsweek*, May 9, 1994, pp. 34–39.
3. Ibid.
4. Paul Taylor, "In New South Africa, Pace of Change Has Race Tensions Simmering," *Washington Post*, July 21, 1994, p. A20.
5. F. Scott Fitzgerald, *The Great Gatsby* (New York: Penguin Books, 1983), p. 19.
6. For a fuller discussion of issues raised in this chapter, see Pinar Batur, *Broken Mirrors: Colonialism and Identity Formation* (forthcoming).
7. Zia Sardar, Ashis Nandy, and Merryl Wyn Davies, *Barbaric Others: A Manifesto on Western Racism* (London: Pluto Press, 1993), pp. 8–9.
8. Oliver C. Cox, *Caste, Class and Race: A Study in Social Dynamics* (Garden City, NY: Doubleday, 1948), pp. 331–332.
9. Ibid., p. 334.
10. Albert Memmi, *The Colonizer and the Colonized* (New York: Orion Press, 1965).
11. Ronald Takaki, *Iron Cages* (New York: Oxford University Press, 1990), p. 12.
12. Joseph Arthur de Gobineau, *Selected Political Writings*, ed. M. D. Biddiss (New York: Harper & Row, 1970), p. 136.
13. Pinar Batur, *Broken Mirrors*.
14. Frantz Fanon, "The Pitfalls of National Consciousness" and "On National Culture," in *The Wretched of the Earth*, trans. Constance Farrington (New York: Grove Press, 1963); Anthony Brewer, *Marxist Theories of Imperialism* (New York: Routledge, 1986).
15. Albert Memmi, *The Pillar of Salt* (Boston: Beacon Press, 1992), p. 331.
16. Peter Green, "After Protest, British Halt Screening of Travelers in Prague," *New York Times*, August 8, 2001, p. A4.
17. Pinar Batur, *Broken Mirrors*.
18. Leonard Thompson, *A History of South Africa* (New Haven, CT: Yale University Press, 1990); Nigel Worden, *The Making of Modern South Africa: Conquest, Segregation and Apartheid* (Oxford: Blackwell, 1994); Basil Davidson, *Africa in History* (New York: Collier Books, 1991); Roland Oliver and Anthony Atmore, *Africa Since 1800*, 3rd ed. (Cambridge: Cambridge

University Press, 1989); Joseph Harris, *Africans and Their History* (New York: Mentor, 1987).

19. Leonard Thompson, *Political Mythology of Apartheid* (New Haven, CT: Yale University Press, 1985), p. 71.
20. Thompson, *Political Mythology of Apartheid*, pp. 72–73.
21. Worden, *Making of Modern South Africa*, pp. 11–12.
22. Thompson, *Political Mythology of Apartheid*, p. 75.
23. Ibid., p. 76.
24. Davidson, *Africa in History*, p. 269.
25. Thompson, *Political Mythology of Apartheid*, p. 70.
26. Thompson, *History of South Africa*, pp. 111–112.
27. Allister Sparks, *The Mind of South Africa* (New York: Knopf, 1990), pp. 148–149.
28. The quote is from Thompson, *History of South Africa*, p. 184; see Sparks, *Mind of South Africa*, p. 153.
29. Merle Lipton, *Capitalism and Apartheid: South Africa, 1910–1984* (Totowa, NJ: Rowman & Allenheld, 1985), pp. 14–15.
30. Thompson, *History of South Africa*; Oliver and Atmore, *Africa Since 1800*, p. 295.
31. Thompson, *History of South Africa*, p. 206; Lipton, *Capitalism and Apartheid.*
32. Francis Meli, *South Africa Belongs to Us: A History of the ANC* (Bloomington: Indiana University Press, 1988).
33. Nozipho Diseko, "The Origins and Development of the South African Student's Movement (SASM): 1968–1976," *Journal of South African Studies* 18 (March 1991): 40–62.
34. Howard Barrell, "The Turn to the Masses: the African National Congress' Strategic Review of 1978–1979," *Journal of South African Studies* 18 (March 1991): 64–92.
35. Bill Keller, "In South Africa, A White 'Third Force' of Violence Is Confirmed," *New York Times*, March 20, 1994, section 4, p. 5.
36. Thompson, *History of South Africa*.
37. Bill Keller, "Where Blood Ran and a Tide Turned," *New York Times*, March 27, 1994, section 4, p. 5.
38. Bill Keller, "Rival Visions of a Post-Apartheid Future Divide South Africa's Zulus," *New York Times*, April 4, 1994, p. A1; Tom Masland and Joseph Conteras, "Ballots or Bullets," *Newsweek*, April 11, 1994, pp. 34–37.
39. "Race about Race: South Africa's Racial Election," *The Economist*, December 9, 2000, p. 5.
40. Frantz Fanon, *Black Skin, White Masks*, translated by Charles Markmann (New York: Grove Weidenfeld, 1967), p. 87.
41. "The Colours of Brazil," *The Economist*, May 10, 1986, p. 42.
42. Charles Whitaker, "Blacks in Brazil: the Myth and the Reality," *Ebony*, February 1991, pp. 41, 60–64.
43. Daniela Hart, "Racial Bias Entrenched," *Chronicle of Higher Education*, July 20, 1988, p. A31–32.
44. E. Bradford Burns, *A History of Brazil*, 3rd ed. (New York: Cornell Press, 1993), pp. 23–27.
45. Thomas Skidmore and Peter Smith, *Modern Latin America*, 2nd ed. (Oxford: Oxford University Press, 1994), p. 140; Burns, *History of Brazil*, pp. 216–217.
46. Michael Hanchard, *Orpheus and Power: The Movimento Negro of Rio de Janeiro and São Paulo, Brazil, 1945–1988* (Princeton, NJ: Princeton University Press, 1994). p. 45.
47. Hanchard, *Orpheus and Power*, p. 43.
48. Thomas Skidmore, *Black Into White: Race and Nationality in Brazilian Thought* (Oxford: Oxford University Press, 1974), pp. 48–69; Dain Borges, "Puffy, Ugly, Slothful and Inert: Degeneration in Brazilian Social Thought, 1880–1940," *Journal of Latin American Studies* 25 (1993): 235–256.
49. Thomas Sanders, "Racial Discrimination and Black Consciousness in Brazil," *American Universities Field Staff Reports* 42 (1981); Hanchard, *Orpheus and Power.*
50. Sanders, "Racial Discrimination and Black Consciousness in Brazil," p. 2.
51. George Andrews, "Racial Inequality in Brazil and the United States: A Statistical Comparison," *Journal of Social History* 26 (1992): 234; see also Peggy Webster and Jeffrey Dwyer, "The Cost of Being Nonwhite in Brazil," *Sociology and Social Research* 72 (1988): 136–142.
52. Andrews, "Racial Inequality in Brazil and the United States," pp. 256–257.
53. Howard Winant, "Rethinking Race in Brazil," *Journal of Latin American Studies* 24 (1992): 173–192.
54. Quoted in Whitaker, "Racial Bias Entrenched."
55. Ibid.
56. Jerry Davila, "Expanding Perspectives on Race in Brazil," *Latin American Research Review* 35 (2000): 198.
57. Anthony Faiola, "Yet Another Fresh Start for Brazil," *Washington Post National Weekly Edition*, October 20, 1997, p. 19.
58. "Brazil's Unfinished Battle for Racial Democracy," *The Economist*, April 22, 2000, p. 31.
59. Francisco Oliviera, "A Bible and an Automatic," *Index on Censorship* 28 (January 1999): 115.
60. David Kennedy, "Who are Brazil's Indigenas: Contributions of Census Data Analysis to Anthropological Demography on Indigenous Populations," *Human Organization* 59 (2000): 311; "Threat to Brazil's Indians," *Geographical* 73 (June 2001): 12.
61. Fanon, *Wretched of the Earth*, p. 41.
62. Pierre Birnbaum, *Anti-Semitism in France: A Political History from Leon Blum to the Present*, trans. Miriam Kochan (Oxford: Blackwell, 1992), p. 1.
63. Stephen Wilson, *Ideology and Experience: Antisemitism in France at the Time of the Dreyfus Affair* (Rutherford, NJ: Fairleigh Dickinson University Press, 1982).

64. Alan Riding, "Mitterand's Mistakes: Vichy Past is Unveiled," *New York Times*, September 9, 1994, p. A4.
65. Maxim Silverman, *Deconstructing the Nation: Immigration, Racism and Citizenship in Modern France* (London: Routledge, 1992), p. 10.
66. Douglas Johnson, "The Making of the French Nation," in *The National Question in Europe in Historical Context*, ed. Mikulas Teich and Roy Porter (Cambridge: Cambridge University Press, 1993), p. 59.
67. Silverman, *Deconstructing the Nation*, pp. 3–4.
68. R. D. Grillo, *Ideologies and Institutions in Urban France* (Cambridge: Cambridge University Press, 1985), p. 65.
69. Silverman, *Deconstructing the Nation*, p. 3.
70. Julia Kristeva, *Nations Without Nationalism* (New York: Columbia University Press, 1993), pp. 97–98.
71. Catherine Wihtol De Wenden, "North African Immigration and the French Political Imaginary," in *Race, Discourse and Power in France*, ed. Maxim Silverman (Brookfield, VT: Gower, 1991), p. 108.
72. Daniel Singer, "Liberte, Egalite, Racisme?, *Nation*, October 21, 1996, p. 19.
73. Kristeva, *Nations Without Nationalism*, pp. 13–14.
74. Chris Woodall, "Arabicide in France: an Interview with Fausto Giudice," *Race and Class* 35 (1993): 21–33.
75. Youssef Ibrahim, "France Bans Muslim Scarf in Its Schools," *New York Times*, September 11, 1994, p. 4.
76. Ibid.
77. Letitia Creamean, "Membership of Foreigners: Algerians in France," *Arab Studies Quarterly* 16 (1996): 49–67.
78. Alice Chasan, "Border Skirmishes: European Integration vs. Ugly Atavisms," *World Press Review*, January 2000, p. 2.
79. Anna Frangoudaki, "Reproduction of the Patterns of Interstate Power Relations in the Conceptions of 15-year-old students in EU Countries: the Persistence of Prejudice," *Journal of Modern Greek Studies* 18 (2000): 355.
80. "French TV Executive, former TV Host Fined for Racist Song Performed on Air about Blacks," *Jet*, April 1, 1996, p. 65.
81. Fanon, *Wretched of the Earth*, p. 40.
82. Pinar Batur, "The Discourse of Counterattack: Ethnic Movements and the Formation of Ethnic Identity." (Unpublished Ph.D. dissertation, University of Texas, 1992.)
83. Fanon, *Wretched of the Earth*.
84. Batur, *Broken Mirrors*.

Photo Credits

Preface and Chapter 1: p. xvii, Getty Images, Inc.; p. 3, Esbin Anderson/The Image Works; p. 7, Jonathan Fickies/AP/Wide World Photos; p. 10, Tracy Pick/Stock Boston; p. 17, Bob Daemmrich/Stock Boston.

Chapter 2: p. 22, Kunio Awaki/Corbis/Stock Market; p. 27, Getty Images, Inc.; p. 33, A. Ramey/PhotoEdit; p. 38, Merritt Vincent/PhotoEdit.

Chapter 3: p. 59, United States Capitol Historical Society; p. 61, Corbis; p. 66, Steven Rubin/The Image Works.

Chapter 4: p. 77, Rudi Von Brief/PhotoEdit; p. 80, courtesy of the Library of Congress; p. 85, UPI/Corbis; p. 96, Judy Gelles/Stock Boston; p. 99, Brown Brothers.

Chapter 5: p. 106, David Karp/AP/Wide World Photos; p. 111, AP/Wide World Photos; p. 115, Tannen Maury/The Image Works; p. 121, Corbis; p. 124, AP/Wide World Photos.

Chapter 6: p. 130, Charles Coffey; p. 134, Corbis; p. 150, David Lassman/The Image Works; p. 152, Charles Coffey; p. 155, Martha Cooper/The Viesti Collection, Inc.

Chapter 7: p. 159, David R. Frazier/David R. Frazier Photolibrary, Inc.; p. 169, AP/Wide World Photos; p. 183, UPI/Corbis; p. 185, Maria Mulas; p. 190, Alex Wang/Getty Images, Inc.

Chapter 8: p. 196, Bob Daemmrich/Stock Boston; p. 202, Robert Holmes/Robert Holmes Photography; p. 215, Corbis; p. 219, AP/Wide World Photos; p. 225, Bob Daemmrich/Stock Boston.

Chapter 9: p. 232, Alan Diaz/AP/Wide World Photos; p. 245, Corbis; p. 248, Hazel Hankin/Stock Boston; p. 253, Joe Marquette/AP/Wide World Photos; p. 259, AP/Wide World Photos.

Chapter 10: p. 265, Damian Dovarganes/AP/Wide World Photos; p. 272, AP/Wide World Photos; p. 275, Tim Boyle/Getty Images, Inc.; p. 280, Christian Simonpietri/Corbis/Sygma.

Chapter 11: p. 289, Lia Chang Gallery Collection, copyright Lia Chang; p. 301, AP/Wide World Photos; p. 303, AP/Wide World Photos; p. 306, Stock Boston; p. 311, Lia Chang Gallery Collection, copyright Lia Chang; p. 314, Bob Daemmrich/The Image Works.

Chapter 12: p. 323, Bizuayehu Tesfaye/AP/Wide World Photos; p. 330, Bill Mokdad; p. 332, Justin Sullivan/Getty Images, Inc.; p. 334, Bill Mokdad; p. 335, AP/Wide World Photos.

Chapter 13: p. 340, Corbis; p. 343, AP/Wide World Photos; p. 347, Lara Jo Regan/Getty Images, Inc.; p. 350, AP/Wide World Photos.

Chapter 14: p. 356, Jean-Jaques Gonzalez/The Image Works; p. 362, AP/Wide World Photos; p. 364, Corbis; p. 368, AP/Wide World Photos.

Index